MANCHESTER MEDIEVAL LITERATURE AND CULTURE

RETHINKING THE *SOUTH ENGLISH LEGENDARIES*

Manchester University Press

MANCHESTER MEDIEVAL LITERATURE AND CULTURE

Anke Bernau and David Matthews *series editors*

Series founded by: J. J. Anderson and Gail Ashton

Advisory Board: Ruth Evans (Saint Louis University), Nicola McDonald (University of York), Larry Scanlon (Rutgers University), Stephanie Trigg (University of Melbourne)

The Manchester Medieval Literature and Culture series publishes new research, informed by current critical methodologies, on the literary cultures of medieval Britain (including Anglo-Norman, Anglo-Latin and Celtic writings), including post-medieval engagements with and representations of the Middle Ages (medievalism). 'Literature' is viewed in a broad and inclusive sense, embracing imaginative, historical, political, scientific, dramatic and religious writings. The series offers monographs and essay collections, as well as editions and translations of texts.

Titles Available in the Series

Rethinking the *South English Legendaries*

EDITED BY HEATHER BLURTON AND
JOCELYN WOGAN-BROWNE

Manchester University Press

MANCHESTER AND NEW YORK

distributed in the United States exclusively by Palgrave Macmillan

Published by Manchester University Press
Oxford Road, Manchester M13 9NR, UK
and Room 400, 175 Fifth Avenue, New York, NY 10010, USA
www.manchesteruniversitypress.co.uk

Distributed in the United States exclusively by
Palgrave Macmillan, 175 Fifth Avenue, New York,
NY 10010, USA

Distributed in Canada exclusively by
UBC Press, University of British Columbia, 2029 West Mall,
Vancouver, BC, Canada V6T 1Z2

British Library Cataloguing-in-Publication Data
A catalogue record for this book is available from the British Library

Library of Congress Cataloging-in-Publication Data applied for

ISBN   978 0 7190 8434 8   hardback

First published 2011

Typeset
by Servis Filmsetting Ltd, Stockport, Cheshire
Printed in Great Britain
by TJ International Ltd, Padstow

Dedicated with affectionate respect
to
Sherry L. Reames,
in gratitude both for her own scholarship and
her twenty years of leadership in founding and sustaining
The Hagiography Society

Contents

Part V Performance

Part VI Afterword

List of figures

*All images from Oxford, Bodleian Library, MS Tanner 17
reproduced by permission of the Bodleian Library, Oxford*

List of Tables

Notes on contributors

Tim Ayers is Senior Lecturer in the History of Art Department and a member of the Centre for Medieval Studies at the University of York. He is the author of *The Medieval Stained Glass of Wells Cathedral*, 2 vols (British Academy, 2004), and recently edited the medieval volume in the three-volume *History of British Art, 600–1600* (Tate, 2008). He is completing a study on the stained glass of Merton College, Oxford.

Virginia Blanton is Associate Professor of English at the University of Missouri-Kansas City, where she serves as doctoral faculty in English and Religious Studies. Her research focuses on medieval hagiography and religious ritual, as well as the representations of women in religious culture. She is the author of *Signs of Devotion: The Cult of St Æthelthryth in Medieval England, 695–1615* (Penn State Press, 2007) and co-editor of *Intertexts: Studies in Anglo-Saxon Culture Presented to Paul E. Szarmach* (Arizona Center for Medieval and Renaissance Studies, 2008).

Heather Blurton is Associate Professor of English at the University of California, Santa Barbara and formerly Lecturer in English and Medieval Studies at the University of York, UK. She is author of *Cannibalism and High Medieval English Literature* (Palgrave Macmillan, 2007).

Sarah Breckenridge is a PhD Candidate in English Literature at The Pennsylvania State University. Her dissertation considers literary representations of English landscapes from the twelfth to sixteenth centuries, in texts including the *Gesta Pontificum Anglorum*, the *South English Legendaries*, *The Canterbury Tales*, *Piers Plowman* and *The Faerie Queene*. Her research interests include medieval and early modern place, landscape, identity, history and hagiography.

John Frankis is retired from the School of English, University of Newcastle upon Tyne. He has published widely on the manuscripts and texts of insular literary culture.

Thomas Heffernan is Kenneth Curry Chair in the Humanities and is a faculty member in the English and Religious Studies Departments at the University of Tennessee. He is the author of five books, including *Sacred Biography: Saints and Their Biographers in the Middle Ages* (Oxford University Press, 1988) and (with E. Ann Matter), *The Liturgy of the Medieval Church* (Medieval Institute Publications, 2001), and most recently a critical edition of the *Passio Sanctarum Perpetuae et Felicitatis* (forthcoming, Oxford University Press).

Thomas Liszka is Associate Professor of English, Penn State Altoona. He has published numerous articles on the structure and early history of both the *SEL* and its manuscript contexts. His essay on the dating of the Laud Miscellaneous 108 manuscript of the *SEL*, *Havelok* and *King Horn* texts is published in *The Texts and Contexts of Bodleian Library MS Laud Misc. 108: The Shaping of English Vernacular Narrative*, ed. Kimberley Bell and Julie Nelson Couch (Leiden: Brill, 2011).

Robert Mills is Senior Lecturer in English at King's College London. He is author of *Suspended Animation: Pain, Pleasure and Punishment in Medieval Culture* (Reaktion, 2005), and co-editor of *The Monstrous Middle Ages* (University of Wales Press and University of Toronto Press, 2003) and *Troubled Vision: Gender, Sexuality and Sight in Medieval Text and Image* (Palgrave Macmillan, 2004).

Chloe Morgan has recently gained her PhD 'Brynge hym into my chapelle: sacred space in Middle English Romance', at the Centre for Medieval Studies, University of York. She is author of 'A Life of St Katherine of Alexandria in the chapter-house of York Minster', *Journal of the British Archaeological Association*, 162 (2009).

Oliver Pickering is Honorary Fellow in the School of English, University of Leeds, having previously been Deputy Head of Special Collections in Leeds University Library. He has published widely on Middle English texts and manuscripts, and has been Editor of *The Library: The Transactions of the Bibliographical*

Society and he has also been editor of *The Library: The Transactions of the Bibliographical Society*.

Sherry L. Reames is Professor Emerita of English at the University of Wisconsin-Madison, and founding President of the Hagiography Society (1990–2010). She has published *The Legenda aurea: A Reexamination of Its Paradoxical History* (University of Wisconsin Press, 1985) and many studies of hagiography and liturgy.

William Robins is Associate Professor of English and Medieval Studies, University of Toronto. Recent publications include the critical edition (with Attilio Motta) of Antonio Pucci's *Cantari della Reina d'Oriente* (Testi di Lingua, 2007) and (with Robert Epstein) the edited collection *Sacred and Profane in Chaucer and Late Medieval Literature: Essays in Honour of John V. Fleming* (Toronto University Press, 2010).

Catherine Sanok is Associate Professor of English and Women's Studies at the University of Michigan, and author of *Her Life Historical: Exemplarity and Female Saints' Lives in Late Medieval England* (University of Pennsylvania Press, 2007). She is currently working on a book about fifteenth-century lives of British and English saints.

Anne B. Thompson is Professor Emerita of English, and Euterpe B. Dukakis Professor Emerita of Classical and Medieval Studies, Bates College. She is the author of *Everyday Saints and the Art of Narrative in the South English Legendary* (Ashgate, 2003) and editor of *The Northern Homily Cycle* (TEAMS for Medieval Institute Publications, 2008).

E. Gordon Whatley is Professor at Queen's College and the Graduate Center, CUNY. His recent publications include 'Eugenia before Ælfric: a preliminary report on the transmission of an early medieval legend', in *(Inter)texts: Studies in Anglo-Saxon Culture Presented to Paul E. Szarmach*, ed. Virginia Blanton and Helene Scheck (Arizona Center for Medieval and Renaissance Studies, 2008), and *Saints' Legends in Middle English Collections*, ed. with Anne B. Thompson and Robert K. Upchurch (TEAMS for Medieval Institute Publications, 2004).

Karen A. Winstead is Professor of English at the Ohio State University. She is the author of *Virgin Martyrs* (Cornell University Press, 1997) and *John Capgrave's Fifteenth Century* (University of

Pennsylvania Press, 2007); the editor and translator of *Chaste Passions* (Cornell University Press, 2000), a collection of virgin martyr legends; and the editor of Capgrave's *Life of Saint Katherine* (TEAMS for Medieval Institute Publiations, 1999), with a translation of that book forthcoming.

Jocelyn Wogan-Browne is Thomas F.X. Mullarhey Chair in Literature Fordham University, New York, and author of *Saints' Lives and Women's Literary Culture, c. 1150–1400: Virginity and Its Authorizations* (Oxford University Press, 2001). She has most recently published (with Thelma Fenster) *Matthew Paris: The Life of St Edward the King*, FRETS (French of England Translation Series) 1 and *Matthew Paris, The Life of St Alban* FRETS 2 (Tempe, Arizona: ACMRS, 2008 and 2010), and *Language and Culture in Medieval Britain: The French of England c. 1100-c. 1500* (York Medieval Press, 2009).

Stephen M. Yeager is Assistant Professor of English at Wayne State University. His edition of the SEL *Egwine* is forthcoming in *Traditio* (2011), and he is currently working on his book entitled Rewriting the *Unwritten: Vernacular Law and Vernacular Literature from Wulfstan to Piers Plowman.*

Acknowledgements

We thank the Department of English and Related Literature at the University of York for a Pump Priming Grant towards initial conference sessions and the University of California, Santa Barbara, for a Faculty Research Grant to Heather Blurton. Special thanks to Shannon Meyer for enthusiastic and conscientious research assistance. Much of Jocelyn Wogan-Browne's research on the *South English Legendary* was enabled by a Fordham Faculty Fellowship Grant for which she is grateful to Fordham University.

For permission to reprint we thank The Boydell Press for John Frankis, 'The social context of vernacular writing in thirteenth-century England: the evidence of the manuscripts', originally published in P. J. Coss and S. D. Lloyd (eds), *Thirteenth Century England I* (Woodbridge: Boydell Press, 1986), pp. 175–84; Thomas J. Heffernan for 'Dangerous sympathies: Simon de Montfort, politics, and the *South English Legendary*', originally published in Klaus P. Jankofsky (ed.), *The South English Legendary: A Critical Assessment* (Tübingen: Francke, 1992), pp. 1–18; Four Courts Press, Dublin and Thomas Liszka for permission to reprint Thomas R. Liszka, 'The *South English Legendaries*', originally published in Thomas R. Liszka and Lorna E. M. Walker (eds), *The North Sea World in the Middle Ages: Studies in the Cultural History of North-Western Europe* (Dublin: Four Courts Press, 2001), pp. 243–80; the Society for the Study of Medieval Languages and Literature for permission to reprint material from Oliver S. Pickering, '*South English Legendary* style in Robert of Gloucester's *Chronicle*', *Medium Aevum*, 70 (2001), 1–18, and D. S. Brewer for material from Oliver S. Pickering, 'The outspoken *South English Legendary* poet', in A. J. Minnis (ed.), *Late-Medieval Religious Texts and Their Transmission: Essays in Honour of A. I. Doyle* (Cambridge: D. S. Brewer, 1994), pp. 21–37. Minor changes of convention have been made in reprinting to conform these essays (including their quotations from the *South English Legendary*) to the present volume's house-style, and typographical errors have been corrected.

For permission to reproduce images from MS Tanner 17 we thank the Bodleian Library, Oxford and for permission to reproduce images of York Minster, we thank the Dean and Chapter of York.

The editors are grateful to all who responded to their calls for papers at the Leeds and Kalamazoo International Medieval Congresses of 2007 and to the Hagiography Society, especially Fiona Griffiths and Sherry Reames, for hosting *South English Legendary* sessions. We thank Manchester University Press for their warm reception of the project and their patience while it took shape, and our contributors likewise, especially Professor Anne Thompson, to whose graciousness in writing a response to the volume we are much indebted. We thank our copy-editor John Banks for his skilful and meticulous work and Judith Everard for her vigilance and care over the index.

Abbreviations

AA.SS.	*Acta Sanctorum quotquot toto orbe coluntur. . .*, ed. G. Henschen and D. Papenbroeck, 68 vols (Antwerp and Brussels, 1643–1940) [http://acta.chadwyck.com/].
ANTS	Anglo-Norman Text Society
BHL	*Bibliotheca hagiographica Latina antiquae et mediae aetatis,* Société des Bollandistes (ed.) (Bruxelles: Société des Bollandistes, 1949).
BL	British Library
CCSL	Corpus Christianorum Series Latina
D'Evelyn and Mill	*The South English Legendary, Edited From Corpus Christi College Cambridge MS 145 and British Museum MS Harley 2277*, ed. Charlotte D'Evelyn and Anna J. Mill, 3 vols, EETS OS 235, 236, 244 (London: Oxford University Press, 1956–9).
Dunn-Lardeau	Brenda Dunn-Lardeau (ed.), *Legenda Aurea: sept siècles de diffusion: actes du colloque international sur la Legenda aurea, texte latin et branches vernaculaires à l'Université du Québec à Montréal, 11–12 mai 1983* (Montréal: Bellarmin; Paris: J. Vrin, 1986).
EETS ES	Early English Text Society Extra Series
EETS OS	Early English Text Society Original Series

EETS SS

East Midland Revision

Frederick,
'National identity'

Görlach, *Studies*

Görlach,
Textual Tradition

Hamelinck, 'St Kenelm'

HBS
Horstmann

Jankofsky,
'National
characteristics'

Early English Text Society
Supplementary Series
*An East Midland Revision of the South
English Legendary: A Selection from
MS. C.U.L. Add. 3039*, ed. Manfred
Görlach (Heidelberg: Winter, 1976).
Jill Frederick, 'The *South English
Legendary*: Anglo-Saxon saints and
national identity', in Donald Scragg
and Carole Weinberg (eds), *Literary
Appropriations of the Anglo-Saxons
from the Thirteenth to the Twentieth
Centuries* (Cambridge: Cambridge
University Press, 2000), pp. 57–73.
Manfred Görlach, *Studies in Middle
English Saints' Legends*, Anglistische
Forschungen 257 (Heidelberg:
Winter, 1998).
Manfred Görlach, *The Textual
Tradition of the South English
Legendary*, Leeds Texts and
Monographs NS 6 (Leeds: School of
English, University of Leeds, 1974).
Renee Hamelinck, 'St Kenelm and
the legends of the English saints in
the *South English Legendary*', in N.
H. G. E. Veldhoen and H. Aertsen
(eds), *Companion to Early Middle
English Literature* (Amsterdam: Free
University Press, 1988), pp. 21–30.
Henry Bradshaw Society.
*The Early South-English Legendary or
Lives of Saints*, ed. Carl Horstmann,
EETS OS 87 (London: Trübner and
Co. for EETS, 1887).
Klaus P. Jankofsky, 'National char-
acteristics in the portrayal of English
saints in the *South English Legendary*',
in R. Blumenfeld-Kosinski and T.
Szell (eds), *Images of Sainthood in
Medieval Europe* (Ithaca: Cornell
University Press, 1991), pp. 81–93.

Jankofsky   Klaus P. Jankofsky (ed.), *The*
                                  South English Legendary: A Critical
                                  Assessment (Tübingen: Francke, 1992).
Liszka, *SELS*   Thomas R. Liszka, 'The *South English*
                                  Legendaries', in Thomas R. Liszka and
                                  Lorna E. M. Walker (eds), *The North*
                                  Sea World in the Middle Ages: Studies
                                  in the Cultural History of North-
                                  Western Europe (Dublin: Four Courts
                                  Press, 2001), pp. 243–80, reprinted in
                                  this volume.
Liszka,   Thomas R. Liszka, 'The first "A"
  'The first "A"   redaction of the *South English*
  redaction'   *Legendary*: information from the
                                  "Prologue"', *Modern Philology*, 82:4
                                  (1985), 407–13.
LSE   *Leeds Studies in English.*
MED   *Middle English Dictionary* at http://
                                  quod.lib.umich.edu/m/med.
MGH   Monumenta Germaniae Historica.
Ministry   *The South English Ministry and*
                                  Passion, ed. Oliver S. Pickering,
                                  Middle English Texts 16 (Heidelberg:
                                  Carl Winter, 1984).
Nativity   *The South English Nativity of Mary*
                                  and Christ, ed. Oliver S. Pickering,
                                  Middle English Texts 1 (Heidelberg:
                                  Carl Winter Universitätsverlag, 1975).
OED   *Oxford English Dictionary Online.*
OPS   Occasional Publication Series
Pickering,   Oliver S. Pickering (ed.), 'The
  '"Defence of Women"'   "Defence of Women" from the
                                  Southern Passion: a new edition', in
                                  Jankofsky, pp. 154–76.
Pickering,   Oliver S. Pickering, 'The expository
  'Expository *temporale*'   *temporale* poems of the *South English*
                                  Legendary', *LSE*, NS 10 (1978), 1–17.
Pickering   Oliver S. Pickering, 'The *temporale*
  '*Temporale* narratives'   narratives of the *South English*
                                  Legendary', *Anglia*, 91 (1973), 425–55.
PMLA   *Publications of the Modern Language*
                                  Association of America.

RS   Rolls Series.
Salih (ed.), *Companion*   Sarah Salih (ed.), *A Companion*
   to Middle English   *to Middle English Hagiography*
   Hagiography   (Cambridge: D. S. Brewer, 2006).
Samson,   Annie Samson, 'The *South English*
   'Constructing a   *Legendary*: constructing a context',
   context'   in P. R. Coss and S. D. Lloyd
                            (eds), *Thirteenth Century England I*
                            (Woodbridge: Boydell Press, 1986),
                            pp. 185–95.
SEL   *The South English Legendary.*
SELS   *The South English Legendaries.*
Southern Passion   *The Southern Passion*, ed. Beatrice
                            Daw Brown, EETS OS 169 (London:
                            Oxford University Press, 1927).
Thompson,   Anne Thompson, *Everyday Saints*
   Everyday Saints   *and the Art of Narrative in the*
                            South English Legendary (Aldershot:
                            Ashgate, 2003).

Introduction

1

Rethinking the *South English Legendaries*

Heather Blurton and Jocelyn Wogan-Browne

By number of extant manuscripts alone, the *South English Legendary* (*SEL*) is among the most popular texts of the English Middle Ages, alongside *The Wycliffite Bible*, *The Prick of Conscience*, the *Prose Brut* and *The Canterbury Tales*.[1] Over sixty manuscripts and some three hundred separate items in circulation in various textual combinations and types of books witness to the *SEL*'s presence in insular culture from the late thirteenth to the fifteenth centuries.[2] Before its competitors appeared on the scene, the *SEL* dominated vernacular production of saints' lives in the late thirteenth and earlier fourteenth centuries, and in the South and the Midlands it remained the most popular legendary throughout the fourteenth century.

There are many reasons for paying attention to such a phenomenon. But after much twentieth-century work on the *SEL*'s textual tradition and some recent increasing appreciation of its stylistic, narrative and performative possibilities, the *SEL* still remains largely outside the central canons of Middle English literature. And in spite of excellent recent work that has made hagiography much more intelligible, significant, and respected in modern literary and historical scholarship,[3] the *SEL* has received less critical attention than other works containing saints' lives, with only one book-length study on it to date.[4] In some ways, it has shared the fate of Middle English 'popular romance'. As Nicola McDonald argues, 'popularity', defined as 'the capacity to attract a large and heterogenous medieval audience, as well as [the] ability to provide that audience with enormous enjoyment', can exclude texts from serious and sustained academic consideration: it can also attract class-based social prejudice that denigrates the cultural value of popular works by seeing them as simple and addressed to simple people.[5] Our argument in this volume is for new perspectives on the very considerable ability of the *SEL* to entertain, move and

provoke thought in a range of audiences. We do not argue for a
single approach to so varied and long-lived a congeries of narrative, but we do argue for the importance of applying the paradigms
of manuscript rather than print culture in seeking to understand
the *SEL* as a phenomenon. Welcome new editions are currently
making small selections from the work more readily available:
discussion of how we can usefully conceptualize the *SEL* while
reading its narratives is more than ever needed.[6]

Any rethinking of the *SEL*, such as this volume proposes,
might well begin with its famous Prologue (which is most likely
not really a prologue at all).[7] The *SEL* Prologue is well known to
scholars of medieval literature as perhaps the most artful moment
from this large collection of saints' lives and other narratives, and,
indeed, as one of the most beautiful in Middle English literature.
It begins with an image of gardening: of God planting the seed of
the true faith in harsh ground, of Christ watering it with his life
blood to help it take root, and the blood of the martyrs completing
its cultivation:

> Nou blouweth the niwe frut   that late bygan to sprynge
> That to is kunde eritage   mankunne schal bringe . . .
> God him was the gardiner   that gan ferst the sed souwe
> That was Jesus Godes sone   that tharefore alyghte louwe
> They he seuwe that sed himsulf   so hard was mannes thoght
> That ar it were with reyn ysprenged   hit ne mighte morie noght
> With a swete reines deu   he sprengde this harde more
> With is swete herte blod   and yaf his lyf therfore . . .
> Tho bigan this nyuwe sed   somdel to cacche more
> Ac yute after this manyman   his blod ssade thervore.
>
> (I, 1, 1–16)[8]

(Now the new fruit flourishes that recently began to grow and which
will bring mankind to its true heritage . . . God was the gardener who
first began to sow the seed, which was Jesus, God's son, who came
down low for that purpose. Though God sowed the seed himself,
man's mind was so hard that before it was moistened with rain it
could not ripen. He sprinkled this hard root with his sweet heart's
blood, and gave his life to do so . . . Then this new seed began to take
a little better, but even so, after this many a man shed his blood for
it.)

The martyrs are subsequently metaphorically transformed into
knights in the army of Christ, who courageously follow their
standard bearer even to death and whose histories are contrasted
with the 'lying stories' of secular romance. These two metaphorical

strands – of seeds and gardens on the one hand, and knights and kings on the other – situate the prologue within the very best of Middle English literature. The image of God as a gardener anticipates Julian of Norwich's intuition that the servant of God 'shuld ben a gardiner, delvyn and dykyn, swinkin and swetyn, and turne the earth upsodowne'.[9] The knights on horseback draw on Franciscan imagery even while they anticipate a more secular audience by deploying – and outdoing– tropes from popular romance. 'Men wilneth muche to hure telle of bataille of kynge / And of knightes that hardy were that muchedel is lesynge' (I, 3, 59–60: 'People greatly want to hear stories of kings and of knights who were bold, but these are mostly idle tales'), claims the Prologue: apostles and martyrs, on the other hand, are truly 'hardy' and 'studevast in bataille' (I, 3, 63–4).[10]

As a prologue, however, this opening to the *SEL* is highly unstable, even by the standards of medieval manuscript culture. Thomas Liszka has shown that the *SEL* 'Prologue' is in fact referred to as a 'prologue' in only one manuscript: elsewhere the same lines are called '*Banna Sanctorum*', '*de baptismo qui dicitur nouus fructus*', 'here it spekith of the fruyt called Cristendom', or by still other rubrics, with no agreement among the manuscripts. It surely follows that the function of the 'Prologue' may also have been variously understood. Indeed the modern assumption that this is a prologue to the whole work is, as Liszka shows, a misunderstanding: in some manuscripts, the *SEL* begins not with saints' lives (the *sanctorale*) but with a series of narratives of the holy family and the moveable feasts of the church (the *temporale*).[11] Liszka suggests that the composition of the 'Prologue' was an attempt to unify an evolving work. The processes of compiling the *SEL* are not entirely clear: as Pickering summarizes:

> The composition of the temporale narratives would seem to have taken place after the completed sanctorale was already in circulation. Those manuscripts which contain temporale narratives either assemble them before the sanctorale, distribute them according to calendar date, or position them haphazardly. The original pattern seems to have been the first, suggesting that the temporale narratives were first developed as a separate cycle (or cycles) alongside the saints' lives, unbounded by liturgical models. This separateness, their unrestricted growth, and the consequent latitude in selection and positioning allowed each compiler of a *SEL* collection, help to account for the unpredictability of their occurrence in the surviving manuscripts.[12]

The function of the *Banna sanctorum* prologue, then, was to introduce not the legendary as a whole but the second section of the work dealing with the lives of the saints and their fixed feastdays (the *sanctorale*).[13] Moreover, the *Banna sanctorum* is not present in the earliest extant manuscript of the *SEL*, Oxford, Bodleian MS Laud Misc. 108 (late thirteenth century).[14] The Laud manuscript offers instead lines that announce a different idea of the *SEL*:

> Al this bok is imaked of holi dawes   and of holie mannes lives
> That soffreden for ore Louerdes love   pinene manie and rive
> That ne spareden for none eighe   Godes weorkes to wurche:
> Of hwas lives hwane heore feste fallez   men redez in holi churche.
> Thei Ich of alle ne mouwe nought telle   Ichulle telle of some,
> Ase everech feste after othur   in the yere doth come
>   (Horstmann, 177, 1–6).

(This whole book is composed about holy days and holy people's lives who suffered various and abundant torments for love of our Lord and who did not hesitate to do God's works on account of any fear: their lives are read out in Holy Church when their feast day occurs. Though I cannot tell all of them, I can tell some, as each feast comes one after another in the year.)

The combination here of 'holi dawes' and 'holie mannes lives' perhaps more succinctly describes the project of the *SEL*, since its two categories embrace both the moveable church feasts and holy family narratives (the *temporale*) and the saints' lives (the *sanctorale*) of the church year.[15]

Even without consideration of the *temporale*, the *Banna sanctorum* prologue gives little hint as to the capaciousness of the *SEL*'s interests: of, for instance, the cosmology in the life of St Michael, where 'Eorthe is amidde evene   as the stre amidde an eighe' ('Earth is amidst heaven like the embryo in the middle of an egg'), and where, given the earth's roundness, the sun, revolving round it, shines on only half of it at once, as if it were a 'candel biside an appel' (II, 415, 396 and 411);[16] a trenchant analysis of how misogynistic stereotypes work and are reinforced in the *temporale* narrative of Christ's passion with its 'Defence of Women';[17] St Benedict's rebuke to the jongleur sent to try his powers of perception:

> 'Leve sone, . . .   Kynges clothes thou has on   for he dude the
>   hider sende
> Ac a fol thi sulf hider thou come   and a fol thou sselt hom
>   wende.'
>   (I, 125, 120–2)

('Dear son, . . . you have king's clothes on, for he sent you hither,
but you've arrived here as a fool yourself, and as a fool you'll return
home.');

Nero giving birth to a frog ('lite harm   thei it hadde ibeo a
dogge', 'no harm had it been a dog', I, 273, 268); Mary Magdalene
routing the devils attending her sister Martha's deathbed:

> The o suster to the other com   to helpe hure in hure fere
> Yute heo thoghte in the kunde of blode   in hevene thei heo were
> (I, 352, 101–2)

(The one sister came to the other to help her in her fear: she still
thought of natural blood ties, even though she was in heaven).

the Virgin as the first pilgrim, tracing, in her mourning, the places
where her son had been on earth 'As men doth yute a pilrenage' ('as
people still do on pilgrimage', II, 365, 17); Christopher, the strong
man of Christianity, in the Monty Pythonesque moment when two
hundred terrified Saracen knights sent to capture him offer confid-
ingly 'Yif thou wolt, we wolleth him segge   that we ne mowe
the noght finde' ('If you like, we'll tell him we couldn't find you',
I, 345, 152); the numerous miracle stories from working lives:[18] the
possibilities are endless.

But it is too easy to pull out such moments. The *SEL* is not
a single narrative, incidentally inclusive of charming vignettes
of medieval 'life', but a framed tale collection, in which a plethora of narratives participate. Dryden's exclamation about *The
Canterbury Tales*, 'Here is God's plenty!' should be applied with
proper respect for the pacing, management, structure and desires
of the *SEL* narratives. These narratives rival the generic capaciousness of romance in their inclusion of many different registers
and materials. And yet, although it would be untrue to call the
SEL simply a laicization of hagiography (since saints have never
been owned only by the church), the *SEL* can also be thought of
alongside other great late medieval lay appropriations of material
once considered the preserve of the Latinate – such as the mystery
cycles' taking and reshaping of Scriptural and apocryphal narrative.[19] The generative power of the *SEL*'s framing idea is shown
by the constant ebb and flow of additions, omissions and new
collocations throughout its various manuscript realizations. The
beautiful *Banna sanctorum* 'prologue' provides no definitive thematic or reading key to this narrative universe, but offers rather
one possible orientation.

Indeed, no two existing manuscripts of the *SEL* are exactly alike, and the *SEL*'s texts themselves appear in a wide variety of manuscript contexts.[20] The selection of both *temporale* and *sanctorale* narratives varies from manuscript to manuscript, and although *temporale* and *sanctorale* together might be imagined to form a cycle of Christian history from its beginnings and one continued on through the lives of its most important saints, no extant manuscript of the *SEL* demonstrates this 'complete' form. (The idea that the Christian cycle should be the most perfect instantiation of the *SEL* may then appear evident to us only with the benefit of hindsight.)

Moreover, the apparent miscellaneity with which some manuscripts include saints' lives of varying form and provenance along with *SEL* texts points to a further dimension where, for medieval audiences at least, the boundaries of the *SEL* are indistinct. Alongside its *SEL* texts, London, BL MS Harley 2250, for instance, contains the sole medieval text of *St Erkenwald*. That *St Erkenwald*, although found uniquely among *SEL* lives, is not considered to belong to this work but is sometimes attributed to the poet of *Pearl* and *Sir Gawain and the Green Knight* raises the issue of style and prosody as defining features of the *SEL*. *St Erkenwald* is written in an unrhymed alliterative line, while the *SEL* texts are distinguished by their predominant if not exclusive use of a loose, long, seven-stress (septenary) line in rhyming couplets.[21] Being neither alliterative verse nor syllabic French-influenced verse (such as Chaucer's), the *SEL* is rarely treated in studies of prosody, but this manuscript evidence suggests that medieval audiences may not have made so sharp a distinction between the value of these metres. However, the varied narratives of the *SEL* in fact are beautifully suited to reading aloud and to semi-dramatic performance: the septenary couplet drives the narrative insistently onwards but with considerable flexibility in the run of stressed and unstressed syllables across its seven beats and mid-line caesura.[22]

If the prosody of the *SEL* has been little studied, more attention has been given to dating the work. In spite of Görlach's *tour de force* in examining the manuscripts and reconstructing the development of the *SEL* and the revisions to his conclusions by other scholars, no closer general agreement than 'late thirteenth century' (1270–80, sometimes 1290s) for the period of its conception and initial development has been possible.[23] So too, no precise place of origin is known, though a general provenance for the legendary is usually agreed to be the south-west of England – hence the work's title – and specifically the area of Gloucester or Worcester.

Authorship and audience are the subject of continuing discussion. Modern scholarship's candidates for authors have included religious in several of the monastic orders, as well as secular clerics, and, possibly, an original author, sometimes identified as Robert of Gloucester, who either himself revised, or whose work was revised at an early stage in the manuscript history, by someone with a knowledge of the influential Latin *Golden Legend* (the *Legenda aurea* of c. 1260, by Jacobus de Voragine, Bishop of Genoa).[24] The earliest scholarship on the *SEL* posited a liturgical function for the work: subsequent studies have called this assumption into question, noting the length of some of the legends and their unsuitability for reading aloud in a single church service, the lack of certain universally venerated saints and the collection's adherence to the calendar, rather than the liturgical, year.[25] Nevertheless, a monastic provenance has traditionally been assumed, although an origin among the friars, whether Franciscan or Dominican, has also been proposed. The inclusion of lives of St Francis and St Dominic in the *SEL*, as well as the association of their mendicant orders with popular preaching, has been adduced in support of this claim.[26] An audience composed chiefly of lay persons with an appetite for such preaching, or perhaps of nuns, has generally been assumed for the collection, and, while the *SEL*'s perceived neglect of theological discussion in favour of quick dialogue and dramatic action, as well as the collection's vernacularity, have been adduced in favour of a lay audience, the work cannot be limited to one.[27] Annie Samson has suggested that the collection was intended for 'regional gentry and perhaps secular clergy, and designed either for individual reading or for reading in the chamber', in other words, for the same audience that consumed romance.[28] This analysis suggests that the collection was intended for enjoyment, as well as for education.[29]

In the interpretative criticism of the legendary there has often been a focus on vernacularity, nationalism and populism in the *SEL*. The work supplements its selection of saints with increasing numbers of English and British saints, especially in its later manuscripts, and is often discussed by critics as a nationalizing legendary. Yet the *Banna sanctorum* prologue's implicit emphasis on the universality of the Christian struggle through its crusading imagery suggests that at least one contemporary understanding of the work saw it as having little to do with the Englishness often celebrated by critics as its particular feature.[30] Though the *SEL* frequently locates territories and protagonists as English, the work does not use prologue topoi of linguistic nationalizing (for that matter, like many texts of the period, its lexis is frequently the product of interchange between French and English, and it routinely deploys French vocabulary in both marked and everyday usages).[31] While some modern scholars insist that the *SEL* is purposefully complicit with the ideologies of nationalism, others see it as fundamentally a regional collection.[32]

The *SEL*'s variety in its text selections and their manuscripts together with its constantly changing development suggests that the title by which the collection is known to its modern readers is misleading, as Thomas Liszka has influentially pointed out in his article 'The *South English Legendaries*'.[33] In comparison with the glamour of its chief competitor, the *Golden Legend*, the very title 'South English Legendary' positions the collection as local, provincial, insular and rather dull, while the singular 'legendary' suggests nothing of the variety and flexibility of the contents, time and audience of these manuscripts.[34] We agree with Liszka that the texts have been done a disservice by the accepted title, and we follow his suggestion that the plurality of the work should be reflected by a plural in its title.

We none the less exploit the possibility of using a plural title while continuing to discuss a single 'work' rather than 'works'. For the *SEL* is at the heart of a question that has become of increasing importance with modern scholarship's attention to and new understandings of manuscript culture. We need on the one hand to recognize the plurality of manuscript forms of texts, together with the fact that our print-based models of authors, textual ownership, fixed textual boundaries and identicality as a value in textual reproduction are not the priorities of manuscript culture. But a response that simply said 'each manuscript is a different text' would be inadequate: as William Robins argues below, our conceptual models need to take into account the fact that there is a relationship between the idea of a given work and its plurality of realisations.

In textual criticism before the later twentieth century, variation in manuscripts was ascribed primarily to scribal inadequacy rather than to the demands and cultural priorities of subsequent readers and anthologisers. This left the author as the originator of a whole work, identifiably his or hers, but subject to degeneration in transmission. For works without a presiding author or some other means of assigning high-culture value, textual variance has tended to be equated with absence of cultural capital. Nevertheless, as Bernard Cerquiglini has reminded us: 'In the Middle Ages the literary work is [only] one variable . . . That one hand was the first, sometimes is undoubtedly less important than this incessant rescripting of a work that belongs to whoever rearranges it and gives it a new form.'[35] It is abundantly clear from the *SEL* manuscripts that this was and continued to be a work in progress. The attempt to reconstruct a textual authenticity for the *SELS* cannot deliver a controlling authorial intention: this would have lain as much in the future of what the collection might become as in where it originated. Privileging a text's reproduction rather than its production, together with the abandonment of authorial intention, an attentiveness to the local, to fragmentation, contingency, hybridity, *différance* and the disruption of high art by popular culture, is likewise characteristic of postmodernism. This suggests that the *SEL* is a phenomenon whose time has come, and that the work will repay new paradigms of study and performance.

Study of the *SEL* was predominantly textual throughout much of the twentieth century. A number of article-length studies exist, and more individual legends have been edited in recent years.[36] There is also an important collection of *SEL* studies edited by the late Klaus Jankofsky in 1992 which includes textual, literary and historical studies, usually of individual legends, sometimes as readings of particular lives, sometimes as samples of a methodology that might be brought to bear on the work as a whole.[37] The sole fulllength literary critical account of the *SEL* as a whole is the study of its narrative properties mentioned above, Anne Thompson's *Everyday Saints*, a study which reveals a great deal of the range and vigour of the *SEL*, with regard not only to its *sanctorale* but also to selected aspects of its *temporale*.

What differentiates the present volume is its embrace of the multiplicity of *SEL* manuscripts and its concern to incorporate the malleability and variance of the work's forms into questions of how to approach it. Much previous work has in effect functioned as if there were a single work at issue, its contours effaced by the processes of time and deviant copyists, but fundamentally conceived as a static form, changing principally by degeneration, or contamination (to use Görlach's term) in the textual tradition. As part of its creation of a new platform from which to encourage reading and study of the *SEL*, the present volume takes forward some key studies from earlier work by reprinting them (with some updates) and adds new studies founded on more recent conceptualizations of the work to encourage respect for and more exploration and teaching of the *SEL*. Accordingly, in its first section, *(Re-)situating the South English Legendary*, the volume reprints several essays on the manuscript context of the poem alongside newly commissioned work. Liszka's study of 2001 is foundational to consideration of the *SEL* in its manuscript *mouvance* and is reprinted here. The first study to conceptualize the *SEL* as plural, this essay reviews early editorial practice and the titling of the *SEL*, highlights the omission of the *temporale* as a prefatory group of narratives from Horstmann's and D'Evelyn and Mill's editions and the consequent scholarly tendency to treat the *SEL* as simply a *sanctorale*, and demonstrates the variations in the main *SELS* manuscripts. The thirteenth-century manuscript context is fleshed out by John Frankis's classic study of the social context of vernacular writing, reprinted and updated here. A new essay by Sherry Reames gives a fresh account of the Latin backgrounds of the work. The leading scholar of the *SELS' temporale* narratives, Oliver Pickering, has updated and synthesized two of his important early studies in which detailed stylistic analysis is used to discern different contributions to the *SEL*. Here this enlarged essay serves a dual purpose: it shows the processes at work by which the *SELS* grew and, through its close and informed stylistic study, introduces readers to the rich rhetorical and dramatic possibilities of the *SEL*'s formerly denigrated verse form.

Like most medieval texts, the *SEL* is designed for reading aloud and for hearing as much as for individual or silent reading: indeed it is a difficult text to read silently to oneself, its mode being rather that of vivid semi-dramatized performance. But this does not make it simply oral, earthy, vernacular in some kind of binary opposition to textuality: its sources in so far as they are established lie both in Latin *vitae* of saints and in the apocryphal lives of the holy family together with familiarity with liturgical *lectiones*. The *SEL* is not a stranger to textual culture in either composition or copying. Without denying the flair and immediacy so often shown in its narratives, two essays in the volume's second section, *Manuscripts and textual cultures of the* South English Legendaries, explore the *SELS'* own images of textual culture and the close allegiance of saints' cult and documentary culture (Chloe Morgan, Stephen Yeager). In the final essay of Part II, William Robins offers an important new analysis and reconceptualization of the *SELS'* manuscript situation and proposes a conception of the work that at once preserves the idea of the *SEL* and yet is adequate to the flexibility with which that idea is variously realized in the manuscripts.

Intimately linked with the question of the nature and modes

of the *SEL* has been the issue of what versions of community it addresses or invokes. The volume's third section, *Textual communities and the* South English Legendaries, includes essays looking both conceptually and thematically at the *SEL*. Catherine Sanok's essay, usefully read in tandem with Robins's in Part I, looks at the modalities of community in the *SELS*: not whether the community figured is 'England' but whether it is defined by institutions or practices and in what relation the figure of the saint stands to the community so figured. Virginia Blanton examines the native East Anglian saints of a branch of the *SEL* to argue for the work's ability to serve as devotional reading for nuns. Jocelyn Wogan-Browne argues for the importance of urban cultures in the formation and audiences of *SELS*, and Gordon Whatley considers how the highly selective *SEL* treatment of Gregory rather than Augustine as the apostle of the English reflects the *SEL*'s self-positioning over the foundation of Christendom in England.

So capacious and varied a work as the *SEL* demands study from many perspectives and intertexts, and these are exemplified in the volume's fourth section, *Contexts and discourses*. A classic study of the *SEL* as political commentary by Thomas Heffernan is reprinted here, together with newly commissioned essays. Heather Blurton identifies the discourse and anxieties of conversion in relation to the *SEL*'s constructions of Jewishness and proposes that a simple invocation of anti-Semitism cannot account for the *SEL* treatment. Rather, an epistemic shift in the nature of evidence and proof is one important discourse to which the *SEL*'s stagings of trial and judicial torture respond. Sarah Breckenridge's essay looks at the discourses of cartography to argue for the life of Kenelm's representation of the diocese of Worcester as a spiritual and cultural centre and to consider the application of mapping to devotional practice. Karen Winstead examines the disjunctions between the visual and textual discourse of sanctity in the *SEL*'s only illustrated manuscript. Robert Mills probes the Saracen identity of Thomas Becket's mother and the issues of cultural and linguistic translation in the *SEL*. Jocelyn Wogan-Browne aligns one particular late manuscript realization of the *SEL* against the politics of reformist orthodoxy in the English fifteenth century.

The fifth section is devoted to *Performance*, drawing on recent developments in early performance theory and providing sample extracts from classroom experimentation. Like the liturgy and the sermon, the saint's life is a potentially performative genre

and potentially also a performance text, and, although the extant
evidence for them in England is scarce, saints' plays have long
been assumed to have existed at the interstices of performative
and devotional practices.[38] Some of the characteristics of the *SEL*
that have been held against it in the past as evidence of a lacking
aesthetic unity – its vernacularity, its relative neglect of theological
set pieces, and, above all, its reliance on quick and witty dialogue
– all suggest that the *SELS* have a more intimate relationship to
performance than has heretofore been explored.[39] Performance, of
course, 'is less a knowable phenomenon than a "way of knowing"
in itself', and we intend here to capitalise on the ways in which
performance might be not just a medieval devotional practice, but
also a way of knowing for contemporary students.[40] A new essay
by Oliver Pickering looks closely at a particularly pronounced
form of audience interpellation, the *SEL*'s black humour, while a
collaborative essay (Chloe Morgan, Jocelyn Wogan-Browne, Tim
Ayers) discusses the issues and discoveries of performing *SEL* narratives in York Minster alongside, and in explicit relation to, the
visual narratives of the stained glass saints of York's chapter-house.
Finally, Anne Thompson, author of the most substantial work of
interpretative criticism of the *SEL*, and a pervasive influence in the
essays here, contributes a response and further directions for *SEL*
studies in an *Afterword*.

   Throughout the volume, quotations from the *SELS* have been
transliterated and given modern capitalization and light punctuation as well as modern translations where necessary, so that the
SEL can as readily as possible speak for itself: reading aloud or at
least hearing the *SEL* in the auditory imagination does more than
anything else to reveal its powers.

   Despite its medieval popularity, almost all knowledge about
the provenance, authorship and audience of the *SEL* remains provisional. There remains much work which can only be signalled
rather than carried out here. Nevertheless, as we have argued, it
is time to look at the *SEL* afresh: this volume therefore hopes to
contribute to a greater presence for the *SEL* in our English Middle
Ages and, most of all, to relinquish the quest for the origins of the
SEL, at least for the moment, in favour of attention to the highly
various ways in which this shifting narrative universe developed
and was received. Not *the* or a single *South English Legendary*
provided pleasure and instruction to medieval audiences across the
thirteenth to the fifteenth centuries, but rather, many and varied
South English LegendarieS.

Notes

1 For figures and discussion see Michael Sargent, 'What do the numbers mean?: a textual critic's observations on some patterns of Middle English manuscript transmission', in Margaret Connolly and Linne R. Mooney (eds), *Design and Distribution of Later Medieval Manuscripts in England* (Woodbridge: York Medieval Press, 2008), pp. 205–44. The figures of course depend on exactly what is counted: Sargent gives 250 for the *Wycliffite Bible*, 181 for the Middle English *Brut*, 123 for *Pricke of Conscience*, 81 for *The Canterbury Tales*.

2 Manfred Görlach's fundamental study, *Textual Tradition*, excluded manuscripts with only *temporale* texts, but subsequent research has included them (see further pp. 5–6, 106–9 below). An inclusive count gives 65 manuscripts.

3 For a good introduction to Middle English hagiography, see Sarah Salih, 'Introduction: saints, cults and *Lives* in late medieval England', in Salih (ed.), *Companion to Middle English Hagiography*, pp. 1–23; for a bibliography see John Scahill with Margaret Rogerson, *Middle English Saints' Legends*, Annotated Bibliographies of Middle English Literature 8 (Woodbridge: D. S. Brewer, 2005): *SEL* bibliography is on pp. 39–75.

4 There are useful short introductions to the *SEL* in E. Gordon Whatley with Anne B. Thompson and Robert K. Upchurch, *Saints' Lives in Middle English Collections* (Kalamazoo, MI: Medieval Institute, 2004), and by Manfred Görlach, 'Middle English legends, 1220–1530', in Guy Philippart (ed.), *Hagiographies: International History of the Latin and Vernacular Hagiographical Literature in the West from Its Origins to 1550* (Turnhout: Brepols, 1994), pp. 427–85, and to the manuscript tradition in Görlach, *Textual Tradition*, D'Evelyn and Mill, and Liszka, *SELS* (reprinted below, pp. 23–65). Overviews of scholarly discussion on the *SEL* are offered in Görlach, *Studies*, pp. 27–57: see also his ch. 6 for the *SEL*'s relation to late medieval English legendaries. In addition to exploring and celebrating the narrative possibilities of the *SEL*, Anne Thompson's *Everyday Saints*, the only book-length *SEL* critical study, gives a succinct account of scholarship on the *SEL* in an Appendix.

5 Nicola F. McDonald, 'A polemical introduction', in McDonald (ed.), *Pulp Fictions of the Middle Ages: Essays in Popular Romance* (Manchester: Manchester University Press, 2004), pp. 1–21 (2, 9).

6 The major editions are Horstmann (cited by page and line number) and D'Evelyn and Mill (cited by volume, page and line number): see Abbreviations above. In quoting from these editions we transliterate runic letters, normalize u/v and i/j, replace the mid-line *punctus* and colon by a fixed space, modernize capitalization, and on occasion modify modern editorial punctuation and override medieval scribal morphology. Six lives are edited by Manfred Görlach in *East Midland*

Revision. More reader-friendly selections have begun to appear: see Sherry L. Reames with Martha G. Blalock and Wendy L. Larson (eds), *Middle English Legends of Women Saints* (Kalamazoo, MI: Medieval Institute Publications, 2003); Whatley with Thompson and. Upchurch (eds), *Saints' Lives*. For editions of *SEL temporale* texts, see *Ministry*, *Nativity*, *Southern Passion*, and Pickering, "Defence of Women".

7 Liszka suggests that it was designed to provide a link between the *temporale* and the *sanctorale*: see Liszka, *SELS*, originally p. 257, p. 37 below.

8 Unless otherwise noted, quotations from the *SEL* are from D'Evelyn and Mill. The Prologue is also printed with glosses in J. Wogan-Browne et al. (eds), *The Idea of the Vernacular: Middle English Literary Theory 1280–1530* (University Park, PA: Penn State Press, and Exeter: Exeter University Press, 1999), pp. 195–200.

9 *The Shewings of Julian of Norwich*, ed. Georgia Ronan Crampton (Kalamazoo, MI: Medieval Institute Publications for TEAMS, 1994), ll. 1955–6 (www.lib.rochester.edu/camelot/teams/julianfr.htm).

10 Karen Bjelland, 'Franciscan versus Dominican responses to the knight as societal model: the case of the *South English Legendary*', *Franciscan Studies*, 48 (1988), 11–27; Diane Speed, 'The construction of the nation in medieval English romance', in Carol Meale (ed.), *Readings in Medieval English Romance* (Cambridge: D. S. Brewer, 1994), pp. 135–57, noting that in the Laud MS, the *SEL* is bound with *Havelok* and *King Horn*, suggests: 'We are probably accustomed to allowing this conjunction to remind us of the piety of the two romances, but we might equally allow it to suggest recognition of the romance qualities of the *Legendary*' (143).

11 These include Old Testament History (Creation to Daniel), various versions of the Virgin's conception by Joachim and Anna, and the Nativity of Christ, narratives of Christ's life on earth and the Passion, the Harrowing of Hell and the Assumption of the Virgin, accounts of both fixed and movable feasts (the Circumcision, Epiphany, Septuagesima, Lent, Easter, Rogationtide): for more detail see Pickering, 'The *temporale* narratives'; 'Expository *temporale*'.

12 *Nativity*, p. 37. The relationship of the *temporale* to the *sanctorale* has attracted attention mainly as an issue of editing and textual transmission, rather than for its literary and thematic consequences.

13 Liszka, 'The first "A" redaction', p. 409. See also his 'The dragon in the *South English Legendary*: Judas, Pilate, and the "A(1)" redaction', *Modern Philology*, 100:1 (2002), 50–9.

14 Laud's text is acephalous and so a prologue may have been lost.

15 Liszka has noted that this formulation ignores the Old Testament narratives ('The First "A" Redaction', p. 408). Laud ignores the implications of its own explanation: it does not follow the order there proposed

and, although the lines announce New Year's Day, they in fact occur in the middle of the collection (which begins with St Dunstan on 19 May).

16 Neither yolk nor white but the little thickened white mass anchored by a thread to the yolk – in French 'le germe' – is indicated here (see D'Evelyn and Mill, III, glossary, *stre* n. 1). On St Michael see Gregory M. Sadlek, 'The image of the devil's five fingers in the *South English Legendary*'s "St Michael" and in Chaucer's Parson's Tale', in Jankofsky, pp. 49–64.

17 Pickering, '"Defence of Women"'.

18 *Temporale* narratives are not often enough discussed, but see Thompson, *Everyday Lives*, pp. 129–35, on the *SEL*'s excellent narrative handling of the story of the trapped miner sustained by his wife's attendances at mass.

19 For a succinct treatment of this literature, see Pamela M. King, *The York Mystery Cycle and the Worship of the City* (Woodbridge: D. S. Brewer, 2006), ch. 1.

20 For varying manuscript selections see Liszka, *SELS* below, Appendices 1–15, and the manuscript descriptions in *Textual Tradition*, pp. 70–130. For the earliest extant *SEL*'s inclusion of early Middle English romances and other texts, see Kimberley K. Bell and Julie Nelson Couch (eds), The *Texts and Contexts of Bodleian Library, MS Laud Misc. 108:* The *Shaping of English Vernacular Narrative* (Leiden: Brill, 2011). Cambridge, St John's College MS B 6 contains only *temporale* texts (see *Ministry*, p. 8). Various *SEL* lives appear singly in other manuscript collections: for example Oxford, Corpus Christi College, MS 237 contains the *SEL*'s Life of St Margaret amidst medical recipes, a list of British towns, and Lydgate's 'Life of Our Lady' (Salih, 'Introduction', and Mary Beth Long, 'Corpora and manuscripts, authors and audiences', in Salih, (ed.), *Companion to Middle English Hagiography*, pp. 47–69 (53) and A. S. G. Edwards, 'Fifteenth-century English collections of female saints' lives', *Yearbook of English Studies*, 33 (2003), 131–41). There is a selection of nearly a hundred *temporale* and *sanctorale SEL* narratives in the Vernon Manuscript fols.1r–107r, depending on how narratives are counted: N. F. Blake, 'Vernon Manuscript: contents and organization', in D. A. Pearsall (ed.), *Studies in the Vernon Manuscript* (Cambridge: D. S. Brewer, 1990), pp. 45–59 (47–50).

21 Görlach suggests that the septenary line is not a hard and fast rule: 'the original texts were probably never intended to conform with a strict metrical pattern, and later scribes did not care much about the metre' (Görlach, *Textual Tradition*, p. 11). Certainly there is variation in the *SEL* between the septenary line and lines better read in six beats, as well as occasional hypermetric lines not readily accounted for by local rhetorical effects. But although the varying numbers of unstressed syllables in relation to the stresses in the *SEL* line make for highly flexible

verse of vivid aural effect, most of the verse is none the less regular. Medieval audiences may also have enjoyed metrical variety as between different lives in their manuscript collections: for example, Oxford, Bodleian MS Rawl. Poet. 225 (STC 14716), Görlach's Br, included by him among 'fragmentary' manuscripts (ibid., pp. 109–11), contains, alongside *SEL* texts, a life of Barbara in quatrains (fols 2r–5r), a non-*SEL Theophilus* in stanzaic abbacc tail rhyme (fols 11r–15r), a St Nicholas with a continuation in rhymed prose (fols 34v–42v), and a *Margaret* partly drawn from the *SEL* tradition but with a unique version of the dragon fight in tail rhyme stanzas (fols 117v–120r).

22 An exception is D. A. Lawton, in his 'Middle English unrhymed alliterative poetry and the *South English Legendary*', *English Studies*, 61 (1980), 390–6, where he argues that the origin of the line is as much in the alexandrine as it is septenary and compares it with Langland's verse.

23 Görlach, *Textual Tradition*, pp. 37–8; Liszka, *SELS*, and Robins in this volume.

24 The fundamental study is Sherry L. Reames, *The Legenda Aurea: A Reexamination of Its Paradoxical History* (Madison: University of Wisconsin Press, 1985). See more recently Dunn-Lardeau. For a review of the various possibilities of authorship by religious or by secular clerks, see Görlach, *Studies*, pp. 39–47, and for 'revisers' as opposed to 'authors' pp. 47–55; for the Robert of Gloucester connection, see Pickering, pp. 128–39 below.

25 For a summary and rebuttal of the arguments in favour of a liturgical function for the *SEL*, see Samson, 'Constructing a context'. On the *SEL*'s relation with liturgical sources, see the essay by Reames below.

26 See the arguments presented in Bjelland, 'Franciscan versus Dominican responses', and Warren F. Manning, 'The Middle English Life of Saint Dominic: date and source', *Speculum*, 31 (1956), 82–91.

27 Görlach, *Textual Tradition*, p. 45; Samson, 'Constructing a context', p. 186.

28 Samson, 'Constructing a context', p. 194.

29 For an argument on pleasure as a prime motive in hagiography, see Sarah Kay, 'The sublime body of the martyr: violence in early romance saints' lives', in Richard W. Kaeuper (ed.), *Violence in Medieval Society* (Woodbridge: Boydell Press, 2000), pp. 3–20.

30 Moreover, the *SEL* contrasts with many of its contemporary texts, which play on the themes of Englishness and make a particular point of linguistic Englishness: for example, *Cursor Mundi*'s self-conscious address to 'Englis lede of Engeland' (Wogan-Browne et al. (eds), *Idea of the Vernacular*, p. 270, l. 77), or *Handlyng Synne*'s assertion that 'For lewde men y undyr-toke / On englyssh tunge to make thys boke' (*Handlyng Synne*, ed. Idelle Sullens (Binghamton, NY: Medieval and Renaissance Texts and Studies, 1983), p. 4, ll. 43–4).

31 A few examples taken at random in D'Evelyn and Mill include (with
    marked usage invoking a different register italicized here and French
    words used in English left in roman) *Vincent* I, 25 (priue 4, feble 5,
    apert 6, poer 7, renable 8, aposer (i.e. legally to question, interrogate)
    11); I, 28 (angwise 106, poer 108; I, 29 criant 128, cheisil 131); *Brigid*
    I, 43 (perche 171, angwisse 231); *Agase* I, 55 (gent and freo 37, fran-
    chise 39, swagi 44 (AN suager); *Oswald* I, 72 (per 31, dignete 40), I,
    73 (trauaille 75), *Patrick* I, 89 (*beu frere* 103, 166, *bel amy* 199, sanfaille
    206, *Beu frere* 565), I, 105 (Sire merci 655, *beu frere* 659, *Beu frere* 679);
    Mary of Egypt I, 136 (semlant 12, prest ne queinte 13, queintore . . .
    pointe 14, hant 30), I, 138 (cotes 42, destorbance 78, pavement 83).
    The lexis and registers of the *SEL* deserve a great deal more systematic
    attention than they have yet had.
32 The majority of the English saints in the *SEL* are southern, and, while
    many of them had national or international cults (Becket, Patrick),
    others are more unexpected and much more localized (Kenelm,
    Frideswide, Egwine).
33 Liszka, *SELS*.
34 The title *SEL* is not medieval, but has been borrowed from
    Horstmann's edition. Liszka notes that medieval 'titles' for the collec-
    tion seem to have been similarly descriptive (*SELS*, p. 245, and p. 25
    below).
35 'L'oeuvre littéraire, au Moyen Age, est une variable . . . Qu'une main
    fut première, parfois, sans doute, importe moins que cette inces-
    sante récriture d'une oeuvre qui appartient à celui qui, de nouveau, la
    dispose et lui donne forme' (Bernard Cerquiglini, *Éloge de la variante:
    histoire critique de la philologie* (Paris: Seuil, 1989), p. 57).
36 See n. 6 above for editions, and n. 4 for overviews of scholarship.
37 See e.g. Jankofsky: Bell and Couch, *Texts and Contexts of Bodleian
    Library, MS Laud Misc. 108*, is the only other *SEL* collection.
38 See, for instance, Carolyn Muessig (ed.), *Preacher, Sermon and
    Audience in the Middle Ages* (Leiden: Brill, 2002); Claire Waters,
    *Angels and Earthly Creatures: Preaching, Performance and Gender in
    the Later Middle Ages* (Philadelphia: University of Pennsylvania Press,
    2004); Clifford Davidson, 'The Middle English saint play and its
    iconography', in Clifford Davidson (ed.), *The Saint Play in Medieval
    Europe* (Kalamazoo, MI: Medieval Institute Publications, 1986), pp.
    31–122.
39 But see Karen Bjelland, 'Defining the *South English Legendary* as a
    form of drama', *Comparative Drama*, 22 (1988), 227–43.
40 Richard Schechner, 'What is performance studies anyway?' in Peggy
    Phelan and Jill Lane (eds), *The Ends of Performance* (New York: New
    York University Press, 1998), pp. 357–62 (360) – quoted in Bruce
    Holsinger, 'Cultures of performance', *New Medieval Literatures*, 6
    (2003), 271–311 (274).

Part I

(Re-)situating the *South English Legendary*

2

The *South English Legendaries*

Thomas R. Liszka

Most scholars are familiar with *The South English Legendary* as it appears in the three-volume edition by Charlotte D'Evelyn and Anna J. Mill, published between 1956 and 1959.[1] The edition is based on Corpus Christi College Cambridge MS 145 and British Library MS Harley 2277 (known by their sigla as C and H).[2] The Harley manuscript, dated about 1300, is the second oldest *SEL* manuscript and the earliest orderly text. However, because of some serious lacunae, especially at the beginning of the manuscript, and some careless copying throughout the manuscript, the editors substituted the similar, but later, Corpus Christi manuscript as their primary base text. They then supplemented it from the Harley text.

Before this edition, the only apparently complete edition was that of Carl Horstmann, published in 1887, with the title *The Early South-English Legendary or Lives of Saints*.[3] It was an edition based on the oldest *SEL* manuscript, Bodleian Library MS Laud Miscellaneous 108, usually dated around 1280. Its lacunae were filled from three other manuscripts, including the Harley.[4]

The Early English Text Society, a respected society of folk who usually know what they are talking about, published both editions. In both, the work edited is called the *South English Legendary*, singular, and not the *South English Legendaries*, as I title this article. Nevertheless, I do so to stress the existence and significance of variety among the manuscript texts of the work that collectively have come to be called by the name *South English Legendary*. I will discuss these two editions as points of departure.

I have listed the contents of the familiar D'Evelyn and Mill edition in Appendix 2.1. The collection begins with a prologue, in some manuscripts identified as the *Banna Sanctorum*. It is not so titled in the Corpus Christi College manuscript. But the editors, nevertheless, have supplied the title in square brackets. The edition is of a festial, that is, a collection of readings for the feasts of the church. Most of these feasts, of course, are saints' days, so most of the readings are saints' lives. The cycle of feasts is arranged not according to the church calendar, which begins with Advent, but according to the secular calendar, beginning 1 January. (The dates of the feasts are not indicated in the edition proper or in the edition's table of contents, but I have indicated them in Appendix 1 for reference.) There are also readings for many of the fixed feasts, such as Circumcision and Epiphany, and for the moveable feasts of Septuagesima, Lent and Easter, and there is one combined reading for the Greater and Lesser Litanies, which are fixed and moveable feasts, respectively. (I have marked in bold all of the non-saints' lives in Appendix 2.1.) The readings for the moveable feasts of Septuagesima, Lent and Easter have been placed in an approximately appropriate position, following the feast of the Annunciation, or, as it is often called, St Mary Day in Lent, and the text for both Litanies follows the life of St Mark because the Greater Litany also falls on his feast day, 25 April. The Lesser Litany, or Rogationtide, is a moveable feast which falls on the three days before Ascension Thursday. The collection then runs through the 29 December feast of St Thomas Becket and ends with an apparent appendix of texts for two 'luther briddes' or 'wicked birds', as they are sometimes called, Judas and Pilate. All texts are in rhymed couplets, usually with seven beats per line.

The D'Evelyn and Mill edition is said to be exclusively of a *sanctorale* collection. *SEL* scholars take some liberties with the terms *sanctorale* and *temporale* from the way they are used in the liturgical service books. There the *sanctorale* includes the readings for almost all of the fixed feasts arranged according to their calendar dates, and the *temporale* is a separate, usually preceding collection that includes the readings for the moveable feasts which 'move' around the calendar, in relation to the day of the week that Christmas falls on and the date of the year that Easter falls on. But, as you have seen, the manuscripts on which D'Evelyn and Mill based their edition have most of this content inserted into the *sanctorale* cycle. Thus, we use the term *sanctorale* to refer to all those texts worked into the collection of saints' lives. The term *temporale* refers to all those texts in a separate collection preceding the saints' lives, whether they concern moveable feasts or not. The Corpus Christi manuscript and, consequently, the D'Evelyn and Mill edition lack a separate *temporale* section. But, as we shall see, several *South*

English Legendary manuscripts do have a *temporale* collection preceding the *sanctorale*.[5]

I wish to use these editions by D'Evelyn and Mill and by
Horstmann as starting points for this discussion because – while
they lack the textual authority of the surviving manuscripts – they
present the texts, whether correct, corrected or corrupt, to which
most of us by necessity refer. They present our visual image of the
SEL. They are, therefore, responsible for some basic assumptions
that we make about the *SEL*. I have displayed the D'Evelyn and
Mill edition first, though later in date, because its orderly presentation of texts makes for a clearer image. But I wish to discuss Carl
Horstmann's older edition of the less orderly text first.

Perhaps the most basic assumption we make about a work is
its name. Although I don't believe that Carl Horstmann intended
to do so, his edition gave the collection its modern name, *South
English Legendary*. Horstmann intended his title, *The Early South-
English Legendary*, merely to describe generically, temporally and
geographically what was in his edition, in order to differentiate it
from the northern and Scottish collections of homilies and saints'
lives, and other collections such as Mirk's *Festial*. Other scholars before him, such as Madden and Furnivall, and a few after
him were forced to use similar descriptive, rather than real titles
because the manuscripts themselves preserve only slight evidence
of an accepted medieval title.[6]

There are twenty-five manuscripts that preserve likely places to
look for a title – that is, on folia with a medieval table of contents
and on folia where one can find, or where one might have hoped
to find, an *incipit* or *explicit* for the entire collection. Of these
twenty-five manuscripts, only six preserve possible titles. But the
titles preserved appear to be merely generic descriptions of the
contents of the manuscripts, not unlike the ones Horstmann and
the other early scholars used. 'Vita Sanct*orum*' appears in two
manuscripts, British Library MSS Harley 2277 (H) and Egerton
2810 (M). The Harley manuscript also contains the expanded
description, 'vit*e* s*a*nctorum . . . & Allie Historie'. Magdalene
College Cambridge MS Pepys 2344 (P) twice uses 'Legenda s*a*nc-
t*orum*'. And Bodleian Library MS Laud Miscellaneous 463 (D)
has 'legenda s*a*nctorum in lingua Anglicana'. Finally, because of
the *SEL*'s similarity to Jacobus de Voragine's important Latin
collection, Lambeth Palace MS 223 (G) simply appropriates
Jacobus's title for the *SEL*, calling it 'legenda Aurea'. One manuscript, unique in containing exclusively *temporale* texts, St John's

College Cambridge MS 28 (I), refers to its collection simply as 'temporale in Anglicis'.[7]

Given the manuscript evidence then, or the lack thereof, we are intrigued to find Horstmann's footnote to the very first sentence of the Introduction to his edition. In it, he states that 'The Title of the complete collection was perhaps the *Mirrour of Saints' Lives*'.[8] None of the surviving manuscripts preserves this title, but one might fancy that the nineteenth-century editor was aware of some subsequently lost medieval reference to the collection, which he would reveal at a later date. Horstmann apparently intended to edit all the manuscripts known to him and to write a comprehensive introduction in the last volume.[9] Alas, he did not fulfil that intention. But perhaps had he done so, in his final volume, the long-lost reference to a *Mirrour of Saints' Lives* would be revealed, and, quite possibly along with it, Fermat's proof for his last theorem. But, this flight of fancy aside, in the absence of any manuscript authority for the *Mirrour of* title, we must conclude that Horstmann was merely making a harmless speculation on the analogy of similar medieval works with *Mirrour* or *Speculum* in their titles.

Now, while I am not aware that any subsequent scholar has ever referred to the collection as the *Mirrour of Saints' Lives*, the title *South English Legendary*, taken from Horstmann's title for his edition, has gradually, but completely, caught on. In 1886, the year before Horstmann's edition, F. J. Furnivall referred to Horstmann's forthcoming work as the 'Early English *Lives of Saints*'.[10] In 1901, George McKnight still referred to the collection as 'the Southern Cycle'.[11] And in 1916, John Edwin Wells used the terms 'The Southern Legend Collection' and 'The Southern Legendary' in his *A Manual of the Writings in Middle English*.[12] But references to anything other than the *South English Legendary* or *SEL* after that are rare. The title, of course, was confirmed when Charlotte D'Evelyn and Anna J. Mill entitled their edition simply *The South English Legendary*, without comment or disclaimer. We might note that, in J. Burke Severs's updating of Wells's *Manual*, the names *South English Legendary* and *SEL* appear regularly in place of Wells's generic descriptions.[13] And of course Manfred Görlach in the most extensive modern study of the work and its manuscripts, *The Textual Tradition of the South English Legendary*, uses that name exclusively.

Now the adoption of the name *South English Legendary* may seem like a mere historical curiosity, but with a name comes an identity.

After Horstmann's edition, the collection was no longer merely a group of individual items. It was a whole. Previous editors and Horstmann himself had published various individual *SEL* items (for lack of another name) from the Laud Miscellaneous 108 and other manuscripts. But now for the first time a collection, appearing complete, was published. It could be identified, considered and discussed as a thing with a name, albeit modern. Now I do not mean to suggest that D'Evelyn, Mill, Severs, Görlach and other modern scholars were or are unaware that the *South English Legendary* is a modern title; they certainly are so. Nevertheless, their treatment of the work has been influenced by the identity implicit in that name.

Especially significant to the formation of that identity was Horstmann's decision to exclude certain items from his edition. Appendix 2.2 contains a summarized list of contents for the Laud Miscellaneous 108 manuscript. (In the appendix, summarized contents are identified with italic capitals.) We can be fairly certain that at the beginning of the manuscript seven items have been lost because the items are numbered throughout, beginning with item number 8. The first surviving piece is a fragment of a poem on the *Ministry and Passion of Christ*, which begins and ends imperfectly. Then, in a separate quire, a narrative on the *Infancy of Christ* follows.

After these two texts comes the manuscript's important, but puzzling *sanctorale* collection. (In this appendix and the next several, I use a dotted line to show the place where the *sanctorale* collection begins.) The *sanctorale* of this manuscript has a number of texts, preserved in earlier versions than the more familiar ones available in the D'Evelyn and Mill edition. Also, as has often been noted, although the Laud *sanctorale* appears disorganized, it has a unique prologue located not at the beginning of the collection but in the middle. (Its position cannot be accounted for by a simple misbinding of quires.) Despite its position, the prologue describes an organization according to the calendar year. This organization is not realized in the manuscript as a whole, but there are some clusters of texts that preserve some vestiges of a calendar order. The manuscript ends with some religious didactic works, two romances, three appended saints' lives, the poem 'Somer Soneday', and some assorted scribbles and fragments.[14]

Appendix 2.2 also shows which items Horstmann included in his edition and which ones he excluded. The exclusions are highlighted in bold. For most of the excluded texts, such as the romances *Havelok the Dane* and *King Horn,* Horstmann's decision to exclude is easily defended. On the other hand, the exclusion of the first two items, the *Ministry and Passion* fragment and the poem on the *Infancy of Christ,* seems significant. For these two poems appear to represent remnants of a *temporale* section. And if the *temporale* also included the seven lost items, it would have been of substantial size.[15]

In addition to Laud Miscellaneous 108, there are five other *SEL* manuscripts in which a *temporale* collection precedes a *sanctorale.* But this arrangement of *SEL* texts is not now represented in any edition. British Library MS Egerton 1993 (E) is a good example (Appendix 2.3). Preceding the *Banna Sanctorum,* the first item in the *sanctorale,* we find the *Old Testament History,* a poem that begins with the Creation and Fall and then follows with the stories of important patriarchs and prophets, in this manuscript running from Adam through Habakkuk. After that comes the *Abridged Life of Christ,* a poem on the *Conception of Mary,* and the *Expanded Nativity* version of the *Nativity of Mary and Christ* poem that appears in some other *SEL* manuscripts.

None of the manuscripts beginning with a *temporale* section has the same poems in the same order, but, as you look at them, certain similarities emerge. For example, Trinity College Cambridge Manuscript 605 (R) (Appendix 2.4) has the *Old Testament History* followed again by material associated with Jesus and Mary before the *Banna Sanctorum.* In this manuscript, the beginning of the *Abridged Life of Christ* and one of the Miracles of our Lady, a text that in other manuscripts usually appears in the *sanctorale,* precede the *sanctorale* cycle. On the other hand, some *temporale* items – the conclusion of the *Abridged Life of Christ,* the poem on the *Nativity of Mary and Christ,* and the *Trinity Conception of Mary* – have been worked into the *sanctorale* cycle in December contexts, where they appear to have functioned as texts for Christmas and the Feast of the Conception (25 and 8 December, respectively). And a small portion of the *Ministry and Passion* poem was appended to the collection.

Lambeth Palace 223 (G) (Appendix 2.5) begins atypically with the *temporale* poems on the moveable feasts, which in other manuscripts often appear in the *sanctorale* cycle. It then, however, reverts to the familiar pattern: *Old Testament History,* followed by material of one sort or another on the lives of Christ and Mary, preceding the *sanctorale* cycle.

Two other manuscripts have vestiges of the same order (Appendices 2.6 and 2.7). Each begins with the *Old Testament*

History. The Vernon manuscript (V) follows with the *Vernon Life of Mary* before the *sanctorale*, and Winchester College MS 33a (W) follows its *Old Testament History* with the lives of Pilate and Judas, which frequently appear among texts on Christ's passion, whether presented in *temporale* or *sanctorale* contexts.

And finally, the unique manuscript exclusively composed of *temporale* texts, St John's College Cambridge MS 28 (I) (Appendix 2.8), begins familiarly with the *Old Testament History*, includes the *Nativity of Mary and Christ* and the *Ministry and Passion* poems, and supplements the passion story with the St Longinus and Pilate *vitae*, and the stories of *The Harrowing of Hell and the Destruction of Jerusalem*. The collection is completed with the moveable feasts *temporale*.

The variety among the various *temporale* collections would even today make it difficult, perhaps impossible, for an editor to select one particular collection, if that editor hoped to present a definitive *South English temporale* collection. Nevertheless, it should have been apparent to Horstmann that in many manuscripts some *temporale* collection – with a basic chronological order of *Old Testament History*, followed by material from the lives of Christ and Mary – was clearly part of the complete literary work – by whatever title that work should be called.

If we pay attention to how scribes and readers have referred to these *temporale* texts in the manuscripts – in marginal titles, running titles and titles appearing in lists of contents and in the other marginal indexes to the content of the texts – we will find even more evidence of the homogeneity of the *temporale* and *sanctorale* collections. The medieval reader appears to have accepted the *temporale* texts as much the same kind of thing as the *sanctorale* texts.

Appendix 2.9 shows the contents of Trinity College Cambridge MS 605 (R) again, this time emphasizing its *temporale* collection. The appendix also identifies the titles given in the manuscript for the various texts. It has both running titles and some marginal titles, and there are two lists of contents at the end of the manuscript. Only the first was completed. Its relevant titles appear here in the third column. The middle column has the titles that we find in the body of the manuscript. There, the text that we refer to as *Old Testament History* is identified as several continuous texts with the titles: 'Adam & Eve', 'Noe', 'Abraham', 'Iacob', 'Ioseph', 'Moyses', 'Dauid', 'Salamon', 'Roboam' and 'Daniel'. The selection from the *Abridged Life of Christ* has the title '*Salutatio Marie*'.

Most of these titles appearing in or with the text also appear in the completed list of contents. However, we find there additional references to 'Isaac', 'Sampson', 'Saul', 'Absolon', 'Helise' (that is, Elisha) and 'Helie' (that is, Elijah).[16]

It seems clear that, while the audience probably recognized smaller units and separate sections in the manuscript, they also saw a unity to the whole. They recognized the *temporale* and *sanctorale* as one continuous series of *vitae* of holy people: those living before Christ and Mary, Christ and Mary themselves, and those living after Christ and Mary. Note by comparison that in the margins, running title and list of contents of the *sanctorale* the saints are referred to simply as 'Hillary', 'Wolston', 'Fabian' etc. – not as 'St Hillary', 'St Wolston', 'St Fabian' etc. Thus, the presentations of two groups of holy people are as closely assimilated as they can be.

This manuscript is not alone in its homogeneous presentation of the *temporale* and *sanctorale* texts. Lambeth Palace 223 is also a good example (Appendix 2.10). There is no medieval list of contents, but running titles are used throughout, and marginal titles are frequent (although other referential marginalia are sometimes indistinguishable from the latter). After the manuscript's atypical beginning with the moveable feasts, the scribe gives an especially complete titling or indexing of the *Old Testament History*, using the names of the main characters. The names of 'Loth', 'Esau', 'Iosue', 'Gedeon', 'Ionathas', 'Nathan', 'Ieroboam' and 'Ionas' are added to those we noted in the previous manuscript. In the next part of the manuscript, we find a selection entitled 'Ierome'. At first glance, the selection might seem chronologically inappropriate, in a place where we expect material from the life of Christ and Mary. However, 'Ierome' is a small stand-alone portion of the *Abridged Life of Christ*. Furthermore, although it would better fit the pattern for which I am arguing if Christ's or Mary's name had been used in the title, we should at least note that the content is referred to by the name of a person, the author Jerome, rather than by the thematic title, the 'Fifteen Signs of Judgment', as the text is also called. The texts following 'Ierome' all do include either Christ, Jesus or Mary in their titles.

Winchester College MS 33a's (W) brief selection of *Old Testament History* texts has interlinear or marginal titles (Appendix 2.11). Included are the expected 'Vita de Adam', 'Noe', 'Abraham' and 'Joseph' texts. The text identifying 'Rebecca' as a central character spans the units usually referred to as 'Isaac', 'Jacob', and 'Esau' in the other manuscripts. The unique title suggests that the compiler exercised some subjective judgement as to who the main character in the text was. Nevertheless, the compiler still presents the text as the story of somebody. The 'Vita Pilati' and 'De Iuda Scarioth' are appropriate parts of the story of Christ's passion, which is composed of stories of bad people, as well as good. The pattern continues in the *sanctorale* where the first three titles are 'Vita Sancti Oswaldi', 'Vita Sancti Edwardi regis Anglie' and 'Vita Sancti Cuthberti episcopi'.

I have not supplied an appendix showing the titles used in British Library MS Egerton 1993 (E) and St John's College Cambridge MS 28 (I) because they are exceptions to the pattern. The Egerton manuscript has only one marginal title similar to the ones I have been discussing, the title 'Liber Salamou*n*'. Instead, there are many marginal statements of reference, such as 'Portam auream' and 'Fuit in die Herodes rex'. These do not seem intended as titles. They can appear almost anywhere, and they are usually not near large capitals. Still, the presentation in the *sanctorale* is like that of the *temporale*. No titles accompany the saints' lives. Instead, there are merely reference statements such as 'Mirac*ulu*m', 'Narratio', and 'Lamentatio' next to the text.

The St John's *temporale* manuscript (I) also uses few names of main characters as titles of texts. Instead, 'De creacione mundi' appears to be the main title of the *Old Testament History*, and much annotation and other indexing, such as 'Adam accepit pomum' and 'Nudi erant', appear in the margins. However, a possible title, 'Abraham', does appear next to a major capital at the beginning of his episode, and 'Isakar Ioachym et Anna' (or simply 'Ioachym et Anna', since there is a large space between the words 'Isakar' and 'Ioachym') appears as a title for the *Nativity of Mary and Christ*.

Finally, the Vernon manuscript (V) is deceptive (Appendix 2.12). There are no titles in the collection proper, but there is a large index to the huge book's collection. It appears at first glance to use people's names as titles for the items in the *temporale* only exceptionally. The collection begins with 'de creacione coeli & terre & de aliis operibus sex dierum'. Most titles after that are in English and descriptive of the action, such as 'Hou the devel bygylede Eve' and 'Of the deth of Moyses'. Nevertheless, although they appear to be in the minority, we still find used as titles almost all of the names that we are used to finding. (These appear in bold.) Included are 'Of noe', 'Oof abraham', 'Of Ysaac', 'Of Iacob', 'Off Sampson', 'Of Saul', 'Of Dauid', 'Of Ieroboam', 'Of Helye', 'Of Daniel', 'Of Abacuc the profete', 'Of Ioachim and of Anna' and again 'Of anna'.[17] In all probability then, the compiler of the index started from a list of names used as titles, but then supplemented it in an extremely thorough fashion.

Given then these three facts – the common core and arrangement of *temporale* texts in the manuscripts that have them, the number of manuscripts that begin with or otherwise preserve a separate *temporale* collection, and the consistency of presentation between the *sanctorale* and *temporale* texts – Horstmann's decision not to include the two *temporale* texts beginning the Laud manuscript in his edition of the *Early South–English Legendary* may seem surprising. (See Appendix 2.2 again.) Horstmann knew and, in fact, had described the contents of all but one of these manuscripts. Only the Winchester manuscript was unknown to him.

He also knew that, in the Laud manuscript, at least the first of the two texts in question, the *Ministry and Passion* fragment, was related to the collection he was editing. For in his 'List of Contents' of the Laud manuscript, he specifically identified that first text as a 'fragment of the Temporale'.[18] Indeed, Horstmann had described the contents of this manuscript several times previous to his 1887 *Early South-English Legendary* edition. And, in every instance, the first sixty-one items, including these first two texts and running through to St Hippolitus, were listed and considered together as one continuous work. He did so in 1872, again in 1873, and again in 1875.[19] This last time, he stated explicitly

Ms. *Laud 108* enthält bis *fol. 198* die Hauptmasse der Legenden, im Ganzen *61*, darauf drei religiöse Gedichte, die Epen *Havelok* und *King Horn*, dann *fol. 238b* drei weitere Legenden von einer spätern Hand des 15. Jhdts.

(Ms Laud 108 contains up to folio 198 the main part of the legends, sixty-one in all, after that three religious poems, the heroic poems *Havelok* and *King Horn*, then following folio 238b three further legends in a later hand of the fifteenth century.)[20]

Well then, if these first two items were among the sixty-one items he considered to make up 'the main part of the legends', why did Horstmann exclude them from his edition of the 'Legendary'?

One might speculate that he excluded the first item, *Ministry and Passion*, because it was a fragment, which would therefore have made an awkward beginning for his edition. Had he wanted to include the poem, it would have been possible for him to fill its lacunae since the St John's College Cambridge manuscript preserves a complete version of the poem. (He did supply very long passages of the Dunstan, Austin, Brendan, Nicholas, Eustace and Edmund of Abingdon texts from four other manuscripts.) But then, he would have the embarrassing situation of an edition of the Laud text beginning with several pages of text from another manuscript. Furthermore, he could not supply the seven items lost before this first surviving text.

Another possibility is that Horstmann had previously published editions of several of the omitted items. He published *King Horn* in 1872 and the *Sayings of St Bernard* and the *Vision of St Paul* in 1874, both in *Archiv für das Studium der Neueren Sprachen und Literaturen*. As parts of books, he published the *Ministry and Passion*, under the title *Leben Jesu*, in 1873, and the *Infancy of Christ*, under the title *Kindheit Jesu*, in 1875.[21] So the availability of these texts elsewhere in print may have helped to justify his decision to make this an edition of the *sanctorale* only.[22]

To speculate further and, perhaps, more wildly, it is possible that Horstmann was under some pressure to limit the material in the edition. Almost every scholar who reads his introduction will pause to note Horstmann's long and curious defence of his undertaking. Clearly some negativism must have inspired his statement, which begins: 'I know that most Englishmen consider it not worth while to print all these Legends; I know they regard them as worthless stuff, without any merit.'[23] But most scholars are not aware of a similar disparaging attitude towards the project, expressed by Horstmann's series editor, F. J. Furnivall. In EETS editions published prior to Horstmann's edition, Furnivall described various recently published and forthcoming editions in the EETS series. These descriptions do not accompany later reprints of EETS editions. One version of Furnivall's statement reads:

> The Subscribers to the Original Series must be prepared for the issue of the whole of the Early English *Lives of Saints*, sooner or later. The Society cannot leave out any of them, even though some are dull. The Sinners would doubtless be much more interesting.

Now there is some intentional tongue-in-cheek here, also evidenced elsewhere in Furnivall's statement, and, to his credit, Furnivall concedes some value to the saints' lives. He especially evokes that great justification of most nineteenth-century editions of medieval English literature, that is, the obtaining of *linguistic* information:

> But in many Saints' Lives will be found interesting incidental details
> of our forefathers' social state, and all are worthful for the history of
> our language. The Lives may be lookt on as the religious romances
> or story-books of their period.[24]

Nevertheless, Furnivall's labouring to find an appropriate justification for the work might support the speculation that Horstmann
had some encouragement to limit the size of his edition, while still
presenting a selection that could be defended as complete.

Probably though, the least fanciful and simplest explanation is
that Horstmann planned nothing at all sinister, that I am overre-
acting and that he was simply interested in editing the *sanctorale*
only. Many other editors before and after him have chosen to do
selected editions. He did, after all, give his edition the alternative
title '*or Lives of Saints*'.

Perhaps so. Nevertheless, it is at least regrettable that Carl
Horstmann chose to do so. As a result of his selection, and of his
edition's appearance of completeness, and finally of the *sanctorale*'s
becoming identified as a literary work with a name, most subsequent scholars have accepted the *sanctorale* portion of the *SEL*,
de facto, as the complete collection. Again, it is not that modern
scholars aren't aware that the name is modern and that the *temporale* items are related. But these awarenesses have not stopped them
(and here I include myself among the guilty) from treating the collection as if the *temporale* were not a part of the complete work – a
work worthy of its own name and identity, but which today lacks
both.[25]

Among the most important to so treat the *SEL* are those who are
also most responsible for confirming the impression that the *SEL*
is basically a *sanctorale* collection.

When Charlotte D'Evelyn and Anna J. Mill undertook their
edition in the 1950s, they did so at the behest of the Committee on
Editing Medieval Texts from the Medieval Section of the Modern
Language Association of America. The Committee was composed of such notables as John Edwin Wells, Carleton Brown, Sir
William Craigie and Sanford B. Meech.[26] It is easy to imagine that
the Committee and the editors understood their project as consistent with, but a necessary compromise to, the work planned by Carl
Horstmann.

When Horstmann said that he hoped to 'find my way through
this mass of materials', the numerous and diverse manuscripts

which he had been discussing, 'and to lay open the relation of the principal MSS., in the Introduction to the last volume' he apparently meant that he intended to edit all the manuscripts known to him in separate volumes.[27] While completing that plan would have been impractical, the Committee on Editing Medieval Texts saw an obvious and immediate need for a more representative edition, with only Horstmann's edition of one important, but apparently disorganized and otherwise atypical manuscript in print. They and the editors sought 'to make available for further study the earliest orderly text of *The South English Legendary*'. This was, Charlotte D'Evelyn and Anna J. Mill say, their 'whole purpose'.[28] In doing so, in preparing an edition based on the Harley and Corpus Christi manuscripts, they performed an extremely useful service: they improved our understanding of the *SEL* immeasurably. For, in most of its manuscripts, the *SEL* was not, after all, simply a jumble of texts, as the Laud manuscript may appear to be. Indeed, there are a number of key manuscripts that resemble the D'Evelyn and Mill edition, having an orderly arrangement of *sanctorale* items, and lacking a separate *temporale*. These I shall discuss shortly.

But, as we have already seen, there are also a number of manuscripts in which an orderly *temporale* does precede the *sanctorale*. Now, these later editors agreed with Horstmann that there would still be generations of work to do on the *SEL* after they completed their task. But, if D'Evelyn and Mill weren't going to edit a manuscript with an orderly collection of *temporale* and *sanctorale* texts, such as the Vernon or Lambeth manuscripts, or if they weren't going to complement their own edition with an edition of the St John's College manuscript's *temporale* collection, why didn't they at least call for such editions? One must wonder if D'Evelyn and Mill might not have recognized a need for the availability of the *temporale* collection, if there were not already in print an edition of something called *The South English Legendary* from which the *temporale* had been excluded.

Manfred Görlach's work is monumental in scope. By collating or sample collating each *sanctorale* item in each of the more than sixty *SEL* manuscripts known at the time of his study and by surveying each of these manuscripts for evidence relevant to date, dialect and provenance, Görlach has given us useful working hypotheses as to the early history of the collection and its subsequent development. If Horstmann, D'Evelyn and Mill agreed that 'it will require more brains, the brains of several generations to come, before every question relative to this collection can be decided',[29] clearly Manfred

Görlach accomplished one or two generations' shares of the work single-handedly. Nevertheless, Görlach has systematically studied only the *sanctorale* items. Moreover, in his list of the manuscripts, he classifies several manuscripts which have a single *sanctorale* text among other items as 'Manuscripts Containing Single Items of the SEL'. (One such is National Library of Scotland MS Advocates 23.7.11 (Az). It has an excerpt from a *sanctorale* item, the St Michael legend, set among various medical and astrological texts.) But he classifies manuscripts such as Bodleian Library Laud Miscellaneous 622 (Lx), which contains *temporale* items in non-*SEL* contexts, among the 'Miscellanies Erroneously Claimed to Contain SEL Texts'.[30] Again, one wonders if either the scope of Görlach's study or his classification of manuscripts would have been different if Horstmann had not excluded the *temporale* from his edition.

Let us now revisit the D'Evelyn and Mill edition (Appendix 2.1). Even though they did their work in an era when more scholars thought such things possible, Charlotte D'Evelyn and Anna J. Mill knew that they were not preparing a 'definitive edition' of the *South English Legendary*. They based their edition on only four of the manuscripts known to them, with some additional attention to the Laud text edited by Horstmann. They were simply trying to present something more representative of the texts preserved in several important manuscripts, texts whose arrangement is consistent with the plan for the work described both in the Laud prologue and in the *Banna Sanctorum*, a collection arranged according to the calendar year. The editors wished to give the scholarly world something better to work from than Horstmann's edition of an apparently disorganized text, and of course my point is that, for better or for worse, scholars have done so.

Although among the surviving *sanctorale* collections, just as in the *temporale* collections, no two manuscripts preserve the same texts in the same order, a fact which Charlotte D'Evelyn notes,[31] there are a number of manuscripts with collections or fragments of collections reasonably similar to her and Anna J. Mill's edited text. It is indeed an edition representative of these manuscripts. Of the twenty-six major manuscripts, six begin their collection with the *Banna Sanctorum*, and several of the acephalous manuscripts appear to have done so as well.[32] Twenty-two of the manuscripts, including most of the manuscripts with separate *temporale* collections, are largely in calendar order, despite some variations, breakdowns, lacunae etc.[33] Of the three remaining manuscripts having *sanctorale*, all – including the Laud manuscript – contain at least some groups of texts arranged in calendar order.[34]

British Library Cotton Julius D. ix (J) is a good example of the kind of collection represented by the D'Evelyn and Mill edition (Appendix 2.13). It is a *sanctorale* collection, beginning with the *Banna Sanctorum*, here identified, though not in the main scribe's hand, as the 'Prologus libri', and having the moveable feasts inserted into the cycle. It is arranged in calendar order, beginning 1 January. And its contents are similar to those of the edition. Depending upon how we count them, it has about eighty of the same texts, and its differences are relatively minor. Only nine D'Evelyn and Mill texts are lacking. In the cycle proper, there are eleven saints' lives not in D'Evelyn and Mill, all of them in the July through December part of the cycle. Only two texts appear in a different calendar position. (In D'Evelyn and Mill, the three parts of Michael appear together, but here the second part of Michael is in its proper calendar position, commemorating the feast of Michael in Monte Tumba. Conversely, in D'Evelyn and Mill, the Exaltation of the Holy Cross appears in its proper September position, but here the three Holy Cross texts appear together in the May position of the Invention or Finding of the Holy Cross.) Finally, as in many *SEL* manuscripts, texts that obviously came to hand after the scribe had completed the cycle are appended after the December section. Here, seven are appended.

But what kinds of manuscripts and what phenomena are not represented well by the D'Evelyn and Mill edition?

As I have argued elsewhere, because the *Banna Sanctorum* came to function as a prologue in many of the manuscripts that lack a *temporale* section and because we have become accustomed to thinking of the *South English Legendary* as a *sanctorale* collection, the fact that the *Banna* was written to be a transition from the *temporale* to the *sanctorale* became obscured. In one of two elaborate metaphors that make up the major part of the poem, salvation history is compared to a battle. When a king goes into battle, first, he sends his archers; then, he enters himself; finally, he sends his knights of the rear guard. The poem explains that the three groups correspond to the patriarchs and prophets, Christ himself, and the martyrs who followed, all going to battle against the devil. The metaphor nicely unites the three parts of the collection in those manuscripts that have *Old Testament History* and material from the lives of Christ and Mary preceding the collection of saints' lives.[35] However, in the D'Evelyn and Mill edition and the manuscripts it resembles, the point is lost.

Furthermore, in comparison to the eleven items in the Cotton Julius manuscript but not in the D'Evelyn and Mill edition, there are among the various *SEL* manuscripts more than thirty *sanctorale* texts not in D'Evelyn and Mill.[36] These deserve to be better known.[37] Nevertheless, since most manuscripts are like the Cotton Julius manuscript in that they typically contain only a small number of these legends, the absence of most of these thirty-plus texts from the D'Evelyn and Mill edition does not seriously compromise it as a representative edition.

On the other hand, a most significant absentee from the D'Evelyn and Mill edition is the piece known as the *Southern Passion*. It was derived from the *temporale* text known as the *Ministry and Passion*, probably for incorporation into the *sanctorale*.[38] The *Southern Passion* is a very long poem, which has been the subject of a separate EETS edition by Beatrice Daw Brown where it runs to 2566 lines.[39] Curiously, the poem does appear in the Harley manuscript, the oldest orderly manuscript, about which D'Evelyn and Mill originally planned their edition. In that manuscript it occupies more than twenty folia. But when they changed their plan, by substituting the Corpus Christi manuscript as their base text, the *Southern Passion* disappeared from the *Legendary*, making the *temporale* even less conspicuous in the collection. Its appearance out of context in a separate edition makes its text accessible to scholars. However, the *Southern Passion* is a poem that exists in a context. It survives in twelve manuscripts. Eleven of these are major *SEL* manuscripts in which the poem forms the largest part of the series of moveable feasts inserted into the *sanctorale* Easter cycle. The other is a miscellany in which the *Southern Passion* follows the *SEL* St Michael, Annunciation, Septuagesima and Lent texts.[40] In other words, the *SEL* Michael and Easter cycle texts are included in the miscellany. Thus, while we have a *Southern Passion* edition, we lack an edition of the *South English Legendary* with the largest portion of its Easter cycle intact.

Also obscured from view in the D'Evelyn and Mill edition of an orderly *SEL* text is the existence of largely disorderly manuscripts in which the processes of collecting and arranging were ongoing. I have referred already to those manuscripts that have an appendix of a few texts after what is or appears to have been a reasonably consistent *sanctorale* cycle. There are twelve such manuscripts.[41]

But look again at Trinity College Cambridge 605 (R) (Appendix 2.14). After the *temporale*, its *sanctorale* begins in typical D'Evelyn and Mill fashion with a forty-three-item January to July section in which calendar order is followed. But then eighteen texts follow which either were copied from sources, one or two at a time, or were taken from a source in which that kind of collection occurred. In either case, when this second group of texts was added, the compiler abandoned any hope of producing a calendrically organized finished product in this manuscript. Then follow twenty-eight items presented in calendar order from May through December, when again the compiler appears to have had an extensive orderly source at hand. The texts following next either began an appendix to that orderly source and were copied here along with the orderly content, or come from new sources and begin here an appendix to the Trinity manuscript. (Note that the Brendan and Patrick texts appear consecutively at the beginning of this section, a subject I will discuss below.) The manuscript continues in and out of calendar order, with 17 and 18 March, 9 July and 1 August, three November texts and two Miracles of the Virgin before a final series of October to December texts, concluding with texts that are frequently appended after December.

A more extreme example is Bodleian Library Bodley 779 (B) (Appendix 2.15). It has more *sanctorale* items than any other *SEL* manuscript. And it begins with the aforementioned Brendan and Patrick duo; then, after eleven additional randomly collected items, it has nine English saints in calendar order from January to July, eight November saints and one December saint in calendar order, six saints in random order, five January saints, thirteen March through May items in order (counting the Exaltation of the Holy Cross as a May item), two random items, six August through September items in order, five random items (including a portion of the *Southern Passion* misbound), twelve October items in order interrupted by one November item, thirty-one items mostly in random order but including many unique items (indicated with italics) and a long collection of popes and several English saints, nine December items in order, and finally seventeen randomly collected items including a stretch of four English saints' lives and a small November section. It is clearly not an accident that, if we ignore the randomly ordered sections of this manuscript, we see that the collector passed through the calendar twice: (1) January to July, November to December, and (2) January, March to May, August to September, October and December.

There are two similar manuscripts in which the processes of collecting and arranging are apparent. One of them is the important, but enigmatic Laud Miscellaneous 108 manuscript.[42] I submit that its relative state of order or disorder would not seem such an anomaly to scholars if the similarly ordered or the disordered *SEL* texts were better known.

For example, we can see in these manuscripts and in the more organized manuscripts having a single appendix that certain texts such as Brendan and Patrick either circulated independently of the *SEL* or formed the cores of circulating *SEL* booklets. In four manuscripts Brendan and Patrick follow one another, and in three of these (the other being non-determinable) the two texts begin the entire collection or begin an appendix.[43] They never fall in the middle of an appendix. In three other manuscripts, one or the other text begins an appendix,[44] and only once does a single text fall in a non-calendrical and nondescript location.[45] Similar observations could be made of other longer *SEL* texts, such as the Thomas Becket and the Michael texts, as well.

These kinds of facts about the arrangement and development of *SEL* collections in manuscripts and sections of manuscripts that appear disorganized, as well as the fact of alternative calendrical arrangements, beginning with Advent in two manuscripts, Christmas in one and September in two others are not available to scholars working from the orderly D'Evelyn and Mill edition.[46]

Of course, one edition can't do everything. And we touch now upon the debate raging among editors in medieval studies and, indeed, in literary studies generally. Should an editor attempt to correct and present an ideal text, one consistent with an author's final intentions? Or should an editor simply present a text that actually existed in some point in time? Nowadays, more textual critics argue that editors should do the latter. There are many technical dimensions to the argument, but most of them reduce to: how can we ever really know what someone intended? And even if we guess right on the first seven disputed readings, our having done so is not a guarantee that we won't guess wrong on the next seven, or even that the author intended the non-disputed readings, which we do not see a need to question. Furthermore, the assumptions on which the 'science' of stemmatics and the newer alternatives to it are based have been questioned.

But there is one basic difference between the editorial situation in, say, Chaucer studies and the *SEL* that, in the case of the *SEL*, makes the argument moot. If I am editing a Chaucer text, even if I despair that I never can know what Chaucer 'wrote' or 'intended', even if I don't think that either the surviving materials or the science to analyse them can be trusted, I still know that at the head of the manuscript tradition, at the top of the stemma, stands a literary genius, whose accomplishments justify our efforts, ingenuity and good intentions.

But the *SEL* is not such a work. The earliest manuscript is in such a state that, unless new materials are discovered, not even the most optimistic recensionist could ever hope to recreate the original state of the text. Furthermore, from what we can guess about that original state, it is clear that greater geniuses reside further down on the stemma than at the top. I would prefer to have recreated, for example, the *SEL* text intended by whoever wrote the *Banna Sanctorum* or the one on which the reviser whom O. S. Pickering dubs the 'Outspoken Poet' worked.[47] These were or would have been superior artistic achievements to the original state of the text. But more relevant than my personal preferences is the fact that – as we have seen – later compilers of the *Legendary*, unlike those later authors who tried to pass their own work off as Chaucer's, did not respect the genius of those who came before them. To the later *SEL* compilers, the *SEL* was an open text, one that not merely could, but should be improved, adapted, and suited to local use. As a result, there were produced many *South English Legendaries* that deserve to be better known.

APPENDIX 2.1

Contents: *The South English Legendary*, ed. by D'Evelyn and Mill

		Prologue / [Banna Sanctorum]
1	January	**Circumcision/Yeres Day**
6	January	**Epiphany**
14	January	Hillary
19	January	Wulfstan
20	January	Fabian
20	January	Sebastian
21	January	Agnes
22	January	Vincent
27	January	Julian the Confessor
29	January	Julian the Hospitaller
1	February	Bridget
3	February	Blaise
5	February	Agatha
10	February	Scolastica
14	February	Valentine
16	February	Juliana
24	February	Mathias
28	February	Oswald the Bishop
2	March	Chad
12	March	Gregory
15	March	Longinus
17	March	Patrick
18	March	Edward the Martyr
20	March	Cuthbert
21	March	Benedict
25	March	**Annunciation**
		Septuagesima
		Lent
		Easter
2	April	Mary of Egypt
19	April	Alphege
23	April	George
25	April	Mark
		Rogationtide / Litanies
29	April	Peter the Dominican
1	May	Philip and James
3	May	**Holy Cross: Early History and Invention**
4	May	Quiriac
16	May	Brendan
19	May	Dunstan
25	May	Aldhelm
26	May	Austin
11	June	Barnabas

APPENDIX 2.1 continued

		Theophilus / Miracles of the Virgin
22	June	Alban
24	June	John the Baptist
29	June	Peter
29	June	Paul
9	July	Swithun
17	July	Kenelm
20	July	Margaret
22	July	Mary Magdalene
24	July	Christina
25	July	James the Great
25	July	Christopher
29	July	Martha
5	August	Oswald the King
10	August	Lawrence
15	August	**Assumption**
24	August	Bartholomew
1	September	Giles
14	September	**Holy Cross: Exaltation**
21	September	Matthew
29	September	Michael I, II, III
30	September	Jerome
9	October	Denis
18	October	Luke
21	October	Ursula / 11,000 Virgins
28	October	Simon and Jude
31	October	Quentin
1	November	**All Hallows**
2	November	**All Souls**
6	November	Leonard
11	November	Martin
16	November	Edmund the Bishop
20	November	Edmund the King
23	November	Clement
25	November	Katherine
30	November	Andrew
6	December	Nicholas
13	December	Lucy
21	December	Thomas
25	December	Anastasia
26	December	Stephen
27	December	John
29	December	Thomas Becket
		Judas
		Pilate

APPENDIX 2.2

Contents: Bodleian Library MS Laud Miscellaneous 108 (L) and *The Early South-English Legendary*, ed. by Carl Horstmann

ITEMS 1–7, LOST	
Ministry and Passion, *imperfect at beginning and ending*	excluded
Infancy of Christ, *in a different metre*	excluded
Holy Cross, Invention, *imperfect at beginning*	HORSTMANN'S *EARLY SEL*
St Quiriac	
Holy Cross, Exaltation	
St Dunstan	
15 SAINTS' LIVES	
St Thomas Becket	
Prologue, *unique*	
Circumcision	
Epiphany	
St Fabian	
St Sebastian	
39 SAINTS' LIVES	
St Mary Magdalene	
St Hippolitus	
Sayings of St Bernard	excluded
Vision of St Paul	excluded
Debate of Body and Soul	excluded
Havelok the Dane	excluded
King Horn	excluded
St Blaise, *in second hand*	HORSTMANN'S
St Cecelia, *in second hand*	*SEL* APPENDIX
St Alexius, *in second hand, a different metre and rhyme scheme*	excluded
Somer Soneday, *in second hand*	excluded
Miscellaneous lines of verse	excluded

APPENDIX 2.3

Contents: British Library MS Egerton 1993 (E)

Old Testament History
Abridged Life of Christ, *lines 1–480*
Conception of Mary
Expanded Nativity [of Mary and Christ]

Banna Sanctorum
St Andrew (30 Nov)
St Nicholas (6 Dec)
  5 SAINTS, December/Advent
  74 SAINTS and OTHER LEGENDS, January–October
  END OF MS LOST

APPENDIX 2.4

Contents: Trinity College Cambridge MS 605 (R)

Old Testament History, *with insertions*
Abridged Life of Christ, *beginning*
Miracle of Our Lady: Oxford Scholar

Banna Sanctorum
Circumcision (1 Jan)
  33 SAINTS' LIVES, January – May
  47 SAINTS' LIVES, mostly out of order
St Lucy (13 Dec)
St Thomas the Apostle (21 Dec)
St Stephen (26 Dec)
Nativity of Mary and Christ
Abridged Life of Christ, *ending*
St Thomas Becket (29 Dec)
St Brendan (16 May)
St Patrick (17 Mar)
St Edward the Martyr (18 Mar)
  15 SAINTS' LIVES, mostly November and October, but out of order
St Birin (3 Dec)
Trinity Conception of Mary
St Sylvester (31 Dec)
Ministry and Passion, *Pater Noster portion*
Judas
Pilate

APPENDIX 2.5

Contents: Lambeth Palace MS 223 (G)

Moveable Feasts / Septuagesima
Lent
Easter
Rogationtide

Old Testament History
Abridged Life of Christ, *conclusion*
Vernon Life of Mary, *Prologue*
Nativity of Mary and Christ
Lambeth Assumption of Mary

Banna Sanctorum
Circumcision (1 Jan)
   SAINTS' LIVES, January – December
St Eustace (1 Nov)

APPENDIX 2.6

Contents: Bodleian Library MS English Poetry a.I (the Vernon MS) (V) *SEL* contents only

---

Old Testament History
Vernon Life of Mary

Banna Sanctorum
Circumcision (1 Jan)
   SAINTS' LIVES, January – December, with some losses
St Thomas Becket (29 Dec), *ending lost*
St Sylvester (31 Dec), *lost*
   APPENDIX OF VARIOUS SAINTS, lost

APPENDIX 2.7

Contents: Winchester College MS 33a (W)

Old Testament History
Pilate
Judas

   16 SAINTS' LIVES, mostly February – June, disorganized
Banna Sanctorum
Circumcision (1 Jan)
Epiphany (6 Jan)
Sts Fabian & Sebastian (20 Jan)
St Agnes (21 Jan)
  NON-SEL MATERIAL

APPENDIX 2.8

Contents: St John's College Cambridge MS 28 (I)

Old Testament History
Nativity of Mary and Christ
Ministry and Passion

St Longinus
Pilate
Harrowing of Hell and the Destruction of Jerusalem

Movable Feasts / Septuagesima
Lent
Easter
Rogationtide

APPENDIX 2.9

Titles of Contents: Trinity College Cambridge MS 605 (R)

Modern title	Title in text	Title in list of contents
Old Testament History	Adam & Eve	Adam & Eve
	Noe	Noe
	Abraham	Abraham
		Isaac
	Iacob	Iacob
	Ioseph	Ioseph
	Moyses	Moyses
		Sampson
		Saul
	Dauid	Davyd
		Absolon
	Salamon	Salamon
	Roboam	Roboam
		Helise
		Helie
	Daniel	Daniel
Abridged Life of Christ, *beginning* **Miracle of Our Lady: Oxford Scholar**	Salutatio Marie	Salutatio Marie
Banna Sanctorum		Banna Sanctorum
Circumcision (1 Jan)		Yeres Day
Epiphany (6 Jan)		Twelthe Day
St Hilary (14 Jan)	Hyllary	Hilary
St Wulfstan (19 Jan)	Wolston	Wolston
St Fabian (20 Jan)	Fabian	Fabian
	ETC.	

APPENDIX 2.10

Titles of Contents: Lambeth Palace MS 223 (G)

Modern title	Title in text
Moveable Feasts / Septuagesima	ffestes mevable
Lent	Lentoun
Easter	Aster
Rogationtide	Holy Thoresday; **Also** Rogacionis
Old Testament History	Adam
	Noe
	Abraham
	Loth
	Isaac
	Iacob
	Esau
	Ioseph
	Moyses
	Iosue
	Gedeon
	Sampson
	Saul
	Ionathas
	Dauid
	Kyng Dauid
	Nathan
	Salomon
	Ieroboam
	Elye
	Ionas
	Helisee
	Danyel
Abridged Life of Christ / XV Signs of Judgment	Ierome
Vernon Life of Mary, *Prologue*	Concepcio Sancte Marie
Nativity of Mary and Christ	Concepcio Sancte Marie
	Vita Beate Marie
	Concepcio Xpisti
	Natiuitas domini nostri Ihesu Xpisti
	Purifacatio beate Marie
	Puericia domini nostri Ihesu Xpisti
Lambeth Assumption of Mary	Assumpcio beata Marie

THEN *SANCTORALE* CYCLE

APPENDIX 2.11

Titles of Contents: Winchester College MS 33a (W)

Modern title	Title in text
Old Testament History	Vita de Adam
	Noe
	Abraham
	Rebecca
	Joseph
Pilate	Vita Pilati
Judas	De Iuda Scarioth
St Oswald (19 Feb)	Vita Sancti Oswaldi
St Edward Martyr (18 Mar)	Vita Sancti Edwardi regis Anglie
St Cuthbert (20 Mar)	Vita Sancti Cuthberti episcopi
	ETC.

APPENDIX 2.12

Titles of Contents: Bodleian MS English Poetry a.I (Vernon MS) (V)

Modern title	Title in list of contents
Old Testament	De creacione coeli & terre & de aliis operibus sex dierum
	Qualiter deus posuit adam in paradiso & precepit ei ne comederet &c
History	Hou the devel bygylede Eve How adam knew hym self naked aftur is trespas
	How god reprovede Adam and Eve ant the devel
	Hou adam gat caym and abel
	Of noe and of the flood
	Oof abraham Of Ysaac Of Iacob
	Hou rebecca sende iacob to laban
	Hou iacob wrastlede wyt the angel
	Of iosepes Swyfnes and he was sold
	Hou the chyldren of israel wente into Egypte
	Off the burthe of moyses
	How god aperede to moyses in the busk
	Hou god sende moyses to kyng pharao forto delyvere his people
	De plagis egipti
	Hou moyses yaf the lawe in the desert
	Off the prophecie off balaam
	Of the deth of moyses
	Off Sampson Of Saul Of Dauid
	Hou absolon pursuwede his fader
	Hou dauid made sorwe for absolones deth
	Hou dauid noumbrede the people off israel
	Of the coronacioun of kyng Salomon
	Of the dom of salomon bytwene tweye commun wymmen
	Of salomones ded **Of Ieroboam**
	Of Helye And hou he was rapt in to the eyr
	Hou heliseus multeplyede oyle
	Of Daniel Of Abacuc the profete
Vernon Life of Mary	that alle the profetes prophecieden of crist
	Of the feste of the concepcion of vre lady
	Of ioachim and of Anna
	Hou the angel tolde ioachym that he scholde gete vre lady Of ioachimmes offrynge **Off anna** Of the natiuite off vre lady And hou vre lady was offred in to the temple

APPENDIX 2.12 continued

Modern title	*Title in list of contents*
	Hou vre lady ladde heore lyf in thee temple
	Hou vre lady was wedded to ioseph
	De legacione gabrielis & incarnacone ihesu christi
	Hou ioseph wolde ha forsake vre lady
	Of the nativite of vre lord ihesu crist
	Of his circumcision Hou he was offred in the temple to Symeon Hou he was baptised Off the sorwe that ovr lady hadde when heo say vr sone on the cros
	Hou crist on the cros bytok hys moder to seynt Jon to kepe
	ETC.

APPENDIX 2.13

Contents: British Library MS Cotton Julius D. ix (J)
(D & M = the D'Evelyn and Mill edition of the *South English Legendary*)

		Prologus Libri (later hand) / [Banna Sanctorum]	
1	January	Circumcision / Yeres Day	
6	January	Epiphany	
14	January	Hillary	
19	January	Wulfstan	
20	January	Fabian	
20	January	Sebastian	
21	January	Agnes	
22	January	Vincent	
27	January	Julian the Confessor	
29	January	Julian the Hospitaller	
1	February	Bridget	
3	February	Blaise	
5	February	Agatha	
10	February	Scolastica	
14	February	Valentine	
16	February	Juliana	
24	February	Mathias	
28	February	Oswald the Bishop	
2	March	Chad	
12	March	Gregory	
17	March	Patrick	
18	March	Edward the Martyr	
20	March	Cuthbert	
21	March	Benedict	
25	March	**Annunciation**	
		Septuagesima	
		Lent	
		Easter	
2	April	Mary of Egypt	
19	April	Alphege	
23	April	George	
25	April	Mark	
		Rogationtide / Litanies	
29	April	Peter the Dominican	
1	May	Philip and James	
3	May	Holy Cross: Early History and Invention	
14	**September**	**Holy Cross: Exaltation**	**MOVED to Invention**
4	May	Quiriac	
16	May	Brendan	

APPENDIX 2.13 continued

19	May	Dunstan	
25	May	Aldhelm	
26	May	Austin	
11	June	Barnabas	
24	June	John the Baptist	
29	June	Peter	
29	June	Paul	
20	July	Margaret	
22	July	Mary Magdalene	
24	July	Christina	
25	July	James the Great	
25	July	Christopher	
27	**July**	**Seven Sleepers**	not in D & M
10	August	Lawrence	
15	August	Assumption	
24	August	Bartholomew	
1	September	Giles	
21	September	Matthew	
26	**September**	**Justine**	not in D & M
29	September	Michael I	
2	**October**	**Leger**	not in D & M
4	**October**	**Francis**	not in D & M
6	**October**	**Fides**	not in D & M
9	**October**	**Denis**	
16	**October**	**Michael II**	MOVED to M. in Monte Tumba
18	October	Luke	
21	October	Ursula / 11,000 Virgins	
28	October	Simon and Jude	
31	October	Quentin	
20	**May**	**Ailbright / Ethelbert in twice**	not in D & M
1	November	All Hallows	
2	November	All Souls	
6	November	Leonard	
1	**November**	**Eustace**	not in D & M
11	November	Martin	
13	**November**	**Brice**	not in D & M
16	November	Edmund the Bishop	
20	November	Edmund the King	
22	**November**	**Caecilia**	not in D & M
23	November	Clement	
25	November	Katherine	
27	**November**	**Jakes**	not in D & M
30	November	Andrew	
3	**December**	**Birin**	not in D & M

APPENDIX 2.13 continued

6	December	Nicholas	
13	December	Lucy	
21	December	Thomas	
25	December	Anastasia	
26	December	Stephen	
27	December	John	
29	December	Thomas Becket	
30	December	Egwine	
31	December	Sylvester	

APPENDIX

20	May	Ailbright / Ethelbert	**in twice not in D & M**
1	**February**	**Ignatius**	**unique text not in D & M**
19	October	Frideswide	**not in D & M**
29	September?	Michael III	
5	January	Edward the Confessor	**not in D & M**
11	April	Guthlac	**not in D & M**
		Theophilus / Miracles of the Virgin	**miracles first**

In D & M. Not in Cotton Julius D. ix

15	March	Longinus	
22	June	Alban	
9	July	Swithun	
17	July	Kenelm	
29	July	Martha	
5	August	Oswald the King	
30	September	Jerome	
		Judas	
		Pilate	

APPENDIX 2.14

Contents: Trinity College Cambridge 605 (R)

		Old Testament History	*TEMPORALE*
		Abridged Life of Christ, part 1	
		Miracle of the Virgin: Oxford	
		Scholar	
		Banna Sanctorum *SANCTORALE*	**JANUARY TO JULY**
1	January	Circumcision / Yeres Day	
6	January	Epiphany	
14	January	Hillary	
19	January	Wulfstan	
20	January	Fabian	
20	January	Sebastian	
21	January	Agnes	
22	January	Vincent	
27	January	Julian the Confessor	
29	January	Julian the Hospitaller	
1	February	Bridget	
2	February	Candlemas, Purification	
3	February	Blaise	
5	February	Agatha	
10	February	Scolastica	
14	February	Valentine	
16	February	Juliana	
24	February	Mathias	
28	February	Oswald the Bishop	
2	March	Chad	
12	March	Gregory	
15	March	Longinus **in twice**	
20	March	Cuthbert	
21	March	Benedict	
25	March	Annunciation	
		Septuagesima	
		Lent	
		Easter	
2	April	Mary of Egypt	
19	April	Alphege	
23	April	George	
25	April	Mark	
		Rogationtide / Litanies	
29	April	Peter the Dominican	
1	May	Philip and James	
19	May	Dunstan	
25	May	Aldhelm	

APPENDIX 2.14 continued

		Theophilus / Miracles of the Virgin	
17	June	Botulf	
17	July	Kenelm	
25	July	Christopher	
27	July	Seven Sleepers	
1	September	Giles	**SUPPLEMENTING & FILLING GAPS: 1, 2 or 3 at a time**
29	July	Martha	
29	September	Michael I, II, III	
6	October	Fides	
9	October	Denis	
18	October	Luke	
3	May	Holy Cross: Early History, Invention	
14	September	Holy Cross: Exaltation	
4	May	Quiriac	
15	August	Assumption	
24	August	Bartholomew	
27	December	John	
24	June	John the Baptist	
29	June	Peter	
29	June	Paul	
6	December	Nicholas	
30	November	Andrew	
15	March	Longinus **in twice**	
26	May	Austin	**MAY TO DECEMBER**
11	June	Barnabas	
22	June	Alban	
20	July	Margaret	
22	July	Mary Magdalene	
25	July	James the Great	
1	August	Athelwold **in twice**	
4	August	Dominic	
10	August	Lawrence	
13	August	Hippolyt	
21	September	Matthew	
30	September	Jerome	
2	October	Leger	
4	October	Francis	
1	November	Eustace	
16	November	Edmund the Bishop	
13	November	Brice **slightly out of place**	
20	November	Edmund the King	

APPENDIX 2.14 continued

24 July	Christina **out of place, but from a virgin section?**	
22 November	Caecilia	
25 November	Katherine	
13 December	Lucy	
21 December	Thomas	
26 December	Stephen	
25 December	Nativity of Mary and Christ Abridged Life of Christ, part 2	
29 December	Thomas Becket	
16 May	**Brendan**	**APPENDIX?**
17 March	**Patrick**	
18 March	Edward the Martyr Miracles of the Virgin: Devil in Service	
9 July	Swithun	
1 August	Athelwold **in twice**	
6 November	Leonard	**NOVEMBER**
11 November	Martin	
23 November	Clement	
	Miracles of the Virgin: BV comes to the Devil Miracles of the Virgin: Saved by Learning Two Words	
19 October	Frideswide	**OCTOBER TO DECEMBER**
21 October	Ursula / 11,000 Virgins	
28 October	Simon and Jude	
31 October	Quentin	
20 May	Ailbright **out of place?**	
1 November	All Hallows	
2 November	All Souls	
3 December	Birin	
8 December	Trinity Conception of Mary	
31 December	Sylvester	
	Ministry and Passion/ Pater Noster Judas Pilate	**APPENDIX**

APPENDIX 2.15

Contents: Bodleian Library Bodley 779 (B)

16	May	Brendan	
17	March	Patrick	
24	July	Christina	**RANDOM**
5	August	Oswald the King	
1	January	Circumcision / Yeres Day	
25	December	Expanded Nativity Extract, Christmas portion In Principio **Southern Passion, part 1**	
29	December	Thomas Becket	
29	December	Michael I, II	
1	November	All Hallows	
2	November	All Souls	
3	February	Blaise	
19	January	Wulfstan	**JANUARY TO JULY, ENGLISH SAINTS**
28	February	Oswald the Bishop	
18	March	Edward the Martyr	
19	April	Alphege	
19	May	Dunstan	
25	May	Aldhelm **in twice**	
26	May	Austin	
17	July	Kenelm	
9	July	Swithun **in twice**	
6	November	Leonard	**NOVEMBER TO DECEMBER**
11	November	Martin	
16	November	Edmund the Bishop	
20	November	Edmund the King	
23	November	Clement	
25	November	Katherine	
27	November	Jakes	
30	November	Andrew	
6	December	Nicholas	
25	July	Christopher	**RANDOM**
27	July	Seven Sleepers	
1	May	Philip and James	
29	June	Paul	
29	January	Julian the Hospitaller	

APPENDIX 2.15 continued

1	February	Bridget	
21	January	Agnes	**JANUARY**
14	January	Hillary	
20	January	Fabian	
20	January	Sebastian	
22	January	Vincent	
20	March	Cuthbert	**MARCH TO MAY**
21	March	Benedict	
25	March	Annunciation	
		Septuagesima	
		Lent	
		Easter	
2	April	Mary of Egypt	
23	April	George	
25	April	Mark	
		Rogationtide / Litanies	
29	April	Peter the Dominican	
3	May	Holy Cross: Early History and Invention	
14	September	Holy Cross: Exaltation	
27	January	Julian the Confessor	**RANDOM**
12	March	Gregory	
10	August	Lawrence	**AUGUST TO SEPTEMBER**
13	August	Hippolyt	
15	August	Assumption	
24	August	Bartholomew	
1	September	Giles	
26	September	Justine and Ciprian	
11	April	Guthlac	**RANDOM**
1	November	Eustace	
4	August	Dominic	
24	February	Mathias, **beginning Southern Passion, part 2, misbound**	
24	February	Mathias, **ending**	
4	October	Francis	**OCTOBER, with unique texts in italic**
6	October	Fides	
9	October	Denis	
11	October	*Nicasie and his Companions*	

APPENDIX 2.15 continued

14	October	*Calixtus*	**POPE**
3	November	*Vonefreda*	
18	October	Luke	
22	October	*Hillarion*	
25	October	*Crissaunt and Dariye*	
21	October	Ursula / 11,000 Virgins	
25	October	*Crispin and Crispinyan*	
26	October	*Euarist*	**POPE**
28	October	Simon and Jude	
			RANDOM, many unique texts in bold
25	September	*Firmim*	
28	April	*Vital*	
25	May	Aldhelm **in twice**	**ENGLISH**
20	July	Margaret	**ENGLISH**
20	August	*Oswin*	**ENGLISH**
24	June	John the Baptist	
26	June	*John and Paul*	
28	June	*Leo*	**POPE**
19	February	*Marius and his wife and two sons*	
29	June	Peter	
9	July	Swithun **in twice**	**ENGLISH**
22	June	Alban	
?		*Illurin*	**POPE**
15	January	*Paulin the ermyte*	
31	December	*Sylvester*	**POPE**
1	October	*Remigi*	
11/17?	April	*Anicet*	**POPE**
22	April	*Sother*	**POPE**
22	April	*Gay*	**POPE**
23	January	*Emerinciane*	
11	January	*Hyginus*	**POPE**
10	December	*Melchiades*	**POPE**
11	December	*Damas*	**POPE**
29	November	*Saturnin and Cicin*	
31	July	*Innocent*	**POPE**
30	May	*Felix*	**POPE**
29	July	*Simplice and Faustine*	
30	July	*Abdon and Cemen*	
30	July	*Ierman*	
1	August	*Athelwold*	
29	July	Martha	

APPENDIX 2.15 continued

8	December	Conception of Mary	**DECEMBER**
13	December	Lucy	
21	December	Thomas	
25	December	Anastasia, **beginning, cancelled**	
25	December	Nativity of Mary and Christ	
25	December	Anastasia	
26	December	Stephen	
27	December	John	
28	December	*Holy Innocents*	
22	July	Mary Magdalene	
3	December	Birin	
8	December	Conception of Mary, **extract**	
2	October	Leger	
5	January	Edward the Confessor	**ENGLISH**
23	June	Aeldri / Etheldred	**ENGLISH**
19	October	Frideswide	**ENGLISH**
15	June	Edburga	**ENGLISH**
31	October	Quentin	
4	May	Quiriac	
13	November	Brice	
22	November	Caecilia	
27	November	Barlaam and Josaphat	
13	July	Mildred	
11	June	Barnabas	
31	May	Petronella / Parnel	
17	June	Botulf	

Notes

1 Hereafter D'Evelyn and Mill.
2 In the following discussion, especially the notes, I make some use of the sigla established in Görlach, *Textual Tradition*, pp. viii–x, and in O. S. Pickering and Manfred Görlach, 'A newly-discovered manuscript of the *South English Legendary*', *Anglia*, 100 (1982), 109–23.
3 Hereafter Horstmann.
4 The others are British Library Cotton Julius D.ix and Bodleian Library English Poetry a.1 ('The Vernon Manuscript').
5 O. S. Pickering, 'The *temporale* narratives', and his 'Expository *temporale*'. I refer to the *temporale* texts as they have been defined and titled

by O. S. Pickering in 1973, rather than using the older definitions and titles.

6 See below.

7 H: fol. 227r (explicit) and fol. 232v (contents). M: fol. 3v (contents). P: p. [iii] (contents) and p. 1 (above first item, a title in place?). D: fol. 157r (explicit). G: fol. 297r ('here endeþ'). I: fol. 79r (explicit).

8 Horstmann, p. vii.

9 Horstmann, p. vii. The title page of his edition also identifies this edition as Volume 'I'. However, the series was not continued.

10 F. J. Furnivall, 'Early English Text Society: statement for 1887 and 1888', in Carl Horstmann (ed.), *The Lives of Women Saints of Our Contrie of England*, EETS OS 86 (London: Trübner, 1886), the second of four unnumbered pages prior to p. i.

11 *King Horn, Floriz and Blauncheflur, the Assumption of Our Lady, First ed. in 1866, by J. Rawson Lumby, and now re-ed. from the manuscripts*, ed. George McKnight, EETS OS 14 (London: Oxford University Press, 1901), p. xxviii.

12 John Edwin Wells, *A Manual of the Writings in Middle English: 1050–1400* (London: Oxford University Press, 1916), pp. 292, 317 etc.

13 J. Burke Severs (gen. ed.), *A Manual of the Writings in Middle English 1050–1500*, II, Section IV.4 'The Southern Temporale' by Laurence Muir, pp. 403–7, Section V 'Saints' Legends' by Charlotte D'Evelyn and Frances A. Foster, pp. 410–57 (Hamden, CT: Connecticut Academy of Arts and Sciences, 1970).

14 Thomas R. Liszka, 'MS Laud Misc. 108 and the early history of the *South English Legendary*', *Manuscripta*, 33 (1989), 75–91. Previous scholarship is also summarized there.

15 Pickering, 'Expository *temporale*', pp. 4–5.

16 The completed table of contents is on fol. 275r; the incomplete table, on fol. 275v. Its *temporale* titles appear to be the same as those in the completed table. However, much of its text is illegible on my microfilm copy, and I have not seen the manuscript itself.

17 Mary S. Serjeantson, 'The index of the Vernon manuscript', *Modern Language Review*, 32 (1937), 222–61.

18 Horstmann, p. xiii.

19 Carl Horstmann, 'Die Legenden des Ms. Laud 108', *Archiv für das Studium der Neueren Sprachen und Literaturen*, 49 (1872), 395–414; *Leben Jesu, ein Fragment und Kindheit Jesu*, ed. Carl Horstmann, I. Theil, *Leben Jesu* (Münster: Regensberg, 1873), pp. 3–7; *Altenglische Legenden*, ed. Carl Horstmann (Paderborn: Schöningh, 1875), pp xi–xiii.

20 Horstmann, *Altenglische Legenden*, p. xi. Translation mine.

21 Carl Horstmann, 'King Horn nach Ms. Laud 108', *Archiv für das Studium der Neueren Sprachen und Literaturen*, 50 (1872), 39–58. Carl Horstmann, 'Die Sprüche des h. Bernhard und die Vision des h. Paulus nach Ms. Laud 108', *Archiv für das Studium der Neueren*

Sprachen und Literaturen, 52 (1874), 33–38. Horstmann, *Leben Jesu, ein Fragment und Kindheit Jesu*, I. Theil, *Leben Jesu*. It does not appear that the second volume was published. *Kindheit Jesu* was published in Horstmann, *Altenglische Legenden*, pp. 1–61.

22 Of course, Horstmann also edited elsewhere the life of St Mary Magdalene and St Patrick's Purgatory from this manuscript, but included them in *Early South-English Legendary* edition as well. 'Magdalena' in *Sammlung Altenglischer Legenden*, ed. Carl Horstmann (Heilbronn: Gebr. Henniger, 1878), pp. 148–62. 'IV Das Fegefeuer des h. Patrick [. . .] c. aus Ms. Laud 108 Purgatorium sci Patrici abbatis' in Horstmann, *Altenglische Legenden*, pp. 177–211.

23 Horstmann, p. xi.

24 F. J. Furnivall, 'Original and Extra Series books, 1893–5', in Carl Horstmann (ed.), *The Minor Poems of the Vernon Manuscript*, EETS OS 98 (London: Trübner, 1892), p. 5 (of 10 numbered pages prior to p. i). A similar version appears in F. J. Furnivall, 'Statement for 1887 and 1888', in Horstmann (ed.), *The Lives of Women Saints of Our Contrie of England*, pp. 2–3 (of 4 unnumbered pages prior to p. i). For the tongue-in-cheek tone, compare Furnivall's comment on the many recent editions with German rather than English editors: 'Members will also note with pleasure the annexation of large tracts of our Early English territory by the important German contingent under General Zupitza, Colonels Kölbing and Horstmann, volunteers Hausknecht, Einenkel, Haenisch, Kaluza, Hupe, Adam, Holthausen, &c. &c.', in 'Original and extra series books, 1893–5', p. 5.

25 I refer to the *Banna Sanctorum* as a 'Prologue' in Thomas R. Liszka, 'The *South English Legendary*: a critical edition of the Prologue and the Lives of Saints Fabian, Sebastian, Gregory the Great, Mark, Quiriac, Paul, and James the Great' (PhD dissertation, Northern Illinois University, 1980), *passim*.

26 D'Evelyn and Mill, I, p. v.

27 Horstmann, p. vii.

28 D'Evelyn and Mill, I, p. v.

29 Horstmann, p. vii. D'Evelyn and Mill, I, p. v.

30 Görlach, *Textual Tradition*, pp. ix–x, 51–63, 118, 128 and *passim*. His subsequent major work on the *SEL* continues to be thorough studies focused on the *sanctorale*. See, most recently, Görlach, *Studies*, especially pp. 25–57.

31 Charlotte D'Evelyn, 'Introduction' in D'Evelyn and Mill, III, p. 3.

32 MSS DCJQTY.

33 MSS GFVSUAJCQNTPKYHODMXERZ.

34 MSS BLW.

35 See Pickering, 'Expository *temporale*' and Liszka, 'The first "A" redaction'.

36 The exact number is difficult to calculate since deciding what is and what is not an *SEL* item becomes a factor. Görlach identifies most of the items with a '+' in *Textual Tradition*, pp. vii–viii and *passim*.

37 Görlach has announced an intention to edit the texts that do not appear in either D'Evelyn and Mill or Horstmann: *East Midland Revision*, p. 7.

38 *Ministry,* pp. 33–5.

39 *Southern Passion.*

40 MSS BDHKNOPTVYZ and the miscellany Uz.

41 MSS ACDGHJ(M/Bd)NO(Q/Qa/Ba)VZ. MSS M and Bd were originally parts of the same manuscript, as were MSS Q, Qa and Ba. See Görlach, *Textual Tradition*, pp. 90, 95–7, 107–8, 115. The Q/Qa/Ba manuscript appears to have had a lengthy appendix, including *sanctorale* and *temporale* items and the romance *Gy of Warwick*.

42 The other is MS W.

43 In MSS LRB, Brendan and Patrick begin units. The scribe of Wa made an obvious error in copying Brendan. On the same folio, after 24 unique lines from Julian the Hospitaller, the Brendan text continues, beginning with line 661. Brendan, thus, does not begin a unit in Wa. It is uncertain how it appeared in Wa's exemplar. See Görlach, *Textual Tradition*, pp. 115–16.

44 MSS VZU.

45 Patrick appears in a June context in V.

46 MSS EP begin with Advent. MS Y begins with the *Banna Sanctorum*, referred to as 'De Natiuitate', followed by the legends of Sts Stephen, John, and Thomas Becket (26, 27 and 29 December, respectively). MSS US each begin with the September feast of St Michael.

47 See, respectively, Liszka, 'The first "A" Redaction', and O. S. Pickering, 'The outspoken *South English Legendary* poet', in A. J. Minnis (ed.), *Late-Medieval Religious Texts and Their Transmission* (Cambridge: D. S. Brewer, 1994), pp. 21–37 (revised version printed in this volume). It is doubtful, but unknown, if either revision was ever finally realized. It is also possible that these were the same people and perhaps the same person responsible for Görlach's 'A' redaction. See Görlach, *Textual Tradition*, *passim*, and Görlach, *Studies*, pp. 47–8.

3

The social context of vernacular writing in thirteenth-century England: the evidence of the manuscripts[1]

John Frankis

The social context of medieval vernacular literature has received a good deal of scholarly attention in recent years, but this has been particularly concentrated on the later period because evidence of all kinds becomes steadily more abundant after the mid-fourteenth century.[2] For the thirteenth century the evidence is more scanty and the whole position is less clear, and although various approaches have been adopted, much remains uncertain. There is for example still room for a study based on statements about entertainments at court or about the performances of singers and narrators (to avoid the controversial term 'minstrels') in great households; that the consideration of such familiar kinds of evidence might still lead to new conclusions has been demonstrated by Dr Bullock-Davies.[3] Another approach is reflected in the conjectures about poetic composition and performance that have grown out of the theory of oral-formulaic composition.[4] Different again is the approach exemplified in the late Professor Dobson's studies of *Ancrene Wisse*, in which the conclusions extend far beyond matters of social context, though that is involved too.[5] Something of the social context of thirteenth-century vernacular writing may also be deduced from a consideration of the manuscripts in which texts have been preserved, though it is in the nature of this material that the social context that emerges is almost exclusively clerical.

The overwhelming majority of manuscripts preserved from thirteenth-century England are in Latin, and a considerable majority of the manuscripts containing vernacular writing cannot be ascribed to any one particular milieu or place of origin; for texts in English, linguistic evidence may indicate a general geographical locality, which is important, but it can do little to illuminate the social context. For the period between the Conquest and 1200 there is even less evidence, so the position may be summarized very briefly: localizable vernacular manuscripts are exclusively clerical,

especially those in English (some later copies of Old English homilies, the *Peterborough Chronicle* and, clearly clerical though not
precisely localizable, the *Ormulum*), and even Anglo-Norman
writing that we know to have been composed in the twelfth century
for secular patrons, like Gaimar's *L'estoire des engleis* or Benedeit's
Voyage of St Brendan, tended to be written by clerical authors and
to be preserved in clerical manuscripts, often of later date, like BL
Cotton Vespasian B.x from Durham Cathedral Priory (Benedeit)
and BL Royal 13.A.xxi from the Premonstratensian Abbey at
Hagnaby (Gaimar). The *Comput* and *Bestiaire* of Philippe de
Thaun, dedicated to the second queen of Henry I, survive in a
twelfth-century manuscript from the Cistercian Abbey of Holme
Cultram (now BL Cotton Nero A.V.).[6]

There is a growing body of vernacular writing in both French
and English after 1200, and the number of thirteenth-century manuscripts that can be ascribed to particular religious houses enables
us to see that there was a concern for vernacular writing in many
monasteries, especially in some of the great Benedictine houses. In
some cases this was an inheritance from the Anglo-Saxon period:
the pre-Conquest foundations had libraries that included manuscripts in Old English, and in some cases the study and copying of
Old English texts continued into the thirteenth century: the case of
Worcester is well known,[7] but one might also mention BL Cotton
Vespasian A.xxii from Rochester Cathedral Priory, which contains
thirteenth-century copies of homilies by Ælfric.[8] Continued interest in a range of kinds of vernacular writing may be illustrated from
a few selected manuscripts, beginning with those from Benedictine
houses. Perhaps the most extraordinary of these is BL Harley 978:
this consists of thematically unrelated booklets, but with no signs
that any of them ever circulated separately (i.e., no dirt and wear
on what would have been the outer leaves of independent booklets: on the contrary, there is perhaps some indication of linking
between sections in the form of overlapping ruling of lines and
the decoration of initial letters). The first and last sections contain
indications that the manuscript was in use at Reading Abbey and
there can be little doubt that these sections were compiled there;[9]
the intervening sections are likely to have been at Reading too,
though the actual place of writing is less certain; the mixture of
hands is bewildering, but no more so than might be expected
in a manuscript from a large religious house. The contents are
varied: the first section contains music, mostly liturgical, but also
including the famous 'Cuckoo Song', which is the only English

text in the manuscript; a substantial central portion contains an important collection of Latin goliardic poems.[10] Other sections contain the French verse fables of Marie de France and, more surprisingly, her Breton lays; moreover, this is the only complete manuscript of all Marie's lays and is the basis of all modern editions. It is striking to find such courtly secular poetry, with traces of moral ambiguity and of paganism, preserved in a Benedictine abbey, and this may conceivably lend support to the theory, now generally abandoned, that the author of the lays was the Abbess of Shaftesbury.[11] A rather more conventional anthology is that in BL Arundel 292 from Norwich Cathedral Priory; here the contents are predominantly religious: the opening section contains English verse translations of liturgical texts, short religious poems and the only extant copy of the Middle English *Bestiary*; the other contents are some Latin prose texts (mostly religious, but also *Apollonius of Tyre*, the *Prophecies of Merlin* and some scientific material) and some Anglo-Norman poems, including a translation of the *Distichs of Cato*; the items added about 1400, including the famous poem on blacksmiths, do not concern us here, though they tell their own story about later medieval monasticism.[12] The Norwich manuscript thus reflects a fairly relaxed humane approach to piety, but not so alarmingly so as the Reading manuscript. More exclusively religious is Lambeth Palace MS 522 from St Augustine's Canterbury, which contains only French writings, mostly Anglo-Norman, including Grosseteste's *Chasteau d' Amour*, St Edmund's *Mirour de Seinte Eglyse* and a French verse *Gospel of Nicodemus*. This is a more obviously pious collection than either the Reading or the Norwich manuscript, and the use of the French language for religious literature is a long-recognized aspect of English monasticism.[13] Each of the main pieces in this manuscript is preceded by an illustration that relates in a general way to the following text and represents either the contemplative or the active aspect of the religious life; the contemplative figures, usually prostrate before the Cross or the Virgin, are generally Benedictine monks, but the active figures, shown preaching, are mostly friars, Dominicans in three cases and Franciscans in two: the implication, that the inhabitants of a Benedictine monastery might take a sympathetic interest in the activities of the newly founded mendicant orders, is noteworthy.[14] Some other Benedictine manuscripts have thirteenth-century English poems added peripherally to Latin texts (e.g., BL Royal 2.F.viii from St Albans, and Bodleian Tanner 169 from Chester) and in these cases the English inscriptions are likely to have had a more or less private personal mnemonic function for some monastic reader.[15]

The monasteries of the Augustinian canons are also important for the encouragement of vernacular writing. This appears in the first instance in the fact that at least one house, Southwick Priory, acquired and preserved some Old English manuscripts. A pre-Conquest copy of the Old English Bede was obtained, directly or indirectly, from Winchester (now BL Cotton Otho B.x–xi), and a twelfth-century copy of other Old English texts (now BL Cotton Vitellius A.xv, part I) was also at Southwick by the late thirteenth century but is unlikely to have been written there.[16] An early Augustinian interest in vernacular writing may also appear in the fact that Osney Abbey held what is now the best manuscript of the *Chanson de Roland* (Bodleian Digby 23), while by 1180 the *Ormulum*, an English verse gospel-paraphrase, was being written by a man who identifies himself as a canon named Orm living under the Augustinian rule, but does not say at which monastery.[17] Vernacular manuscripts held by Augustinian houses in the thirteenth century include a French translation of Gregory's *Dialogues* at St Frideswide's, Oxford (now Paris, BN f.fr. 24766), while the oldest extant collection of Welsh poetry, the Black Book of Carmarthen (now National Library of Wales, Peniarth 1), was held by the Augustinian priory in Carmarthen. The *Ancrene Wisse*, a treatise of spiritual guidance for female recluses, one of the outstanding masterpieces of medieval English prose, was long thought on theological grounds to be of Augustinian origin and is now generally believed to have been composed in Wigmore Abbey in the early thirteenth century.[18] Finally, by the end of the century Peter de Langtoft, canon of Bridlington, was compiling his Anglo-Norman chronicle. One may note in passing that Augustinian literary activity in the English language continued vigorously to the end of the Middle Ages.[19]

The role of nunneries in fostering vernacular writing becomes more conspicuous in the later Middle Ages, but a striking early example is provided by BL Cotton Claudius D.iii, from the Cistercian nunnery at Wintney, which contains a thirteenth-century copy of the Old English translation of the Benedictine Rule. This is of particular interest in that the compiler evidently made no attempt to make or acquire a new translation, but copied an existing one in a form of language that may well have posed some problems of comprehension to the nuns who were to use it; it is one of the latest extant copies of an Old English text.[20] Other thirteenth-century manuscripts with vernacular texts from nunneries are Fitzwilliam, McClean 123, from the Fontevrault house at Nuneaton, an important collection of religious poems in English and French,[21] and BL Egerton 2710 from the Benedictine nunnery at Derby, with contents exclusively in French.

Conspicuously absent from the foregoing list is any reference to the vernacular literary activity of friars: there are in fact no known thirteenth-century English manuscripts of mendicant origin with vernacular texts, a deficiency that can be only partly explained by the suggestion that vernacular texts used by Franciscans may have been written on rolls, which were much more perishable than books.[22] Among thirteenth-century manuscripts of unknown provenance, however, there are four, containing some of the most outstanding English poems from the period as well as a good deal of French material, which are often grouped under the heading of 'Friars' Miscellanies'. These are Trinity College, Cambridge B.14.39 (James Catalogue no. 323, henceforth cited as TCC 323), BL Cotton Caligula A.ix, Jesus College, Oxford 29 and Bodleian Digby 86. The discovery of the Franciscan contribution to vernacular writing, especially to religious lyrics, is largely due to a number of scholars in America in the first half of the twentieth century, notably Carleton Brown, R. L. Greene and R. H. Robbins; their work was of outstanding importance and as regards the period after 1300 it was reasonably firmly based.[23] The later Franciscan contribution to vernacular writing is obviously of great interest, and it is perhaps not surprising that the case was sometimes overstated, some poems and manuscripts being ascribed to Franciscans on rather inadequate evidence. Influential statements on the alleged Franciscan origin (or at least mendicant origin, for the Dominicans were, perhaps rather implausibly, drawn into the matter) of the Trinity, Caligula, Jesus and Digby manuscripts appeared especially in the 1930s and 1940s, and one would be content to let them lie in honourable retirement if they had not been resurrected for repetition in a number of recent publications.[24] Summarized briefly, the main arguments were as follows. TCC 323 was ascribed to Dominicans because it contains a laudatory anecdote about a *predicator*; Jesus 29 was held to be Franciscan because it contains one poem by a known Franciscan (the *Luve Ron* of Thomas of Hales); Caligula A.ix has so much in common with Jesus 29 that whatever applies to one was assumed to hold good for the other; and Digby 86 was alleged to be Franciscan because it includes a French prayer ascribed to St Francis, has a calendar that includes the feasts of Dominic and Francis among other saints' days, and because it came to Digby from Thomas Allen, who is known to have acquired manuscripts from the Franciscan house at Oxford among other places. None of these arguments, of course, can carry much weight, and underlying most of them there seems to be a tacit assumption, no doubt encouraged by later fourteenth-century attacks on friars, that no one but a friar would ever speak well of friars or take a sympathetic interest in their works or writings, so that any manuscript that contains commendation of friars or writing by friars was liable to be classed as the work of friars. Furthermore, other texts in such manuscripts might then be classed as mendicant compositions, and other manuscripts containing any of these texts, like the celebrated Harley 2253, were then said to be at least influenced or even dictated by friars. In this way a considerable body of alleged mendicant writings was compiled in order to boost the slender evidence summarized above. The argument that Jesus 29 must be a Franciscan manuscript because it contains a poem by Friar Thomas of Hales is best evaluated in the light of the fact that another work by him, an Anglo-Norman sermon, is uniquely preserved in a thirteenth-century manuscript from the Benedictine Abbey of Westminster (now St John's College, Oxford 190).[25] Reference has already been made to the Benedictine interest in friars reflected in the illustrations of Lambeth 522, and one need think only of the enthusiasm for Franciscans reflected in such diverse forms as the patronage of Bishop Grosseteste and the commendation expressed by the author of *Ancrene Wisse*.[26]

Arguing the origin of a manuscript from the nature of its contents is not unreasonable, but it is full of pitfalls and any conclusions can be only tentative. This may be exemplified in Jesus 29: looking at its contents, one is struck by the one outstandingly anomalous text, *The Owl and the Nightingale*. Whereas the other pieces, English and French alike, are devotional texts that would appeal to any pious reader, *The Owl and the Nightingale* is uniquely learned, witty and urbane, full of jokes about music, poetry and ecclesiastical politics. Its appeal for preferment for Nicholas of Guildford indicates an origin in the world of the secular clergy, and the whole poem takes us much closer to Walter Map than to St Francis. One might therefore be inclined to deduce that the men who copied *The Owl and the Nightingale* into the Jesus and Caligula manuscripts must surely have been secular clerics, and this deduction might seem to receive weighty, even overwhelming, support from the fact that the Caligula manuscript is dominated (194 out of 261 folios) by one long poem, Laȝamon's *Brut*, which declares itself to be the work of a secular cleric. That both manuscripts might be from the world of the secular clergy (perhaps parish priests, but more probably a college of secular canons or the familia of a bishop) seems intrinsically plausible, and it is therefore salutary that the researches of Betty Hill have cautiously been directing our attention to the Premonstratensian Abbey at Halesowen (which accords well enough with the linguistic evidence).[27] In the absence of conclusive evidence it is wise to keep an open mind about the provenance of all four of these manuscripts, and moreover we limit our own capacity for observation if we treat all four manuscripts as being of the same kind simply because a small number of texts occurs in two or three of them and a very small number is common to all four. Certainly they have common features: they are all from the same period, c.1260–80, and on linguistic grounds may be assigned to the same general area (the south-west Midlands; more specifically, the diocese of Worcester, or perhaps the dioceses of Worcester and Hereford); they all contain a mixture of languages (English and French in Jesus and Caligula; English, French and Latin in the other two), and all are in some sense religious, though this point needs further explanation. Each, however, is also a highly individual collection with its own special nature. Jesus and Caligula have most in common, and may even in part have been copied from a common exemplar. They are both strikingly literary collections and should be classed as anthologies rather than as miscellanies; they cater for an interest in poetry, but the presence of Laȝamon's *Brut* and an Anglo-Norman prose chronicle in Caligula gives it a historical dimension that Jesus does not have. It is not merely that the *Brut* would have been accepted as in some sense a record of history: a concern for the past of England is even more tellingly indicated in the apparent care with which at least one of the copyists preserved the linguistic archaisms of Laȝamon's text.[28] Caligula thus reflects a society that not only encouraged religious faith through the use of poetry but also cared about its past and fostered legends that assert some sense of national identity. In both these manuscripts there are individual English poems that are close in spirit to the evangelical puritanism of the early Franciscans, but when the French pieces are taken into account the dominant tone of each collection is rather one of religious sobriety and conformity, with the further historical element in Caligula. On the other hand, Jesus and Caligula are relatively homogeneous collections when compared with the wide-ranging imaginative fertility reflected in

BL Additional 46919 and BL Harley 913, two authentic Franciscan miscellanies from about half a century later, in which in fact a characteristic Franciscan element is not easy to isolate.[29] The most likely milieu for the production and readership of Jesus and Caligula seems to me to be the world of the secular clergy, but a house of regular canons would be equally conceivable.

TCC 323 is a different matter altogether. This too is an anthology, in one sense narrower in that all the contents are strictly religious, in one sense broader in that it contains both verse and prose in Latin, French and English. Its most recent editor follows older opinion in taking it to be a preaching-book and cautiously concludes that it may be Franciscan.[30] Its nature as a preaching-book is, however, far from certain. One cannot deny that the texts in it might well be useful to a preacher, but the material is not obviously arranged in any systematic way. There is no trace, for example, of the alphabetic arrangement found in fourteenth-century preaching books like that of the Franciscan John Grimestone,[31] nor is there any apparent thematic arrangement. It seems in fact to be a rather haphazard collection, with various kinds of text being entered as they came to hand. Preaching a sermon from it could be a perplexing task: many of the texts are very long (like the Middle English verse life of St Margaret), extended works for reading aloud rather than sermons, and certainly not illustrations to a sermon. Some of the short vernacular poems admittedly resemble those in Grimestone's book or in the *Fasciculus Morum*, but these are only a small part of the whole. Reichl very reasonably argues that the large number of contributors (he distinguishes six major and six minor hands) points to compilation in a religious house, and clergy who had dealings with the laity are perhaps more likely compilers than members of an enclosed order, though the latter cannot be ruled out, particularly if one thinks in terms of a nunnery, but there seems no obvious reason for preferring a mendicant convent to a house of regular or secular canons.

Digby 86 is different again, and it is in many ways the most eccentric and revealing of the four manuscripts.[32] It is more truly a miscellany than the others, less exclusively a literary anthology. It begins with material for practical use (notes for the confessional, medical material, prayers, notes on prognostications, on the interpretation of dreams and on the signs of doomsday, and a calendar for religious use, very much the kind of material in fact that one finds in commonplace books of the later Middle Ages) but it goes on to become rather more literary, without quite losing sight of practicality in the form of interspersed prayers, proverbs and the like. The selection of literary texts is extraordinarily wide (the contents are roughly half French and a quarter each Latin and English), including verse and prose, religious and secular, from the pious to the scurrilous. It has more secular material than any of the other three manuscripts. Among the French contents, works of moral instruction like the *Doctrinal Sauvage*, of continental origin, stand side by side with fabliaux like the Anglo-Norman *Le Lai du Cor*, while the scurrilous *La Vie d'un Vallet Amerous* immediately precedes *Des Quatre Files Deu*, an extract from Grosseteste's *Chasteau d'Amour*. The English pieces include numerous religious poems, as well as unique texts of the earliest extant English fabliau, *Dame Siriz*, and beast-epic, *The Fox and the Wolf*, a bird-debate on women, *The Thrush and the Nightingale*, and the remarkable poem on *The Names of a Hare*, which gives an unparalleled insight into medieval rural superstition.[33] Emphasis on the variety of the material should not of course obscure the fact that the collection is predominantly religious, and it is especially the shorter English religious poems that link this manuscript with the others in the group, but these few shared poems should not lead us into classifying this extravagantly heterogeneous collection with the neat anthology for churchmen that we find in Jesus 29.

Carleton Brown, who first tentatively ascribed the Digby manuscript to friars in 1932, himself drew attention to the signatures that appear at various points in the margins and deduced from them that by the mid-fourteenth century the manuscript was in private lay hands.[34] In 1963, B. D. H. Miller amplified this in a carefully argued study to show that the manuscript had probably always been in lay hands and was likely to have been compiled for a lay household.[35] Miller's study ought to have put an end to the classification of Digby 86 as a 'friar's miscellany'; of course, one cannot rule out the possibility that some of the poems in it may have been transmitted by friars, but there is no positive evidence that this was so. Nevertheless, the manuscript still has in parts a distinctly clerical appearance. While the religious poems, saints' lives and works of meditation and instruction might appeal to any ordinarily pious reader, lay or clerical, the notes for the confessional, the psalms and prayers in Latin and especially the professional-looking calendar, also in Latin, all look like items for the practising cleric. So, while accepting Miller's suggestion that the manuscript was compiled in and for a lay household, I would see the compiler (the manuscript is almost entirely in one hand) as a cleric, perhaps the local parish-priest, more probably a private chaplain in a manorial household, at any rate a member of the secular clergy. Support for the suggestion that the compiler was a domestic chaplain to one of the Worcestershire families named in the marginal inscriptions may perhaps be seen in the fact that the contents of the manuscript indicate that he had a dual function, to· provide both spiritual guidance and also what one might call book-based entertainment. That the secular pieces, as much as the religious ones, had a social function, rather than reflecting a purely private literary interest, is strikingly demonstrated by the Anglo-Norman poem entitled *Ragemon le Bon*.[36] This is the text for a parlour-game, a comic fortune-telling by the drawing of lots, and, as Långfors pointed out, the Digby version is decidedly ribald and even malicious by comparison with its continental French counterpart; so much so that it, or some very similar version, provoked a religious parody that is recorded in TCC 323. Moreover, where the French original is addressed to men, the Digby version is intended for mixed company: most of its stanzas, at least forty, are addressed to men, but the last ten or twelve are addressed to women. One may note in passing that the fifteenth-century English version of the same game is addressed exclusively to women, a point with interesting social implications.[37] *Ragemon le Bon* thus gives us some insight into the society for whom the Digby manuscript was compiled: sexually mixed, though predictably male-dominated (the poem has familiar jokes about women and cuckoldry), requiring entertainment, somewhat naive and even coarse in taste, rustic rather than urban, at any rate lacking in the refinement and sophistication that one might expect to find in an aristocratic court (not to mention a Benedictine monastery, if one thinks of the contents of Harley 978), but, on the evidence of other texts, fundamentally devout, responsive to spiritual guidance as well as to fun. Thus Digby 86, more than any other manuscript of the period, gives us an insight into what one might loosely call the upper middle class of thirteenth-century rural England.

What has emerged from the foregoing sketch of selected thirteenth-century manuscripts is a picture of the clergy, at that date the literate section of the community, mediating vernacular writings, partly to other clergy and partly to the laity; in the latter case religious instruction shades off into the provision of entertainment. Writing in French seems to have run somewhat ahead of that in English in the sense that the provision of texts for lay patrons and readers occurs at an earlier date for texts in the French language, whether Anglo-Norman or continental, than for those in English, and there may even have been some professional production of books with French texts for a lay readership before the end of the thirteenth century.[38] The first example of a professionally produced volume with English texts is presumably the Auchinleck Manuscript from the next century, c. 1330–40. Whether any extant thirteenth-century manuscripts that include English contents were professionally produced for lay use is not known; in this, as in so many other matters, the important division is less that between clergy and laity than that between regular clergy on the one hand and secular clergy and laity on the other, for the latter groups shared so much common experience of life. There is perhaps nothing unreasonable in the supposition that thirteenth-century manuscripts of romances and other secular poems in English were prepared for laymen by clerics, and Digby 86 probably provides the closest we can get to positive evidence of this; for similar texts in French the evidence of clerical origin is stronger, though the intended audience remains uncertain.

Postscript 2008

The foregoing article from 1986 inevitably contains some accidental omissions. Note 10 (on BL MS Harley 978) should have referred to Christopher Hohler, 'Reflections on some manuscripts containing 13th-century polyphony', *Journal of the Plainsong and Medieval Music Society*, 1 (1978), 2–38. Note 29 overlooked the description of BL Additional MS 46919 in *Catalogue of Additions to Manuscripts 1946–1950*, Part I, *Descriptions* (London: British Library, 1979), pp. 197–206. On pp.71–2 above my reference to the contents of BL MS Cotton Caligula A.ix should have cited as the authority for the unity of the manuscript Ker's comments in *The Owl and the Nightingale, Reproduced in Facsimile from the Surviving Manuscripts*, introduction by N. R. Ker, EETS OS 251 (1963), pp. ix–xi; the unity of what had previously been regarded as two separate manuscripts is further supported by the lack of signs of wear on the final verso of the Laȝamon section and the initial recto of the second part (contrasting with the badly worn opening page of Laȝamon's text).

Subsequent publications on the subjects touched on in the article are too numerous to list here; any consideration of the Digby manuscript must now of course take into account the introduction to *Facsimile of Oxford, Bodleian Library, MS Digby 86*, with an introduction by Judith Tschann and M. B. Parkes, EETS SS 16 (Oxford: Oxford University Press, 1996).

Addendum: the social context of Oxford, Bodleian Library, MS Laud Misc. 108

MS Laud Misc.108, probably the oldest surviving manuscript of the *SEL*, is of obvious concern to the present volume; at the time of writing the foregoing article my work on this manuscript was too inconclusive to receive mention, but some points may be briefly made here, especially as my conclusions broadly support the study by Annie Samson that accompanied my own article.[39]

It has long been recognized that the Laud MS was compiled in three stages; part 1 contains a somewhat eccentric text of *SEL*, part 2 contains the romances *Havelok* and *King Horn*,[40] and part 3 contains some supplementary saints' lives added as a continuation of part 2 in the late fourteenth or early fifteenth century; the implications of this structure deserve further consideration. There seems to be general agreement that parts 1 and 2 are broadly contemporary (late thirteenth or early fourteenth century) but are of unrelated origin: part 1 was written in the south Midlands, probably west Oxfordshire, and part 2 was written in west Norfolk.[41] The place where the two parts were united is presumably shown by the linguistic localization of part 3, which is said to be 'from a western (probably Gloucs) original with East Anglian overlay'; part 3 may thus have been compiled in the same general area as part 2, though perhaps a century later.[42] From these localizations one can construct the following tentative sequence of events. First, somewhere around 1300 two scribes were independently at work in widely separated places, one copying saints' legends in Oxfordshire, the other copying romances in West Norfolk. Subsequently the Oxfordshire manuscript was taken to East Anglia (probably to the same area or even the same place where part 2 was written) and combined with the manuscript of the romances, perhaps even bound in its present position preceding the romances (some of the decorative flourishing of initial letters in both parts seems to be in the same hand). Finally, a good deal later, a third scribe inserted after the romances some more saints' lives as a supplement to the opening legendary, in effect treating the romances as part of the legendary (the heading *Incipit Vita Havelok* on fol. 204 may have assisted this process).

Neither part 1 nor 2 is likely to have been compiled in a monastic scriptorium: in terms of subject (but perhaps not language and style) *SEL* might well have appealed to a monastic copyist but west Oxfordshire has no obviously appropriate religious houses: the Cistercian abbey at Bruern (Oxfordshire), the only monastery in the right linguistic area, is unlikely to have found *SEL* relevant to the monastic life practised there about 1300. Conversely, although western Norfolk (the area immediately east of Ely) is extraordinarily rich in religious houses, the *Havelok–Horn* manuscript does not seem the kind of compilation that would have been judged appropriate to monastic activities about 1300. These circumstances suggest that the two manuscripts that make up the Laud MS circulated, and were probably produced, in a secular environment, possibly among layfolk, more probably among secular clergy (whether parish priests or clergy in minor orders). An inscription on the final flyleaf shows that the manuscript was in lay hands (probably London merchants) by the mid-fifteenth century[43] and this also supports the suggestion of a secular origin for the manuscript (on the assumption that a monastic book is unlikely to have found its way into lay ownership so long before the Reformation).

This conjectured history of the Laud MS would fit well with the proposal that *SEL* was an enterprise that had its origins among secular clergy, but it accords less well with Görlach's suggestion of a Benedictine enterprise for use either in nunneries or in parish churches whose priests were appointed by Benedictine monasteries.[44] These speculations are of course highly tentative but it is of interest that they broadly support the arguments for a non-monastic origin for *SEL* advanced on other grounds in Annie Samson's study.

Notes

1 This study aims to take into account a wide range of kinds of writing, but does not touch on business and administrative documents. For writing in the widest sense of the term, including the latter, see M. T. Clanchy, *From Memory to Written Record* (London: Arnold, 1979).

2 Important recent studies are R. F. Green, *Poets and Princepleasers* (Toronto: Toronto University Press, 1980); J. Coleman, *English Literature in History, 1350–1400* (London: Hutchinson, 1981); *English Court Culture in the Later Middle Ages*, ed. V. J. Scattergood and J. W. Sherborne (London: Duckworth, 1983); P. R. Coss, 'Aspects of cultural diffusion in medieval England', *Past and Present*, 108 (1985), 35–79. A narrower field is surveyed in Anne Hudson, *Lollards and Their Books* (London: Hambledon, 1985), and in *English Wycliffite*

Sermons I, ed. A. Hudson (Oxford: Clarendon Press, 1983), introduction, esp. pp. 189–202. The seminal study by M. B. Parkes, 'The literacy of the laity', in *Literature and Civilization: The Medieval World*, ed. D. Daiches and A. Thorlby (London: Aldus, 1973), deserves special mention.

3 C. Bullock-Davies, *Professional Interpreters and the Matter of Britain* (Cardiff: Wales University Press, 1966); a general introduction to this aspect of literary study is J. Burrow, 'Bards, minstrels and men of letters', in *Literature and Civilization*, ed. Daiches and Thorlby, pp. 347–70.

4 For the thirteenth century, see W. A. Quinn and A. S. Hall, *Jongleur* (Washington, DC: University Press of America, 1982), which is centred in a stylistic analysis of *King Horn* and gives full references to the seminal studies of Parry, Lord and Magoun, as well as subsequent publications. The whole subject of oral tradition is notoriously problematic and the relevance of modern practices to the Middle Ages remains uncertain. See, e.g., R. Finnegan, *Oral Poetry* (Cambridge: Cambridge University Press, 1977); a rare survival from the thirteenth century is noted by R. A. B. Mynors, *A Catalogue of the Manuscripts of Balliol College* (Oxford: Clarendon Press, 1963), p. 242; see Iona and Peter Opie, *The Singing Game* (Oxford: Oxford University Press, 1985), pp. 44–6.

5 E. J. Dobson, *The Origins of Ancrene Wisse* (Oxford: Clarendon Press, 1976).

6 See J. Morson, 'The English Cistercians and the Bestiary', *Bulletin of the John Rylands Library*, 39 (1956–57), 146–70; C. R. Cheney, 'English Cistercian libraries', in his *Medieval Texts and Studies* (Oxford: Clarendon Press, 1973), pp. 328–45.

7 Basic information is in N. R. Ker, *Medieval Libraries of Great Britain* (London: Offices of the Royal Historical Society, 1964), pp. 205–15; Ker, *Catalogue of Manuscripts Containing Anglo-Saxon* (Oxford: Clarendon Press, 1957), pp. lvi–lx and under separate manuscripts, esp. no. 398; the latter refers to the activities of the thirteenth-century scribe with the 'tremulous hand', who wrote glosses in several Old English texts.

8 See Ker, *Catalogue*, xix; M. P. Richards, 'BL MS Cotton Vespasian A.xxii, the Vespasian Homilies', *Manuscripta*, 22 (1978), 97–103.

9 B. Schofield, 'The provenance and date of *Sumer is icumen in*', *Music Review*, 9 (1948), 81–6.

10 Most of the Latin poems were printed in T. Wright, *The Latin Poems of Walter Mapes*, Camden Society OS 16 (London: J. B. Nichols, 1841); see A. G. Rigg, 'Golias and other pseudonyms', *Studi Medievali*, 18 (1977), 65–109. The contents of the manuscript are listed in C. L. Kingsford, *The Song of Lewes* (Oxford: Clarendon Press, 1890), pp. xi–xvii.

11 For references see C. Bullock-Davies, 'Marie, Abbess of Shaftesbury, and her brothers', *English Historical Review*, 80 (1965), 314–22, which sheds light on the abbess but does not strengthen the connection with the authoress of the lays.

12 See E. Salter, 'A complaint against blacksmiths', *Literature and History*, 5 (1979), 194–215.

13 See M. D. Legge, *Anglo-Norman in the Cloisters* (Edinburgh: Edinburgh University Press, 1950); Legge, *Anglo-Norman Literature and Its Background* (Oxford: Clarendon Press, 1963). One may also note the widespread monastic use of French for works on estate-management, such as those by Walter of Henley and Grosseteste. See Dorothea Oschinsky, *Walter of Henley and Other Treatises on Estate Management and Accounting* (Oxford: Clarendon Press, 1971), esp. the list of manuscripts on pp. 51–5.

14 The illustrations are accurately described in M. R. James, *A Descriptive Catalogue of the Manuscripts in the Library of Lambeth Palace* (Cambridge: Cambridge University Press, 1932), pp. 715–23.

15 See Carleton Brown, *English Lyrics of the XIIIth Century* (Oxford: Clarendon Press, 1932), nos 32.C, 63, 64.

16 Ker, *Catalogue*, pp. 230–4, 279–81 (nos 180, 215).

17 On the date and provenance of the autograph manuscript see most recently M. Parkes, 'On the presumed date of the manuscript of the *Orrmulum*', in *Five Hundred Years of Words and Sounds for E. J. Dobson,* ed. E. G. Stanley and D. Gray (Cambridge: D. S. Brewer, 1983), pp. 115–27.

18 Dobson, *Origins*.

19 Ker, *Medieval Libraries*, lists about a score of manuscripts in English or French, or with vernacular entries, from Augustinian houses. The contribution of Augustinian canons to writing in English surpasses the better publicized Franciscan contribution.

20 M. Gretsch, 'Die Wintney-Version der *Regula Sancti Benedicti*', *Anglia*, 96 (1978), 310–48, suggests that the text was copied from a manuscript from Winchester.

21 B. Hill, 'Cambridge, Fitzwilliam Museum Manuscript McClean 123', *Notes and Queries*, 210 (1965), 87–90.

22 B. Hill, 'The *Luue-Ron* and Thomas de Hales', *Modern Language Review*, 59 (1964), 321–30. In support of Hill's identification of Hales with the modern Halesowen one might note that Hailes, Gloucestershire, often suggested as Thomas's place of origin, is excluded by the fact that in Middle English *Hailes* and *Hales* were not homophones and there is no possibility that the spellings were interchangeable in the thirteenth century.

23 Important publications on the Franciscan contribution to the composition and circulation of English poems, particularly religious lyrics, appeared in the introductions to Carleton Brown, pp. xx–xxxiii;

The Early English Carols, ed. Richard Leighton Greene (Oxford: Clarendon Press, 1935), pp. cxi–xviii, cxxi–xxxviii; and R. H. Robbins, *Secular Lyrics of the Fourteenth and Fifteenth Centuries* (Oxford: Clarendon Press, 1952), pp. xvii–xviii; the latter summarized fuller statements published in *Modern Language Notes*, 53 (1938), 239–45, and *Journal of English and Germanic Philology*, 39 (1940), 230–8. From the late thirteenth and early fourteenth centuries come the Anglo-Norman writings of Nicholas Bozon, which constitute a major Franciscan contribution to vernacular literature.

24 Especially D. L. Jeffrey, *The Early English Lyric and Franciscan Spirituality* (Lincoln: University of Nebraska Press, 1975), pp. 205–8, but also Derek Pearsall, *Old English and Middle English Poetry* (London: Routledge & Kegan Paul, 1977), pp. 94–102 (on 'Friars' Miscellanies'). D. Brewer, *English Gothic Literature* (London: Macmillan, 1983), p. 46, accepts the probable Franciscan origin of Digby 86 and, more tentatively, the likely Dominican origin of TCC 323. It may be mentioned that *Verses in Sermons: Fasciculus Morum and Its Middle English Poems*, ed. Siegfriend Wenzel (Cambridge, MA: Medieval Academy of America, 1978), pp. 90–3, is very cautious about the alleged Franciscan connection, while the scholarly study of J. B. Allen, *The Friar as Critic* (Nashville: Vanderbilt University Press, 1971), scrupulously avoids alleged mendicant vernacular lyrics; cf. also Coss, p. 63.

25 M. D. Legge, 'The Anglo-Norman sermon of Thomas of Hales', *Modern Language Review*, 30 (1935), 212–18.

26 *Ancrene* Wisse, ed. J. R. R. Tolkien, EETS OS 249 (London: Oxford University Press, 1962), pp. 36, 213; and see the comments in Dobson, *Origins*.

27 B. Hill, 'Oxford, Jesus College MS 29', *Notes and Queries*, 220 (1975), 98–105, points to numerous correspondences between texts in the Jesus and Caligula manuscripts and works recorded in the catalogue of Titchfield abbey, a daughter-house of Halesowen. Whether either manuscript was ever in Halesowen abbey is not known, but either may well have been copied in that area from Halesowen manuscripts now lost.

28 E. G. Stanley, 'Laȝamon's antiquarian sentiments', *Medium Aevum*, 38 (1969), 23–37; see 25–8 for the preservation of authorial spellings in Caligula.

29 The fullest description of Additional 46919 is still that of P. Meyer in *Romania*, 13 (1884), 497–541; for Harley 913 see W. Heuser, *Die Kildare-Gedichte* (Bonn, 1904; repr. Darmstadt: Wissenschaftliche Buchgesellschaft, 1965); both manuscripts are predominantly religious, but the former also contains texts on hunting, falconry and chivalry, and the latter various comic and satirical pieces.

30 K. Reichl, *Religiöse Dichtung im englischen Hochmittelalter* (Munich: Fink, 1973), esp. pp. 49–58.

31   National Library of Scotland, Advocates MS 18.7.21, ed. E. Wilson, *A Descriptive Index of the English Lyrics in John of Grimestone's Preaching Book* (Oxford: Blackwell, 1973). See also H. G. Pfander, 'Medieval friars and some alphabetical reference-books for sermons', *Medium Aevum*, 3 (1934), 19–29.

32   The fullest published account is still in E. Stengel, *Codicem Manu Scriptum Digby 86* (Halle: Libraria Orphanotrophei, 1871). My work on Digby 86, on which I am drawing here, has been made possible by a grant from the University of Newcastle upon Tyne Research Fund for the purchase of photostats of the manuscript.

33   Most of the texts here mentioned are unique to Digby 86, but the Anglo-Norman *Disciplina Clericalis* and the *Doctrinal Sauvage* are both preserved in a large number of manuscripts, while *The Thrush and the Nightingale* is also in the Auchinleck MS. The extract from Grosseteste is unique to Digby in this form.

34   Brown, pp. xxviii–xxxiii.

35   B. D. H. Miller, 'The early history of Bodleian MS Digby 86', *Annuale Medievale*, 4 (1963), 23–56.

36   Edited together with its continental precursor and the religious version in TCC 323 by A. Långfors, *Un jeu de société du moyen âge, Ragemon le Bon* (Helsinki: Annales Academiae Scientiarum Fennicae, 1920).

37   Edited by Freudenberger, *Ragman Roll, ein spätmittelenglisches Gedicht* (Erlangen: Junge, 1909); both manuscripts of this poem are now available in facsimile: *Bodleian Library MS Fairfax 16*, ed. J. Norton-Smith (London: Scolar Press, 1979), and *Manuscript Bodley 638: a Facsimile*, ed. P. Robinson (Norman, Oklahoma: Pilgrim Books, 1982).

38   Coss, pp. 60–1 and n. 95. R. Vaughan, *Matthew Paris* (Cambridge, 1958), pp. 159–81, gives information about the French religious texts, mostly saints' lives, composed by Matthew Paris for aristocratic readers. This does not of course constitute professional book-production (there seems to be no evidence of any related financial transactions), but it is presumably in some sense a precursor of the professional book trade, which seems to have begun in England with the supply of texts in French for wealthy readers.

39   Samson, 'Constructing a context'.

40   I apply the term 'romance' to *Havelok* and *Horn* as a matter of convention and convenience but I acknowledge that the copyist may not have thought of them as belonging to a category that was radically different from many religious narratives, whether or not saints' lives. On the subject of 'romances' juxtaposed with religious texts (including *SEL*) see A. S. G. Edwards, 'The contexts of the Vernon romances', in Derek Pearsall (ed.), *Studies in the Vernon Manuscript* (Cambridge: D. S. Brewer, 1990), pp. 159–70; but *Havelok* and *Horn* present different

problems from the Vernon romances (*Robert of Sicily*, *The King of Tars* and *Joseph of Arimathea*).

41 Margaret Laing, *Catalogue of Sources for a Linguistic Atlas of Early Medieval English* (Cambridge: D. S. Brewer, 1993), pp. 136–7.

42 *A Linguistic Atlas of Late Mediaeval English*, ed. Angus McIntosh et al., 4 vols (Aberdeen and New York: Aberdeen University Press, 1986), vol I, p. 149; this agrees with the conclusion of Görlach, *Textual Tradition*, p. 89.

43 On the note of ownership see Jane Roberts, *Guide to Scripts Used in English Writings up to 1500* (London: British Library, 2005), p. 160.

44 Görlach, *Textual Tradition*, pp. 45–50.

4

The *South English Legendary* and its major Latin models

Sherry Reames

Scholarship on the *SEL*'s relationship to its Latin predecessors has retreated considerably from the premature verdict of Minnie Wells, who took the *Legenda aurea* to be the source of almost everything in the *SEL* except the accounts of British saints.[1] Manfred Görlach, whose heroic research on the manuscripts in 1974 laid the foundation for all subsequent work on the *SEL*'s textual traditions, contributed enormously to our knowledge of its Latin sources and models as well, concluding that (as he would sum it up later) 'the *SEL* shows unmistakable [*Legenda aurea*] sources only in some 20% of its legends' and suggesting that the primary influence probably came instead from a liturgical legendary in southern England:

> As I have tried to show in detail (Görlach 1974 . . .), it makes much better sense to assume that for the original SEL a liturgical collection of the Sarum type, and close to the surviving Exeter Ordinale of 1337, was reworked into a rhymed legendary, including some very short and imperfect stories; this 'Z' collection could have originated at Worcester, around 1270.[2]

Görlach's instincts seem to have been wonderfully accurate, but he had not done enough research on liturgical manuscripts to give more than scattered hints about the complexity of English liturgical traditions and the significance of their influence on the *SEL*. The second part of the current essay will summarize my own findings about the connections between the *SEL* and the liturgical versions of three specific legends. First, however, I want to fill in the general picture more clearly and completely than Görlach did. As I hope to demonstrate, the more we learn about the ways in which saints' legends were abridged and adapted for the liturgy in the time of the *SEL*, the stronger the case becomes for seeing this tradition as having provided not just the source material for

individual chapters but the principal models and precedents for the
SEL (or multiple *SEL*s) as a whole.

Hagiographical texts for the liturgy: the tradition(s) in southern England

Görlach's unspecific reference to 'a liturgical collection of the
Sarum type' reflects his awareness that the hagiographical texts in
Sarum manuscripts often differ from those that would be printed
in the sixteenth century and reproduced in the supposedly standard edition of the Sarum breviary by Procter and Wordsworth.[3]
Besides the Exeter Cathedral lectionary, compiled by Bishop John
de Grandisson in 1334–37, Görlach had closely examined at least
one other early Sarum lectionary of saints, BL Cotton Appendix 23
(c. 1340?, diocese of Worcester).[4] And he had begun to realize that
the differences between those manuscripts and the later printed
editions represent just the tip of the iceberg. In fact, the secular
breviary and lectionary manuscripts that identify themselves as
'Sarum', by either explicit statement or close adherence to the
distinctive Sarum calendar and rubrics, are so far from having
standardized hagiographical texts that one can often identify ten
or more different textual families in their lessons for a particular
saint.[5] And there is no compelling reason to confine one's attention
to these Sarum-identified manuscripts, since many related traditions are preserved in English manuscripts for monastic services
and non-Sarum secular ones.

The historical reasons for all this diversity are important to
understand. By the time the Sarum rite was codified in the early
thirteenth century, most of the great monasteries, cathedrals and
collegiate churches had developed their own divine office lectionaries (that is, their own collections of lessons for use at Matins),[6] and
the lessons derived from hagiographical sources were much likelier
to differ than the rest. As the editors of the Hereford Breviary
noted a century ago, 'There never seems to have been a standard
[liturgical legendary] set out, analogous to the Homiliary of Paul
[the Deacon]'.[7] Instead, those responsible for the liturgy in each
institution chose the lessons from whatever accounts they had or
could borrow on the saints they wished to commemorate. They did
not necessarily begin with the same sources, then; and, even when
they did, there was nothing to make them select exactly the same
episodes to be read, or treat those episodes in exactly the same way.
Major differences thus emerge even among the handful of surviving

English Benedictine breviaries, although Tolhurst's edition might create the impression that the exemplar from Hyde Abbey typifies them all.[8] In the case of Cecilia, for example, the breviary from Muchelney Abbey (now BL Add. 43406) takes the most conservative approach, just reproducing the beginning of the saint's standard *Passio*; its eighth and last lesson breaks off before the end of the first episode. Although the Hyde Abbey breviary also has eight lessons and starts in an almost identical way, it abridges the *Passio*, ingeniously combining several dozen brief excerpts to retell all the key events except the martyrdoms of Tiburce, Valerian and Maximus (who had a saint's day of their own) and Cecilia's problematic trial, which it reduces to a refusal to deny her faith despite the persecutor's ultimatum.[9] A third Benedictine breviary, the one from Ely Cathedral priory (Cambridge, CUL Ii.iv.20), gives a condensed version with new summary wording and such different priorities that it devotes six of its eight brief lessons to the trial and martyrdom of Tiburce and Valerian.

Although the homogenizing influence of the Sarum liturgy eventually prevailed in southern England, it never completely uprooted the more localized traditions on saints that had preceded it. Remnants of those competing traditions can be seen even in Sarum manuscripts from the very end of the Middle Ages and in the printed editions.[10] And so many unexpected texts for saints survive in the fourteenth-century manuscripts as to suggest that many dioceses and individual churches adopted the Sarum liturgy piecemeal, accepting its calendar and ceremonial while retaining non-Sarum feasts that had local importance and continuing to use whatever legendary or lectionary of saints they already had.[11] Retaining many of the old traditions and service books made good practical sense, of course, and the early ordinals had ambiguities which invited compilers of breviaries to do just that, incorporating local options within (mostly) Sarum Use.

The Sarum agenda in the thirteenth century may not have included any idea of a standardized lectionary. By 1260 the Dominicans were already pursuing an ideal of liturgical uniformity that extended to the lessons, as they demonstrated by authorizing a single lectionary for public celebrations of the divine office in all Dominican houses; they even accompanied the authorized lectionary with explicit warnings that copyists were not to alter or omit anything.[12] But the Dominicans were far ahead of both the secular clergy and other religious orders in their concern for uniform texts. The strengths of the Sarum rite lay elsewhere – in its clear organization and in its ceremonial. Early Sarum ordinals consequently have much to say about the processions, ritual gestures and blessings for each occasion, and they carefully identify every psalm, prayer and sung text to be used; but they give no such attention to the lessons. About the lessons for St Sylvester's feast day on 31 December, for example, the thirteenth-century ordinal in BL MS Harley 1001 says only that there are to be nine, with the middle three devoted to Christ's Nativity and the last three to a homily on the gospel 'Homo quidam peregre'; the content of the first three lessons is left entirely to the user's discretion (fol. 17v). For many other saints' days either the original version of this ordinal or later revisions go one small step further, specifying the *incipit* of the first lesson as well as the total number of lessons; thus for Margaret, nine lessons beginning 'Adest nobis dilectissimi' (fol. 66v); for Christina, three lessons beginning 'Erat temporibus Dioclitiani' (fol. 67); for Laurence, nine lessons beginning 'Post passionem' with a specific gospel in the third nocturn (fols 68v–69).[13] The added *incipit*s tell the user that the lessons should be drawn from the saints' legends, but say nothing about their length or even their particular content, since dozens of different liturgical abridgements could and did begin with the same words. And the brevity and vagueness of all the directives on lessons invite users to interpret them more broadly than the directives on processions and sung texts.

Such loopholes in the Sarum ordinal did not go unheeded. The Exeter Cathedral lectionary frequently pauses to explain that it is disregarding the ordinal's instructions on such matters as the number of lessons for each saint because they conflict with established practice at Exeter.[14] Another fairly early Sarum manuscript, Edinburgh University MS 26 (c. 1350), cites no particular local precedents but encourages its users to follow their own customs and preferences by suggesting alternatives to the ordinal's directives on lessons.[15] Exeter supplies its own (or Grandisson's own) distinctive retellings of saints' legends, which tend to preserve more historical details than most and don't necessarily have the *incipit*s prescribed in the ordinal. A third Sarum or quasi-Sarum manuscript from this period, Cambridge, Gonville and Caius MS 394/614 (early fourteenth century, Ely?), also goes its own way, supplying lessons that are unpredictable in their *incipit*s and often surprising in their sources and textual affiliations.

As I have shown elsewhere, successive revisions of the Sarum ordinal during the later fourteenth century added new directives

on the lessons, closing some of the earlier loopholes, and two sizeable families of Sarum manuscripts eventually emerged that are
consistent and uniform enough to suggest genuine efforts in some
locations to standardize the lessons entirely.[16] But total standardization of the Sarum lectionary was not achieved even in the printed
editions. And the first signs of such effort cannot be seen until c.
1370 – nearly a century after the estimated date of the earliest *SEL*
manuscript, Oxford, Bodleian MS Laud Misc. 108.

Envisioning the kinds of liturgical collections that would have
been available to the original author(s) of the *SEL* requires some
extrapolation from the kinds of evidence I have been citing. No
identifiably Sarum manuscript with lessons for saints has survived
from the period before c. 1300, and very few English lectionaries
and breviaries of any kind can reasonably be dated that early. None
the less, it seems safe to conclude, on the basis of the earliest such
manuscripts we have and the loose instructions on lessons in the
thirteenth-century Sarum ordinal, that English compilers of liturgical collections in this period had remarkable freedom to shape
the collections to their own specifications or those of their intended
audience. They could keep using local sources about the saints,
if they so chose, or they could supplement or replace them with
desired sources from other institutions, apparently regardless of
use or rite, religious order, geography or the distinctions between
monastic liturgies and secular ones.

The eclecticism of the surviving breviaries and lectionaries is
worth pausing to illustrate, since it violates some modern assumptions about the boundaries between different kinds of ecclesiastical
institutions in medieval England. One may be surprised to dis-
cover, for example, that the lessons on St Laurence in Cambridge,
Gonville and Caius MS 394/614, a Sarum breviary that seems to
follow the Ely calendar, are less closely related to other Sarum
sources than to the lessons in the monastic breviary from Chertsey
Abbey, Surrey (Oxford, Bodleian MS Lat.lit.e.39) and the earliest
surviving Hereford breviary. The lessons for both Sylvester and
the Translation of Thomas Becket in that early Hereford manuscript look most closely related to those from another Benedictine
monastery, Hyde Abbey, Winchester. Hyde Abbey's lessons for
Margaret seem to be drawn from the same source as the lessons in
an earlier secular manuscript, Bodleian Lat.lit.c.36, which follows
neither Hereford nor Sarum use; an anonymous catalogue description at the Bodleian connects it tentatively with the collegiate
church of Penkridge, Staffordshire, where the clergy were canons.

Besides the ability to supplement the local lectionary with texts from other institutions, compilers of early English breviaries clearly retained considerable freedom to make changes in the hagiographical texts they had inherited or borrowed. The surviving manuscripts are full of examples. Sometimes earlier accounts are supplemented with material from additional sources, to bring out a newly desired lesson or theme. But the dominant direction of change is towards further abbreviation. This is not just an English phenomenon but a trend noted elsewhere in western Europe by Pierre Salmon, who describes the apparent anarchy thus created:

> From the 11th century on, . . . it seems, everyone enjoyed a great liberty in this regard. Cathedral chapters, abbeys, collegiate churches, priests, whether regular or secular, and even copyists of manuscripts – everybody hacked away [at] the texts as he pleased, without authorization or control . . . Each one made up his office book to suit himself, or almost so, abridging or lengthening the texts – especially shortening them – as seemed good to him.[17]

By 'hack[ing] away' Salmon apparently refers to the practice of truncating the lessons – just giving the beginning of the text verbatim, whether it made sense alone or not. This was the standard method of shortening lessons from the Bible and patristic sources, whose wording was too sacred to be changed, and some breviaries used it also for non-canonical sources like anonymous saints' legends. In extreme cases a single paragraph of the source might be divided into as many as eight or nine lessons – reducing the lessons in effect to mere cues between the sung texts. Of the English breviaries I have seen, those from Cluniac abbeys are most likely to use this convention, but one also finds it elsewhere. Although it looks strange, the convention makes sense if one can assume that the Matins service will always be performed in choir, and that only the designated lector needs to see the full texts that will be read aloud.

More interesting, of course, are the many manuscripts that adopt more innovative and radical ways of abbreviating the lessons – using selective omissions, the replacement of long passages with efficient summaries, and even extensive rewriting, to produce lessons that make sense on their own, despite their brevity. In England, at least, these methods of abbreviation seem to have become the norm before the end of the thirteenth century, especially in secular breviaries. Such breviaries may have been designed for private reading, or for readers who were busier or less literate than their predecessors, or for practical use in sermons or other forms of lay instruction. The crucial point in connection with the *SEL* is that even breviaries with very brief lessons increasingly prioritize the stories, boiling the legends down to narratives that are coherent and give some sense of completeness despite their brevity. Sometimes these breviaries retell a single dramatic incident from the saint's life – for example, Katherine's defeat of the fifty philosophers. More often, especially with martyrs, they simplify or omit earlier episodes in order to get to the saint's death. They may sacrifice most of the legends' original symbolism, Biblical allusions and doctrinal instruction along the way, as well as historical complexity, but they attempt to tell meaningful stories.

As I have been attempting to suggest, the parallels between the *SEL* and the retellings of saints' legends in contemporary English liturgical manuscripts, especially secular ones, are too numerous and compelling to be coincidental. As the *SEL* would do, these liturgical manuscripts freely abridged and recast earlier Latin legends to adapt them to new audiences and circumstances, often simplified their language as well as their content and generally emphasized basic narrative elements more than doctrine or symbolism or historical detail. Nor is it just coincidence that the liturgical collections took multiple forms, as would the *SEL*. Most liturgical collections were still 'open texts' – unregulated, unofficial, largely anonymous, amenable to local variations, and sufficiently flexible and unpretentious to encourage further changes and revisions. Such openness, together with the extent to which the legends had already been made accessible to less learned audiences, might easily have suggested the further step of vernacularization. If the principal model had been a work like the *Legenda aurea* instead – a single, systematic text, aimed at a relatively homogeneous and well-educated readership, and protected against extensive rewriting by the textual discipline of the Dominicans – the *SEL* would almost certainly have originated a good deal later than it did, and turned out quite differently.

Rereading the *SEL* in the context of the liturgical sources: three case studies

Given the enormous diversity of English liturgical manuscripts and the small proportion of them that have survived, it may be impossible to find a collection that could have served as the source for more than a few chapters of the early *SEL*. Even the search for the source of an individual chapter can look like a daunting challenge when one realizes the number of Latin retellings that might possibly be relevant – not just those in the *Legenda aurea* and the printed Sarum and Hereford and Hyde Abbey breviaries but also those in all the manuscript versions of English breviaries and lectionaries and in the monastic and cathedral legendaries from which the liturgical abridgements came. My experience so far suggests, however, that comparing the *SEL*'s retelling of a given legend with a good sample of the liturgical retellings is always worthwhile, whether it leads to the discovery of an actual source or not. Hence the following brief case studies.

The Translation of Thomas Becket. Görlach suggests, following Thiemke, that the *SEL*'s account of this event (which immediately follows its long retelling of the Becket legend) is derived from the Appendix to the *Quadrilogus* rather than a liturgical source.[18] So far as I can see, however, the Q-Appendix and the *SEL* account have only one significant parallel that is not shared by the large printed editions of the Sarum breviary: they both describe the private exhumation of the saint's body that preceded the public ceremony.[19] Apart from this episode, the *SEL* account has less in common with the Q-Appendix than with the Sarum lessons commemorating the translation. Unlike the Q-Appendix, for example, both the printed Sarum lessons and the *SEL* acknowledge Pope Honorius's grant of indulgences to pilgrims who witnessed the translation (Sarum lec. 4; *SEL* 176, 2421–2), list the seven momentous Tuesdays in St Thomas's life (Sarum lec. 5; *SEL* 177, 2457–72), name the justiciar, Hubert de Burgh, as a participant in the public ceremony (Sarum lec. 8; *SEL* 176, 2449), and explain that Henry III was still too young to help carry the relic-chest to the new shrine (Sarum lec. 8; *SEL* 177, 2455–6).[20]

As for the exhumation, there is an earlier version of the Sarum lessons, partially preserved in many manuscripts and most completely in BL Cotton Appendix 23, which includes this episode too, along with virtually everything in the printed editions and several additional passages that they omit.[21] In this longer Sarum text (which I will call Cotton), even the exhumation scene is a good match for the *SEL*'s version, whereas the Q-Appendix gives many extra details and neglects to mention Prior Walter as a participant (*SEL* 176, 2435; Cotton lec. 6). Both Cotton and the *SEL* also include a passage, unparalleled in both the Q-Appendix and printed Sarum lessons, which dates the translation and gives a politically inflected explanation of the fifty-year delay since Thomas's canonization. Cotton makes the political points tactfully, alluding only indirectly to the troubled reign of King John, whose battles with church leaders had led to his own excommunication by the pope, a long interdict on his realm and periods of exile for both the monks of Canterbury Cathedral and Stephen Langton, the archbishop who would eventually carry out Thomas's translation:

> lec. 5) Anno quinto pontificatus piissimi patris Honorii tertii et [etatis] Henrici tertii illustris Anglorum regis tertiodecimo, temporibus sanctissimi patris Stephani Cantuariensis archiepiscopi, translatio est gloriosissime consummata. Et merito talium temporibus, quia qui innocenter vixerat, decens erat et honestum ut ab innocentibus et temporibus [innocentium] transferetur, ac si prius aliquid digni non fuissent, qui tantum martirem honore tanto debito possent honorare.[22]

> (The translation was most gloriously carried out in the fifth year of the pontificate of the holy father Honorius III, when Henry III, the illustrious king of England, was in the thirteenth year of his life and the holy father Stephen was archbishop of Canterbury. And deservedly in the times of such rulers, since he had lived so innocently that it was fitting and honourable that he be translated by innocent ones and in the times of innocent ones – whereas to some extent those before this had been unworthy to honour such a martyr as he deserved.)

This passage is still recognizable in the *SEL*, although the political message has been simplified and the indirection replaced with blunt language about King John's wickedness:

> Seint Thomas, this holi man,   onder eorthe he lay,
> Are that he ischrined were,   wel mani a long day;
> He lai there nine and fourti yer   and half a yer therto
> And aboute ane eighte dawes   are he were of eorthe ido.
> God wolde abide ane guode tyme   to don so noble thing:
> That thare weren bothe guode   erchebischop and king.
> For the king Johan, that longue was   evere of luthere rede,
> Luyte thoughte bi is daie   to don so guode dede.
>
>   (175, 2405–12).

> (This holy man St Thomas lay in the earth for many a long day before he was enshrined: he lay there for forty-nine years plus half a year and about a week before he was taken up from the earth. God wanted to wait for a propitious time for so noble an event, when there was both a good archbishop and a good king. For King John, who for a long time was constantly of wicked intent, little thought of doing so good a deed in his time.)

Recognizing the correspondences between the early *SEL*'s account of the translation and the lessons preserved in Cotton not only supports the general hypothesis about the use of liturgical sources, but also (and more important) gives us a better chance of accurately seeing what was distinctive about the *SEL*'s version.[23] One interesting change in the passage just quoted is the way the *SEL* identifies the king as the key figure determining whether the saint is translated. The pattern continues in the ensuing lines, which implausibly insist on attributing Thomas's 1220 translation to the eagerness of a good young king, Henry III, to do this noble deed; the actual architect of the translation, Archbishop Stephen, is demoted to a subordinate role and the pope's support reduced to an afterthought:

Ake the king Henri, is yonge sone,   nolde nought longe afine,
After that he was king imad,   are Seint Thomas were in schrine.
He nas nought threttene yeres old   tho he dude this noble thing,
And it was in the feorthe yere   that he was imad yong king.
The guode Erchebischop Stevene   radde faste therto,
So that bi hore bothe redes   this dede was ido.
The pope, Honorie that was tho,   hidere he gan sende
Ane legat fram Rome that het Pandulf   to bringe this dede to ende.
                                                    (175–6, 2413–20).

(But King Henry, his young son, did not want to delay long after he was made king before St Thomas was in a shrine. He was not yet thirteen years old when he did this noble thing, and it was in the fourth year after he was made the young king. Good Archbishop Steven strongly advised it, so that this deed was done through the resolve of them both. Honorius, who was then pope, sent hither a legate from Rome called Pandulf to see this deed through.)

Two larger differences between the Cotton-Sarum and early *SEL* accounts of Thomas's translation also deserve notice. The *SEL* tries to explain the private exhumation of the saint's body, reordering the narrative so that it follows the description of the enormous crowds that had gathered for the public translation, and presenting it as a response to the problem they posed:

                    [the crowds]   so thicke thudere drowe
That al the contreie thare-aboute   the tounes wide and longe
Unnethe mighten al that folk   that thudere cam afonge;
So that this heighe men   that scholden this dede do
Weren in care hou heo mighten   for prece comen therto;
So that Erchebischop Stevene,   of hwam ich er ou seide,

> And the bischop Richard of Salesburi   tharof heom nomen to
> rede,
> And Prior Water of the house   and the covent also,
> Wenden heom in privete   this dede for to do.
> Bi nighte, tho men weren aslepe   and luyte tharon thoughte,
> Heo nome[n] op the holi bones   and in one cheste broughte.
>
>   (176, 2428–38)

([The crowds] gathered in such numbers that the whole region and the spacious towns could hardly hold all the people who came there: so that the leaders who were to perform the translation were concerned as to how they could accomplish it amid the throngs. So Archbishop Steven, whom I mentioned before, and Bishop Richard of Salisbury, and Prior Walter of the monastic house and the convent [monks] with them, decided to carry out this deed privately. By night, when people were asleep and not expecting it, they took up the holy bones and placed them in a reliquary.)

Although this explanation was presumably intended to justify the secrecy surrounding the exhumation, one wonders if it aroused rather than allayed suspicion by creating such a vivid contrast between the prelates' hidden activity and the unsuspecting sleep of the people.

The other large change involves another reordering of the source material. In the *SEL*, the listing of Thomas's momentous Tuesdays is not found near the start, where the liturgical texts place it, but moved to the end, where it becomes the springboard for a distinctive conclusion about the custom of a Tuesday fast in St Thomas's honour:

> Theos seven auntres bi Tiwesday   him comen at the leste.
> Tharefore we iseoth manie men   makien one biheste
> To bileve flesch thene Tiwesdai   othur to o mel faste
> Forto heo comen to Caunterburi   othur the hwyle heore lif
>   ilastez.
>
>   (177, 2473–6)

(These seven events, moreover, all happened to him on Tuesdays. Thus we see many people make a promise to abstain from meat or to fast with just one meal on Tuesdays before they come to Canterbury, or for as long as they live.)

The suggestion that the narrator and his audience have witnessed this custom among their neighbours makes the kind of connection with everyday life that Anne Thompson has noted as a distinguishing feature of the *SEL*,[24] and it also represents a significant departure from the convention (followed by nearly all the Latin sources) of ending a translation narrative with the miracles that surrounded the great event. Instead of leaving the audience with an advertisement for the saint's power to save them, the *SEL* account ends with the implicit suggestion that they emulate his self-sacrifice by voluntarily making a small weekly sacrifice of their own.

Saint Wulfstan. Theodor Wolpers pointed out the close parallels between the *SEL* account of Wulfstan and the set of nine liturgical lessons from BL MS Cotton Vespasian E.9 that Darlington had published as the 'Short Life' in his edition of the *Vita Wulfstani.*[25] Görlach did not find a better Latin source for this part of the *SEL*, and neither have I. None the less, I have noticed something interesting by looking more carefully at those Latin lessons and comparing them with some of their own sources and analogues. Görlach characterized the anti-Norman polemic in the *SEL* account of Wulfstan, which receives its strongest expression in MS Laud Misc. 108, as a departure from the known Latin sources and suggested that it might be an innovation by the vernacular poet.[26] Rereading the lessons in the Vespasian manuscript, however, I see a polemical account of the Conquest that is as remarkable in its context as the more vehement and fully developed version in the *SEL*.

The Conquest narrative in Vespasian's lesson five stands out from its surroundings because it seems to derive from a different source. Nearly everything in the preceding lessons was evidently borrowed from the abridged Life of Wulfstan by the Worcester monk Senatus or from a closely related text; Vespasian even shares Senatus's distinctively worded summaries of material from William of Malmesbury's standard Latin *Vita Wulfstani.*[27] The close parallels with Senatus resume after the first few lines of lesson six. But when it comes to the Conquest itself, Vespasian refuses to follow Senatus and William of Malmesbury in attributing the Norman victory to God's punishment of the English for their sins or a lack of manly courage in the English forces or the justice of William's claim to the crown. Rejecting all such mitigating arguments, Vespasian offers a pro-English narrative that insists on the united strength and virtue of the English warriors, blames their defeat only on Harold's personal shortcomings and the foreigners' guile, and laments the Norman victory as an unalleviated and continuing disaster for England:

[Willelmi] adventus fama ad aures Haroldi, et principum regni allapsa decurrens, una omnes et unanimiter ad bellum incitavit.

Accinguntur, in prelium congregiuntur, et a rege universi virtutis suscipiunt incentivum. Juventus Anglorum sane insignis, juventus strenua et nulli cessura victori, si consultius ausa, si capud nacta incolume, perjurii regis penale fatum non sensissent. Set heu hominum mens, venturi nescia. Arte hostium et irrupcione acies intercisa prorumpitur, et nostrorum virtus sui prodiga et vite contemptor impetus succubuit, totumque robur regni cum rege mactator gladius sic assumpsit, quod nunquam denuo resumptis viribus ad libertatem assurgere attemptarentur. (lec. 5, ed. Darlington)

(When the news of William's landing reached Harold and the princes of the realm, every one of them hastened to war. They armed themselves, met together on the battlefield, and were all roused to valour by the king. The truly excellent young men of England, those valiant young warriors, would not have submitted to any conqueror if they had been used more skilfully, if they had found their leader uninjured, if they had not experienced the destined punishment of the king's perjury. But alas, the human mind does not know the future. By the enemies' stratagem, the vanguard of the invasion was sent forth divided, and the courage of our men, lavish and heedless of life, fell before their assault; and the murderous sword so claimed all the flower of our realm, along with the king, that never again did they strive to rise up for freedom with restored powers.)

Two motifs in the final lines of this lesson – that the whole strength of the English fell with Harold and that it has never recovered – echo the 'never again' passage at the end of Book II of William of Malmesbury's *Gesta Regum Anglorum*; [28] but the tone and most of the wording are different, suggesting the possibility that both descend from an earlier source.

The early *SEL* is more explicit about identifying Harold as the rightful king, and it admits no fault whatever on his part, shifting the blame for the English loss to some traitorous barons who betrayed themselves and the king who trusted them (lines 79–80). But its Conquest narrative is surprisingly close to the Vespasian account in most other respects. As in Vespasian, the king responds to the enemy's invasion by gathering a united army of Englishmen that should never have been defeated:

Harold heorde herof telle,   the king of Enguelonde,
He liet greithie faste is ost   agein him for to stonde.
The baronie of Enguelonde   redi was wel sone
The king to helpe and heomsulve,   ase right was for to done . . .
No strencthe ne hadden this straunge men   that were icome so
                                                                                                   newe

Ageinest heom of Enguelonde,   the hwyle huy wolden beo
                                  trewe.

                                  (72, 69–72; 73, 75–6)

(Harold, king of England, heard about it; he had his army strongly
equipped to stand against him. The barons of England were very
soon ready to help the king and themselves, as was right to do . . .
These foreign men, so recently arrived, had no strength against the
men of England for as long as they remained loyal.)

And as in Vespasian the unexpected defeat of Harold and his forces
is lamented as the disastrous fall of the whole of England, from
which it has never recovered:

. . . he was bineothe ibrought   and overcome at the laste
And to grounde ibrought, and alle his,   and al Enguelond also,
Into unecouthe mannes honde   that no right ne hadden tharto;
And never eft [it] ne cam agein   to righte eyres none . . .
Never eft to is cuynde heritage   ne cam it, Ich onderstonde.

                                  (73, 86–89, 94)

(he was defeated and overcome at last and brought down, and all his
troops and all England too, [brought] into the hands of strangers that
had no right to it, and it never afterwards returned to the rightful
heirs . . . Never again did it come back to its natural inheritors, as I
understand.)

In Vespasian, as in the early *SEL*, the tendentious Conquest
narrative leads directly into the popular legend of Wulfstan's staff.
With England defeated, in almost total servitude to the invaders, the attempt to depose Wulfstan (which they both attribute to
William the Conqueror himself) becomes a further act of Norman
aggression, an attempt to destroy the last remnant of Anglo-Saxon
authority in the church. Only the *SEL* takes the further step of portraying Wulfstan as an outspoken critic of the new regime, whom
William wants to silence. In both retellings, however, Wulfstan's
miraculous vindication and the humbling of his foreign opponents
takes on unusual political weight, becoming a powerful symbol of
national pride and hope in the face of Norman tyranny.

Despite all the parallels, I do not believe the Vespasian lessons
were the immediate source of the early *SEL* account of Wulfstan,
anti-Norman rhetoric and all. Rather, I would suggest that these
lessons indicate the existence of a larger tradition of nationalistic
Latin writing about Wulfstan and his era that must have begun
soon after the Conquest and survived for more than two centuries, at least in some parts of western England. Görlach was

probably right in connecting the lessons with the Worcester area, but the physical manuscript is less helpful than he and Darlington believed. Although Cotton Vespasian E.9 also includes a cartulary from Westwood Priory in Worcestershire, the texts were originally separate items and may just have been bound together by the Cotton librarian.[29] But other evidence sheds further light on the origins and use of the Vespasian lessons themselves. The fourth lesson includes some details about Wulfstan's election as bishop of Worcester that are not found in Senatus or even William of Malmesbury, and gives an unflattering portrayal of his predecessor Ealdred, who was locally resented for having kept some lucrative diocesan estates when he left Worcester to become archbishop of York. Such details suggest that whoever compiled the lessons had an unusual interest in the see of Worcester, as well as access to its sources.

Commemorations of Wulfstan were not confined to Worcester, however, and neither apparently was the circulation of these particular lessons. I have not encountered any complete copies except in the Vespasian manuscript, but excerpts survive in many Sarum and quasi-Sarum breviaries, including BL Stowe 12 (1322–25, Norwich), Bodleian Auct. E.1.1 (c. 1400, diocese of Salisbury?) and even the printed editions of the Sarum breviary. The excerpts chosen tend to come from the most conventional sections of the Vespasian text, often just describing the saint's early virtues, holy death and a few of his miracles. But a handful of breviaries also include excerpts from Vespasian's distinctive account of Wulfstan's election, and at least one – the printed Hereford breviary of 1505 – includes part of its Conquest narrative, showing that these potentially controversial parts of the text must sometimes have circulated with the rest and continued to find some readers who appreciated them.

St Laurence. Although Görlach suggested the *Legenda aurea* as the source of the *SEL* account of Laurence, he obviously had some misgivings about that hypothesis, having noticed resemblances to 'liturgical epitomes' in one episode that raise the alternative possibility that 'a detailed pre-LgA source' was used in combination with the *Legenda*.[30] Having studied more unpublished Latin versions, I see no reason to assume that the *SEL* author(s) used the *Legenda* retelling at all. In fact, the *Legenda* lacks much of the dialogue found in the *SEL* account and adds a great deal of distinctive material, all of which the *SEL* lacks. A closer match to the *SEL*'s content is provided by full-length versions of BHL 4753, the traditional legend, copies of which were available in Worcester and Salisbury by the middle of the eleventh century.[31]

The ideal source, however, would be an abridged descendant of BHL 4753 that omits all the episodes and speeches that don't appear in the *SEL* while retaining all the episodes and speeches that do. Although I have not found exactly that ideal source, I have found parts of it in a branch of the liturgical tradition best repre- sented by BL Add. 32427, a fifteenth-century Sarum breviary from the diocese of Worcester. Since space is limited, I will confine the demonstration to two examples of the parallels.

Whereas the *Legenda aurea* and most breviary accounts hurry past the details introducing Laurence's first meeting with the emperor Decius, BL Add. 32427 takes time to explain that Decius has just learned that Laurence received the church's treasure from the recently martyred Bishop Sixtus; hence it is clear what he is thinking at this point:

> Parthemius tribunus nunciavit Decio imperatori quod Laurencius, archidiaconus beati Sixti pape qui habebat thesauros ecclesie recon- ditos, in custodia tenebatur. Tunc Decius gavisus est valde et fecit sibi beatum Laurencium presentari. (lec. 1)

> (The tribune Parthemius informed Emperor Decius that Laurence, the archdeacon of blessed Pope Sixtus who held the hidden treasures of the church, had been arrested. Then Decius greatly rejoiced and had St Laurence presented to him.)

The *SEL* version gives the same details, expanding on them to convey Decius's character and motivation even more clearly:

> The aumperoure huy [the officers] senden word   al hwat huy hadden ido,
> And hou Seint Laurence in prisone was   in strongue bendes also,
> And hou he al that tresor hadde   of churchene to him idrawe
> [That the bissop him hadde itake   ar he were ibroght of dawe.]
> The aumperou[r] iheorde this;   he was glad tharof and fawe,
> For he thoughte that tresor al habbe,   thei it were agen lawe.
> Thane holie man he liet fette   and bifore him lede.
>   (340, 19–24)[32]

(The officers sent word to the emperor about everything they had done, and how St Laurence was in prison, strongly shackled, and how he had gathered to himself all the treasure of the churches that the bishop had entrusted to him before he lost his life. The emperor heard this and was glad and eager about it, for he intended to have all that treasure, even though it was against the law. He had the holy man fetched and led before him.)

Once imprisoned by Decius's officer Hippolytus, Laurence baptizes and heals the blind prisoner Lucillus – a fairly long scene in BHL 4753, which both the *Legenda* and most breviaries abbreviate more drastically than the *SEL* does. But BL Add. 32427 retains a selection of speeches and details that closely corresponds with the selection in the *SEL*. Here is the Latin version:

> Erat autem in custodia quidam homo gentilis nomine Lucillus, qui plorando amissis oculis cecus factus fuerat. Cui dixit beatus Laurencius, 'Crede in dominum nostrum Jesum Christum et baptizare, et illuminabit te'. Respondit Lucillus cum fletu, dicens, 'In Christum credo, et ydola vana respuo'. Cumque eum Laurencius baptizaret, aperti sunt oculi eius et cepit clamare dicens, 'Benedictus Dominus Jesus Christus, qui me illuminavit per beatum Laurencium, qui cecus fui et modo video.' (lecc. 2–3)

> (Also in the prison was a pagan named Lucillus, who had wept away his eyesight and become blind. Laurence told him, 'Believe in our Lord Jesus Christ and be baptized, and he will give you light.' Lucillus tearfully replied, 'I believe in Christ and renounce vain idols.' When Laurence baptized him, his eyes were opened and he began to shout, saying, 'Blessed be the Lord Jesus Christ, who through blessed Laurence has given me light; I was blind and now I see.')

The *SEL* version is so similar in both order and content that one can easily spot its additions (italicized here), which serve not only to clarify the action and intensify the drama but also to humanize both main characters, making it easier to identify and sympathize with them:

> On hethene man thare was inne,   Lucille was is name,
> That hadde thareinne so muche iwope   *for seoruwe and for schame*
> That he weop out bothe is eiyene   and al blynd was bicome.
> *Seint Laurence hadde reuthe   that is sight him was binome;*
> 'Bilief', he seide, 'on Jesu Crist   *that for us schedde is blod,*
> And afong Cristinedom,   ant thou schalt habbe thi sight wel guod'.
> 'Ich bilieve', this othur seide,   'on him *with al mi thought,*
> And forsake alle theos false godes   *that ne mowen me helpe nought.'*
> Seint Laurence baptizede him,   and *anonright* with the dede
> His sight him cam *wel cler and guod*;   tho began he anon to grede,

'Ihered beo *swete* Jesu Crist,   *that here hath icud is mighte*
And thorugh is serjaunt, Seint Laurence,   me hath isent mi
                                                            sighte!
For *ase ye wuten everechone,*   mi sight me was binome,
And thorugh Jesu Crist and Seint Laurence   it is me agein
                                                            icome.'
                                                        (341, 38–51)

(A heathen man was inside – his name was Lucillus, – who had wept
so long in there *for sorrow and shame* that he wept both his eyes out
and had become quite blind. *St Laurence felt pity that his sight had
been taken from him.* 'Believe', he said, 'in Jesus Christ, *who shed his
blood for us,* and receive baptism, and you will have your sight fully
restored.' 'I believe', said the other, 'in him *with my whole mind,*
and I forsake all these false gods *who lack any power to help me.*' St
Laurence baptized him, and *as soon as* it was done, his sight was
restored to him, *completely distinct and good.* Then he began to cry
out, 'Praised be *sweet* Jesus Christ, *who has made his power known
here* and, through his servant St Laurence, has sent me my sight!
For *as you all know,* my sight was taken from me, and through Jesus
Christ and St Laurence, it has returned to me.')

Unfortunately, BL Add. 32427 allots only six lessons to
Laurence's legend, rather than the eight or nine for which this
particular abridgement must have been designed.[33] Lessons five
and six, on the saint's ordeal and his intrepid responses, are disordered and full of gaps, as if the compiler was rushing to include
the most memorable lines, and the lessons end in the midst of
Laurence's tortures. As a result, this manuscript offers only spo-
radic opportunities for comparison with the second half of the
SEL account. Partial copies of the same abridgement survive,
however, in several other Sarum manuscripts and the early
printed editions of both the Hereford and York breviaries. And
further research may identify a fuller and more satisfactory copy
than BL Add. 32427.[34]

As I hope this essay has suggested, there is a wealth of unpublished material on saints in English liturgical manuscripts which
still remains to be discovered and put to use in studies of the *SEL*
and in a variety of other projects. I am preparing a descriptive
inventory of the hagiographical lessons in Sarum breviaries and
related manuscripts and would be glad to share information with
other researchers.

Notes

1 Minnie E. Wells, 'The *South English Legendary* in its relation to the *Legenda aurea*', *PMLA*, 51 (1936), 337–60.

2 Manfred Görlach, 'The *Legenda aurea* and the early history of the *South English Legendary*', in Dunn-Lardeau, p. 304. The 1974 study to which he refers is of course *Textual Tradition*.

3 *Breviarium ad usum insignis ecclesiae Sarum*, ed. Francis Procter and Christopher Wordsworth, 3 vols (Cambridge: Cambridge University Press, 1879–86). This edition was based primarily on the last and most comprehensive of the early printed editions, 'Breviarium seu horarium domesticum: sive choro ecclesiastico deserviens ad usum insignis ecclesie Sarum' (1531; STC 15830). The other major early editions were the 1516 folio breviary with the same title (STC 15812), and the 1518 lectionary, 'Legende totius anni . . . secundum ordinem Sarum' (STC 16137).

4 The Exeter lectionary was published as *Legenda Exon.*, vol. 3 of the *Ordinale Exon.*, ed. J. N. Dalton, HBS 63 (London, 1926). Cotton Appendix 23 has often been overlooked by students of English liturgies, probably because the old catalogue of Cotton manuscripts identifies it only generically as a book of 'Lectiones in festis diebus sanctorum', but it is an important source for the history of Sarum lessons about saints.

5 Breviaries were very efficient compilations that provided all the rubrics and texts needed for celebrating the divine office; sometimes they included the music as well. Lectionaries had much more space for the lessons (used at matins) and sometimes gave longer versions of them. The term 'secular' in reference to such books means just they were designed for liturgies that used either three or nine lessons, whereas the maximum in monastic liturgies was twelve.

6 The term 'lectionary' applies whether or not the designated lessons had been copied into a single book. Initially, the legendary and homiliary existed as separate volumes, with the lessons just marked off in the margins.

7 *The Hereford Breviary, Edited from the Rouen Edition of 1505 with Collation of Manuscripts*, ed. Walter H. Frere and L. E. G. Brown, 3 vols, HBS 26, 40, 46 (London: Harrison and Sons [for the Society], 1903–15). Unlike the nineteenth-century editors of the Sarum and York breviaries, Frere and Brown became well aware of the unpredictability of the hagiographical lessons because they tried to include all the variants from the surviving manuscripts. They discuss this problem in HBS 46, pp. xxxv–xl; the quotation here appears on p. xxxvii.

8 *The Monastic Breviary of Hyde Abbey, Winchester*, ed. John B. L. Tolhurst, 6 vols, HBS 69–71, 76, 78, 80 (London: Harrison and Sons, 1932–42).

9 Tolhurst prints these lessons on Cecilia in HBS 78, at fols 384r–385v.

10 Sherry L. Reames, 'Lectionary revision in Sarum breviaries and the origins of the early printed editions', *Journal of the Early Book Society*, 9 (2006), 95–115.

11 Sherry L. Reames, 'Unexpected texts for saints in some Sarum breviary manuscripts', in George H. Brown and Linda Ehrsam Voigts (eds), *The Study of Medieval Manuscripts of England: A Festschrift in Honor of Richard Pfaff* (Tempe, AZ; MRTS, 2010 pp. 163–84).

12 On this lectionary, see esp. Leonard Boyle, 'Dominican lectionaries and Leo of Ostia's *Translatio S. Clementis*', *Archivum Fratrum Praedicatorum*, 28 (1958), 362–94.

13 Here and throughout this essay, my quotations from medieval texts use modernized capitalisation, word division and punctuation, and distinguish between u/v and i/j. Translations are mine unless otherwise noted.

14 These departures are not only made in the 1330s version of the Exeter lectionary, but also reaffirmed with increased explicitness in the revised version (Exeter Cathedral MS 3505B) that was produced around the end of the fourteenth century.

15 Introducing the lessons for St Egidius or Giles, for example, Edinburgh 26 explains that according to Sarum Use the three middle lessons should be taken from the Common of one martyr, to commemorate the secondary saint of the day, but 'ex devotione' it is supplying nine proper lessons for Egidius and the reader may choose whichever he prefers: 'Eligat qui voluerit unum modum vel alium' (fol. 523).

16 For the ordinal changes, see esp. Reames, 'Unexpected texts for saints'; for the standardization efforts, Sherry L. Reames, 'Late medieval efforts at standardization and reform in the Sarum lessons for saints' days', in Margaret Connolly and Linne R. Mooney (eds), *Design and Distribution of Late Medieval Manuscripts in England* (Woodbridge and York: York Medieval Press, 2008), pp. 91–117.

17 Pierre Salmon, *The Breviary Through the Centuries*, trans. Sister David Mary (Collegeville, MN: Liturgical Press, 1962), p. 160 n. 226.

18 Görlach, *Textual Tradition*, p. 216. The Translation narrative is presented as a separate chapter in D'Evelyn and Mill, but it just comprises lines 2405–78 of the Becket chapter in Horstmann. Except as noted, I rely on Horstmann for quotations and line numbers from the *SEL*.

19 For the text of the Q-Appendix, see *Materials for the History of Thomas Becket*, ed. James C. Robertson and J. B. Sheppard, 7 vols, RS 67 (London: Longman, 1875–85), vol. 4, pp. 428–30.

20 The Sarum references here are based on Procter and Wordsworth's edition (cited above in n. 3); the fuller lessons in the Cotton manuscript, described hereafter, are numbered differently.

21 For an edition and detailed discussion of this previously unpublished text, see Sherry L. Reames, 'Reconstructing and interpreting a thirteenth-century office for the Translation of Thomas Becket', *Speculum*, 80 (2005), 118–70.

22 The bracketed words are missing from Cotton, but found in the three medieval manuscripts that have most of the same text: two later Sarum breviaries from Norwich and Bodleian Laud Misc. 666, a collection of texts about Becket dating from c. 1300.

23 Although we can't know for certain that no intermediate Latin or vernacular source came between the liturgical text preserved in Cotton and the retelling in Bodleian MS Laud Misc. 108, I have done enough research on the Latin manuscripts to be sure that the Cotton text represents the dominant branch of liturgical texts for this feast; so the *SEL*'s departures from it were at the very least unusual, though not necessarily brand new.

24 Thompson, *Everyday Saints*.

25 Theodor Wolpers, *Die englische Heiligenlegende des Mittelalters* (Tübingen: Niemeyer, 1964), p. 231 and n. 73; cited by Görlach, *Textual Tradition*, p. 265, n. 25. For the text of these lessons, see *The Vita Wulfstani of William of Malmesbury*, ed. Reginald R. Darlington (London: Royal Historical Society, 1928), pp. 111–14.

26 Görlach, *Textual Tradition*, pp. 136–7.

27 Senatus's abridgement is also found in Darlington, *Vita Wulfstani*, pp. 68–114.

28 William of Malmesbury, *Gesta Regum Anglorum*, ed. and trans. R. A. B. Mynors, R. M. Thomson and M. Winterbottom (Oxford: Clarendon Press, 1998), II. 228.11. Despite the similar motifs, William was making a different argument: 'it was God's hidden and stupendous purpose that never again should Englishmen feel together and fight together in defence of their liberties, as though all the strength of England had fallen away with Harold' (ibid., p. 423). William used these motifs again in his *Vita Wulfstani*, II.1, arguing there that the English collapse validated Wulfstan's prophecy about the kingdom's weakness at the time of the Conquest.

29 William of Malmesbury, *Saints' Lives*, ed. and trans. M. Winterbottom and R. M. Thomson (Oxford: Clarendon Press, 2002), p. 4, n. 2.

30 Görlach, *Textual Tradition*, p. 187.

31 E. Gordon Whatley gives a helpful discussion of these early sources in 'Acta Sanctorum', in Frederick M. Biggs, Thomas D. Hill, Paul E. Szarmach and E. Gordon Whatley (eds), *Sources of Anglo-Saxon Literary Culture*, vol. 1 (Kalamazoo, MI: Medieval Institute Publications, 2001), pp. 289–92. For BHL 4753, I relied on Hippolyte Delehaye's edition, 'Récherches sur le légendier romain', *Analecta Bollandiana*, 51 (1933), 72–98.

32 The bracketed line, apparently omitted by mistake from Laud Misc. 108, is inserted here from D'Evelyn and Mill.

33 Some other breviaries complete the story of Laurence's martyrdom by continuing the narrative in either the remaining three lessons on the saint's feast day or the extra three lessons devoted to Laurence during his Octave; the latter group includes Bodleian MS Auct. E.1.1 and the 1505 printed Hereford breviary, both mentioned earlier in this essay.

34 Although Cotton Appendix 23 is also a Worcester manuscript, it gives a different abridgement of the Laurence legend. Likewise, while BL Add. 32427 has excerpts from the Vespasian lessons on Wulfstan, Cotton Appendix 23 follows another tradition.

5

Outspoken style in the *South English Legendary* and Robert of Gloucester

Oliver Pickering

I

Widespread evidence of textual revision has always been one of the fascinating aspects of the late thirteenth-century *SEL* collection. It is a feature of many individual poems of both *sanctorale* and *temporale* – broadly, lives of saints and lives of Christ – and holds the key to understanding the relationships between them. The multiplicity of extant manuscripts, preserving poems in different stages of development, provides ample raw material for detailed study of the phenomenon. The rewriting of existing verse is at times so striking that it is clear that a poet other than the original author was responsible. The mixture of styles within the *SEL* corpus suggests in any case that more than one writer was active. The task of disentangling the contribution of different poets is, however, immense, because of the scores of manuscripts and thousands of lines of verse involved.[1] It might also not be thought worth it, given the pedestrian nature of much of the *SEL*, were it not for evidence, throughout the collection, of the presence of a more than usually competent writer. There are also compelling stylistic reasons to think that this same poet was closely involved in the composition of Robert of Gloucester's *Chronicle*.

Evidence of revision in the *temporale* narratives reveals this poet's hand at work with particular clarity. It has been shown (to use their modern titles) that the *Expanded Nativity* was developed out of the *Nativity of Mary and Christ* (*Nativity*), and the *Southern Passion* out of the *Ministry and Passion* (*Ministry*), very likely written as a sequel to *Nativity*.[2] *Nativity* and *Ministry*, at least, were almost certainly written to stand outside the *SEL* cycle, and were perhaps composed independently of it. *Southern Passion*, in contrast, was probably written to fill a place within the *SEL*, and it became the standard Passion poem of the collection.

It seems certain that the same writer was responsible for both *Expanded Nativity* and *Southern Passion*. The two poems are, in content, closer to the gospels than are *Nativity* and *Ministry*, and the reviser achieves this both by fresh gospel translation and by cleverly adapting lines and phrases from the earlier compositions for his own purposes.[3] *Expanded Nativity* and *Southern Passion* also have in common instances where the poet speaks in a more personal voice with considerable intensity, seemingly because his feelings are strongly engaged. Two examples from each poem may be given here. The first of those from *Expanded Nativity* asks how it was that the ox and ass knelt down before the Christ child, and then answers its own question:

> Now was this a wonder dede   and aghe kunde inow;
> Vor wel Ichot that oxen kunne   bet now drawe ate plow,
> And asses bere sackes   and corn aboute to bringe,
> Than to make meri gleo   and knele bifore a kinge . . .
> How couthen heo here legges bowen   and here knen so to
> wende,
> To knele bifore a king?   who made hem so hende?
> Now weren hit wonder gleomen to,   who broughte hem such
> mod?
> Ac whan we habbeth al ido,   that child ibore was God.
> (*Expanded Nativity*, 331–4, 337–40)

(Now this was a wonderful thing to do, and against their nature, for I know well that oxen are more fitted to pulling ploughs, and asses to carrying sacks and bringing corn, than to rejoicing and kneeling before a king . . . How were they able to bend their legs and move their knees so as to kneel before a king? Who made them so gracious? It might seem a miracle to minstrels: who put them into such a state of mind? But when all is said and done, the child who was born was God.)

The second example from *Expanded Nativity* is from slightly further on in the poem, where the writer strongly criticizes those who maintain that St Anastasia could have been present at the birth of Christ:

> The lesinge of mani foles   telleth of Seint Anastase,
> That heo scholde with Oure Ledi beo;   hit nis bote the mase:
> Vor heo ne seigh never Oure Ledi her,   vor to hundred yer
> bifore
> And more, ar heo come an erthe   oure Lord was ibore.
> Som wrecche bifond this lesinge   with onrighte,

> Vor as muche as me maketh of hire munde   a midewinter nighte.
>
> (*Expanded Nativity*, 355–60)

(The lies of many fools relate of St Anastasia that she attended Our Lady, but that is nothing but fantasy, because she never saw Our Lady, for the reason that Our Lord was born more than two hundred years before she lived on Earth. Some wretch made up this lie without any basis of truth, on the grounds that she is commemorated on Christmas night.)

In the first example from *Southern Passion* the writer contrasts Judas's plain dealing with the Jews with the over-pricing practised by medieval merchants, but still concludes bitterly that he was a *luther chapman*:

> Goed chep the shrewe him grauntede   that him so solde;
> He ne axede nought a ferthing more   than the Gywes him tolde.
> He ne lowede him nought to deore   as this chapmen wolleth
>   echon
> Thing that is deoreworth   ak he axede ham anon
> 'What wolleth ye for him give'   as who seith 'beode ye
> And as goed chep ich wolle him give   as ye wolleth bydde me.'
> Now luther thrift upon his heved   'Amen', seggeth alle!
> For luther chapman he was   and also him is byfalle.
>
> (*Southern Passion*, 779–86)

(The villain who sold him granted them a good bargain: he asked for not a farthing more than the Jews specified. He did not set too high a price on him, as every merchant will in the case of something precious, but he asked them straight out, 'What will you give for him?', as if to say, 'You make the offer, and I shall give as good a bargain for him as you will ask me for'. Now ill luck fall on his head – everyone say Amen! For he was a wicked merchant, and a bad end befell him.)

The second example is from the end of *Southern Passion*'s outspoken defence of women from slanderous attack; 146 lines long in the complete version, it occurs immediately after Christ's post-resurrection appearance to Mary Magdalene, Mary being taken as a model of love and faithfulness:[4]

> And whanne we habbeth alle isede,   God geve hem alle chame
> That witoute enchesoun   seyth wommen eny blame.
> For more myldehede ne goodnesse   in non erthelyche beste nys,
> Ne more mylce ne treunesse   than in good womm[a]n is.
> Ye seith Mary Magdalene   oure Lord she sought alone
> Tho the apostlis that wit hym were   lete hym lygge echone.
> Wheyther was here a [pert]ere love?   Seggeth that ye ne lyghe!

Was ther eny stabelere   than [was] this holy Marye?
(Southern Passion, 1983–90)

(And when all is said and done, let God shame all those who blame
women without reason. For there is no greater gentleness or goodness, or kindness or truth, in any being on Earth than there is in a
good woman. Mary Magdalene, as you see, sought out Our Lord by
herself after the apostles who had been with him left him lying [in
the tomb], without exception. Was there a more manifest instance of
love? Take care not to lie! Was there anyone more faithful than this
holy Mary?)

In these extracts we see the poet ranging from gentle tender-
ness to strong invective, the latter a result of his uncompromis-
ing attitude to flawed or wicked behaviour – he does not suffer
gladly either fools or villains, who in consequence are mocked
scornfully or condemned outright. Particular aspects of his style
are the direct, colloquial way in which he addresses his audience,
frequently supplying or anticipating their reactions; lively illustrations from contemporary life, often including direct speech;
expressions of wonder, and of imaginative sympathy with individuals (or, as in the first example, animals); and repeated, often
exclamatory, rhetorical questioning. He also possesses the ability
to round off a passage with a striking, summarizing line, and to
escape the limits of the couplet by constructing longer or shorter
units of sense. Certain phrases recur as a further mark of individual
style; we may compare 'Ac whan we habbeth al ido', from line 4 of
the first example, with 'And whanne we habbeth alle isede', from
line 1 of the fourth.[5]
    This poet's manner of writing in *Expanded Nativity* and
Southern Passion is so marked that it would be surprising if it were
not identifiable elsewhere in the *SEL* collection, assuming he had
a hand in it. Further examples will demonstrate that he was in
fact more widely involved, but something may first be said about
'normal' *SEL* verse style.
    Critics over the years, notably Theodor Wolpers, have drawn
attention to the simplicity and transparency (arising from devotional and homiletic impulses) of much of the writing in the saints'
lives, and to its success in communicating emotion; the style has
been characterized by Gregory Sadlek as 'basically light and child-
like', and as giving an 'impression of primitive lucidity'.[6] There
have also been a number of publications demonstrating that the
SEL contains a considerable amount of effective dialogue.[7] We

may take as a rewarding example of these studies an article by Anne Thompson which analyses the narrative style of the life of Mary Magdalene.[8] Thompson shows convincingly that the author is good at conveying the feelings of the protagonists (partly through attention to detail) and good at involving our feelings as readers. She remarks on 'the skill with which narrative and dialogue, direct and indirect speech are mingled',[9] and quotes one particular passage of dialogue between the king and queen in the story, which may be reproduced here as typical:

> To is wif he wend anon,   'Dame, Ichelle,' he sede,
> 'In alle manere to Peter wende,   he ssel me bet rede.'
> 'Certes, sire,' quath this wif,   'thou ne sselt noght fram me
>   wende
> That Inelle the siwy vot with vot,   sende wat God me sende.'
> 'Dame,' quath the other,   'thou spext folie, thi red is wel wilde,
> Thou mightest adrenche in the se,   noste thou ert mid childe?'
> This god wife fel to hure loverdes fet,   wepinge wel sore,
> 'Ichelle,' heo sede, 'with the wende   thegh I necome aghe
>   namore.'
>
>   (I, 307, 129–36)

(He went immediately to his wife and said, 'Madam, I intend in every way to make a journey to [St] Peter; he shall teach me more fully.' 'Be assured, sir', said this wife, 'you shan't leave me without my following you foot by foot, whatever [fate] God may send me.' 'Madam', said the other, 'you're speaking foolishly, your plan is crazy – you might drown in the sea, don't you realize you're pregnant?' This good wife fell to her lord's feet, weeping bitterly. 'I shall', she said, 'go with you even if I never come back.')

This extract is undoubtedly successful in combining narrative and speech economically – it is not claimed that the reviser who is the subject of this essay is the only *SEL* poet capable of writing well – but the language is noticeably plain, without any expressive variety. Thompson praises 'the simple, almost spare quality of the redactor's diction . . . with its emphasis on nouns and verbs and its lack of rich or varied descriptive terms' as enhancing 'the expressive qualities of the narrative'.[10] Effective it may be, but the point to be made here is that the words and phrases used are ones which occur again and again throughout the bulk of the saints' lives. Unlike the language employed by the author of *Expanded Natitivity* and *Southern Passion* when his feelings are aroused, they are not special in themselves.[11]

The sentences in the above passage from *Mary Magdalene* also keep carefully within the couplet framework.[12] Such writing has a leisureliness characterized not only by the length of line and, as Thompson remarks, 'the need to find only one rhyme for each couplet (i.e. no midrhyme)',[13] but by the expectation of a syntactic pause each time the second line of a couplet comes round. *SEL* couplets, as Sadlek comments when discussing the style of the 'Prologue' or '*Banna sanctorum*', are usually complete units of thought.[14]

Strikingly different is the following passage of narrative, taken once again, though at random, from *Southern Passion*:

> A man was while an hosebonde   that sette a gret vyne,
> And by-wallede hit aboute   and suthe atte fyne
> He dalf theron and arerede   al a tour amydde,
> And hurede him eorth-tylyers   and so that hit bytydde
> That he wente a pilgrinage   and tho the tyme was ney
> Of the frut to gadery   of hynen he him by-sey,
> And sende to tho eorth-tylyers   that frut to underfonge.
> The eorth-tylyers this hinen nome   and some in pyne stronge
> Hi bete and some slowe   and with stones hevede therto.
> The lord sende yut mo hynen   and me dude ham also.
>
>   (*Southern Passion*, 233–42)

(There was once a householder who planted a large vineyard and walled it about, and then afterwards dug in it and erected a tower in the middle, and hired husbandmen. And it so happened that he went on a pilgrimage, and when it was nearly time to pick the fruit he employed servants and sent them to receive the fruit from the husbandmen. The husbandmen seized these servants, and beat some of them very painfully, and killed some, and hurled stones [at others]. The lord sent more servants, and they did the same to them.)

Even though the poet is not here speaking in his 'personal' voice, but translating from the gospel, it is clear that the verse moves in a much more fluid way than is normal in the *SEL* saints' lives, overflowing the couplet boundaries with ease. It is the work of a writer who is quite happy to stop one idea part-way through a couplet and begin at once on a different one.

In order to illustrate this further we may return again to this poet's lengthy defence of women. In all manuscripts except one this passage is basically ninety-two lines long, which is how it was published by Beatrice Brown in her EETS edition of *Southern Passion*. But in one manuscript, Oxford, Bodleian MS Bodley 779, there are an extra fifty-four lines which occur as five separate blocks within the standard text. Brown printed these lines in her Notes (pp. 99–100), evidently believing them not to be original, and indeed Bodley 779 is a fifteenth-century manuscript written well over a hundred years after the date of composition of the piece. There is, however, no doubt that these fifty-four lines are part of the poet's original composition, partly because they are at times integral to his closely reasoned argument but also because they are in his habitually unrestrained verse style. There is ample evidence, but a single example must suffice.[15]

The passage in question consists of six lines of the standard text (*Southern Passion* 1953–58) followed by eighteen of the 'extra' lines, which are here italicized. The poet is asking whether men or women are more lecherous: the answer is men, which he illustrates at length by explicit comparison of the sexual behaviour of male and female animals:

If lecherie is so lethir dede,   and so lethir to do,
As the Gospel us seyth and the bok,   and Oure Lord sulf therto,
Wheyther is thenne more to blame   that the dede deth so,
Other thilke that ne deth here nought   ac soffreth that me here
do?   4
Wel ye wete that the man hit is   that the dede deth:
Whoso seyth that nere nought ryght,   he lyghth thorwghout his
teth
– Bot he be al tothles,   as God geve that he were!
The kynde ek of alle other bestis   us wolle yit soth lere   8
That the goodnesse of women   is more of [worth] inough,
And the clennesse also, [than] of men,   and that me hem blameth
wit wough:
Ye seth wel chip and rotherin   and houndis yit therto,
Hennis and ges and ek hors   and ech maner beste also,   12
That the she best halt here stille   as non soche thyng nere,
Alle in pes but as hit falleth   in here tyme of the yere;
And yut somme of hem, but yif hy be   in good lese ido,
From soche thyng stille beth   yere and other to.   16
How thenketh you of the he bestis?   Fareth h[y] alle so?
Nay, forsothe, nought mony,   yif hy mowe come therto,
Ac beth alle evere yare   when h[y] mowe here make fynde,
Bothe somer and winter ek;   ther bleveth fewe behynde.   20
And yif hy habbeth son a smel   at then tounnis ende
Of folye of here make,   yit hy wolleth thedir wende,
And so synful beth in here dede that chame hit is to thenche;
Here mou folis neme ensaumple   and here lethir wordis quenche!   24

(If lechery is such an evil deed, and such a wicked thing to do, as the gospel and mass book (?) tell us, and Our Lord himself also, who is more to blame, the person that performs the deed or the one that

doesn't do it but suffers it to be done to her? You know well that it's
the man who performs the deed. Whoever says that's not the case,
he's lying through his teeth – unless he's completely toothless, as
God grant that he were! The nature of all other animals will teach
us the truth, that women's goodness and virtue are of greater worth
than men's, and that they are blamed unjustly. You see clearly in the
case of sheep, oxen and dogs, hens, geese and also horses, every kind
of animal, that the she-beast behaves quietly as if there were no such
thing [as mating], and stays completely placid unless she happens
to be in season; and some of them, unless they're put to excellent
pasture, even abstain from such a deed for a year or more. How do
the he-beasts strike you? Do all of them behave like this? No, indeed,
not many, if they have the opportunity. If they encounter their mate
they're always ready for it, both summer and winter; few hang back.
If they so much as catch a sexual whiff of their mate, even at the end
of the village, they will go there, and are so sinful in the way they go
about it that it's shameful to think of. Foolish people should learn a
lesson from this and cease their wicked words!)

The poet begins the comparison at 1. 8, half-way through a
couplet, after an extra piece of invective (1. 7) that wittily continues
the mention of teeth in the preceding line. There can be no doubt
that the 'additional' passage is original, as a different writer inter-
polating the animals comparison would naturally have begun with
a new couplet following immediately on 1. 6. Lines 1–4, 11–16, in
particular, illustrate the long, discursive sentences that come naturally to this poet, but 8–10, 18–20, 21–3 demonstrate equally his
disregard of couplet boundaries.

II

The examples of the 'outspoken' poet's work so far discussed have
all come from the *temporale* narratives of the *SEL*, predominantly
Southern Passion. I show now that the same style of writing can
be found elsewhere in the collection. It will have become apparent that the poet is at his most characteristic when commenting,
expounding or 'preaching', and it is in certain expository sections
of the *sanctorale* that his voice most clearly reappears.

We may look first at two passages from *All Souls Day*, which is
largely about purgatory, preparation for death, and the fate of the
soul. Throughout the legend the explanatory writing overflows
couplet boundaries as need arises, making the outspoken poet's
authorship at once a possibility, but the vocabulary used is generally plain. It is the illustrative anecdotes from contemporary life

that reveal his presence, for (as in *Southern Passion*) it is the opportunity to denounce real specimens of sin and folly that moves his
verse on to a different level. In this mode he fiercely exposes the
dangers of going to a bad priest for confession and penance:[16]

> Hwat, hou is hit thanne of Janekin   and of Robinet the wilde,
> Of Annot and of Malekin   that wollez habbe thene preost so
>   milde,
> And huy seggez, 'Thilke preost is to hard   God schilde us fram
>   is loth;
> Go we to Sire Gilbert the preost   he nis nevere wroth,
> He wollez schrive us nessche inough   and ore sunnes al forgyve'.
> Bi God, hwane huy habbez al ido   hom huy goth unschrive;
> For heore penaunce schal beo so luyte   that Sire Gilbert and
>   huy also
> Schullen gon a-develewey   bote God nime yeme heom to.
>   (421–2, 45–52)

(What is then the situation with Jankin and wild Robinet, with
Annot and Malekin, who would like the priest to be lenient, saying,
'This priest is too severe, may God preserve us from his harshness.
Let us go to Sir Gilbert the priest, he is never angry. He will hear
our confession gently and wholly forgive our sins.' By God, when
they've done all that, they'll go home unshriven, because their
penance will be so small that both Sir Gilbert and they will go to the
devil, unless God takes heed of them.)

It is noteworthy that the phrase 'hwane huy habbez al ido' in l. 50
occurs in very similar form ('Ac whan we habbeth al ido') in l. 340
of *Expanded Nativity*, quoted earlier.

Sir Gilbert crops up again later in *All Souls* as an example of a
priest who has said mass while in a state of sin:[17]

> Ake thei the Masse ne beo the worse   the preost, bi mi swere,
> That hire singuth in dedlich sunne   acorie it schal ful deore!
> For hwane Sire Gileberd imassed hath   his lif he wole so dighte
> At the taverne to beon a-day   and bi is quene bi nyghte;
> He seith, hwane men cleopiez him preost   'Sittez stille, mine
>   guode ifere,
> The preost hanguez at churche   and Ich am nouthe here'.
> His cope othur is surplis   the preost he seith it isse:
> Ake his cope schal bileve at hom   hwane he schal to helle, iwisse!
>   (430, 339–46)

(But although the Mass is none the worse, I swear that the priest
that sings it while in a state of deadly sin shall pay a severe penalty!
For when Sir Gilbert has finished the Mass he arranges his life so as

to be in the tavern during the day and beside his mistress at night. When people address him as priest he says, 'Relax, my good friend. The priest is hanging in the church and I myself am here.' By 'the priest' he's referring to his cope or surplice, but his cope will remain at home when he goes to hell!)

Similar colloquial or conversational comment, drawing in the audience either directly (by addressing them) or indirectly (by force of language), occurs at lines 123–6, 190–4, 304–5, and 374–9 of *All Souls*. But much of the legend comprises tales – *narraciones* – told in a straightforwardly plain style, and it has therefore to be considered that the poet merely revised a pre-existing composition, retaining its narrative elements. However, we cannot rule out that a writer of such demonstrable versatility was capable of adopting the 'normal' *SEL* style if he wished, particularly for simple didactic purposes. Illustrative tales are of course found alongside exposition and invective in prose sermons, and lines 187–94, which move from story to characteristic address in mid-couplet (189–90), support the theory that the outspoken poet wrote the whole legend. The tale is of a clerk attacked by thieves, who is rescued by dead bodies that rise from their graves and beat off the assailants:

> Aboute this theoves hi come echon   and gonne hem to dryve
> To here put hi wende sithe aghe   the clerk hamward blyve
> And thus his beden were iyulde   that he bad er ofte
> Ich am siker aweiward the theoves   ne makede here pas noght softe
> For Ich wot non of you ne scholde   hem habbe so sore agaste
> A wonder bataille hit was on   hadde hit longe ilaste
> For Ich wene ther nis no champioun   that hadde ther ibeo
> That nadde sone ynome his red   hamward forto fleo.
>
> (II, 470, 187–94)

(They surrounded these thieves and chased them away. Then they returned to their graves and the clerk quickly went home. In this way the prayers that he had often said were answered. I'm certain the thieves wouldn't have run away quietly [in normal circumstances], for I know none of you would have frightened them so badly. It would have been quite a battle if it had gone on long, and I can't think that any champion who'd been present wouldn't soon have listened to his own advice to run away home.)

Our poet's hand is again clearly evident in *Michael*, which is only partially a saint's life. The first of its three sections, recounting tales of Michael's guardianship of Mount Gargano, is mainly narrative in what is apparently the usual style, but there are two distinctive passages of amused, almost gloating comment on the fate of 'bad' characters. After the story of a miraculous arrow which turns back against its archer, we find:

> Nou was that a wonder arwe   and wonder wei he soghte
> I ne kepte noght leorni so to ssete   ne such arwe that me broghte
> A wonder ssere wind he was on   wonder wat he thoghte
> Ac evere he that him sset   me thincth the game aboghte.
>
> (II, 403, 23–6)

(Now that was a miraculous arrow, which took an extraordinary path. I've no desire to shoot like that or to have any such arrow. It was [blown by] a marvelously perfect wind – what it intended is astonishing (?). But it seems to me the game was up for the person who shot it.)

The expression of wonder is typical of this poet – we may compare 'Now was this a wonder dede' from the first extract from *Expanded Nativity* quoted earlier (p. 107 above) – but here it's a sardonic wonder that makes fun of the man who suffered by debunking him ironically, bringing the whole miracle down to earth with a splash of realism. Soon afterwards we find reference to another 'game' after Michael and his angels have helped defeat the Saracens: the latter, says the poet, would have done better to have stayed at home picking their toes:

> A wonder game hi pleide ther   that mighte segge hor fo
> Hom hadde betere be[o] atom   and ipiked hore two.
>
> (II, 404, 67–8)

(Their enemies [i.e. the Saracens] might well say they'd played a wonderful game there – they'd have been better staying at home picking their toes.)

Michael part II also commences with miraculous narrative, and again we find a characteristic comment (noticeably beginning in mid-couplet) following the story of a woman and her new-born child who were saved from the sea:

> For Gode ther nis non of you   that hure couthe habbe iwest so wel
> Ne so ived hure ne hure child   that ne costnede worth a strau
> For thei he[o] hadde viss and drinke inou   ye witeth wel it was rau
> And to fleote so in the grete se   wonder that heo nas ded
> Sein Michel was a god wardein   wanne we habbeth al ised.
>
> (II, 407, 150–54)

(By God, there is none of you who could have preserved her so well, or have fed her and her child like this – which cost nothing, because although they had plenty of fish and drink you know well that it was uncooked. And to float in this way in the deep sea! – it's a marvel that she didn't die. When all is said and done, St Michael was an excellent guardian.)

As often, this passage encompasses wonder, sympathy, down-to-earth realism, an address to the audience (involving them by contrasting their abilities unfavourably, as in *All Souls* 191) and once more the phrase 'wanne we habbeth al ised'.

The real subject of *Michael* II is Lucifer and the devils of hell, a subject with which the poet does not find it hard to get involved. His account of the fall of Lucifer is marked by strikingly unusual imagery and vocabulary:[18]

Fram the hexte stude that is   with one swenge he com
To the lowest iwis   a wonder wei he nom
[Now wo to him] wat was him?   Wi verde the ssrewe so?
He pleide mid the valling torn   to wel he couthe it do
Jambeleve he com swenge   into helle gronde
A murgore in he hadde er   that worse there he fonde
A wonder sweng me thincth he made   is bigete was wel lute
Acorsi he may everemo   is misfaringe prute.

(II, 407–8, 173–80)

(He fell from the highest place there is to the lowest in a single swoop – he took an extraordinary path. Now misfortune befall him! What was he thinking of? Why did the villain act as he did? He tried a falling manoeuvre, and performed it too well, so that he came swinging headfirst into the depths of hell. He had a happier lodging beforehand – he found a worse one there! It seems to me he made an extraordinary swoop; his reward was very small. May he forever curse his sinful pride.)

Lucifer 'swings' down into hell; *valling torn* apparently refers to a fall at wrestling; *Jambeleve* 'headfirst' is from Old French *jambes levees*.[19] And once again we see the evil characters described in terms of losing at games, and as being better off if they hadn't done what they did.

The remainder of *Michael* II can be attributed without difficulty to our poet, comprising, as it does, strongly written homily enlivened with graphic illustrations and his idiosyncratic colloquialisms. Devils are said to visit wicked men in their sleep ('Hi of liggeth as an hevi stok   as hi wolde a man astoffe / That he ne ssel wawy fot ne hond   ne unnethe enes poffe', II, 409,

233–4: 'They oppress them like a heavy stump of wood as if they
wanted to stifle a man so that he can't move foot or hand or barely
draw breath'); the devil himself is compared in detail to a guard-
dog who will bite those who come near him; and there is in particular a long and expert exposition of the devil's five fingers, with
which he entices men to sin in different ways ('The devel stont
and fawe wolde   hente him bi the polle / With liteman is leste
finger   he ginth him ferst to t[o]lle', II, 412, 323–4: 'The devil
stands and would gladly seize him by the head / With "Little man",
his smallest finger, he first begins to lure him').[20] The whole of
Michael II could profitably be analysed in detail as an example of
combined poetic and homiletic skill.

The third part of *Michael* is different again, being the relatively
well-known scientific treatise which leaves the subject of Michael
altogether, and discourses in great detail and with impressive
knowledge on the subjects of cosmology, the world, weather,
the elements and humours, the development of the human foetus
and the relationship of the body and the soul. It appears to have
enjoyed a popularity separate from that of the *SEL,* as it occurs
out of context in a range of non-*SEL* manuscripts.[21] Once again
it is highly likely that our poet was responsible. The treatise is
consistently strongly argued, and interestingly written, but it
continues for some four hundred lines. There is the feeling that
the poet, taking the opportunity to instruct an audience at length
on matters that interest him, gets somewhat carried away on his
flow of words. It has recently been well argued that the subject
matter of *Michael* III is not inappropriate for the saint in question, and that the tripartite legend possesses, if not unity, at
least thematic coherence;[22] but *Michael* III is a digression from
the saint's life in the same way that the long defence of women
is a digression from *Southern Passion*'s narrative of Christ's
resurrection.

Much of *Michael* III is patiently explanatory in style, but the
audience is kept involved (e.g. 497–8, 593), and there are typical
exclamations and occasional personal touches. Thus when the poet
explains the origin of hoar frost:

> He cleveth in hegges al aboute   and in weodes also
> And Ichot in my vortop   he hath ofte ido.
>
> (II, 422, 623–4)

(It clings to hedges all around and to weeds also, and I know it's
often affected the top of my head.)

The most striking passage stylistically is 717–28, which describe in great detail the undignified position of the foetus in the womb, comparing it to a hare lying bent in its form and proceeding as a result to warn against human pride:

Al round it lith in the wombe   and ibud as an hare
Wanne he in forme lith   for is in is somdel nare
And ibud the legges beoth   it nolde noght elles veie
The helen atte bottocs   the knen in either eiye
That heved ibuyd adonward   the armes ek withinne
The elbowes toward the ssere   the vestes to the chinne
Al i[b]ud him is the rug   so that nei rount it is
Man ware of comth al thi prute   for ther nis non iwis
Thou makest the so hei her   and to man nelt abowe
Loke hou crokcd thou were there   and to wan thou might the powe
Thou nemightest noght holde up thin heved   ne enes undo thin eiye
Wannene com it suthe to bere   thin heved so heie?
(II, 425–6, 717–28)

(It lies curled up in the womb and bent as a hare when lying in its form, for its lodging-place is restricted. The legs are bent round – otherwise it wouldn't fit – with the heels against the buttocks and the knees in either eye. The head is bent downwards, and the arms are tucked inside, with the elbows towards the groin and the fists against the chin. The back is completely bent, so that it's almost circular. Man, where does your sense of pride come from, for there is none here! Here [on earth] you give yourself high status, and won't bow to anyone. Consider how crooked you were there, and to whom you were able to cry! (?) You weren't able to raise your head, or even open your eyes. Where does it come from that you now hold your head so high?)[23]

Such a precise account of the relative position of a baby's limbs in the womb would suggest specialist knowledge on the part of the author.

An examination of *All Souls* and *Michael* has clearly revealed the outspoken poet's presence in these two predominantly expository and homiletic *sanctorale* legends. Before we turn to consider his possible part in the narrative saints' lives it can be shown that his hand is also distinguishable in certain of the *temporale* poems that expound the feasts and fasts of the church year.

Of these *Rogationtide* is one likely candidate, being full of couplet *enjambement* and sermon-like distinctions; there is also an anecdotal explanation of the custom of blessing people when they sneeze,[24] and a typically testy dismissal ('And noght as seith many fol', I, 161, 9) of those who have the wrong idea about why one fasts at the time of year in question. But it is in the much longer *Lent* that our poet's voice is particularly audible. It has been suggested that the extant text is composite, with the lively section on fasting and confession (the bulk of the item) representing an intrusion after the 'dry technical' lines 1–40 which explain how the length of Lent is calculated.[25] The style certainly appears to change at line 41, and there soon follows a vivid passage on gluttons – who should be fasting – breaking wind uncomfortably from all parts of their body:

> Hi goth up and doun and bolketh   with wel dreori chere
> Hi nolleth ete a mossel more   bote hore mawe amti were
> Hi bolketh and bloweth above   ac I ne segge noght elles ware
> Hi poffeth and meneth hore stomak   that mot nede uvel vare.
>
> (I, 130, 51–4)

(They walk up and down and belch with a very sad face. They don't want to eat a scrap more except on an empty stomach. They belch and break wind from the upper part of the body – but I don't say from where else. They pant and moan about their stomach, which must needs continue in a bad way.)

When the fast-breaker tries to excuse himself, says the poet, he can give only 'A balled [i.e. "threadbare"] reson' (68) – an evocative and unusual phrase found also in *Southern Passion*'s defence of women passage.[26] The section on shrift continues in similar style, with tell-tale lines such as 'And wanne ye seoth reson wy   ne with seggeth me noght' (I, 133, 151), and memorable comparisons of a residue of sin, left over after confession, with a hen's nest egg (I, 134, 163–72), and of those who forget about fasting as soon as Easter comes with a bloodhound who loses his sense of smell in springtime:[27]

> Ac hi vareth as deth the blod hond   at bigynnynge of the yere
> The smul hath wel of everich best   of hare and ek of dure
> Ac wanne the hauthorn bigynneth to blowe   al it is forlore
> For swotnesse of thulke flour   the smul that was bivore
> Thei lesyn thanne al here smel   and here cours ecchon
> And the hunte sitt at hom   hym lest not to felde gon
> So it farith be suyche men   that al here thought don geve
> For to smelle Oure Lordis grace   qwan thei ben wel schryve

But anon as lente is don   that is here soulys bote
Thei etyn flesch wol hertylyche   the smak is ful sote.

(They behave like bloodhounds at the beginning of the year, when
they easily discern the smell of every animal, both hare and deer. But
when the hawthorn begins to blossom, the sense of smell they previously had is totally lost, because of that flower's sweet scent. They
lose all their sense of smell and impetus, so that the hunter sits at
home, not wanting to go out into the field. It's the same with people
who concentrate on sniffing Our Lord's grace when they've been well
shriven, but who tuck into meat with a hearty appetite, finding the
smell so pleasing, as soon as Lent, our soul's salvation, is over.)

III

The question of the outspoken poet's involvement in the narrative
saints' lives is a difficult one, which can only be touched on here.
Much more research is needed to resolve the matter. On the one
hand there is extensive evidence for his presence, as the following
characteristic couplets will testify:

For it was god inou to him   withinne and eke above
Wat segge ye? segge ich soth?   ne lieth noght for is love!
                                                    (*Juliana*, I, 67, 135–6)

(For it was good enough for him, from every point of view. What do
you say? Do I speak the truth? Don't tell a lie, for the love of God.)

Nou was this a sori couple   and also him mote bivalle
And luther thrift uppon hore heved   'Amen', seggeth alle!
                                                    (*John the Baptist*, I, 242, 21–2)

(Now this was a wretched couple. May a bad end befall him, and ill
luck fall on their head – everyone say 'Amen'!)

Nou an alle develwey   and ne come he nevere agen
Wy sitte ye so stille?   wi ne segge ye amen?
                                                    (*Peter*, I, 260, 391–2)

(Now may he go wholly to the devil and never come back! Why do
you sit so still, why aren't you saying amen?)

Ye yolle mote he everemo   and uvel him mote betide!
The ssrewe fond is macche tho   Ichot he ssolde abide.
                                                    (*James the Great*, I, 339, 363–4)

(Yes, let him howl for evermore, and may he suffer misfortune! The
villain met his match then – I'm sure that's how it should stay.)

A, ye, ye, wel was that   such gleo Ich wolde ihure:
An hard puf him was blowe agen   to teche him pleie with fure.
                                        (*Matthew*, II, 401, 137–8)

(Ah, yes, yes, that was good – I like to hear of such sport. A strong
puff was blown against him, to teach him to play with fire.)

Nou wo worthe is pol so wis   and sorwe him come to!
Ichot ther nys non of you   that couthe aposy so.
                                        (*Andrew*, II, 549, 213–14)

(Now may misfortune fall on his devious head, and sorrow afflict
him! I'm sure there is none of you that could put such questions.)

Nou uvele itheo that him hath   such lesing ibroght
Ye mowe iseo hou me lieth   on wymmen for noght.
                                        (*Clement*, II, 517, 67–8)

(Now may he that told such a lie do badly! You may see how people
tell baseless lies about women.)

It may be noted that the last-quoted couplet displays the same attitude as *Southern Passion* towards the unjust treatment of women.

Similar couplets or longer passages can be found in, for
example, *Scholastica, Chad, Benedict, Alphege, Theophilus, Alban,
Swithun, Margaret, Jerome, The Eleven Thousand Virgins, Lucy,*
and *Anastasia*. The problem of the extent of our poet's involvement arises from the frequent isolation of such exclamations and
asides in the midst of sober, straightforward storytelling in apparently normal *SEL* mode. Has the poet, acting as a reviser, simply
inserted his comments into existing legends, or did he in many
cases compose the surrounding narrative in the traditional style,
as was suggested for the *narraciones* in *All Souls*? In the following
passage from *Swithun* plain story and 'outspoken' comment alternate, exemplifying the problem particularly well:

A day as this werkmen   aboute this worke stode   55
And the contreiemen to chepinge   come mid muchele gode
Mid a bagge vol of eiren   a womman ther com
A mason sone this womman   in is folie nom
And biclupte hure in ribaudie   as foles doth yute ofte
And brak hure eiren nei echone   he ne handlede hure noght
                                                      softe   60
Tho the womman hure harm ysei   reulich he[o] gan bygynne
For he[o] is hadde igadered longe   som selver to wynne
He[o] weop and made deol inou   and cride also anhey
Sein Switthin com tho ther vorth   and this deol isey

Of this womman he hadde reuthe   he nom up his hond anon   65
And blessede the eiren tobroke   and hi bicom hole echon
Ase sonde as hi evere were   hi bicome attelaste
Glad was tho this sely womman   and thonkede him wel faste
Mighte eirmangars fare nou so   the baldeloker hi mighte
Hup[p]e over diches ware hi wolde   and bothe wraxli and
                                 fighte   70

(I, 276)

(One day as these workmen stood around this construction work, and the country folk were making their way to market with quantities of goods, a woman came by with a bag full of eggs. A lecherous mason took hold of this woman and embraced her coarsely, as sinful men often do, and broke almost all her eggs – he didn't treat her gently. When the woman saw the damage that had been done, she began to [cry out] sorrowfully, for she'd spent a long time collecting them, to earn money. She wept and greatly lamented, and cried out loudly. Then St Swithun came along and observed this grief, and he took pity on the woman. He raised his hand and blessed the broken eggs, and they all became whole, and as sound as they ever were. The poor woman was delighted, and thanked him profusely. If this could happen to egg-sellers these days, they might more confidently leap over ditches wherever they wanted, and both wrestle and fight.)

Lines 61–8, in particular, use phrasing and vocabulary found throughout the *SEL*, while the *foles* of 59b, the ironical understatement of 60b and the extravagant fantasy of 69–70 immediately identify the outspoken poet. The final couplet might be a later addition, not being structurally connected, but 59–60 are so closely bound up with the foregoing lines, completing the sentence begun in 58, that this passage would seem to be the work of a single writer.

We are assisted somewhat by the existence of different manuscript traditions, as not all of the lines to be attributed to our poet are found in all manuscripts. On the face of it this would seem to add weight to the theory that isolated comments surrounded by 'ordinary' narrative are likely to represent a reviser's interpolations. The split between the 'Z' and 'A' traditions of the *SEL*, identified by Manfred Görlach, can often be equated with the textual differences between MS Laud Misc. 108 (=L) and MSS Cambridge, Corpus Christi College 145 and London, BL MS Harley 2277, the manuscripts used for the two main *SEL* editions.[28] Görlach more precisely associates L with a tradition 'L', deriving partly from 'Z' and partly from 'A'; from 'L' in turn derive traditions 'G' and 'F', of which prominent representatives are the Vernon manuscript

(Oxford, Bodleian MS English Poetry a. I, =V) and London, Lambeth Palace Library, MS 223 (=G).[29]

Of the seven couplets quoted above, *Juliana* 135–6 are not in GV (the legend is omitted from L); *John* 21–2 are not in LV (the legend is omitted from G); *Peter* 391–2 are not in GV, which diverge from the main 'A' tradition after l. 195 (the legend is not in L); *James* 363–4 are not in LGV;[30] *Matthew* 137–8 are not in LGV; *Andrew* 213–14 are not in GV (the legend is omitted from L); and *Clement* 67–8 are not in LG (lines 1–326 are lost in V). On this evidence there appears to be a strong possibility that the outspoken poet interpolated his comments into existing compositions.

The matter is in fact more complex. *John* 65–6 – a curse – are not in LV, but this couplet merely concludes a strongly written passage on Salome which they *do* have. *Alban* has a markedly unrestrained sequence (85–90) on the gruesome fate that befell the saint's executioner (discussed below, pp. 427–8), of which LGV possess the first four lines but not the final two. *Jerome*, not present in L, has a passage that brings together several of the outspoken poet's features of style with which we have become familiar (sympathy with animals, imagined direct speech, a challenge to the audience, expression of wonder, questioning), but the second half (73–6) is not in GV:

The lion bigan to vauni tho   as wo seith Ichelle vawe
Fram daie to daie as youre [asse]   youre wode hom drawe
Bothe on rugge and on carte   bocsomliche inou
Mildore thanne the asse dude   hare wode hom he drou
And natheles it bicom him uvele   such mester to do
Ich wene there nis non of you   that him ssolde bringe therto
A wonder cartare he was on   ware were is wilde pas?
Wanne we habbeth al itold   a vair miracle ther was.

(II, 431, 69–76)

(The lion then began to show compliance, as if saying, 'I shall gladly fetch your wood home each day, as your ass did, both on my back and in a cart, with perfect obedience'. He brought their wood home more tamely than the ass did, and yet it was most unfitting for him to perform such a task – I can't think any of you could have made him do it. He was an exceptional carter: what had happened to his wild way of walking? When all is said and done, a wonderful miracle had occurred.)

In these three examples it is comment rather than narrative that is absent from the control manuscripts, but it does not seem likely that the comment was added later by a different writer. In the case of *Lent* it is GV and other manuscripts representing the presumed earlier tradition that preserve the fullest text – preserving in effect more of the work of the outspoken poet – and the 'A' tradition that has what seems to be an abridgement.[31] Similarly, the full text of *Southern Passion*'s defence of women exists (as was said) in only a single manuscript, Bodley 779; and *Southern Passion* as a whole more often than not survives in shortened rather than complete form.[32] The reason for such abridgement may well have been that later redactors or scribes wished to tone down, or reduce the extent of, the poet's asides, digressions and general 'outspokenness', and this may also explain some of the differences in the textual transmission of the saints' lives; it may be that curses and personal comments are at times being excised rather than interpolated.

In this connection it may be noted that *All Souls* and *Michael*, full-scale legends that I attributed with some confidence to the outspoken poet, occur in MSS LG and LGV respectively, and not merely in manuscripts of the 'A' tradition. In both cases L possesses texts equivalent to those in 'A', whereas G is noticeably divergent.[33] Its *All Souls* begins quite differently; thereafter a number of typically outspoken lines are omitted, including the distinctive 304–5 (not quoted earlier) –

Away mi child saith the dame   that snyveleth bi the wowe
Bi Crist, heo aughte thonki God   that nom hit for his owe

('Alas, my child!', cries the woman snivelling beside the wall. By Christ she ought to thank God, who took it for himself.)

– and lines 344–9 (but not 342–3) of the second 'Sir Gilbert' passage. Of the quotations given earlier from *Michael*, G completely lacks 23–6, 67–8 and 623–4; leaves out 151–4 after a different version of 150; leaves out 175–8 while preserving 173–4, 179–80; omits not only 323–4 but the whole passage on the devil's fingers; and retains 233–4 and 717–28. The balance of the evidence here is that G contains abridged versions of *All Souls* and *Michael* rather than texts free of later interpolation.

It is in fact likely that our poet treated different *sanctorale* subjects in different ways. More work is needed, but when *SEL* style is thoroughly investigated it may prove to be the case that on some occasions he left existing legends scarcely altered whereas on others he composed virtually from scratch. Certainly the strength and variety of writing in (for example) *Alban, John the Baptist,* and

Peter (not to mention *Michael* and *All Souls*) suggest that the outspoken poet was primarily responsible for the extant texts.

Meanwhile it can be shown that he was an active reviser of *sanctorale* legends (in the same way that he revised *Ministry* into *Southern Passion*, and *Nativity* into *Expanded Nativity*), although the evidence is not extensive because the presumed 'Z' layer of the *SEL* survives only partially, if at all, in manuscripts like L and G. As has become obvious, there is plentiful minor variation between different texts of the same legend, much of which may be said to represent revision in the sense of being deliberate; but there are comparatively few legends of which two different versions survive, particularly in the second half of the calendar year.[34]

Two rewarding examples, however, are *Dunstan* and *Bridget*, of which the revised versions contain clear examples of our poet's style. *Dunstan* is the more straightforward case. Görlach records that the 'A' redactor 'added the dates of Dunstan's birth and death in 21–4, 203–4, the episode of the temptation in the smithy 59–92, and replaced [the original 41–8, as in L] by a completely new passage on the antiquity of Glastonbury, 45–58'.[35] Whereas the additions are self-contained (which potentially opens their status to dispute), it is evident that the last change is the work of a reviser. L says wrongly (and vaguely) that Dunstan founded Glastonbury Abbey. The 'A' version is clearly concerned to put things right, and spends six lines establishing very precisely – in effect contradicting the other – that the abbey existed 453 years earlier, before the time of either St Patrick or St Augustine. The smithy episode, in which the devil comes to Dunstan in woman's form, is a typically skilful anecdote in the outspoken poet's liveliest style. At the climax the saint applies red hot tongs to the devil's nose, so that:

He yal and hupte and drou agen	and made grislich bere
He nolde for al is bigete	that he hadde icome there
With is tonge he strok is nose	and twengde him evere sore
Forte it was withinne nighte	that he ne mighte ise[o] namore
The ssrewe was glad and blithe inou	tho he was out of is honde
And flei and gradde bi the lift	that me hurde into al the londe,
'Out, wat hath this calwe ido?	wat hath this calwe ido?'
In the contreie me hurde wide	hou the ssrewe gradde so
As god the ssrewe hadde ibe[o]	habbe ysnut atom is nose
He ne highede namore thuderward	to tilie him of the pose.

(I, 207, 83–92)

(He howled and hopped about and pulled away, and made a horrible uproar. Notwithstanding all the reward [he might have had?], he wished he'd never come there. [Dunstan] pulled his nose with the tongs and tweaked it painfully again and again until it was night-time, when he couldn't see any longer. The villain was happy enough when he'd escaped from his hands, and flew up into the sky shrieking (which was heard in all the country round about), 'Alas, what has this baldy done, what has this baldy done!' – people far and wide heard how the villain shrieked in this way. He had as well have been blowing his nose at home. He didn't hurry that way any more to cure himself of a head-cold.)

Bridget is rewritten much more extensively, L's fifty-eight lines being expanded to 270. Görlach describes the 'A' redactor's procedure in some detail, and his analysis need not be repeated here.[36] Most of the new material is narrative of a generally ordinary *SEL* kind; given that our poet's hand is clearly apparent elsewhere in the rewritten legend, as will be seen, this is presumably good evidence that he could indeed turn his hand to basic *SEL* style when necessary (unless, of course, there was a stage of intermediate narrative revision, which cannot wholly be ruled out).[37] Otherwise, various short miracles from L's text are reused at appropriate points, and the way in which the first of these is adapted is, as Görlach points out, evidence that a reviser is at work. It is the characteristic couplets (161–2, 171–2) inserted after each of the first two miracles that reveal the poet in his 'outspoken' mode; in each case the effect is somewhat to devalue the miracle by suggesting that it could be repeated for everyday benefit. Thus after Bridget has been enabled to hang her wet clothes to dry on a sunbeam:

> Me thingth he[o] ne dorste carie noght   perche forto finde
> Wanne he[o] wolde hure clothes honge   and the sonne ssinde.
> (I, 43, 171–2)

(It seems to me she didn't need to be concerned about finding a pole if the sun was shining when she wanted to hang out her clothes.)

In the second main block of added story (173–252) the poet's presence is perhaps betrayed by a single complex sentence stretching over six lines (203–8). Not long afterwards there is a characteristic comment on Bridget's willingness to lose an eye rather than marry:

> Wel leover hure was to leose hure eiye   ye, parde, bothe to
> Thanne to be[o] iwedded wif   folie forto do

Were wymmen ivare nouthe so   wo so wolde yeorne crie?
As wel we mowe segge nay   wat halt it to lye?

$$(I, 45, 235-8)$$

(She was much more willing to lose an eye – indeed both of them –
than to be a married woman and have sexual relations. Do women
behave like this nowadays? Is there anyone who'd want to call out
enthusiastically? We may as well answer negatively – what's the
point of lying?)

L's text has only four lines on Bridget's refusal to marry. As
Görlach comments about the 'A' version, 'the stress is much more
on the details, which often serve for sensation rather than piety'.[38]
From the accumulated evidence we now have about our poet's contributions to the *SEL,* there is little doubt that he is a sensationalist.

Manfred Görlach says that *Bridget* is 'the best example of the
"A" redaction in the *SEL* corpus'.[39] This essay has refrained from
identifying the outspoken poet as *the* 'A' reviser, but it has become
clear that he must, at least, have played a major part in fashioning the *SEL* that has come down to us.[40] It has been shown that
he was active in both *temporale* and *sanctorale* portions, and now
that the most striking features of his style have been recognized it
may become possible to trace him at work in less obvious places.
Certainly the full extent of his activity is still very unclear, particularly the degree to which he involved himself in composing *sanctorale* narrative. He is most naturally a preacher, and his principal
talents appear to be those of a lecturer, homilist, anecdotalist, and
social and ecclesiastical critic.

IV

I showed in 2001 that the characteristic features of the outspoken
poet's style were also widely evident in Robert of Gloucester's
Chronicle, a contemporary work that had long been known to have
intimate textual connections with the *SEL*.[41] The consensus, as
summarized by Manfred Görlach, was that Robert was the bor-
rower, to the extent of having taken over more than five hundred
SEL lines, most significantly from the legends of the English saints
*Kenelm, Dunstan, Athelwold, Edward the Elder, Alphege, Edward
the Confessor* and *Thomas Becket*, but Görlach demonstrated that
the textual relationships are not always clear cut.[42]

On the whole the shared passages (in the *SEL*'s case always from
the 'A' version) do not display the characteristics of the outspoken

poet, and it would seem as if Robert made no effort to incorporate the liveliest material; for example, the lines shared with *Dunstan* – few enough in number – do not include the episode in which the saint is tempted by the devil in the smithy. However, another episode in the life of Dunstan is inserted by Robert between two passages of narrative taken from *Edward the Elder*. The lines in question (5828–39) do not occur in the *SEL*, yet they could on stylistic grounds have been written by the outspoken poet. Here it is not the concluding comment (5836–9) that is striking,[43] but the long and involved sentence that describes the floor breaking under the participants in a council being held in Calne, Wiltshire:[44]

> And hii velle and to brusede   some anon to dethe
> And some ymaymed and some yhurt   so that eny unnethe
> Withoute gret harm ofscapede   bote Sein Dunston bi cas
> That hente him by a bem   and ysaved was.
>
> (5832–5)

> (And they fell and were badly injured, some at once fatally, and some maimed and others hurt, with the result that scarcely any escaped without great harm except for St Dunstan, who, as it happened, caught hold of a beam and was saved.)

There is a more extensive example of the same phenomenon in Robert's treatment of the *SEL*'s *Edward the Confessor*, which is unusually long and undoubtedly to be attributed to the outspoken poet, on account both of the vitality of some of its *narraciones* and of the extremity of the personal comment at lines 521–8.[45] Most of the correspondences appear to show that Robert borrowed selectively, and that he avoided the most striking stories (for example that in which the king allows a poor man to steal from him three times), with the result that much of the *Chronicle*'s narrative is relatively pedestrian. The relationship between the two texts is not, however, straightforward. The *Chronicle* has a longer and better version of Edward's striking appeal to God for assistance (6726–47, *SEL* I, 116, 189–206), including an introductory couplet lacking in the saint's life. Slightly later the latter strangely omits, after its line 230, any equivalent of the *Chronicle*'s 6756–61, a seemingly central part of the narrative in which Edward is brought back from Normandy and taken to Winchester to be crowned.

But the passage most deserving of attention is another that is present in the *Chronicle* and absent from the *SEL*, namely the lengthy account of Queen Emma's trial by ordeal after being accused of lechery with Bishop Aelwine.[46] This occupies lines

6850–7009, and the detail and sense of involvement on the part of the poet transform the previously rather pedestrian narrative; in fact it would appear that a writer with qualities and characteristics at the least very similar to those of the outspoken poet was responsible. The episode in effect takes the place of the healing miracles that occupy a good part of the saint's life, and the underlying Latin source is also different: instead of Ailred of Rievaulx's *Vita Edwardi Regis*, on which the *SEL* appears to depend throughout, Robert bases his account on the Winchester Annals.[47]

His account of Queen Emma's trial is characterized first by the lengthy, complex passages of direct speech on the part of both the accusing archbishop (6880–99) and the queen when pleading her innocence (6925–37). Couplet enjambement is common, as in the following passage in which Archbishop Robert, in a single ten-line sentence, lays down the rules under which the defendants must walk over burning ploughshares (cf. also 6927–33, 6934–6 and 6949–50):

Lat nime foure yrene ssares   vor hiresulve al afure
And five vor the bissop   and yif heo it mai dure
Wanne hii liggeth in the flor   to steppe up echon
After other barevot   that heo ne bileve noght on
[And that heo] steppe mid folle vot   withoute quakinge
And yif hire vet beth thanne sauf   withoute wemminge
Graunteth hom alle quit   ac yif heo quakieth out
Other stepth biside other hire vet   in eny wemme be ybroght
Holdeth hom gulti of the dede   and lateth hom also
Al hor lif as wikked men   in strong prison be ydo.

(6890–9)[48]

(Prepare four burning iron shares for her, and five for the bishop, and if, when [the shares] are lying on the floor, she succeeds in stepping barefoot on each of them in turn, without missing any out – and with the whole of her foot, without trembling – and if her feet remain unharmed, without injury, then acknowledge them wholly innocent. But if she trembles in any way, or steps to one side, or her feet suffer any injury, adjudge them guilty of the deed and let them in consequence, as criminals, be committed to a secure prison for the rest of their lives.)

Although Robert follows the narrative of the Annals fairly closely, he decisively changes the character of the female protagonist, turning her from a morally ambiguous figure into a wholly good person whose complete vindication leads to an extravagant appeal for forgiveness on the part of her son the king, who does penance for his unjust actions (6966–97). The poet's sympathies for the queen are revealed also in his affecting description of the removal of her outer garments before her ordeal, about which he protestingly exclaims:

> Hire riche clothes were of ydo   bote that heo was biweved
> Hire bodi with a mantel   a wimpel aboute hire heved
> Hire legges bare binethe the kne   that me mighte ech stape ise
> A wey uvele bicom it quene   so bar vor to be.
>
> (6940–3)[49]

(Her fine clothes were removed except for those which covered her: a shift over her body, a wimpel on her head, her legs bare beneath the knee so that each step could be observed. Alas, it was wickedly unfitting for a queen to be so unclothed.)

Particularly fine are the lines, mainly of dialogue, in which the queen is afterwards taken outside, not realising that she has already undergone the ordeal:

> . . . An[d] ladde ire outward of the chirche   the quene bigan to
>   crie
> 'Vor the love of Jhesu Crist   ne doth noght the vileinie
> To do my penaunce withoute,   ac in alle manere
> As it me it iloked was,   in holi chirche here'
> 'Ma dame', quath this bissopes,   'Thou it ast ido iwys'
> 'So helpe me God', quath the quene,   'I nuste noght er this
> No fur I ne velede   ne ne sei in this place
> Bote nou Ich it verst ise   ihered be Godes grace.
>
> (6956–63)

(. . . and led her outside the church. The queen began to cry out, 'For the love of Jesus Christ, don't shame me by making me do my penance outside, but let it be performed in every way as it was ordained, here in the holy church.' 'Lady', said these bishops, 'you have done it already.' 'So help me God', said the queen, 'I didn't know that until now. I neither felt nor saw any fire in this place, but now that I have seen it, may God's grace be praised.')

But Robert, exactly like the outspoken poet, cannot resist an opportunity for irreverent and indeed wholly inappropriate comment when one presents itself. After enumerating the twenty manors given to St Swithin's (Winchester Cathedral) by a grateful queen, king and bishop for the saint's part in the miracle, he jokes feelingly that that should keep the abbey in vegetables for a good while:

> That wolde be tuenty under al   and that nas noght lute there
> Vor it wolde finde hom lec and worten   inowe bi the yere.
>
> (6998–9)

(Which made a total of twenty, and that wasn't a small amount, for it would provide them with sufficient leeks and other vegetables from one year to the next.)

Immediately afterwards he goes further out on a limb by contrasting, with an oath and a sarcastic allusion, the very different attitude to the clergy taken by the next King Edward, who can be no less than the seemingly reigning monarch, Edward I:

> Vor Gode the nexte king Edward   that after him suthe com
> Ne gef hom noght folliche so muche   withinne is kinedom.
>
> (7000–1)

(By God, the next King Edward after him didn't give them fully as much [anywhere] within his kingdom.)

Another example of a complex relationship between the two works is the description of the madness and death of the emperor Nero, shared by the *SEL*'s *Paul* (I, 273, 249–81) and lines 1542–85 of the *Chronicle*. The passage has been closely analysed by Manfred Görlach, who first brought the parallel to attention and who demonstrates that while there are few wholly identical lines in the two texts, the overall 'agreement in the wording, in some rhymes and in the structure of the sentences forbids one to regard the texts as independent translations of identical or related sources'. It is clear that there is an intimate relationship between the two passages, but, as Görlach says, 'who borrowed from whom?'[50]

How can such textual relationships be resolved? How many authors were there? Görlach prefers not to draw a firm conclusion in the case of Nero, arguing that 'the passage in question, then, adds to the warning that the alleged stylistic homogeneity of the *SEL* collection need not indicate unity of authorship', and adding that 'Many people in the 13th century must have been able to compose verses like those found in the *SEL* and *RGl*, and some probably did'. As a general statement this view is not to be disregarded, but the easiest solution to the problem of the passages discussed above is to conclude that they were composed by the same author, who in some cases adapted what he had first written for a different purpose at a later date. A possible conclusion is that we are dealing with a single, prolific poet who was responsible for a large body of versified narrative, both historical and hagiographical, and who

– depending on what was needed or appropriate – either composed
new verses or drew on previously written material, sometimes verbatim, sometimes adapting.

Evidence of the outspoken poet's style is equally discernible
in passages from Robert of Gloucester's *Chronicle* not paralleled
in the extant legendary, although there are few obvious examples
before the period surrounding the Norman Conquest, at which
point the writer appears to become more involved with his narrative. However, in the immediate pre-Conquest period, between
the lives of those Anglo-Saxon kings for which Robert found
material in the *SEL*, occurs an account of Canute, whose pompous
address to the rising waves, though closely based upon Henry of
Huntingdon's Latin chronicle, ends with an absurd threat to the
sea which is not found in the source: 'Other bi the fey ich owe to
God   Icholle rekeni [the] mitte' (6575, i.e. 'Or, by the faith I
owe to God, I shall get even with you').

The description of the battle of Stamford Bridge illustrates other
features of the distinctive style in question, especially the fluid
method of handling couplets. In the following passage the stratagem to defeat the hitherto all-powerful Danish champion begins
in the second half of the first line of a couplet, with a subordinate
clause, and climaxes at the beginning of the following couplet. The
poet then uses the first line of the next couplet to praise the man
who did the deed, before starting the narrative going again in the
second line:

> . . . vor te on mid gile nom
> A ssip and [under him   bynethe] the brugge com
> And smot him ar he were ywar   under the fondement lowe
> Mid a spere and so an hey   that he deide in an throwe
> A stalwarde pece that was   nou God cuthe is soule love
> Tho thoghte the Englisse vor is deth   that hii were al above
> And passede the brugge anon . . . (7310–16)

(. . . until someone cunningly took a boat, and passed under the
bridge below him, and – before he realised – struck him beneath the
buttocks with a spear, and thrust upwards so that he died instantly.
The man who did this was a brave fellow: may God show mercy on
his soul. Then the English, on account of [the enemy champion's]
death, were convinced that they had the upper hand, and they
crossed the bridge immediately.)

For instance, the writer forcibly expresses his loathing of Harald
('vor he was evere a ssreward', 7323), and puts similar sentiments

into William the Conqueror's mouth during his long, rhetorically powerful speech to his men before Hastings (7,423–53). It is a passage that combines strong language with a mastery of the couplet format.

The poet reserves his most personal remarks, of the kind associated with the outspoken poet, for the Normans themselves. His fiercest attack comes when describing the church-building activities of William and his barons, which they undertook, he says, in consciousness of their sins. This is made the occasion for extreme anti-Norman sentiment, as he contrasts the barons' outward piety with their savagery towards their Saxon underlings:

> So varth monye of this heyemen   in chirche me may yse
> Knely to God as hii wolde   al quic to him fle
> Ac be hii arise and abbeth iturnd   fram the weved hor wombe
> Wolves dede hii nimeth vorth   that er dude as lombe
> Hii todraweth the sely bonde men   as hii wolde hom hulde ywis
> They me wepe and crie on hom   no mercy ther nis.
>
> (7606–11)

(Many of these nobles behave in this way: in church you may see them kneel before God as if they were desperate to hasten to him, but once they've stood up and turned their stomachs away from the altar, they, who had earlier behaved like lambs, start performing the deeds of wolves. They cut the innocent serfs to pieces, as if they wanted to flay them. Although the latter weep and cry out to them, they show no mercy.)

The strength of expression here is very characteristic of the outspoken poet.

All the passages so far discussed have come from the part of Robert's *Chronicle* common to its two extant versions, which diverge completely after the death of Henry I in l. 9137. The longer one carries on in considerable detail, eventually ending (in the most complete manuscript, which itself ends fragmentarily) almost three thousand lines later with an event in 1271.[51] The shorter version continues for only 592 lines, quickly running over the years following the death of Stephen in 1154, and terminating with a mention of Edward I's conquest of Wales in the 1280s.[52] Scholars have noted that the two continuations treat the events of Stephen's reign at almost identical length (440 and 438 lines) but quite differently, and have taken this as proof that they are by different authors.[53]

As for the *Chronicle* as a whole, it has often been suggested that *three* authors may have been involved, that is to say that the two continuations were each by a writer different from that of the pre-Stephen narrative.[54] After some hesitation both Wright, the *Chronicle*'s nineteenth-century editor, and Edward D. Kennedy, in the *Manual of Writings in Middle English*, adopt this position, as a result of which they take the view that 'Robert of Gloucester' wrote only the longer continuation, i.e. the one in which he names himself as having witnessed the eclipse that accompanied the battle of Evesham in 1265 ('Roberd / That verst this boc made', 11,748–9).[55] The alternative theory is that the author of the original narrative wrote one of the two continuations. This would require his narrative of events up to 1135 to have passed into other hands presumably before the chronicle as a whole was 'finished' – thus enabling a different ending to be written – but this is hardly an impossible occurrence.

Wright and Kennedy are surely too cautious in their judgements, and the former is wrong to say that there is 'no positive evidence for one or the other' theory. Thorlac Turville-Petre, discussing the content of the *Chronicle*, has convincingly demonstrated that the work (by which he means up to and including the longer continuation) was 'written from a single and coherent ideological standpoint'. Although he feels bound to acknowledge that more than one writer may have contributed – despite there being 'no particular grounds for assuming it' – his discussion takes as its premise that the original author's narrative carries on into the longer continuation. He argues strongly that among this author's chief concerns, in the pre- and post-Conquest period alike, is the English people's struggle for their ancient liberties in the face of rulers who would repeatedly take these away.[56]

This consistent ideological standpoint is paralleled by positive evidence of an even stronger kind, that of individual style, for it is immediately apparent that the stylistic features exemplified throughout this article also characterize the narrative of the battle of Evesham in the longer continuation. After the account of the failure of Simon de Montfort's rebellion at Evesham occurs a passage describing the slaughter of the Welsh infantry in Tewkesbury: the poet's laconic comment on the piles of corpses is a typically ironic 'And grace nadde non of hom   to fighte ne to fle' (11,763, i.e. 'none of them had the grace either to fight or to flee'). Then follow lines on Simon de Montfort the younger in a style which has become familiar, and which the poet brings into play when he feels, as very evidently here, some sympathy for his subject:[57]

> Tho the bataile was ido   and the godemen aslawe were
> Sir Simond the Yonge com   to mete is fader there
> He mighte tho at is diner   abbe bileved al so wel
> As me seith 'Wan ich am ded   make me a caudel'
> And tho me tolde him bi the wei   wuch the ende was ther
> He turnde agen to Keningwurthe   wel longe him thoughte e[r]
> He mighte segge wan he com   'Lute ich abbe iwonne
> Ich mai honge up min ax   febliche ich abbe agonne'.
>
> (11,764–71)[58]

(When the battle was over and the good men were slain, Sir Simon the younger came to meet his father there. He might at that time as well have remained at his dinner; as one says, 'When I am dead, make me a caudel'.[59] And when he was told along the way what had been the outcome [of the battle], he turned back to Kenilworth – it seemed to him a very long journey. He might say when he arrived, 'I've achieved little. I may as well hang up my axe – I've acted feebly.')

There are other places in the longer continuation's detailed narrative of thirteenth-century events to which attention could also be drawn for evidence of similar poetic style, notably the detailed account of the deeds of the de Montfort supporter, Sir John Giffard (11,060–185), the very fluent description of the town and gown riots in Oxford in 1263 (11,186–233), and the comment on oppressive bailiffs (11,162–3).

But from a stylistic point of view it will be most useful to compare the account of the reign of Stephen in the longer continuation (hereafter continuation A) with that in the shorter (hereafter continuation B). The former contains only occasional lines that recall the *SEL* reviser's particular turns of phrase, but these are distinctive enough, one being a comment occasioned by the ruthlessness of the Empress Maud – 'Wanne wimmen al maistres beth   hii beth uvel to knowe' (9487, 'When women are in power they're bad to know') – and another, following her flight from London and subsequent defeat, being a characteristic (and world-weary) 'she might say': 'Heo mighte wanne heo come hom   segge "si haut si bas"' (9499, 'She might say when she came home, "Now high, now low"').

The reign of Stephen in continuation A is, however, notable for the very large amount of space (9280–465) allotted to the speeches before the battle of Lincoln and to the hand-to-hand fighting there. The rallying speech of Robert, Earl of Gloucester, is fifty lines in length (9294–343), and includes long passages of difficult argument that ignore the usual couplet boundaries, as in:

> Ac o thing ich you segge soth   that thoru the luther weye ywis
> That ye come unnethe hider thoru   non hope ther ne is
> Vor to fle he is so luther   as ye alle iseye
> Thanne ne beth ther bote tueye weyes   other her right deye
> Other overcome ur fon as we ssolle   and bringe hom ther doune
> Make we thanne mid ur suerdes   ur wey to the toune.
>
> (9310–15)

(But one thing I tell you truly, that there's no hope to be placed in the bad road by which, with difficulty, you came here, for it is also bad for escaping, as you can all see. Therefore there are only two choices: either to die here justly, or to overpower our enemies, as we shall, and defeat them. Let us then, with our swords, make our way to the town.)

The account of Stephen's reign in continuation B is markedly different, both in content and in style. This version gives space to episodes wholly or largely ignored in A (notably Stephen's early campaign against Maud in Normandy, and the future Henry II's campaigns in England before Stephen concedes defeat), and in turn it neglects the siege and battle of Lincoln almost completely. One event which it treats at greater narrative length is Maud's famous escape in the snow over the frozen Thames, and it is here that continuation B achieves its most memorable effect ('glymsede on hare eyghen', 252):[60]

> Temese was tho ifrore   hard and thicke ynou
> And was swithe whit above   of the snywede snou
> Snou whyte clothes   the lefdi dude hure on
> And forth over Temese   quyt gan awey gon
> Hure fon were loth to loke   on snou that was so whit
> That glymsede on hare eyghen   therfore heo yeode quyt
> After the bleo of snou   hure wede ywrout was
> That gilede eke hare eyghen   that heo yseyghe nas.
>
> (247–54)

(The Thames was frozen hard and thick at that time, and was extremely white on the surface from the snow that had fallen. The lady put on snow-white clothes and went away across the Thames without hindrance. Her enemies were reluctant to gaze at snow that was so white that it dazzled their eyes, therefore she went unchallenged. Her clothing was made to match the colour of snow, so that it deceived their eyes with the result that she wasn't observed.)

This is more detailed than the corresponding passage in A (9510–17), where the effect on Maud's enemies is not described. But it is also wholly bound by the expectations of couplet closure, and it is more ponderous and decidedly more repetitive than A's fluid, casual lines, in which comment and comparison are ever-present:[61]

> So gret vorst ther com in Avent   that men mighte of agrise
> That me mighte bothe ride and go   in Temese upe the yse
> And gret snou ther was also   thervore an quointyse
> The emperesse bithoghte   and dude as the wise
> Wite clothes heo dude hire on   as wo seith ilich the snowe
> That me ne ssolde hire vor the liknesse   ise ne iknowe
> And upe the ise of Temese wende vorth   and so out of Oxenford
> Al southward in to the med   and so to Walingford.
>
> (9510–17)

(Such a great frost occurred in Advent – of a kind to terrify people – that it was possible both to ride and walk on the Thames over the ice. And there was a large amount of snow also, for which reason the empress thought of a trick and acted cleverly: she put on white clothes, as one might say like the snow, so that, as a result of this similarity, she shouldn't be observed or identified, and went away over the ice on the Thames, and so out of Oxford southward into the meadows, and thus to Wallingford.)

In B only a sarcastic comment some lines later – 'The amperesse me soute   me seide heo was igo afeld' (260, 'They tried to find the empress; people said she's gone to the fields') – is at all reminiscent of the *SEL* reviser.[62]

B's account of Stephen's reign is in addition almost entirely narrative, quite devoid of passages of dialogue or direct speech of any kind. And it is followed, as this version works towards its conclusion, by a bare, prosaic summary of subsequent events, in which the writer baldly justifies not recounting the battles of Lewes and Evesham by saying that they are often narrated and still remembered:

> That were ihurd ilome   and ne buth foryute nout
> Therfore on this boke   ne buth hi nout ywrout.
>
> (585–6)

(Which were often heard about and are not forgotten, therefore they are not included in this book.)

Robert, as we may now securely call the author of the stylistically consistent *Chronicle* and longer continuation, claims in contrast to have been present at Evesham in 1265, and indeed gives a detailed account of the battle.[63] Questions of date are naturally

of importance in determining his writing career. The longer continuation is usually dated c. 1300 on the basis of a reference to
the sainthood of St Louis of France, who was canonized in 1297
('Thulke gode Lowis is nou seint [canonized] and ileid in ssrine',
10,943). The pre-continuation narrative appears to refer to Edward
I (1272–1307) as the reigning monarch, as was noted above in
discussion of lines 7000–1, and Wright proposed a date after 1294
for this passage on the basis that this was 'when the king exacted
of the clergy half their revenues'.[64] Line 7001 is, however, wholly
unspecific, alluding to what is presumably taxation by the sarcastic device of accusing Edward of not giving the clergy anywhere
near as much as did his earlier namesake. It could just as plausibly
have been written in the 1280s, given the extent to which Edward
demanded money from the church in 1282 and 1283.[65]

Robert may have been only young in 1265, and may not have
begun his writing career until the 1270s. Given that it would have
taken no little time to compose the *Chronicle*, it is quite possible that
he was still at work in the later 1290s, especially if there had been
a break in composition after reaching the end of Henry I's reign;
one interpretation of 'That verst this boc made' is that Robert is
deliberately emphasizing, after the passage of time, his authorship
of the original pre-Stephen narrative, especially if that had meanwhile been continued by another writer. This span of years, which
may thus have included a period when the *Chronicle* was set aside,
would have allowed him to make extensive contributions, perhaps
in the mid- or later 1280s, to the *SEL* also. The *Southern Passion*,
one of the lives of Christ attributable to the outspoken poet, refers
to Jews as being allowed to live in England, which would date the
poem to before 1290, the year of their expulsion;[66] the *SEL* as a
whole is dated by Görlach to c. 1270–90, with the reviser likely to
have been active in the latter part of that period.[67] This evidence
from dates fits well with what I hope to have demonstrated on the
basis of stylistic evidence, that there is a strong likelihood that
Robert of Gloucester can be equated with the outspoken poet.

Notes

Parts I–III of this essay are a slightly refashioned version of my 'The
outspoken *South English Legendary* Poet', published in A. J. Minnis
(ed.), *Late-Medieval Religious Texts and Their Transmission: Essays in
Honour of A. I. Doyle* (Cambridge: D. S. Brewer, 1994), pp. 21–37. A
small amount of text has been transferred to notes, other notes have

been slightly reformulated, and occasional typographical errors have been corrected. Translations of all Middle English passages have been inserted. Part IV of the essay is an abridged version of my '*South English Legendary* Style in Robert of Gloucester's *Chronicle*', *Medium Aevum*, 70 (2001), 1–18, with some parts reworked for the new context. The translations originally presented in footnotes now appear in the body of the text. I am grateful to the publishers of the original essays for allowing me to base the present text closely upon them.

1 Work on the collection was transformed by the publication of Görlach's *Textual Tradition*, in which he pointed to unambiguous evidence of revision in some twenty saints' lives, and posited a general development from what he called the 'Z' version, compiled in Worcestershire possibly in the 1270s, to the 'A' version, compiled in Gloucestershire possibly in the 1280s. It has subsequently become clearer (as Professor Görlach always acknowledged was likely) that the development into 'A' was the result of more than one rewriting. See Pickering. 'Expository *temporale*', and Liszka, 'The first "A" redaction'. The 'A' version is broadly represented by D'Evelyn and Mill, while the manuscript edited by Horstmann partially preserves 'Z' texts.

2 For editions of *Nativity*, *Ministry*, and *Southern Passion*, see Abbreviations, above: for the *Expanded Nativity*, Carl Horstmann (ed.), *Altenglische Legenden* (Paderborn: Schöningh, 1875), pp. 81–109, from which editions I quote. For general information, see Pickering, '*Temporale* narratives'.

3 See O. S. Pickering. 'Three *South English Legendary* nativity poems', *LSE*, NS 8 (1975), 105–19, and 'The *Southern Passion* and the *Ministry and Passion*: the work of a Middle English reviser', *LSE*, NS 15 (1984), 33–56.

4 This second quotation from *Southern Passion* is based on Pickering, '"Defence of Women"', p. 172. The line numbers from Brown's edition are however given here for ease of comparison.

5 The quality of writing in *Southern Passion* has been remarked on by earlier commentators, notably by Brown in the Introduction to her edition (pp. xv–xvi) and by Derek Pearsall, *Old English and Middle English Poetry* (London: Routledge & Kegan Paul, 1977), pp. 105–6.

6 Theodor Wolpers, *Die englische Heiligenlegende des Mittelalters* (Tübingen: Niemeyer, 1964), pp. 209–58; Gregory M. Sadlek, 'Three basic questions in literary studies of the *South English Legendary*' (PhD dissertation, Northern Illinois University, 1983), pp. 221, 242, when analysing the life of Vincent. Wolpers, p. 215, also notices what is in effect the outspoken poet's style, but does not suggest that such passages are the work of a separate writer.

7 For example, Klaus P. Jankofsky, 'Entertainment, edification and popular education in the *South English Legendary*', *Journal of Popular Culture*, 11 (1977), 706–17, and 'Personalized didacticism:

the interplay of narrator and subject matter in the *South English Legendary'*, *Texas A & I University Studies*, 10 (1977), 69–77, in both of which he also stresses what he calls the *SEL*'s pervasive tone of compassion; and Karen Bjelland, 'Defining the *South English Legendary* as a form of drama', *Comparative Drama*, 22 (1988), 227–43.

8 Anne B. Thompson, 'Narrative art in the *South English Legendary'*, *Journal of English and Germanic Philology*, 90 (1991), 20–30. A later version of her argument is included in her *Everyday Saints*, pp. 90–8. Thompson's quotations from the poem are from D'Evelyn and Mill, but with altered punctuation.

9 Thompson, 'Narrative art', p. 23.

10 Ibid., p. 29.

11 Sadlek, 'Three basic questions', also stresses the *SEL*'s typical plainness of style and repetition of core vocabulary (see, for example, pp. 178, 243–4 and 277).

12 This is also largely the case with a passage of pure narrative (I, 307–8, 145–50) quoted by Thompson, 'Narrative art', p. 24.

13 Ibid., p. 28.

14 Sadlek, 'Three basic questions', p. 181. The appropriateness of the slow-moving septenary couplet for the clarity of style and devotional-didactic purpose of the *SEL* is remarked on by Wolpers, *Die englische Heiligenlegende*, p. 214.

15 The matter of the 'additional' lines is fully discussed and illustrated in Pickering, '"Defence of Women"', from where the quotation is again taken (see pp. 160–1, 169–70).

16 Quotations are henceforth normally from D'Evelyn and Mill, but the first two passages from *All Souls* are quoted from Horstmann, pp. 421–2, 430 (where they are lines 45–52 and 339–46), because of corruption in the text printed in the former edition. A lesser degree of corruption occurs in other quotations from D'Evelyn and Mill, but emendation has only rarely been attempted.

17 *Southern Passion*, pp. c–ci, quotes both of the Sir Gilbert passages as examples of *SEL* denunciations of less than perfect priests, and compares a short passage in *Southern Passion* itself (175–8) criticizing avaricious clergy. Brown does not mention the much more strongly worded *Southern Passion* 2249–54 on the consequences at Doomsday for priests (like Sir Gilbert here) who through their own deficiency cause other men to fall into sin; the passage is discussed in Pickering, 'The *Southern Passion* and the *Ministry and Passion'*, pp. 48–9.

18 In the third line I have emended D'Evelyn and Mill's 'No wonder' (from Cambridge, Corpus Christi College, MS 145) on the basis of the variant reading in MS Harley 2277, 'No wo him'. MS Laud Misc. 108 (in Horstmann, p. 304) reads 'Nov sori beo he'.

19 *MED*, s.v. *falling*, ppl., 2(f), and *jaumb-leve* n., (b).

20 This episode is discussed and praised in Gregory M. Sadlek, 'The image of the devils's five fingers in the *South English Legendary*'s "St Michael" and in Chaucer's Parson's Tale', in Jankofsky, pp. 49–64.

21 See Görlach, *Textual Tradition,* p. 288 (n. 278), and Thomas R. Liszka, 'MS Laud Misc. 108 and the early history of the *South English Legendary*', *Manuscripta,* 33 (1989), 75–91 (86, n. 17).

22 Gregory M. Sadlek, 'The archangel and the cosmos: the inner logic of the *South English Legendary*'s "St Michael"', *Studies in Philology,* 85 (1988), 177–91.

23 D'Evelyn and Mill, III (glossary), p. 66, and the *MED,* s.v. *puen* v. (with no other attestations), tentatively suggest the meaning 'lean, support oneself' for *powe* at the end of l. 726, but it is perhaps more plausibly an unnoticed early form of *Oxford English Dictionary, pew* v.1, (of a bird), 'to cry in a plaintive manner', found in John Trevisa's *De proprietatibus rerum* in the form *pewynge* (see *MED,* s.v. *peuen* v., 'of a kite, to cry plaintively', recording only this occurrence). D'Evelyn and Mill and the *MED* cite the forms *pue* and *puye* from other *SEL* manuscripts bearing witness to l. 726.

24 Most of this passage is omitted from the 'A' tradition as a result of archetypal homoeoteleuton (see Görlach, *Textual Tradition,* p. 162), and so is not included in the version of *Rogationtide* printed in D'Evelyn and Mill. For the text, printed from Cambridge, St John's College, MS B.6, fol. 83v, see Pickering, 'Expository *temporale*', p. 8.

25 Görlach, *Textual Tradition,* p. 156.

26 In a line unique to MS Bodley 779, and so not printed as part of the main text in *Southern Passion.* See Pickering, '"Defence of Women"', where it occurs in l. 133 of the full text there printed.

27 Lines 5–10 of this passage are quoted from Cambridge, St John's College, MS B.6, fol. 81v, as some thirty lines of *Lent,* including these, are omitted from the version of the poem printed in D'Evelyn and Mill; all are very likely the work of the outspoken poet. See Görlach, *Textual Tradition,* p. 156, and Pickering, 'Expository *temporale*', pp. 7–8. Lines 1–4 of the passage are lines 113–16 in D'Evelyn and Mill.

28 See n. 1 above.

29 See Görlach, *Textual Tradition,* pp. 51–60 and the chart of affiliations on p. 304. I am indebted to Görlach's analysis of the texts of the different legends for what follows, which is, necessarily, a simplification of the total manuscript evidence. The inclusion or omission of individual lines in the numerous different manuscripts of the *SEL* is an extremely complex matter, as Görlach shows.

30 Görlach, *Textual Tradition,* p. 183, accidentally fails to note the omission from MSS GV.

31 See n. 27 above. MS L contains none of the expository *temporale* poems.

32 See *Southern Passion,* pp. xvii–xxx, summarized in Pickering, '*Temporale* narratives', pp. 444–5.

33 As before, I am indebted to Görlach, *Textual Tradition*, for the details
    that follow.
34 Görlach, *Textual Tradition*, does not list these legends as such, but for
    references see pp. 11 and 52–4.
35 Ibid., p. 168.
36 Ibid., p. 142.
37 Görlach, *Textual Tradition*, pp. 169, 142, shows that the reviser
    consulted fresh, presumably Latin, sources, for the new material
    he inserted into *Dunstan* and *Bridget*. It may be that there is a link
    (for this writer) between the activity of translation and the use of a
    plain, unadventurous style. It is certainly the case that the conscien-
    tious gospel translations included in *Expanded Nativity* and *Southern
    Passion* are normally stylistically unexceptional.
38 Görlach, *Textual Tradition*, p. 142.
39 Ibid., p. 141.
40 The evidence of abridgement in the 'A' text of *Lent,* and the archetypal
    homoeoteleuton in the 'A' *Rogationtide,* suggest that he was working
    at a stage before the version represented by the Corpus Christi and
    Harley manuscripts printed in D'Evelyn and Mill.
41 O. S. Pickering, '*South English Legendary* style in Robert of
    Gloucester's *Chronicle*', *Medium Aevum*, 70 (2001), 1–18.
42 See Görlach, *Studies*, pp. 48–55, which include a summary of and ref-
    erences to earlier scholarship on this matter.
43 Quoted by Görlach, *Studies*, p. 52, when discussing the interpolation.
    Görlach entitles this legend *Edward the Martyr*.
44 I quote from *The Metrical Chronicle of Robert of Gloucester*, ed.
    William Aldis Wright, 2 vols, RS 86 (London: HMSO, 1887), hereaf-
    ter cited as 'Wright'.
45 This saint's life does not occur in the standard version of the *SEL*, and
    was edited separately by Grace Edna Moore, 'The Middle English
    Verse Life of Edward the Confessor' (PhD dissertation, University
    of Pennsylvania, 1942), from BL, MS Cotton Julius D.ix, fols
    281r–297v. Moore carefully lists the many parallels between chronicle
    and legend, and analyses some of Robert's adaptations (pp. lvii–lxii).
    Edward the Confessor is extant in only three *SEL* manuscripts; see
    Görlach, *Textual Tradition*, pp. 134–5.
46 This episode was analysed by Marianne O'Doherty in a 1997 MA
    research project for the Centre for Medieval Studies, University of
    Leeds, under the title: 'Old stories and new contexts: constructions of
    the figure and reign of Edward the Confessor in Robert of Gloucester's
    Verse *Chronicle*'. I am indebted to this study for some of what follows
    here. See also Thorlac Turville-Petre, *England the Nation: Language,
    Literature, and National Identity 1290–1340* (Oxford: Clarendon
    Press, 1996), pp. 92–3, for an account of Robert's portrayal of Edward
    the Confessor as a kingly saint rather than a saintly king.

47 I.e. the *Annales Monasterii de Wintonia*, printed in *Annales Monastici*, ed. Henry Richards Luard, 5 vols, RS 36 (London: HMSO, 1865), II, pp. 1–125 (20–4).

48 Line 6894 has been emended with reference to the reading of Bodleian MS Digby 205, quoted in Wright's textual apparatus. Other emendations to Wright's text are similarly based on his variant readings.

49 The passage is reminiscent of lines in the *Expanded Nativity*, in which the poet reflects on the inappropriately humble circumstances of a king being born in a stable: 'Whar was as al the nobleye,   that fel to a quene, / At a kinges burthtime,   whar was hit isene? / Ledies and chamberleins,   scarlet to drawe and grene, / To winden ynne the yonge king?   Al was lute, ich wene' (*Expanded Nativity*, 315–18).

50 Görlach, *Studies*, pp. 50–1 (51). The quotation from Görlach in the next paragraph is also from p. 51.

51 This manuscript is BL, Cotton Caligula A.xi, the base text for Wright's edition. For an account of the manuscripts, see Anne Hudson, 'Tradition and innovation in some Middle English manuscripts', *Review of English Studies*, NS 17 (1966), 359–72 (359–60).

52 Wright prints in his appendix to vol. II all the passages found in the shorter version that do not occur in the longer, including the shorter version's different continuation (Appendix, section XX).

53 This is the view summarized by Edward Donald Kennedy, 'Chronicles and other historical writings', in Albert E. Hartung (ed.), *A Manual of the Writings in Middle English VIII* (Hamden: Connecticut Academy of Arts and Sciences, 1989), p. 2618.

54 It is assumed that the author of the shorter continuation was also responsible for the interpolations in the pre-King Stephen narrative occurring in the shorter continuation manuscripts; see Kennedy, ibid.

55 Wright, I, pp. viii–ix; Kennedy, 'Chronicles', p. 2618. The same three-author view is adopted in C. E. Wright, *English Vernacular Hands from the Twelfth to the Fifteenth Centuries* (Oxford: Clarendon Press, 1960), p. 10.

56 Turville-Petre, *England the Nation*, pp. 91–6 and 98–100. The above quotations are from p. 73. Cf. also Sarah Mitchell, '"We englisse men": construction and advocacy of an English cause in the Chronicle of Robert of Gloucester', in Erik Kooper (ed.), *The Medieval Chronicle: Proceedings of the 1st International Conference on the Medieval Chronicle, Driebergen/Utrecht, 13–16 July 1996* (Amsterdam: Rodopi, 1999), pp. 191–201.

57 On this matter cf. the essay by Heffernan reprinted in this volume.

58 This passage, the comment on the slaughter in Tewkesbury, and Robert's statement of authorship all occur within the facsimile reproduction of MS Cotton Caligula A.xi, fol. 165r (lines 11,746–83), contained in Wright, *English Vernacular Hands*, plate opposite p. 10.

59 I.e. a hot fortified drink, or broth (*MED*). The proverb is associated with the idea of help arriving too late; see Morris Palmer Tilley, *A Dictionary of the Proverbs in England in the Sixteenth and Seventeenth Centuries* (Ann Arbor: University of Michigan Press, 1950), C196, and B. J. and H. W. Whiting, *Proverbs, Sentences and Proverbial Phrases from English Writings Mainly before 1500* (Cambridge, MA: Belknap Press, 1968), C117 (and cf. C116).

60 I quote from Wright, II, appendix, section XX.

61 These two passages also illustrate that the lines in continuation B are, as a rule, metrically shorter than those in A, their first half-line frequently having no more than three stresses. An extreme case is 163–4: 'The castel of slede   he huld eke al so / Tho nuste the king   what he myte do', but there are other lines and couplets almost as short.

62 Occasional lines elsewhere in the shorter continuation show that its author has perhaps caught something of the style, notably the ironic 'Wel dure he aboute   his mede that day' (30), said after the sudden death of a man who desecrated Henry II's corpse.

63 The stylistic homogeneity appears to rule out interpreting 'That verst this boc made' as a reference by a later writer to Robert as the original author of the *Chronicle*.

64 Wright, I, p. x.

65 See, for example, Sir Maurice Powicke, *The Thirteenth Century, 1216–1307*, 2nd edn (Oxford: Clarendon Press, 1962), pp. 505–06.

66 See *Southern Passion*, p. xi, and also *Ministry*, pp. 46–7.

67 See most recently Görlach, *Studies*, pp. 27–9.

Part II

Manuscripts and textual cultures of the *South English Legendaries*

6

'Lite bokes' and 'grete relikes': texts and their transmission in the *South English Legendary*

Chloe Morgan

Introduction

Ever since Beatrice Daw Brown observed that 'certain aspects' of the *SEL* 'would have no application for those whose lives were ordered by monastic rule', scholars have interpreted the collection's attitude towards learned, clerical culture in rather ambivalent terms.[1] Few emphasize its hostility as forcefully as Michael Robertson, who has argued that it displays a 'remarkable suspicion of learning'.[2] But a number of studies have stressed its 'simple, practical tone' and its 'vigorous, down-to-earth' approach to its material.[3] Such statements tend to imply that the *SEL* operates as a written form of oral discourse: its use of dialogue is often noted, and its narrative voice has been compared to 'a parent patiently reviewing a lesson for a young child'.[4] Composed in the English vernacular, and therefore distanced from a written culture dominated by Latin and Anglo-Norman, the *SEL* is seen to privilege homespun wisdom over bookish learning, and speech-like rhythms over poetic flair. 'Nothing', Anne Thompson remarks of the collection's prologue, 'suggests an interest in writing, but allusions to speaking and hearing abound'.[5]

Reading through the *SEL*, however, one is struck by the degree to which it does, in fact, engage with the written word. Its rhyming septenaries may be perfectly pitched for oral performance, but the *SEL* poet does not reject what Katherine O'Brien O'Keeffe has called the 'technology of writing' as a means of conveying information.[6] Variations on the verb to 'wite', or to know, are regularly rhymed with 'write', while exclamatory remarks and references to oral delivery are counterpointed by offhand invocations of 'bocs' and other textual sources. On occasion, the two are even mentioned in the same breath: 'the swetenesse that is mid God   in tale and in boke' (I, 60, 50).[7] The legends themselves show the saints reading, writing and handling a wide variety of texts, from gospel books and charters to inscriptions on tombs and altars. Some are rather ordinary, others are endowed with miraculous powers. Some are Scriptural, others are composed by the saints themselves, and a significant number are divine in origin, either written by Christ during his time on earth or, as heavenly letters, miraculously delivered during mass.

In this article I will explore the collection's attitude towards the written word by considering a few of the lives which directly describe the production, transmission and reception of texts. Theorists from Augustine to Derrida have highlighted the multiple ways in which Latinate Christianity, always a religion of the Word, uses images of text and textual reception to explain complex metaphysical concepts. Others have shown how later vernacular authors, including Chaucer and Dante, used similar images to develop a sophisticated sense of authorial self-consciousness.[8] With its vast circulation and remarkable longevity, the *SEL* has repeatedly frustrated attempts to place it in terms of geographical origin, target audience or ideological allegiance. Although it does not always offer a systematic programme of representation, and although the majority of texts that it features are also present in its sources, I will suggest that the *SEL* also uses the image of the written word to articulate important theological concepts and to explore its own, inherently written, status. Far from being ambivalent, the *SEL*'s approach to the textual sign is consciously and intimately related to its status as both hagiography and vernacular text.

'Literacy' or 'textuality'?: interacting with the unread text

Recent scholarship has emphasized that the lines between literacy and illiteracy were far from clearly drawn in the Middle Ages. People interacted with text in a range of different ways, and being unable to decipher the precise contents of a text did not automatically preclude a sophisticated pattern of interaction with textual objects. By the close of the thirteenth century, text and letters had come to play a fundamental role in the lives of most groups of lay society, and exerted a powerful influence over many aspects of their day to day existence. The role of texts in structuring religious devotion was apparent 'to literate and illiterate alike', while the growth of 'practical literacy' meant that the written word played an important part in social and commercial transactions, including land ownership, where the symbolic function of a deed could be as

important as the detailed information that it contained.[9] Outside
the church, particular prayers, Biblical verses and invocations to
saints were thought to hold medico-magical properties, and were
worn as apotropaic amulets or used to cure a diverse range of afflic-
tions, from epilepsy to labour pains. Laypeople were familiar with
the concept of texts playing a number of different roles which did
not depend on what we would see as conventional reading. Texts
were useful tools, indicators of different kinds of significance,
repositories of memory and power.

The legend of St Barnabas provides a good example of how
the *SEL* presents issues surrounding the transmission of text to
its audience. After briefly relating the saint's conversion and his
acceptance of St Paul, the legend focuses on Barnabas's apostolic
mission to Cyprus. It describes how he carries 'the gospelles of
Sein Mattheu [. . .] in a bok as God wolde' (I, 219, 61–2) with him
wherever he goes, and how he uses it to heal the sick:

> Of oure swete Louerd of hevene   Sein Barnabe hadde such grace
> That yif he eny sik man fonde   as he wende in eche place
> He leide uppon him is bok   that so holy and god was
> Of the gospelles of Sein Mattheu   so strong siknesse non nas
> That he thoru oure Louerdes grace   ne held of anon.
> Ther thoru he made many o man   to Jesu Crist gon
> Thoru vertu of this holyman   and of this holy boc also
> (I, 219, 67–73)

(St Barnabas had such grace from our sweet Lord of heaven that, if
he came upon any sick man as he went from one place to another, and
he laid on him his book of St Matthew's gospel that was so holy and
good, there was no sickness so strong that he did not immediately
heal it through our Lord's grace. By these means he caused many a
man to go to Jesus Christ, through the virtue of this holy man and of
this holy book too.)

Perhaps surprisingly, given that the saint spends much of his
time preaching to the 'wisoste' (I, 218, 24) men in the land, there
is nothing in the legend to suggest that this 'bok' is ever read or
even opened: Barnabas and the people that he heals interact with it
through touch alone.

This reticence about the contents of the volume could be taken
as evidence of the *SEL*'s reductive approach to textual culture, a
Latinate, written object presented in the simplest possible terms
for Jankofsky's 'unlettered English listeners'. But this would be
to pass over the lengthy traditions with which this image engages.

Jocelyn Wogan-Browne has remarked that 'even very bookish saints' Lives' show an interest in modes of transmission which do not rely on straightforward reading, a phenomenon that she describes as 'the hagiological valorization of seeing, wearing, touching, carrying and eating as modes of textual transmission'.[10] The image of the unread but miracle-performing volume was by no means limited to vernacular literary productions anxious about their own relationship to Latin textuality. Gregory of Tours, for instance, describes how a blind man is restored to sight by a life of St Nicetius 'de quo virtus divina procedens' ('from which divine power flowed').[11] John of Salisbury likewise relates how, rather like Barnabas, St Cuthbert healed an invalid with the Gospel of St John, a volume which itself became a relic, buried with the saint and then preserved in the treasury of Durham cathedral.[12]

In their ability to convey their messages instantaneously, these miracle-performing unopened volumes invoke important debates about the ability of the material, written sign to transmit the divine Word. Human writing, as Augustine observed in his commentary on the Psalms, depended on linear time and physical space, and was fundamentally different from the ineffable truth which it sought to express:

> In scripturis enim scribitur littera post litteram, syllaba post syllabam, verbum post verbum; nec ad secundum transitur, nisi primo perscripto. Ibi autem nihil velocius, ubi non multa sunt verba, nec tamen aliquid praetermissum est, cum in uno sint omnia.[13]

Paradoxically, the intensely physical image of the closed codex could work to control what Derrida has called the 'aphoristic energy' of writing.[14] Though formed from disparate folios inscribed with individual words and letters, it presented its contents as a unified totality, echoing the divine Word, where 'all may be in one'.[15] Jewelled bindings and ornamental book shrines also emphasized the iconic status of the closed volume, presenting it as a material expression of the ineffable, a single sign which potentially encompassed all others within it.[16] Like Christ, and like the Eucharist, it seamlessly combined the material and the spiritual, offering the possibility of communing with the divine through physical experience.[17]

Although they were entrenched in Latinate culture, these kinds of interactions would naturally hold a particular appeal for audiences whose own relationships with text did not depend exclusively on reading. 'By iconic principles', as Wogan-Browne remarks, 'textuality embraces the un-Latinate and the illiterate'.[18] The power and significance of St Barnabas's gospel is not revealed through a complex process of interpretation or exegesis, interpreting signs *literam post literam*. Nor is it only accessible to those who have the knowledge and skills to approach it in this way. Instead, it is available to all those who come into contact with it, or, in the *SEL*'s own words, 'many o man' (I, 219, 72). These two elements – positive physical and visual interaction with icon-like texts, and the relationship between the saint and the textual sign – are key aspects of the *SEL*'s particular textuality.

Heavenly letters and useful books: spiritual and worldly textuality

The famous bibliophile, Richard de Bury (d. 1345) expressed horror at the thought of the laity coming into contact with books.[19] Sullied by physical labour, they could not touch 'librorum lilia' ('the lily leaves of books') without defiling them, and were 'omni Librorum communione penitus . . . indigni' ('utterly unworthy of any communion with books').[20] Even worse, they would treat the book as an object rather than a text, turning it this way and that, and looking 'librum aeque respiciunt resupine transversum sicut serie naturali expansum' ('at a book turned upside-down just as if it were open in the right way').[21] For the highly literate de Bury, this kind of interaction compromised the essential nature of the written word, rendering it base and meaningless.

In the *SEL*, however, the kind of positive, physical interaction with the closed volume described in *Barnabas* is also possible with texts that have their contents on display. These texts can be read, but also transmit their meaning in a range of different ways, creating a broad and inclusive textual community. One of the *SEL*'s most famous lives, *St Kenelm*, provides a good example of the different modes of interaction with text, shading between literacy and textuality, which the *SEL* authorizes. In this story, the body of the saint, a boy-king of the Marches of Wales who has been murdered by his jealous sister, lies hidden in the valley of Clent, venerated only by a pure white cow. When God decides that it is time for the body to be discovered, he sends a dove to deliver a 'lite writ', written in his own hand, to the Pope in Rome, depositing it on 'Seinte Petres weued' ('St Peter's altar') just as he is performing mass. But when the pope has finished officiating and takes up the letter, he finds that he is unable to read it:

> The pope nom this holi writ   tho the masse was ido
> He nuste wat it was to segge   ne in wit neccuthe iwite
> For he ne couthe Engliss non   and an Engliss it was iwrite
> (I, 288, 258–60)

(The pope took up this holy writ when the mass was finished: he did
not know what it said nor could he understand anything in it, for he
knew no English, and it was written in English.)

The pope is clearly expecting the act of reading to transform his
relationship with the text from one of wonder and veneration to
one of direct communication. But the fact that the letter is written
in a language other than Latin has the rather satisfying effect of
placing the pope, the figurehead of the Christian world, in the
position of one of de Bury's laity. Faced with a text that he cannot
read, but which is presented to him as an object of veneration, he
has no choice but to understand its divinity in purely physical and
visual terms.

   This is emphasized by the form of the text, which is said to
be 'wight and ssinde brighte   the lettres al of golde' ('white
and shone brightly, the letters all golden', I, 288, 256) and which
forges a clear visual link between the 'writ' and its heavenly author.
However, the use of golden letters did not guarantee an immediate relationship between the physical existence of the written sign
and its divine meaning.[22] Jerome, for instance, commented on the
disjunction between the material pleasure gained from the beautifully written text and the Christian message which it failed to
represent: 'Aurum liquescit in litteras, gemmis codices vestiuntur,
et nudus ante fores earum Christus emoritur' ('gold is melted for
lettering, manuscripts are decked with jewels: and Christ lies at
their door naked and dying').[23] An eleventh-century Latin version
of St Kenelm seems to embrace the possibility of this disjunction,
emphasizing just how disorientating the unfamiliar and intensely
materialized text is for the pope: 'At sacer apostolicus cum tremore
respiciens novam scedulam, ignotis verbis ac litteris editam' ('The
holy and apostolic father looks with trembling at the strange crisp
white sheet written all over with unfamiliar words and letters').[24]
The A-redaction of the *SEL*, on the other hand, does not present
the document as inspiring fear.[25] Of course the Englishness of the
letter is not an issue for the audience of the vernacular life, and the
idea that God might be an Englishman would certainly have added
to the appeal of the episode.[26] But Renee Hamelinck's gleeful
observation that 'the Pope cannot understand the divine message

but the people can!' does not fully convey the delicate layering of
different textual interactions which takes place in this scene.[27] For
an audience familiar with the concept of interacting with texts on
visual and physical levels, the distinction between divinely created
golden letters and more mundane, human script would have made
perfect sense in a way that it would not, perhaps, for the pope.
It is this kind of interaction, the conveyance of textual meaning
through a wide variety of different means, as much as the use of the
vernacular, that the *SEL*'s version of the legend works to justify.

The letter's physical presence remains central to its function even after it has been transformed into a 'readable' text by
some English pilgrims who, interestingly, 'understode wel that
writ   tho hi it *hurde* rede' my emphasis:

> This writ was wel nobliche   iwest and up ido
> And iholde for grete relike   and yute it is also
> The nobleste relike it is   on therof of al Rome
> As it aghte wel, wo so understonde   right wel wanne it come
> For wanne it out of hevene com   and of oure Louerdes honde
> Wat noblore relike mighte beo   I ne can noght understonde.
> Thervore Sein Kenelmes day   as the pope made is heste
> At Rome hi holdeth heiliche   and maketh swuthe gret feste
> (I, 288, 269–76)

(This writ was very splendidly kept and put away and considered a
great relic. And so it still is: it is one of the noblest relics of all Rome,
as it well ought to be, for anyone who understands rightly where it
came from: for, given that it came out of heaven and from our Lord's
hand, what nobler relic there might be I cannot understand. For this
reason, they hold St Kenelm's day as a high feast in Rome as the
pope promised and make a very great feast of it.)

The way in which the legendary describes the continued existence of the letter differs significantly from the Latin life. In the
Latin text, the letter is said to be read 'per totam patriam' or
throughout the whole land. This presumably involves the text
being read, meditated on, copied and circulated, participating
fully in the textual culture of highly literate communities. In the
SEL, on the other hand, the letter remains firmly in one location
and in its original form. As a relic, a divinely created object, the
text preserves its close relationship with its heavenly originator.
Permanently white and gold, interaction with it continues to be
determined by veneration rather than by interpretation: the pope's
original reaction is constantly reprised by those who visit it. So

this heavenly letter in *St Kenelm* is written, seen, held, read, heard and worshipped, and all of these contribute equally to its meaning within the narrative.

So far, I have discussed texts which have a particularly close relationship with the divine, expressed through their physical form, either as an iconic unopened codex or golden writing, and which can convey their message through modes of reception other than traditional reading. There are a number of similar texts which appear throughout the legendary, many of them written, like the letter in St Kenelm, in a divine hand.[28] All of these texts work to forge close links between Christ, the Word made flesh and the written sign. These links are made evident by their powers, their appearance or even the fact that, like the heavenly letters in St Giles and St Kenelm, they are placed on an altar and thus visually linked with the Eucharist.[29] Simply looking at them or touching them can be a devotional act for, like the Host itself, they represent a union of the physical and spiritual sign, expressed in unequivocal terms. Their message can be accessed through reading, but they can also, through being displayed or handled, function as material signs representing the power of God. The legend of St Simon and St Jude, for instance, features another letter written by Christ, addressed to King Agbar, the leprous king of Odessa. When 'irad', the letter has the power to protect a town from invaders (II, 450, 49–54). But when Christ sends St Jude to heal Agbar, in a move that would have horrified de Bury, Agbar 'nom that holy writ . . . and roddede therwith is sike lich' ('took that holy writing . . . and rubbed his diseased face with it', II, 451, 67).[30]

But divinely authored and miraculous texts are not the only kind of written objects which feature in the *SEL*. To discuss them in isolation, as I have been doing, is to give something of a one-sided impression of the collection's treatment of the written word, and to pass over one of its most interesting features. Many of the *SEL*'s legends centre on scholarly saints who find themselves involved in textual production, or on ecclesiastical saints whose earthly power is negotiated through charters and other legal documents. As one would expect from a narrative-driven collection, individual lives tend to minimize or even omit to mention the numerous written works of saints such as Wulfstan or Hilary.[31] When the *SEL* does mention these texts, however, they are not portrayed in a way that confirms Robertson's accusation of a suspicion of learning.[32] The knowledge that Aldhelm's computational treatise imparts to its owner, for instance, is explained clearly and succinctly:

So that seint Aldhelm made   a lite boc tho
Forto knowe Esterday   and Leinte evere mo
That wo so hath thulke bok   he may evere iknowe
Hou he ssel nyme thulke tyme   heie other lowe.

(I, 212, 53–6)

(So that Aldhelm made a little book at that time to determine
Easterday and Lent for evermore, so that whoever has that book may
always know when he should set that time, high or low.)

The *SEL* does, however, preserve a distinction between texts
which are composed by human hands and those which have a more
direct relationship to the divine. Aldhelm's 'lite boc' does imbue its
reader with power, but that power consists in the specific knowledge of the complex but quantifiable issue that is the *temporale*
festivals of the church year. It is not the miraculous knowledge of
the divine imparted by Barnabas's apostolic gospel book, nor the
direct expression of divine will that we found in Kenelm's heavenly
letter.[33] Even those texts endowed with the highest human authority remain limited in their significance. To draw an example from
the same life, the charter which Aldhelm brings back from Rome
confirming the privileges of Malmesbury Abbey is very much a
product of power mediated and negotiated through human agency:

Chartre he broghte god inou   fram Rome of alle theos thinge
And suththe he com to Engelonde   and ssewede hom the kynge
  . . .
The privileges forthwith the pope   confermed bothe to:
Wanne popes and kynges hath imad   ne may no man undo

(I, 212, 41–6)

(He brought a good enough charter from Rome concerning all these
things, and then he came to England and showed them to the king
. . . The pope at once confirmed the privileges to both of them when
popes and kings have done something, no man can undo it.)

The implication is that the audience of the *SEL* would not have
any difficulty understanding why these texts were necessary, and
the kinds of functions that they performed, even if they would have
had no contact with them themselves. But although it acknowledges their existence, the *SEL* carefully mediates their ability to
provide communion with the divine. Earthly writings, even those
of the saints, are bounded in their significance and are untempered
by the quasi-Eucharistic presence of the spiritual within the physical that is found in divinely authored texts. There is no sense of the

christo-mimetic scribe, effecting salvation through his labours.[34]
Miraculous events hardly ever accompany the human creation of
texts, the sole exception being the work of the Evangelists, particularly John, whose divinely inspired act of textual creation leaves a
lasting legacy on the environment:

> He bad also that ther ne ssolde   thoru oure Louerdes grace
> Wind ne rein ne other weder   come in thulke place
> To lette him of his holy dede   the wile he there aboute were.
> Oure Louerd hurde is bone wel;   ne reinde it nevere eft there,
> Ne no wind com yute to this daie   as this holyman it bad,
> Ne no tempest in thulke stude   that this bok ymad.
> Holy is the holy bok   wanne so holy is the stude
> That ther ne may no tempest come   as this holiman it hadde
> ibede.
> (II, 598, 137–44)

(He also prayed that, through our Lord's grace, no wind or rain or any
other (bad) weather should come to that place and hinder him in his
holy occupation, while he was busy with it. Our Lord certainly heard
his prayer: it never again rained there, nor has any wind yet come to
this day, nor any tempest in that place, just as this holy man who made
this book prayed for it to be. Holy is the holy book when the place is
so holy that no tempest may come there, as the holyman had prayed.)

This careful distinction between the material and the spiritual
emphasizes that the legendary's response to texts is not just a
reflection or simplification of that of its sources. Instead, it is a
carefully constructed reaction to longstanding tensions about the
creation and transmission of text, designed to help a particular
audience configure their own particular relationship to the written
word in devotional terms. The role of text in conveying the divine
message is not just based on composition, copying and reading,
but can take place in other ways. Text does not automatically gain
magico-mystical powers, but is involved in the transmission of
earthly knowledge as well as the divine will. Aware of its audience's
ability to recognize and relate to different registers of text in different ways, the A-redaction of the *SEL* is able to circumnavigate
some of the tensions and anxieties raised by the transmission of the
spiritual via a material text.

Hagiographic textuality: the saint as holy sign

The association between the saint and the text as a physical
object endowed with spiritual import was well recognized in

hagiographical tradition. The hagiographical text, its main function being to 'prove' and confirm the sanctity of the saint by recounting their miracles, virtue and often grisly death, was itself central to that system of proof. In the words of Gail Ashton, 'belief in the various miracles and symbols demonstrating [the saint's] worth extends to belief in the *vita* itself . . . the hagiographical text brought together body, book and divine word'.[35] T. J. Heffernan describes how the development of a cult became interwoven with the hagiographical text which validated it. This reciprocity produced a phenomenon which he terms the 'iconicity of the text'.[36] As a text became disassociated from 'a unique historical author', it received 'approbation from the community as a source of great wisdom'.[37] Endowed with this status it evolves into something similar to Earle's *imago non manufacta*, eventually becoming 'a document revered as a symbol (viz. icon) of the deity'.[38] In his influential article, Earle discusses the phenomenon of the *imago non manufacta*, an image or text which 'displays no human imaginative artistry'.[39] Used to distinguish between non-Christian holy images, which are 'made by hands' and therefore 'idols', and the Christian icon, this term can be usefully applied to the distinction made by the *SEL* between human texts and those created by divine agency.[40]

The vast majority of *SEL* manuscripts were not high-status textual productions themselves. Though several are rubricated and have illuminated letters, only one manuscript has a sustained programme of figurative illustration.[41] There is, in short, no attempt to reconstruct the shining textuality of St Kenelm's heavenly letter. But the *SEL*'s careful representation of motifs of textual transmission relates closely to its own project, both as hagiography and as vernacular literature. In particular, the distinction that it maintains between the man-made and the divinely created text has implications for an understanding of the role played by writings about the saints, and their ability to convey devotional messages.

The idea that the saint himself or herself functioned as a sign which, like the *SEL*'s divinely authored texts, worked simultaneously on material and spiritual levels had been current for centuries. The late fourth-century poet Prudentius, for example, compared St Emeterius and Chelidonius of Calahorra to a divinely created text:

> Scripta sunt in caelo duorum martyrum vocabula
> Aureis quae Christus illic adnotavit litteris
> Sanguinis notis eadem scripta terris tradidit.[42]

Crucially, Christ himself is the instigator of this privileged written discourse, the saint the sign through which he expresses himself. Poised between the intense physicality of their wounds and the blissful spirituality of their heavenly reward, the figure of the martyr is figured as an inscribed sign which functions simultaneously on two levels, the earthly and the divine. Both golden and bloody, their wounds forge a typological connection between the saint, the written word and the earthly manifestation of the divine Word, or Christ's wounded body, which was itself often compared to a parchment inscribed with bloody letters.[43]

In the *SEL*'s legend of Edmund Rich, Archbishop of Canterbury, the body of the saint likewise functions as a site for textual transmission, forming an intersection between the materiality of the earthly text and the potential of the saint to function as divine sign. The legend relates how, in his youth, the saint takes a course in mathematics 'for to beo more profound' (II, 500, 224). While he is studying, his dead mother, 'Dame Mabille' (II, 493, 23), always a model of holiness in life and performer of miracles in death (II, 497, 144), appears to him in a vision and rebukes him:

'Leove sone', quath the moder   'betere figurs ther beoth
Wherto thu most thin hurte do   and thenche her on nomore'.
Heo nom forth his right hond   and wrot ther on his lore:
Threo rounde cerclen heo wrot   in the paume amidde
In the tueye heo wrot 'Fader' and 'Sone'   and 'Holi Gost' in the
                                                          thridde
                                                    (II, 500, 232–6)

('Dear son', said the mother, 'there are better figures on which you must set your heart and think on these others no more.' She took his right hand and wrote his learning on it for him. Three round circles she wrote in the middle of his palm: in two of them she wrote 'Father' and 'Son' and in the third, 'Holy Ghost'.)

Robertson suggests that this tripartite diagram is fundamentally opposed to clerical, textual culture, a rejection of book learning in general in favour of less formal modes of communication. Its three carefully labelled circles would certainly be easy for a lay audience to understand and to remember.[44] But it is important to note that its 'lore' (II, 500, 237) is not presented as an alternative to the kind of complex theological texts written by Aldhelm and Jerome. Instead, it is offered as an orthodox substitute for Edmund's foray into 'ars-metrike'; science which is described as 'a lore   that of figurs al is / And of draughtes as me draweth in poudre' ('a learning consisting only of figures and of diagrams such as one draws in the dust', II, 500, 227–8). It is these 'draughtes' (lines) scratched into 'poudre' (dust) which are contrasted so strongly with both the diagram drawn on to the flesh of the holy man and the advice given Edmund in his youth by the Christ child: 'In mi foreheved iwrite   mi name thu schalt iseo / Signe therwith thi forheved   and thi breost also / Anewe whan thu to bidde gost   and aday whan thu risest therto' ('You will see my name written on my forehead: sign your own forehead with it and also your breast each time when you go to pray and each day when you get up to pray', II, 495, 68–70). Making signs on the body of the saint is infinitely preferable to scratching them into the base earthly material of dust. Edmund's body functions as a site on which the material processes of writing can take place in ways that are straightforward and unproblematic. As sign, Edmund exists in time and space; he inscribes himself with the holy name in particular locations, 'thi forheved and thi breost' and at particular points in the day, 'Anewe . . . and aday'. As saint, however, his actions confirm not only his typological relationship to Christ, but the ability of the saint, and, by extension, writings about the saint, to convey the divine message.

A variation on this trope, which would have been particularly thought-provoking for an audience in whose lives legal and administrative texts played an increasingly important role, occurs in the proto-Faustian legend of 'St Theophilus'. The *SEL* is unusual in granting Theophilus a *vita* of his own. His narrative is more often found as part of Marian miracle collections or in readings on Mary's Life. However, this legend seems to have had considerable appeal, appearing in a number of stained glass windows, sculptures and illuminations.[45] At the centre of this narrative is a text which is emphatically non-hagiographical, the pact with the devil which Theophilus 'writ with his owe honde', an intensely materialized, man-made text, which visual sources often represent as a contemporary legal document.[46]

When Theophilus takes the charter to church it is read out to the congregation 'right as the gospel was irad' ('just as the gospel was being read / in just the same way as the gospel', I, 226, 171). Its meaning and function are shifted by the community's participation in reading and venerating the document in a devotional context: 'Th chartre bivore al that folk   the bissop let rede / That echmon iseie is luther sunne   and oure Leuediis milde dede' ('The bishop had the charter read before all those people / so that each one could see [Theophilus's] wicked sin and our Lady's deed

of mercy', I, 226–7, 177–8). Echoing the association between text
and the mass which is found in *Kenelm*, the diabolic text undergoes
a process of transubstantiation as it is read out at the altar. As a
manufactured text, however, it is denied the status of becoming
a 'grete relike' (I, 288, 270) celebrated as an *imago non manufacta*.
Theophilus's insistence, contrary to the desire of the 'folk' to preserve it 'for miracles' (I, 227, 179) that the charter be 'to doust
ibarned' ('burned to dust', I, 227, 182), emphasizes its material
nature and provides a counterpoint to the trope of the relic-text.

Instead, Theophilus's repentance turns him into a saint, or a
sign created by the divine. He himself becomes a testimony to the
power of Mary over Satan. The blaze of the fire which destroys the
charter is eclipsed by the divine light 'brightore than the sonne'
(I, 227, 187), which shines from his face. Like the golden script in
Kenelm, this is an unproblematic visual representation of his holiness, emphasizing the presence of the spiritual within his physical
form. In renouncing the unholy narrative and physicality of the
'chartre', Theophilus becomes a representation of the superiority
of the divinely sanctioned sign over the manufactured, earthly one.
The new narrative he adopts is one of highly visible and public
holiness, performed in front of the assembled congregation: 'He
gaf and delde poure men is god wel and clene / And swor that
out of churche he nolde   the wile he alive were' ('He gave and
shared out to poor men his goods, wholly and completely, / And
swore that he would never go out of the church while he was alive',
I, 227, 189–90). After three days of fasting and prayer he enters
the company of heaven, and the *SEL* narrator affords him a hagiographical source-text to prove his status:

> To hevene wende is soule anon . . .
> For seint he is in hevene hey   and is day falth in the yere
> Litel bivore Averil   as the bok us doth lere
>
>   (I, 227, 196–98)

(His soul then went to heaven . . . for a saint he is in high heaven, and
his day falls a little before April in the year as the book teaches us.)

Through this 'bok' and the *SEL* account itself, the audience of the
vita is positioned with the congregation who observe Theophilus's
renunciation of the 'chartre', his public repentance and his elevation to saintly status. As the narrative unfolds, their relationship to
the 'chartre' and to Theophilus himself undergoes a series of shifts.
These culminate in a celebration of the figure of the saint and a

renunciation of the material diabolic text in favour of a sign which truly participates in hagiographical discourse.

When he is blessed by heaven, Theophilus replaces the mendacious textual sign, written in his own hand, with the sign of the saint. In exploring the relationship between the figure of the saint and the process of creating a hagiographical text, the legendary is validating its own status as a text which, although it exists and is transmitted in time, from c. 1265 to c. 1440, and in space, from Somerset to Yorkshire, has a real ability to communicate a devotional message to its audience. It involves its audience in the communal validation and veneration of hagiographical narratives, enhancing an understanding of the way in which texts in all their forms, but particularly hagiographical text, can play in devotion.

Conclusion

An exploration of the *SEL*'s treatment of motifs of textual transmission reveals a subtle reinterpretation of longstanding traditions and anxieties about the role of the written word in communicating important spiritual material. Like many hagiographical texts, the *SEL* legitimizes modes of textual transmission other than reading.[47]

Here, however, this emphasis on the visual and tactile properties of textual objects is coupled with a consistent distinction drawn between man-made texts and those which constitute an *imago non manufacta*, being of divine origin. This enables the *SEL* to circumnavigate many of these tensions while encouraging its audience to consider the nature of their own relationships with texts in devotional terms. Rather than a hostility towards textual culture, the *SEL*'s use of the motifs of textual transmission seems to express a willingness on the part of a lay audience to consider its implications in many areas of their lives.

The *SEL*, thus, does not dismiss textual culture but, rather, grapples with the problems which had faced generations of theologians and hagiographers. Sensitive to the nature of its audience's textual consciousness, the *SEL* represents these motifs in a way particularly resonant for a community beginning to learn about the religious rituals in which it participated. Links between the Eucharist and the written sign, for example, are made explicit and rendered in visual terms. The motifs of textual transmission which occur throughout the *SEL* are thereby connected to its wider devotional and educational purposes.

Translating, reworking and popularizing narratives which had, in many cases, been circulating for centuries, the *SEL* provides a crucial point of interaction between clerical, textual culture and communities that were not, in the modern sense of the word, fully literate, but on whose complexly oral and written culture it sheds much light.

Notes

1 *Southern Passion*, p. xx.
2 Michael Robertson, 'The shallow clerk: a morphology of *The South English Legendary*', *Comparison*, 10 (1970), 36–65 (62).
3 Brown, *Southern Passion*, p. cx; Klaus P. Jankofsky, '*Legenda Aurea* materials in the *South English Legendary*: translation, transformation, and acculturation', in Dunn-Lardeau, pp. 317–30 (329). Theodor Wolpers remarks on the *SEL*'s 'schlichten, menschlichen Frommseins' ('simple, human piety'): *Die Englische Heiligenlegende des Mittelalters* (Tübingen: Niemeyer, 1964), p. 251.
4 Gregory M. Sadlek, 'The image of the devil's five fingers in the *South English Legendary*'s St Michael and Chaucer's Parson's Tale', in Jankofsky, pp. 49–64 (59).
5 Thompson, *Everday Saints*, p. 46.
6 Katherine O'Brien O'Keeffe, *Visible Song: Transitional Literacy in Old English Verse* (Cambridge: Cambridge University Press, 1990), p. 4.
7 All quotations are from D'Evelyn and Mill. For the suggestion that references to oral transmission and direct addresses to a listening audience are 'an illusion within an already written text' see Samson, 'Constructing a context', p. 191.
8 Rita Copeland, *Rhetoric, Hermeneutics, and Translation in the Middle Ages: Academic Traditions and Vernacular Texts* (Cambridge: Cambridge University Press, 1991). R. Evans, A. Taylor, N. Watson and J. Wogan-Browne, 'The notion of vernacular theory' in Wogan-Browne et al. (eds), *The Idea of the Vernacular* (University Park, PA: Penn State Press, and Exeter: Exeter University Press, 1999), pp. 314–30.
9 Lesley Smith, 'The theology of the twelfth and thirteenth-century Bible', in R. Ganeson (ed.), *The Early Medieval Bible: Its Production, Decoration and Use* (Cambridge: Cambridge University Press, 1994), pp. 223–32; M. B. Parkes, 'The literacy of the laity', in D. Daiches and A. Thorlby (eds), *Literature and Civilization: The Medieval World* (London: Aldus, 1973), pp. 555–77; M. T. Clanchy, *From Memory to Written Record: England 1066–1307*, 2nd edn (Oxford: Blackwell, 1993), pp. 8–42.
10 Jocelyn Wogan-Browne, 'The apple's message: some post-Conquest

hagiographic accounts of textual transmission', in A. J. Minnis (ed.), *Late-Medieval Religious Texts and their Transmission: Essays in Honour of A. I. Doyle* (Cambridge: D. S. Brewer, 1994), pp. 39–53 (40).

11 Gregory of Tours, 'Vita patrum', in B. Krusch (ed.), *Gregorii Episcopii Turonensis Opera*, MGH: Scriptores Rerum Merovingicarum (Hanover: Hahn, 1885), pp. 661–743 (p. 701, l. 27); trans. E. James as *Life of the Fathers*, Translated Texts for Historians 1 (Liverpool: Liverpool University Press, 1986), p. 77.

12 Cited in D. Marner, *St Cuthbert: His Life and Cult in Medieval Durham* (Toronto and New York: University of Toronto Press, 2000), p. 46.

13 'For in writings, letter is written after letter, syllable after syllable; word after word; nor do we pass to the second except when the first is written out. But nothing can exceed the swiftness, where there are not several words and yet there is not anything omitted, as all may be in one': Augustine, *Ennarrationes in psalmos I*, CCSL 38 (Turnhout: Brepols, 1956), psalm 44:6, 1.24–8, p. 498: trans. James Tweed in James Tweed, Thomas Scratton, Henry Musgrave Wilkins et al. (eds), *Expositions on the Book of Psalms*, Library of the Fathers of the Holy Catholic Church nos 24, 30, 32, 39 (Oxford: John Henry Parker, 1847–57), vol. 2, p. 234.

14 Jacques Derrida, *Of Grammatolgy*, trans. Gayatri Spivak, 2nd edn (Baltimore and London: Johns Hopkins University Press, 1999), p. 18.

15 J. M. Gellrich, *The Idea of the Book in the Middle Ages: Language Theory, Mythology and Fiction* (Ithaca: Cornell University Press, 1985), esp. ch. 1; Andrew Taylor, *Textual Situations: Three Medieval Manuscripts and Their Readers* (Philadelphia: University of Pennsylvania Press, 2002), pp. 22–4.

16 See M. P. Brown, *The Lindisfarne Gospels: Society, Spirituality and the Scribe* (London: University of Toronto Press, 2003), pp. 66–9.

17 On the connection between the book and the Eucharist see Smith, 'Theology of the twelfth and thirteenth-century Bible', p. 230.

18 Wogan-Browne, 'Apple's message', p. 43.

19 On De Bury's relationship to books, see Michael Camille, 'The book as flesh and fetish in Richard de Bury's *Philobiblon*', in Dolores Warwick Frese and Katherine O'Brien O'Keeffe (eds), *The Book and the Body* (Notre Dame, Indiana: University of Notre Dame Press, 1996), pp. 34–77.

20 *The Philobiblon of Richard de Bury*, ed. and trans. E. C. Thomas (Oxford: Blackwell, 1960), p. 134; trans. p. 240.

21 Ibid.

22 Brown, *Lindisfarne Gospels*, p. 76.

23 Jerome, *Ep.* 22 in *Select Letters of St Jerome*, ed. F. A. Wright, Loeb Classical Library 262 (London: Heinemann, 1954), pp. 132–3.

24 Rosalind C. Love (ed.), *Three Eleventh-Century Anglo-Latin Saints'*

Lives: Vita S. Birini, Vita et Miracula S. Kenelmi and Vita S. Rumwoldi (Oxford: Oxford University Press, 1996), p. 64; trans. p. 65.

25 The St Kenelm life in MS Laud 108 does suggest the Pope's disorientation (Horstmann, 352, 252–3: see further Wogan-Browne, below, pp. 257–8).

26 Jankofsky, 'National characteristics' pp. 87–8.

27 Hamelinck, 'St Kenelm', p. 29.

28 See for example St Martha, in D'Evelyn and Mill, I, 354, 165–72.

29 For *Giles* see D'Evelyn and Mill, II, 384–9, esp. 135–6, 389. On heavenly letters see Emily Steiner, *Documentary Culture and the Making of Medieval English Literature* (Cambridge: Cambridge University Press, 2003).

30 Görlach sees a strong *Legenda aurea* influence in this legend (*Textual Tradition*, p. 27).

31 So too, the *SEL Wulfstan* makes little of the saint's own writings, though as against the charge that that he knows too little 'of lore' (I, 12, 111) to be bishop of Worcester, it shows his habitual relation with learning in the claim that he would sleep with his head on the altar step or 'is bok therunder do' ('put his book under [his head]'), I, 8, l.17. The point is made in relation to St Hilary by Thompson, *Everday Saints*, p. 11.

32 Robertson, 'Shallow clerk', p. 62. On the *SEL*'s use of charters see further Yeager in this volume.

33 Jerome's writings are similarly portrayed as a means of ordering 'the servise of churche' (D'Evelyn and Mill, II, 428, 4), arranging what already exists rather than directly transmitting messages from the heavens.

34 Examples of the salvific capacity of scriptural writing include Orderic Vitalis's account of the sinful scribe saved by having transcribed one more letter of Scripture than the number of his sins during his life (*Historia Ecclesiastica*, ed. and trans. Marjorie Chibnall, 7 vols (Oxford: Oxford University Press, 1980), vol. 2, pp. 50–2). For the Evangelists as authors credited with direct powers of divine transmission, see, e.g., in addition to St John, Bede's description of Luke 'spiritu sancto calamum regente nullatenus falsum scribere potuit' ('who, being controlled like a pen by the Holy Spirit, could by no means write anything false'): Bede, *Exposito Actuum Apostolorum*, ed. M. L. W. Laistner, CCSL 121 (Turnholt: Brepols, 1983), Praefatio ll. 38–9; trans. L. T. Martin as *Commentary on the Acts of the Apostles*, Cistercian Study Series 117 (Kalamazoo, MI: Cistercian Publications, 1991), p. 4.

35 G. Ashton, *The Generation of Identity in Medieval Hagiography: Speaking the Saint* (London: Routledge, 2000), p. 2.

36 Thomas Heffernan, *Sacred Biography: Saints and Their Biographers in the Middle Ages* (New York: Oxford University Press, 1992), p. 35.

37 Ibid., p. 16.

38 Ibid., p. 36.

39 J. W. Earle, 'Typology and iconographic style in early medieval hagi-ography', *Studies in the Literary Imagination*, 8 (1977), 15–46, p. 26.

40 Ibid.

41 See the essay by Winstead below.

42 Aurelius Prudentius Clemens, 'Peristefanon Liber', *Carmina*, ed. M. P. Cunningham, CCSL 126 (Turnholt: Brepols, 1966), pp. 251–389, p. 251, l.1–3; trans. Sister M. Clement Eagan as 'The martyrs' crowns' in *The Poems of Prudentius*, The Fathers of the Church Series (Washington: Catholic University of America Press 1962), pp. 95–274, p. 95: 'Written fair on Heaven's pages are the names of martyrs twain / Christ Himself in golden letters has engraved them there on high / And on Earth they are recorded in bright characters of blood.' The martyrs referred to are Emeterius and Chelidonius of Calahorra, little known Spanish saints (Eagan, p. 95).

43 M. J. Carruthers, 'Reading with attitude, remembering the book', in Frese and O'Keeffe (eds), *The Book and the Body*, pp. 1–33 (4–5).

44 Compare e.g. the devil's five fingers (see Sadlek, 'Image of the devil's five fingers' in Jankofsky, pp. 49–64) and see Robertson, n. 2 above.

45 See A. Freyer, 'Theophilus the penitent as represented in art', *Archaeological Journal*, 92 (1935), 287–333, and M. W. Cothren, 'The iconography of Theophilus windows in the first half of the thirteenth century', *Speculum*, 59 (1984), 308–41.

46 See for example the de Brailes hours (c. 1240) where it is depicted with a large and pendulous wax seal (Claire Donovan, *The de Brailes Hours: Shaping the Book of Hours in Thirteenth-Century Oxford* (Toronto and Buffalo: University of Toronto Press, 1991), pp. 69–77 and figs 39, 44, 45): Nigel Morgan, *The Lambeth Apocalypse: Manuscript 209 in Lambeth Palace Library* (London: Harvey Miller, 1990), pp. 55–6 and fols 46r–47r.

47 Outside the *SEL*, see e.g. lives of St Margaret (Wogan-Browne, 'Apple's message', p. 40); Wendy Larson, 'Who is the master of this narrative? Maternal patronage of the cult of St Margaret', in Mary C. Erler and Maryanne Kowaleski, *Gendering the Master Narrative: Women and Power in the Middle Ages* (Ithaca: Cornell University Press, 2003), pp. 94–104.

7

Documents, poetry, and editorial practice: the case of 'St Egwine'

Stephen M. Yeager

The version of the *Life of Egwine* in the *SEL* or *SELS*[1] seems, on its surface, to provide a relatively conventional account of a minor saint. The historical Ecgwine[2] was the third bishop of Worcester and the founder of Evesham abbey; the record does not tell us much about him beyond these basic facts. In this essay, I will show how the *SEL Egwine* is also an 'account' in the more bureaucratic sense of the term, as its hero is remembered mostly for confirming the possessions and privileges of the monastery he founded. I will argue that this documentary function of the text has influenced its manuscript transmission in ways that traditional literary editing techniques do not quite take into consideration. My reading of the *Egwine* tradition will thus examine its particular generic ambiguities to identify some of the limitations of both literary-critical and legal-diplomatic interpretative methodologies in describing the full complexities of this text and its source tradition, in order to reveal how these methodologies have shaped our understanding of the *SEL* materials generally.[3]

The *SEL Egwine* can be divided into two roughly equal parts, each of which focuses on one main miracle. In the first half of the poem (lines 1–92), Egwine takes holy orders (8–10) and is appointed bishop against his wishes (11–14); his incessant preaching inspires resentment, which leads the most unrepentant sinners to call for his removal from office (15–22). Egwine must travel to Rome to defend himself, an indignity he accepts with humility (23–30). He locks himself in iron chains, and throws the key into the nearby River Avon; he then travels to Rome (21–38). After his arrival, he sends one of his servants to the market to buy a fish; in the belly of the fish is the key that Egwine threw into the Avon at the start of the journey (51–6). As the narrator observes in line 58, 'nadde never the keie so fer wit oute miracle icome' ('The key would never have come so far without a miracle'). Egwine stays in

Rome for a time, then returns to England (63–86). The poem here particularly emphasizes the privileges and franchises bestowed on Egwine by the pope (76) and confirmed by King Atheldred (83).

The second half of the poem (93–160) focuses on the foundation of Evesham abbey. When Evesham was still a wilderness, it was inhabited by a shepherd named Eoves, who incidentally gave Evesham its name (93–105). Eoves has a vision one night of three beautiful women walking through the wood, singing; the woman leading the other two is the most beautiful, and she is holding a book (106–14). Eoves immediately tells Egwine about his vision (115) and Egwine goes to see for himself, visiting the spot and praying for a vision (116–21). When his prayer is answered, the leader of the three women, who is the Virgin, instructs Egwine to found a monastery in her honour on that very site (121–6). Egwine immediately complies, first acquiring the land from Atheldred, then building a church (127–32). Shortly thereafter, Atheldred gives up his throne to enter a monastery; he is succeeded by Kenred (133–8). Kenred is evidently dissatisfied with the poor state of Evesham's endowment, and Egwine suggests that they should travel to Rome (139–42). When they arrive, Pope Constantine gives them many franchises; they return to England, and the franchises are confirmed by Brightwold, the archbishop of Canterbury (143–50). Satisfied, St Egwine retires to become a monk in the newly endowed Evesham abbey, where he remains until his death on St Sylvester's Eve (153–6).

Such a biography may seem to split into obviously 'literary' and 'historical' components, with the fish and key motif (found in other hagiographies, such as that of St Gregory the Penitent) and the vision of the three women functioning as romantic and literary validations of the legend's two documentary cores, the papal and royal confirmations of Ecgwine as bishop in the first half of the poem and of the rights and privileges of the monastery he founds at Evesham in the second. But the 'documentary' here is neither straightforwardly historical nor textually stable. Katherine Lewis has compellingly argued that the modern disciplines of history and literary criticism arose in part as an explicit rejection of hagiography as a valid historical genre, a rejection that has skewed both the reading and the subsequent textual criticism of hagiographic texts.[4] Given the complexities of St Ecgwine's hagiographic tradition, we need, in reading the *SEL Egwine* and its tradition, to move beyond the limitations of modern literary-critical and historical methodologies, and particularly of literary and diplomatic textual criticism, in order to pursue a fuller engagement with the kinds of information that the tradition actually contains. All of the *Egwine* witnesses are manifestations not of a *text*, but of a *claim*, whose hypothetical 'best' or most 'complete' version is thus not an 'authorial' series of words and phrases, but rather a future in which the claim continues to be recognized. The specific readings of the text, and even key narrative details, are preserved as a means towards this more pragmatic end. At the same time, such claims are made within an always already religious and sacralized construction of ends and means. One result of this, as will be further argued below, is that the illocutionary and performative force of even so apparently documentary a genre as the charter is stronger than we might think. And an important implication here is that, as against our persistent tendency to conceptualize the vernacular as oral and Latin as written, the *SEL* and its Latin sources share more with each other in their attitude to the written word and its valences than either does with our secularist editorial methods and practices.[5]

Variation and authentication: S-1251

In order to conduct this fuller consideration of the nature and specifics of the Ecgwine tradition, it is necessary to look at particular aspects of the Latin materials. The two episodes in which Egwine obtains documents validating his purposes originate in the earliest surviving version of the *Vita S. Ecgwini*, attributed to the pre-Conquest eleventh-century author Byrhtferth of Ramsey.[6] This *Vita* includes several long digressions that fill out the story of a man mostly forgotten by local lore and barely mentioned in the historical record. In this the *Vita* is typical of many high medieval monastic Latin *vitae* and their use of conventional scenes and motifs to claim and defend particular territories and rights.[7] Among the few available documents consulted by Byrhtferth,[8] the most important here is the (now lost) charter later catalogued by Sawyer as 1251 (hereafter S-1251), a first-person account by Ecgwine describing how Evesham monastery came to be founded.[9] In it, Ecgwine recounts the vision of the Virgin Mary, the trip to Rome and the circumstances surrounding the endowment. Byrhtferth even appears to transcribe the charter into his text, though as Lapidge notes 'it is clear that Byrhtferth was paraphrasing, not quoting verbatim' from the putative original (because this paraphrase will be important to discussion below, it will be hereafter referred to as an independent entity, B-1251).[10] For the moment, it is worth noting that Byrhtferth's reliance on legal documents is indicative of the close relationship between his text's claims for Ecgwine's sanctity and Evesham's claims for its endowed properties.[11]

Byrhtferth's *Vita* was heavily revised and redacted after the Conquest by Dominic of Evesham into a version upon which all subsequent accounts of Ecgwine are based, including that found in the *SEL*.[12] In accordance with Norman tastes, Dominic eliminates Byrhtferth's 'hermeneutic' Latin and most of his digressions, and he also alters details to historicize the text's claims.[13] For example, Dominic follows Byrhtferth's text when he says that Ecgwine's second journey to Rome was a part of the famous pilgrimage undertaken by the two Kings Coenred and Offa, but he adds to his sources (and to the importance of Ecgwine) by locating the saint's meeting with Coenred and Offa at St Aldhelm's funeral.[14]

Many of the changes to B-1251 made by Dominic in his own citation/paraphrase of Ecgwine's charter (hereafter D-1251) appear to be his own additions, rather than corrections with reference to a lost original copy of S-1251.[15] D-1251 is also filled out with details apparently borrowed from Byrhtferth's hagiographic narrative, even as it eliminates some of the 'silly anachronisms' of B-1251 noted by Lapidge.[16] In these respects Dominic's *vita* and Byrhtferth's are alike: both participate in the construction of saints' lives to represent the needs of a particular monastic house at a particular time, and the required fictionalizing (as it would seem to modern critics working with the historical and literary binary noted above as analysed by Katherine Lewis) becomes yet more intense in Dominic's version of Egwine's life. As Lapidge points out, Dominic was undertaking this project just after the Conquest and during the 'Golden Age' of English forgery, at a monastery that has become particularly notorious among modern historiographers for its forged documents.[17] After the Conquest new pressures to prove proprietary rights to monastic possessions resulted in the large-scale monastic production of history as it ought to be, and many 'pre-Conquest' charters were produced in this cause in the late eleventh and twelfth centuries. Ancient deeds of privilege were by this time 'essential' for maintaining rights, and a charter written by a local saint would have been especially useful in this capacity.[18] However, as historians have increasingly recognized, the practices of modifying or even inventing documents that are now called 'forgeries' were not by nature illicit. Rather, such practices ought to be understood as reflecting the different aims and standards of document production and maintenance in the eleventh and twelfth centuries. These are influenced not only by political circumstances but more fundamentally by the archivists' medieval conceptions of what a document was for, and of how it related to other historical sources.[19]

Of the several redactions and revisions of Dominic's *Vita*, the most pertinent to this consideration of the Latin tradition and notions of textual authentication is a particular reworking of Dominic's text (and of its citing and paraphrasing of Ecgwine's charter): the redaction by Thomas of Marlborough.[20] Thomas rewrites Dominic's *Vita S. Ecgwini* extensively, adding and changing substantive details in both the prose narrative and the charter.[21] The relationship of Thomas's text to those of Dominic and Byrhtferth, and in particular the relationship of T-1251 to D-1251 and B-1251, allows the identification of patterns of variation and revision in the different treatments of this document which will in turn form a basis for comparing similar patterns identifiable in the witnesses of the *SEL Egwine*.

Charters and the nature of Thomas of Marlborough's witness

Thomas of Marlborough's account of Ecgwine's life could not possibly be considered the 'best' version of the *Vita S. Ecgwini*, in that it is clearly a revised version of Dominic's text, based in turn on Byrhtferth's. Accordingly, Sayers and Watkiss's edition of Thomas's *History of the Abbey of Evesham* collates T-1251 against D-1251, along with the rest of the text that Thomas borrowed from Dominic. And yet, to historians, T-1251 is the most 'complete' witness of the document S-1251, because its transcriber apparently took the greatest care to employ the appropriate forms that make the document's claims to authenticity seem historically plausible.[22] Hence the confusing discrepancy that in the on-line 'Electronic Sawyer' catalogue, the earliest witness of S-1251 listed is T-1251.[23] Because B-1251 and D-1251 do not quite seem like diplomatic transcriptions to modern historians, their narratives do not qualify as charters for the purposes of cataloguing. In other words, even though Dominic's and Thomas's respective versions of the *Vita S. Ecgwini* are considered by their literary editors to witness the same literary text, the portions of those texts that quote or paraphrase the document S-1251 are not considered by diplomatic editors to witness the same document.

The editorial problem posed by these texts is made still more interesting and complicated by the genre of the Anglo-Saxon charter itself. Charters are no more straightforwardly factual than *vitae* and have a surprising range of generic affiliations and functions. So for instance, in Stephen of Ripon's *Life of St Wilfrid*, site of the earliest known account of an Anglo-Saxon charter's use, the saint's charter is described as a performed liturgical text:

> Stans itaque sanctus Wilfrithus episcopus ante altare conversus ad populum, coram regibus enumerans regiones, quas ante reges pro animabus suis et tunc in illa die cum consensu et subscriptione episcoporum et omnium principium illi dederunt, lucide enuntiavit necnon et ea loca sancta in diversis regionibus quae clerus Bryttannus, aciem gladii hostilis manu gentis nostrae fugiens, deservit.

> (Then St Wilfrid the bishop stood in front of the altar, and, turning to the people, in the presence of the kings, read out clearly a list of the lands which the kings, for the good of their souls, had previously and on that very day as well, presented to him, with the agreement and over the signatures of the bishops and all the chief men, and also a list of the consecrated places in various parts which the British clergy had deserted when fleeing from the hostile sword wielded by the warriors of our own nation.)[24]

The phrase 'cum consensu et subscriptione episcoporum et omnium principium', which sounds like a reference to a witness list, suggests that Wilfrid's 'sermon' here is a charter.[25] The formal and thematic influence of sermon literature on Anglo-Saxon charters has long been acknowledged, and it is not coincidental that such a substantial number of Anglo-Saxon charters should survive in gospel books and liturgical manuscripts.[26] Like the gospel books, the text of Wilfrid's 'signatures' seems to have functioned as a prop in the performance of a ritual, with a purpose that 'resided less in the information it contained than in its function as a potent symbol of ownership'.[27] As Finberg notes, 'a Testament left by the founder would serve this [sermon-like] purpose very well, if only as the beginning of a memorial or register to which additions could be made from time to time'.[28] It thus seems likely that the various versions of the lost charter S-1251 were written in a more homiletic rhetorical mode than the term 'charter' implies, and, moreover, that this aspect of the text reflects a probable performance context where it was integrated into the liturgy on occasions of institutional importance.

The generic ambiguity of charters illustrates the paradox imposed on Ecgwine's hagiographic tradition by the divergent organizational principles of different scholarly disciplines. If T-1251 is to be considered an extended citation of a literary, homiletic text, then an editor ought to follow the lead of Sayers and Watkiss by collating it against the readings of D-1251, as a part of Thomas's text which is based on a part of Dominic's *Vita*. On the other hand, if we consider T-1251 to be a transcription of a legal document, then the importance of comparing it with Dominic's text is diminished. For example, where T-1251 identifies a subking who donated twenty hides at Twyford as 'Osweard', it appears to be correcting the 'Oshere' of D-1251 with reference to B-1251.[29] For the diplomatic editor, the question of where Thomas found 'Osweard' is secondary to the question of whether the subking actually *was* Osweard, and whether an error on this point would have invalidated the document; from this perspective, the combination of Thomas's agreement with Byrhtferth and his greater credibility in general gives scholars a reason to prefer T-1251 to D-1251, even though the former is clearly based on the latter.

A focus on historical fact thus discourages full consideration of the possibility that T-1251 was not always 'corrected', but in some places was simply changed.[30] After all, Thomas of Marlborough was the chief litigant in a legal battle between Evesham and the see of Worcester over monastic privileges, a dispute that he ultimately won in arguments based on his close textual analysis of T-1251 and similar documents.[31] He was also a member of the new generation of Bologna-trained canon lawyers, whose sophisticated grasp of the textual features required by a papal court to verify a document's claims would have given him both the means and motivation to generate a formally consistent text.

There is ample evidence that Thomas edited the text for just such a legal audience, most obviously in the passages where events from Dominic's *Vita* appear in T-1251, though they are not witnessed in either D-1251 or B-1251. For example, Ecgwine briefly discusses his first journey to Rome in T-1251, though this episode appears only in the narrative, not the charter portion of Dominic's *Vita S. Ecgwini*.[32] T-1251 also replaces a mention of St Wilfrid 'archbishop' of York (Wilfrido Eboracensi archiepiscopis) found in D-1251 with the simplified 'Bishop Wilfrid' (Wilfridus episcopus).[33] Here Thomas also contradicts Byrhtferth's version, where the corresponding passage of B-1251 calls Wilfrid archbishop of York (archipresbytes Eborace civitatis).[34] The claim that St Wilfrid of York was present at the synod described in the various versions of S-1251 is highly suspect.[35]

Given that Thomas had a strong motive to change the text to bolster the document's value as proof for his claims, there is little reason to hypothesize that a 'Wilfridus episcopus' should have appeared in the version of the charter consulted by Byrhtferth. Thomas's modification (which keeps the famous name) gives us the most strategic version of the evidence, and not necessarily the most accurate.[36]

In the remainder of this essay, I will explore the implications of these circumstances for editorial methodologies through an analysis of the *SEL Egwine* manuscripts. I will apply a 'disjunctive' editorial approach (to adapt William Robins's term)[37] to the text, looking at it as both a historical record and as a literary text, in order to show how the pressures on the tradition created by its quasi-legal, quasi-literary authenticating strategies make themselves manifest in some of the more substantial textual variants.

The *SEL Egwine* manuscript tradition: a diplomatic approach

Five extant manuscripts witness the *SEL Egwine*: Görlach's E (London, BL, Egerton 1993, fols 221v–222v, s. xiv);[38] J (London, BL, Cotton Julius D.ix, fols 266v–268r, s. xv);[39] Qa (London, BL, Add. MS 10626, fol. 7a (incomplete), s. xiv);[40] S (London, BL, Stowe 949, fols 142v–144r, s. xiv[2]);[41] and V (Oxford, Bodleian MS English Poetry A.1 (the 'Vernon Manuscript'), fols 52v–53r, s. xiv[2]). The E and S manuscripts' witnesses of *Egwine* (hereafter *E-Egwine* and *S-Egwine*) both seem to bear witness to a separate branch of the poem's tradition from *V-Egwine* and *J-Egwine*. Most crucially, neither *E-Egwine* nor *S-Egwine* contains passages found in *V-Egwine* and *J-Egwine*, which have clear analogues in the Latin sources. (*Qa-Egwine* is incomplete, and does not witness the key variants found among the other witnesses.)

In his interpretation of this evidence, Görlach asserts that *V-Egwine* is the 'best' version of the poem, on the grounds that the additional lines found in *J-Egwine* are 'obviously unoriginal'.[42] However, this argument works from the assumption that the translator is copying a literary text, and thus that his or her faithfulness to the source will typically manifest as an attempt to render the 'content' of the source text into a new language. This characterization of the unique *J-Egwine* passages, however, closes off as much as it clarifies: other comparative methodologies taking account of the textual assumptions discussed above can lead to new interpretations.

There are fourteen lines unique to *J-Egwine*, divided into three passages: 35–8, 41–6 and 89–92.[43] The most likely site of interpolation is the passage at lines 41–4, describing Egwine's decision to stop at Aldhelm's funeral on his first journey to Rome in chains:

> And yut, yvetereth as he was,   un even wei he nom.
> From the toun of Evesham   by Malmesbur he com.
> Seint Aldelme he fond do deth,   the masse he song do,
> And burethe then holiman   ar he wolde from him go.

> (And yet, fettered as he was, he took an even path. He came from the town of Evesham by Malmesbury. He found St Aldhelm dead, sang the mass, and buried the holy man before he would leave him.)

These lines contradict Dominic's version of events, in which Ecgwine's second trip, following his vision of the Virgin, begins with Aldhelm's funeral.[44] In Byrhtferth's account, Ecgwine travels to Rome with the two kings to confirm the privileges of the monastery of Evesham.[45] According to the *Historia ecclesiastica gentis Anglorum*, Aldhelm died in 709, the same year as the trip to Rome by the Kings Coenred and Offa.[46] Thus if Egwine went to Aldhelm's funeral on his first trip to Rome as described in the *J-Egwine* passage, then it would mean that he arrived in Rome, experienced the miracle, befriended the pope and advised him in everything, came back to England, had the vision of the Virgin, and returned to Rome with Coenred and Offa within a single year.

To a literary-critical editor, then, the passage seems to have been added to *J-Egwine* by a scribe who was not familiar with St Ecgwine's hagiography and its supporting documentation, but who wanted to reconcile the poem with lines 87–90 of the *SEL Aldhelm*, where Egwine comes to the more famous saint's funeral in chains:

> So that the bissop of Wircestre   Seint Edwine tho com
> Al yve[te]red toward Rome   and there vorth thene wei nom
> And Seint Aldelm at Malmesburi   faire an eorthe broghthe
> And suthe wende forth to Rome   and deore thane wei aboghte.[47]

> (Thus the bishop of Worcester, St Egwine, then came all fettered towards Rome, and then took the way forth, and beautifully brought St Aldhelm into the earth at Malmesbury and afterwards went forth to Rome, and dearly paid for that passage.)

This passage, which bears a close resemblance to *J-Egwine* lines 41–4, is based in turn on William of Malmesbury's assumption that Egwine went to Rome with Coenred and Offa *before* he went to Aldhelm's funeral in chains, an emendation perhaps based on William's belief that Coenred and Aldhelm died in the same year.[48]

However, as outlined above, it cannot be presumed that consistency with the source narrative is strong evidence for the 'originality' of any reading of this poem. In fact there are discrepancies between all of the poem's witnesses and their putative sources, which allow for alternative ways of reading these unique *J-Egwine* lines. In this regard, it is noteworthy that all of the various Latin versions of the *Vita S. Ecgwini* claim that Coenred returns to England with Ecgwine to sign the charter, though Bede clearly states that the king stayed in Rome after his journey 'to his last day' ('ad ultimam diem').[49] Given the untenability of the narrative witnessed by the primary sources, it might be argued that the version of events found in *Egwine* could witness an attempt by the translator to reconcile his text with knowledge of Coenred's death in Rome. Hence, perhaps, the failure of every version of the *SEL Egwine* to mention Offa; in each manuscript, Egwine travels to Rome with King Kenred alone.[50] Further, at line 139, *Egwine* claims that this journey happened when Kenred was a 'newe kinge.' Æthelred abdicated in 704, and it is debatable whether his successor Coenred would still be a 'newe' king in 709, five years into his reign.[51]

A closer look at the text suggests, however, that these modified details are part of a comprehensive, if subtle, change to the source narrative. The *SEL* poem also includes the detail that Atheldred gave up his throne to become a monk, at a point in the narrative parallel to the inclusion of this detail in the versions of the charter S-1251. However, the sequence of events in *J-Ecgwine* is slightly different from that of the charter. For example, in the charter, Ecgwine starts with his vision of the Virgin. He then alludes to possessions that Æthelred gave him before his abdication, and how they were supplemented over time by other regional kings. Then, Ecgwine tells us that, two years after the last of the endowments described, Ecgwine met Coenred and Offa at Aldhelm's funeral.[52] Implicitly, then, a good deal of time elapses between Ecgwine's vision and the journey to Rome.

In the *SEL Egwine*, on the other hand, Atheldred's donations seem to happen immediately after the miracle, as can be seen in lines 125–8:

Tho he hadde iseie the suete sighte   and there maidens thenne wente,

The bischop thonkethe Jesu Crist,	that such holi sighte him sente.
To the king he wente, Atheldreth,	that king was the yut tho
And ar he yeue him thilke place	from him he nolde go.

(When he had seen the sweet sight and the maidens went from there, the bishop thanked Jesus Christ, that had sent him such a holy sight. He went to the King Atheldred, who was still king at that time, and [Egwine] would not go before [the king] gave him that place.)

Thus the miracle, Atheldred's abdication and the trip to Rome with Kenred seem to happen in relatively rapid succession, a narrative change that not only quickens the pace of events but makes them reach their conclusion earlier. In this version, it is well within the realm of possibility that Kenred and Egwine were able to travel to Rome and back before 709, so that Kenred's famous trip to Rome with Offa could have been his second pilgrimage. In this case, then, the translator's licence to remove unnecessary detail from the narrative also happens to have eliminated the historical inconsistencies that threaten Evesham's claims to its own endowment. Thus in the *SEL Egwine*, it is problematic to suggest that the movement of Aldhelm's funeral to the first trip is a clear example of interpolation, especially when there is an authoritative source for the *J-Egwine* passage in not only the *SEL Aldhelm* but also the *Gesta pontificum*.

A second passage worthy of reappraisal is *SEL* lines 35–8. These lines do not match the content of Dominic's Latin; nor do they vary substantially from the hagiographic narrative, in a way that suggests historical correction. None the less, they respond to a more 'diplomatic' reading of the poem, in that they suggest an imitation of the *form* of Dominic's text. In the quotation below, the lines unique to *J-Egwine* are marked in bold; as the italics indicate, these lines also witness four continuously rhyming lines:

Egwine 31–40, 45–6

His leggs wit strong feteris	hi gyvethe faste,
And the keie biside Evesham	in the water of Haven caste.
Al ygyveth he wente ford	in sorue and pynes stronge;
To Rome he com, wit alle wo,	thei hit were er longe.
Thou esi wei he hadde	**on nymeth god *gome***
To wende from Evesham	**al yfetereth to *Rome***
For mighte his leggis ake	**he spurude eft *lome*.**
He aboghte hevene somedel dere	**ar he thuther *come*.**
Tho that folc y seie him come	yvetereth so faste,

For wonder hi come abouten him   and wer somdel agaste;
. . .[53]

Tho he was to Rome icome,   wonther ther was ynou;
To Seinte Petres cherche   Seint Egwyne ferst drou.

(He bound his legs fast with strong fetters, and threw the key in the
water of Avon beside Evesham. All bound, he went forth in sorrow
and strong pains; he came to Rome with every misery, though it did
not take long. **Though the good man had taken a slow path to
go all fettered from Evesham to Rome, and though his legs
might ache, he hurried afterwards earnestly. He bought
heaven quite dearly before he came there.** When that people
saw him come fettered so fast, they came around him for wonder and
were very frightened; . . . when he came to Rome, there was much
wonder; St Egwine first approached St Peter's church.)

That the lines could in fact be 'original' is suggested by their correspondence to a relatively purple passage in Dominic's Latin,
marked in bold below. This homiletic aside makes an ornamental
use of anaphora and homoeoteleuton, indicated by italics:

Dominic of Evesham, *Vita S. Ecgwini* 5.23–9, 6.1–15
Et quamuis coram hominibus se immunem ab illatis sciret et
confiteretur, tamen – quia coram Deo peccatis se obnoxium esse
non diffitebatur – proficiscendo tamen in superni arbitris et divini
examinis iudicio necnon et pro peccatis populi sui, pedes suos vinculis ferreis astrinxit que clave poterant ligari et reserari, ipsamque
clavem in fluvium Aven proiecit.
   Vinctus ergo Iesu Christi Domini nostri Ecgwinus, emulatus
Petrum fluctus calcantem et Paulum in vinculis gloriantem, tanta
difficultate tantisque laboribus pervenit at apostolicam urbem, apos-
tolicis etiam vinculis triumphantem. **O fortissim*um* victor*em*
labor*um*! O contemptor*em* humanar*um* exprobration*um*! O
homin*em* angel*is* et homin*ibus* admirand*um*, et tot popul*is*
et gent*ibus* spectacul*um* fact*um*! O virum cunct*is* imitabi-
lem: *nec* terror*ibus* concuss*um*, *nec* blandiment*is* seduc-
t*um*, *nec* labor*ibus* vict*um*, qui inter corpor*is* sui pressur*as*
et abiection*es* *nec* mundan*as* laud*es* captavit *nec* aspectus
homin*um* recusavit!** Denique vir sanctus, secundum apostulum
'stigmata Iesu Christi in corpore suo portans' [Gal. 6:17], in con-
spectu populorum vinctis ferro pedibus Romam ingreditur, et –
quod maxime quesierat – in ecclesia Petri apostolorum principis ad
orationem prosternitur.

(Although the man of God had confessed and knew he was immune
to accusations in the presence of men, none the less – because he was
unable to deny in the presence of God that he could be guilty of sin

– with judgement approaching in accordance with divine decision and heavenly witnesses, and also for the sins of his people, he girded his feet with iron chains, which could be bound and unbound with a key, and he threw that same key into the Avon river.

Chained therefore by Jesus Christ our Lord, and emulating Peter walking on water and Paul glorying in chains, Ecgwine arrived with much difficulty and many labours at the apostolic city, which indeed triumphed in the apostolic chains. **Oh bravest victor over toils! Oh disdainer of human reproach! Oh man admirable to men and angels, and deed spectacular to so many peoples and nations! Oh man imitable to all men; neither shaken by fears, nor seduced by flattery, nor conquered by labours; who, with pressures and humiliations upon your body, neither strove after worldly praise, nor rejected the gazes of men!** And so the holy man, who was (as the apostle says) 'carrying the signs of Christ on his body', entered Rome in the sight of the people, with his feet chained in iron, and – as he had dearly wished – he prostrated himself to pray in the church of Peter, prince of the apostles.)

Four-line repetitions of rhyme-endings are not uncommon in the *SEL*, and in at least some cases they seem to be intended as moments of heightened ornamentation.[54] In the present instance, the correspondence of a four-line rhyme to the ornamental Latin passage suggests that the 'content' of the passage imitated by the translator was in fact its 'form'; both passages use the occasion of the saint's triumphant entry into Rome rhetorically to emphasize his holiness, and thus call attention to the divine (and apostolic) authority underlying any charters that list him as a witness.[55]

It is worth reiterating that this interpretation of the evidence does not suggest *J-Egwine* to be in fact the 'best text' of the poem. On the contrary, these variant possibilities exemplify a suggestive richness obscured by the critical division between 'original' and 'unoriginal' readings, with its tendency to read manuscript variants as features of the tradition that either distort the text or create new texts. In the present instance, the impact of poetic form and narrative structure on the texts' claims for Evesham abbey is indicative of the need for both historians and literary critics to find new ways of reading between the manuscripts of the *SEL*. New kinds of fine-grained and respectful attention to the treatment of source material, both within Latin traditions of monastic hagiographies and in the *SEL Ecgwine*'s own use of sources, can further illuminate their paradigms of textual power and value, together with the valence within the Latin and vernacular manuscript culture of the *SEL*'s formation and development.

Notes

1 The plural title is suggested by Liszka, *SELS*. All citations of the *SEL Egwine* come from the edition included as an appendix to Stephen M. Yeager, 'Poetic properties: legal forms and literary documents in early English literature' (PhD dissertation, University of Toronto, 2009), pp. 249–55, lightly modified by use of the present volume's conventions.

2 I will use the *SEL* spelling in the name 'Egwine' when referring to the *SEL* text or its protagonist, and the Old English 'Ecgwine' in reference to the historical figure or the character in the *SEL*'s possible sources.

3 For a fuller treatment of the distinction between 'literary-critical' and 'historical-diplomatic' methodologies, see Yeager, 'Poetic properties', esp. pp. 1–28.

4 Katherine J. Lewis, 'History, historiography and rewriting the past', in Salih (ed.), *Companion to Middle English Hagiography*, pp. 122–40, esp. pp. 123–6. See also Felice Lifshitz, 'Beyond positivism and genre: hagiographical texts as historical narrative', *Viator*, 25 (1994), 95–113.

5 See also the essay by Morgan in this volume.

6 The *Vita Ecgwini* is anonymous in its only surviving manuscript, London, BL, MS Cotton Nero E.i, fols 24v–34v (Worcester, xi^2), but has been attributed to Byrhtferth of Ramsey, partly because of its florid 'hermeneutic' Latin: see Michael Lapidge (ed.), *The Lives of St Oswald and St Ecgwine* (Oxford: Oxford University Press, 2009), pp. xciii–xcix.

7 Lapidge (ed.), *Oswald and Ecgwine*, pp. lxxxiii–lxxxiv; Michael Lapidge, *Anglo-Latin Literature, 900–1066* (London: Hambledon Press, 1993), pp. 293–315. A similarly manufactured cult is that of St Swithun; see M. Lapidge, J. Crook, R. Deshman and S. Rankin (eds), *The Cult of St Swithun* (Oxford: Clarendon Press, 2003). See also recent studies of the record-keeping practices at St Albans: Julia Crick (ed.), *Charters of St Albans* (Oxford: Oxford University Press for the British Academy, 2007), esp. pp 56–90; Crick, 'St Albans, Westminster, and some twelfth-century views of the Anglo-Saxon past', *Anglo-Norman Studies*, 25 (2003 for 2002), 65–83.

8 Authentic charters by Ecgwine include S 64, 102, 1177 and 1252; spurious ones include S 22, 54, 78, 79, 97, 248, 1174, 1175, 1250 and 1251.

9 Peter Sawyer's original 1968 catalogue has since been updated and digitized as 'The Electronic Sawyer', www.esawyer.org.uk, accessed 19 September 2009.

10 Lapidge, *Anglo-Latin*, 305. For a full summary of Byrhtferth's style, see Lapidge (ed.), *Oswald and Ecgwine*, pp. xliv–lxv. Because the text of Ecgwine's first-person account 'quoted' in the various versions of the *Vita S. Ecgwini* changes along with the surrounding texts, I will refer to the passage of Byrhtferth's *Vita* corresponding to the hypothetical charter by the abbreviation B-1251, the corresponding passage

of Dominic of Evesham's *Vita S. Ecgwini* as D-1251, and Thomas of
Marlborough's version as T-1251. 'S-1251' is thus the title given to
the hypothetical original document which was perhaps the source for
some or all of these paraphrases and transcriptions.

11 This aspect of the tradition also demonstrated by the fact that
Byrhtferth's account of one of Ecgwine's *miracula* happens to be
the only existing description by a pre-Conquest author of an Anglo-
Saxon-era land dispute between a monastery and its tenant; see
Lapidge (ed.), *Oswald and Ecgwine*, IV.10. On the relevance of this
scene to Old English legal history, see Patrick Wormald, *The Making
of English Law: King Alfred to the Twelfth Century* (Oxford: Blackwell
Publishers, 1999), pp. 158–61.

12 Dominic's version survives in Dublin, Trinity College, MS 172 (s.
xiii) and Hereford, Cathedral Library, MS P.7.vi (s. xii²). Again, the
Vita is anonymous in the manuscripts, and the attribution to Dominic
is Lapidge's: see Michael Lapidge, 'The medieval hagiography of
St Ecgwine', *Vale of Evesham Historical Society Research Papers*, 6
(1977), 77–93. All citations of this text are from Michael Lapidge
(ed.), 'Dominic of Evesham: *Vita S. Ecgwini Episcopi et Confessoris*',
Analecta Bollandiana, 96 (1978), 65–104.

13 Lapidge, 'Medieval hagiography', p. 85. See also William of
Malmesbury's similar treatment of Coleman's *Vita Wulfstani*: Andy
Orchard, 'Parallel lives: Wulfstan, William, Coleman and Christ', in
Julia Barrow and Nicholas Brooks (eds), *St Wulfstan and His World*
(Aldershot: Ashgate, 2005), pp. 39–58.

14 I.9.43–51; for fuller discussion see Lapidge (ed.), 'Dominic of
Evesham: *Vita S. Ecgwini*', pp. 72–3.

15 For example, one phrase from his version of the charter, *in posterum
eidem ecclesie omnimodam libertatem ab episcoporum exactionibus obti-
nere satagebam*, uses a language to describe exemption that is 'very
unlikely to belong to 714': see Jane Sayers, '"Original" cartulary
and chronicle: the case of the Abbey of Evesham', in *Fälschungen
im Mittelalter. Internationaler Kongress Der Monumenta Germaniae
Historica, München, 16 19 September 1986*, MGH 33 (Hanover:
Hansche Buchhandlung, 1988), vol. IV, pp. 371–95 (375).

16 Lapidge, 'Medieval hagiography', p. 84; Lapidge (ed.), 'Dominic of
Evesham: *Vita S. Ecgwini*', p. 100, n. 9.1.

17 Hart argues that Evesham forged 'an extensive group of charters . . .
during the abbacy of Walter at the end of the eleventh century', specifically 1097 to 1104, a period that corresponds with Dominic's literary
activity: C. R. Hart, *The Early Charters of Northern England and the
North Midlands* (Leicester: Leicester University Press, 1975), p. 63.

18 Sayers, '"Original"', p. 374. Compare St Wulfstan's promotion of
the cult of St Oswald, and its probable relation to the claims
for Worcester's exemption from royal oversight under *Oswaldslow*:

Patrick Wormald, 'Lordship and justice in the early English kingdom: Oswaldlaw revisited', in his *Legal Culture in the Early Medieval West: Law as Text, Image and Experience* (London: Hambledon Press, 1999), pp. 313–32; F. Tinti, 'From episcopal conception to monastic compilation: Hemming's Cartulary in context', *Early Medieval Europe*, 11:3 (2002), 233–61; Stephen Baxter, 'Archbishop Wulfstan and the administration of God's property', in Matthew Townend (ed.), *Wulfstan, Archbishop of York: The Proceedings of the Second Alcuin Conference* (Turnhout: Brepols, 2004), pp. 161–205.

19 For a survey of late medieval forgery and its causes, see Alfred Hiatt, *The Making of Medieval Forgeries: False Documents in Fifteenth-Century England* (Toronto: University of Toronto Press, 2004). For post-Conquest examples and discussion, see further Crick, 'St Albans, Westminster'; Crick (ed.), *Charters of St Albans*, pp. 3–13.

20 This *vita* prefaces Thomas's history of Evesham Abbey in Oxford, Bodleian Library, MS Rawlinson A.287 (xiii[1]). All citations of this text are from Thomas of Marlborough, *History of the Abbey of Evesham*, ed. Jane E. Sayers and Leslie Watkiss (Oxford: Clarendon Press, 2003), pp. 6–40. See also Lapidge (ed.), *Oswald and Ecgwine*, pp. xci–xcii.

21 Lapidge (ed.), 'Dominic of Evesham: *Vita S. Ecgwini*', p. 75.

22 Thomas, *History*, p. 32 n. 1.

23 'The Electronic Sawyer', accessed 21 September 2008. On the versions of the charter, see also Thomas, *History*, pp. xxvii–xxxix.

24 Stephen of Ripon, *The Life of Bishop Wilfrid*, ed. Bertram Colgrave (Cambridge: Cambridge University Press, 1927), pp. 36–7.

25 On this point see also *The Latin Charters of the Anglo-Saxon Period*, ed. F. Stenton (Oxford: Clarendon Press, 1955), p. 32. Sermon literature has been appropriately characterized by Kienzle as a 'fluid genre', and, as Chaplais demonstrated, document production was largely controlled by the Church throughout the Anglo-Saxon period (Beverley M. Kienzle, 'The typology of the medieval sermon and its development in the Middle Ages: report on work in progress', in X. Hermand and J. Hamesse (eds), *De l'Homélie au Sermon: Histoire de la Prédication Médiévale: Actes du Colloque International de Louvain-la-Neuve (9–1 Juillet 1992)* (Louvain-la-Neuve: Institut d'Études Médiévales de l'Université Catholique de Louvain, 1993), pp. 83–101 (86): also F. Ranger (ed.), *Prisca Munimenta: Studies in Archival and Administrative History Presented to A. E. J. Hollaender* (London: University of London Press, 1973), pp. 28–42, 43–62, 88–107; Simon Keynes, *The Diplomas of King Æthelred 'the Unready' (978–1016): A Study in Their Use as Historical Evidence* (Cambridge: Cambridge University Press, 1980), pp. 19–39 (22–8).

26 See also Dorothy Whitelock, *English Historical Documents Volume 1, c. 500–1042* (London: Routledge, 1996), pp. 383–4; N. R. Ker,

English Manuscripts in the Century after the Norman Conquest (Oxford: Clarendon, 1960), pp. 19–20; David N. Dumville, *Liturgy and the Ecclesiastical History of Late Anglo-Saxon England: Four Studies* (Woodbridge: Boydell Press, 1992), pp. 123–6.

27 Susan Kelly, 'Anglo-Saxon lay society and the written word', in R. McKitterick (ed.), *The Uses of Literacy in Early Medieval Europe* (Cambridge: Cambridge University Press, 1990), p. 44. See also M. B. Bedingfield, *The Dramatic Liturgy of Anglo-Saxon England* (Woodbridge: Boydell Press, 2002).

28 H. P. R. Finberg, *Early Charters of the West Midlands* (Leicester: Leicester University Press, 1961), p. 214. Finberg is making a case for the plausibility of S-1251's version of events in Ecgwine's charter in the context of this larger argument about the charter genre. As regards the documentary status of the various versions of the charter, he has 'little' confidence in S-1251 and 'less' in S-1250 (an Evesham charter of which historians have thought the lost first-person narrative charter S-1251 posited as Byhrtferth's source to have been an expansion). Finburg none the less argues that a valid claim might underlie them (pp. 89–90). Hart, however, points out that S-1251's account is most likely based on a misreading of the charter S 1252 (Hart, *Early Charters*, pp. 74–5).

29 Thomas, *History*, p. 34, n. 6.

30 Sayers and Watkiss list the changes: Thomas, *History*, p. xxxi. They speculate that he must have made them because the privileges otherwise were 'not precise enough' (p. xxxix).

31 Alain Boureau, 'How law came to the monks: the use of law in English society at the beginning of the thirteenth century', *Past and Present*, 167 (2000), 59–60. See also Sayers, '"Original"', pp. 371–95, and M. T. Clanchy, *From Memory to Written Record: England 1066–1307*, 2nd edn (Cambridge MA: Blackwell, 1993), pp. 324–5.

32 Thomas, *History*, pp. 40–1.

33 10.32; Lapidge (ed.), 'Dominic of Evesham: *Vita S. Ecgwini*', p. 88.

34 Lapidge (ed.), *Oswald and Ecgwine*, III.4.

35 York became an archbishopric only in 735, and thus could have no 'archbishop' before that date. Moreover, Wilfrid died in 709, the same year as Aldhelm; there was not time for Ecgwine and Coenred to leave Aldhelm's funeral for Rome and return before Wilfrid's death: see William of Malmesbury, *Gesta pontificum Anglorum*, ed. and trans. M. Winterbottom and R. M. Thomson (Oxford: Clarendon Press, 2007), V.231.

36 Sayers and Watkiss suggest that this Wilfrid could be the bishop of Worcester chosen to succeed Ecgwine during his lifetime: Thomas, *History*, p. 20, n. 4. Meanwhile, the *Sanctilogium* redactor appears to have modified Thomas's text to read 'sanctum Wilfridum episcopum': *Nova Legenda Anglie*, p. 18.

37 See William Robins, 'Towards a Disjunctive Philology', in Sîan Echard and Stephen Partridge (eds), *The Book Unbound* (Toronto: University of Toronto Press, 2004), pp. 144–77.

38 Görlach, *Textual Tradition*. On manuscript 'E', see ibid., p. 80; Horstmann, p. xviii; Laurel Braswell, 'Saint Edburga of Winchester: a study of her cult, A.D. 950–1500, with an edition of the fourteenth-century Middle English and Latin lives', *Mediæval Studies*, 33 (1971), 292–333 (319); Michael S. Nagy, 'Saint Æthelberht of East Anglia in the *South English Legendary*', *The Chaucer Review*, 37:2 (2002), 159–72 (165); Lapidge et al., *Swithun*, p. 718.

39 Görlach, *Textual Tradition*, pp. 6, 86–7; D'Evelyn and Mill, pp. 1, 8–9.

40 Görlach, *Textual Tradition*, pp. 95–6; Carl Horstmann (ed.), *Altenglische Legenden. Neue Folge* (Heilbronn: Henninger, 1881), pp. xxviii–xxx; Lapidge et al. (eds), *Swithun*, p. 719.

41 Görlach, *Textual Tradition*, pp. 98–9; British Museum, *Catalogue of the Stowe Manuscripts in the British Museum*, 2 vols (Hildesheim: Olms, 1973), pp. 632–4.

42 Görlach, *Textual Tradition*, p. 216.

43 *J-version* lines 45 and 46 differ from the other manuscripts, but are not wholly unique like lines 41–4. In my edition, all citations of this text retain the scribe's frequent confusion of 'd' and 'ð': see Yeager, 'Poetic properties', pp. 162–4.

44 For a recent summary of Aldhelm's career, see Michael Lapidge, 'The career of Aldhelm', *Anglo-Saxon England*, 36 (2007), 15–70.

45 Lapidge (ed.), *Oswald and Ecgwine*, III.3.

46 *Bede's Ecclesiastical History of the English People*, ed. Bertram Colgrave and R. A. B. Mynors (Oxford: Clarendon, 1969), V.19.

47 D'Evelyn and Mill, I, 213, 87–90.

48 V.231; 'Distinction was added to [Coenred and Offa's] company, as I said, by the blessed bishop Ecgwine, who, after performing the funeral rites for Aldhelm, of his own free will completed that difficult journey in shackles', William of Malmesbury, *Gesta pontificum*, ed. and trans. Thomson, pp. 576–9. Note that William's mention of Ecgwine's presence at Aldhelm's funeral merely explains who Ecgwine is, and thus does not necessarily imply that Ecgwine's journey in chains and his journey with Coenred and Offa were one and the same.

49 Bede, *Historia ecclesiastica*, V.19.

50 I use the *SEL* spellings Kenred and Atheldred to name the characters in the *SEL*, and the standard Coenred and Æthelred to discuss the historical figures and characters in the Latin hagiography.

51 However, the account of D-1251 specifies that Aldhelm died only two years after Coenred became king, which might suggest that Dominic's date for Coenred's ascendancy was 707 (Lapidge (ed.), 'Dominic of Evesham: *Vita S. Ecgwini*', I.9.52). If the *J-Egwine* translator(s)

followed this date (as the *Egwine* reference to Constantine (1.143), who became pope in 708, might suggest), then there would be even more pressure to truncate the narrative into a relatively rapid succession of events, as Kenred would have to leave for Rome with Offa almost immediately after returning to England with Egwine.

52 *J-Egwine*, lines 29, 34–5.

53 As discussed above, lines 41–4 of *J-Egwine* are not witnessed in the Latin text.

54 See Yeager, 'Poetic properties', pp. 181–5.

55 On form and diplomatic criticism, see R. Sharpe, 'Charters, deeds, and diplomatics', in F. A. C. Mantello and A. G. Rigg (eds), *Medieval Latin: An Introduction and Bibliographic Guide* (Washington, DC: Catholic University Press of America, 1996), pp. 230–40 (230).

8

Modular dynamics in the *South English Legendary*

William Robins

A central issue for the study of the *SEL* is the relationship between, on the one hand, individual textual items such as saints' lives or expository poems and, on the other hand, collections of those items in larger wholes. Indeed, because the enigmas surrounding this interplay are so vexed, it remains unclear just what we refer to when we use the modern title *SEL*: as Gregory Sadlek puts it, 'is the *SEL* a single work, or is it merely a collection of smaller works?'[1] In order not to foreclose this question, I will use the modern title and its abbreviation *SEL* to refer to a Middle English textual domain rather than to designate a particular work. This domain includes many poems which share the basic thematic and formal features of a clearly defined genre (they deal with episodes in the history of the church, including the lives of saints, explanations of feast days, stories from the Old Testament and narratives from the lives of Mary and Christ; they employ a common metrical pattern, based on loose seven-beat lines arranged in rhyming couplets; their stories are presented in an uncomplicated style with stark characterization and strong narrative emphasis). Moreover, these poems also constitute a textual system that is fairly well integrated and demarcated, in so far as they tend to circulate alongside other poems in the group (the tradition comes down to us in a large number of manuscript compilations, which range from sizeable volumes that contain only items from the *SEL* corpus to small miscellanies that include a small sampling of *SEL* material). The pre-eminent philological fact of this textual tradition is that no two manuscripts present the same items in the same order; this fact raises all sorts of puzzling questions about the kind of coherence that was expected in this domain.

Most philological analysis of the *SEL* has been governed by the idea that there have been a few distinct redactions of the collection. In 1936, Minnie Wells argued that a well-ordered form of the

collection, now lost, must have predated even the earliest manuscripts, and since then several scholars have offered hypotheses
about missing stages that could account for the variability of the
extant manuscripts.[2] The strongest redactionist arguments are put
forward in Manfred Görlach's important 1974 monograph, *The
Textual Tradition of the South English Legendary*, a study which
remains fundamental for philological study of the *SEL*. Görlach
defined fourteen different 'redactions', hypothetical stages in the
history of transmission of the *SEL*. The relations among these
redactions are highly complex: very few of the major extant manuscripts are located within a single redaction, since most show conflation, with their different items traceable to different redactions;
most of the redactions, too, show a conflation of prior redactional
stages. Görlach, in a subsequent publication, offered this synopsis
of his main arguments:

> once the main (Gloucestershire?) 'A' redaction of the 1290's had
> substantially added to the content [of an earlier 'Z' redaction], by
> drawing on the *Legenda Aurea* and, in the case of some English
> saints, English historians, the legendary was normally left unaffected
> by further large-scale revision. What variation there is in the extant
> MSS is due either to the survival of early pre-'A' versions and their
> fusion with the revised texts, or to somewhat inconsistent efforts
> to replace dialect forms, improve the rhymes ('P'), regularise the
> metre ('E'), or cut down on the repetitions ('M') – just enough vari-
> ation to distinguish the different strands of the textual tradition, but
> nothing compared with what one finds in romances, or even indi-
> vidual legends from the east of England. This stability well into the
> 14th century can possibly be explained by the assumption that the
> legendary was usually copied as a collection, and its contents treated
> with a reverence that stopped scribes and revisers from interfering
> with the text.[3]

In strong formulations, such as this one, the redactionist approach
considers (whenever possible) notable modifications to individual
SEL poems to be parts of a revision of an entire compilation. It
assumes that transmission occurred through a series of major
manuscript compilations ('the assumption that the legendary was
usually copied as a collection'), with new 'redactions' generated out
of earlier redactions, either through a process of revision and rear-
rangement or through a process of conflation.

As a theory to account for the general history of the *SEL*, the
case for thinking in terms of redactions presents some methodological problems. In usual philological parlance, a 'redaction' is a state

of a text that was established through a concerted process of revision and that also serves as the hypothetical ancestor of a discrete branch of the extant witnesses. A redaction is both a revision and a recension. In the complex situation of the *SEL*, however, these two aspects do not map on to each other very well. The evidence for recension is to be found at the level of the individual item, for each item will have its own stemma; to complicate matters further, the unambiguous presence of 'conjunctive and separative errors' is so rare in this kind of tradition that stemmatic conclusions for most items can really only be provisional. As for revision, the working assumption here is that major revision would have been introduced at the level of the collection as a whole; moreover, because revision is understood not only as textual alteration but also as changes in the selection and arrangement of individual items within the larger whole, the great variability of manuscript contents complicates matters. The notion of a 'redaction' as introduced by Görlach serves to bridge the gap between the evidence of textual filiation garnered from individual items and the evidence of arrangement garnered from the extant compilations. Where stemmatic evidence is inconclusive, hypotheses about the changing shape of the collection are brought in; where those hypotheses seem inconclusive, recourse is made to stemmatic evidence. Görlach is fully aware of the 'circular reasoning' this involves.[4]

The pressure thereby put on the notion of a 'redaction' reveals itself in a crucial passage from Görlach's monograph and its accompanying note:

[Text:] Wherever there is clear evidence that the SEL collection was consistently revised, and the principle of the revision can be formulated with some precision, I shall speak of 'redactions'. As long as a redaction is only postulated as a help for the classification of the manuscripts or parts of these (and thus is equivalent with a hyparchetype), the principle is neither complicated nor controversial: a redaction ends where the evidence from the different texts end, and the only important consideration is whether the affiliations remain persistent. If these redactions are considered as successive stages in the development of, preferably, a single legend, the principle can still be employed with a high degree of probability. Only where successive redactions are used for a total reconstruction of the history of the SEL may the hypothesis become overcharged
[Note:] A revision of the legendary may of course have been partial or have been attempted with varying degrees of success or thoroughness; a redaction is therefore not necessarily persistent throughout

the SEL. My following discussion includes redactions ('A', 'E', 'M', 'P') and compilations ('L', 'G') as well as archetypes defined by conjunctive errors ('J', 'C', 'Q', 'H').[5]

The terminology grows tortuous here, especially when the note is read alongside the text, undercutting it at every turn. The text states that a redaction is equivalent with a hyparchetype, but the note acknowledges that only some of the posited entities are archetypal; and, bafflingly, 'redactions' are considered as a sub-set of 'redactions'. The text defines a 'redaction' as an occurrence of consistent revision, but the note admits that such revision tends to be partial, unsuccessful and non-persistent. The text cautions that the principle of redactions would be 'overcharged' if used for reconstructing the history of the *SEL*, and yet it is precisely this goal that animates the monograph as a whole, and that is material- ized in the stemma, map and summaries provided.

Such terminological slippage betrays either some methodologi- cal fuzziness or else a propensity for overstating the case, perhaps both. In response, I treat Görlach's conclusions about redactions rather gingerly. His arguments that an initial 'Z' collection was revised into 'L' and 'A' redactions have been found useful by other scholars, with Oliver Pickering and Thomas Liszka proposing yet other intermediary stages in this development.[6] Yet even when consideration is limited to such early stages, the demonstration of distinct redactions requires so much cross-conflation as to make for philological vertigo. The claims about later redactions have not received much subsequent philological scrutiny. The hypothetical existence of some of these stages is plausible, such as the general outlines of 'H' and 'D', which are posited as hyparchetypes of closely related witnesses. The positing of 'U' as a redaction in the fullest sense – a stage of revision that serves also as a hyparchetype of two surviving witnesses – is not certain, but Görlach's argu- ments in his 1976 edition are careful and credible.[7] By contrast, the cases made for other redactions, such as 'E', 'G' and 'M', are meth- odologically and evidentially weak. Redaction 'E', for example, is supposedly characterized by manuscript groupings, but these are not at all persistent; by the inclusion of some rare legends which, however, seem more likely to have been transmitted along inde- pendent avenues; and by a tendency to shorten the lines of verse which, however, is a common practice among many copyists of septenary poems in the fifteenth century.[8] Görlach here welds together discordant information about transmission (persistent groupings), compilation (selection and order) and revision (metrical change) in order to posit an artificial construct, redaction 'E', that is unlikely to correspond to reality.

The great debate about *SEL* textuality that never occurred would have been between Görlach and Beverly Boyd. In a series of articles surprisingly overlooked, Boyd offered a radically different conceptualization of the relationship between items and compilations, seeing the textuality of the *SEL* as chaotic, protean and shifting. In a 1958 article, she introduced the notion of free-floating blocks of text (she calls them 'fragments') that might include only one or a few items, and which were transmitted in unpredictable ways so as to generate many different selections and arrangements:

> Certainly, the strangely garbled and incomplete nature of the manuscripts we have been discussing . . . and the hitherto unexplainable variation of their contents, suggests that the materials which Horstmann called *The Early South-English Legendary or Lives of Saints* stem from fragments involving a *liber festivalis*, and at least one revision of it, and that neither the original nor its revision was known in complete condition to the scribes of any of the extant manuscripts.[9]

In a 1968 article, Boyd abandoned the notion of a coherent original collection, and argued that we should rather think of the *SEL* as a large corpus of items which had a certain traditional quality to them; these items circulated fitfully, subject to accidents of availability, their transmission animated by an 'ingredient of change'. 'In summary', she writes, 'the ecclesiastical writings now called the *South English Legendary*, extant in many manuscripts which differ in contents, arrangement, style, and dialect, are better described as a corpus of versified Middle English writings for the ecclesiastical year than as a single work'.[10] Boyd was writing before Middle English philology had really theorized the qualities of openness and *mouvance*, yet her approach anticipates the sense articulated by current students of the *SEL* that it 'was a diffuse and open text, relentlessly modified and adapted to suit the locations in which it was copied and the historical circumstances in which it was disseminated'.[11]

Where Görlach emphasizes the surviving compilations, seeing them as different redactions of a unified work, each redaction animated by a consistent purpose, Boyd emphasizes the individual items that together make up a corpus, with the make-up of compilations a much more open and unpredictable affair, subject to

vagaries of accidental survival and copyist intervention. Their differences derive in large measure from relying on contrasting ways
of construing the nature of a 'collection'. In the *SEL*, there are at
least three levels of textual coherence in play: that of the item, that
of the compilation and that of the ensemble (the cultural text of
the *SEL* taken as a whole). There are accordingly several different relationships at stake: between item and compilation, item and
ensemble, compilation and ensemble. The notion of a 'collection'
has been variously used in *SEL* criticism to signify either the level
of the compilation or that of the ensemble. Görlach's approach
gives precedence to the compilation: items are considered above
all as elements in compilations, and the *SEL* as a larger whole is
pictured as a series of compilations (extant manuscripts as well as
hypothesized redactions). By contrast, Boyd's approach privileges
the relation of the item to the ensemble as a whole, which is seen
as a corpus of discrete texts; compilations are seen as provisional
clusterings of such items according to local exigencies.

Görlach and Boyd refused opportunities to debate their differences. Görlach's 1974 study dismissed Boyd's work in passing. Her
first article 'consists of a summary of earlier research and does not
contribute materially to the discussion'. Her doubt about recover-
ing the collection's original form is the consequence of 'insufficient
consideration of the manuscripts and of the textual evidence'.[12]
The dismissiveness was returned when Boyd penned a terse
review of *The Textual Tradition of the South English Legendary*:
'Unfortunately, the author's conclusions are lost in an obscure
style and in a critical apparatus so complicated as to defy readability . . . As matters stand, it is difficult to find in his data evidence
for his conclusions; indeed, the conclusions are not easy to identify.
Once identified, they do not seem greatly innovative.'[13] And thus
instead of conducting a lively debate about the textuality at work
in the tradition of the *South English Legendary*, each scholar dismissed the other's work with an accusation of that most damning
of scholarly faults: adding nothing new. In this regard, they wil-
fully misrepresented the challenges posed to their diagnoses of the
relationship between item and collection (or more specifically, of
the relationships among item, compilation and ensemble) within
the *SEL*'s textual domain.

In what follows, I hope to revive the potential for dialogue
between Görlach's redactionist principles and Boyd's notion of a
more chaotic corpus. I aim to do justice to the concerns expressed
from both vantages, not in order to steer a middle way between

them so much as to suggest that a dynamic interplay between item
and collection is an ineluctable aspect of the textual domain that we
call the *South English Legendary*. To do so, I will draw attention
to a few aspects of *SEL* textuality that were given short shrift in
Görlach's monograph and that still remain relatively understudied.

The first of these features I will consider is the existence, for
several saints and a few feast days, of more than one *SEL* legend,
each produced independently. There are nine saints for whom
two or three distinct legends survive: Athelwold (2), Benedict (2),
Fides (2), Franciscus (2), Frideswide (2), Gilbert (2), Kenelm (2),
Mary Magdalene (2) and Sylvester (3). Their cases are not all of
the same sort. For Mary Magdalene, we possess one legend in the
familiar *SEL* style, as well as another where a non-*SEL* poem in
a different metre has been partly adapted to the *SEL*'s rhyming
septenary couplets. A similar situation obtains for Gilbert, made
more confusing by later conflation of the two poems. To this tally
one might add the case of Guthlac, for whom we possess three different legends, although because they all share a common opening
it is uncertain to what extent we are dealing with revision or with
new, independent composition. Besides these nine instances from
the *sanctorale*, there are also distinct and independent compositions
for the prologue, and for three *temporale* feasts: the Ascension, the
Assumption and Circumcision-Epiphany. (The narrative *temporale* sequences are somewhat more complicated, with revision,
rewriting and perhaps independent composition at work in the
various poems on the lives of Mary and Jesus.)[14]

Because Görlach considers the basic unit of coherence to be the
compilation (with a normative arrangement provided by the order
of the liturgical calendar) his study counts 'individual items' not in
terms of discrete poems but rather in terms of slots in the liturgical cycle. Thus the two poems on St Benedict are considered not
as separate 'items' but as different fulfilments of a single exigency;
accordingly both are grouped under item number 26, a classification
that renders the phenomenon of multiple poems inconspicuous.
Sometimes the lesser-attested poems are spoken of, misleadingly,
as variant 'versions', rather than as independent poems. Also in line
with the emphasis on compilations, Görlach's preferred explanation for independent compositions is that there must have been
something defective about an exemplar which a copyist patched
to make sure his new compilation wasn't faulty. Typical is the
appraisal of the shorter poem on St Kenelm: 'probably the legend
was independently supplied because "G" did not contain it'.[15]

A different valuation would emerge if we accorded less authority to the idea of the compilation; we could consider the multiple versions as produced by poets whose aim was not primarily (or not at all) to patch up a redactional 'emergency', but rather to contribute to the general ensemble of *SEL* texts. A poet may have wanted to versify in *SEL* style the life of a saint for a variety of reasons: to disseminate information about the saint, to encourage devotion, to celebrate a feast day, to add to the memorials of local customs etc. Production of an *SEL* poem might be seen, in the first instance, as an event distinct from its incorporation into a particular compilation. At the very least, these cases of plural lives demonstrate that many poets found in the *SEL* an implicit invitation to collaborate, an invitation to extend the repertoire of vernacular religious poetry in this distinctive style. These cases illustrate that a degree of textual proliferation animated the *SEL* tradition.

St Frideswide attracted at least two poets who felt she deserved a legend in *SEL* style: a shorter life is extant in three manuscripts and a longer life, translated from a different Latin source, is extant in four. The conventionality of *SEL* style is well illustrated in their opening verses:

> Seint Frethesyde, that holy mayde,   was of Engelonde;
> Atte Oxenford heo was ybore,   as ich understonde.
> Hir fader hete Kyng Didan   and Sefreth hete the quene –
> This were hire eldren,   that hure gotten hem bytwene.[16]

(St Frideswide, the holy maiden, was from England; she was born at Oxford, as I understand. Her father was called Didan, and Sefreth the queen was called; these were her parents, who together begot her.)

> Seynte Fredeside was   her of Englonde.
> At Oxenford heo was ibore,   as ic understonde.
> Aboute seve hondred yer   and sevene and twenti right
> After that God was an erth   in Is moder alight,
> This holi womman was ibore –   Seynte Fredeswide.
> Didan was hire fader name;   hir moder het Saffride.[17]

(St Frideswide was from here in England; she was born at Oxford, as I understand. Just about seven hundred and twenty-seven years after God alighted in his mother on earth, this holy woman was born – St Frideswide. Didan was her father's name; her mother was called Saffride.)

One immediately notices that the opening couplets are nearly identical. This is not due to any textual filiation, for the lines are thoroughly formulaic. Their basic pattern, as well as the rhyme *Engelonde : understonde*, is found at the start of dozens of other *SEL* legends, for example the life of St Swithun: 'Sein Swithin the confessour was   her of Engelonde / Biside Winchestre he was ibore   as ich understonde' ('St Swithun the confessor was from here in England; he was born at Winchester, as I understand').[18] Conventionality, in fact, is everywhere evident in these passages, from the rhyming tags to the reinforcing repetition of information, the balancing of half-lines, the co-ordination of syntax and rhythm, and the uncomplicated lexical register. These common elements ground the participation, by each poem, in the larger endeavour of the *SEL*, harnessing the *SEL*'s replicable style in order to contribute to its mode of cultural expression.

Yet at the same time these opening lines do something else. They mark the start of a new, separate poetic unit – acting like chapter headings, or like a 'Once upon a time' commencement in storytelling. The closing lines, equally formulaic, similarly establish where these units end: the shorter life's 'Now God ous bring to the blysse   that He broght that may!' ('Now may God bring us to the bliss where he brought that maiden') has the same pattern and function as the longer life's 'Nou bidde we God, vor hire love,   that He to hevene ous bringe!' ('Now let us ask God that, for her love, he might bring us to heaven').[19] Lines like these show a crucial dynamic of the *SEL* at work. Poets strive to align their work as much as possible with the characteristics of *SEL* hagiography, even as they establish clear demarcations of the textual autonomy of their own compositions.

This interplay of conventionality and autonomy works itself out in other ways, too. For instance, it is manifest in the way that the two legends of Frideswide, while equally conventional, strike out with divergent narrative emphases and poetic tones, as Sherry Reames has described in her edition of the two poems.[20] It also establishes a basic pattern for the proliferation of saints' legends within the *SEL*, providing mechanisms whereby poets can produce an independent poem and contribute to a larger ensemble at the same time. Mechanisms for proliferation are somewhat different in the *temporale* narratives of the *SEL*, where individual episodes involving Mary and Jesus are also assimilated within larger narratives of their lives.

This force of proliferation, as it plays itself out in composition of saints' lives, occurs not only in the cases of saints with plural legends. The poets writing all *SEL* legends were responding to its unspoken invitation to participate; the composition of legends was not necessarily always determined by the exigencies of particular compilations. The proliferation of texts seems to have occurred at all phases in the tradition's history. It served as a counter-tendency to an opposing principle of consolidation, whereby the ensemble could come to seem closed, or whereby particular configurations could be taken as normative. Such consolidation is what Görlach, in a quotation above (p.188), speaks of as the relative 'stability' of basic forms of the collection over time, underpinned by the copyists' 'reverence' for the text. Textual proliferation and textual consolidation stand in an uneasy balance throughout the history of the *SEL*. Just as the pressure of consolidation might often have put a brake on the generation of new texts, the possibilities for proliferation unsettled any tendency for the collection to achieve stability.

Another under-examined aspect of the *SEL* is the fact that there are so many extant legends that survive in only a single witness. To give an indication of their range, I provide in Table 8.1 a list of the clear-cut cases of 'unique texts' (I have not included instances of heavily revised versions attested in single manuscripts, or of related items in different metres). This checklist includes the Laud prologue, eleven *temporale* items and thirty-seven *sanctorale* items (which amounts to about one-quarter of the items in the *sanctorale* repertoire). Seven manuscripts preserve one or more unique texts.

Of the thirty-four unique texts in Oxford, Bodleian MS Bodley 779 (*B*), twenty-nine are not listed (nor are they anywhere named) in Görlach's *Textual Tradition of the South English Legendary*, although no reason is given for their exclusion. Perhaps there seemed little to learn about manuscript filiations from these texts; perhaps privileging early moments in the collection's history rendered the late *B* manuscript suspect; perhaps the information would have swelled an already large volume. The resulting distortion undercounts the total number of poems involved in the *SEL*, and in doing so it also downplays the extent of textual proliferation. These items, however, can help us see how the textuality of the *SEL* involves not only a principle of proliferation – an aspect of the production of new texts – but also a principle of dispersal – an aspect of their material circulation.

Take the life of St Oswin, left uncatalogued by Görlach. It is a lengthy, crafted narrative, with many scenes in dialogue, with sentence structures that often extend well beyond the rhythmical unit of the couplet, and with many touches of storytelling that recall Middle English historical romances. The accommodation of

Table 8.1 Unique items in the SEL corpus

MS[1]	Fols	Vv.	Subject	Feast	Type	Index[2]	Görlach[3]
B	177r–183r	618	St Franciscus	4 Oct.	O.F.M.	3494	Cf. 66.2
B	183v–184v	128	St Fides	6 Oct.	Virgin	1397	Cf. 66.3
B	186r–187r	108	Sts Nicasius, Quirinus and Scubiculus	11 Oct.	Martyrs	125	
B	187r–188v	176	St Calitus	14 Oct.	Pope/Martyr	1553	
B	189r–v	112	St Winifred	3 Nov.	Virgin [Welsh]	4176	
B	190v–192r	152	St Hilarion	22 Oct.	Patriarch	902	
B	192r–195r	354	Sts Chrysanthus and Daria	25 Oct.	Martyrs	2761	
B	197r–198v	167	Sts Crispin and Crispinian	25 Oct.	Martyrs	2225	
B	198v–199v	108	St Evaristus	26 Oct.	Pope/Martyr	733	
B	201v–202v	148	St Firmin	25 Sept.	Bishop/Martyr	2898	
B	203r–v	108	St Vital	28 Apr.	Martyr	3855	
B	208r–212v	512	St Oswin	20 Aug.	King/Martyr [English]	1531	
B	216r–217r	120	Sts John and Paul	26 June	Martyrs	1790	
B	217r–v	42	St Leo II	28 June	Pope	3624	
B	217v–218v	118	Sts Marius, Martha, Audifax, and Abacuc	19 Jan.	Martyrs	2126	
B	225r–226r	96	St Silverius	20 June	Pope	1445	
B	226r–227r	90	St Paulus	15 Jan.	Hermit	2679	
B	227r–229v	308	St Sylvester	31 Dec.	Pope/Confessor	318	Cf. 88.2
B	229v–231r	232	St Remigius	1 Oct.	Bishop	3383	
B	231r–v	68	St Anicetus	17 April	Pope/Martyr	2852	

Table 8.1 continued

MS¹	Fols	Vv.	Subject	Feast	Type	Index²	Görlach³
B	231v–232r	76	St Soter	22 Apr.	Pope/Martyr	3202	
B	232r–233r	88	St Caius	22 Apr.	Pope/Martyr	901	
B	233r–v	78	St Emerentiana	23 Jan.	Virgin Martyr	2851	
B	233v–234r	56	St Hyginus	11 Jan.	Pope	2913	
B	234r–235r	86	St Melchiades	10 Dec.	Pope	2143	
B	235r–v	62	St Damasus	11 Dec.	Pope	2881	
B	235v–236v	120	Sts Saturninus and Sisinius	29 Nov.	Martyrs	87	
B	236v–237v	98	St Innocent I	31 July	Pope	3386	
B	237v–238r	76	St Felix III	25 Feb.	Pope	794	
B	238r–239r	102	Sts Simplicius and Faustinus	29 July	Martyrs	3814	
B	239r–240r	132	Sts Abdon and Sennen	30 July	Martyrs	2836	
B	240v–241r	180	St Germanus	31 July	Bishop [French]	2919	
B	241r–242v	178	St Athelwold	1 Aug.	Bishop [English]	446	Cf. 57.1
B	265r–266v	234	Holy Innocents	28 Dec.	Temporale	2660	Cf. 60
G	43–48r	364	Assumption	15 Aug.	Temporale	1092	
I	73–79r	542	Harrowing of Hell		Temporale	3706	
J	272v–273v	46	St Ignatius	1 Feb.	Bishop/Martyr	2914	12.1
L	88	6	Prologue		Prologue	224	
L	88	16	Circumcision and Epiphany	1–6 Jan.	Temporale	224	

M	94r–99r	402	St Teilo	9 Feb.	Bishop [Welsh]	3061	14.1
M	164v–170v	514	St Sylvester	31 Dec.	Pope	Cf. 3053	Cf. 88.2
M	171r–173r	180	Advent and Christmas	25 Dec.	Temporale	3336	Cf. 34.1
M	173r–174v	114	Ascension		Temporale	3335	
M	174v–176r	116	Pentecost		Temporale	3338	
M	176r	30	Trinity		Temporale	3337	
R	1r–6v	528	Adam and Eve		Temporale	Cf. 3973	xr
R	261v–269v	740	Conception of Mary	8 Dec.	Temporale	74	xk
R	38v–39r		Candlemas	2 Feb.	Temporale	586	
S	145v–154r	641	St Fremund	11 May	King/Martyr [English]	3192	39.2

Notes:

1 Manuscript sigla: B = Oxford, Bodleian Library, Bodley 779; G = London, Lambeth Palace, MS 223; I = Cambridge, St John's College, MS 28; J = London, British Library, MS Cotton Julius D.IX; L = Oxford, Bodleian Library, MS Laud Misc. 108; M = London, British Library, MS Egerton 2810; R = Cambridge, Trinity College, MS 605; S = London, British Library, MS Stowe 949.

2 Item numbers in Julia Boffey and A. S. G. Edwards, *A New Index of Middle English Verse* (London: British Library, 2005).

3 Item numbers in Manfred Görlach, *The Textual Tradition of the South English Legendary* (Leeds: University of Leeds School of English, 1974).

conventional *SEL* style to a more dilatory pace is evident from the poem's opening verses:

> In som tyme weren in Ingelonde   kingus swythe ryve,
> For, so Ich finde in bok iwrete   at onus ther weren fyve,
> And everich hadde his kindom   and al his pouer to welde,
> And moche werre was hem betwene   and pes swythe selde –
> For ofte ye seth this iwis,   pride, envye and tresoun
> Sleth wel many a gret lorde   and bringeth hem adoun
> And dryveth hem of londe   and doth hem wel gret wo –
> For ofte to sothe hit is iseye   that they fareth so.
> For so was Seint Osewin   somtyme idreve by cas,
> That after Edwinis day the king   that of Northombirlond was.[21]

(At one time in England there were numerous kings, for, as I find written in a book, there once were five, each with his own kingdom and wielding his own power, and there was much war amongst them, and peace very rarely for indeed one often sees this, that pride, envy and treason slay many great lords, and bring them down, and drive them from their land, and deal them great woe, for in truth it is often seen that they fare so; for thus was St Oswin often beset by fortune, who after Edwin's day was king of Northumberland.)

Besides its occurrence in *B*, there is no evidence that the legend of St Oswin ever made it into any large compilations of the *SEL*. In *B* there is no obvious reason for placing the life of St Oswin alongside its neighbouring texts. The series of poems around it – *St Vital* (28 April), *St Aldhelm* (25 May), *St Margaret* (20 July, a non-*SEL* poem), *St Oswin* (20 August), *St John the Baptist* (24 June) – seems unmotivated by consideration of feast day, type of saint or nationality.[22] In effect, the legend of St Oswin seems to have come to the compiler of *B* as a more or less stray text, and there are grounds for suspecting that it may at times have circulated on its own. After all, we can infer the independent circulation of other *SEL* items (such as the legends of St Patrick and St Michael, and perhaps some of the other legends occasionally found on their own in non-*SEL* manuscripts). Furthermore, the legend of St Margaret that precedes the poem in *B* is a non-*SEL* poem in quatrains that also 'seems to be a "floating" saint's life incorporated intermittently into hagiographic collections as well as circulating separately'.[23] The dilatory expression of the *SEL* style suggests that the life of St Oswin might have been composed so as to be able to be read either as a part of the *SEL* collection or independently. It could have easily circulated as part of a miscellany or as a separate entity. For its 512 lines, a small pamphlet of four bifolia ruled with thirty-two lines per page would accommodate the text exactly.

The unique poems also allow us to make inferences about how some *SEL* texts might have circulated in mini-compilations grouped according to one or another type of legend. British Library, Egerton 2810 (*M*) includes a series of unique poems on *temporale* feasts: Advent and Christmas – Ascension – Pentecost – Trinity – Corpus Christi (this last is not fully unique, for it is attested also in *B*); this is followed by a series of more widely attested *temporale* poems: Septuagesima – Quadragesima – Pascha – Letania.[24] The set of unique items suggests that the compiler of *M* made use of one or two separate booklets or small gatherings concentrating on such feasts. We have direct evidence of such a practice in Cambridge, St John's College 28 (*I*), a compilation of eighty-four folios dedicated to *SEL temporale* poems (only one of them, on the Harrowing of Hell, is a unique text); it closes with the Septuagesima – Quadragesima – Pascha – Letania series. The arrangement into which the unique items in *B* are disposed suggests that several mini-compilations were used as exemplars, for the manuscript shows clusters of lives of martyrs, of lives of popes (also a series of lives of martyred popes), and, more diffusely, of lives of French and English bishops. We have direct evidence that booklets of selected *SEL* texts circulated in manuscripts such as Cambridge University Library Ff.5.48 (*Uz*), College of Arms, Arundel 127 (*Ax*), and the two separate booklets in Winchester College 33 (*W*). In these cases the selection of items seems to be based partly on type of saint and partly on an overarching thematic concern.[25]

The circulation of legends in a variety of small-format copies, such as parchment rolls, unbound loose leaves, stitched pamphlets or custom-made booklets, demonstrates how a principle of dispersal could animate the *SEL*. Such dispersal works in an ever-changing balance with a principle of gathering, whereby *SEL* texts also accumulate together into collections that are often of considerable scope. The ephemeral nature of the smaller-format copies means that direct evidence is scarce – there are, for instance, no surviving parchment rolls with *SEL* texts on them, which is unsurprising given that there are very few literary rolls of any sort despite their importance for the traffic of texts in the late Middle Ages. The unique texts add a special twist, for they suggest that many texts could have circulated in small formats without ever

making it into the large compilations. In other words, there may
well have been, alongside the transmission of texts in well-ordered
compilations, a parallel practice of transmission in small formats.
The two practices intersect occasionally, as the inclusion of unique
texts in manuscripts like B and M demonstrates.

Görlach's study downplays the evidence of circulation in small
formats: 'Even if the loss of booklets must have been disproportionately high, the small number of surviving booklets seems to
indicate that a) the SEL was usually copied as a collection, and b) it
had lost much of its popularity in the 15 C, when the habit of taking
excerpts or selections appears to have been more common.'[26] The
argument that small-format selections are only a late phenomenon
has been challenged by more recent studies. As for the argument
that the SEL was usually copied as a collection, this working
assumption overemphasizes the principle of gathering while downplaying the principle of textual dispersal. And it should be pointed
out that even just a few such intersections of small-format and
large-format traditions suffice to throw stemmatic deductions
about redactions into disarray.

For decades scholars had assumed that the only natural way
for arranging SEL texts in a compilation was to follow the order
of the saints' feast days in the liturgical calendar, and accordingly
sections that did not follow the calendar cycle were thought of as
random or disordered. A dissertation of 1964 by Laurel Braswell,
however, showed that some of the apparently disordered portions of Bodleian Library, MS Laud Misc. 108 (L) group saints
according to 'hierarchical' type: a series of apostles, for instance,
and a series of virgin-martyrs.[27] The implications of this were
explored in a pair of innovative articles by Thomas Liszka. He suggests, in an article from 1989, that the compiler of L worked from
several smaller exemplars, some of which were organized cycli-
cally (including one with a prologue announcing such an arrangement), and some of which presented groups of saints according to
kind, either by hierarchical type or by nationality (English saints,
Irish saints). Because of interweaving material from different
exemplars, because of co-existing rationales for organization and
because of the compiler's shifting intentions, the order of L is idiosyncratic: 'the Laud manuscript is one in which the processes of
collecting and arranging material were ongoing'.[28] In an essay of
2001, Liszka demonstrated that similar processes are at work in
other idiosyncratic collections, including B, W and Cambridge,
Trinity College 605 (R): 'I submit that its [i.e. L's] relative state

of order and disorder would not seem such an anomaly to scholars if the similarly ordered or the disordered *SEL* texts were better known.'[29] Where his earlier study of *L* suggested that the compiler intended eventually to integrate all materials in calendar order in a subsequent draft, the later study makes no mention of such an ulterior intention. After all, if idiosyncratic ordering is not anomalous, then it follows that these compilers need not have been particularly anxious about whether or not their material was subjected to the dictates of liturgical order.

Passing from questions of circulation (the material embodiment of these texts) to related questions of transmission (the process of generating new copies), I wish to home in on some mechanisms for rearranging *SEL* items during the course of transmission, and to do so I turn to a small example taken from the unique legends found in *B*, namely the short legend of Sts Saturninus and Sisinius. This legend may have come to the *B* compiler as part of a mini-compilation of *SEL* poems focussing on the lives of martyrs, for several other martyr legends occur in its general vicinity. However, in its immediate context in *B*, the legend of Sts Saturninus and Sisinius is interposed among a series of lives of popes, a series which probably indicates that the *B* compiler also used a gathering of papal lives as one of his exemplars. This reshuffling may have been occasioned by a copyist's error. The preceding two legends of Pope Miltiades (10 December) and Pope Damasus (11 December) are in the proper liturgical sequence; however, a copyist of the life of Damasus has erred in writing the date of Damasus's death, giving not the third ides of December (11 December) but the third kalends (29 November): 'the thridde calendir of Decembir out of world thisse / Damas wente, out of this lif in to heven-blisse'[30] ('the third kalends of December out of this world went Damasus, out of this life to heavenly bliss'). The feastday for Sts Saturninus and Sisinius is 29 November, i.e. the kalends of December, as their legend correctly has it: 'the thridde calendre of desembre here hevedin were of ismete'[31] ('the third kalends of December their heads were smitten off'). One viable explanation for the placement of this poem, then, is that the *B* compiler experimented sporadically with different ways of linking legends, maintaining or rearranging items sometimes according to type of saint and sometimes according to liturgical calendar, sometimes blending these modes. In this case, the experiment, based upon an error generated within one of the texts, was not checked against a martyrology or breviary. In other words, in this instance the compiler is not so much aligning two legends with proper liturgical order as he is toying around with that possibility on the basis of a provisional hunch.[32]

What we see here is a process of recombination that often occurs in the transmission of the *SEL*. In the course of copying out a new collection, an item from an exemplar might be omitted, a new item might be supplied from elsewhere, while an item that in one manuscript context had been grouped with one set of items might now be clustered with a different set. Such recombination could, theoretically, generate utterly heterogenous selections and arrangements at every stage of copying, but in practice the free movement of items tends to be kept in check. Recombination is encouraged by the fact that there is more than one legitimate way of grouping these texts together. Liturgical calendars, hierarchical typologies of saints, national historical consciousnesses, chronologies of salvation history, relations between fixed and moveable feasts could all affect the sequencing of legends, as could aesthetic interests such as shared themes among poems, and material interests such as their length. Competing rationales of arrangement enabled individual items potentially to exist in an 'unmarked' state, circulating on their own or included in a collection in a more-or-less random placement. Nevertheless, rival rationales simultaneously channelled the recombinatory energy of the *SEL* into more-or-less established configurations. One of those configurations – that which followed the liturgical cycle – came to dominate the sequencing found in most compilations. But other rationales also exerted pressure on compilers, both early and late in the collection's history. The volatility of the shape of the collection as it moved from one manuscript to another, and the persistence of well-established configurations, are equally conspicuous aspects of how recombinatory poetics affected the transmission of the *SEL*.

The handful of saints with plural lives, the numerous unique legends and, to a lesser extent, the co-existence of different rationales of arrangement are features that have received only minimal consideration in the study of the *SEL*. What happens if we treat these as legitimate, persistent, salient features of *SEL* textuality, rather than as epiphenomena that can be safely ignored? Regarding practices of composition, these features demonstrate a fluid rapport between a principle of consolidation (the stabilization of a traditional *SEL* ensemble) and a principle of proliferation (the generation of autonomous poetic texts). Regarding circulation in material formats, they reveal an ongoing tension between techniques for gathering texts together and techniques of textual dispersal. And as for the transmission of texts into new manuscript contexts, they show that a basic logic of recombination was guided, but also made volatile, by the potential for reconfiguration. Taken together, these practices and their effects show that the textual domain of the *SEL* is decisively informed by what we might call modular dynamics. Individual poems exist as modules, to the extent that they possess an integrity and an autonomy of their own (with the potential to exist outside of any particular configuration) and are, at the same time, conformable to being clustered with other items in assorted configurations.

Such modular dynamics unsettle schemes that attempt to account tidily for the way individual items relate to *SEL* collections. I suspect that redactionist accounts of the *SEL* have been overstated: their central claims, which are presented as philologically based deductions, often seem fore-ordained by methodological assumptions; privileging the well-ordered compilation as the basic textual unit tends to lead to self-validating results. These suspicions do not, however, lead me to accept wholeheartedly Boyd's argument that the *SEL* should be considered a corpus of individual items. The textual domain of the *SEL* is more than a corpus of discrete poems. It encompasses those poems, but it also encompasses protocols for joining those items into groups. It encompasses, moreover, the way these poems belong to a large repertoire, the way they tended toward certain usable configurations, the way they made themselves available in manuscript compilations of various sorts.

The textual domain of the *SEL* takes shape in the first instance as an ensemble. To a large degree, this ensemble is energized by the unremitting friction between individual items on the one hand and the grouping of those items into compilations on the other. Thus, if we were to ask whether a particular *SEL* saint's life is a distinct work in its own right or rather the component of a larger work, the answer is that it is both. Similarly, if we ask whether an extant compilation counts as a unified work, or rather simply as an assemblage of smaller works, the answer here, too, is that it is both. The point to make is not just the easy one that our modern terminology regarding 'works' is anachronistic. These contrasting descriptions are not simply the consequence of different perspectives according to which an object might be described. They register two different states of being for these texts, which always are, simultaneously, both coherent textual units in their own right and incomplete fragments of a larger enterprise.

Thomas Liszka has rendered the convincing verdict that we confront no single entity identifiable as the *SEL*, but rather a set of different compilations which are so many different *SELS*: 'To the later *SEL* compilers, the *SEL* was an open text, one that not merely could, but should be improved, adapted, and suited to local use. As a result, there were produced many *South English Legendaries* that deserve to be better known.'[33] To this important observation a corollary might be added: there are at the same time manifold *SEL* legends. The textuality of the *SEL* is constituted not only by practices of compilation but also by the autonomy (whether potential or realized) of individual items whose meaning is only partly shaped by the compilations through which they travelled. One implication of Liszka's argument is that a primary editorial task should be to produce editions of individual manuscript compilations, not presuming to excavate some more originary redaction. Another implication, this time for the corollary I have added, is that an equally fundamental task is to focus on individual legends one at a time, producing, where possible, critical editions based on all of their extant witnesses (and not using the manuscript filiations of one poem to predetermine the analysis of any other).

Anne Thompson, in her 2003 book on the *South English Legendary*, argues that the 'idea of a collection' that runs so strongly throughout the *SEL* is generated above all by the formal and thematic dimensions of the *SEL* itself, rather than by any homologies with the liturgy:

> The underlying principle of the SEL is indeed additive: one story gives way to another, then to another, and then to yet another, and authors approach each with anticipation and delight, not tiring of the multiple possibilities inherent in the creation of yet another fictional world. The stories do not get better although some *are* better than others; it is enough that each one takes its place within – and submits to the influence of – the idea of a collection, whereby narrative itself is the unifying thread that knits up the whole.[34]

Thompson's point about the aesthetic possibilities of narrative could also be applied to the poetic features of these poems (septenary couplets, rhythmic divisions, uncomplicated and flexible lexis and syntax), for these also influenced how writers might participate in this cultural enterprise. Perhaps it is above all at the level of the ensemble – the *SEL* understood as a larger cultural text – that such an idea of a collection seems to be operative; the idea of an ensemble exceeds its instantiation in any particular manuscript compilation, expanding the repertoire through processes of proliferation and dispersal as well as consolidating it in manageable gatherings. The upshot is that the *SEL* is not simply a batch of individual poems, nor simply a set of manuscript compilations, but is also, in important ways, a larger cultural text. The way that features of the *SEL* facilitate participation are worth further study, for they may help us understand how late medieval writers, readers and copyists began to think of themselves as contributing to the even more diffuse project of establishing a widespread, vernacular, Middle English, literary culture.

Notes

1 Gregory M. Sadlek, 'The *South English Legendary* as rose window', *Ball State University Forum*, 25:4 (1984), 3–17 (4).

2 Minnie E. Wells, 'The *South English Legendary* and its relation to the *Legenda aurea*', *PMLA*, 51 (1936), 337–60.

3 *East Midland Revision*, p. 9.

4 Görlach, *Textual Tradition*, p. 220 n. 14.

5 Ibid., p. 51, and p. 237 n. 179.

6 See especially Pickering, 'Expository *temporale*'; Liszka, 'The first "A" redaction'; and Manfred Görlach, 'The *Legenda aurea* and the early history of *The South English Legendary*', in Dunn-Lardeau, pp. 301–16.

7 *East Midland Revision*, pp. 29–32.

8 Cf. Görlach, *Textual Tradition*, pp. 55–6.

9 Beverly Boyd, 'New light on the *South English Legendary*', *Texas Studies in English*, 37 (1958), 187–94 (193).

10 Beverly Boyd, 'A new approach to the *South English Legendary*', *Philological Quarterly*, 47 (1968), 494–8 (498).

11 Robert Mills, 'Violence, community, and the materialisation of belief', in Salih (ed.), *Companion to Middle English Hagiography*, pp. 87–103 (87).

12 Görlach, *Textual Tradition*, p. 220, nn. 12, 13.

13 Beverly Boyd, review of *The Textual Tradition of the South English Legendary* by Manfred Görlach, *Speculum*, 52 (1977), 678.

14 See Pickering, '*Temporale* narratives'.

15 Görlach, *Textual Tradition*, pp. 179–80.

16 'Shorter *South English Legendary* life of St. Frideswide', lines 1–4, in Sherry L. Reames with the assistance of Martha G. Blalock and Wendy L. Larson (eds.), *Middle English Legends of Women Saints* (Kalamazoo, MI: Medieval Institute Publications, 2003), p. 27. All translations are mine.

17 'Longer *South English Legendary* life of St. Frideswide', lines 1–6; in Reames et al. (eds), *Middle English Legends of Women Saints*, p. 37.

18 'De sancto Switthino', D'Evelyn and Mill, I, 274, 1–2.

19 'Shorter *South English Legendary* life of St. Frideswide', v. 118; 'Longer *South English Legendary* life of St. Frideswide', v. 188.

20 Reames et al. (eds), *Middle English Legends of Women Saints*, p. 24.

21 'Seint oswin the king the holy marter', lines 1–10, in Carl Horstmann (ed.), 'Des Ms. Bodl. 779 jüngere Zusatzlegenden zur südlichen Legendensammlung', *Archiv für das Studium der neueren Sprachen und Literaturen*, 82 (1889), 369–422 (369, 1–10).

22 For the contents of *B*, see Carleton Brown, *A Register of Middle English Religious & Didactic Verse. Part I: List of Manuscripts* (Oxford: Oxford University Press, 1916), pp. 29–37; and Liszka, *SELS*, pp. 276–81 (pp. 23–65 above)

23 A. S. G. Edwards, 'Fifteenth-century English collections of female saints' lives', *Yearbook of English Studies*, 33 (2003), 136.

24 For the contents of *M*, see Brown, *Register*, pp. 293–7.

25 Görlach, *Textual Tradition*, p. 118, suggests an interest in cosmology and history for *Ax*. Ralph Hanna suggests a concern for salvation history in general and for the Easter cycle in particular for the booklets in *W*; Ralph Hanna III, 'Miscellaneity and vernacularity: conditions of literary production in late medieval England', in Stephen G. Nichols and Siegfried Wenzel (eds), *The Whole Book: Cultural Perspectives on the Medieval Miscellany* (Ann Arbor: University of Michigan Press, 1996), pp. 37–51. On the interests manifested in MS *B*, see further Wogan-Browne in this volume.

26 Görlach, *Textual Tradition*, p. 71.

27 Laurel Nichols Braswell, 'The South English Legendary collection: a study in Middle English religious literature of the thirteenth and fourteenth centuries' (PhD dissertation, University of Toronto, 1964).

28 Thomas R. Liszka, 'Ms. Laud Misc. 108 and the early history of the *South English Legendary*', *Manuscripta*, 33 (1989), 84. Cf. Beverly Boyd, 'The enigma of Bodleian Library MS Laud Misc. 108 (circa 1300)', *Manuscripta*, 39 (1995), 131–6.

29 Liszka, *SELS*, p. 259 (p. 40 above).

30 'Seint damas the pope', v. 57; in Horstmann (ed.), 'Des Ms. Bodl. 779', p. 408.

31 'Seint saturnin and cicin, twey holy marterus', v. 115, in Horstmann (ed.), 'Des Ms. Bodl. 779', p. 410.

32 A more erudite reason for aligning the two legends – that Pope Damasus composed a poetic Latin epitaph for Saturninus's tomb – is attractive but highly unlikely. See Damasus I, *Epigrammata Damasiana*, ed. Antonio Ferrua (Rome: Pontifico Istituto di Archeologia Christiana, 1942), pp. 188–92.

33 Liszka, *SELS*, p. 261 (p. 41 above).

34 *Everyday Saints*, p. 124.

Part III

Textual communities and the *South English Legendaries*

9
Forms of community in the *South English Legendary*

Catherine Sanok

For the *SEL*, questions about form are usually pitched at the level of the line (the septenary verse that is its hallmark) and sometimes at the level of the legend (in, for example, the debate about the influence of sermons on the legends' length and narrative style). In this essay I want to make a category shift, to think about form on the level of the legendary itself, especially as the first multi-part narrative in Middle English.[1] This is, of course, a tricky line of enquiry because it assumes the existence of the 'South English Legendary', despite its various textual tradition. An important essay by Thomas Liszka has restored a sense of that variety and called for a scholarship responsible to it.[2] I understand my project here as a complement, not challenge, to the one Liszka advocates and to the growing *SEL* bibliography that has advanced our understanding through close attention to particular legends and particular manuscripts, even as I want to take seriously the idea of the *SEL*. By this I mean not a putative ideal form of the work abstracted from its textual instantiations but the formal principles that define the work, however flexibly, such that we can identify a hugely various textual tradition by a single title. It is easy to dismiss such an 'idea' as a fiction, but this fiction is not only an artefact of modern scholarship or editorial practice. It is also a poetic conceit, announced in the *Banna sanctorum* and elaborated in the two extended metaphors that initiate the *sanctorale*, and it informs the ways in which the materials assembled in Bodleian MS Laud Misc. 108 (which Carl Horstmann edited as the *Early South-English Legendary*) were reordered.[3] Significantly, this idea does not *inaugurate* the textual tradition we call the 'South English Legendary': it is a response to early stages of that tradition, evidence, we might say, of meditation on the formal possibilities presented by a single work that comprises many individual short narratives. This meditation can be credited to the so-called A redactor responsible for the *Banna sanctorum*, which concludes by specifying the calendar order, beginning with 1 January, that organizes the collection. This is of course roughly the text represented by D'Evelyn and Mill.[4] Despite the risks that attend discussing the *SEL*, it is only by addressing the text at the level of the whole that we may recognize how the *SEL*, too, is interested in category shifts and how its variousness as a multi-part narrative compels this interest.

The *SEL* as a multi-part collection and the question of community

My basic argument in this essay is that the *SEL*'s formal concerns as a multi-part narrative are closely correlated to its interest in community. It is significant that the prologue, identified as the *Banna sanctorum* in several manuscripts,[5] at once transforms the miscellaneous texts of the *SEL* into a collection and addresses a community defined in relationship to this collection. This double purpose is served by each of the prologue's central conceits: the agricultural metaphor in which the 'new fruit' of Christianity is grown in a sacrificial garden, watered first by Christ's blood and then by the blood of generations of martyrs, and the military metaphor in which Christ is a king arrayed for battle, attended by ranks of archers and backed by his hardy knights. These violent metaphors are the ground on which the prologue establishes a community defined by their (prescribed) affective response: 'Wel aghte *we* lovie Cristendom   that is so dure iboght' (I, 3, 57: 'Well should we love Christendom that is so dearly bought'). The metaphors also ground the formal features of the collection as such, which exemplifies and extends them. Most obviously, the serried ranks of Christ's knights find a close analogue in the stories about them, told 'bi reuwe' (I, 3, 66) in the *sanctorale* that follows. The order of this series, in turn, recalls the garden of the 'new fruit': it follows calendar order, 'as hare dai valth in the yere' ('as their day falls in the year'), a seasonal and cyclical order commemorating the 'herte blod' that waters the seed that Christ has sown.[6] The metaphors that compel the community addressed by the *SEL* ('Wel aghte we lovie Cristendom') also figure the form of the collection, the narratives that represent an ordered procession of Christ's saints, organized by the cycle of the year, itself defined by both agricultural seasons and the ritual celebration of the life of Christ.

Even fashioned into a collection, however, the constituent parts of the *SEL* retain their striking variety, and this variety challenges the way we might be tempted to conceptualize the collection through the logic of synecdoche, the part standing for the whole. It is a logic suggested both by the structure of the *SEL* as a multi-part narrative and by its primary subject: saints, who are often imagined as holy metonyms for the communities formed or addressed by their cults. This is true at times in the *SEL* itself: it is at the heart of the idea of community developed, for example, in the legend of Alphege, in which the saint stands for an urban community and that community, in turn, stands for England. Although Alphege is associated with specific places throughout the legend – Deerhurst, where he first becomes a monk; Bath, where he lives as a hermit and then prior; and then Winchester, where he serves as bishop before he is made archbishop of Canterbury – he is introduced as having been born in 'Engelonde', the first indication that the local places he inhabits stand as synecdoches for a national community. This figural structure is at the narrative and thematic center of his martyrdom. When the Danes invade England seven years after Alphege is made archbishop – 'For Deneis and men of Engelond   selde beoth ysome' (I, 150, 52: 'For Danes and English men are rarely joined together') – and the townspeople of Canterbury are threatened, Alphege offers himself as a substitute: he 'propherede is owe lyf   forto give for hore' (I, 151, 87: 'offered his own life in exchange for theirs'). His ability as one man to stand for this urban community is, in a crossing of religious and secular forms of community, a function of his exceptional status as archbishop. This representative function is, through another category shift made possible by the legend's figural logic, constitutive of a still larger and more imaginative community: both Alphege and the devil understand his sacrifice in terms not of Canterbury but England. The devil, disguised as an angel, successfully tempts Alphege to escape from prison by claiming that God wants him to do so in order to 'saui Engelond' (I, 151, 102). Alphege ultimately realizes that he has been tricked. His error is not, as we might expect, the hubris of believing the devil's account of the potential significance of his life, much less the folly of privileging a political community over a religious one, but the mistaken strategy proposed to realize the sacrifice he wants to make 'For the love of Engelond' (I, 154, 186).

The legend of Alphege, then, understands category shifts through the logic of synecdoche. It is the figural structure by which the individual represents a local community (Canterbury), and by which that local community, in turn, represents a larger one (England) in a graduated scale. It is, not incidentally, a scale that assumes and asserts that religious and secular community are coextensive. This logic could inform the collection as a whole, as it does, for example, in the much later *Kalendre of the New Legende of Englande*, printed by Richard Pynson in 1516.[7] That collection seeks to establish a national *sanctorale*, with a necessary relationship between Pynson's representation of a homogeneous national community and the capacity of every saint in the collection to represent England. Individual institutional and regional affiliations of individual legends are not erased, but the *Kalendre* subordinates them to their national affiliation through its very form, which establishes England as the privileged category through which identity and history are understood.

In the *SEL*, the remarkable heterogeneity of its narratives prevents any one part from standing for the whole, and this resistance to synecdoche on the level of form – the failure of any one legend to stand for the collection – correlates with a resistance to synecdoche as a privileged model for representing community. Local categories of identity and community only rarely point to larger ones: they are themselves too heterogeneous. Indeed, the *SEL* recognizes the synecdochic structure of English community explored in the Alphege legend itself as only one form of community among others – a particular, not paradigmatic, form in a collection that comprises many different forms.[8] The various ways in which community is represented in the *SEL* quickly multiply: while, for example, the legend of St Kenelm defines community in terms of geography,[9] *Wulfstan* imagines it in terms of historiography,[10] and other legends, such as *Aldhelm*, give prominent attention to genealogy.[11] While *Alphege* takes affect as a structure of community, as we have seen, *Oswald*, with its central story about his care for the hungry, emphasizes ethics.[12] We might contrast, too, Thomas Becket's exemplarity – Edmund Rich's life is imagined importantly as an *imitatio Thome* – with Rich's own exceptionality, as evidenced by his miraculous birth without the blood and 'hore' (muck) of childbed (II, 492, 8–10).[13]

These are all figures who help to define England, but there are many other communities represented or addressed by the *SEL*, of course, and in their heterogeneity they render the collection still more resistant to the logic of synecdoche. The legend of Edmund Rich famously invokes a feminine audience, when the narrator, after describing Edmund's devotion to the Virgin, teases: 'Wele whare eni of you couthe   such an hosebonde fynde' (II, 496, 100: 'Any of you would be lucky to find such a husband'). There are also intriguing moments of attention to very specific groups, such as eggmongers, for whom the story of St Swithun's miraculous reconstitution of a woman's broken eggs has special significance. At the same time, the many legends in the *SEL* that find analogues in the *Golden Legend* (that is, that show a rough correspondence with the Dominican *sanctorale*) point to a broad Christian community, defined by a shared liturgical tradition.

For both the collection and its idea of community, the category shift from the individual to the collective is defined not by synecdoche but by multiplicity. Indeed, the *SEL* uses its multi-part structure to develop a fascinating exploration of overlapping, non-exclusive, non-coterminous communities. Its heterogeneity does not index discrete communities, neither dividing one reader from another according to a privileged category of identity nor subordinating one category to another. After all, a member of the *SEL*'s audience may be a woman and an eggmonger, a resident of Worcestershire and an 'English' subject. She would share some of these categories of identity with her husband, some with other women, some with all (or most) members of her town. She participates in many communities: some are larger and some smaller in scale, but they cannot therefore be coordinated with, or made to stand for, one another.

This is true even for regional, national and supranational community, which are imagined in the *SEL* not as category shifts from the particular to the general but as shifts between incommensurable categories, defined not by quantitative but by qualitative differences. This is thematized in the collection's final legend, the Life of Thomas Becket, in the story of Becket's father Gilbert, a Crusader who is captured in Jerusalem and becomes a favourite of the Saracen prince, Amiraud. One day, Amiraud asks Gilbert about 'the manere of Engelond . . . and of the lawe' (II, 611, 18). The prince's interest in English practice is echoed by his daughter, who also 'esste him (Gilbert) of Engelond   and of the maner there / And of the lif of Cristendom   and wat hare bileve were' (II, 611, 29–30: 'asked him about England and the manners there and about the life of Christians and what their beliefs were'). Unlike her father, the girl recognizes that Gilbert hails from two communities, England and Christendom – the first sign of the perspicacity and sympathy that will make her worthy to be his wife and mother to the holy Thomas. The category shift from England to Christendom may seem privileged by the narrative: the girl, after all, does not need to adopt English manners, but

she must convert. Yet Gilbert's own answer moves, oddly, in the
other direction, toward a local, rather than supranational, frame:
he tells the girl about England and Christianity, as she has asked,
and also about 'the toun het Londone   that he was inne bore'
(II, 611, 32: 'the town called London where he was born').[14] Later,
when she secretly follows him after his escape, 'London' is the only
English word she knows and she uses it to arrive at Gilbert's house
and prove her love for him: in so far as community is a phenomenon of affect, it requires a local habitation even if it is not limited
to this place.

The story insists that the local, national and supranational communities are different not only in scale but in structure: London is
defined by place, England by manners and law, and Christendom
by faith.[15] They cannot, therefore, be understood in terms of category shifts between the particular and the general – from hyponym
to hypernym, to borrow terms from linguistics – or as a species
of synecdoche, as they are in *Alphege*. Indeed, all three function
differently in the story: the union of Gibert and his Saracen bride
depends on the intimacies of urban space (its practical condition)
and shared faith (its ideological condition), while the question of
English custom and law is suspended in this genealogical back
story in order to become the narrative's central problematic. I will
return later to the Becket legend and its interest in how the conflict
between ecclesiastical and royal jurisdiction – the conflict between
England as a religious and as a political community – is complicated by its relationship to both local and supranational communities. Here let me simply underscore how thoroughly the legend
challenges the synecdochic relationship linking local, national and
supranational communities in *Alphege*. In *Becket*, as in the legendary as a whole, these categories cannot be co-ordinated into a hierarchy of value or even stable relationship; instead they coexist as
separate, but non-exclusive and overlapping, categories of identity.

This layered representation of community, presented by the
Becket legend on the level of theme, is, as I argued above, presented in the *SEL* itself on the level of form. Its multi-part narrative offers an image of diversity and complexity without pretending
to a comprehensive accounting or a representative sampling, which
also implies a finite set. From this perspective, the fact that the
collection betrays a regional orientation, or that the native saints
remain a minority, may be seen to strengthen, rather than dilute,
the force of the *SEL*'s representation of a national community,
which is, after all, defined not only by that category of identity and

history but by its complicated relationship to many categories. The nation becomes reified as the primary form of community and affiliation in a later period, of course, but it is not offered as such here.

Indeed, the form of community imagined by the *SEL* resonates strongly with the recent accounts of culture and community in a post-national frame. Arjun Appadurai in an influential analysis of the accelerated pace of global media and the experience of migration argues that cultures are now 'fractal' and 'overlapping' rather than 'isomorphic'.[16] For Appadurai, this is a consequence of the multiple factors that structure global culture – technology, media, finance, ethnic identity and ideology – in their variable relation to one another and in the complicated patterns of their confluence and divergence. In proposing an analogous definition of community from a premodern perspective, the *SEL* suggests the truly theoretical nature of Appadurai's paradigm and its general applicability: material, expressive and ideological formations produce a variety of communities, of markedly different scales, that proliferate and overlap in ways that challenge fictions of unified and bounded cultures in general and the scalar fiction of the nation, in particular, as the privileged form that mediates between the local and the supranational.[17]

The *SEL* arrives at this insight through the formal principle of the multi-part narrative collection, a collection that puts 'regional' saints such as Kenelm in relationship with saints who represent a national community – Becket or Edmund or Alban – and with so-called universal saints – Katherine or John the Baptist or Sebastian. The relationship between them is not defined by a hierarchy of scale or value. It is defined instead in terms of time, through the calendar figured by their feast days and those of the *temporale*.

'As hare dai valth in the yere'

Our hypothetical eggmonger from Worcestershire inhabits different categories of time, just as she participates in different communities: liturgical time, defined by the sequence of holy days; the time of the Christian era, which records her distance from the birth of Christ; the cycle of the seasons, which we might call agricultural time; regnal time, as defined by the king's reign; and the time of her own life span and place in a sequence of generations. The *SEL* is conspicuously indebted to the first: as the Prologue announces, in most manuscripts the legends are told 'bi reuwe' according to their place in the liturgical calendar. The *SEL* produces its individual narratives as a collection through the formal technology of the calendar. The individual legends relate to the whole primarily as temporal phenomena: individual feast days that together fashion a year.

It is tempting for this reason to privilege liturgical time in readings of the *SEL*, especially when we attend to the collection's form. We might contrast, for example, Klaus Jankofsky's reading of the native saints' lives and that of Thorlac Turville-Petre. Jankofsky argues that the audience of the *SEL* inhabits a double sense of time. The emphasis on sacrificial violence in the legends of the 'Latin' martyrs, Jankofsky argues, structures a typological relationship to Christ and thus points to a transcendent, extra-historical temporal frame. As such, they stand in contrast to the Anglo-Saxon saints' lives, characterized by a 'more concrete, historical framework, often with reference to political struggles in which the saints took part or to social injustices and ills that they tried to redress'. For Jankofsky, the ahistorical and historical do not so much contradict as complement one another: 'all' he argues, 'contribute to create on the audience's part an awareness of the continuum of this world and the next'.[18]

Jankofsky's reading is thematic rather than formal: it contrasts one set of legends to another, defined by their subject matter, without regard to the form of the collection as a whole. Turville-Petre's understanding of the same questions of temporality and community, in contrast, depends very much on the calendrical ordering of the text, which he argues obscures a historical rendering of English community; without a chronological structure linking these individual texts, the collection can provide 'only isolated glimpses of the political development of the relationship between Church and Crown'.[19] Unlike Jankofsky's argument that the *SEL* bridges the temporal and atemporal as it places England in the context of Christianity, Turville-Petre suggests that both inhabit a shared atemporality.

The two temporal models at issue here – sometimes juxtaposed as 'liturgical time' and 'historical time' – are generally understood as antitheses, especially in the work of early modern scholars who contrast the cyclical liturgical time of the Middle Ages to the 'steady advance of historical time' in post-Reformation religious and humanist discourses.[20] It is true that, to the extent that the *SEL* adopts a calendrical order, it troubles and obscures the historical nature of the communities it represents. But the *SEL*, if affiliated in important ways with the liturgy, is not itself properly liturgical.[21] Even its temporal paradigm deviates from liturgical practice, as its very form should remind us. The liturgical year traditionally begins with Advent and so therefore does Jacobus de Voragine's *Legenda aurea*, for example, which explicitly theorizes the liturgical calendar in its preface.[22] But the *SEL* follows neither the liturgical year nor, as we might expect, the English year, which began on 25 March, the feast of the Annunciation.[23] Both the liturgical year and the English year take Christ's coming as a starting point, and for obvious reasons; his human life marks a decisive split with the past, inaugurating a temporal difference that structures the otherwise arbitrary annual marking off of one year from another. As we will see, the choice of 1 January, the feast of the Circumcision, does something similar: as the *SEL* emphasizes, it marks the first time Christ's blood is shed. But the effort necessary to establish this temporal boundary betrays the oddness of 1 January as the start of the year in a paradigm of Christian time.

It is also strikingly unusual in vernacular culture. The *SEL*'s term for this day is 'yeresday', and the *Middle English Dictionary* lists three instances from three different moments in the legendary's own textual history (MS Laud 108; MS Corpus Christi 145, and MS Egerton 1993) as the first three uses of the term; the next witness given by the *MED* is Trevisa's translation of the *Polychronicon* (1387). 'New Year's day' is used as early as the *Ormulum* (1200), but that is the only witness given by the *MED* until *Sir Gawain and the Green Knight*. So, on the evidence of the *MED*, the idea of 1 January as the start of the new year is rare outside of the *SEL* until the end of the fourteenth century. In England, the primary narrative context in which 1 January serves as the start of the year is in historiographic traditions that depend on the Julian calendar.[24] What modern scholarship has understood as antithetical temporal frames – the liturgical and the historical – are simultaneously invoked in the *SEL*'s form, poised between the calendar, with its strong allusion to liturgical time, and historiography, as it marks out the years from 1 January.

One practical effect of this order is that the year is inaugurated by the feast of the Circumcision, the first time Christ's blood is shed, as the legend notes (I, 3, 5). As with a year beginning with the Annunciation or the season of Advent, a year that begins with the Circumcision follows Christ's life as the deep structure of the year. The Circumcision, however, draws special attention to typology (unlike the Annunciation, say, with its emphasis on prophecy). Jesus is circumcised according to the 'olde lay', as the legend has it, a phrase it repeats conspicuously four times in its brief twenty-eight lines. Even this new beginning is set in relation to what precedes it. And, of course, it sets this new beginning in pointed, if only implicit, relation to what will follow; as the *first* time Christ's blood is shed, it heralds the Passion and Crucifixion. Time here is caught between past and future, suspended by the atemporal structure of typology, even as the Circumcision stands for the radical division of old and new through the logic of supersession, a cut in time.[25]

If the Circumcision points backward and forward, curiously evacuating the event itself, the second feast in this calendrical organization, Epiphany or Twelfth Day, heaps event upon event. It is not only the day on which the kings visit the infant Christ: it is also the day of his baptism twenty-nine years later ('to bygynne the niwe lay', I, 5, 5–6: 'to inaugurate the new law'), the day he turned water into wine a year after that, and, a year later, the day on which he fed five thousand men with five loaves. Here the *SEL* uses the cyclical nature of the calendar precisely to describe – not deny – chronology, the progress of time, with 6 January standing for a series of dates in Christ's life linked by ideas of transformation but not fully typological in nature. In the conjunction of the Circumcision and Epiphany as the first two narratives of the *SEL* we can see a paradigm for the paradoxical or complementary presence of historical and ahistorical time, grounded not only in the difference between England and Christendom, as Jankofsky has it, but as endemic to Christendom itself – indeed, to the incarnate Christ.[26]

It is also endemic to the form of the legendary, which marries narratives of the past with an annual cycle that obtains in the present, and points to the future. Alison Chapman, in a brilliant discussion of the calendars in Foxe's *Acts and Monuments* and the Book of Common Prayer, argues that 'when . . . a historical narrative is accompanied by a calendar . . . the history makes a far more pressing claim on the experience of time. While the narrative itself shows the unspooling events of times past, the calendar provides a framework for times to come and makes clear the text's intent to shape the future'.[27] The Twelfth Day narrative is closely relevant here: Christ models the progress of time for the reader, for whom the cycle of the liturgical year may also encourage an awareness of such forward movement in the context of their own lives and that of the communities they inhabit.[28] Chapman's argument may be the best framework for understanding the odd choice of 1 January as the start of the year, which may be informed primarily by calendars found in breviaries, which often start with January.[29] The text maps out time the way a calendar itself does: formed by feast days, it is nevertheless a flexible instrument that can accommodate all kinds of time: not only liturgical time but also the structure of national history that puts the stories of England's past in relationship to the present, and even the unfolding of personal or familial histories which inform more local kinds of community.

From this perspective, the calendrical order of the collection is evidence for Anne Thompson's suggestion, made on the grounds of narrative thematics, that the temporal horizon of the *SEL* is less history or eternity than the day.[30] If historical time alienates the past through its relentlessly progressive nature, and liturgical time uses the cycle of the year to point to a time outside the forward movement of chronology, a calendar that marks an intersection between the two provides a paradigm of time to be filled by the individual, who may – like the Christ of the Twelfth Day feast – mark significant events and chart the passing of the years against the calendar.[31] The temporal suspension of typology, emphasized in the brief account of the Circumcision, holds a space open for those who inhabit the present (exclusively, it must be noted, for members of Christian community). Importantly, this is at once an individual and communal paradigm: individual experiences are charted against feast days known to all. Perhaps the most important category of time in the *SEL* is the quotidian, which for medieval Christians has an important relationship to both history and eternity, but also includes all manner of mundane and personal categories of time.

The temporal form of the *SEL* is then a correlative of its representation of community. It, too, is layered, accommodating many different forms of time, from the seasonal time of agrarian community, with its intimate cycles of human family and local affiliation, to the historical frameworks invoked to understand national community, to the eschatology invoked in the *Banna sanctorum*'s trope of transhistorical spiritual warfare. Less bounded and fixed than communities defined as phenomena of geography or blood, communities understood as phenomena of time can borrow from it, as the *SEL* does, an open extension that admits simultaneous frameworks – national and Christian history, human generations and regnal years, agricultural and liturgical seasons etc. This simultaneity is a crucial limit on the logic of synecdoche. The use of time as a structural principle of the *SEL* is thus closely related to its representation of multiple, non-exclusive communities, which is the central insight of the *SEL*, and the central problem of its final legend.

Engelond glad thou beo . . . for one monnes dethe

Unfixed by the graduated ordering of synecdoche, England emerges as a community in its own right, neither the hypernym of regional community nor the hyponym of Christendom. But the *SEL* does not simply celebrate the lack of co-ordination among the various kinds of communities it acknowledges, and its final legend is an extended investigation into the crisis this lack can provoke. The legend of Thomas of Canterbury addresses the irreconcilable claims of ecclesiastical and regnal authority – that is, competing definitions of national community as fundamentally religious or political – a conflict compounded by the coexistence of and intricate relationship among many other kinds of community that cannot be co-ordinated with the nation, including local ones such as Canterbury and supranational ones such as the Cistercian order. Whatever the discursive context for the use of 1 January as the start of the annual cycle, it is clear that a key impetus behind this choice is the prominence it gives to the legend of Thomas Becket, which – like the *SEL* as a whole – acknowledges community as a complicated, layered phenomenon, this time in a tragic register.[32]

The Becket legend plays an important role in the form of the *SEL* in other ways as well. Critics have often noted that its 'length and literary ambition' serve to conclude the whole.[33] More specifically, the legend offers extended echoes of the metaphorics of spiritual knighthood in the *Banna sanctorum* and so creates a thematic frame for the collection. These echoes surface initially in the account of Thomas's Crusader father, Gilbert, and then in the figuration of Thomas himself as a knight of Christ. The formal significance of this thematic frame may point to an important genealogy for the *SEL*'s thinking about community in the cult of Thomas Becket, as it figured in coincident and contested frameworks for local, regional, national and international identity.

Most obviously, the story of Becket's father – the Crusader who marries a Saracen princess whom he has met while imprisoned by her father – recalls, in the idiom of romance, the presence of English Christian communities in the contested territories in the Holy Land. More specifically, it may index contemporary interest in the

English Crusading order dedicated to Thomas of Canterbury, the Knights of St Thomas of Acon. The romance account of Becket's parentage is invented in the early thirteenth century,[34] closely contemporary with the foundation of the order, originally restricted to English canons, after Acre was taken in 1191. One of its central concerns was to raise money to ransom Crusaders imprisoned by Saladin.[35] The order was refashioned as a military order in the first quarter of the thirteenth century, and it had soon amassed enough property in England for a master of the order to be installed in London to administer their possessions. This period of ascendancy was short-lived, however. Forced to relocate to Nicosia after the fall of Acre and at times in danger of being subsumed into the Knights Templar, the order faced significant challenges in the fourteenth century, when disputes over the relative authority of the London master and his counterpart overseas erupted. The changing fortunes of the Order during the course of the *SEL*'s textual history prevent us from assigning any one meaning to its interest in the romance account of Becket's parentage, which reads like an etiological myth for the order's early commitment to succour imprisoned Crusaders.[36] But the very existence of the Order of the Knights of St Thomas of Acon opens questions about England's status as a national and religious community that ramify across its brief history in relation to both local and supranational politics, in broad parallel to the Becket legend itself.

If Crusaders such as Becket's father and the Knights of St Thomas are knights of Christ in a literal sense, Becket becomes one in a metaphoric register once he abandons his secular career. When the knights in Thomas's company leave him amid his trial before the council at Northampton, Becket declares that the poor men whom he serves are truly 'Godes knights'. 'Other men me habbeth forsake / theose knightes ich lovie more' (II, 639, 889–90). So is Thomas himself. In the scene that anticipates his martyrdom, his vestments are elaborately imagined in military terms:

> Tho sein Thomas hadde is masse ido   is chesible he gan of weve
> Ac alle the othere vestemens   he let on him bileve:
> Other armure nadde he non   for Holy Churche to fighte
> . . .
> A crois he nom in is hond   and wende forth baldeliche
> The vestemens [were] is armure   as fel to suche knighte
> The crois was is baner   for Holy Churche to fighte
> Forth wende this gode knight   among al is fon.
>
>   (II, 641, 953–61)

(When St Thomas had finished his mass, he began to take off his
chasuble, but all of his other vestments he kept on. He had no
other armour in which to fight for Holy Church . . . He took a
cross in his hand and boldly went forth. The vestments were his
armour, appropriate to such a knight. The cross was his banner,
to fight for Holy Church. Forth went this good knight, amidst all
his enemies.)

In a clear echo of the *Banna sanctorum*, Thomas declares that he is
'hardiore' because armed with the cross (II, 641, 968).[37] Indeed,
Becket is so frequently identified as a spiritual warrior in religious
and historiographic discourses – particularly those with some connection to the politics of the Barons' War – that the *SEL*'s first
audience may have recognized the commonplace military metaphor of the *Banna sanctorum* as a reference to him above all. In the
Life of St Thomas Cantilupe, the young Thomas is asked by his
uncle, the Bishop Walter of Worcester, about his future, and the
boy responds that he hopes to be a knight. Walter counters that he
will be a knight of Christ, the champion of God and of St Thomas
of Canterbury.[38] This affiliation points to more politicized uses of
the trope to link Becket to Simon de Montfort's victory at Lewes.[39]
Chronicle accounts – arguing that the victory should be attributed
to divine rather than human agency – claim that Thomas Becket
and St George intervened. The *Chronicle of St Martin of Dover*,
in an influential and widely disseminated passage, tells the story of
a boy from Canterbury who saw Thomas in a dream. The boy is
surprised and wonders how Thomas can participate in the conflict
since he is long dead. The saint responds that he is not dead, only
resting in peace, but has risen to fight 'pro patria mea Angliae'.[40]
Becket's association with spiritual knighthood, a framing trope of
the *SEL*, points to internal contests over the nature of national
community, especially the politics and local affiliations of the
Barons' War, as well as to the place of England in Christendom's
ongoing struggle to define itself in the face of Muslim military
power.

The trope of Christian knighthood also, of course, points to
the crisis in English community provoked by the overlapping
jurisdictions of royal and ecclesiastical authority. It does so most
immediately as a figure for Becket's martyrdom on behalf of the
Church's right, but the constitutive tension between the tenor and
vehicle of the metaphor also insists more broadly on the incompatible claims of secular community (chivalry and the loyalty to
the king that it demands) and religious community (the church as

an institution with special prerogatives that devolve from Christ himself). This conflict is given a history in the *SEL*: as Renee Hamelinck has noted, the Becket legend represents the end point of the contest between church and state, the origins of which lie in the Norman Conquest, first introduced in the Wulfstan legend, the inaugural English saint's life in the collection.[41] Wulfstan's legend spans the time before and after the Norman Conquest, and, like the Circumcision with which the *SEL* opens, it speaks to a new beginning. But in English history, authority is retrogressive: the legitimate Old Law of English rule is superseded by the New Law of Norman overlordship. As we have already seen, pre-Conquest England is presented as a unified, coherent community, in which a figure like Alphege can stand for local and national identity, for England as a spiritual community (as archbishop of Canterbury) and as a secular one (as a martyr for 'England'). The Wulfstan legend shows how this coincidence of spiritual and secular authority is compromised by the Conquest: when William dismisses Wulfstan as bishop on the grounds that he is too ignorant, Wulfstan takes his crosier and strikes the tomb of Edward the Confessor, where it sticks fast. When no one else is able to remove it, William and his archbishop repent and urge Wulfstan to reclaim his staff of office. With sly impertinence, Wulfstan replies, 'ich mot nede do   mine sovereines wille' (I, 13, 155: 'I must do my sovereign's will'). In its careful demonstration that the legitimacy of the bishop depends on the authority of the sovereign who appoints him, the legend at once tracks the pre-Conquest coincidence of spiritual and political community and identifies their difference under Norman rule.

As we have seen, the Becket legend stages the question of community from the start, and it elaborates the question through the central conflict between the king and Becket, rendering the terrible verdict that it is impossible to negotiate the intersections of ecclesiastical and regnal jurisdiction in post-Conquest England. But it does not evince the simple anti-Norman bias of the Wulfstan legend. The Becket legend is surprisingly sympathetic to the king's concerns about his own power and authority, even as Becket's sanctity is defined in terms of his willingness to die for the 'righte of Holy Churche' (II, 679, 2114). Instead, the legend – at remarkable length given the narrative expectations set by the rest of the legendary – presents Becket's death as the inescapable consequence of the profound difference between religious and political community, despite Becket's own loyalty and the king's basic goodness. Here too, through the irresolvable conflict between Becket and the king, the *SEL* explores coincident, non-exclusive but sometimes incompatible, categories of community. As recent criticism has taught us, the *SEL* is acutely aware of contemporary medieval contests over how to define England: the constitutionalism of the Barons' revolt, the question of ecclesiastical jurisdiction, the consequences of the Conquest and evacuation of an ethnic definition of what it means to be English. The interest in 'England' in the *SEL* is symptomatic of these contests, but cannot be reduced to any one of them. The refusal to represent England as the hypernym of a set of local communities or as the hyponym of Christendom voids any fixed definition of national community, even as it recognizes the instability, and sometimes violence, that attends such a fragile and fragmented collective.

The end of the Becket legend offers an apparently compensatory image of a seamless, single community formed through devotion to the martyr's body in the ritual of his translation. Not only is the king reconciled to his erstwhile enemy but a markedly diverse community is brought together, a local and living analogue to the kind of procession that the *Banna sanctorum* offers as the structure of the legendary:

> Vorto honoury thys holy man   ther com volk ynowgh
> Of bysscopes and of abbo[te]s   monyon thuder drowgh
> Of pryoures and parsons   and of other clerkes also
> Of heorles and barouns   and many a knyght therto
> Of seriauns and squyers   and hosebondes ynowe
> And of simple men eke of the lond   so thykke thuder drowe
> That al the contrey ther aboute   and toune wyde & longe
> Myghte unnethe al that folk   that ther com undervonge.
>
> (II, 690–1, 19–26)

(To honour this holy man, there came plenty of people. There were many bishops and abbots who came: priors and parsons and other clerks too, earls and barons and many a knight as well, serjeants and squires and householders in plenty, and also simple men of the land so thronged there that all the country around and the spacious town could barely accommodate all the people who came there.)

Here the *SEL* indulges in the fantasy of a community, unified in its devotion to Becket, comprising secular and spiritual estates, rich and poor, rural and urban. Interestingly, the co-ordination of such diversity into a community is associated with temporal repetition in a striking echo of the Epiphany narrative. The translation of Becket's body occurred on a Tuesday, the legend twice insists (II,

693, 38, 53), and it was on Tuesdays that most of the consequential events of his life happened:

> Alle hys chaunces that he hadde   by Tywesdawes hii come
> By Tywesday he was ibore   and of hys moder wombe com
> And also as me bryngeth a theof   vorto vonge hys dom
> Byvore [the] kyng at Northhamthone   by a Tywesday
> Wyth greot sschame he was ibrought   as al that folk ysay
> Vyloker than eny theof   that folk him ther sschende.
>
> (II, 691–2, 54–9)

(All the events of his life fell on a Tuesday. On Tuesday he was born, and came from his mother's womb and, like someone bringing a thief to receive his sentence, before the king at Northampton on a Tuesday, with great shame he was brought, as all people say, more degradingly than any thief, so that people humiliated him there.)

Translated on a Tuesday, martyred on a Tuesday, Becket was also exiled on a Tuesday, informed by God of his impeding martyrdom on a Tuesday and returned to England from exile on a Tuesday (II, 694, 60–8).[42] He is thus to be honoured by a Tuesday fast – a ritual commemoration that can re-enact the community formed during his translation.

The collection, then, closes by co-ordinating the diverse communities of the legendary through the sacrificial body of the saint. But this is less a fiction of a national community founded on Becket's sacrifice than a reminder that this unity exists only in the temporary – even extra-temporal – performances of ritual. Even the weekly commemoration of Becket's martyrdom, while seeking to re-enact this unity, recalls a death that symbolizes the impossibility of fashioning a fully representative, fully integrated national community, given the contested jurisdictions, the local and supranational affiliations, and the irreconcilable commitments of its constituents. Defined in relation to so many different categories of community – ecclesiastical, royal, monastic, chivalric – England has complex and capacious boundaries which resist any literal or material instantiation: hence the symbolic value of Becket's death.

The Becket legend underscores the remarkable way in which the *SEL* imagines English community as defined by what it does not have in common, rather than by what it does: by the particular categories of identity and community that structure the lives of individuals, by the various kinds of time that pace social, historical and religious existence, and by the different ways in which communities are imagined – through a representative or exceptional exemplar, or the mapping of place, or an expression of feeling, by the presence of a sacred object or the performance of a shared ritual. The Becket legend – in the translation story at least – privileges these last two, but it also provides a kind of conspectus of the rest, and so also a confirmation of the heterogeneity that it pretends to unify.

In the way that it theorizes community, the *SEL* may also suggest how we might think about its own status as a text. Liszka has made a powerful argument for the conceptual work that the title has done, encouraging us to treat the 'South English Legendary' as a stable term, despite the various and contingent features of its many redactions. Liszka closes his essay with a brief meditation on the competing claims of the idea and the particular, the *SEL* and *SELS* – the latter rubric still, as he demonstrates, inadequate owing to the way that it erases the *temporale* material. This essay has insisted on the importance of the *SEL*, that is, the idea of the work, as we can identify it in its formal concerns, shared broadly by many of the texts that make up the tradition. But this *SEL*, I hope to have shown, itself insists that particulars, while participating in a whole, are not subsumed by it: one exemplar cannot simply stand as a synecdoche for the general category. It gives us a way to think about heterogeneity as the correlative of the category shift we must make in order to think about a literary work in a manuscript culture, or human community in any era.

My reading of the *SEL* affiliates it with what Emily Steiner has called the 'political aesthetic' of the late Middle Ages: the contribution that poets made through formal experimentation to explorations of the nature of political community.[43] For the *SEL*, the formal provocation for thinking anew about community is the multi-part narrative collection, whose constituent parts are too heterogeneous for any one part to stand for the whole. Itself organized through an open paradigm of time, the *SEL* may encourage us to think about its idea of community not as the prehistory of more fully national texts like the *Kalendre of the New Legende of England*, but as a challenge to the synecdochic logic that imagines the nation as subsuming and co-ordinating the diverse communities that inhabit and extend beyond it.

Notes

I am grateful to the editors of this volume, to Micheal Vaughan and Claire Waters, and to the audience at the 'Rethinking the *South English*

Legendary' panel (Kalamazoo, 2007) for insightful and generous responses to earlier versions of this essay, and to Angela McClain for diligent assistance with research.

1 On the *SEL* as the first multi-part narrative collection in Middle English, see Christopher Cannon, *Middle English Literature* (Cambridge: Polity Press, 2008), p. 160, and Thompson, *Everyday Saints*, pp. 115–35.

2 Liszka, *SELS*.

3 As Liszka argues, the Prologue supplies a 'unity and theme to the collection' still not fully explored, and this notional unity is preserved in the later revision. Indeed, it is in some ways enhanced by the incorporation of *temporale* material into the calendrical ordering that follows the Prologue (Liszka, 'The first "A" redaction', p. 407).

4 D'Evelyn and Mill set out to present the earliest 'orderly' text of the *SEL* (D'Evelyn and Mill, I, p. v). This represents only part of the manuscript tradition, and, as Liszka suggests, may distort our sense of the *SEL* (Liszka, *SELS*, pp. 255–60, pp. 35–40 above).

5 According to D'Evelyn and Mill, p. 1. Görlach, *Textual Tradition*, does not supply information about the title given to this item.

6 This metaphor thus also embraces the *temporale* material. I suggest some of the ways in which this material is important to the representation of time and its relationship to community below (pp. 217–2), but this essay focuses primarily on the *sanctorale*.

7 *The Kalendre of the New Legende of England*, ed. Manfred Görlach (Heidelberg: Carl Winter Universitätsverlag, 1994).

8 On the 'vernacular heterogeneity' of the *SEL* and the 'diversity of interests and polities' with which it is correlated, see Lesley Johnson and Jocelyn Wogan-Browne, 'National, world and women's history: writers and readers of English in post-Conquest England', in David Wallace (ed.), *Cambridge History of Medieval English Literature* (Cambridge: Cambridge University Press, 1999), p. 106.

9 *Kenelm*, I, 280–1, 10–74: see further Breckenridge in this volume; Hamelinck, 'St Kenelm', 26–7, and Frederick, 'National identity', p. 67.

10 I discuss briefly below how the legend addresses the nature of English community through its representation of the consequences of the Conquest. Its historiographical interests extend to the causes of the Conquest (I, 10, 75–80).

11 I, 211, 1–4. On the role of genealogy see Paul Acker, 'Saint Mildred in the *South English Legendary*', in Jankofsky, pp. 140–53, at p. 143.

12 D'Evelyn and Mill, II, 357–8, 17–28.

13 On the *SEL*'s parallels between Edmund and Henry III and Becket and Henry II, see Thompson, *Everyday Saints*, p. 51.

14 This scene is significantly different in what Hermann Thiemke identifies as the 'a' version of the prologue to the Becket legend, found in MS

Laud 108, Stowe 949, Lambeth 223 and the Vernon manuscript: there, the princess asks Gilbert all at once about his name, his faith and his land: Thiemke, *Die me. Thomas Beket-legende des Gloucesterlegendars* (Berlin: Mayer and Müller, 1919), p. 3.

15 In making this argument, I assume that the Amiraud's use of 'lawe' points primarily to secular law, as contrasted to the princess's interest in Christianity. But the term can also refer to religion, and the ambiguity here is thematically important: the Becket legend addresses precisely the question of religious and secular jurisdiction in England, as if in an extended historical response to the Saracen prince about the nature of English law.

16 Arjun Appadurai, *Modernity at Large: Cultural Dimensions of Globalization* (Minneapolis: University of Minnesota Press, 1996), esp. chap. 2, pp. 27–47.

17 Appadurai contrasts the scalar or spatial understanding of community to a 'contextual' one, defined by intimate webs of sociality and 'technologies of interactivity' (p.178). He suggests how a scalar understanding is essential to the nation, which produces local communities as 'exemplars of a generalizable mode of belonging to a wider territorial imaginary' (p. 191).

18 Jankofsky, 'National characteristics', p. 91.

19 Thorlac Turville-Petre, *England the Nation: Language, Literature and National Identity* (Oxford: Clarendon Press, 1996), p. 66.

20 Alison Chapman, 'Now and then: sequencing the sacred in two Protestant calendars', *Journal of Medieval and Early Modern Studies*, 33 (2003), 91–123 (100).

21 Cf. Samson, 'Constructing a context', which argues against reading the *SEL* as a *liber festivalis* (pp. 187–90).

22 Jacobus explains that the calendar begins with Advent, the time of renewal, even though in 'sequence of time' it is preceded by the time of 'deviation', the period from Adam to Moses, represented in the liturgy by the interval between Septuagesima and Easter. The Church is not bound by temporal sequence, as Jacobus reminds us; rather, because the season of Advent 'is designated the time of renewal and recall . . . it is proper for the Church to renew the sequence of her offices with this season': Jacobus de Voragine, *Golden Legend*, trans. William Granger Ryan (Princeton: Princeton University Press, 1993), I. 4.

23 Samson also notes the unusual choice of 1 January, 'Constructing a context', p. 189n. See also Thomas Heffernan, 'Additional evidence for a more precise date of the "South English Legendary"', *Traditio*, 35 (1979), 345–51 (348n) for three *SEL* manuscripts beginning with the first Sunday of Advent (348n).

24 See R. T. Hampson, *Medii Aevi Kalendarium* (London: Henry Kent Causton, 1841), 2.408–9; cf. Heffernan, 'Additional evidence', 348n.

25 See Kathleen Biddick, *Typological Imaginary: Circumcision, Technology, History* (Philadelphia: University of Pennsylvania Press, 2003).

26 The role of these two Christic feasts in establishing a framework for the relationship between the native and non-native saints' lives is one way we might recognize the significance of the A redactor's co-ordination of *temporale* and *sanctorale* material in the collection.

27 Chapman, 'Now and then', p. 94.

28 Chapman bases her argument on Cranmer's non-typological structuring of readings in the Book of Common Prayer ('Now and then', pp. 110–11). The *SEL*, whose calendar form also eschews typology as the structure of time, produces a similarly open temporality.

29 On the calendar tradition, see Hampson, *Medii Aevi Kalendarium*, pp. 389–472.

30 This is a central argument of Thompson, *Everyday Saints*.

31 Chapman, 'Now and then' argues that such a conjunction makes space for secular time.

32 His study of Laud 108 has led Thomas Liszka to argue that the Becket legend was initially intended as the first item in the *sanctorale* section and to read the Laud prologue as a 'supplement' to *Becket*. Liszka's analysis suggests how crucial the placement of the Becket legend is to the conception of the *SEL* in both its early and late stages. Liszka discerns another provisional order, beginning with the more expected 25 November, in MS Laud 108: Liszka, 'MS Laud Misc.108 and the early history of the *South English Legendary*', *Manuscripta*, 33 (1989), 75–91.

33 Görlach, *Textual Tradition*, p. 217. Görlach notes that the legend of Sylvester, celebrated on 31 December, is not included in most of the A MSS and suggests that it is omitted because it would be an 'anticlimax' after the Becket legend.

34 According to Anne Duggan, the Saracen legend surfaces in the early thirteenth century, not long after Thomas's translation: Duggan, 'The Lyell Version of the *Quadrilogus* Life of St Thomas of Canterbury', *Analecta Bollandiana*, 112 (1994), 107, 112–13.

35 My account of the Order of St Thomas depends on A. J. Forey, 'The military order of St Thomas of Acre', *English Historical Review*, 92 (1977), 481–503.

36 Lawrence Warner suggests that Londoners' curiosity about the Church of St Thomas of Acre explains the origin of the legend: 'Becket and the hopping bishops', *Yearbook of Langland Studies*, 17 (2003), 107–34, at 124. To my mind, the legend provides a more specific association with the devotional protocols of the order than with the London church, but Warner's demonstration of the continuing interest in Becket's affiliation with the Muslim east in *Piers Plowman*, in the waning days of the Order of Thomas of Acon, suggests how central that affiliation may have been for early audiences of the *SEL*.

37 The scene of martyrdom also develops this trope: see Cannon, *Middle English Literature*, p. 159.
38 'Dixit idem episcopus, quod esset miles Christi, et pro Deo et S. Thoma martyri, Cantuariensi archiepiscopo, in clericali ordine militaret', AA.SS October 1, col. 544D, cited by Anne Duggan, 'The cult of St Thomas Becket in the thirteenth century', in *Thomas Becket: Friends, Networks, Texts and Cult* (Aldershot: Ashgate, 2007), p. 44.
39 On the *SEL*'s political affiliation with the Barons' Revolt, see Heffernan, 'Dangerous sympathies', in Jankofsky, pp. 1–17, reprinted below pp. 295–312.
40 See C.L. Kingsford, *The Song of Lewes* (Oxford: Clarendon Press, 1890), p. 85 n. 358. The belief that Becket offered saintly assistance at Lewes may inform the selection of materials in British Library MS Harley 978, the miscellany that contains the Song of Lewes, the most important political poem about the Barons' Revolt. The book also contains Latin and French versions of the story of Becket's parentage, as well as other texts regarding the saint, in implicit analogy between Becket's opposition to Henry II and Simon's opposition to Henry III. Kingsford provides a list of the manuscript's contents, pp. xi–xvii. For a recent discussion of this book and representations of Simon de Montfort himself as a 'second Becket', see Andrew Taylor, *Textual Situations: Three Medieval Manuscripts and Their Readers* (Philadelphia: University of Pennsylvania Press, 2002), p. 125.
41 Hamelinck, 'St Kenelm', p. 24.
42 On the tradition of Becket's Tuesdays, see Kay Brainerd Slocum, *Liturgies in Honour of Thomas Becket* (Toronto: University of Toronto Press, 2004), pp. 247–55. Slocum shows that the liturgical celebration of Becket's Tuesdays – of which there are seven – emphasizes their numerological significance in the context of post-Conquest thought about the special role of England in the Apocalypse.
43 Emily Steiner, '*Piers Plowman*, diversity, and the medieval political aesthetic', *Representations*, 91 (2005), 1–25.

10

Counting noses and assessing the numbers: native saints in the *South English Legendaries*

Virginia Blanton

Thomas R. Liszka has shown that the collection known as the *South English Legendary* is not a united whole but more an amorphous grouping of feast days, one that shifts and changes depending upon the manuscript in which it is preserved.[1] A concentrated thematic focus in one manuscript might look very different in another grouping, from which fixed or moveable feasts have been omitted and legends of other saints added. Of course, fragments of manuscripts confuse the issue further. Thus, it is difficult to speak generally about the whole collection, especially when some lives appear only in a few manuscripts. My interest in the *SELS* centres on the native saints included therein, some of whom may have been incorporated when the source text, *Legenda aurea*, was translated into English while others may have circulated in an English legendary before the advent of Jacobus de Voragine's collection.[2] When frequency of appearances is considered, the most compelling legends are epitomes of native female saints, such as Æthelthryth and Mildred: simply because they appear in very few copies of the *SEL*, one wonders about the reasons for their inclusion. Little attention has been directed at these native figures, even though several scholars have provided readings of native male saints as evidence of an interest in a 'nationalist agenda', sometimes for the *SEL* as a whole.[3] This essay seeks to bring into the conversation the native female saints' legends in the *SELS*, to challenge the essentialist arguments put forward about male saints as representative, and to suggest another way to view the inclusion of the legends of native saints in the *SEL*. In particular, I aim to consider what the presence of epitomes about native women (and about the native men who appear alongside them in particular manuscripts) offers when we think about how the *SELS* originated, developed and evolved into a complex set of manuscripts. The first section below provides some data about the occurrences of native saints in the *SELS*, indicating the relatively common appearance of legends of native males and the particularly rare appearances of legends of native females. The second section then discusses the native male and female saints featured within what Manfred Görlach has termed the 'E' branch of the *SEL* stemma, where some of the rarest native legends survive. I demonstrate below how the calendar order of each native feast and the geographical location of each cult provide some indication of a regional focus in this small grouping of manuscripts. This work is not intended as a definitive discussion of these native legends; instead, it is designed to offer new avenues of inquiry and to issue a call for further work on the native legends in this collection.[4]

The sum of its parts

Within the surviving twenty-six manuscripts, nineteen 'fragmented' collections, and twenty single items of the *SEL*, there is considerable variation among the contents, which makes an assessment of the native saints featured in them difficult.[5] Table 10.1 provides a list of the known native figures featured (or lost), their feast days and the locations where they were principally culted, as well as the manuscripts in which they appear.[6] Hamelinck notes that nearly one-fifth of all the legends of the *SEL* are about English saints.[7] Of these, twenty-four are about native males and seven are about native females (although we might also include Helen, Augustine and Birin, non-native saints whose cults were celebrated as if they were native; as a point of interest these are marked out by angle brackets in the table). The great majority of the native saints are figures of the Anglo-Saxon church. Outside of the two native males who were regularly included in the *Legenda aurea* (Thomas Becket and Patrick), the native males most commonly celebrated include episcopal and royal figures. The list below provides some examples of the most popular saints, as evidenced by the appearance of their legends in multiple copies of the *SEL*. Included next to each saint's name is the number of manuscripts or fragments in which the legend occurs.

Wulfstan, bishop of Worcester	21
Edward the elder, king of Wessex	20
Bishop Oswald, archbishop of York	20
Dunstan, archbishop of Canterbury	18
Edmund, king of East Anglia	16

Table 10.1 Native saints' legends in the collective *SEL* manuscripts and fragments[1]

Date	Saint	Sigla	Place
5 January	Edward the Confessor	AJB	Westminster
19 January	Wulfstan		Worcester
1 February	Brigid	*Legenda aurea*	Kildare
19 February	Oswald bp		Worcester
2 March	Chad		Lichfield
17 March	Patrick	*Legenda aurea*	Dun, Saul
18 March	Edward k&m		Shaftesbury
20 March	Cuthbert		Lindisfarne, Durham
11 April	Guthlac*	#JBC+	Repton, Crowland
19 April	Alphege		Winchester
<3 May	Helen	GHxM+	Colchester>
11 May	Fremund	V²S	Cropredy, Dunstable
16 May	Brendan		Ardfert, Iona, Clonfert
19 May	Dunstan		Glastonbury, Canterbury
20 May	Æthelberht*	ERVJJ+	Hereford, East Anglia
25 May	Aldhelm		Malmesbury, Sherborne
<26 May	Augustine		Canterbury>
15 June	Eadburh	EVB	Winchester
17 June	Botulf*	EVRB	Boston
22 June	Alban		St Albans
23 June	Æthelthryth*	EVB	Ely
9 July	Swithun		Winchester
13 July	Mildred*	EVBWa	Thanet
17 July	Kenelm	#	Winchcombe
1 August	Æthelwold*	#QaVGRR+WaB	Winchester
5 August	Oswald k&m		Durham
20 August	Oswin	B	Tynemouth
19 October	Frideswide	#V²AJPBSRWa	Oxford
21 October	Ursula	*Legenda aurea*	Cologne
3 November	Winifred	B	Shrewsbury
16 November	Edmund bp		Abingdon
20 November	Edmund k		Bury St Edmunds
<3 December	Birin	ODBJRWa	Winchester>
29 December	Thomas Becket	*Legenda aurea*	Canterbury
30 December	Ecgwine*	VESQaJ	Ramsey, Evesham, Worcester

Notes:

1   The shaded lines indicate those saints included in the 'E' branch of the *SEL*. An asterisk marks the saints whose cults are attested in East Anglia and Kent. A number sign notes that more than one version of a legend exists. Angle brackets set off those non-native saints who were culted in England as if they were native. The sigla used here are from Manfred Görlach, *The Textual Tradition*.

2   Fremund and Frideswide are lost from V, as indicated by its index.

By comparison, Thomas Becket, archbishop of Canterbury, whose feast was celebrated throughout western Europe, is featured in twenty-three separate manuscripts. That some of the native male legends appear nearly as often in recensions of the *SEL* as Becket's legend indicates that there was a particular interest in adding them.

When we compare the number of native males to native females in these manuscripts, the female saints are far less frequently honoured, a fact that parallels the whole collection of *SEL* manuscripts where males outnumber females four to one.[8] Not including Brigid of Ireland or Ursula, who were featured in copies of the *Legenda aurea* on the continent and who seem to appear in the *SEL* (in twenty-one and thirteen manuscripts respectively) because of a more universal devotion, the native women of the *SEL*, who are almost entirely women religious of aristocratic or royal status, rarely appear: Frideswide, abbess of a nunnery in Oxford, is included in seven manuscripts and one fragment; Mildred, abbess of Minster-in-Thanet, in three manuscripts plus one fragment; Æthelthryth, abbess of Ely, and Eadburh, abbess of Nunnaminster, Winchester, merit three manuscripts each; and Winifred, abbess of Holywell, is featured in only one manuscript.[9] A comparison between the universal female saints honoured in the *SEL* and the local women illustrates a considerable difference, suggesting that female saints were not neglected wholesale but that native females were: Katherine of Alexandria and Margaret, the most popular saints in late medieval England, appear in eighteen manuscripts each; Faith, another well-regarded saint from France, appears in eleven. By contrast, the disparity between the universal and native male saints is negligible: Peter and Paul appear in seventeen manuscripts and the martyrs Stephen and John the Baptist are featured in sixteen. This simple accounting leads to several important conclusions regarding this form of textual devotion to the saints:

- When adapting universal lives from the *Legenda aurea* for inclusion in the *SEL*, English clerics demonstrate a significant interest in including native male saints and their focus seems to have been on Anglo-Saxon episcopal and royal figures.
- The 4:1 ratio of all male to female saints in the *SEL* is significantly better than the ratio in one source text, the *Legenda aurea*, which is 6:1; the ratio of native males to native females remains the same at roughly 4:1.

- Individual native male saints appear as regularly as the universal saints, both male and female, in these manuscripts (Wulfstan, who is in twenty-one of the extant manuscripts, seems to have been copied as often as Katherine at eighteen appearances and John the Baptist at sixteen), which is suggestive about the measure of local devotion being reflected or encouraged by the compiler and revisers of the *SEL*; but
- Native female saints are featured sporadically at best and appear in only a few branches of the *SEL* stemma as outlined by Görlach; the majority of these legends are included in the 'E' branch.

These observations are suggestive about the nature of devotion to native saints as the *SEL* was first compiled and later as it was circulated in multiple recensions among various audiences. We might conclude that in addition to, or instead of, a nationalist agenda, the multiple manuscripts are providing information about the popularity of individual cults. That is, if a native saint appears multiple times, it is evidence of a highly attested cult. When we compare the number of church dedications (often seen as a register of 'popular devotion') to those saints who appear in the largest number of *SEL* manuscripts – and I fully grant that church dedications may be an entirely different kind of register of devotion from *vitae* and thus not comparable – we see only one exception to that theory: Botulf, abbot of Icanho, who is featured in only four *SEL* manuscripts, has sixty-four church dedications.[10] A comparison between appearances and church dedications shows, with this exception, a decided correlation: Eadburh with six dedications appears in three manuscripts and Ecgwine, bishop of Worcester, with two dedications appears in four manuscripts. Likewise, Frideswide appears in eight manuscripts but has only two church dedications. At the other extreme, male saints who were most commonly attested saints in church dedications (Cuthbert, Bishop Oswald, King Edmund, Swithun, Chad and Dunstan) are those featured most often in the *SEL* manuscripts.

The disparity between male lives and female lives in the *SEL* and male and female saints as dedicatees of parish churches might indicate that the shrine cults of these female saints were not as significant to lay devotees or that the narratives about native females were less popular among religious and lay readers. Other collections of saints' lives, however, demonstrate that a more complex series of considerations may exist for some, if not all of these, cults. As I note elsewhere, the cult of Æthelthryth was densely attested throughout East Anglia, and shrine receipts from 1300 to 1400 illustrate an impressive pilgrimage cult, one that exceeded the receipts for seemingly more 'popular' male saints such as Cuthbert.[11] Similarly, the multiple narratives written about Æthelthryth (in Latin, Anglo-Norman and Middle English) demonstrate that her story was widely circulated among various groups. Other legendaries also support the view that readings about native women were valued, particularly in collections intended for female houses. In a thirteenth and early fourteenth-century vernacular collection owned by the nuns at Campsey Ash Priory in Suffolk (London, British Library Add. MS 70513), Anglo-Norman lives of native saints are presented alongside the lives of universal saints and two regional saints from other European countries. Of the thirteen lives in this manuscript, more than half are native figures: Thomas Becket, Edward the Confessor, Edmund Rich, Richard of Chichester, Æthelthryth, Osith and Modwenna.[12] Likewise, the fourteenth-century Latin legendary owned by the nunnery at Romsey (London, British Library, Lansdowne MS 436) features lives of forty-seven native saints of whom one-third, or sixteen, are native women. The contents of these two legendaries indicate that attention to native women was important in fourteenth-century nunneries, where texts were read in Latin and in French. Evidence from John of Tynemouth's *Sanctilogium Angliae*, a collection of native lives written in Latin and circulated among Benedictine monasteries, confirms that, when legendaries were almost entirely focused on native saints, interest in reading about native women continued but not at the same level. Of the 172 total saints featured, only thirty-three are female (a 5:1 ratio).[13] Still, legendaries such as Osbern Bokenham's *Legendys of Hooly Wommen* (London, British Library MS Arundel 327), which contains thirteen female lives, indicate that female readership, both lay and religious, helped to drive interest in female saints. Likewise, of the twenty-two lives included in Cambridge University Library Add. MS 2604, nineteen are about female saints. Like Bokenham's collection, we can tie this collection to an East Anglian community of nuns.[14] Thus, the evidence from other legendaries suggests that when female saints appear in a given collection, the intended readership was female, and one wonders if we might conclude, as Görlach has done, that the *SEL* manuscripts in which native females appear were intended for a female audience. He has suggested that the earliest versions of the *SEL* were produced for the devotional reading of nuns, speculating that many of the English lives were included when the collection was first organized near Worcester. Görlach contends that over time, as a lay audience was targeted, these female saints (who were aristocratic nuns) were weeded out to meet the requirements of non-monastic female readers.[15] This suggestion would account for the relative paucity of native females in the *SEL* overall and their rare appearance in the individual manuscripts. Might we also conclude, therefore, that the many recensions of the *SEL* were intended for a male audience, since most do not include native female legends?

The existing data allow us to pose some additional possibilities. In one case, native women seem to have been added to the *SEL* when there was a deliberate effort to represent many native saints (such as the sole appearance of Winifred and Oswin in Oxford, Bodley MS 779) or when local devotion prompted the writer to include a favoured saint (such as Helen in London, Lambeth Palace MS 223, which was produced for an individual).[16] The eight manuscripts that feature Frideswide suggest that locale also mattered. Her cult at Oxford lay in close proximity to the region of production for the *SEL* (Worcestershire and Gloucestershire), and it may be the reason she was honoured more frequently than other native women (about which I will say more below). Or, the contexts of each life might hold the key, as the lives of the women featured are fairly similar: they resist marriage and devote themselves to the monastic life. All of these are strong possibilities, ones that will require a corporate effort to study the lives individually and collectively before making a claim about their value. That said, I would like to suggest that the geography of the native cults provides some evidence about the nature of the survivals, for the 'E' branch shows a strong affinity with the cults of East Anglia and Kent, and may indicate that a regional association informs the production and dissemination of these manuscripts, as the following demonstrates.

The parts of the sum

Column four of Table 10.1 provides a list of the principal locations where the native saints were culted. The third column highlights the manuscripts in which these native lives appear, using the sigla set out by Görlach. If a legend was included in recensions of the *Legenda aurea*, as are those of Brigid, Patrick, Ursula and Thomas Becket, it is noted in order to distinguish these lives from those added after the *Legenda aurea* arrived in England and, thus, to distinguish these legends from those that are indicative of a particularly English devotion. A blank in column three indicates that the legend is repeated in a significant number of manuscripts in various branches of the *SEL* and for most this blank is also an indication that they were included in the *Legenda aurea*. While an analysis of the patterns in which these more common legends of native figures in the *SEL* is warranted, the popularity of these legends is not the focus here.

Instead, I am centring my attention on the thirteen saints whose feasts are highlighted by a shaded line. This notation means that the saint does not appear in the *Legenda aurea* and is featured in only a few copies of the *SEL*. These manuscripts are listed in the third column. Edward the Confessor, the first name that is shaded, features in only three manuscripts: A, J and B. Guthlac, the second name so highlighted, is found in J, B and C[+]. Because these thirteen occur rarely in the *SEL* manuscripts, the presence of one of these saints' legends in any given manuscript provides some indication of localized interest, for it means that it was intentionally added to the collection at some point. Studying the patterns and considering the connections among the manuscripts may help us uncover more information about devotion to these saints, both about the intentions of the copyists and about the reading practices or preferences of the readers of the *SEL*.

When the manuscripts for each of the thirteen legends are examined, we see that these saints generally appear in related manuscripts of the 'E' branch, which includes four manuscripts dated to the fourteenth century:

> E = London, British Library MS Egerton 1993, c. 1325–50
> V = Oxford, Bodleian Library MS Eng. poet.a.1, c. 1385 (the 'Vernon Manuscript')
> B = Oxford, Bodleian Library MS Bodley 779, c. 1400
> R = Cambridge, Trinity College MS 605 (R.3.25), c. 1400

Of these manuscripts, Bodley 779 is 'a copy of a late collector, who drew upon three of the known textual traditions of the SEL, but also included some 37 unique items. Script and make-up of the book suggest that it was assembled by a non-professional scribe and made for private reading'.[17] I might add that it seems to have been compiled to feature native saints, for it contains ten of the thirteen shaded in Table 10.1; Æthelberht (king of East Anglia), Ecgwine (bishop of Worcester) and Fremund (archbishop of Canterbury) are not included, but all five of the female saints are. It is also exceptional in that the ratio of native males to native females in the manuscript is 3:1, better than any other compilation. If Görlach is correct about the intended audience, this would be an interesting conclusion regarding an individual's interest in native saints at the beginning of the fifteenth century. Still, Görlach notes that a good number of the additions to this manuscript are of legends of popes, so it may be the collector was trying for representative coverage, rather than focusing on a particular devotional interest

The other manuscripts in the 'E' branch have fewer native females: the Vernon manuscript has four; Egerton 1993 has three, and Cambridge, Trinity College MS 605 has one, Frideswide. Of interest, Egerton 1993, which is the earliest manuscript in this family, has Æthelberht, Eadburh, Botulf, Æthelthryth, Mildred and Ecgwine, or six of the thirteen saints under discussion. The Vernon manuscript is quite similar to Egerton 1993, adding Æthelwold and Ecgwine for a total of eight saints from this list. Trinity College MS 605 contains the fewest native saints from this list, only four: Æthelberht, Botulf, Æthelwold and Frideswide.

This table shows that most of the thirteen legends are featured only in three or four manuscripts, several in only one or two. Frideswide, then, is exceptional in that her life is attested in seven copies, with an eighth now lost from the Vernon manuscript. This number is a bit misleading, since there are two distinct versions of the Middle English life, both drawn from Latin accounts. Sherry Reames has edited both Middle English versions, identifying them as the 'shorter' and the 'longer' versions.[18] The shorter is included in two manuscripts and one fragment;[19] the longer version is attested in four manuscripts.[20] Reames demonstrates that the shorter version, which focuses on Frideswide's royalty, her virginity and her vocation as a nun, seems oriented towards a monastic audience, and that the longer version, which 'provides clear lessons on good and bad conduct for laymen',[21] seems to be more appropriate for a lay audience. This division shows that, when a version was disseminated, it had a limited circulation similar to other legends of native female saints. It also provides some suggestion about a legend now lost. The index to the Vernon manuscript indicates that a legend of Frideswide was originally included. Reames's assessment of the audiences for the two versions of Frideswide's life suggests that this lost version was most likely the shorter one, since the Vernon manuscript seems to have been used in a nunnery and the shorter life would have been more appropriate to an audience of nuns. Such a conclusion would confirm Görlach's finding of a tangential connection between the 'G' branch, where the shorter lives of Frideswide appear, and the 'E' branch, where the majority of the other native females are featured, even as it would push us to think further about the possible connections between the 'E' and 'G' branches.

As the example of Frideswide demonstrates, we need to compare the copies of individual lives to establish the nature of each. Are they exact copies, slight modifications or completely different versions? Is an intended audience clear? Do modifications suggest an alternative audience? What are the sources for the life? Or for different versions of the same life? Do the lives follow the pattern for liturgical texts, such as lections for a feast day? Do they provide material that informs other native lives? Do they help us see connections among the branches of the *SEL* stemma? To begin to answer these questions, it is important that we edit the native saints' lives that were not included in the D'Evelyn and Mill volumes, published in 1956. Only a few editions of these native legends have been published, all independently.[22] If all were to be edited and published collectively, we would be in a better place to examine the source texts and consider when these native lives came into the *SEL*, even as we could then think about the relationships among the native legends and their collective contributions.

Görlach initiated some of this work, when he examined the native lives in relation to other liturgical texts. He found that the lives in the 'E' branch show 'distinct non-Sarum affiliations, including as [the 'E' branch] does a great number of Hereford/ Worcester saints', those whose relics were in Worcester or those whose feasts were highly celebrated in Worcester.[23] Where comparisons between the lessons of the Sarum Use and legends in the *SEL* have proved moderately successful for some of the native saints, no legendary or liturgical text has been found that could be the source text for the native legends in the 'E' branch.[24] Discovering the source texts then seems to be a requirement and one that may have to be accomplished on a case-by-case basis. My own work on the cult of Æthelthryth shows that there are four distinct Middle English versions of her life: one written in quatrains contained in a manuscript owned by Wilton Abbey (London, British Library MS Cotton Faustina B.iii); the second, a translation of John of Tynemouth's Latin prose life, (Cambridge University Library MS

Add. 2604); the third, a prose translation from the *Liber Eliensis* (Oxford, Corpus Christi College MS 120) and the fourth, the metrical version in the *SEL*.[25] The source for the *SEL* version seems to be Bede's Latin life, which is stripped down to its essential details. The source for John of Tynemouth's version is Bede but indirectly via Goscelin of St Bertin. By contrast, the Wilton Abbey version is extensively elaborated, including dialogue and a theological argument about the benefits of chastity that do not appear elsewhere.[26] This seems to indicate that the *SEL* version was directly adapted from Bede's Latin narrative and was not influenced by another Middle English version. Could this mean that some or all of the native legends of the 'E' branch come directly from Latin sources? Or, does it mean that the native female legends may have done so? If so, it may well help to determine which monastic libraries had copies of all of the native legends included in the 'E' branch. Perhaps this would help us sort out where the adaptations could have been made – and by extension where these manuscripts were copied and for whom. We would also have to revisit Görlach's idea that these native legends were circulating in a legendary prior to the appearance of the *Legenda aurea* in England and consider which, if any, seem to show evidence that would prove or disprove his suggestion.

I want to point out two other possible lines of enquiry. Returning to Table 10.1, we see that this collective grouping of feast days presents celebrations throughout the calendar year. Collectively, there is a certain regularity between the feasts, roughly every ten to fourteen days, which likely means little since all do not appear together in these manuscripts (with the exception of Bodley 779). There is a tiny gap between 20 March and 11 April and another between 26 May and 15 June. There is a significant gap between 20 August and 19 October. Particularly interesting about this list is the cluster of ten saints specific to the 'E' branch between 11 April and 3 November. While two fall outside of this period, the great majority are grouped in a range that is often termed the summer calendar, which runs from Easter to Advent (and which is variable depending on the dating of Easter).[27] Æthelberht, Eadburh, Botulf, Æthelthryth, and Mildred, moreover, appear in regular combinations in the 'E' branch, which seems to indicate some original interest in adding native feasts to the summer calendar when Egerton 1993 was compiled. It has been noted that the summer calendar is not as full in the *Legenda aurea* and this might be one reason for this concentration of native legends. The large gap

Table 10.2 Native saints whose feasts might reasonably have been in the
         SEL[1]

3 April	Richard bp	Chichester (canonized 1262)
30 April	Erkenwald	London
7 May	John of Beverley	Hexham, York
8 June	William bp	York (canonized 1227)
12 September	Eanswyth*	Folkestone
16 September	Edith	Wilton
3 October	Thomas bp	Hereford (canonized 1320)
7 October	Osyth*	Chich
11 October	Æthelburh	Barking
12 October	Wilfrid	York
17 November	Hild	Glastonbury, Durham
17 November	Hugh bp	Lincoln (canonized 1220)

Note: 1 * indicates those saints whose cults are attested in East Anglia and Kent

following 20 August, the feast of King Oswin, is also intriguing, as
this leaves no devotion to native saints until 19 October, the feast
of Frideswide. The cluster of summer feasts, therefore, may be
an indication of how native legends were added when the *Legenda
aurea* was introduced into England. Or, it may be representative of
a previously circulating summer calendar.

Looking at which saints' legends are included is one way of proceeding, but thinking about which legends are not featured in manuscripts of the *SEL* is also revealing. Table 10.2 presents the feasts
of several native saints that could easily be included in the calendar.
All of these feasts were attested in late medieval English devotion.
Seven are Anglo-Saxon figures, the majority female saints. The
others are all episcopal saints who were canonized between 1220
and 1320, just as the *SEL* collection was produced and disseminated. We might reasonably assume that these new cults would
be celebrated in a legendary produced in Middle English, yet
none of these new saints is included. Equally pertinently, saints
such as Edith of Wilton and Æthelburh of Barking were culted at
very prominent female houses both before and after the Norman
Conquest, yet their legends are not featured either. Why are these
female saints not included? Were the universal feasts in this part
of the calendar so concentrated they were not needed? Were these
cults just not as important at the time? Or might there be some
connection between cult location and legends included that would
indicate why the saints of the 'E' branch were chosen?

The location of the cults that had feasts during the summer months is suggestive, for the great majority of them were culted in eastern England, either in East Anglia or in Kent. By culted, I mean here that these saints were celebrated in this area, either because of the location of their relics or because churches and guilds were dedicated to them. In both Table 10.1 and Table 10.2, these cults are indicated by an asterisk. These include Guthlac, Æthelberht (who was murdered near Hereford but whose cult was highly attested in East Anglia where he had been king), Botulf, Æthelthryth, Mildred and Æthelwold (the bishop of Winchester who refounded the East Anglian monasteries of Ely, Peterborough and Ramsey in the late tenth century). In addition, Ecgwine, whose feast of 30 December lies outside of this temporal range, was also culted at Ramsey in East Anglia. Eadburh, whose feast was celebrated at Winchester, had a mother from Kent, and her cult might well have been celebrated in the fenland monasteries refounded by Bishop Æthelwold. Figure 10.1 shows the locations of these cults. To be sure, the cults of eastern England were less likely to have been included in the original compilation or in the multiple recensions of the *SEL*, since it originated in the Gloucester/Worcester region. As noted above, Görlach suggests that a now-lost breviarium from Worcester, which included lections for many of these saints, may be the source for these lives. Given the geographical locations of these cults, we might also look for an East Anglian source text, one that included these lives and, by extension, a monastery that was associated with them. We might also search for an East Anglian monk relocated to the western Midlands whose allegiances to his regional saints were manifested in his compilation of an *SEL* manuscript that already featured saints in some type of 'nationalist agenda'. I note that the lives of Æthelthryth, Eadburh and Mildred stress their regional homes in East Anglia, Wessex and Kent as much as if not more than, their identities as women 'ibore in Engelonde'.[28] There is not enough evidence here to indicate whether or not these native cults were featured in the earliest version of the *SEL* or were included in later redactions. We would need to trace further the veneration of these cults in the Hereford area, seeking evidence that shows these saints were important when the *SEL* was first developed or somewhat later as redactions were made. In either case, the present evidence suggests there was a compiler who had a strong interest in the so-called eastern cults, an interest, therefore, in regional identities rather than (or in addition to) national ones. If so, it might explain why other Anglo-Saxon

Figure 10.1 Locations of native saints' cults included in manuscripts of the 'E' branch

saints whose feasts would fit in the eleven-week gap between 20 August and 19 October were not included: the great majority of these feasts were not culted in eastern England (only Osyth and Eanswyth's feasts were, and these were relatively minor cults in the later Middle Ages).

One final point about the saints included or not is about the native saints who were canonized between 1220 and 1320: Richard of Chichester, William of York, Thomas of Hereford and Hugh of Lincoln, all bishops whose cults were emerging just before or during the compilation of the *SEL* manuscripts. There is one 'eastern' saint among them, Hugh. We might expect that his canonization in 1220 situated him well to be included as the *SEL* was translated and disseminated between 1300 and 1400. This did not happen, so we are left to wonder if the compiler of the 'E' branch was interested only in Anglo-Saxon or 'ancient' saints from the past, if he was particularly interested in royalty and sanctity, as many of these legends stress, or if he was working from a source text of native lives that dates to before 1220. It is all very puzzling, but I think we can assert that there was far more at work in adding native saints to the *SEL* than an interest in 'nationalism'. As I have stressed here, we have much work to do, teasing out the associations among various legends and among various branches of the *SEL* stemma. Looking more closely at regional associations might well prove to be a significant way to learn more about the copyists and readers of the particular manuscripts that make up the *SEL*, even as investigations into the legends of native saints may offer crucial new insights into the production of this collection.

Notes

1 Liszka, *SELS*. Liszka notes too that we tend to frame the *SEL* as a collection of saints' lives, neglecting the *temporale* completely, a truism that requires additional consideration. While it lies outside of the parameters of this discussion, it would be instructive to examine how and when the *temporale* is adjusted as native saints were added to the collection.

2 Manfred Görlach, 'The *Legenda aurea* and the early history of *The South English Legendary*', in Dunn-Lardeau, pp. 301–16. This essay summarizes his longer discussion in *Textual Tradition*.

3 Hamelinck, 'St Kenelm'; Jankofsky, 'National characteristics'; and Frederick, 'National identity'.

4 Some of these details about the *SEL* are taken from a shorter introduction to the *SEL* in my *Signs of Devotion: The Cult of St Æthelthryth in Medieval England, 695–1615* (University Park: Penn State Press, 2007), pp. 237–41.

5 I am very grateful to Thomas Liszka, whose expertise on this point is invaluable. Dr Liszka provided the first complete accounting of the various fragments and manuscripts (see his 'The dragon in the *South English Legendary*', *Modern Philology*, 100: (2002), 50–9, at 50–1 n. 2). He slightly revised that data in a private communication (August

2009), when I wrote to confirm the total number of manuscripts and manuscript fragments. He writes, 'There are 26 "major" manuscripts known (including the Takamiya), 19 fragments of *SEL* collections, and 20 single items in non-*SEL* contexts (including two fragments of Michael identified since Görlach's book). Then, I'd like to include three mss with temporale texts in non-*SEL* contexts, but Görlach doesn't. Thus, depending on how and what you count, the correct answer is 26, 65, or 68. When I made my totals, then, even though I mentioned the two Michael fragments in the footnote, I apparently didn't count them when I came up with 63 or 66 as a final total . . . Of course, if you count the fragments of the *SEL* mss plus the major mss you get 45. However, if you put mss back together that were once part of the same ms (M+Bd, Q+Qa+Ba, Pr+Wm, and Ua+Wa), you get 40. Then, of course, plus 20 and plus or not plus 3, gives you 60 or 63!'

6 To develop this table and to arrive at the numbers discussed in this section, I have relied on Liszka *SELS*, Görlach, *Textual Tradition*, as well as O. S. Pickering and Manfred Görlach, 'A newly-discovered manuscript of the *South English Legendary*', *Anglia*, 100 (1982), 109–23. For each saint he includes, Görlach indicates the number of appearances in full manuscripts and fragments, as well as notices of saints that appear in indices but whose lives are missing from the manuscript. He also notes manuscripts that likely had a legend that is now missing. I have included only the manuscripts, the fragments, and the notices of indices as evidence for the totals used here. There are other lists of saints in the *SEL* available, which have also been of use: Charlotte d'Evelyn and Frances A. Foster, 'Saints' legends', in J. Burke Severs (ed.), *A Manual of the Writings in Middle English, 1050–1500*, vol. 2 (New Haven: Connecticut Academy of Arts and Sciences, 1970); Carleton Brown, *A Register of Middle English Religious & Didactic Verse*, vol. 1 (Oxford: Oxford Bibliographical Society, 1916); and Horstmann. In addition, I extend my heart-felt thanks to Dr William Robins, who generously shared his unpublished work on the unique items in the *SEL* corpus, provided several important details that have enriched this discussion and corrected my list of saints. Any remaining errors are my own.

7 Hamelinck, 'St Kenelm', p. 21. The ratio of six males to every female in the *Legenda aurea* also shows this disparity.

8 Thompson, *Everyday Saints*, p. 153.

9 Worth noting is that even though Brigid and Ursula were included by Jacobus de Voragine, the inclusion of these figures in the *SEL* is not universal. There is a long and short version of the *Life of Brigid* and, collectively, she is honoured in nineteen manuscripts. Ursula is presented in only fourteen. These figures are significant when compared to the other native female saints, but they illustrate that the desire to represent native women in this collection was not a strong one.

10 Francis Bond, *Dedications and Patron Saints of English Churches: Ecclesiastical Symbolism, Saints and Their Emblems* (London: Oxford University Press, 1914).

11 Blanton, *Signs of Devotion*, pp. 248–9. For details on shrine receipts, see Benjamin J. Nilson, *Cathedral Shrines of Medieval England* (Woodbridge: Boydell Press, 2001), p. 239.

12 The thirteen lives occur in this order: Elizabeth of Hungary, Paphnutius, Paul the Hermit, Thomas Becket, Mary Magdalene, Edward the Confessor, Edmund the Confessor (Archbishop of Canterbury), Æthelthryth (here Audrée), Osith, Faith, Modwenna, Richard of Chichester, and Katherine of Alexandria. For a full description of the manuscript, see Delbert Russell, 'The Campsey collection of Old French saints' lives: a re-examination of its structure and provenance', *Scriptorium*, 57 (2003), 51–83.

13 The surviving manuscripts of this collection include: London, BL MS Cotton Tiberius E.i; London, BL MS Cotton Otho D.ix; Oxford, Bodleian MS Tanner 15; and Karlsruhe, Badische Landesbibliothek, MS St Georgen 12.

14 Several scholars have demonstrated the importance of female saints' lives among female readers, including: Karen A. Winstead, *Virgin Martyrs: Legends of Sainthood in Late Medieval England* (Ithaca: Cornell University Press, 1997), Sheila Delany, *Impolitic Bodies: Poetry, Saints, and Society in Fifteenth-Century England, the Work of Osbern Bokenham* (Oxford: Oxford University Press, 1998), Jocelyn Wogan-Browne, *Saints' Lives and Women's Literary Culture, c. 1150–1300: Virginity and Its Authorizations* (Oxford: Oxford University Press, 2001) and Katherine J. Lewis, *The Cult of St Katherine of Alexandria in Late Medieval England* (Woodbridge: Boydell, 2000). Cambridge University Library Add. MS 2604 is currently being edited by Veronica O'Mara and Virginia Blanton, and it features twenty-two lives in Middle English, half of which are native female saints' lives translated from John of Tynemouth's collection.

15 Görlach, *Textual Tradition*, pp. 32–8.

16 Ibid., pp. 82–3.

17 Ibid., p. 61.

18 Sherry Reames, with the assistance of Martha G. Blalock and Wendy R. Larson (eds), *Middle English Legends of Women Saints* (Kalamazoo, MI: Medieval Institute Publications, 2003), pp. 23–5. See also D'Evelyn and Foster, *Manual*, p. 588.

19 London, BL MS Stowe 949 (S); Cambridge, Trinity College MS 605 (R); plus a very fragmentary third copy, Aberystwyth, National Library of Wales MS 5043 (Wa).

20 Oxford, Bodleian MS Ashmole 43 (A); London, BL MS Cotton Julius D.ix (J); Cambridge, Magdalene College MS Pepys 2344 (P); and Oxford, Bodleian MS Bodley 779 (B).

21 Reames et al. (eds), *Middle English Legends*, p. 24.

22 Individual legends that have been edited include: Laurel Braswell, 'Saint Edburga of Winchester: a study of her cult, A.D. 950–1500, with an edition of the fourteenth-century Middle English and Latin lives', *Mediaeval Studies*, 33 (1971), 292–333; 'The Middle English "Life of Adelwolde"', in Michael Lapidge and Michael Winterbottom (eds), *The Life of St Æthelwold* (Oxford: Clarendon Press, 1991), pp. 87–92; Paul Acker, 'Saint Mildred in the *South English Legendary*', in Jankofsky, pp.140–53, Diane Speed, 'Text and meaning in the "*South English Legendary* Lives of Æthelwold"', *Notes and Queries*, 41.3 (1994), 295–301; Michael S. Nagy, 'Saint Æþelberht of East Anglia in the *South English Legendary*', *The Chaucer Review*, 37:2 (2002), 159–72; and Reames's edition of the lives of Frideswide in *Middle English Legends of Women Saints*, noted above.

23 Görlach, *Textual Tradition*, pp. 32–7.

24 Ibid., pp. 15–17.

25 Blanton, *Signs of Devotion*, pp. 235–63.

26 See now for this life, Mary Dockray-Miller, ed. and trans., *Saints Edith and Æthelthryth: Princesses, Miracle Workers, and Their Late Medieval Audience: The Wilton Chronicle and the Wilton Life of St Æthelthryth*, Medieval Women Texts and Contexts 25 (Brepols: Turnhout, 2009).

27 John Harper, *The Forms and Orders of Western Liturgy from the Tenth to the Eighteenth Century* (Oxford: Clarendon Press, 1991), pp. 192–3.

28 Blanton, *Signs of Devotion*, pp. 240–1.

11

Locating saints' lives and their communities

Jocelyn Wogan-Browne

The legend of St Kenelm, Anglo-Saxon prince and child martyr, seems often to be one of the first by which modern readers are drawn into the *SEL*. That this saint is invoked by Chaucer's Chantecleer in *The Nun's Priest's Tale* as a precedent visionary has perhaps made Kenelm's name unusually visible.[1] But, by whatever route readers find their way to his legend, the power by which it first engages and then detains them has, as Sarah Breckenridge demonstrates elsewhere in this volume, much to do with *Kenelm*'s vigorous interchange between universal (i.e. Rome-centred) Christendom and regional ecclesiastical geography. In its opening lines narrating the shires, rivers and dioceses of England, and in its work creating a spiritual topography for the diocese of Worcester, *Kenelm* draws with particular imaginative force on the narrative potentials of medieval cartography and topography. According to the early *SEL* version, the seven-year-old prince Kenelm is killed by his tutor before he can inherit the kingdom of Mercia.[2] The killing takes place in the Clent Hills forests of the West Midlands at the instigation of Kenelm's wicked sister Quendritha who wants the throne herself. Kenelm's body is buried and hidden for a while in Clent in north Worcestershire, but the murder is eventually announced as a martyrdom, by a dove that drops a document from heaven on the pope's altar in Rome. Kenelm's body is exhumed, and, after a contest between the men of Gloucestershire and Worcestershire for his relics, brought back along routes that map a strongly referential topography through the region. He is finally enshrined at Winchcombe (in Gloucester*shire*, but also in the *diocese* of Worcester),[3] which then becomes the centre of the cult.

The story of Kenelm as a child martyr has almost no basis in fact. The early *SEL* legend exemplifies a well-established template of Anglo-Saxon sanctity, that of the murdered royal infant

as martyr: this was much favoured from the eleventh to the thirteenth centuries, and typically deals with figures for whom there
is, at best, slight earlier documentation and whose lives, or rather
deaths, are thoroughly reinvented.[4] Kenelm died as an adult, and
cannot be tied beyond doubt into the lineage of Coenwulf (king of
Mercia, d. 821, and Kenelm's father in the legend), while Kenelm's
'wicked sister' Quendritha was in fact an abbess, not the lover of
his tutor.[5] But *Kenelm* elaborates its central figure's meaning by
a rich plethora of hagiographic conventions. Many motifs of the
legend (Kenelm's dream of himself in a fruiting tree bedecked with
lights; the sprouting of a great ash tree from his tutor's staff at the
place where Kenelm is killed; the honour done to Kenelm's secret
burial site by a white cow, who stays by it rather than pasturing,
but whose milk yield is miraculously large each day; the curse that
recoils on his wicked sister Quendritha) have also been noted as
having mythical and folkloric elements, their power and resonance
of course all the greater for that.[6]

In addition to its striking opening cartography, *Kenelm* has
another particular asset, highly generative in saints' lives. The
heart of the legend has with justice been seen to be the document
brought by the dove to the pope's altar, in which Kenelm's death is
announced in in an early English alliterative couplet. This couplet
has a semi-independent life which suggests how powerfully it
embodies the legend.[7] The Latin *vita* and twelfth-century historiographers cite it, often in English as well as in Latin, as does Ranulf
Higden in his fourteenth-century *Polychronicon*; for that matter,
Milton translates the couplet in his *History of England*.[8] Produced
directly by God rather than human hand, the dove's heavenly letter
not only brings Kenelm's narrative but divinely manifests Kenelm's
celestial and enduring career: the material document bearing the
couplet and the inscribed letters function as a form of contact relic.[9]
The dove's document has always been a source of fascination in the
development and reception of the legend. The fact that its couplet
announces Kenelm's death not in thirteenth-century long alliterative lines but in shorter verses closer to late Old English (see below,
p. 257) has also made it something of a linguistic relic, seeming to
offer direct contact with a pre-Conquest English cult.

The combination of specific referentiality in *Kenelm*'s narrative
cartography and topography and this early cult document have
been important in making his life seem hermeneutically key to a
number of scholars. If the *SEL* originated in the 1270s–80s in the
Worcester–Gloucester area as Görlach argued, and set out from

there on its long career of being copied, excerpted, added to and reconfigured throughout the fourteenth and fifteenth centuries, *Kenelm*'s own association with that region seems to promise particular opportunities of anchoring the *SEL* in a specific English community (although, as Görlach points out, it is not possible to determine the relations and priority between its early versions and their inclusion – or not – of the contest between the people of Worcester and of Gloucester).[10] More generally, among the *SEL*'s English saints, Kenelm has been thought important to how the English nationalism which many have detected in the *SEL* is believed to function.[11]

In their teaching anthology of *Early Middle English Verse and Prose*, for instance, Bennett and Smithers represent the *SEL* through the *Kenelm* life from the earliest extant manuscript, Oxford, Bodleian MS Laud 108.[12] Their notes include an ordnance survey map reference for the spot on the combe where St Kenelm's bier was set down and a holy well sprang up (with a chapel to follow), and careful annotation of the probability of the bier's processional route following the old local saltways.[13] As Bennett later wrote, evoking the rhetoric of Blake's 'Jerusalem', 'It was something to learn that saints like Kenelm had walked these clouded hills not so many centuries ago'.[14] So too, for Hamelinck, the cartographic introduction to *Kenelm* provides a 'history [an English audience] can be proud of' and the life itself expresses 'the longing for the old Anglo-Saxon times when God's grace so openly rested upon England and its inhabitants', while, for Frederick, Kenelm is an example of 'loyal – indeed *patriotically* self-sacrificial – behaviour' (italics mine).[15] The mutual validation of topography and narrative becomes an expression of a time-transcending English community rooted in the West Midlands countryside. The power of pastoral in English constructions of identity is very strong and seductively geared to landscape, so that it is not entirely unsurprising to see this hypostasized eternal and rural England emerging from readings of the legend. For some, language and territory appear further to cohere in specifying Englishness as a value and a performance carried out by *Kenelm*: so, for instance, Frederick argues that *Kenelm*'s alliterative couplet is itself a demonstration that the English language has 'salubrious traits'.[16] But such mutually validating nationalisms ignore, as I shall argue, a more complicated and multifarious relation to literatures, languages and places, one which is better elicited by setting aside the retrospective pull of linear and nationalizing accounts of English literature.

In this essay, I want to try to prise apart the construction of place and language in *Kenelm* as mutually interlocking testimony to an emergent English nationalism. Then I will draw on Sarah Rees Jones's important recent work on how saints' narratives offer civic definition and a sacralizing of urban powers and identities to the developing town cultures of the high Middle Ages, in order to pursue the question of what happens if we add to *Kenelm*'s literacies and locations an understanding of them as urban and civic.[17]

Location, location

Much discussion of *Kenelm* overlooks the central place of the early *SEL* life. In the journey of Kenelm's body, as in the opening cartography of England, all roads lead to the city of Winchcombe, now a small country town in Gloucestershire but once the capital of Anglo-Saxon Mercia. It is here that *Kenelm*'s two earlier cited features – its cartographic promise of place and its empowered version of documentation – unite, as the town and the bodily relics produced by the document come together.

In the prologue description, Winchcombe abbey features as the necropolis of Kenelm's line:

> Kyng Kenulf his fader hiet   he was kyng thare also
> The *abbeie* of Wynchecoumbe he *liet arere*   and thare inne
>   monekes do;
> And after is dethe he was thare ibured   and yeot he liith there
> In the *abbeiye* that yeot stant   that he himseolf *liet arere*.
>
>   (345, 3–6, my italics).

(King Kenwulf was his father, who was also king there and who built the abbey of Winchcombe and had monks placed there After his death he was buried there and still he lies there, in the abbey that still stands which he himself had built.)

But Winchcombe abbey, contained here in the rhetorical chiasmus of the couplets that describe it, is only part of the meaning of Winchcombe. Another focus of interest emerges in the next line –

> Tho was Wynchecombe gret cite   and mest of inouh
> Of al thulke half of Engelonde   so feor so his lond drouh.
>
>   (345, 7–8)

(Winchcombe was a great city then, and certainly the biggest in all that half of England as far as its hinterland extended).

– a point which frames the whole description of the March: 'And Wynchecoumbe of al this lond [i.e. Mercia]   chef cite tho was' (346, 42) (And Winchcombe was at that time the chief city of all this land).

This alternation between monastery and city makes a civic location (inclusive of, but not restricted to the monastic past) the ground of *Kenelm*'s action. Winchcombeshire was taken into Gloucestershire by 1017, and Winchcombe, the heart of its heartland, the ancient royal vill of the Hwicces and subsequently the mausoleum of the Mercian kings, was apportioned to the Worcester church.[18] The town itself was founded in the eighth century, and by 1086 was, together with Gloucester, one of only two boroughs belonging to the king in the county of Gloucestershire.[19] Winchcombe thus had a considerable career as a royal and monastic administrative centre, and a continuing history of interaction, of shifting allegiances and oppositions between townspeople, monastery and crown. By the thirteenth century, Winchcombe (although it retained one of the five principal markets in Gloucestershire and had a crown-authorized fair) had not recovered its ninth-century status as the centre of a Mercian sub-kingdom, or the prestige of its older role as a royal vill, though it was known to the kings of England.[20] As Rees Jones has argued, one function of the royal Mercian history evoked by *Kenelm*'s setting of Winchcombe in the prologue's display of the five kingdoms is to revalorize Winchcombe's civic present. The town already had vital interests in the cult of Kenelm: civic amenities, such as a water supply and an annual fair were provided in Kenelm's name and related to the stories of his miracles, and in 1206 the abbot of Winchcombe established a new patronal feast and a new charity for feeding the poor of the town in the name of Kenelm, Mary and all the saints.[21]

Comparison with the second version of *Kenelm* in Görlach's 'G' redaction (here represented by the Vernon manuscript) reveals a much less intensely localized text in which there is no cartographical prelude and the translation of Kenelm's body is entirely a clerical affair.[22] Winchcombe is mentioned only in the penultimate line of the legend ('At Winchecumbe is that bodi   idon in one schrine', fol. 39v, col. b, 41). The scene at the pope's altar is witnessed *only* by clerks ('that seghen the clerkes alle', col. a, 11); the dove's message is decoded by 'Englissche *clerkes*' (col. a, 20), specifically sent for (there are no lay witnesses at Rome in this version); cardinals are despatched to Archbishop Wulfrid to enquire for the body; and the pope further sends 'clerkes . . . wel eihte other nyne' to carry out the papal command 'to leggen [the body] in schrine' (col. b, 1–2). When the body is discovered and taken up, 'the bisschops that ther were / And abbodes setten theron hond and toward *toun* hit beere' (col. b, 27–8, 'the bishops who were there and the abbots set their hands to it and carried it towards town'). This is the only mention of a town apart from the equally generic 'widewe . . . of the *toun*' who owns the white cow that pastures on Kenelm's grave, but who is not herself seen directly in the text. There is no Gloucester–Worcester contest for Kenelm's relics: the local people play no part in this divinely assisted clerical invention and translation of the saint. Clent in Coubach is mentioned (fol. 39v, col. a, 15) but only as the focus of the cleric's search and the location of the numinous sign represented by the white cow. The version of the legend in the Laud manuscript by contrast affords striking room to lay agency and to spaces and places inhabited by royal and common lay people.

Civic literacies, relics, multilingualism

The *SEL Kenelm*'s awareness of monastery and city takes on particular significance in the context of thirteenth-century civic literacies. As Sarah Rees Jones has shown, in the thirteenth century those who own land by burgage tenure do not need a lord's permission to buy and sell.[23] Title deeds enable entry to a city community and show one's status, defining one as a householder (versus a landless tenant). So we have moved, in the terms of Clanchy's famous study of medieval literacies, from memory to written record: identity is no longer entirely an agreement with your lord, held in the communal memory of witnesses, and embodied not so much in the charter itself as in the seal, knife or other object appended to it (quite as important a commemoration of the transaction as any writing within the charter).[24] Now documents have power not only as memorial objects but as themselves constitutive. Writing creates trust and status, a status which in this context defines the legal and literary world of the burgess as distinct from the peasant and the aristocrat. The city and writing become associated as marks of inclusion as a civic literary and legal culture distinct from agrarian and aristocratic life develops. (So for instance, in the Corpus-Harley *SEL*, the young Becket, refused the prospect of university by his widowed father, is sent instead to serve 'a borgeis of the toun' where he 'is acountes wrot / So longe that he come to court and was in god offis', II, 616, 164–5).

Divergent responses already throng *Kenelm*'s narrative at the moment when the dove drops its document on the pope's altar at Rome:

> Ase the pope stod at Rome   in his masse a day
> At Seint Peteres weovede   ase muche folk that isai,
> A colvere hwiht so ani snou   cam fram heovene fleo
> And leide on the wevede a luyte writ   and seththe ayen gan steo;
> He fleuh op into heovene an heih   ase ore Louerd it wolde.
> That writ was hwiit and schon wel brihte   the lettres weren of
> golde.
> The pope thonkede Jhesu Crist   and that folk dude also:
> He nam the lettre on his hond   and tho heo was ondo,
> He nuste hwat it was to segge   ne non insiht he ne couthe iwite,
> For he ne couthe Englisch non   and on Englis it was iwrite.
> He liet cleopie eche manere men   of eche diverse londe
> Yif eny couthe of this holie writ   ani thing onderstonde.
> Tho weren thare men of Engelonde   that wusten hwat it sede
> And onderstoden wel that writ   tho heo iheorden it rede.
> That writ was puyr on Englisch iwrite   ase men it radden there,
> And for to tellen withoute ryme,   theos wordes it were:
> 'In Klent Coubache   Kenelm kyngues sone
> Liith onder ane thorne   is heved him bireved'.
>
> (352, 245–62)

(For as the pope stood in Rome and sang his mass one day at St Peter's altar in the church, as a great crowd of people saw, a dove whiter than any snow came flying down from heaven, and laid on the altar a little writ and then turned back to heaven and flew up again into heaven above, as our Lord ordained. The writ was white and shone brightly, its lettering all in gold: the pope gave thanks to Jesus Christ as did the people too. He took the letter into his hand and when it was opened he did not know what it said, nor could he recognize anything in it for he did not know English and it was written in English. He had summoned every kind of person from all the different lands to see if anyone could understand anything of this holy writ. Then there were men of England there, who knew what it said, and well understood the writ when they heard it read out. The writ was written purely in English as people interpreted it there, and to tell it in unrhymed verse, these were its words: 'In Cowbach [Valley] in Clent, Kenelm, son of a king, lies under a thorn [bush], deprived of his head'.)

Exhumation parties in the Clent Hills are at once arranged in the English West Midlands through diocesan networks from the Archbishop of Canterbury downwards, while the dove's writ is

carefully treasured in Rome as a 'grete relike'(352, 263) and a
saint's feast day instituted for Kenelm. Thus absorbed into Roman
institutions, the letter's role as a contact relic allows its illegibil-
ity as text to be subordinated to its pedigree as a heavenly letter.
But what is notably *un*absorbed by the politically and religiously
transcendent centre of Rome is the hermeneutic status of the vernacular in this liturgical setting. A supra-national Christian Latin
community, sung and performed in the Pope's mass, receives
but has no direct access to the English narrative in the dove's
writ. This boundary is emphasized in the passage quoted above
by extensive and precise variation on verbs of knowledge and
understanding – '*couthe, understode, witen*': English is not known
('*couthe*' i.e.'familiar, known to') the pope and therefore he does
not know (*iwite*: '[intellectually] understand') what the writ says.[25]

For all the narrative's stress on the Englishmen in the congregation who understand the writ – without seeing its script – when
they hear it read aloud, this is not a nationalizing representation.
For one thing, as Morgan points out (pp. 155–6 above), the issue
of vernacular hermeneutics *per se* is as much emphasized as that
of English: the materiality of the letter, the complexities of signi-
fication and reception are stressed. Not only is there the lexis of
comprehension (or rather, incomprehension on the pope's part)
already noted, but there is an intralingual pun, by which the dove's
writ is said here to be 'puyr on Engliss' ('*purely* in English'? 259),
and, in another early version, to be 'iwrite pur Engliss' (D'Evelyn
and Mill, I, 288, 265). Does this mean 'written in pure English'
or perhaps (with '*pur*' = French '*for*' rather than '*pure*' = 'written
for the English'?). Moreover, in the life as a whole, English is not
represented as hermetically sealed from Latin in its own territory
(as he is beheaded in the Worcestershire hills little Kenelm recites
the *Te Deum*; Latin is also the environment of the wicked sister's
curse as she recites a psalm backwards only to have her eyes fall
out on to what, the narrative claims, is a still inspectable, bloodied
psalter page).[26] Latin is thus acknowledged as routinely part of life,
but lay knowledge and perspectives are counterpointed against the
boundaries of the pope's knowledge (a point, unsurprisingly, *not*
made in the Vernon text). Lay linguistic territories may be as much
the point here as a patriotic celebration of English.

Kenelm's terminology for the dove's document is significant in
the early *SEL* manuscripts. Rather than the obvious term 'lettre'
with its echo of the genre of the heavenly letter, the dove's document is a 'writ'.[27] Although 'writ' has a general sense of 'writing',

it is also, from the early twelfth century on, used to mean 'a legal instrument'.[28] The literacy of the text and its foundational letter, that is, speaks simultaneously to the developing burghal legal cultures of the thirteenth century and to monastic and liturgical literacies. Later, in the *Gilte Legende*'s version of Kenelm (also based on the Latin *vita*), for instance, the document is a 'scrow' (scroll), like the label- and speech-scrolls of religious iconography, not like a legal instrument.[29] Just as the dove's writ functions in relation to communal identity in the life of Kenelm, so too, argues Rees Jones, the idea of the charter functioned within borough society. Borough charters conferred privileges on the entire community of burgesses, while an individual charter affirmed the private possession of property but became fully constitutive only when it was registered within the public borough court. In this way the charter moves towards a role as a contact relic, mattering (like the dove's English writ in the papal curia) as an object, as well as for the legal Latin in it.[30] Rees Jones's discussion illuminates the urban resonance of documents in saints' lives by extending the argument to civic identity as a whole: just as charters replaced the need for kinship-based lineage and dynasty – so the life of Kenelm compensates for the lack of a stable lineage in Winchcombe's foundation mythology for its town and its monastery.[31] Both have something to gain from further vernacular propagation of the cult.

The ideas and practices of literacy to which *Kenelm* appeals then, can be seen as civic as well as monastic/clerical, lay as well as religious. The languages of that literacy are however no straightforward expression of English*ness*, even in the literacy of a burghal class. The great period of town and market development in England, whether under monastic or secular overlordship or both, is from the twelfth to the end of the fourteenth centuries, overlapping the period in which the *SELS* began circulating. The civic imaginary that begins to form over this period draws, as one would expect, on a wide range of England's multilingual culture. Earlier chorographies of Britain and England tend to be monastic (but none the less exist in French and English as well as Latin, as in the case of the 'Lists of Saints Resting Places' in which Kenelm is mentioned from the early eleventh century on).[32] But in the late twelfth-century, cities as well as monasteries and saints' resting places increasingly become nodal points for imagining topographies, and their onomastic transitions are a frequent topos in British historiography. Following Geoffrey of Monmouth's *Historia regum Britanniae*, a vernacular tradition of cities as markers both of transcience and development is powerfully

developed in Wace's *Brut* and the many French, English and Latin
versions of the *Brut* history of Britain it influenced.[33] The celebration of cities and towns also features in the late twelfth-century
Anglo-Norman *Description of England*, which remarks of Kenelm's
Mercia:

> Cum nus recunte li legistres,
> Des Mercïens fu fait li sistes;
> Citez i ot asez plusurs,
> Viles, chastels, riches burcs.
> Cest realme riche esteit
>
> (37–41)

> '(As the lawyers tell us
> The sixth [shire] was that of the Mercians;
> There were plenty of cities there,
> Towns, castles and rich boroughs,
> This was a powerful kingdom.)[34]
> [MS L: registres 'roll books']

Here the manuscript variants as between earlier *legistres* and later
registres emblematize a dual definition of identity: through authority (*legistres*) and through awareness of documentation (*registres*).[35]
Rees Jones's point that both the life of Kenelm and the *Landboc*
or registry of the abbey and town were composed in the mid- to
later thirteenth century is significant in this context.[36] Towns also
begin to be listed by their occupational attributes, much as monasteries had been and continued to be: Black Monks at Worcester
and White Nuns at Westwood are joined by 'Savoun de Coventre'
(Soap[makers] of Coventry), Furur de Cestre (Furriers of Chester)
and so on.[37] But towns and monasteries are (sometimes fractious)
partners, not alternatives. The iconographic convention that shows
walled cities as defined by their saints is a good example.[38]

These signs that urban place is part of the thirteenth-century's
imaginary seem already to have been assimilated in the *SEL*.
Urban spaces and places, such as the market, are a routine setting:
a deacon who is annoyed with St Martin for giving his 'kurtel'
away and being indecorously clad for mass goes crossly off 'to
chepinge' II, 490, 215, ('to the market') to buy some clothing for
the saint; ignoring the roars and pleas of the devil not to shame
him, St Juliana drags her demon 'thorou the chepinge' (I, 66, 130);
St Swithun exemplifies a good bishop by 'amending' 'the toun' of
Winchestre: he has a bridge built and protects trade (a woman eggmonger is sexually harrassed by a mason working on the bridge as

she brings her wares 'to chepinge' (I, 276, 56): Swithun makes her broken eggs whole again (I, 276, 66); the king of India's messenger seeking a master carpenter meets 'oure Loverd' and St Thomas the apostle 'amidde the cheping' as he 'com furst up of the see' (II, 572, 36). For *Mary Magdalene*, Jerusalem is 'the boru of Jerusalem' (I, 303, 5; 309, 203).

As we have seen, civic literacies were multilingual and included French and English as well as Latin.[39] My argument is not that burgesses in towns needed to be able to read French at large (indeed, as the *SEL* itself suggests, English is already a major language of reading and audition alongside French), though they may well have wanted and needed to understand some genres of document that were likely to be in French as well as in Latin. My point is rather that the idea of civic identity is an idea multilingually recorded and in part mediated and practised through French as well as Latin, even for English speakers: that the documentary and literary cultures of civic identity were connected and a context for each other, and that any one of these languages was practised in a web of multilingual contacts and interactions.[40] Neither composers or audiences of the early *SEL* were likely to have had a wholly monoglot identity, though they may have had very different ranges of English, French, Latin (and perhaps Welsh).

Arguments for the language of *Kenelm* as signifying a monoglot, proto-nationalizing English risk overlooking not only the multilingual matrix of the text's production but the specificity of linguistic politics in different *SEL* lives. It could seem difficult to deny the intention to inscribe a nationalizing community in, for example, the *SEL Wulfstan* (though one might think that this inscription subserves this legend's strenuous validation of the local Worcester saint against the Westminster cult-centre for Edward the Confessor, much adorned and enriched as this was by Henry III's rebuilding and propagation of Edward).[41] But in any case, whatever the specific effects of this one legend, there is no guarantee that they apply to other saints. So, for instance, the English famously spoken by the head of St Edmund of East Anglia ('her, her, her', II, 514, 79) to guide those seeking his body in the *SEL*, as in most other versions of his life, need be there not because the life promotes Englishness or the English language, but because it promotes Edmund. In the *inventio* story for his martyrdom, Edmund's Old English words are as likely to function as an authenticating auditory contact relic as they are as linguistic patriotism. When, in his *SEL* life, Edmund of Canterbury is said specifically

to use English (II, 510, 574), he is on his deathbed: unsurprisingly
the Paris-educated meritocratic courtier saint who is in exile at
Soissons at the time might be supposed normally to use French:
but his deathbed usage is because English is his mother tongue, not
because his legend is being patriotic.[42] (It is earlier observed, with
equal appropriateness, that his favourite prayer 'O intemerata big-
ynneth a Latyn', II, 499, 205 ('begins "O undefiled one" in Latin').
Examples need not be multiplied further to argue the point that
even marked uses of English vary in their significance according to
their particular contexts.[43]

Rather than seeing *Kenelm* as testifying to a backward-looking
nostalgia for an older pre-Conquest England, we could see *Kenelm*'s
power as lying in the way it does something new. *Kenelm*'s confi-
dent invocation – and relegation – of the transcendant Roman
centre confirms the significance of the legend's diocesanal and
regional terrritory and its chief city. The early *SEL* version seems
particularly to reflect a moment of emergent civic literacy and
identity: not only does it focus on Winchcombe in comparison
with other versions, but it also, as we have seen, gives the most
lay-inclusive version of the scene at the pope's altar (itself not
included in all versions of the life of Kenelm).[44] When the narrative action shifts to the Clent Hills forest 'that in Wyricestre-schire
is' (Horstmann, 353, 280) and the people of Worcestershire and
Gloucestershire contend for Kenelm's exhumed body, it is less
clear that this is a hurrah for the English countryside than that it is
a powerful hagiographic topos, put to the service of a specific region
and a community of shire and city inhabitants.[45] The *SEL* characteristically omits such *translatio* stories, whether for its native or its
universal saints: they are more usually found in monastic dossiers
where *inventiones* and *translationes* are frequently used in updating
and reviving cults.[46] The contest in the early *Kenelm* and its use
of Winchcombe as its approved goal thus seems especially striking. But the energies of the legend come not from topographically
coded nostalgia but from the new energies of borough culture.

In *Kenelm*, then, we do not have a precocious leap to nationalism and the associated pastoral of the English countryside, still
less a trace of plucky English's underground continuity, cropping
up in a linguistic relic. Rather, a polyglot culture's Anglo-Saxon
saint, already adopted along with the other saints of England in
Latin and Norman historiography, chorography and chronicles
(themselves often used, as Robert Stein has argued, to construct
the Englishness of English history – in Latin and French – for

the Anglo-Normans as against the continent),[47] is the centre of an account focusing vernacularity against Rome while celebrating a civic awareness whose documentary culture is French and Latin and emergently English. The place of this saint's life and its own conception of its place and community is more complicated than that of a gesture towards 'England, the nation'.

There are implications here for the audience of the early *SEL*. The already contested twentieth-century conception of the *SEL* as a substitute liturgy for laypeople or nuns stands more than ever in need of modifying.[48] Bella Millett has cast doubt on the legendary as proto-liturgical reading for nuns; Oliver Pickering has argued that the great majority of *SEL* copies were used for private reading, Annie Samson has urged the overlap between *SEL* and romance audiences.[49] The *SEL* manuscripts include different combinations of varying selections of saints' lives not necessarily in calendrical sequence, and combine them with romances, scientific and cosmological information, religious and political history, vision and debate literature.[50] The very diversity of materials within and accompanying the *SEL* make it as much like the *Canterbury Tales* as a translated Latin lectionary. Its versions of Christian histories and identities can be seen as representing and not just didactically forming lay interests.

It may be, then, that when we see English toponyms in *Kenelm*, we should not automatically think of 'Englishness', and that when we see 'Wynchecombe' we should think of 'Winchcombe'. And the role of the inhabitants of the borough, not only of religious houses and rural communities, needs consideration for their interests in and influence on saints' cults and various kinds of engagement in their performance. The *SEL* constitutes some of the first bourgeois, or better, borough, reading we have in English: it is, among much else, audition and reading for those who own burgages.

Notes

I am grateful to Heather Blurton for her insight and excellent suggestions regarding this essay, and to my colleague Sarah Rees Jones, to whose work on saints' cults and urban culture I am much indebted. Some of the material here draws on our joint paper at Kalamazoo 2007.
1 See Robert Boenig, 'Chaucer and St Kenelm', *Neophilologus*, 84 (2000), 157–64.
2 The early version of *Kenelm* is represented in MS Laud 108 (c. 1300) and (with minor variation) in Corpus Christi College Cambridge 145 (now thought to be mid-fourteenth century) and Harley 2277 (c. 1300

or later), as well as in later *SEL* manuscripts (see Görlach, *Textual Tradition*, p. 308). It is quoted here from MS Laud 108 (edited by Horstmann, cited by page and line number).

3 The diocese of Worcester was created in 680 and included Winchcombe. The diocese of Gloucester was created after the dissolution in 1541: E. B. Fryde, *Handbook of British Chronology*, 3rd edn repr. with corr. (Cambridge: Cambridge University Press, 1996), p. 227.

4 For the *Vita et miracula* (composed between 1066 and 1075) see Rosalind C. Love (ed.), *Three Eleventh-Century Anglo-Latin Saints' Lives: Vita S. Birini, Vita et Miracula S. Kenelmi and Vita S. Rumwoldi* (Oxford: Oxford University Press, 1996), pp. 49–89. For other examples of Anglo-Saxon child martyrs, see D. W. Rollason, 'The cult of murdered royal saints', *Anglo-Saxon England*, 11 (1983), 1–22; Paul Hayward, 'The idea of innocent martyrdom in late tenth- and eleventh-century English hagiology', in D. Wood (ed.), *Martyrs and Martyrologies*, Studies in Church History 30 (Oxford: Basil Blackwell, 1993), pp. 81–92.

5 There is no evidence of a formal cult of Kenelm before c. 969: Love (ed.), *Three Eleventh-Century Anglo-Latin Saints Lives*, pp. cxi, cxiii. A Cynhelm *princeps* and *dux* recorded in the early ninth century died in adulthood after 811 and was probably a kinsman but not a son of Coenwulf: see Simon Keynes, 'Mercia and Wessex in the ninth century' in Michelle P. Brown and Carol A. Farr (eds), *Mercia: An Anglo-Saxon Kingdom in Europe* (Leicester: Leicester University Press, 2001, repr. Continuum, 2005), pp. 310–28 (315, 316 n. 25). On Quendritha 'filia regis' and abbess of (probably) Minster in Thanet by 824 see Love (ed.), *Three Eleventh-Century Lives*, p. 54, n. 1: for her capacity to inherit from her father Coenwulf, see Pauline Stafford, 'Political women in Mercia, eighth to early tenth centuries', in Brown and Farr (eds), *Mercia*, pp. 35–49 (41–2).

6 See e.g. E. S. Greenhill, 'The child in the tree: a study of the cosmological tree in Christian tradition', *Traditio*, 10 (1954), 323–71. On the Kenelm *vita*, see Catherine Cubitt, 'Folklore and historiography: oral stories and the writing of Anglo-Saxon history', in Ross Balzaretti and Elizabeth Tyler (eds), *History and Narrative* (Turnhout, Brepols, 2006), pp.189–223 (190–6, 222–3); Love (ed.), *Three Eleventh-Century Lives*, pp. 70–3. For the argument that such oral tales originate with the laity and their local clergy, see Catherine Cubitt, 'Sites and sanctity: revisiting the cult of murdered and martyred Anglo-Saxon royal saints', *Early Medieval Europe*, 9:1 (2000), 53–83.

7 According to the eleventh-century *Vita et miracula*, the couplet was widely disseminated: see Love (ed.), *Three Eleventh-Century Lives*, pp. 50–1: see p. 66 for the couplet; for its dissemination, pp. cxvii–cxix, 51, n. 9; 52–3, n. 1; 66. There is a possible trace of it in the English, Latin and French 'Lists of Saints' Resting Places' (D. W. Rollason,

'Lists of saints' resting-places in Anglo-Saxon England', *Anglo-Saxon England*, 7 (1978), 61–93: for Kenelm, see Love, p. cxviii and n. 147; for a late thirteenth-century Anglo-Norman List see Gaimar, *Lestorie des Engles*, ed. T. D. Hardy and C. T. Martin, 2 vols, RS 91 (London: Eyre and Spottiswode, 1888–89), vol. I, pp. xxxix–xlii (with Kenelm at p. xli).

8 See *Landboc sive Registrum monasterii beatae Mariae virginis et sancti Cenhelmi de Winchelcumba*, ed. David Royce, 2 vols, Bristol and Gloucestershire Archaeological Society Publications (Exeter: William Pollard, 1892, 1903), pp. vii–viii, for the variant medieval forms in which the couplet circulates. For Milton's version see *The History of England* (London: R. Chiswell, 1695), book IV, p. 219 (EEBO, accessed 22 May 2010). A Latin translation of the couplet is given in the margin of the Corpus-Harley *SEL* text (D'Evelyn and Mills, I, 288, n. to 269).

9 See further J. W. Earle, 'Typology and iconographic style in early medieval hagiography', *Studies in the Literary Imagination*, 8 (1977), 15–46, and the essay by Morgan in this volume, p. 159.

10 Görlach, *Textual Tradition*, p. 35: on Robert of Gloucester's borrowings from the *SEL*, see Görlach, *Studies*, pp. 48–55; Oliver S. Pickering, '*South English Legendary* style in Robert of Gloucester's *Chronicle*', *Medium Aevum*, 70 (2001), 1–18 (7), revised and reprinted in this volume (pp. 106–45).

11 See Frederick, 'National identity'; Jankofsky, 'National characteristics'; Hamelinck, 'St Kenelm'. For a different approach see Katherine J. Lewis, 'Anglo-Saxon saints' lives, history and national identity in late medieval England', in Helen Brocklehurst and Robert Phillips (eds), *History, Nationhood and the Question of Britain* (New York: Palgrave 2004), pp. 160–70; 'History, historiography and rewriting the past,' in Salih (ed.), *Companion to Middle English Hagiography*, pp. 122–40. For a broader discussion of the English context of the *SEL* and a defence of thirteenth-century English literature, see Thompson, *Everyday Saints*, pp. 21–57.

12 J. A. W. Bennett and G. L. Smithers, *Early Middle English Verse and Prose* (Oxford: Clarendon Press, 1966; 2nd edn, 1968; 2nd rev. edn, 1982), VII (notes on pp. 312–16).

13 Bennett and Smithers, p. 315, n. to 247–56.

14 J. A. W. Bennett, completed by Douglas Gray, *Middle English Literature* (Oxford, Clarendon Press, 1990), p. 60.

15 Hamelinck, 'St Kenelm', pp. 27, 30; Frederick, 'National identity', pp. 60–1.

16 Frederick, 'National identity', p. 64.

17 Sarah Rees Jones, 'Cities and their saints in England, c. 1150–1300: the development of bourgeois values in the cult of Saint William of York', in Caroline Goodson, Anne E. Lester and Carol Symes (eds),

Cities, Texts, and Social Networks, 400–1500 (Aldershot: Ashgate, 2010), pp. 193–214.

18 See Steven Bassett, 'In search of the origin of Anglo-Saxon kingdoms', in his (ed.), *Origins of Anglo-Saxon Kingdoms* (Leicester: Leicester University Press, 1989), pp. 3–27 (and on Winchcombe as mausoleum, ibid., pp. 6–7). For an outline history of the town and monastery, see *Landboc*, ed. Royce, I, pp. i–cxxii.

19 *Landboc*, ed. Royce, p. iii.

20 On Winchcombe's fairs, see *Landboc*, ed. Royce, I, pp. xl–xli. Henry III visited the town in 1232, in 1251 with Eleanor of Provence and in 1265 (ibid., pp. xx–xxii): for later kings' dealings with Winchcombe see ibid., pp. xxvi, xxvi–xxx, xxxix).

21 'Houses of Benedictine monks: the abbey of Winchcombe', *The Victoria History of the County of Gloucester*, ed. William Page (London: Constable, 1907), II, pp. 66–72.

22 See Görlach, *Textual Tradition*, pp. 51, 53 and pp. 103–4: here transcribed from *The Vernon Manuscript: A Facsimile of Bodleian Library, Oxford, Ms Eng. Poet A.1*, ed. A. I. Doyle (Cambridge: D. S. Brewer, 1987), fol. 39v, cols a and b. On the provenance and history of Laud 108 as non-monastic, see Frankis, 'Addendum', pp. 77–8 above.

23 I am indebted again to Dr Rees Jones, part of whose book on *York between the Conquest and the Black Death* (Oxford: Oxford University Press, forthcoming) I heard at 'The Book in the Medieval Town' conference in York, July 2002.

24 M. T. Clanchy, *From Memory to Written Record: England 1066–1307*, 2nd edn (Oxford: Blackwell, 1993).

25 This kind of play occurs elsewhere in the legend, notably in the distinction between the 'witti' (i.e. rational) humans, not daring to speak of Kenelm under Quendritha's crack-down, and the better informed white cow, 'A doumb best, that is withoute witte', who remembers Kenelm and after whom the valley of Kenelm's grave-site is eventually named (213–15, 216, 351; 238–9, 352).

26 Like the dove's writ, these traces in the psalter developed a life of their own as material and documentary witnesses to the legend: see further Love (ed.), *Three Eleventh-Century Lives*, p. 72, n. 3.

27 The *Vita*'s terms are *menbranam, scedulam, epistola*: ibid., pp. 64, 66.

28 See *s.v.* writ *OED* sense 3, *MED* 2a. *MED* gives the *Kenelm* document a special sense presumably derived from the use of 'writ' for Scripture, as 'A writing held to have uniquely elevated status or significance for prophecy, confirmation of beliefs, revelation, or divination', citing both the Harley 2277 and Corpus 145 texts. This is certainly a sense towards which the dove's document moves at Rome, once its status has been decided, but not necessarily its only resonance.

29 *Supplementary Lives in Some Manuscripts of the Gilte Legende*, ed. Richard Hamer and Vida Russell, EETS OS 315 (Oxford: Oxford University Press, 2000), p. 209/100: so too Trevisa's translation of Higden's *Polychronicon* (with a variant *epistolle* in MS Harley 2261) for the Latin's 'chartam': *Polychronicon Ranulfi Higden monachi Cestrensis*, ed. J. R. Lumby, 9 vols, RS 41 (London: Longman, Green, Longman, Roberts and Green, 1865–86), VI, pp. 306–7. In Pynson's *Kalendre* of 1516, the document is a *byll*: *Kalendre of the Newe Legende of Englande*, ed. Manfred Görlach (Heidelberg: Carl Winter Universitätsverlag, 1994), p.128. In the Vernon version discussed above, the dove's document is a 'writ' ('A whit coluere his nome brouhte to Rome in one write / uppe seint petres aulter that writ heo lette falle', fol. 39v, col. a, 9–10), but there is no lay presence and no play made on the pope's own 'wit', very little visualizing of the scene, and no focus on the material document as document ('writ' could very readily be translated in this version as 'a piece of writing').

30 Rees Jones also notes that Sabbatarianism was successfully preached by Eustace, abbot of Flay, in English towns in the early thirteenth century, but only at his second preaching tour – when, repairing his initial failure, he claimed his work to have been authorized by a heavenly letter ('Cities and their saints', p. xxx). See also *Landboc*, ed. Royce, I, p. 19. On earlier versions of the Sabbatarian letter from heaven, a possible influence on the dove's appearance in the Kenelm *vita*, see Love (ed.), *Three Eleventh-Century Lives*, p. 65, n. 5.

31 See more generally Emily Steiner, *Documentary Culture and the Making of English Literature* (Cambridge: Cambridge University Press, 2003), ch. 2 (on charters of Christ).

32 See n. 8 above, and Henry of Huntingdon, *Historia Anglorum*, 'De sanctis modernis commemoratio': *Historia Anglorum: The History of the English People*, ed. and trans. Diana Greenway (Oxford: Clarendon Press, 1996), bk ix, cap. 51, pp. 686–95, pp. 687–8.

33 *Historia Regum Britannie*, ed. Neil Wright, vol. I (Woodbridge and Dover, NH: D. S. Brewer, 1985), pp. 14–15: see also Henry of Huntingdon, *Historia Anglorum*, ed. and trans. Greenway, bk i, cap. 3, pp. 12–15; *Wace's Roman de Brut: A History of the British*, ed. and trans. Judith Weiss (Exeter: University of Exeter Press, 1999), e.g. on London, pp. 33, 1,217–46; 95, 3,745–96, 3,780; for some two hundred prose *Brut* manuscripts in French, English, Latin and Welsh see L. M. Matheson, *The Prose 'Brut': The Development of a Middle English Chronicle* (Tempe, AZ: MRTS, 1998).

34 Alexander Bell (ed.), 'The Anglo-Norman *Description of England*: an edition', in Ian Short (ed.), *Anglo-Norman Anniversary Essays*, ANTS OPS 3 (London: ANTS, 1993), pp. 31–47 (39), and, for its chief source, Henry of Huntingdon, *Historia Anglorum*, ed. and trans. Greenway, bk i, cap. 3–5, pp. 14–20 (cf. William of Malmesbury (*Gesta*

268 Textual communities

Regum Anglorum, ed. and trans. R. A. B. Mynors, R. M. Thomson and
M. Winterbottom, 2 vols (Oxford: Clarendon, 1998), vol. I, bk i, cap.
99–105), identified by Görlach as *Kenelm*'s source (*Textual Tradition*,
p. 34, n. 111)). See further Lesley Johnson, 'The Anglo-Norman
Description of England: an introduction', in Short (ed.), *Anglo-Norman
Anniversary Essays*, pp. 11–30.

35 The *Description* forms part of the epilogue to Gaimar's *Estoire
des engleis* in MSS D (Durham Cathedral Libarary C iv. 27, fols
137r–138v, late twelfth or early thirteenth century) and L (Lincoln
Cathedral 104, olim A iv. 12, fols 155v–157v, later thirteenth century).
A *registre* (register) is a roll or book: *legistres* a lawyer (*AND*): 'legist,
(civilian or Roman) lawyer', J. H. Baker, *Manual of Law French*, 2nd
edn (Aldershot: Scolar Press, 1990).

36 The *Landboc* was compiled in the reign of Henry III: *Kenelm* appears
in the earliest extant *SEL* versions of the late thirteenth century. Until
the mid-thirteenth century, the *Landboc* was the record of authenti-
cated land transactions for the lay tenants of Winchcombe abbey: Rees
Jones, 'Cities and their saints', p. xxx; *Landboc*, ed. Royce, vol. II, pp.
xlv–xlviii.

37 For a monastic chorography see e.g. Gervase of Canterbury's 'Mappa
mundi' in W. Stubbs (ed.), *The Historical Works of Gervase of
Canterbury*, 2 vols, Royal Society 73 (London: Longman, Brown,
Green, Longmans & Roberts, 1879–1880), vol. II, pp. 414–49 (434 for
Kenelm and Winchcombe). For an urban chorography, see C. Bonnier,
'List of English towns in the fourteenth century', *English Historical
Review*, 16 (1901), 501–2, from which the examples quoted here are
taken. *Mappulae* using saints continue (cf. e.g. Osbern Bokenham's
well-known fifteenth-century *Mappula Anglie*).

38 See e.g. the map of York in London, BL MS Harley 1808, fol. 45v,
reproduced in Catherine Delano-Smith and Roger J. P. Kain, *English
Maps: A History* (London: British Library, 1999), p. 180.

39 See e.g. *Borough Customs*, ed. Mary Bateson, Surtees Society 18
(London: Quaritch, 1904–6), for many instances of Latin and French
documentation of borough identity: for a bibliography of French in
English historical documents, see Maryanne Kowaleski, bibliography
of *Town Records* at www.fordham.edu/frenchofengland/ bibliography.
html.

40 Richard Britnell places the loss of French as a civic language in the
fifteenth century: see his 'French in towns', in Jocelyn Wogan-Browne
et al. (ed.), *Language and Culture in Medieval Britain: The French of
England c. 1100–c. 1500* (Woodbridge: York Medieval Press, 2009),
pp. 81–9.

41 See D'Evelyn and Mill, I, pp. 8–15: the account of the Conquest as a
terrible effect of Edward's death and Harold's treason is at ll. 60–90. On
Henry III and the thirteenth-century cult see Paul Binski, *Westminster*

Abbey and the Plantagenets: Kingship and the Representation of Power (New Haven: Yale University Press, 1995).

42 For other examples see Christopher Baswell, 'Multilingualism on the page', in Paul Strohm (ed.), *Middle English* (Oxford: Oxford University Press, 2007), pp. 38–50.

43 For an extension of the discussion on class lines, see Thompson, *Everyday Saints*, p. 49 (apropos Simon de Montfort in the *SEL Dominic*: see also Heffernan, reprinted in this volume).

44 Compare the Vernon version discussed above, pp. 255–6. A variant tradition of Robert of Gloucester's *Chronicle* has Kenelm's severed head speak forty years after its burial to announce the presence of Kenelm's body: *The Metrical Chronicle of Robert of Gloucester*, ed. William Aldis Wright, 2 vols, RS 86 (London: HMSO, 1887), vol. II, appendix X, p. 823, ll. 3–5. For a later *Kenelm* using the same source (the twelfth-century Latin *vita*) as *SEL*, but nevertheless varying its details, see the *Gilte Legende*: Hamer and Rusell (ed.), *Supplementary Lives*, p. 205 and pp. 500–1, nn. to ll. 19, 49, 129.

45 As the *vita* writer notes, the relic contest evokes a typological parallel with St Martin's relics and the dispute between the people of Tours and Poitiers: Love (ed.), *Three Eleventh Century Lives*, pp. 68–9: see also Patrick Geary, *Furta sacra: Thefts of Relics in the Central Middle Ages* (Princeton: Princeton University Press, 1978, repr. 1990).

46 So for instance the *SEL Martin* (Horstmann, 449–456; D'Evelyn and Mill, II, 483–92) does not include the struggle between Tours and Poitiers, nor does Laud in the case of *Faith* (Horstmann, 83–6). Edward the Martyr's several translations (from his unknown grave to Wareham to Shaftesbury and subsequently to a new shrine at Shaftesbury) are, however, narrated in *Edward the Elder* (D'Evelyn and Mill, I, 110–18; Horstmann, 51–3, 145–224).

47 Robert M. Stein, 'Making history English: cultural identity and historical explanation in William of Malmesbury and Laȝmon's *Brut*', in Sylvia Tomasch and Sealy Gilles (eds), *Text and Territory: Geographical Imagination in the European Middle Ages* (Philadelphia: University of Pennsylvania Press, 1998), pp. 97–115.

48 Görlach, *Textual Tradition*, pp. 32–38. Thomas R. Liszka, 'Manuscript G (Lambeth Palace 223) and the early *South English Legendary*', in Jankofsky, pp. 91–101, queries the assumed early presence of the L prologue (posited by Pickering as well as Görlach for the early stages of collection) as a programme for the earliest intended structure for the *SEL* (92); see also Introduction above, pp. 5–6.

49 Bella Millett, 'The audience of the saints' lives of the Katherine-Group', in *Saints and Saints' Lives: Essays in Honour of D. Hugh Farmer, Reading Medieval Studies*, 16 (1990), 12–56; Oliver S. Pickering, 'The *South English Legendary*: teaching or preaching?', *Poetica*, 45 (Spring 1996), 1–14; Samson, 'Constructing a context'.

Samson's category of 'regional gentry' (p. 94) could be widened to include urban aspirant and elite laypeople.

50 Liszka, *SELS*. Oxford, Bodleian MS Laud 108 itself contains the 'Sayings of St Bernard', 'Vision of St Paul', 'Debate between Body and Soul', *Havelok* and *King Horn*, as well as the Middle English poem here entitled *Le enfaunce Jesu Crist*, then the *SEL* Blaise and Cecilia, *Alexius*, *Somer Soneday* and two verse scraps on the flyleaf. Only eighteen of the 'full' manucripts described by Görlach have *SEL* alone.

12

Pope Gregory and St Austin of Canterbury in the *Early South English Legendary*

E. Gordon Whatley

Among the factors encouraging renewed attention to some long-neglected areas of Middle English literature, including the *SEL* collection, is the realization that such texts express in various ways an emerging late medieval sense of English nationhood and of English ethnic, cultural and linguistic identity.[1] Although gender continues to dominate recent work on Middle English saints' lives, some important studies have drawn attention to the self-consciously historical, political and nationalistic character of the legends of native English saints in *SEL*.[2] My aim in the present essay is to contribute to this ongoing exploration by examining the legends of two saints with obvious relevance to early English history – Pope Gregory the Great and Archbishop Augustine ('Austin') of Canterbury – who are largely bypassed in *SEL* studies (although Anglo-Saxonists have more than compensated).[3] The original *SEL* narratives that I will refer to henceforth as *Gregory* and *Austin* deal closely with English 'origins': Gregory conceived the mission to Christianize the English ('the furste man that Cristindom to hem bisoughte', 358, 103, 'the first person that prayed for Christianity [to come] to them'), which Austin carried out ('Erchebischop of Caunterbury: the furste that evere cam', 26, 79).[4] While neither was English, their stories, as retold in *SEL*, are none the less vehicles of national self-consciousness. They also reflect the discrepant standing of Gregory and Austin as English saints: whereas Gregory was generally seen as 'Apostle of the English', Austin's reputation was problematic. Their legends together illustrate something of the variety of the *SEL* collection's narrative modes,[5] craftsmanship and textual complexity.[6] I will begin with *Gregory* as probably the earlier of the two legends to be composed and certainly more typical in terms of its construction of a saintly character.

Gregory, like many *SEL* legends, is much shorter than its equivalent Latin *vitae*. Brevity is achieved partly through bland

summary of significant aspects of the saint's life, as in 'gret clerk
he was and guod prechour' (355, 3a, 'he was a great scholar and
a good preacher'), distilling Gregory's fame as learned doctor of
the church and homilist, but without itemizing or describing his
written works, as Bede does, or incorporating a sample sermon,
as do the two most widely circulated *vitae*.[7] But the distinctive
character of *SEL* legends lies less in the use of broad epitome than
in drastic reduction of episodes. In the case of *Gregory*, the entire
legend comprises a mere handful of anecdotes, ignoring dozens
of episodes and themes in the extant *vitae*. For example, we learn
nothing about Gregory's service as papal legate (*apocrisiarius*) in
Constantinople, where he wrote his *Moralia on Job* and debated
the resurrection of the body with the patriarch Eutychius; there is
no mention of the bubonic plague in Rome or of Gregory's institution of the Rogation-tide penitential observances, both of which
figure largely in his elevation to the papacy in the Latin *vitae*.[8] Also
absent are the familiar stories of the dove that hovered near the
saint's mouth while he was composing his Ezekiel homilies, and of
his intercession for Emperor Trajan.[9]

While intermediary Latin sources may be partially responsible
for this abridgement, the poet also deserves some credit. Manfred
Görlach believed that a breviary must have been the earliest
Latin source used by *SEL* poets for many of their legends, but he
could never identify it among extant breviaries. The late medieval
York Breviary, for example, contains an office for Gregory with
Proper and Common responsories and anthems, to accompany
the prescribed psalms and nine narrative lections, featuring select
episodes from the saint's life, closely paralleling those in *Gregory*.
But there are significant and instructive differences. Such a highly
selective abridgement, commonly found in breviaries from the
thirteenth century, may well have been one sort of *model* for *SEL*'s
approach to the Gregory legend, rather than the determinative
source. My impression is that the *SEL* poets read widely among
Latin legendaries, not just breviaries, and adapted their material at
will.[10] Görlach cites York as a close analogue to the Middle English
version, because, like *Gregory*, it foregrounds the saint's involvement in the English mission, but he rejects it as a source because
Gregory is 'completely independent in wording' and in choice of
other episodes.[11] As we shall see below, the differences also extend
to the poet's structuring of the narrative and his creative amplifica-
tion of certain themes in ways that are not characteristic of breviary
lections in general.

SEL's *Gregory* as a whole consists of six main sections (355–9, 1–117). The introductory section (1–18) briefly but skilfully celebrates Gregory's piety and learning (2–3), his early monastic fervour (3–6) and, in more detail, his asceticism, devotional zeal and work ethic (7–14), all of which lead to his elevation to the rank of cardinal and a leadership role in the Roman hierarchy (15–18). Following this introduction is the narrative core of *Gregory*, a linked series of four episodes directly or indirectly concerned with Gregory's role in the origins of English Christianity: first, Gregory's famous encounter with the English slave children in Rome (19–38); second, his abortive effort to lead a mission to England himself (39–55); third, his election as pope (56–74), which in effect empowers him to delegate to others the missionary task he was not destined to fulfil himself; fourth, a somewhat cursory account of the actual mission to England under Augustine's leadership (75–94). After this comes the conclusion (95–117), in three parts, of which the first (95–101) celebrates Gregory as 'Apostle of England', mentions the English custom of putting children to school on his feast day and asks God to allow the English to protect and cherish the teaching Gregory sent with St Austin; the second part (102–11), as if to acknowledge, somewhat awkwardly, that Gregory was important not just for England but for all Christendom as teacher of 'righte bileve' (358, 102, 'true faith'), retells one of his miracles verifying the doctrine of trans-substantiation;[12] the final few lines (112–17) comprise a prayer for the intercession of Gregory, 'apostle of Engelonde', who is now in heaven because he 'sende us into Engelonde   the lawes of Cristindome' (359, 113).

The four central episodes (19–94), as our summary implies, form a coherent narrative sequence celebrating not only Gregory's saintly goodness and greatness as a churchman but also the charisma and promise of the 'fair folk' of 'Engelonde' to whom he is instinctively drawn and whose conversion from heathendom to a Christian identity results from his profound sympathy for the distant land. One source of dramatic tension within the story is Gregory's sanctity itself, out of which springs not only his prophetic and humane longing for England's salvation but also the saintly wisdom and authority that render him indispensable in Rome itself and prevent him from fulfilling the English mission personally. But this saintliness in turn secures his eventual election to the papacy, with the authority to delegate the mission to others, thus establishing the English church from afar, and earning in the end the title of 'apostel of Engelonde'. The poet eliminates

everything else from the Gregorian source traditions. Space limitations do not permit a thorough analysis of all four episodes in this
central section; to illustrate the *SEL* legend's creative representation of the Gregory figure in relation to the source traditions, I will
focus briefly on the introduction and in more detail on the first of
the central episodes, involving Gregory and the English slaves, but
each of the other sections offers comparable evidence of the poet's
narrative skills and agendas.

The deftly economical introductory section (1–18) prepares
for the central anecdotes proper by first constructing Gregory as
a 'holie man', idealized not so much as a mythic figure from the
remote past of sixth-century Rome, but rather as a type of noble
ecclesiast familiar to late thirteenth-century readers of *SEL* in
their own day[13] – wise, learned, righteous and clean living, and
in 'Regular' orders, a dedicated ascetic, tireless in prayer and
work, eminently worthy of the high office he reluctantly accepts
and performs with distinction. The poem establishes this image
of 'Seint Gregori' before his crucial encounter with the heathen
English slaves, thereby imbuing what he does and says in that
episode with more authority, credibility and, for English readers
surely, grounds for patriotic pride that their Christian origins
were due to such a distinguished saint. The initial portrait in this
section, especially of Gregory's asceticism, is more detailed than
its equivalent in any of the breviary lections, such as York's,[14] and
appears to make creative use of passages from the Latin *vitae*, especially JD, but condensing his rather elaborate anecdote into a few
pithy verses, and altering its tone and significance so as to render
Gregory's asceticism both more wonderful (even humorously so),
and at the same time more familiar.

The first few lines about Gregory's capacity for fasting (7–14)
are adapted by the poet freely from the beginning of JD 7 and end
of 8, eliminating any trace of the original context, which concerns
Gregory's notorious stomach complaint and the ability to 'forget
about' food and ignore his stomach complaint, acquired one Easter
through the prayers of St Eleutherius.[15] The English writer converts this temporary and *ad hoc* loss of bodily appetite into a perma-
nent trait ('al is wille he forles   of drinke and of mete', 356, 8, 'he
lost all his desire for food and drink'), and surely intends his readers
to chuckle at the suggestion that Gregory would rather starve to
death before he would even *feel* hungry ('For defaute he scholde
rathur deie   thane beo ofhoungred ene / So he was to fastingue
iwoned   his liif he ladde so clene', 356, 9–10, 'He would be more

likely to die of starvation than get hungry even once, so accustomed was he to fasting: he led such a pure life'). In other words, his 'clene' living has rendered him immune to bodily needs. Similarly creative is the quatrain beginning 'Wel sielden for al is feblesse   idel he beo scholde' (356, 11, 'very seldom, in spite of all his feeble state, would he be idle'), and concerning Gregory's aversion for idleness, which seems again to reflect JD's wording ('although he was afflicted almost every day with physical weakness, he had no desire to allow his body any rest and thereby lessen the time he spent praying or reading, or writing or dictating').[16] In *SEL*'s *Gregory* this is amplified as if to represent the saint more in terms of thirteenth-century norms. Thus JD's rather vaguely worded 'Praying or reading' (*aut oraret aut legeret*), is formalized as 'of ore Louerdes servise rede othur singne . . . / Othur he wolde bidde is beden   the hwyle he mighte wake' (356, 12, 'to read silently or chant our Lord's service'; 356, 14, 'Or he would pray his rosary for as long as he could stay awake'), as expected of clergy in general by the poet's time.[17] *Aut scriberet aut dictaret* is rendered first, literally, as 'Writen othur telle' (356, 13a, 'write or dictate') but the poet then adds a further gloss to *dictaret* (which in medieval Latin commonly also meant 'versify'[18]) as 'rimes thareof make' (356, 13b, 'compose a poem about what he had written'). Versifying was not something traditionally associated with Gregory the Great, but it was characteristic of English clerics in the thirteenth century.[19] It is a small detail, but typical of the poet's skill in creating what Anne Thompson dubs the 'Everyday saints' of *SEL,* by rendering his subjects more familiar and more vividly contemporary.

Also 'updated' is the terminology of papal government into which Gregory is drawn in recognition of his piety. His appointment as *levita septimus* (lit., 'deacon of the seventh district of Rome') is rendered as the more familiar 'cardinal' ('The pope is guodnesse underyat . . . At Rome he made him cardinal'; 356, 15–16, 'The pope perceived his goodness . . . He appointed him a cardinal at Rome'). When Gregory later asks to undertake his mission to convert the English, in the Latin sources he petitions the pope alone, but in *SEL* it is at a meeting of the 'commuyn conseil' (an early English term for the Roman college of cardinals) that 'seint Gregori aros sone / And bad the pope and is cardinales   graunti him ane bone' (357, 39–40). Later still, Gregory's own election to the papacy (58ff.) is similarly embellished and updated by the poet, apparently to reflect the election procedures instituted at the Council of Lyons in 1274.[20]

The poet's reworking of the Latin sources thus establishes Gregory early in his legend as not only a holy ascetic but also a force to be reckoned with at the centre of Christendom. This Rome with its anachronistic 'conseil of holie churche' (356, 18) and up-to-date elections would no doubt seem to late thirteenth-century English readers more like the internationally powerful Vatican of their own time than the historical Gregory's marginalized and beleaguered outpost of Byzantium, all traces of which the English poet has eliminated. So when Gregory steps out of his 'paleys in a day' (356, 19) and encounters the English slaves, the immediate and positive response they elicit from this holy and powerful man would appear to English readers all the more impressive and gratifying, as 'England' becomes the focus of Gregory's carefully constructed sanctity and he is inspired, at the sight of the children, to create in his prophetic imagination a paradisiac vision of their homeland.

The various Latin accounts of the 'slave boys' episode differ in minor details but share the same basic structure, namely, a description of the shining hair and white bodies and faces of some slave boys for sale in the Forum, followed by Gregory's five-part dialogue with the merchants, in which he asks a question, the merchants answer, and Gregory responds (except to their first answer), as follows: 1. What is their country? Britain, where everyone looks like them. 2. Are they Christians or pagans? Pagan. Gregory sighs and laments that the prince of darkness has power over such brightness! 3. What people? English (*Angli*). Gregory says, yes, they are indeed like *angeli* (angels) with 'angelic faces' (*angelicos vultos*) and are fit to live with the angels in heaven. 4. What province? Deira. Gregory prophesies they will be 'freed from wrath' (*de ira eruendi*). 5. Who's their king? Ælle. Gregory prophesies that *Alleluia* will be sung there.

The York lections abbreviate the five-part dialogue by conflating the merchants' first two replies ('. . . He was told they were from the isle of Britain, where all the inhabitants, though pagans, shone with such beauty'),[21] cutting Gregory's lament, and closing with the third exchange, with its puns on *angli* and *angeli*, omitting questions 4 and 5 about *Deira* and King Ælle.[22] *SEL* likewise omits these, which would mean even less to a southern English audience, but treats the rest with characteristic freedom, relating how Gregory encounters 'marchauns' (merchants) with their 'mercerie' (imported luxury textiles) as he is leaving his 'paleys' one day (356, 19–20), like a typical high ecclesiast in the late 1200s. He is transfixed by the sight of the children. He 'yeorne heom biheold' ('beheld them earnestly')[23] and, in a rhetorically playful addition, 'a stounde he gan atstonde' (356, 23, 'for a while he just stood still'), comprising a pun on 'a stounde' (for a while) and 'astouned' (astonished, amazed), and an alliterative half-rhyme formed by 'a stounde' ('a while') and 'atstonde' (stood still). The homoerotic connotations possible in the Latin sources' descriptions of the bodies, hair and faces of the *pueri venales* (boys for sale)[24] disappear in the gender-neutral phrasing of 'swete children threo'('three sweet children') [25] and 'Fairore thingus[26] thane huy weren   ne mighte no man iseo' (356, 21–2, 'No one could look upon creatures more beautiful than they were'). Likewise the racism implicit in the 'English corporeality' on which, as Lavezzo argues, Ælfric invites his readers to 'gaze',[27] seems to me a non-issue here: the adjective 'fair' in early Middle English is not used to specify skin or hair colour, only beautiful appearance.

As the dialogue develops, the focus also shifts from the children and the people to the country of 'Engelonde', which the poet substitutes at the outset for the Latin *Britannia*, reversing and conflating questions 1 and 3 ('Gregori . . . axede hwat the childre weren   and of hwuche londe'; 356, 23–4, 'Gregory . . . asked what the children were and from which land'), so that the merchants' reply mentions both the people and the country in the same line, and alludes to it again in the next: 'Englische huy beoth   of Engelonde inome, / And swuch is the kuynde of alle the men   that of that lond doz come' (356, 25–6, 'English they are, from England taken / And of similar kind are all the men that come from that land').

Gregory's punning reply is likewise less about children than country:

'Wel aughte', seide this holie man   'that lond beo guod and
                                       riche,
For huy beoth Englische swythe wel icleoped   engles huy buth
                                       iliche.
Yif that [lond] is swuch ase [the] men beoth[28]   name it havez
                                       with righte,
Englene lond it aughte wel beo   and engles thareinne alighte;
And swuch folk aughte in heovene   beon englene ifere'
                                           (356, 27–31)

('That land must surely be good and rich', said this holy man, 'for they are very rightly called 'English': they are like angels. If the land is like its people, it is rightly named. A land of angels it must surely

be, with angels alighting there, and such folk ought to be the companions of angels in heaven'.)

Nothing in the Latin sources corresponds to this exuberant
flight of fancy. Whereas in the *vitae* the saint envisages the angelic
English becoming 'fellow-citizens' or 'joint heirs'[29] of the angels
in heaven (i.e., posthumously), *SEL*'s Gregory imagines first
their earthly homeland as itself a sort of paradise on earth, 'a land
of angels' (*Englene lond*), frequented by angels. One cannot help
wondering if the poet's enigmatic 'swete children *threo*' a few lines
earlier is perhaps a veiled allusion to Abraham's three angelic visi-
tors by the oak of Mambre in Genesis 18. In any event, the name
'Engelonde' recurs no fewer than twelve times in the next eighty
lines, which keeps Gregory's inspired word play ringing in our ears
throughout the legend.

The final exchange between merchants and saint, however, in
which he learns that 'al Engelond   is puyr hethenesse' (356,
33, 'England is totally heathen'), ends with Gregory lamenting,
'alas, the sorienesse' (356, 34, 'alas, the sadness!') and returning
to his palace, 'with wel dreorie chere / And carede muche that in
Engelond   Cristinedom ibrought nere' (356, 37–8, 'with a truly
gloomy countenance, and was greatly saddened that Christianity
had not been brought to England'). In all the *vitae* Gregory learns
the English are heathen *early* in the dialogue, not at the end as here
in *Gregory*, a deliberate structural change that effectively emphasizes the saint's profound sympathy for England, and motivates the
next episode, where he requests the 'commuyn conseil' (357, 39,
'general council') of the pope and cardinals to send him to England.
But this episode likewise ends with Gregory disconsolate, as he
is ordered to abandon his mission and return to Rome 'With wel
dreorie chere' (357, 55, 'With a truly sad face'), after the Roman
people's noisy demonstrations force the pope to recall ('of-sende')
the man 'that halt op the conseile of Rome' (357, 51, 'on whom
depends the council [or 'wise government'] of Rome'). After he
has been elected pope, in episode three of the central section of the
legend, the motif of Gregory's sadness for England's predicament
is repeated at the beginning of the fourth episode ('Of the misbi-
leve of Engelonde   gret deol and care he hadde'; 358, 75, 'He
had great sadness and anxiety about England's lack of Christian
faith'), but this time the traveller who has to return to Rome from
the mission to England is St Augustine, bearing the good news
that 'alle the men of Engelonde   Cristindom nome' (358, 87, 'all

the men of England have accepted baptism'). Overjoyed, Gregory sends Austin back with authority to organize the dioceses and appoint the first twelve bishops.

As will be discussed further below, a later *SEL* poet, Görlach's 'A' reviser, saw fit to excise this account of Austin's mission from *Gregory*, and use part of it to expand the account of the mission in *Austin*,[30] but its original appropriateness to *Gregory* is undeniable, both aesthetically and thematically. Austin's journey to England and back in this fourth episode is foreshadowed by Gregory's abortive round-trip in the second episode and the two are linked by verbal echoes.[31] That Austin reports back to Gregory is also important in the context as a reminder that England's conversion, while carried out by Austin, is really due to Gregory, who is 'ibrought in grete blisse' (358, 88) by the news (Austin's feelings are not recorded!) and it is Gregory's instructions about organizing the dioceses that Austin needs to complete his work.[32] All this further serves to justify the poet's concluding celebration of Gregory as the 'Apostul of Engelonde' (358, 97),[33] highlighted by a reminder of the custom of putting English 'children to lore   the hwyle huy beoth luyte' ('starting children in school while they are young') on St Gregory's day (12 March), in commemoration of the 'lore', i.e., Christian doctrine, that he sent to England with Austin (358, 99–101). Thus the central episodes of Gregory's apostledom begin in Rome with English children for sale and end in England with English children going to school. This allusion appears to be the earliest English evidence for Gregory as patron of school children,[34] and the existence of such a custom, whatever its origins or currency outside the poet's locale, affirms Gregory's special place in English tradition. The legend we have been examining is pervaded with a sympathy and abiding respect for this Roman who never set foot in his (and the poet's) beloved 'Engelonde'.

The *SEL Gregory*'s carefully constructed sense of familiarity and warmth of devotion to the saintly Roman 'Apostle of England' is conspicuously lacking in the corresponding legend of the missionary, Augustine of Canterbury, despite the fact that, on the formidable authority of Bede, he really came to England, preached, baptized, performed miracles, died in Canterbury and bequeathed his relics to the abbey he originally dedicated to Sts Peter, Paul and Mary (later to be known as St Augustine's).[35] *SEL*'s *Austin* is barely a saint's life at all. This difference in the character of the two portrayals is partly the result of their respective sources. Whereas *SEL*'s *Gregory* is based (directly or indirectly) on hagiographic

sources and reads like a saint's life, *Austin* is based on the historical
rather than the available hagiographic tradition. A lengthy, floridly
ambitious Latin life of Augustine was composed by the Flemish
hagiographer Goscelin in the early twelfth century,[36] replete with
typically hagiographical episodes before and after the missionaries'
arrival in England. At Cerne in Dorset, for example, Augustine,
after a difficult encounter with the heathen locals, has a heavenly
vision and plants his crozier in the ground to produce a 'fountain
of life' for his thirsty comrades, then christens the spot 'Cernel',
which Goscelin imaginatively explains as deriving from Latin
cerno, I see, and Hebrew *El*, God.[37] But in *SEL*'s *Austin* there is
no such attempt at legendary associations between place and saint.
Apart from the use of the Dorset episode by Wace and Layamon,
Goscelin's work apparently had little impact on the vernacular
tradition until the fifteenth century, when Augustine's cult seems
to have enjoyed a sort of late flowering.[38] After some introductory
verses reviewing the role of Pope Gregory in initiating Austin's
mission (with some echoes of *Gregory* itself),[39] *Austin* becomes
primarily a quite detailed account of the early days of the mission
in Kent leading up to the baptism of King Ethelbert. It is essentially the story first told in Bede's *History* and drastically abridged
in the breviaries.[40] *Austin* follows their example in omitting all the
papal letters, the bulky *Libellus Responsionum* and the problematic encounters between Augustine and the Welsh bishops. But
Austin includes some Bedan details that the breviaries suppress
(e.g., the missionaries' fears) and omits others that the breviaries
do include (e.g., the litany the missionaries sing approaching their
new lodgings; Augustine's visit to Arles to be consecrated; and
the subsequent founding of Canterbury's cathedral and abbey).
Such differences between *Austin* and the breviaries underscore the
poet's apparent agenda of focusing attention closely on the English
king rather than the Roman missionary as the central figure in the
conversion narrative. Another major difference is that whereas the
breviaries compress and rearrange the order of events surrounding
the king's conversion, making it appear that he is the *first* to convert
and the rest follow him,[41] in *Austin*, Ethelbert's crucial conversion
comes *last*, as the climax of a more complex and credible process,
only partly suggested by Bede, which in the end reflects as well on
the people as on Ethelbert. In general we might say that the poet
has reduced, refocused and reshaped the conversion of the English,
this originary moment of contact between England and Rome, so as
to minimize the foreign missionaries' performance and accentuate

the role of the English king and his people in their own salvation. Although salvation comes to them from afar, it seems to emanate as much from within, from the intrinsic character and worth of king and people, as from without, which accords with Gregory's vision of Anglo-Saxon England as an earthly paradise.

The *Austin* poet ensures that the king, speaking in *oratio recta* each time, is prominent at the beginning, middle and end of the conversion story proper, whereas Bede gives Ethelbert's actual words only once (in the middle episode). In *Austin* we hear him respond to the Romans' messenger promising everlasting benefits to Ethelbert and his people (24–8). Ethelbert is presented here as the prudent monarch, pausing to think, then replying that the message from Rome certainly sounds like good news (29–30), and giving orders ('underfongeth . . . honoureth . . . fyndeth'; 24, 31–2, 'welcome . . . honour . . . provide for') to his attendants for the missionaries to be treated well,

> 'fforte Ich habbe with hem ispeke   and heore message seo;
> God leve, as heo me bihoteth   that hit mote to my prou beo.'
>
> (25, 33–4)

(until I have spoken with them and seen their message; God grant that it may be to my benefit, as they promise.)

In Bede and the extant breviaries there is no thoughtful pause, and the king's reply is given in indirect speech, without personal references. The *Austin* poet with a few small additions has created a character for the king, as both royally generous and courteous to the well-meaning strangers, but also with a shrewd eye to possible personal advantage.

Ethelbert's second speech in *Austin*, responding to the missionaries' sermon on eternal life, at the conference on the island, is similarly nuanced. In Bede's version the king, although courteous to the newcomers, is a traditionalist, unwilling to abandon his nation's ancient beliefs in favour of such a new, untried (*nova . . . incerta*) doctrine.[42] In *Austin*, however, he is both more approving of their 'message' and more thoughtful: he says he would indeed accept this 'swythe fair thing'[43] (25, 57, 'very fine proposal') if he could be 'siker that hit sothth were' (25, 58, 'sure that it was true'). But because the message is so new he cannot 'concenti' ('consent') to it '"Are ich habbe more underyite   hwethur this message beo trewe"' (25, 60, 'until I have better ascertained that the message is true'). The Ethelbert of *Austin*, in other words, delays his conversion not, as in Bede, out of unexamined loyalty to the past but in his zeal for the truth. At the same time he promises to provide for the missionaries' needs, generously acknowledging that they have '"itravailede . . . fram so ferre londe / . . . for ore guode, ase . . . ye dothth me onderstonde"' (25, 61–2, 'travelled . . . from such a distant land . . . for our good, as . . . you give me to understand') and assures them they are free to preach their gospel and win converts: '"for I nelle no man weorne"' (25, 66, 'for I won't prevent anyone'). With such sentiments and language Ethelbert is individualized and humanized in the most positive sense, while the Romans, whose 'foreignness' is subtly conveyed in various ways, remain more at a distance from the action and the reader. The English king is, effectively, impresario of this second phase of the establishment of English Christianity (the first phase being Gregory's encounter with the English slaves).

The missionaries' role is further reduced in the final stage of the conversion narrative, where the *Austin* poet drastically abridges Bede's famous account of the apostolic life led by the missionaries in Canterbury. The poet's emphasis is more on the people's response than on the missionaries' preaching or their monastic lifestyle, which in Bede is the crucial factor. We are told in *Austin* that the king gave them a 'swithe fair woniingue' (26, 67, 'very nice lodgings') and that Austin and his companions 'bigonne to prechie faste' (26, 69, 'began preaching in earnest'). But immediately the focus switches to some 'guode' English people who 'to heom heore heorte caste' (26, 70, 'gave them their hearts') and were baptized. The poet's account of the crowds increasingly thronging about the missionaries ('evere the leng the mo . . . ase thicke ase huy mighten go'; 26, 71–2, 'more and more as time passed . . . filling the place to capacity') is adapted from Bede's 'coepere plures cotidie ad audiendum Verbum confluere' ('every day more and more flocked to hear the Word'),[44] but in the *History* this occurs *after* the king's conversion; in *Austin* it is shifted to *before*, implying that Ethelbert's decision to hear the preachers again, and finally make up his mind, is prompted as much by his 'folk' as by the behaviour and 'faire miracles' of the missionaries.

> He wende and heorde eft heore prechingue   and seigh that hit
>   was guod;
> 'To longue', he seide, 'ich habbe abide   ar ich this understod.'
>   (26, 75–6)

(He went and heard their preaching, and saw that it was good. 'Too long,' he said, 'I have waited, before I accepted this'.)

The king's ingratiatingly humble one-liner, his third piece of *oratio recta* in *Austin*, beautifully rounds off his portrait. The last word, 'understod', sums up his conversion as a conscious, reasoned process, and integrates this climactic moment into a sophisticated verbal game involving repeated use of ME *understonden* to mean, by turns, recognise (2), interpret (16), accept (48), understand (62), accept (76) and remember (82).

Amidst such rhetorical moves to personalize and foreground the image of King Ethelbert, the poet of *Austin* does virtually nothing to individualize the saint himself. Jill Frederick remarks on *SEL*'s general tendency to link English saints with English kings as part of a strategy to 'redefine and reclaim the saints as particularly English',[45] but in *Austin* the titular saint is not so much linked with as overwhelmed by the English king. Austin's consecration as the 'furste' ('first') archbishop of Canterbury gets only brief passing reference after Ethelbert's baptism, with no mention of who performed the consecration or where (79–80). This was a bit too much for the 'A' reviser of *SEL*. At this point in the revised *Austin*, he appears to have interpolated a block of verses from *Gregory*, to the effect that Austin, after the mission's first successes, returns to Rome to report to Gregory, who consecrates him archbishop with the authority to create twelve English dioceses.[46]

The overall treatment of the missionary saint in the original *Austin* contrasts markedly with the careful hagiographical construction of the saintly pope in the *Gregory* legend. Austin is regularly dubbed 'Seint', it is true, throughout the eighty-six-line legend in Horstmann's edition, but neither the epithet 'holie man' nor any of the other more clearly saintly attributes (e.g. goodness, counsel, wisdom, purity) lavished on the pope in *Gregory* is ever bestowed on Austin, an omission all the more pointed because, at the beginning of the legend, where a few lines are devoted to an epitome of Gregory's role in initiating Austin's mission, the pope is dubbed 'the holy Mon' who loved England much (24, 3–4). Even Bede's occasional use of *vir domini, servus domini, sanctus pater* and *dilectus Deo pater* lacks any echo in *SEL*.

If there is anything approaching a 'saint' in *Austin* it is the missionaries as a group. In Bede, Augustine is himself credited with specific miracles (e.g. healing a blind man to the discomfiture of the British bishops), but in *Austin*'s only reference to miracles the agent is plural ('The faire miracles that huy duden'; 26, 74, 'the fine miracles that they performed'). Similarly it is the missionaries collectively who are described twice as 'goode men' (24; 9, 20)[47]

Much of the other action of the mission, in fact, is performed collectively by Austin's 'fellawes', from whom he is rarely differentiated. This is, admittedly, a feature of Bede's account of the first stage of the mission, but, as we have seen, the poet is certainly capable of departing from his sources, and in this case he chooses not to.

One unfortunate exception to the tendency for Austin to disappear within the missionary group is the poet's drastically abbreviated version of Bede's account of an incident on the missionaries' journey to England. Fearing rough treatment from the fierce barbarians and the potential difficulty of communicating with them, they decided to send their leader back to Rome to plead with Gregory to call off their mission. The pope, of course, would have none of this, but renewed their resolve by enlisting Frankish interpreters and the good offices of the archbishop of Arles. The breviaries suppress this episode completely. Most of it is omitted in *SEL* also, except for the anxiety about language difficulties, which, however, the poet attributes to Austin alone:

> He dredde him sore for he ne couthe   the speche of Engelonde:
> He nom men with him that couthen   the speche undurstonde.
> (24, 15–16)

> (he was full of dread because he did not know the English language;
> he took men with him who could understand the language.)

Austin's fear of the foreign tongue surely distances him further, in the reader's mind, from Gregory, in whom the foreign words for the slave boys' identity and distant land inspire only a visionary delight and zealous longing to go there. Austin's inability to 'undurstonde' ('interpret') also contrasts with Ethelbert's later decision to 'understand' (26, 76), meaning 'accept,' the missionaries' teaching.

Comparison of the saints' obits at the end of *Gregory* and *Austin* only reinforces the blatant disparity between the two architects of England's conversion as commemorated in *SEL*.

> Thus the holie man seint Gregori   pope was in Rome,
> And sende us into Engelonde   the lawes of Cristindome.
> Holi churche and Cristindom   thorugh him was so iloked here,
> That he is nouthe in heovene   with aungles ifere.
> Bidde we thanne thene holie man   apostle of Engelonde,
> That he bifore Jhesu Crist   ore neode ounderstonde.
> (359, 112–17)

(Thus the holy man, St Gregory, was pope in Rome, and sent us in England the laws of Christianity. Holy Church and Christianity through him were so securely fastened here, that he is now in heaven, a companion of the angels. Let us then beg this holy man, apostle of England, that he remember our need, while in the presence of Jesus Christ.)

The repetition of 'holie', the distinctive locking image, the final pun on angels and 'Angles', the epithet 'apostle', and the intimacy implied in 'oure neode oounderstonde',[48] together imply the warm devotion to Gregory as a special saint of the English. But Austin even at the end receives no such special epithets or imagery. In addition to indicating Austin's feast day, rather off-handedly ('toward the ende of May', 26, 83), as if expecting readers to be unfamiliar with it, the poet makes matters worse with an awkwardly oblique and grammatically conditional recommendation to celebrate it: 'Wel aughte we his dai anouri   yif we weren wel understonde' (26, 82, 'we certainly should honour his feast day, if we were properly reminded of it').[49]

Augustine should have become a major English saint. As mentioned earlier, Bede's *History* provided plenty of information about the mission, Augustine's leadership, miracles and place of burial. But Bede also ensured that the apostle of the English would always be Gregory, not Augustine. *Inter alia*, he interrupts his account of Augustine's mission to devote the first chapter of Book II of the *History* to an effusive encomium of Gregory, climaxing with the story of the slave boys. He then follows this up with a dramatic and detailed episode in which Augustine *is* the main protagonist. In his supposedly triumphant encounter with the native British bishops, resulting in the slaughter of around twelve hundred unarmed Welsh monks, Augustine's display of saintly power has a cold, unsympathetic quality, which Bede does nothing to ameliorate.[50] He rounds out Book I, furthermore, with the mind-numbing bulk of the *Libellus Responsionum*, comprising Augustine's questions to Gregory and the latter's lengthy replies, on issues and problems arising from the monks' pastoral work among their new congregation, including marital customs, menstruation patterns and wet dreams, which are generally agreed to detract more than a little from the greatness of the occasion, and from the potential greatness of Augustine himself. According to one late Victorian scholar, William Bright, some of the questions themselves indicate 'a certain want of elevation of character . . . One feels a . . . sensation akin to disappointment

. . . even to repulsion, in reading of his "difficulties".'[51] In Bede, Augustine is made to play the straight man to Gregory's charismatic sanctity. Much the same might be said of their respective portraits in *SEL*, where, as we have seen, Austin is upstaged by King Ethelbert.

SEL's *Gregory* and *Austin* together constitute a study in contrasts. The former, set mainly in Rome, flatters English readers with an idealized portrait of Gregory as a strenuous ascetic and holy pope, whose sanctity and authority powerfully validate his spontaneous rapport with the English and their name. English readers would be buoyed also by the saint's inspired recognition of England as a kind of Promised Land, albeit one that must be rescued from heathendom.[52] The *Austin* legend depicts the rescue itself, and the initiation of England's Christian history, in terms that are again as flattering as possible to the readers' English self-image, in that the rescue is less a Roman than an English act, or, rather, a series of 'speech acts' by the dominant figure, a king, displaying secular rather than saintly virtues, although the poet also creates a crucial role for the people, who in effect collaborate and even lead their king by example to ensure the success of the mission from faraway Rome. The Romans, including their leader Austin, are little more than 'messagers', their foreignness emphasized by some choice clusters of French loanwords[53] and their preaching conveyed only in reported speech, as a sort of poetic justice, given their leader's anxious reliance on interpreters. The relative insignificance of Austin's cult outside Canterbury and his lack of a distinctive hagiographic tradition certainly facilitated the poet's nationalist agenda, as did his principal source, Bede, but the poet must take the credit, or the blame, for so completely subordinating the cleric to the king.

Notes

1   See, e.g., Susan Crane, *Insular Romance: Politics, Faith, and Culture in Anglo-Norman and Middle English Literature* (Berkeley: University of California Press, 1986); Diane Speed, 'The construction of the nation in medieval English romance', in Carol Meale (ed.), *Readings in Medieval English Romance* (Cambridge: D. S. Brewer, 1994), pp. 135–57; Thorlac Turville-Petre, *England the Nation: Language, Literature and National Identity 1290–1340* (Oxford: Clarendon Press, 1995); Robert Allen Rouse, *The Idea of Anglo-Saxon England in Middle English Romance* (Cambridge: D. S. Brewer, 2005).

2 E.g., Jankofsky, 'National characteristics'; Heffernan, 'Dangerous sympathies', in Jankofsky, pp. 1–17, repr. pp. 295–312 below; Thompson, *Everyday Saints*, pp. 46–57; Frederick, 'National identity'.

3 See Clare A. Lees, 'In Ælfric's words: conversion, vigilance and the nation in Ælfric's *Life of Gregory the Great*', in Hugh Magennis and Mary Swan (eds), *A Companion to Ælfric* (Leiden: Brill, 2009), pp. 271–96.

4 Quotations are from Horstmann. Subsequent *SEL* references are to Horstmann, and occasionally to equivalent texts in the 'A' revision (see Görlach, *Textual Tradition*, pp. 54–5 and *passim*), D'Evelyn and Mill, I, pp. 81–4 (St Gregory) and pp. 214–17 (Augustine of Canterbury).

5 See Thompson, *Everyday Saints*, pp. 11–12.

6 Limitations of space (and expertise) preclude any attempt here to untangle the intricate textual relationship between the two legends and their successive versions: see Görlach, *Textual Tradition*, p. 148 and pp. 171–2, p. 268 (note 61) and p. 278 (note 180).

7 *Bede's Ecclesiastical History of the English People*, ed. Bertram Colgrave and R. A. B. Mynors (Oxford: Clarendon Press, 1969), II.i, pp. 122–35 at pp. 126–9; the 'interpolated' version of Paul the Deacon's *Sancti Gregorii Magni Vita* (BHL 3640), henceforth *Interpolata*, chapters 8 and 14 (*PL* 75: 41–59, at 45 and 48); and the long *Vita*, in four books, by John the Deacon, henceforth JD (BHL 3641), I.41 (*PL* 75: 59–242, at 79–80).

8 *Interpolata* 8–11 and JD I:34–44 (*PL* 75: 45–7, 77–81). The Rogation-tide origin story is however narrated in the *SEL temporale* account of this feast.

9 *Interpolata* 27–8 (*PL* 75: 56–8); JD II.44 and IV.69 (*PL* 75: 104–6, 221–2), from the Anonymous Whitby life, chapter 27, *The Earliest Life of Gregory the Great*, ed. Bertram Colgrave (1968; rpt Cambridge: Cambridge University Press, 1985), pp. 121–3.

10 On the eclectic use of sources in other *SEL* narratives, see E. Gordon Whatley, with Anne B. Thompson and Robert K. Upchurch (eds), *Saints' Legends in Middle English Collections* (Kalamazoo, MI: Medieval Institute Publications, 2004), pp. 175–7, 257–65. On liturgical sources see the essay by Reames in this volume.

11 Görlach, *Textual Tradition*, p. 148.

12 This miracle occurs in *Interpolata* 23, shortly after the English mission in *Interpolata* 21; it forms lection viii in the *Sarum Breviary* (*Breviarium ad usum insignis ecclesiae Sarum*, ed. Francis Procter and C. Wordsworth, 3 vols (Cambridge: Cambridge University Press, 1879–86)), following the English mission in lection vii: Procter and Wordsworth (eds), *Breviarium . . . Sarum*, 3: 212–13.

13 Three thirteenth-century Englishmen – Archbishop Edmund Rich, Bishops Richard Wych and Thomas Cantiloupe – were canonized; Stephen Langton, Robert Grosseteste, John Pecham (a Franciscan)

and Robert Kilwardby (a Dominican) were exemplary by any other
criteria.

14 *Breviarium ad usum insignis ecclesiae Eboracensis*, ed. Stephen W.
    Swayley, 2 vols, Surtees Society 71, 75 (Durham: Andrews, 1880–83),
    2: 215–19.

15 JD 7 is adapted from Gregory's *Dialogues* III.33 (*The Dialogues of
    Saint Gregory, Surnamed the Great . . .*, ed. and trans. Edmund G.
    Gardner (London: Warner, 1911), pp. 160–1).

16 'Verum quanquam pene quotidiano languore tabesceret, nullam tamen
    corpori suo cupiebat commodare quietem, quo minus aut oraret, aut
    legeret, aut scriberet, aut dictaret' (JD I.8; *PL* 75: 65–6).

17 Robert F. Taft, *The Liturgy of the Hours in East and West*, 2nd revised
    edn (Collegeville, MN: Liturgical Press, 1993), pp. 297–300.

18 R. E. Latham, *Revised Medieval Latin Word-List from British and Irish
    Sources* (London: British Academy, 1965), p. 145.

19 Rosemary Woolf, *The English Religious Lyric in the Middle Ages*
    (Oxford: Clarendon Press, 1968), p. 377; *English Lyrics of the XIIIth
    Century*, ed. Carleton Brown (Oxford: Clarendon Press, 1932), pp. 1
    and 165.

20 In *Gregory* the 'conseil' members fast for three days and nights, hoping
    for divine guidance as to which is worthiest to be elected (58–63). In
    contemporary practice, if the conclave failed to reach a two-thirds
    majority vote in three days, progressively severe fasting was imposed.
    On Gregory X's canon, *Ubi periculum* and the Council of Lyons
    in 1174, see J. A. Watt, 'The papacy', in David Abulafia (ed.), *The
    New Cambridge Medieval History, V: c. 1198 – c. 1300* (Cambridge:
    Cambridge University Press, 1999), pp. 155–8.

21 'Dictumque est illi quia de britania insula essent: et cuius incole
    quamvis pagani tamen omnes tali decore niterent' (Swayley, *Breviarium
    . . . Eboracensis*, 2: 216).

22 Ibid., 2: 216, adapted from JD II.21; PL75: 71–2.

23 'Beheold yeorne' is probably suggested by 'quos cum aspiceret' ('when
    he noticed them') in Bede and *Interpolata*; JD has simply *cernens*.
    Yeorne in EME frequently connotes religious zeal or devotion.

24 For queer and post-colonial commentary on the treatment of this
    episode by other medieval and later writers, see Allen J. Frantzen,
    Before the Closet: Same-Sex Love from Beowulf *to* Angels in America
    (Chicago: University of Chicago Press, 1998), pp. 264–92, and Kathy
    Lavezzo, *Angels on the Edge of the World: Geography, Literature, and
    English Community, 1000–1534* (Ithaca: Cornell University Press,
    2006), pp. 27–45.

25 Besides *SEL*, only Layamon's *Brut* (14701) specifies that there were
    'three' boys (*Layamon, Brut or, or Hystoria Brutonum*, ed. W. R. J.
    Barron and S. C. Weinberg (Harlow: Longman, 1995), pp. 756–7).

26 See *OED*, 'thing', n.[1], 10b., for other similarly positive contexts.

27 Lavezzo, *Angels on the Edge*, p. 35.

28 As emended by Horstmann. Cf. D'Evelyn and Mill, I, 82, 29: 'yif the lond is such as the men'.

29 *Concives* in JD I.21 (*PL* 75: 71) and Swayley, *Breviarium* . . . *Eboracensium* 2:216; *cohæredes* in Bede, *History*, II.i (Colgrave and Mynors, 134–5) and *Interpolata* 17 (*PL* 75: 50). Cf. Romans 8: 17, Ephesians 3:6.

30 D'Evelyn and Mill, I, 83, at 78–9 and 80–1; I, 216–17, at 81–90.

31 E.g., 'ayen wende' (357, 55) and 'wende . . . ayen' (358, 86); 'into engelond   to prechie Cristinedom' (357, 41) and 'into Engelonde   to prechi Cristindom' (358, 77). Similarly linked are Gregory's fasts and prayers as a monk (7–14) and during the papal election (60–70).

32 The basic information behind this episode is common to Bede, *History*, I.xxix (Colgrave and Mynors, 104–7) and JD II.37 (*PL* 75: 100), but only JD has *laetificatus*, corresponding to 'ibrought in grete blisse' (*Gregory* 358, 88); in Bede, the instructions about the bishoprics occur in one of Gregory's letters, in JD and *Gregory* they are presented in third person narrative.

33 'Tharefore we cleopiez him in holie bok   Apostul of Engelonde' (358, 97). *Apostolus anglorum* is regularly bestowed on Gregory in the breviaries and *vitae*; 'holie bok' could refer to either or both. On early medieval contexts of the title 'apostle', see Paul Hayward, 'Gregory the Great as "Apostle of the English" in post-Conquest Canterbury', *Journal of Ecclesiastical History*, 55 (2004), 22–6.

34 Bonnie Blackburn and Leofranc Holford-Strevens, *The Oxford Companion to the Year: An Exploration of Calendar Customs and Time-Reckoning* (Oxford: Oxford University Press, 1999), pp. 114–17. See also Nicholas Orme, *Medieval Schools from Roman Britain to Renaissance England* (New Haven: Yale University Press, 2006), p. 155 and n. 183.

35 Bede, *History* I.xxxiii (Colgrave and Mynors, 114–15). On late Anglo-Saxon promotion of Augustine's cult at Canterbury, see Alan Thacker, 'In Gregory's shadow? The pre-Conquest cult of St Augustine', in Richard Gameson (ed.), *St Augustine and the Conversion of England* (Stroud: Sutton, 2000), pp. 383–4.

36 *Vita Sancti Augustini* (*BHL* 777), *Acta Sanctorum*, Maius 6: 375–411; shorter version (*BHL* 778; *PL* 150: 743–64); new ed. in preparation by Richard Sharpe (*A Handlist of the Latin Writers of Great Britain and Ireland before 1540*, Publications of the Journal of Medieval Latin 1, corrected edition (Turnhout: Brepols, 2001), p. 152). See also Fiona Gameson, 'Goscelin's *Life* of Augustine of Canterbury', in Richard Gameson (ed.), *St Augustine and the Conversion of England* (Stroud: Sutton, 1999), pp. 391–409; and Richard and Fiona Gameson, 'From Augustine to Parker: the changing face of the first Archbishop of

Canterbury', in Simon Keynes and Alfred P. Smyth (eds), *Anglo-Saxons: Studies Presented to Cyril Roy Hart* (Dublin: Four Courts, 2006), pp. 17–20; Hayward, 'Gregory the Great', pp. 32–3.

37 *Acta Sanctorum*, Maius 6: 391–2 and *PL* 150: 760.

38 Kenneth H Tiller, *Laʒamon's Brut and the Anglo-Norman Vision of History* (Cardiff: University of Wales Press, 2007), pp. 147–66; for fifteenth-century examples, see *Supplementary Lives in Some Manuscripts of the* Gilte Legende, ed. Richard Hamer and Vida Russell, EETS 315 (Oxford: Oxford University Press, 2000), pp. 171–2, 369–80, and E. Gordon Whatley, 'John Lydgate's *Saint Austin at Compton*: the poem and its sources', in Siân Echard and Gernot Wieland (eds), *Anglo-Latin Literature and Its Heritage: Essays in Honour of A. G. Rigg on his 64th Birthday*, Publications of the Journal of Medieval Latin 4 (Turnhout: Brepols, 2001), pp. 191–227.

39 E.g., Gregory is 'tolde that the lond was good   and that hit hethene was' (*Austin 24,* 5); cf. 'that lond beo guod and riche' and 'Engelond is puyr hethenesse' *Gregory 356,* 27 and 33); 'Wel sori was seint Gregori   that hit Cristene nas' (*Austin 24,* 6); cf. 'alas the sorienesse' and 'that in Engelond   Cristinedom ibrought nere'(*Gregory* 356, 34 and 38).

40 Bede, *History* I.xxiii, xxv–xxvi (Colgrave and Mynors, 68–9, 72–9). Cf. Swayley, *Breviarium . . . Eboracensis*, 2: 286–8; Procter and Wordsworth, *Breviarium . . . Sarum*, 2: 303–6. The *Hereford Breviary* (*The Hereford Breviary, Edited from the Rouen Edition of 1505 with Collation of Manuscripts*, ed. Walter H. Frere and L. E. G. Brown, 3 vols, Henry Bradshaw Society 26, 40, 46 (London: Henry Bradshaw Society, 1904–15), 2: 183–4) is identical to *Sarum*, but ends abruptly after the missionaries' first meeting with Ethelbert, i.e., before any conversions!

41 In Bede, *History* I.xxvi (Colgrave and Mynors, 76–7), a few Canterbury people convert before the king, but after him many more flock to hear the preaching and convert, as the missionaries begin performing miracles.

42 *History*, I.xxv, Colgrave and Mynors, 74–5.

43 Cf. 'Fairer thingus' (*Gregory* 356, 22) in reference to the English slave boys.

44 *History*, I.xxvi, Colgrave and Mynors 76–7.

45 'The *South English Legendary*', 60–1.

46 The 'A' version of *Austin*, D'Evelyn and Mill, I, pp. 216–17, 81–90. One sign that these verses are interpolated is that the initial phrase in 81, 'So longe so this holymen', is syntactically awkward here but fits more coherently in *Gregory* 84.

47 The monks are characterized as 'holymen' twice in the 'A' *Austin* (12 and 81).

48 See *MED*, understonden, v., 7.b, and 13.a.

49 For *understonde* as past participle, used as here in a passive construction, and meaning either 'remember, be reminded of' or 'be knowledgeable about something' see *MED*, understonden v., 5.(b), and
   7.(b); also *OED*, understand, vb. 8.a. Similarly luke warm is *Austin*'s
   difficult opening couplet (1–2), alluding to 'other' missionaries, like St
   Birinus who converted the West Saxons.

50 *History*, II.i (encomium of Gregory), II.2 (Augustine and the Britons);
   Colgrave and Mynors, 122–43, on which see Richard and Fiona
   Gameson, 'From Augustine to Parker', pp. 14–15; on Bede's pos-
   sibly Celtic sources and sympathies, see Ian Wood, 'The mission of
   Augustine of Canterbury to the English', *Speculum*, 69 (1994), 4.

51 Bede, *History*, I.xxvii (Colgrave and Mynors, 78–103); William
   Bright, *Chapters of Early English Church History*, 3rd edn, revised
   and enlarged (Oxford: Clarendon Press, 1897), p. 72. On the authorship of the *Libellus*, see Malcolm Godden, 'Were it not that I have
   bad dreams: Gregory the Great and the Anglo-Saxons on the dangers
   of dreaming', in Rolf H. Bremmer, Jr, Kees Dekker and David F.
   Johnson (eds), *Rome and the North: The Early Reception of Gregory
   the Great in Germanic Europe*, Mediaevalia Groningana, NS 4 (Paris;
   Sterling, VA: Peeters, 2001), pp. 99–105.

52 Lavezzo remarks that Ælfric's homily on Gregory 'encourages the
   Anglo-Saxons to . . . imagine themselves as belonging to a chosen
   people' (*Angels on the Edge*, p. 35).

53 E.g., *Austin* 23–6, where satirical intent is possible in the deadpan
   symmetrical repetition of the French loanwords *message* and *messager*
   in three consecutive *a*-verses, and the ambiguous connotations of
   another French adjective, 'qweynte' (24, 24), as epithet for the first
   messager.

Part IV

Contexts and discourses

13

Dangerous sympathies: political commentary in the *South English Legendary*

Thomas J. Heffernan

The battle was a rout; it was shortlived but fierce. Dead and dying, both baron and commoner, rebel and royalist, fell at Green Hill, a small rise in the fertile Vale of Evesham just north of the city proper.[1] According to the *Flores Historiarum*, Simon de Montfort, the earl of Leicester and leader of the rebellious barons, lost both life and cause in the Battle of Evesham on Tuesday 4 August 1266, shortly after 9 o'clock in the morning.[2] The fight at Evesham on that August morning was seen by contemporaries as, not surprisingly, no less than Armageddon. Chroniclers reported that terrible storms preceded the battle and the sun itself disappeared from the sky on 4 August. The anonymous author of the pro-baronial verse panegyric in MS Cotton Otho, D.VIII (fol. 219r) typifies this extreme reading of the consequences of the loss at Evesham:

> Coelum signa dabat, quoniam sol non radiabat,
> Et motum terrae dedit hora ferissima guerrae.
> Dum sic bellatur, Domini gens dum cruciatur,
> Tunc pluit et tonuit, imbres dedit aetheris ira
> Ingens grando fuit, quo possis dicere mira.[3]

> (The sky gave signs, seeing that the sun was not shining and the most dread hour of war caused an earthquake while the battle was waged, while the people of God were crucified; then it rained and thundered, the anger of the heavens caused the rain; there was huge hail, which you could call marvellous.)

Rishanger's *Chronicle* reported that the sky was so dark that the monks of Evesham, undeterred in their practice of the monastic *horae*, were unable to read the words of the day's choir lesson *propter opacitatem*.[4]

While both sides interpreted these natural signs as prophecies of their impending victory, the rhetoric of the chronicles sympathetic to de Montfort – the overwhelming majority – insinuated that the storms and dark sky marked the death of righteousness and in that regard were like the great storm which followed the death of Christ.[5] There is an entry in a copy of the St Albans *Flores Historiarum* which viewed the incidents of the battle as comparable to the Crucifixion with Earl Simon portrayed as dying a martyr's death.[6] The Chronicle of Worcester which uncritically supported de Montfort and his reform programme referred to de Montfort as a Maccabee and called him *Gigas*, one of the fabled giants, the son of earth and Tartarus. The leader of the rebellious forces, Earl Simon de Montfort, is said to have cried out 'Dieu merci' as he fell fatally wounded.[7] The earl of Leicester was so regarded by the regular clergy that a divine office was composed in his memory honoring the 'new Maccabaeus'.[8]

Simon de Montfort was a bold charismatic leader: he was the first man in English history to lead single-handedly a political movement; to oppose the king, seize power and hold the monarch captive, and rule in the king's name.[9] His evidently considerable personal gifts combined with idealism, ambition and ability have made de Montfort a subject of controversy from his own day to the present.[10] My purpose in this essay is to illustrate the manner in which that political and military reputation was transformed by certain of his contemporaries into a sacral one, and to point to an allusion in the *SEL* as evidence of the cult's tenacity despite royal edicts prohibiting any form of reverence to be given to de Montfort. Hagiographic collections, like the *SEL*, could easily therefore be the vehicle for political commentary. Although he did not consider vernacular materials like the *SEL* as vehicles for political protest, J. C. Russell was the first to examine the manner in which political opponents of the king were transformed into 'saints' so as to serve an anti-monarchial movement. Contemporary scholarships focus on the exemplary characteristics of the hagiographic legends in collections of *libri festivales* which, like the *SEL*, tend to blunt the social and political edge of this genre. The present essay redresses this aspect of these saintly epitomes in order to suggest that such vernacular legendaries were perfectly suited for political commentary, since they could shield themselves from retribution beneath the cloak of religion.[11]

A veteran soldier of Simon de Montfort's calibre must have known that his outnumbered and exhausted troops could not overcome the two armies before him.[12] He was trapped: Prince Edward's greatly superior troops (reckoned at eight thousand foot soldiers) were at his front, his recent supporter Gilbert de Clare, eighth earl of Gloucester, would block his flank with his men along the west bank of the River Avon, and Roger de Mortimer, baron of Wigmore, would cross the River Avon and block de Montfort's attempts to reach London and the south-east, possibly via the Offenham or Bengeworth bridges. A veteran of innumerable battles, de Montfort prepared to fight gallantly, perhaps knowing it would be to the death.[13] On that doomed Tuesday 4 August 1266, in the company of his captive king, he first celebrated mass. He then marched his small troop of supporters two miles north of the walls of monastic Evesham into the green meadows of the Vale of Evesham.[14] He there met the brunt of Prince Edward's superior forces. Edward's troops flung themselves at the rebels, yelling 'death to the traitor' as they came.[15]

The savagery of the attack caused the small contingent of Welsh guards in de Montfort's service to flee. Shortly after Edward's frontal assault, Gilbert de Clare attacked from the rear. Although the battle would be lost, de Montfort and a small band of retainers which included his sons, Henry and Guy, the Justiciar Hugh Despenser and Peter de Montfort, actually managed to breach the enemy's forward line. But this was a pyrrhic victory, more important for the later hagiographer than for the military success of the earl of Leicester. Soon his horse would be felled from under him. And at the end, although the chroniclers tell that he continued to fight on foot, the fifty-seven-year-old earl fell to the earth bleeding from many wounds, commending his soul to God's mercy. The battle was lost and the baronial cause suffered an irreparable defeat.

The royalists considered de Montfort a traitor and treated his remains with savage barbarity. His hair shirt was stripped from his body. Roger de Mortimer is said to have been first to brutalize the earl's corpse: his head, hands, feet and genitals were cut off.[16] His headless trunk was thrown to the dogs, his genitals possibly stuffed into his mouth.[17] The earl of Leicester's youngest son Simon, coming late to his father's assistance, saw his head borne on a pike and carried towards Wigmore Castle where it was prominently displayed during a night of revelry.[18]

The chronicles differ on precisely what parts of his body were mutilated and the ultimate disposition of his corpse. Prince Edward was said to have been repulsed by the barbarity shown to his uncle's body and ordered the monks of Evesham abbey to collect the remains for burial. The continuation of William of Newburgh's *Historia Rerum Anglicarum* in the entry for 1265 reported that, following the dismemberment, the body parts were sent throughout

England but owing to a miracle were brought together again and buried at Evesham.[19] The *Chronicle of London*, possibly reflecting events some time after the battle, states that the monks of Evesham gathered up the mutilated corpse and buried it in the monastic church. The *Waverly Chronicle* is the most specific, remarking that he was buried along with his son and Hugh Despenser under the high altar of the abbey 'in ecclesia conventuali de Evesham, ante magnum altare, scilicet ante gradum inferius'.[20]

But for his enemies even a mutilated corpse in the tomb was a threat. They argued that someone who had been excommunicated and had humiliated Henry through forced renunciation of kingly prerogatives did not warrant consecrated burial. Their opposition against sacred burial may have been successful: the *Oseney Chronicle* states that his body was exhumed and cast into an open sewer which is secret and unknown at the time of the writing.[21] These implacable enemies of the earl of Leicester had precious little interest in whether de Montfort was buried in consecrated ground. That was merely the rationale used to get rid of his body. The royalists were prescient. They knew that de Montfort's popularity in life with the people of England could easily be transferred to his place of burial. And that the very place of his defeat could become a shrine, a rallying place for an anti-royalist faction and thus a continuing threat to the kingdom's stability. Indeed this is exactly what appears to have taken place as the *Historia Rerum Anglicarum* recorded 'in loco ubi nunc habetur honorifice sepultus . . . et in loco ubi occisus est fontem nunc esse amoenissimum, et cunctis infirmantibus inde gustantibus saluberrimum' ('and now in this place he is said to have been honourably buried, and in the place where he was slaughtered (it is said) that there now is the most beautiful fountain, and it is very healthy for all the infirm who drink from there').[22]

For example, the earl of Leicester's fellow rebel, John de Vesey, seigneur of Alnwick Castle, Northumberland, was involved in an action which represents a populist attempt to make of the earl a saviour figure interceding on the side of the commons against an oppressive ruling class. Shortly after the Battle of Evesham, de Vesey obtained the amputated foot of the earl. He took it with him to Alnwick Castle and had a silver shoe reliquary made for it. Such movement gives credence to the chronicler's statement in the continuation to William of Newburgh's *Historia Rerum Anglicarum* concerning the dispersal of the body parts. De Vesey on his expulsion from Alnwick and its subsequent confiscation by the royalists

– his punishment for rebellion and supporting de Montfort – may himself have removed the relic of the earl to Alnwick abbey where it was revered secretly for generations.

The severe mutilation of the earl's body points to the depth of the division between the royalists and the rebels: the royalists wished to humiliate and decimate the baronial cause. The barons' attempts to keep his memory green through efforts like that of de Vesey's coincide with their continued struggle for their cause. In addition, in the royalist triumph at Evesham many saw an opportunity not only for the extirpation of the rebels but also for personal gain. On 6 August, just two days after the Battle of Evesham, Gilbert de Clare began to seize the estates of those he defeated (called by the royalists the *exheredatorum* –'the Disinherited') and those of their known sympathizers. Canon 7 of the *Dictum de Kenilworth* promulgated on 31 October 1266 declared that all ordinances passed by Simon de Montfort, when the earl of Leicester held the royal seal, were null and void *penitus adnichilentur et cassentur*.[23]

The parliament meeting in Winchester on 14 September 1266 declared that the lands of the rebels were to be seized throughout the kingdom. Despite some resistance to such measures from a more moderate faction who aligned themselves with Prince Edward's party, the Crown supported punitive measures against the rebels closely aligned to de Montfort. The effect of these measures abetted an undercurrent of political dissatisfaction which Henry typically did not foresee. In rewarding those who supported him against de Montfort through the confiscation of baronial properties (reclaimable through ransom), Henry exacerbated the potential for further class conflict. For example, the eviction of hereditary baronial families from lands they had held since the Conquest created severe social dislocation for the vassals who lived on these lands. The vassals could not be counted on to welcome their new masters, who, after all, were the representatives of a sovereign whom they did not hold in high regard.[24] Their discontent coalesced at times into new outbreaks of rebellion in which men like Adam Gurdon and Henry of Hastings became types of de Montfort *redux*. And thus Henry unwittingly added to the intense feeling which celebrated the memory of the political saint martyred in the Battle of Evesham.

The papacy was quick to support Henry since it did not wish to jeopardize a regnal system which contributed a sizeable revenue to its upkeep. The newly elected Pope Clement IV, formerly Cardinal

Guy of Saint Sabina, was an old antagonist of the earl of Leicester.
Clement did everything in his power to bolster the king and seek
to ruin the Countess Eleanor, the widow of the earl and mother of
his surviving children. Indeed, he went so far as to empower his
newly appointed legate (4 May 1265), Cardinal Ottobuono Fiesco,
to preach a crusade against the rebels, stating in a letter of 14
October 1265 that he might enter England 'preaching, if necessary,
a crusade, or causing it to be done if he cannot enter the realm'.[25]
After the debacle of Evesham, certain areas like the City of London
resisted for a short while. The names of those Londoners who
fled after Evesham and thus escaped the royalists were entered
on a roll deposited in the Wardrobe. This roll was read publicly
on Christmas 1269 and those named were prohibited from ever
returning to the realm on pain of death. The earl of Leicester's
surviving namesake Simon was exiled to the continent and forbidden to return to England. The king's enmity caused him to have his
sister, the countess, exiled to France. She retired to the Convent
of Augustinian nuns of St Dominic at Montargis, dying in 1275
deprived of her status, her good name and her estates.

A cult devoted to sanctifying the memory of de Montfort appears
to have begun within weeks of his death. This cult appears to
have had a wide populist base with numerous devotees. Further,
it appears that the worship of de Montfort increased rapidly in
the years following his death and persisted for some time despite
severe prohibitions. There is some documentary evidence to argue
that the cult had broad popular support. This evidence is chiefly
the narratives written by the monks of Evesham reporting approximately two hundred miracles performed through the intercession
of de Montfort.[26] These records are brief, many no longer than
a few lines, and they are chiefly concerned with illustrating the
nature of the petition and the physical benefit received by the peti-
tioner. In short, they exist to bolster the claim that de Montfort
was indeed an efficacious patron, saint and martyr. Aside from
their brevity, they are little different than the cultic records used to
support any individual for whom a case for canonization was being
pursued.

   However brief the entries are, they do provide important historical information. For example, we learn the penitents' names,
sometimes their social class, their gender and city or village of
origin. We can thus identify devotees of diverse social classes,
representing the wealthy, the knightly (sometimes accompanied

by *armigerus*), and the villager. Both the secular and regular clergy are represented, from the humble parish priest to clerics of importance. A great number of women and children also came to Evesham and sometimes the date of the benefaction was recorded, as in the following example:

> Emma mulier de villa de Auburne, de comitatu Lincolniae, habuit filiam nomine Elianore, de aetate fere duorum annorum, quae casu, die sanctae Trinitatis anno gratiae MCC septuagesimo secundo, cecidit in quodam vivario, et submarsa est, et mortua. Mater reperiens postea filiam suam ita submarsam, statim extraxit eam de aqua, et mensuravit ad comitem Symonem; statim puella pristinae sanitati, divina gratia opitulante, restituitur. De hoc omnes vicini sui perhibent testimonium.[27]

> (Emma, a woman from the village of Auburn in the County of Lincolnshire, had a daughter by the name of Eleanor who was twelve years old. It happened that on the day [feast?] of the Holy Trinity in the year of grace 1272, she [Eleanor] fell in a certain pond under the water and died. The mother discovering later that her daughter was submerged immediately drew her out of the water and measured her with [the string of] Lord Simon. Immediately, the child was restored to her former health with the help of divine grace. All of her neighbours bear testimony about this.)

The pilgrims came from many English counties, many travelling from cities as distant as Canterbury, and from abroad, Spain, Ireland, e.g., 'Ricardus Seypo, miles Hiberniae'. And as the case quoted above of the child Elianore from Auburn in Lincolnshire makes perfectly clear, the cult of de Montfort appears to have flourished in spite of and years after the harsh prohibition promulgated by Henry III which threatened 'bodily harm' against those who would give reverence to de Montfort. That the perception of physical danger was palpable for those who wished to invoke the name of de Montfort in times of need is made clear in the *Furness Chronicle*. This chronicle, kept for the Cistercian Abbey in Furness, Lincolnshire, until 1298, makes the threat of physical danger appear very real when it records that 'no one dared speak of such things [the cures granted by Simon de Montfort's corpse] for fear of the king and his men'.[28]

With certain singular exceptions, like that of the Westminster continuation of the St Albans *Flores Historiarum*, the contemporary chronicles were sympathetic to the baronial movement against the royalists.[29] Although such leanings could no doubt have caused

them difficulties had they been public, their sentiments were virtually all private, that is intended for the brethren of their particular
religious house and order. An entry written shortly after the Battle
of Lewes in the moderately pro-baronial chronicle of Osney abbey
well illustrates the self-censoring mechanism which fear of reprisal
brought to bear on the monastic historian: 'and we have omitted
from this history much else that was done in these days, for the
sake of the readers' peace, because what perhaps might please the
king's men would displease those who favoured the barons'.[30] It
would appear to be a bolder act of political rhetoric, and possibly a
very foolish one, to make pro-baronial sentiments in a more public
setting and in English. And yet this is what I believe we can see
being undertaken in the West Midlands *SEL*.

The *SEL*'s 'Vita sancti Dominici confessoris' contains certain
carefully chosen remarks about Simon de Montfort which, I
believe, point to the existence of his cultic status with the com-
moners of the West Midlands a generation after his death; the
generation during which both Henry III and Edward I deliberately
made repeated efforts to extirpate sympathy for de Montfort and
his cause. Such a transformation of the ambitious, tough-minded
political warrior into a martyred saint, although invested with all
the trappings of medieval hagiography, served a politically dangerous end – to perpetuate the memory of the dead earl as a means of
keeping the reformist movement alive. What is arresting in this
present instance is that a *liber festivalis* like that of the *SEL* is the
chosen vehicle for such political commentary.[31]

In the present essay I wish to examine a brief but hitherto
unexamined remark made about Simon de Montfort in the *SEL
Dominic*. The lines read:

An Eorl thare was in the londe tho   that guod Man was inough:
Sire Symon de Mountfort   that to alle guodnesse drough,
His fader that was here aslawe   among us in Engelonde
At the batayle of Evesham   that longue worth onderstonde.
This guode knyght Sire Symon   strong knyght was inough
And agein this uvele cristine men   to batayle al day he drough.
                                                    (279, 39–44)

. . .

And Sire Symon de Mountfort   that guod knight was and
                                                    hende,
Sosteinede this holie men   to bringue this dede to ende.

| Ich wene, Ich may for sothe it segge | yif huy nadden ibeo bifounde, |
| The world hadde for grete sune ibeo | are this ibrought to grounde! |

(282, 156–9)

(There was an earl in that country who was a good man, Sir Simon de Montfort, who showed forth all virtue. He was the father of the one slain here in England at the battle of Evesham, whose worth we well knew. This good knight Sir Simon was a strong knight and true and clashed always against corrupt Christians [39–44] . . . This Sir Simon de Montfort, chivalric and worthy, helped the holy men to accomplish their goal. I believe that I may truly say, if they had not been found the world for great sin would ere now been brought ground. [156–9])

The Simon de Montfort whom the author is singling out for praise is, as the text is careful to point out, the father of the Simon who was slain at Evesham. It was this elder Simon, also earl of Leicester, who was the military leader who assisted St Dominic in his efforts to crush the Catharists in the Midi and died leading the destructive siege of Toulouse in September 1217.[32] The Cathars were seeking religious freedom, but it is well to underscore that they were also seeking more autonomy from the dominance of the north. Simon de Montfort's struggle with St Dominic against the Cathars was both religious and political. Dominic's evangelization of the Midi would not have achieved the success it did without the assistance of the elder de Montfort. But having accounted for the importance of de Montfort in Dominic's evangelistic programme, we still need to enquire into the pertinence of these lines in our text. Why do the lines in the *SEL* single out the heroism of Dominic Guzman's military confidant? To be sure, de Montfort senior was an important player in the historical record: he was primarily responsible for the military reestablishment of Catholicism in those areas of the Midi under the sway of Catharism; he was the hero of the Battle of Toulouse, and worked closely with Dominic to establish the rule of orthodoxy. There is ample reason then for mentioning their friendship in the *SEL*.

Aside from their correctness in the historical record, however, there is the equally important concern as to whether these remarks function effectively in the *SEL*. The *SEL* is very deliberately an English, one might almost say local, *liber festivalis* and as such was principally designed to create in the listener a reverence for the matter of that particular liturgical day. How pertinent given this

West-Midland audience is the anecdote of St Dominic and Simon de Montfort, the crusader against the Cathars? The life of St Dominic is filled with legendary materials which would underwrite Dominic's sanctity and that of the Dominicans more adroitly and have a broader appeal to what was, I believe, a semi-literate audience, than these lines celebrating his military colleague. Moreover, would such historical incidents justify the homage given to him in the above lines for this particular English audience, an audience for whom the struggle against the Cathars more than half a century earlier had little personal consequence? And what of the mention of his son, Simon? Why is he cited in the above quotation from the life of St Dominic? There is no record which suggests that the child de Montfort ever even met Dominic. Moreover this Simon, who led the rebellious barons of England, is mentioned only obliquely, rather referentially. It is difficult to explain with certitude the allusion to the seigneur of Kenilworth Castle in these lines. Perhaps the mention of the son is an attempt on the scribe's part to avoid having the English listener confuse the two men, the one well-known to the audience and the elder foreign.

Since the *vitae* in the *SEL* are essentially translations of existing Latin *vitae sanctorum*, a preliminary way to address the issue of emphasis is to examine the sources of the Dominic *vita* used in the *SEL*. If the lines quoted above are present in an exemplar used by the *SEL* scribe, then he may simply be reflecting the authority of his source. However, if these lines are not present, and we can identify the sources from which the Dominic life in the *SEL* is taken, then we may provisionally see them as a commentary designed for this particular English community. Many of the narratives in the *SEL* are taken from the *Legenda aurea* with little attempt to adumbrate de Voragine's influential work. And such compelling influence from the *Legenda aurea* is clearly evident in the *SEL Dominic*. Indeed, a close inspection of this English *vita* of St Dominic with its counterpart in the *Legenda aurea* illustrates that the English text is essentially a translation of the text in the *Legenda aurea*. However, there is a small but compelling difference between the *SEL* text and its Latin exemplar. Significantly, the lines above attesting to the heroism of Simon de Montfort against the heresy of Catharism – and the reference to his son – are not in the life of St Dominic in the *Legenda*. Furthermore, I have been unable to find a Latin or earlier English exemplar which might have supplied these references to the de Montforts.[33]

If the scribe of the Dominic *vita* in the *SEL* is responsible for
the addition of these lines, the homage being paid to Simon de
Montfort senior takes on a rather more complex political motive.
If my argument about the uniqueness of the de Montfort anecdote
in the English text is correct, I believe we can conclude, first, that
this brief account was written specifically for this English audience; second, it is more likely that this audience was interested in
Simon of Evesham and his role in history than that of his father;
third, the references are intentionally oblique and have a double
meaning because expressions of praise for Simon de Montfort were
not politically shrewd during the closing years of the thirteenth
century. Although Edward I understood the need to initiate a
programme of reform, he was also intent, as Anthony Tuck says,
on asserting 'the jurisdictional supremacy of the crown' and had
little sympathy in the first decade of his reign for the de Montforts
or those whom he suspected still retained sympathy for the causes
which gave rise to the Provisions of Oxford.[34] Thus the scribe may
have intentionally used the references to Simon and Dominic in a
guarded manner because the political climate was yet hostile.

The allusion to the de Montforts provides the listener with the
resources necessary to make the following interpretative move: all
the references to Simon de Montfort senior are a type of metaphoric displacement and should be understood as references to the
son. There is no formal rhetorical figure or trope to identify the
particular narrative strategy being used. However, it is a commonplace of richly contextual arguments and can be best identified as
an extrapolative trope. To wit, the encomiastic remarks which are
said about the father should be understood as being said about the
son. Furthermore, the expression 'that longue worth onderstonde'
appears to refer appositionally to the phrase 'At the batayle of
Evesham', thus pointing by indirection to the heroism of Simon de
Montfort of Evesham.

Lastly I would ask that we consider that the feast of St Dominic
is celebrated on 4 August. This is the very date of the Battle of
Evesham, a date which had become the unofficial feast day of the
revered but uncanonized Simon de Montfort – since it was on this
day that so many of the chronicles celebrate his spiritual victory.
For example, the copy of the *Flores Historiarum* in the Chapter
Library of Westminster (James MS. 24) remarked that Simon
'will be received in heaven as a reward for his labours'.[35] It strains
even historical scepticism to presume that the scribe of the *SEL*
writing in Gloucestershire within a generation of Evesham was

unaware of these two singular moments. Indeed, the coincidence of these two dates for the scribe was undoubtedly something that he would have believed providential. If we can assume with some plausibility that the scribe of the *SEL Dominic* could have believed that the occurrence of the two events on the same day was indeed providential, then we can imagine him – despite the hostile political climate – believing that the feast day of Dominic and the death of de Montfort were ordained by God for 4 August and thus he was obliged to celebrate the memory of both. Furthermore, some of the incidents discussed about Earl Simon, the hero of Toulouse and St Dominic, would have enabled the congregations to extrapolate about their Simon de Montfort, the martyr of Evesham, and his ever faithful cleric, that man of God who celebrated mass for him on the morning of the Battle of Evesham, Bishop Walter de Cantilupe.

It is one of history's grand ironies that de Montfort was defeated by the nephew whom he had tutored in the tactics of warfare. As recently as 15 October 1259, Prince Edward swore to aid his uncle Simon against all men except his father the king, to whom both owed their fealty. Although we will never know how the political system of England might have changed had de Montfort lived, we do know that his death at Evesham was crucial in establishing a cult dedicated to revering his memory. With a lightning swift convergence of the collective will, the common people of the West Midlands turned his defeat into their triumph. Theirs was a triumph which transformed the ambitious, battle-scarred spokesman for constitutional reforms into a religious hero. The royalist forces won the day but the commons of England gained a martyr saint and a political saviour around whose cause political dissent could continue to seek legitimacy. The *Brut Chronicle* illustrates this depth of feeling on the part of the commons:

> Wanne king Herry hadde the victori at Evesham, and Simonde the erle was y-sley by the helpe of Gilberte off Claire, erle of Gloucestre, the wiche was in the warde of the foreseid Simon by the assignemente of kynge Herry. And afterward the same Gilberte was with king Herry in the forseide bateille of Evesham, were-thurgh the forseide Simon was destroiedde; and thatt was grete harme to the comens of Englonde, thatt so gode man was destroiedde, ffor he was dede for the comenne profite of the same ffolke, and therefore God hathe schewed ffor him many grete miracules to diverse ffolkes of her maladies and grevawnce, werefore thei have be heledde.[36]

The de Montfort heirs – with some exceptional privileges granted to wives and widows of the rebels – were pariah from their defeat at Evesham and throughout part of the reign of Edward I.[37] The royalist party considered all who supported the de Montforts as traitors to the Crown and harried these individuals with special vehement 'bodily harm' during the last ten years of Henry III's reign. It would appear that one of the reasons that Gilbert of Clare, the youthful Earl of Gloucester, deserted de Montfort prior to the debacle at Evesham was his hatred for special privileges afforded the de Montfort sons. Obvious expressions of sympathy for the baronial cause in the English language, no matter how oblique, suggest a larger current of sympathy. Such public sympathy was not without risk and could lead to serious consequences. Thus the few lines in the *SEL*, a text designed for public recitation, written perhaps within a generation of Evesham, and in the very region where the war between king and baron was so hotly contested, beg our attention.

Why are these words of praise for Simon – a man, no matter how noble his intention, who was demonstrably a traitor to his king – in an English *liber festivalis* like the *SEL*? They are there to give voice to the popular imagination as it gives homage to politico-religious heroes in opposition to the wishes of the ruling classes. Surely the compiler knew of the attendant risks for any remarks which could be read in a flattering manner. It is entirely possible that reverence for the cult of Simon reached such proportions during Edward's reign that it had achieved some legitimacy in the Midlands and the populace fully approved the mention of his name in a collection of saints' lives. It is interesting to note that, although the apparatus of canonization had long become centralized in the Roman curia, the English continued to nurture local cults for some time, e.g., the worship given to 'Saint' Richard Rolle in the 1350s in Yorkshire. Ostensibly it was hoped that efforts like that afforded to the memory of de Montfort would assist formal petitions for sanctity and further serve as a vehicle for political protest.

Simon de Montfort did have the support of those members of the church hierarchy who believed in his reformist policies, reformist bishops of England, like the bishop of Worcester, Walter Cantilupe, his most passionate episcopal backer, and the bishops of Winchester, London, Lincoln, Salisbury and Coventry. De Montfort also received some support from certain influential mendicants, men like Adam Marsh, whose sagacity was respected by many including Henry III. Yet, at the same time, Simon's

movement against Henry was perceived by many as an attempt
to destroy the very hierarchial fabric of the medieval social order:
the king was the Lord's secular champion and the pope his vicar.
Aquinas argued that a prince could not be coerced by the law;
rather, the law has coercive force only from the power of the prince.
Viewed from this theological perspective, de Montfort's actions,
although one might argue that they were directed at bringing about
socially redemptive behaviours, violated both civil and canon law.
Indeed, de Montfort died as an official excommunicant ostensibly
because he reneged on his vow to accept Louis IX's ruling concerning the legitimacy of the Provisions of Oxford. The great curse
was legitimated by Pope Urban IV on 21 February 1264.[38] Urban,
a Frenchman and royalist, supported King Louis IX, ruling, in
the *Mise of Amiens*, to remove all restraints on Henry III's royal
prerogatives negotiated by the provisions of Oxford. Urban's successor Clement VI, nursing old grievances against de Montfort, in
a letter of August 1265 to his legate in England, Ottobuono Fiesco,
warned him 'not to admit a treaty of false peace until the pestilent
man with all his progeny be plucked out of the realm'.[39]

Yet the people of England so continued to revere his cause that
Henry III, through his counsellors in the eighth canon of the
Dictum de Kenilworth, published 31 October 1266 and addressed
to the papal legate, Ottobuono Cardinal of St Adrian, ordered
that the church should see to it that Simon de Montfort 'should
not be regarded a saint or a just man (*pro sancto vel iusto reputetur*)
since he died excommunicate according to the tenets of the Holy
Church; and the vain and fatuous miracles (*et mirabilia*) attributed
to him by others (*ab aliquibus*) shall not pass any lips; and let the
Lord King strictly forbid this under threat of bodily harm (*sub
pena corporali*)'.[40] Canon 8 should be read with care: first, although
but a scant ten weeks since the Battle of Evesham, the *Dictum* finds
it necessary to sanction those who call de Montfort a saint and to
proscribe miracles attributed to him; second, by implication and
the threat of *sub pena corporali* it underscores the king's realization
that this popular movement was directed as much against himself
and towards those of the official church hierarchy who supported
the royalist position as it was towards reverencing the earl of
Leicester's memory. Despite such threatening official pronounce-
ments against de Montfort, his cult as evidenced in works like the
SEL continued to grow both with the clergy and the laity.

Although Edward I characteristically acted with more pru-
dence and political wisdom than his father, he nonetheless

sought to keep the de Montfort family from re-establishing any
legitimacy in England.[41] For example, Edward resented the
repeated attempts on the part of Simon's youngest son, Amaury
de Montfort, to have the sentence of excommunication removed
from his father.[42] Edward wrote a letter remonstrating with
Clement IV requesting that the sentence be maintained. Indeed,
the animosity between the cousins, Edward I and Amaury de
Montfort, continued unabated at least through 1285. Given the
continuity of such royal displeasure for the de Montfort heirs
through much of the 1280s, it makes enormous sense, if the scribe
of the *SEL* – a text composed and circulated not too terribly far
from Evesham where we might expect support for de Montfort to
be strong – wishing to applaud the merits of Simon the martyr of
the Battle of Evesham, did so indirectly through encomia about
his father.

Notes

1 N. M. Trenholme, 'Evesham: a history of the borough', in J. W.
   Willis-Bund and William Page (eds), *The Victoria History of the
   County of Worcester* (London: Constable & Co., 1906), vol. II, pp.
   371–96 (371).

2 *Flores Historiarum*, ed. Henry Richards Luard, RS 95 (London: Eyre
   & Spottiswode for HMSO, 1890), vol. III, p. 5 and note: 'bellum
   intulit hora diei tertia . . .'. The greatest detail concerning time and
   place of the battle of Evesham is in the *Osney Chronicle*, in *Annales
   Monastici*, ed. Henry Richards Luard, 5 vols, RS 36 (London: HMSO,
   1864–69), vol. IV, p. 174: 'gestum est hoc praelium extra oppidum
   Eveshamiae die Martis proxima post festum S. Petri ad Vincula,
   quarto die mensis Augusti, pridie scilicet nonas eiusdem mensis'.

3 *The Chronicle of William de Rishanger, of the Barons' Wars*, ed. J. O.
   Halliwell (London: Camden Society, 1840), p. 142. These remarks
   about the storms preceding the Battle of Evesham occur in many of the
   chronicles which treat the incident.

4 Halliwell, *Chronicle*, p. 47.

5 Antonia Gransden, *Historical Writing in England c. 550 to c. 1307*
   (Ithaca: Cornell University Press, 1974), p. 421.

6 Ibid.

7 Luard, *Annales* IV: 170.

8 George Prothero, *Life of Simon de Montfort, Earl of Leicester* (London:
   Longmans, 1877), appendix.

9 D. A. Carpenter, 'Simon de Montfort: the first leader of a political
   movement in English history', *History: The Journal of the Historical
   Association*, 246 (1991), 3–23.

10 B. Wilkinson, *The Later Middle Ages in England 1216–1485* (New York: McKay, 1969), p. 72.

11 Josiah Cox Russell, 'The canonization of opposition to the king in Angevin England', in C. H. Taylor and J. L. La Monte (eds), *Haskins Anniversary Essays in Medieval Studies* (Boston: Houghton Mifflin, 1929), pp. 279–90. See also J. W. McKenna, 'Popular canonization as political propaganda: the cult of Archbishop Scrope', *Speculum*, 45:1 (1970), 608–23. While I know of no work of scholarship which has focused so deliberately on the political nature of the hagiographic texts in the *SEL*, Jankofsky has underscored the overt nationalist sentiment in a number of these legends, e.g., the anti-Norman spirit in the *Wulfstan* epitome; see his 'National characteristics', p. 85, and his '*Legenda Aurea* materials in the *South English Legendary*: translation, transformation, and acculturation', in Dunn-Lardeau, pp. 317–30 (322).

12 Wilkinson, *Later Middle Ages*, p. 79.

13 Halliwell, *Chronicle*, p. 45: 'Hortabatur Hugonem Dispensatorem et Radulphum Basset caeterosque fideles ut fugerent, tempora expectantes meliora . . .'

14 Trenholme, 'Evesham', pp. 372–3.

15 Charles Bemont, *Simon de Montfort Earl of Leicester, 1208–1265*, trans. E. F. Jacob (Oxford: Clarendon Press, 1930), p. 242.

16 Halliwell, *Chronicle*, p. 46: 'Comes Leyc., capitaneus eorum, capite truncatus, pedibus et manibus amputatis . . .'

17 Bemont, *Simon de Montfort*, p. 243, n. 2.

18 Halliwell, *Chronicle*, p. 46: 'cuius capud uxori Rogeri de Mortuo Mari, in castro Wigorniae praesentatur'.

19 *Chronicles of the Reigns of Stephen, Henry II and Richard I*, ed. Richard Howlett, RS 82 (London: Longman & Co., 1885), vol. II, p. 548.

20 Luard, *Annales* vol. II, p. 365.

21 Luard, *Annales* vol. IV, p. 177.

22 Howlett, *Chronicles*, p. 548.

23 *Documents of the Baronial Movement of Reform and Rebellion 1258–1267*, ed. R. E. Treharne and I. J. Sanders (Oxford: Clarendon Press, 1973), p. 322.

24 The supporters of de Montfort were equally rapacious towards certain groups, notably the Jews. See P. R. Coss, 'Sir Geoffrey de Langley and the crisis of the knightly class in thirteenth-century England', in T. H. Aston (ed.), *Landlords, Peasants and Politics in Medieval England* (Cambridge: Cambridge University Press, 1987), pp. 193–5.

25 *Calendar of Entries in the Papal Register Relating to Great Britain and Ireland: Papal Letters, A.D. 1198–1304*, ed. W. H. Bliss (London: Eyre & Spottiswoode, 1893), vol. I, p. 419.

26 Halliwell, *Chronicle*, pp. 67–110.

27 Ibid., p. 101. The word *mensuravit* is interesting and is first used in England at approximately this date (see R. Latham, *Revised Medieval*

Latin Word-List from British and Irish Sources (London: British Academy, 1965), p. 295). 'Mensuravit' refers to a piece of string which was first used to measure the corpse of the recently deceased saint. This cord was then saved and used as a sacral object in its own right. For example, in the present instance, the mother would have placed the string lengthwise on the child Elianore's body thereby hoping to revive the child. The example of Emma and her daughter Elianore presents a problem since the precise location of the child's putative death is not given. How did the mother avail herself of the miraculous string? The miracle suggests that she had immediate access to the string of the Earl of Leicester. Did the child die having accompanied her mother on pilgrimage to Evesham or alternatively did she die near her home and the mother travelled to Evesham for the relic? There is one other possibility and that is that pilgrims to Evesham might return to their home with bits of string which were then kept as sacred relics. While I have no evidence for this last suggestion, it does make it easier to account for the chronicler's use of the word 'statim' on two occasions, suggesting immediate access to the string, and 'vicini', her neighbours.

28 Howlett, *Chronicles*, pp. 548: 'Sed non [ausus] est quisquam huiusmodi [aliquid] propolare propter timorem regis et suorum.'
29 Gransden, *Historical Writing*, p. 420.
30 Ibid., p. 431.
31 Horstmann, pp. 278–88.
32 M. H. Vicaire, *Saint Dominic and His Times*, trans. Kathleen Pond (New York: McGraw Hill, 1964), p. 233.
33 For a discussion of the relationship between the Life of St Dominic in the *Legenda aurea* and that in the *SEL*, see Warren F. Manning, 'The Middle English life of Saint Dominic: date and source', *Speculum*, 31 (1956), 82–91. Although Manning was not concerned with Simon de Montfort, it is clear from his analysis that the references to de Montfort were not contributed to the *SEL* by the *Legenda aurea*. Manning makes the interesting suggestion that the author of the Life of St Dominic was a Dominican resident in their house at Gloucester. While I think such a suggestion would require more rigorous examination, the mendicants were strong supporters of the de Montforts' reformist efforts and thus Manning's suggestion (made for other reasons) is plausible. Manfred Görlach concurs with Manning on the relationship of the *SEL Dominic* and the *Legenda aurea* as well as on the possibility of Dominican authorship; see his *Textual Tradition*, pp. 186, 286, and more recently his 'The *Legenda Aurea* and the early history of the *South English Legendary*', in Dunn-Lardeau, pp. 301–16 (304–6). For a discussion of the material which went into the Life of St Dominic and the *Legenda aurea*, see Sherry L. Reames, 'The legacy of the founder', in *The Legenda Aurea: A Reexamination of Its*

Paradoxical History (Madison: University of Wisconsin Press, 1985), pp. 164–95.

34 *Crown and Nobility 1272–1461: Political Conflict in Late Medieval England* (Oxford: Blackwell, 1986), p. 14.

35 Gransden, *Historical Writing*, p. 421.

36 Another English chronicle which shares this pro-baronial sentiment which we see in the *Brut* is *The Metrical Chronicle of Robert of Gloucester*, ed. William Aldis Wright, 2 vols, RS 86 (London: HMSO, 1887), vol. II p. 764; notice the similarity of the verb used to describe Simon de Montfort's death and that used in the *SEL*: 'Tho was the bataile strong   in either side alas/Ac atten ende was binethe   thulke that feblore was/And Sir Simond was *aslawe* and is folk al to grounde/More murthre yare nas   in so lute stounde/Vor there was werst Simond   de Mountfort *aslawe* alas' ll. II, 714–8.

37 Clive H. Knowles, 'Provision for the families of the Montfortians disinherited after the Battle of Evesham', in P. R. Coss and S. D. Lloyd (eds), *Thirteenth Century England I* (Woodbridge: Boydell Press, 1986), pp. 124–7.

38 Bliss, *Calendar*, pp. 410–11.

39 Bliss, *Calendar*, p. 419.

40 Treharne, *Documents*, p. 322.

41 Edward was still seeking to disinherit those who were 'rebels' as late as May 1275. For evidence see the *Calendar of the Patent Rolls, Edward I A.D. 1277–1281* (London: Eyre & Spottiswoode, 1901), p. 119; the entry for 19 May reads: 'Commission to Stephen de Penecestre and Ralph de Sandwico to enquiry by jury of the counties of Kent, Surrey and Sussex what lands and tenements of those who took part against the King and Henry III in the late disturbance in the realm have not yet been seized into the king's hands, and who the said persons were and in whose hands the said lands and tenements now are, and what is their yearly value, and to seize all such lands and tenements into the king's hands, according to the provision formerly made'. See Sir Maurice Powicke, *King Henry III and the Lord Edward: The Community of the Realm in the Thirteenth Century*, 2 vols (Oxford: Clarendon Press, 1947), esp. chapters x–xii.

42 Bliss, *Calendar*, p. 434.

14

'His right hond he liet of-smite': Judas/ Quiriac and the representation of Jewish identity in the *South English Legendaries*

Heather Blurton

In the earliest of the extant *SELS*, that found in the Laud manu-script (Oxford, Bodleian MS Laud Misc. 108) and dated to the end of the thirteenth century, the *passio* of St Quiriac appears as an element of the *Invention of the Holy Cross* which opens the incom-plete text.[1] St Quiriac is the (apocryphal) first bishop of Jerusalem, who, when the evil emperor Julian the Apostate comes to town, is duly martyred, and subsequently remembered on 4 May. His nar-rative is linked to that of the *Invention of the Holy Cross* because, before he became the bishop of Jerusalem, Quiriac was Judas, the Jew whose grandfather helped bury the cross after the crucifixion, and in whose family the information about the location of the cross has been passed down from generation to generation. As a result of his experiences with St Helen and her discovery of the True Cross, Judas is converted to Christianity, takes the new name of Quiriac, becomes bishop and is martyred.

This study will resituate the version of Quiriac's story told in the earliest manuscript of the *SEL* from liturgical to cultural history, by considering it in the context of the contemporary coin-clipping scandal of the late thirteenth century, and of the punitive actions against English Jews subsequently taken by Edward I. In the thirteenth century, coin-clipping was increasingly associated with Jewish moneylenders: as early as 1247 Matthew Paris complained that the kingdom's coinage was being 'circumcised by the circum-cised',[2] and the association is epitomized at the end of the four-teenth century in Coveteise's oft-quoted lines from *Piers Plowman*: 'I learned among Lumbardes a lesson, and of Jewes / To Weye pens with a peis, and pare the hyeste' (B.V.238–9, 'I learned a lesson from Lombardes and Jews: to weigh pennies with a scale and to pare down the highest').[3] In the *SEL*, Quiriac himself is clipped, as his hand is 'of-smite' in the course of his martyrdom. This torture obliquely figures the traditional punishment for coin-clipping: the loss of a hand. Admittedly, these connections are circumstantial: a strange torture in the passion of a converted Jew, the resemblance of that torture to a traditional punishment for coin-clipping, and the further coincidence of the implication of the Jews in a coin-clipping scandal that was contemporary in time and location to the probable origin of the *SEL*. But if the connections hold, they may reflect contemporary anxieties about the Jews as counterfeiters, not only of coins but, through conversion, of Christian identity. I will suggest that the discourse of counterfeiting that originates in false coins is imaginatively transformed in this narrative into a discourse of counterfeit identity; specifically, the *SEL passio* of St Quiriac articulates cultural anxiety about whether the conversion of Jews to Christianity can ever achieve more than a counterfeit Christian identity.

If it is correct that the version of the *SEL* in the Laud manuscript was initially preceded by a now-lost collection of *temporale* material, the Passion of St Quiriac that ends the *Invention of the Holy Cross* would then be the first proper saint's life of the collection, forging a link of sorts between the *temporale* and the *sanctorale* material.[4] Rather than following the chronological narrative of the history of the holy rood, its discovery and exaltation common to most of the *SELS* as to the *Legenda aurea*, the Laud *SEL* begins with the discovery of the cross, followed by its history, and ends with a short adaptation of the *Exaltation* followed by a series of *exempla* in which Jews attack the cross.[5] Although the narrative organization of the Laud manuscript may be due to scribal confusion,[6] its effect is to enfold the entire history of the cross, from its creation, through its triumphant role in the making of a Christian empire, within the life story of one Jew. The consideration of Jewish identity that is central to Quiriac's story is thus foregrounded at the very beginning of the Laud *SEL* manuscript.[7]

The *Inventio* narrative also functions as a *vita* for Quiriac, while his martyrdom is brief, taking only thirty-four lines. The action of the martyrdom begins almost immediately. Quiriac refuses the demands of the emperor that he give up Christianity, and first his hand is cut off, then he is forced to drink molten lead, is roasted on a griddle and finally boiled in oil before being stabbed through the heart, at which point his soul goes directly up to heaven. In this context, the amputation of the hand stands out: of the tortures, the description of this moment is the lengthiest, and it is the first scene in the *passio* where the saint and his persecutor interact. The *passio* begins,

Seint Quiriac, that Bischop was   prechede Godes lawe.
The luthere Aumperour Julian   broughte him of dawe,
For the holie rode that he fond   and for he men thereto drough
To bilieven on Jesu Crist –   for he heold it al wough.
Tho the Aumperour hadde Seint Quiriac   biforen him ibrought,
He bad him bilieve on heore maumates   and tho he nolde
                                                                                       nought,
His right hond he liet of-smite   and seide, 'Ich do the this
For tho hast tharewith iwrite   agein ore lawe, iwis.'

                                                                       (11, 357–64)

(St Quiriac, the bishop, preached God's law. The evil Emperor
Julian brought him to trial, because of the holy cross that he found,
and because he drew men to it to believe in Jesus Christ – because he
thought it was very wicked. So the Emperor had St Quiriac brought
before him. He asked him to believe in their idols, and when he
would not, he had his right hand cut off, and said, 'I do this to you
because you have often written therewith against our law, I know.')

This torture suggests the exhortation of Matthew 5:30: 'And if
thy right hand scandalize thee, cut it off, cast it from thee: for it is
expedient for thee that one of thy members should perish, rather
than thy whole body be cast into hell.' Even allowing for the justification that the hand has been targeted because it has written
against 'our law', the amputation of the hand seems an odd torture
in this context – so many of the saints' lives in the *SEL* draw on a
common repertoire of torture and execution that the loss of a hand
stands out. Of Quiriac's three tortures, the last two are characteristic of saints' passions. However, the loss of Quiriac's hand has
significance beyond a literal attack on the offending hand. The
amputation of Quiriac's hand is symbolically reminiscent of a specifically judicial punishment: indeed, it is reminiscent of what was,
by the end of the thirteenth century, an old-fashioned punishment
for coin-clipping – that is, counterfeiting money.

   The amputation of a hand had been the traditional penalty for
counterfeiting since the Anglo-Saxon period. In the late twelfth
century, the legal theorist Glanville 'classed *crimen falsi,* or counterfeiting, along with sedition, robbery, rape and homicide, among
others' as treason 'and stated that these crimes were to incur the
extreme penalty or amputation of members'.[8] Thus Henry of
Huntingdon notes with satisfaction: 'It is rewarding to hear how
severe the king was towards wicked men. For he had almost all the
moneyers throughout England castrated and their right hands cut
off for severely debasing the coinage.'[9] As the image of the king on

the coin became increasingly associated with the person of the king, counterfeiting money began to approach *lèse-majesté*, and thus to merit capital punishment, and by the end of the thirteenth century the more common punishment for counterfeiting money, as for other forms of treason, was hanging.[10] Ironically, the persistence of the connection between coin-clipping and the amputation of the guilty clipper's hand in the popular imagination is succinctly demonstrated by a Jewish response to allegations of the crime. Condemning the practice in a letter of c. 1276–86 to a London rabbi, Rabbi Meir of Rottenburg expostulates: 'Cut off their hands! . . . How much blood has been spilled by these and others like them who invalidate the currency. These are the ones who have brought destruction upon the Jewish inhabitants of France and England.'[11] Hanging, however, may not have been as rhetorically useful in the signifying economy of hagiography as was the deeply symbolic punishment of amputating the hand of a counterfeiter.

Hanging, nevertheless, was the fate of 269 Jews and twenty-eight Christians who were caught up in the notorious coin-clipping scandal between Easter 1276 and May 1279.[12] Edward I found a solution for dealing with a debased currency through a mass arrest of the Jews of England on 18 November 1278.[13] The homes of the Jews – and some Christians – who had been arrested were subsequently searched, and evidence against them was discovered. While there is no record of the trials, the evidence suggests that genuine trials did take place as not all those accused received the same punishment: some were hanged, others exiled, and some acquitted. The king, of course, profited enormously from the resultant forfeitures:

> According to the conventional wisdom, the fate of the Jews was sealed a decade before their expulsion. Edward I had what he wanted, at least for the moment, because the judicial campaign and recoinage had restored monetary integrity, while a substantial fiscal bounty of forfeited property, heavy fines and coerced gifts helped finance a protracted Welsh war.[14]

The situation in the south-west of England became increasingly volatile for the Jews throughout the second half of the thirteenth century. The Jewries there were particularly hard hit during the Barons' Wars in the 1260s, not only because of the indebtedness of many of the nobility to the Jews but also because they recognized that the Jews were useful to the king financially and wanted to disrupt this service. This was also a time of forced conversions as the Jewries of Canterbury, London, Northampton and Winchester were attacked by the baronial parties.[15] In 1275, however, Edward I pronounced the 'Statutes of Jewry', which prohibited Jews from lending money at interest,[16] and there is surely a correlation between the prohibition of usury in 1275 and the rise in prosecution of coin-clipping cases in 1276–78.[17] Also in 1275 Jews were expelled from the dower lands of the queen – Bath, Gloucester, Worcester and some other smaller towns – interestingly, precisely the locale and the time period most often associated with the earliest versions of the *SEL*.[18]

Like all good saints, when Quiriac's hand is lopped off, he has a snappy comeback for his tormentor:

'Thou luthere hound,' this othur seide   'wel hast thou idon bi me,
Of mine guode thou were wel onderstonde   Ich aughte wel
                                                                          blesci the:
For thou me hast that lime binome   that me hath ofte to sunne
                                                                          idrawe,
And ofte Ich habbe tharewith iwriten   agein Jesu Christes lawe,
The hwyle ich was a luther Giu   and on God biliefde nought.'
                                                                          (11–12, 365–9)

('You evil hound,' the other said, 'You've done well by me, you understood well what would be good for me, I really ought to bless you: for you've taken from me that limb which often drew me to sin, and with which I have often written against the law of Jesus Christ, while I was an evil Jew and didn't believe in God.')

The paradoxical nature of this response is such that it serves to remind the audience that Judas/Quiriac is a converted Jew. And this reminder brings with it a narrative discomfort – it disturbs the standard pagan/Christian dynamic of these scenes – because, if Quiriac succumbs under the pressure and renounces Christianity, he assumedly will not then revert to being pagan like the emperor who questions him; rather, he will revert to being Judas the Jew, who comes from a distinguished family with a genealogy that runs parallel to that of Christianity, and whose very name brings with it a host of negative associations. The fact that Judas's persecutor is himself an apostate from Christianity raises the stakes here, as it highlights the potential instability of religious identity. Judas/Quiriac's double identity is again gestured to when the Emperor, sensing himself in a losing battle with the soon-to-be martyr, abandons hope of conversion and simply entreats: 'Seighe that thou art Cristine nought' (12, 381, 'say that you are not a Christian'). Here, he might be read as either asking Quiriac to recant or to simply admit to the truth about himself: that he is not really a Christian in any case. Judas/Quiriac has a double identity, and, while within the economy of the legendary the amputation of the hand serves to demonstrate that his true identity is that of a Christian, in a late thirteenth-century context of reception, his Jewish identity may have been taken as the essential one. The hand thus functions dually: on one level, its amputation gestures to the traditional penalty for coin-clipping. Simultaneously, explicitly positioned as the locus of sin, the hand functions as a literalization of the fear that conversion is never complete, and that a vestige of essential identity always lingers. In this context, Quiriac's response links the act of losing a hand with the fact of being a Jew.

Throughout the Middle Ages, the Augustinian call to preserve the Jews as a people was experienced in tension with the desire to convert and thus to 'save' individual souls.[19] The latter was complicated by the concern that some irreducible element of Jewish identity will inevitably survive baptism – even perhaps in spite of the best intentions of the convertor and the converted.[20] A case in point is that of Henry of Winchester, a converted Jew close to the royal court. Still engaging in business with Jewish communities of the south-west after his conversion, Henry played a key role in the coin-clipping scandals by giving evidence against some of the accused. Either he had been caught counterfeiting himself and arranged to give evidence in exchange for amnesty, or he had perhaps been working under cover for the royal government in an elaborate sting operation.[21] Whichever the case may be, Henry subsequently was rejected from sitting on a panel that was to judge those accused of coin-clipping – Jewish and Christian – because of his status as a Jewish convert. The knight who later recalled this incident – as evidence in the canonization proceedings of Bishop Thomas Cantilupe who had registered the protest – characterized Henry as 'a certain knight who was a Jew and called Henry of Winchester, the Convert'.[22] Despite the fact that Henry had close ties to the royal court, had possibly worked under cover on its behalf against the Jews and had been named and knighted by no less a patron than Henry III, he is nevertheless described as a 'convert' and a 'Jew' rather than a Christian. Nor can this attitude be accounted for as the prejudice of one man. On the contrary, as Steven Kruger writes:

> Jews and Saracens, thought of as both religiously and racially different and as possessing bodies somehow essentially other than

Christian bodies, are often depicted as strongly resistant to conversion, with Jewish 'stubbornness' becoming a platitude in medieval
Christian depictions of Jews.[23]

Throughout the thirteenth century the sense that Jews could never
be fully converted deepened its roots in the Christian West. The
case of Henry of Winchester suggests that, to thirteenth-century
eyes, the converted Jew, at best, counterfeits Christian identity.

Thus Quiriac's double identity is also potentially counterfeit:
only one identity can be authentic. This sense of doubling, of the
attempt to distinguish the real from the inauthentic, or counterfeit, structures the narrative of the *Inventio*. In the moment when
Quiriac offers his own interpretation of the loss of his hand ('ofte
Ich habbe tharewith iwriten   agein Jesu Christes lawe' 12, 368)
to subvert that of his tormentor, he overdetermines its significa-
tion, because both interpretations are ultimately true: the hand has
written both for and against Christianity. In this moment, we recall
that Quiriac's story is embedded in a narrative that is predicated
on the quest to establish the truth of Christianity through the discovery of its chief relic, the True Cross. The moment of Quiriac's
conversion from Judas the Jew is closely aligned to the discovery
of proof of Christ's life through the miracle that distinguishes the
True Cross from the others found with it: three crosses are discovered, but only the True Cross is able to raise the dead. The miracle
of raising the dead performed by the True Cross situates Quiriac's
conversion as simultaneous to the distinction of the authentic from
the counterfeit.

The necessity of distinguishing between the three crosses buried
on Golgotha notwithstanding, the True Cross is unique in so
far as any copy of it participates fully in its authenticity. This is
the lesson demonstrated by the pair of miracles that follow the
Invention of the Holy Cross in the Laud *SEL*.[24] In these miracles,
one Jew attacks the True Cross which responds by bleeding, and
another Jew attacks a cross which responds identically: thus,
through their identical response to Jewish violence, all crosses are
demonstrated to be the True Cross. These miracles simultaneously reveal suspicion of the Jews, whose imagined predilection
towards attacking the cross is both reviled and relied upon: Jewish
perfidy is increasingly depended upon in medieval *exempla* as the
guarantor of Christian truth. Moreover, they are also a reminder
that the crime coin-clippers commit is not simply one of devalu-
ing the currency or of traducing the king's image. With the issue

of Edward I's long-cross pennies, designed so that the arms of the cross reached the edge of the coin, any Jew clipping a coin is simultaneously engaged in an attack on the cross. Thus, the revelation of widespread coin-clipping in the arrests of November 1278 must have simply reaffirmed what was already known about the dangerous relationship between Jews and the cross.

So the *Invention of the Holy Cross*, like Quiriac's *passio*, is fundamentally about articulating a true, as opposed to a counterfeit, identity. Moreover, this entire version of events is identified as counterfeit by the contemporary – and competing – account of *Cursor Mundi*, originating in the north of England c. 1300. *Cursor Mundi* knows the Judas/Quiriac legend, but it does not acknowledge the *SEL*'s version of his life as authoritative. *Cursor Mundi*, after its redaction of the *Invention of the Holy Cross* is finished, indicates that there are, in fact, other versions of the story:

> Qua-sum this tale can beter tende,
> For Cristis love he hit amende;
> This tale, quether hit be il or gode,
> I fande hit writen of the rode.
> Mani tellis diverseli,
> For thai mai finde diverse story,
> That fande the crois he hight Judas;
> Made bissop of the toun he was,
> And his name was turnid thus.
> That he was calde Quiriacus.[25]

(Whoever can tell this tale better, for the love of Christ he may amend it; this tale, whether it be bad or good, I found it written of the cross. Many tell it different ways, for they may find a different story, that he who found the cross was called Judas; he was made bishop of the town, and his name was changed so that he was called Quiriac.)

The story about Quiriac that *Cursor Mundi* goes on to tell is common to the *SEL,* where the devil appears to challenge Quiriac directly after the correct identification of the True Cross. Some, *Cursor Mundi* notes, think that the cross was found by a Judas who later changed his name to Quiriac, and who is subsequently confronted by the devil who threatens revenge: 'ful wele I sal thi dedis quite' (474, 'I'll get you back for that'). There may be a suggestion of Quiriac's martyrdom at the hands of the Emperor Julian the Apostate ('another kinge gaine the sal rise' (475, 'another king will rise against you'), but instead, this Quiriac simply banishes the devil to hell ('Crist that is lorde myne, / he deme the in-to helle depe / ever in wellande wa to wepe' (484–6, 'Christ, who is my lord, condemns you to the deepest hell, to wail and weep forever'), and the episode ends.

Although *Cursor Mundi* does not make its Quiriac a martyr, nevertheless, like the *SEL*, it draws a connection between the *Invention* narrative and Jewish moneylending. In *Cursor*'s preferred version of events, the Judas who helps St Helen find the cross does so out of an entirely different set of motivations, and he never changes his name, or becomes bishop of Jerusalem. Instead, Judas becomes indebted to two of Helen's messengers who adjudicate a dispute between him and a Christian goldsmith to whom he has lent money and from whom he is now demanding account: 'If he his money mught noght gett, / that he sulde yilde of his awen flesse' (81–4, If he could not return his money, he should pay with his own flesh'). This, of course, is the 'pound of flesh' so memorably demanded by Shakespeare's Shylock. When Helen's messengers ask Judas how he intends to collect the debt, his answer invites the reader to imagine him in the position of hagiography's stock pagan torturer, as he enumerates the body parts he will take:

> 'How,' saide the Iew, 'bot be my lay,
> That werst that ever I can or may
> His eien first putt out I sal
> And his hende smite of with-al;
> Tonge and neise wil I noght save,
> Til atte I al my covenande have.'
>
> (103–8)

('How else,' said the Jew, 'but by my law the worst that I can ever do? First I shall put out his eyes and then cut off his hand; tongue and nose I will not save, until I have all of my covenant.')

In response, his judges insist that he may take his pound of flesh, but no blood, and, when he complains at the inequity of their judgement, they forfeit all his property to Helen. In an attempt to recoup the lost property, Judas agrees to help Helen find the cross.

Thus *Cursor Mundi* reverses the dynamic of the *SEL*: its Judas does not become a bishop, he is the persecutor rather than the martyr, and, whereas in the *SEL* Quiriac loses his hand, in *Cursor Mundi* Judas threatens to amputate the hands of his debtors. The signifying economy of the martyrdom scene is turned inside-out as Judas transforms from tortured to torturer. The *Cursor Mundi* thus turns away from a narrative of Jewish conversion (although in this version Judas does convert upon the discovery of the cross), to turn its focus instead to a literalization of the ways in which Jewish usury represents a physical attack on the Christian body. In its juxtaposition of two versions of the discovery of the Holy Cross, the *Cursor Mundi* foregrounds the problem of identifying the authentic history. It emphasizes that this is a story which is one of many, a story which exists in many versions, and which chronicles a search for a true relic that must itself be divined from a number of false versions.

This concern with authenticity, conversion and identity can be traced through the *SEL* tradition. While there has not been a thorough study of the representation of Jews in the *SEL*, Thomas Renna's discussion of 'The Jews in the Golden Legend' finds that, although produced in a climate of increasing anti-Semitism, the *Legenda aurea*'s 'occasional anti-Jewish stereotypes were not intended to attack Jews – whether thirteenth century, first century, or under the Old Law – but to imply that the Jews are disposed to convert to the Christian faith'.[26] While conversion is indeed the prevailing theme in the *Legenda aurea* as in the *SEL*, I am tempted to identify Renna's conclusion as wishful thinking, given the *Legenda*'s quotation from the repertoire of anti-Semitic *exempla*. In the *SEL* as in the *Legenda aurea*, Jews appear in the *sanctorale* most often in the miracles appended to the saints' lives that serve as proof of the saint's holiness or of his or her power of intercession. Thus *Theophilus*, the story of a man who sold his soul to the devil, but who was mercifully saved through the intervention of the Virgin, concludes with the earliest English-language version of one of the popular anti-Semitic tales that the Virgin attracted in such numbers, 'The Jewish Boy in the Oven'.[27] Like the story of Quiriac and the stories of Jews attacking the cross that normally follow the *Exaltation of the Holy Cross*, this is a story which ends in the conversion of a Jewish boy and his mother to Christianity although, as Robert Mills notes, the boy is never actually referred to as being himself Jewish, but rather as a 'Jew's child', a circumlocution that again speaks to an anxiety about the essence of identity.[28] Another conversion narrative is found in one of the miracles of St Nicholas. Here, too, a Jewish merchant's greed is demonstrated to cause direct physical harm to the saintly body. In this *exemplum*, a Jew beats his wooden statue of St Nicholas after finding the 'god' ('goods') that he had entrusted to its safekeeping stolen. The revelation of St Nicholas's torn and bleeding body to the thieves effects both the return of the merchant's property and his conversion.[29]

In this story as well, the Jewish protagonist's attachment to St Nicholas before his conversion may perhaps be taken to indicate his unstable identity. In addition to these examples, Jews of course appear as persecutors in the *temporale*, they are directly responsible for the martyrdom of the apostle Barnabus in what is perhaps an extension of their role in the *temporale*, and, perhaps most insidious, scattered throughout the *SEL* are many incidental mentions of 'luther Giwes'. Mills makes a point about the *SEL* that seems to me to be equally true of the *Legenda aurea*: that tales of the Jews attacking the cross, or an image of the cross (as in *The Exaltation of the Cross*), or a saint (as in *Barnabas*) or an image of the saint (as in *Nicholas*) anticipate and participate in the underlying rationale of the host desecration accusation, which is more or less contemporary to the earliest production of *SEL* manuscripts.[30]

The *SELS*, of course, are in their very essence mutable: a connotation that may have resonated for a redactor or audience in one time and place may hold less, or even no, meaning for another. So while cultural anxiety about Jewish conversion permeated medieval society even after – and perhaps especially after – the Expulsion of 1290, the more local memory of the coin-clipping scandals of 1276–79 may have lost its position as a flashpoint of cultural memory.[31] The transformation of the Quiriac story across *SEL* manuscripts reflects the shifting interests that this changing historical context suggests. With the later versions of the *SELS*, which tend to integrate the *temporale* into the *sanctorale*, the *Invention of the Holy Cross* is separated from the *Exaltation*, which takes with it the *exempla* in which Jews attack the cross.[32] In this format, Quiriac looks more like a saint's *passio* that follows the *Invention* chronologically, and less like a constituent part of the legend of the *Invention of the Holy Cross*.[33] By the fifteenth century, William Caxton's version of Quiriac's martyrdom in the *Golden Legend* removes the amputation of the hand along with the discussion of its writings entirely. Caxton inserts instead the figure of Quiriac's mother, Anne, who comes to visit her son in prison and is subsequently also martyred, thus taking the *passio* in a new direction altogether.[34]

Indeed, while the earliest extant *SEL* manuscript was produced at a moment of great upheaval in Jewish-Christian relations in the south-west – following closely upon the depredations of the baronial wars, the coin-clipping executions and the expulsion of Jewish residents of the queen's dower lands – the majority of *SELS* were produced *after* the Expulsion of 1290. Nevertheless, this reading of the *passio* of Quiriac offers both an early context of reception for the narrative, and also a suggestion of the ways in which aspects of that early context may have continued to reverberate. Like the narrative in which he is embedded and the Jewish convert whom he figures, Quiriac embodies the very essence of the counterfeit. While this concern with counterfeiting may take on one form when embedded in the historical context of the late thirteenth-century coin-clipping scandals, the metaphoric resonances of conversion, identity and authenticity continue as culturally contested ideals throughout the lifetime of the *SELS*. Indeed, contextualizing Quiriac's passion in this way suggests that the 'Latin' as well as the 'English' saints may be fruitfully interpreted as participating in discourses of national identity.[35] In this way, the message written by Quiriac's amputated hand is one that addresses not only the representation of Jewish identity in the *SELS* but also the problematics of historicizing a text with multiple, shifting and contested historical contexts.

Notes

I would like to thank Jocelyn Wogan-Browne for her very generous and useful suggestions.

1 The text of the Laud *SEL* is generally dated to c. 1280 (Liszka, *SELS*, p. 243, p. 23 above), and the earliest composition of an *SEL* to c. 1270–80. The manuscript is edited by Carl Horstmann. All references will be to Horstmann by page and line number unless otherwise noted. Versions of the *Invention of the Holy Cross* and the legend of Judas Cyriacus had been in circulation in the Latin West from the sixth century, eventually forming by the fourteenth century a cycle that included the discovery of the cross by St Helen, the mother of Constantine the Great, with the help of Judas Cyriacus, the Exaltation of the Cross, and the back history of the wood of which the cross was made. For a comprehensive study of the legend in literature and art, see B. Baert, *A History of Holy Wood: The Legend of the True Cross in Text and Image*, trans. L. Preedy (Leiden: Brill, 2004).

2 Matthew Paris, *Chronica majora*, ed. Henry Richards Luard, RS 57, 7 vols (London, 1872–83), vol. 5, pp. 487–8.

3 William Langland, *Piers Plowman: The B Version, Will's Vision of Piers Plowman, Do-Well, Do-Better, and Do-Best*, ed. G. Kane and E. T. Donaldson (London: Athlone Press,1988), pp. 320–1. Quoted in W. Johnson, 'Textual sources for the study of Jewish currency crimes in thirteenth-century England', *British Numismatic Journal*, 66 (1990), 21–32 (21).

4 On the question of whether St Quiriac belongs more properly to the *temporale* or the *sanctorale* material, see the discussion in Pickering, '*Temporale* narratives', and Pickering, *Nativity*, pp. 36–7.

5 For the relationship between the Laud MS and the rest of the *SEL* manuscripts, see Samson, 'Constructing a context', p. 187. The relationship of the *SEL* to the *Legenda aurea* in general is a complicated one. Horstmann insisted from the first that the earliest versions of the *SEL* were independent of the *Legenda aurea*, and this insistence is confirmed by, among others, Görlach, Pickering, 'Outspoken style in the *SEL* and Robert of Gloucester', and Sherry Reames's essay in this volume. Görlach argued that *Legenda aurea* influence in the *SEL* did not begin to be felt until the summer saints, although he noted a stronger influence of the *Legenda aurea* on the winter saints in the 'A' redaction. He nevertheless singled out Longinus and Quiriac as exceptions to this rule, suggesting that Quiriac had a direct source in the *Legenda aurea* (Görlach, *Textual Tradition*, p.27). However, there are several aspects of the *Invention* narrative as it appears in the Laud manuscript of the *SEL* that seem to me to suggest that there is no direct *Legenda aurea* influence at this stage. The first is the order of the narrative, discussed below. The second is the separation of the *Invention* and the *Exaltation* narratives in the *Legenda aurea* as in later versions of the *SEL*. From these two points it makes sense to follow Görlach's supposition of *Legenda aurea* influence at a later stage in the *SEL*'s evolution. In addition, one point of difference is striking, and this is that the *Legenda aurea* version of Quiriac's martyrdom adds a torture which, to the best of my knowledge, all the *SEL* texts lack: in the *Legenda aurea*, Quiriac is thrown into a pit of snakes, which all miraculously die at contact with the saint. The *SEL*'s omission of this torture seems to defy the logic by which the *SEL*'s modifications of the *Legenda aurea* are usually assumed to proceed: that is, it is neither an overly theological explanation, nor does it detract from the narrative vigour and excitement of the *SEL* text. This suggests to me that it was simply never part of the *SEL* tradition. In the final analysis, it is, of course, impossible to know with certainty.

6 M. E. Wells, 'The *South English Legendary* and its relation to the *Legenda aurea*', *PMLA*, 51:2 (1936), 337–60, argues that the version in the Laud MS has fallen out of order. Samson suggests instead that the Laud scribe began using an exemplar in calendrical order mid-way though his task of copying ('Constructing a context', p. 189).

7 Indeed, it is worth remembering that the addition of Judas to the narrative of the discovery of the cross has the point of giving Helen a Jewish antagonist and, more generally, of imaginarily pitting Judaism against Christianity. The earliest versions of the story had no such character (Baert, *History of Holy Wood*, pp. 42–3).

8 Zefirah Rokeah, 'Money and the hangman in late 13th century England: Jews, Christians, and coinage offenses alleged and real', *Jewish Historical Studies*, 31 (1988–90), 83–109 (95).

9 Henry of Huntingdon, *The History of the English People, 1000–1154*, trans. D. Greenway (Oxford: Oxford World Classics, 2002), p. 58. For an interesting argument about the symbolic connection between coin-clipping and castration, see Willis Johnson, 'Between Christians and Jews: the formation of anti-Jewish stereotypes in medieval England' (PhD dissertation, University of California, Berkeley, 1997).

10 Elsewhere the amputation of the hands of counterfeiters was still the practice in the thirteenth century. See Alan Stahl, 'Coin and punishment in medieval Venice', in R. Mazo Karras, J. Kaye and E. A. Matter (eds), *Law and the Illicit in Medieval Europe* (Philadelphia: University of Pennsylvania Press, 2008), pp. 164–79.

11 Johnson, 'Jewish currency crimes', p. 25.

12 The figure of 269 is Rokeah's ('Coinage offenses', 1990, pp. 96–8): she also notes the numbers given by the chroniclers at p. 108 n. 7. Rokeah has attempted to trace the fate of individuals in Zefirah Rokeah, 'Money and the hangman in late 13th century England: Part II', *Jewish Historical Studies*, 32 (1990–92), 159–218. Another approximately 148 Jews were released from prison after paying a fine, but forfeited their property (Rokeah, 1992, p. 161). Brand suggests that this lesser penalty was for the lesser crime of exchanging good coin for bad: Paul Brand, 'Jews and the law in England, 1275–90', *The English Historical Review*, 115:464 (2000), 1138–58 (1150). Most critics note that *anyone* handling money exchange is likely to engage in a little coin-clipping from time to time. The disproportionate number of Jews accused of coin-clipping may simply indicate that Jews disproportionately handled money exchange. The severity of the punishment, however, seems to have been motivated by prejudice: Rokeah notes that in the fifty-year period leading up to the Expulsion in 1290, 'While about 5.5 per cent of the Christians were executed on coinage charges, about 15 per cent – nearly three times as many – of the accused Jews were executed' (Rokeah, 1992, p. 160).

13 In addition to the series of articles cited above by Rokeah, see Robin Mundill, *England's Jewish Solution: Experiment and Expulsion, 1262–1290* (Cambridge: Cambridge University Press, 1998).

14 Don Skemer, 'King Edward's articles of inquest on the Jews and coin clipping, 1279', *Historical Research*, 72:177 (1999), 1–26 (13).

15 Robert C. Stacey, 'The conversion of the Jews to Christianity in thirteenth century England', *Speculum*, 67 (1992), 263–83 (272).

16 Brand notes that, while closing the door to usury, the Statute at least opened the door to mercantile activity, while at the same time reinforcing pre-existing prescriptions on Jewish activity ('Jews and the law', 1140–2). See also the discussion in Mundill, *England's Jewish Solution*, pp. 119–20.

17 Skemer, 'King Edward's articles of inquest', p. 6.
18 The upper limit of 1290 for the composition of the *SEL* is based on a passage in the *Southern Passion* that is taken to suggest that the Jews were still living in England at the time of the text's composition (*Southern Passion*, 475–6). The passage in question reads that the Jews live 'among us': however, the localization of the early versions of the *SELS* to Worcestershire/Gloucestershire, and the expulsion of the Jews from this part of the country as early as 1275 might suggest a possible earlier date as a *terminus ad quem*. For the expulsion from Eleanor's dower lands, see Joe Hillaby, 'The Worcester Jewry, 1158–1290: portrait of a lost community', *Transactions of the Worcestershire Archaeological Society*, 3rd series, 12 (1990), 73–122 (112).
19 Jeremy Cohen, *Living Letters of the Law: Ideas of the Jew in Medieval Christianity* (Berkeley: University of California Press, 1999).
20 The most recent and comprehensive discussion of medieval cultural anxiety about Jewish conversion is Steven Kruger, *The Spectral Jew: Conversion and Embodiment in Medieval Europe* (Minneapolis: University of Minnesota Press, 2006). For more historical discussions, see Stacey, and Jonathan Elukin, 'From Jew to Christian? Conversion and immutability in medieval Europe', in James Muldoon (ed.), *Varieties of Religious Conversion in the Middle Ages* (Gainesville: University of Florida Press, 1997), pp. 171–89, and Jonathan Elukin, 'The discovery of the self: Jews and conversion in the twelfth century', in M. A. Signer and J. Van Engen (eds), *Jews and Christians in Twelfth-Century Europe* (Notre Dame: University of Notre Dame Press, 2001), pp. 63–76. Some Jews did, of course, convert to Christianity, a movement that governmental policy under Henry III attempted to facilitate through the establishment of the *Domus conversorum*. A much smaller number of Christians converted to Judaism (Stacey, 'The conversion of the Jews').
21 The former argument is that of Skemer, 'King Edward I's articles of inquest', 12, the latter of Brand, 'Jews and the law', pp. 1149–50.
22 Stacey, 'The conversion of Jews', p. 277.
23 Kruger, *The Spectral Jew*, p. 75.
24 Most other versions of the *SEL*, along with the *Legenda aurea*, separate the *Exaltation* from the *Invention* and include these miracles with the former, thus distancing them from the *passio* of Quiriac.
25 The *Invention of the Holy Cross* section of *Cursor Mundi* is extracted in *Legends of the Holy Rood: Symbols of the Passion and Cross-Poems in Old English of the Eleventh, Fourteenth, and Fifteenth Centuries*, ed. Richard Morris, EETS OS 46 (London: N. Trübner for EETS, 1881), pp. 108–21, ll. 455–64, henceforth cited by line number in the text. The entire text is also edited by Morris in *Cursor Mundi*, ed. Richard Morris, 7 vols, EETS OS 57, 59, 62, 66, 68, 99, 101 (London: N. Trübner for EETS, 1874–93). See J. J. Thompson, *The Cursor*

Mundi: Poem, Texts and Contexts (Oxford: The Society for the Study of Medieval Languages and Literatures, 1998), for a discussion of the possible relationship between *Cursor Mundi* and the *SEL*.

26 Thomas Renna, 'The Jews in the *Golden Legend*', in Michael Frassetto (ed.), *Christian Attitudes Toward the Jews in the Middle Ages: A Casebook* (New York: Routledge, 2007), pp. 137 – 150 (144).

27 In the Corpus 145 manuscript. Robert Mills, 'Violence, community and the materialization of belief', in Salih (ed.), *Companion to Middle English Hagiography*, pp. 87–103 (97); see also the discussion in Miri Rubin, *Gentile Tales: The Narrative Assault on Late Medieval Jews* (New Haven: Yale University Press, 1999).

28 Mills, 'Violence, community and the materialization of belief', pp. 97–8.

29 Mills notes the potential play of words here on goods/good/God ('Violence, community and the materialization of belief', p. 96).

30 Ibid., p. 97.

31 On the ubiquitous representation of Jews in the post-Expulsion literature of medieval England see, among others, Anthony Bale, *The Jew in the Medieval Book* (Cambridge: Cambridge University Press, 2007); Kruger, *The Spectral Jew*; Sylvia Tomasch, 'Postcolonial Chaucer and the virtual Jew', in J. J. Cohen (ed.), *The Postcolonial Middle Ages* (New York: Palgrave Macmillan, 2000), pp. 243–60.

32 In this position they create a new narrative logic, as the narrative of the *Exaltation* is largely concerned with questions of Muslim identity and conversion. Pickering has argued that the *temporale* material (lives of the Holy Family and feasts of the church calendar) were added to the *sanctorale* (the lives of the saints) in order to complete the collection of the lives of the holiest men and women. Pickering suggests that initially the *temporale* was placed before the *sanctorale*, but that later this pattern was changed so that the *temporale* narratives were placed among the *sanctorale* in calendrical order (*Nativity*, p. 37).

33 The iconography of Quiriac's role continues in importance, but his role in the discovery of the location of the True Cross rather than his martyrdom is stressed (see Baert, *A Legend of Holy Wood*).

34 F. S. Ellis (ed.), *The Golden Legend: or, Lives of the Saints, as Englished by William Caxton* (London: J. M. Dent, 1900). The *Golden Legend* is Caxton's own translation of the *Legenda aurea* using also the *Gilte Legend* and the *Legende doree*.

35 On the *SEL's* English saints, see Frederick, 'National identity'; Hamelinck, 'St Kenelm'; and Jankofsky, 'National characteristics'.

15

Mapping identity in the *South English Legendary*

Sarah Breckenridge

In early medieval legendaries time and space intersect in complicated ways. In the *SEL*, the frame narrative, which arranges the
saints' lives chronologically according to feast days, intersects with
an emphasis on geographical place in the lives themselves. In his
prologue, the poet of the *SEL* explains that he will 'Telle . . . of
[apostles and martirs]   as hare dai valth in the yere / Verst byg-
ynneth at Yeres Day   for that is the verste feste / And fram on
to other so areng   the wile the yer wol leste' (I, 3, 66–8, 'Tell . . .
[of apostles and martyrs], as their feast day falls in the year; beginning first at New Year's Day, for that is the first feast, and from one
to another in order, so long as the year lasts').[1] Here we are told that
the *SEL* is organized according to time. The poet describes it as a
product of the computus tradition, which from the eighth century
on attempted to align divine and human time by identifying the
date of Christ's resurrection and the number of years elapsed since
his incarnation within a temporal system consisting of twenty-
four-hour days, thirty-day months and 365¼-day years (calculated
arithmetically using measurements of the sun, moon and stars).[2]
Vocabulary related to the progression and demarcation of time
dominates the passage quoted above, and the poet's inclusion of
Easter in the *SEL* confirms his interest in locating Christ's resurrection within the calendar year.

  While time provides the *SEL*'s ordering structure, the *SEL*'s
alignment with the computus tradition suggests that place must
also figure centrally because a computus's geographical origin
determined both its underlying arithmetic and its cultural influence. First, the place where computus manuscripts were calculated
was significant because astrological observations, which provided
the numerical values used to calculate time, were dictated by one's
latitudinal location. Second, the manuscript itself was authorized by the site of its composition – any given embodiment of

the church calendar's cultural influence depended on the socio-political power attributed to its geographical origin. Most texts regarding the calculation of time originated in Greece and Rome: the great centres, both figuratively and cartographically, of ancient civilization. Because the *SEL* poet was operating within the calendrical tradition, we might expect him to claim similar origins for the *SEL* itself, but instead he challenges Roman authority by emphasizing the *SEL*'s composition in Worcestershire. In this study, I examine the *SEL* poet's treatment of Worcestershire to show that the chronological project of the *SEL* is underwritten by an emphasis on regional place. By positioning the *SEL* within the calendrical tradition while disavowing European origins, the *SEL* poet suggests that an English region rather than a continental empire can claim cultural and geographical authority in matters of divine and human time. He begins by using the tradition of Bede's *Historia ecclesiastica* as the dominant paradigm for writing about time and place in the Middle Ages, while denying Bede's emphasis on Rome. He then appropriates narrative and liturgical authority for Worcestershire by using cartographical language in the Legend of St Kenelm to construct a map with the Worcester diocese rather than Rome at its centre.[3]

The authorizing function of place in the SEL and its predecessors

The *SEL* poet is straightforward in his prologue: the Lives contained within the *SEL* are ordered according to the liturgical year. None the less, he repeatedly reminds us that place engenders and authorizes the *SEL*'s chronological structure. This relationship between time and place finds precedent in England's earliest texts and manuscripts concerned with the ordering and meaning of time. Bede's *Historia ecclesiastica* (hereafter *History*) in particular served as a model for future computations by foregrounding place. Presented as a history that instructs readers by encouraging them to imitate historical successes, the *History* also demonstrates the importance of the liturgical calendar by devoting considerable space to the dating of Easter. A letter from Abbot Ceolfrith to King Nechtan of the Picts in book V.21, the longest document in the *History*, contains an exhaustive excursus on the calculation and celebration of Easter; and book III.25 contains Bede's account of the Synod of Whitby (664), where the English pledged to follow the Roman Church's liturgical calendar. Bede further encourages readers to understand the *History* as embodying the ecclesiastical ordering and shaping of time by locating the Synod of Whitby at the very centre of his text, suggesting that the Synod is a critical component of the *History*.

Narrative accounts of the church's attempts to regulate Easter observances in Great Britain also occur regularly in the *History*. In book II, for instance, Bede records Archbishop Laurence's attempt to standardize the date of Easter in Scotland. Having discovered that the Scots did not observe Christ's resurrection on the date prescribed by the Roman Church, Laurence tried to persuade the Scottish bishops to adopt Rome's liturgical calendar by criticizing the Scots' improper dating techniques. In a letter dated c. 605 he writes,

> When, in accordance with its custom, which holds good throughout the world, the apostolic see sent us to the western lands to preach the Gospel to the heathen peoples, we came to this island of Britain. Until we realized the true situation, we had a high regard for the devotion of both the Britons and the Scots, believing that they fol-lowed the customs of the universal Church. On further acquaintance with the Britons, we imagined that the Scots must be better. We have now, however, learned . . . that the Scots are no different from the Britons in their practices.[4]

Significantly, this criticism is based not on innate Scottish inferior-ity but on the fact that the Scots deviate from the norm. They fail as Christians not because they are Scots but because they are *not* Romans. Laurence emphasizes custom twice in the opening two lines of his letter to underscore the importance of conformity in the church, and by demeaning the West while revering Rome he implies that a community cannot be designated Christian until it fully conforms to the traditions held by the Roman church.

By recognizing cultural difference as the underlying problem in Laurence's letter, we can see how place comes to play a significant role in Bede's chronological project. Nicholas Howe argues that 'the reason for setting [the date of Easter] has everything to do with Christendom as a place occupied by believers who maintain them-selves as a community through the simultaneous observance of the same set of liturgical practices across great distances of space'.[5] In this passage Howe pinpoints Bede's fundamental concern: the *History* is troubled more by spatial than by temporal disjunction. The universal acceptance of a standard date for Easter is certainly a source of apprehension in Bede's text, but this problem is merely a symptom of the church's failure to unify disparate places. Bede is not as concerned with the liturgical calendar as he is with the fact that the *same* calendar is recognized across geography.

Bede further establishes the significance of place in the *History* by beginning the text with a chapter on geography, describing Britain's topography, natural resources, fortifications, and its location 'at the end of the world' (I.1). Despite his focus on Britain, though, Bede's perspective is surprisingly *not* British. Instead, he describes the island in terms of its relationship to Rome. Britain lies 'toward the north-west at a considerable distance from the [European] coasts', and the country's days and nights are elongated because of its location 'far north toward the pole' (I.1). By describing Britain as a northern satellite, Bede's *History* grants Rome centrality: Rome and the Roman church endow Britain with value. By positioning the island under a Roman *umbra*, Bede grants Britain an identity based not on intrinsic Britishness but on uniformity with a continental precedent.

While Alan Thacker, A. H. Merrils, Kathy Lavezzo and Fabienne Michelet have all acknowledged this geographical component of the *History*, none has noted this text's influence on the early medieval calendrical tradition.[6] Yet Bede's treatment of Britain's geographical and cultural status in the ecumene proved fundamental to later calendrical concerns, demonstrating how problems regarding the liturgical calendar were ultimately grounded in place. In the *History*, Bede shows that the church was invested in both the calendar's uniform observance across geography, and in designating Rome as the world's geographical and spiritual centre. By comparing these elements of the *History* to the *SEL*'s treatment of time and place, we can make a series of suggestions regarding the *SEL*'s participation in the calendrical tradition. Specifically, we can see the *SEL* adopting the *History*'s attention to place, yet diverging radically from the *History* by identifying the diocese of Worcester rather than Rome as the centre of both Christendom and the world. In a long tradition of texts and manuscripts concerned with place and time, the *SEL* emerges as the first to present a model of English regional authority.

Like Bede, the *SEL* poet presents his audience with a chronologically ordered document that is grounded in and authorised by place. The liturgical calendar and methods of calculating time are significant to the *SEL*, but where the *SEL* was calculated and composed is of greater import. The *SEL* poet makes his interest in geography immediately clear by beginning with a passage that alerts his readers to the importance of place:

Nou blouweth the niwe frut   that late bygan to springe
That to is kunde eritage   mankunne schal bringe.
This nywe frut of wan Ich speke   is oure Cristendom,
That late was an eorthe ysouwe,   and later forth it com.
So hard and luther was the lond   on wan it ssolde sprynge,
That wel unnethe eny more   me myghte theron bringe.
God him was the gardiner   that gan ferst the sed souwe
That was Jesus Godes sone   that tharefore alyghte louwe

(I, 1, 1–8)

(Now blooms the new fruit that lately began to grow, the fruit that
will bring mankind to its true inheritance. This new fruit that I
speak of is our Christendom that was so lately sown on earth, and
afterwards came forth. So hard and wicked was the ground on which
it was to spring up, that it could scarcely be got to take root. God
himself was the gardener who first sowed the seed that was Jesus, the
son of God, who therefore came down to earth.)

In these lines, the site that produces Christianity is presented
as a place that we can physically experience, with topographical
markers including fruit trees and rocky ground loosened by the
blood of Christ and God's martyrs. Because the *SEL* also grows
from this pastoral setting, the legendary is both literally and
figuratively enabled by place: the text itself proceeds from these
geocentric lines, and its 'niwe frut' will blossom only if mankind is
attentive to the soil in which it has been sown.

The *SEL*'s interest in place also extends to its chronological
project. In the Legend of St Michael, for example, the poet grants
place authority by emphasizing the relationship between astrology
and *geography* over the relationship between astrology and *chronology*. This legend contains a lengthy digression on astrology that
provides the *SEL* poet an ideal opportunity to discuss astrology's
role in the calculation of time, and, given the *SEL*'s calendrical shaping, we might expect him to embrace this prospect. Yet
instead of treating the heavens as bodies used to calculate time, the
poet treats them as bodies used to designate place. In part two of
Michael, the *SEL* poet describes how St Michael instructed Bishop
Aubert to found St Michael's church when he reached a site where
'a bole thou . . . finde' (II, 406, 115, 'you find a bull'). *Bole* is best
translated as 'bull' in the *SEL* poet's dialect, and given the poet's
reference to Gargan (whose wandering bull discovered a holy site
in AD 492 that was converted to a church in honour of St Michael)
this translation seems appropriate. A gloss to line 115 in the margin
of Cambridge, Corpus Christi College MS 145 reading 'Taurus',

however, suggests that a second interpretation of *bole* circulated
with the *SEL*. According to this interpretation, Aubert could expect
to see Taurus *the constellation* when he reached the site designated
by St Michael for his church.[7] Taurus traditionally marked the
vernal equinox, or the beginning of the lunar year, and thus played
a critical role in the chronology of computus manuscripts. As Bede
points out in his *History*, 'the moon falling either on or after the
[vernal] equinox itself certainly belongs to the first month; on it the
ancients used to keep the Passover, and on it, when the Lord's day
comes, we should keep Easter' (V.21). The *SEL* poet, however,
supplants the importance of Taurus as a constellation used to calculate the date of Easter. In the legend of St Michael no reference is
made to Easter or the vernal equinox, and Taurus gives Aubert an
idea of *where* to build St Michael's church rather than *when* to build
it: '*There* as thou vinst this bole ihud   mi churche thou sselt rere'
(II, 406, 117, 'Where you find this concealed bull, you shall found
my church'). This attention to place is further emphasized when
the narrator draws attention to the topographical features defining
the site of St Michael's church, one of two churches in *Michael*
located on a hill (the church Aubert founded was located on Mount
Tombe, better known as Mont Saint-Michel):

> Ope hulles bothe this churchen were   and bothe of Sein Michel
> Heymon me thincth he wolde be[o]   he lovede hulles so wel . . .
> In the grete se of occean   the hul of Tombe is
> That geth al aboute the world   in the on ende iwis
> The se geth al aboute the hul.
>
> (II, 406, 121–2, 133–5)

(Both of these churches were upon hills, and both churches of St
Michael. It seems to me he would be a highly esteemed man, he
loved hills so much . . . The hill of Tombe is found in the great sea
of the ocean that, certainly, travels all around one end of the world;
this sea surrounds the hill.)

From the topographical detail in this passage, it is clear that the
SEL poet is primarily concerned with where St Michael's church
is located. Despite the opportunities that both the *bole* and the
lengthy discourse on astrology in *Michael* offer, the poet abstains
from discussing the liturgical calendar, focusing instead on geographical detail and the means by which place authorizes Aubert's
construction of St Michael's church.

The *SEL*'s emphasis on place demonstrates continuity in the
computus tradition, recalling Bede's insistence on geographical

and cultural similitude in the *History*, but it differs significantly from the *History* by defining England as a geocultural entity separate from Rome. The *SEL* poet locates the diocese of Worcester at the centre of the geographical world and Christendom, usurping a site traditionally reserved for Rome in both cartographic and poetic representations of the world. This refocusing makes the *SEL* the first calendrically based text to grant an English diocese authorizing power. Many scholars have acknowledged the *SEL*'s Anglo-centric focus.[8] Klaus Jankofsky argues that the *SEL* was written for a popular English audience by identifying its national characteristics, including references to the existence of Christianity before St Augustine's arrival, the English–Danish conflicts, and national customs.[9] Jill Frederick likewise suggests that the *SEL* served a national agenda by venerating Anglo-Saxon saints at a time when 'Englishness' challenged Anglo-Norman linguistic and cultural authority.[10] These studies have contributed significantly to modern understandings of the *SEL*, but they tend to value nationalism over regionalism despite the *SEL* poet's focused emphasis on the Worcestershire/Gloucestershire region. Moreover, scholarship has failed to recognize cartography's contribution to the emergent regionalism of the *SEL*. Only by examining the poet's cartographical treatment of place in *Kenelm* can we fully realize his intent to grant the diocese of Worcester geographical and cultural authority over its continental predecessors.

Geographical place in *Kenelm*

The Legend of St Kenelm, an Anglo-Latin saint's life translated and amended for inclusion in the *SEL*, is somewhat unconventional: Kenelm is not remarkably religious and the circumstances leading to his death are purely political. The inclusion of Kenelm's life in the *SEL* is crucial to the collection, however, as a means of identifying the significance of place in its model of ecclesiastical time. In *Kenelm*, the *SEL* poet replaces Bede's Rome with Worcester, transferring Rome's monopoly on liturgical matters (including the liturgical calendar) to an English diocese. The poet carefully justifies his focus. As Catherine Cubitt notes, he begins by asserting the authenticity of Kenelm's story.[11] More importantly though, he includes a remarkably long description of England that uses cartographical language to construct a map with Worcestershire and Gloucestershire at its centre. The centres of *mappae mundi* were generally occupied by either Rome or

Jerusalem, and so by redrawing the world map in this way the *SEL* poet positions the diocese of Worcester as the world's spiritual model, and thereby grants the diocese of Worcester the authorizing function once reserved for Rome.

Far from representing geographical reality, medieval maps constituted regional subjectivities. By physically interpreting and manifesting space, maps allowed medieval viewers to envision where they were living and who they were as a people. In the late thirteenth century, rhetorical and diagrammatic representations of geographical space were increasingly influencing English identity. Earlier, many types of maps appeared in influential manuscripts including Virgil's *Georgics*, St Jerome's *Liber locorum*, Isidore of Seville's *De natura rerum* and Bede's *De ratione temporum*. In these manuscripts, the most common cartographical representation of the world was the T-O map, which divided the world into three continents (Asia, Africa and Europe) and labelled cities and dominant features of the landscape. A derivative of the T-O map, and the representation of space most relevant to *Kenelm*, was the list map, which also divided the world into three continents but contained lengthy descriptions of each continent rather then labelling cultural or topographical features. The list map has often been described as simply another way of presenting text, but places are grouped in a geographically significant way, and transitional maps often integrate the list map with more illustrative and geographically accurate representations of space.[12]

In a seventy-five-line digression that does not appear in either of *Kenelm*'s Anglo-Latin sources (*Vita et miracula* and *Vita brevior Sancti Kenelmi*) the *SEL* poet describes England's ninth-century geopolitical division in terms similar to those found on contemporary list maps. First, the poet establishes cartography's relevance to his tale by using the word *drou* on multiple occasions, suggesting that he is *drawing* a map for his audience rather than simply recording a tale. He writes, 'Gret cite was tho Winchcombe   and mest of inou / Of al thulke half of Engelond   as ver as is lond *drou*' (I, 280, 7–8, 'Winchcombe was then a great city, and the very best of all that half of England, as far as land is drawn').[13] In *Kenelm* the contextual meaning of the term is confirmed when the poet refers a second time to the geographical placement of cultural centres using the word *drou*: 'And Somerset that to Wellis   thulke tyme *drou* / Nou it is the bissopriche of Bathe' (I, 281, 55–6, 'And from Somerset to Wells, as it was drawn at that time. Now it is the bishopric of Bath'). By suggesting that his text transcends textual media, the *SEL* poet demands that his geographical division of Anglo-Saxon kingdoms in the opening seventy-five lines be read both rhetorically and diagrammatically; it functions as both a textual description and a pictorial representation of geographical place.

This duality was common among early medieval maps. While today the word 'map' refers primarily to a pictorial or geographical representation of the world or a region, in the early thirteenth century there was not a word that exclusively meant 'map'. The word *mappa* meant cloth, and *carta* meant document. The most common word attached to what we now consider maps was *descriptio*, which could mean either a map or a textual description, and *picture* and *figura* could mean any diagram or drawing.[14] The distinction between what we now call maps and textual descriptions of the world, then, were not so distinct in the medieval period. The *SEL* poet can conceivably present his audience with a textual description of place and expect them to read it as a pictorial representation of that place.

Having aligned his text with the hermeneutic flexibility that characterized medieval maps, the *SEL* poet proceeds to describe the Anglo-Saxon geopolitical division of England according to directional details and measurements. He begins by describing the size of England: 'Engelond was god and long   and somdel brod therto / Aboute eighte hondred mile   Engelond long is / Fram the south into the north   and to hundred brod iwis / Fram the est into the west' (I, 280, 10–13, 'England was good and long, and somewhat wide as well. England is about eight hundred miles long from the south into the north, and two hundred miles wide from the east into the west'). This passage is followed by a description of the country's three major rivers, including the direction in which they flow:

> there inne beoth
> Manie wateres god inou   as ye alday iseoth,
> Ac threo wateres principals   ther beoth of alle iwis:
> Homber and Temese   Severne the thridde is.
> To the north se Homber geth   that is on of the beste
> And Temese into the est se   and Severne bi weste
>
> (I, 280, 13–18)

(There are in [England] many good waters as you can see every day, but there are three principal waters, certainly: the Humber and the Thames; the third is the Severn. The Humber, which is one of the best, flows to the north, and the Thames flows into the eastern sea, and the Severn flows west.)

This sequence is particularly relevant to medieval cartographical practices, as even the earliest maps noted the world's major bodies of water. On T-O maps the continents were divided by rivers or seas (typically the Nile, Mediterranean and Don), and more detailed maps almost always featured the four rivers of paradise (Nile, Tigris, Euphrates and Ganges).

The *SEL* poet also describes the Anglo-Saxon kingdoms in terms of their geographical location. In a passage that will be quoted at length below, the poet describes the location of the March of Wales, followed by a description of the many shires that it contains: 'The kyng that was king of the March   hadde tho the beste / Muchedel he hadde of Engelond   the on half al by *weste*' (I, 280, 21–1, 'The King that was king of the March held the best lands. He possessed much of England, the Western half'). Specific cities are also located geographically on the poet's linguistic map. The poet explains that, relative to Canterbury, the bishopric of Rochester is 'in the west side . . . next' (I, 281, 61–2, 'the nearest [bishopric] to the west'). Here the *SEL* poet maintains his allegiance to geography, accurately describing the relative location of two religious sites. By making a point of including such accurate details in his description of place, the poet suggests that although his analysis of place is partially subjective, as any geographical analysis was in the early medieval period, it is not entirely devoid of geographical observation. He intends to reposition the world's spiritual and cartographical centre, but he still locates the remaining cities or shires accurately with respect to one another. In other words, the map he is *drau*ing is not a subjective fantasy, it is a restructured and reinterpreted reality.

The seventy-five-line narrative digression in *Kenelm* also adheres to medieval mapmaking constructs by emphasizing history. As Evelyn Edson notes, '[Maps] serve to establish the location of actions and the routes of armies, and to show the passage of time as events worked their changes on the countryside . . . In fact, the great Hereford Cathedral map describes itself as an *estorie*, whose modern descendant is the word "history", and its lengthy inscriptions, which blanket its 2.23 square metres, tell a story indeed.'[15] In *Kenelm*, history is manifest in the transformation of place names. The clearest example of this concerns the evolution of Somerset to Bath: 'yute hadde the king of Westsex . . . Somerset that to Wellis   thulke tyme drou / Nou it is the bissopriche of Bathe   ye witeth wel inou' (I, 281, 51, 55–6, 'The king of Wessex possessed land . . . from Somerset to Wells, as it was drawn at that time. Now this region is the bishopric of Bath, as you know well enough'). By acknowledging this transformation of the ecclesiastical landscape the poet distinctly sets his legend in the past, while acknowledging the effect that the past has had on the present. Moreover, he engages the historical function of maps, offering his audience an image of England in the ninth century while pointing to regions that have evolved since then – a practice particularly common in list maps of the period.

One of the most interesting ways the poet engages cartographical language occurs outside of the opening seventy-five-line description of place. In the tale itself the *SEL* poet mentions a number of landmarks that came to define the spiritual landscape of Worcestershire. For instance, the tale recounts how, when Kenelm's body was discovered following his martyrdom, a well emerged at the site of his exhumation:

> Anon so hi nome up this holi bodi   a welle spreng up ther stod
> Of the stude that he lai on   that yute is cler and god
> For ther is a welle fair inou   and evere eft hath ibe[o]
> In the stude that he lay on   as me mai there ise[o].
>
> (I, 289, 293–6)[16]

(As soon as they exhumed this holy body, a well sprang up in that place – the place where he lay – which is still clear and good. For there is a fair well, and it has been there ever since, in the place where he lay, as one may see there.)

The well is not just a textual fabrication alluded to in the legend to make Kenelm's exhumation more fantastic. Instead, it is a topographical feature that the poet insists can still be seen in the late-thirteenth century: 'as me mai there ise[o]'. In fact, regional place lore contends that the well is still visible today at the Romsley church, where wall paintings of Kenelm's martyrdom also survive. The ash tree that marks the location of Kenelm's murder also serves as a landmark. The poet recalls, 'And a gret ass bicom suthe   and yute stont in thulke place / To ssewi the mighte of seint Kenelm   and oure Louerdes grace' (I, 285, 171–2, 'And a great ash appeared afterwards, and yet stands in that place, to demonstrate the might of St Kenelm and our Lord's grace'). On the map constructed in the opening seventy-five lines of St Kenelm's life, these landmarks would be illustrated and briefly annotated in the same way that Gog and Magog's enclosure, the Tower of Babel and Scylla and Charybdis were on contemporary maps. The presence of such landmarks or legends on medieval maps served to emphasize a map's historical function while also mapping a culture's influence on the physical landscape. Both the well and ash tree in *Kenelm*, then, serve as examples of Worcestershire's spiritual reshaping of geographical reality.[17]

While the poet spends a great deal of time integrating the rhetoric of a non-literary medium and adhering to conventions of medieval map making, he also problematizes many common features on medieval maps. On most medieval maps Jerusalem, the world's spiritual hub, was located at the centre (in T-O and list maps it was placed on the point where the vertical and horizontal lines of the T met). When Jerusalem did not occupy a central position, Rome did, thereby providing cartographical validation for Rome's authorizing function in computus and calendrical texts.[18] In *Kenelm*, however, Worcestershire is given a position of dominance. The poet writes,

> The kyng that was king of the March   hadde tho the beste
> Muchedel he hadde of Engelond   the on half al by weste
> Wircetressire and Warwikssire   and also of Gloucestre
> That is nei a bissopriche   the bissops of Wircestre.
>
> (I, 280, 21–4)

(The king that was king of the March held the best lands. He possessed much of England, the Western half: Worcestershire and Warwickshire, and also Gloucestershire, all of which is by a bishopric: the bishopric of Worcester.)

In this passage Worcestershire is defined as the 'beste' kingdom in England, and when Kenelm is introduced we are told 'Kyng he was of Engelond   of the March of Walis' (I, 279, 2, 'he was the king of England, of the March of Wales'). Here 'Engelond' and 'the March of Walis' are working appositively, suggesting that the March of Wales is the locus of England's spiritual and cultural identity. The *SEL* poet also repeatedly emphasizes the ascendancy of Winchcombe, nowadays a small town, that synecdochally represents the March of Wales. Following a laudatory description of the church where Kenelm is buried, we are told: 'Gret cite was tho Winchcombe   and mest of inou / Of al thulke half of Engelond' (I, 280, 7–8, 'Winchcombe was a great city, and the very best of all that half of England'). In this passage Winchcombe is proclaimed to be a 'gret cite', and the partitive genitive 'mest of inou' suggests that its greatness supersedes the combined force of half of England. Following a long summary of the bishoprics in the March of Wales we are also told:

Al this lond was wile icluped   the March of Walis
And of al was sein Kenelm and is fader   kyng iwis
Non of al the otheris thing   agen this kynedom nas
And Winchcombe of al this lond   chef cite tho was.

(I, 280–1, 39–42)

(All this land was called the March of Wales, and it belonged to St
Kenelm and his father, the King. None of the other lands compared
to this kingdom, and Winchcombe was the chief city of this land.)

Again Winchcombe's ascendancy is clear. It is the chief city in the
March of Wales, and, since 'Non of al the otheris thing   agen
this kynedom nas', no city in the remaining four kingdoms can
even come close to Winchcombe's greatness. This description of
Winchcombe suggests that the shire should be centrally featured
on a cartographical representation of England.

The argument for this ascendancy is also substantiated by
the status of the Worcester diocese in the thirteenth century.
Beginning in 890 with the foundation of the *burh*, Worcester blos-
somed as a secular and religious site. One of the diocese's most
distinctive features was its devotion to antiquarian pursuits. As the
Cathedral Priory's extensive collection of Old English manuscripts
suggests, Worcester's residents were interested in preserving and
studying Anglo-Saxon literature.[19] At a time when much of Britain
had been subsumed by the Norman administration, Worcester
distinguished itself as a place devoted to pre-Conquest English
identity. This would have appealed to thirteenth-century sensibili-
ties for a number of reasons. First, in the thirteenth century there
was a continuing movement to reclaim Anglo-Saxon saints who
were removed from liturgical calendars following the Norman
invasion. Both Worcester's extant manuscripts and its landscape
were marked by the presence of these saints. Second, in the centuries following the conquest there was a strong push for monastic
reform. As a conservative Benedictine diocese, Worcester would
have served as a model for reformers.[20] The Cathedral Priory's collection was markedly Benedictine, and the monks' literary studies
demonstrated their commitment to St Benedict's insistence that
'idleness is the enemy of the soul; the brethren, therefore, must
be occupied at stated hours . . . in sacred reading'.[21] The extensive
record of glossing that survives from medieval Worcester, including the Tremulous Hand's famous glosses, is evidence for this
commitment.[22] Because of Worcester's dedication to Benedictine
reform and Anglo-Saxon sanctity, the diocese would undoubtedly

have stood out as a religious site worthy of cartographical and literary acclaim in the thirteenth century.

Worcester's physical landscape was also quite remarkable. Located atop a bluff in between the Severn and Frog Brook, the city was a prominent settlement in midwestern England.[23] In addition to being militarily and commercially viable given its location on one of England's three major rivers, the city was distinguished by its many churches and cathedrals. A cathedral dedicated to St Peter was built as early as 680, and between the seventh and thirteenth centuries more than fifteen additional churches were constructed. St Mary's Cathedral was a particularly notable element of the landscape, and features prominently on John Speed's 1610 map of Worcester.[24] This Benedictine cathedral defined the landscape by providing visual confirmation of the diocese's commitment to the *Rule of St Benedict* and pre-Conquest sanctity. Worcester's religious priorities were further confirmed by the fact that at least nine of the ten parish churches depended on the bishop as a patron. This was unusual in the centuries following the Norman invasion, since the Crown patronized the majority of England's churches (in Gloucester, for example, the Crown patronized at least four of the parish churches). Because of Worcester's unconventional allegiance to what was in the thirteenth century an outdated patronage system, St Mary's cathedral was a significant example of pre-Conquest patronage in Worcester that dominated the landscape.

These landscape features and Worcester's historical condition in the thirteenth century substantiate *Kenelm*'s emphasis on the diocese of Worcester as a geographical site of religious preeminence. Remarkably, this emphasis in *Kenelm* results in the subordination of Canterbury, long acknowledged as the seat of English religion. The most notable reference to Canterbury in *Kenelm* occurs when the Romans deliver a letter to Canterbury that they received from God regarding Kenelm's exhumation and canonization. The authority of Wulfred, archbishop of Canterbury, is set aside immediately upon the letter's arrival. The poet writes, 'Tho this letter fram the pope   to the archebissop com / Of bissops and of is clerkes   conseil therof he nom' (I, 288, 285–6, 'When this letter from the pope came to the archbishop, he took council about it from his bishops and his clerks'). Wulfred's authority alone is insufficient in matters concerning Winchcombe. He is forced to seek counsel, and, even when the committee agrees to search for Kenelm's body, they require the townspeople's aid, 'that underyite this cas / Ortrowede wel war it lay   for the miracle so

vair was' (I, 289, 291–2, 'who understood this case; they knew well
where [St Kenelm's body] lay, for the miracle was so pleasing').

In addition to challenging Canterbury's religious authority, this
passage undermines Rome's authorizing power by suggesting that
the pope himself is unable to interpret the divine Word. The letter
delivered to Rome is in English rather than the standard liturgical
language: Latin. The *SEL* poet is explicit on this point, noting that
the pope

> . . . nuste wat it was to segge   ne in wit neccuthe iwite
> For he ne couthe Engliss non   and an Engliss it was iwrite. . .
> Tho were there men of Engelond   that weste wat is sede
> And understode wel that writ   tho hi it hurde rede
> The writ was iwrite pur Engliss.
>
> (I, 288; 259–60, 263–5)

(knew not what it [the letter] said, nor could reason understand it.
For he did not know any English, and in English it was written . . .
but there were men of England there who knew what it said and
understood that writ well when they heard it read. The letter was
written in English.)

By rendering the pope helpless in his ability to translate God's
word, the mere existence of this letter fortifies England's spiritual
ascendancy. The traditional mouthpiece of the church is rendered
speechless, replaced by the English vernacular in a letter that is
best interpreted by the people of the diocese of Worcester.

From these examples, it is clear that the *SEL* poet intends to
present his readers with both a rhetorical and illustrative depiction
of the world that locates the diocese of Worcester as its spiritual
and diagrammatic centre. Including *Kenelm* in the *SEL* is thus a
significant move. The *SEL* grants Worcester centrality and suggests that the diocese rivals Rome as a site capable of producing
authoritative liturgical calendars. Unlike previous interpretations
of calendrical time, the thirteenth-century legendary grants geographical and cultural authority to an English region over a continental empire. By narrowing his geographical focus, and including
cartographical detail in the *SEL* that could be corroborated by
corporeal experience, the *SEL* poet guarantees that his audience
will recognize the *precise* centre of Christendom. The hub of the
SEL's spiritual world is not located on an island 'far north toward
the pole'; it is located in the diocese of Worcester, where one can
still see the well and the ash tree of Kenelm's legend. This use of
place to regional ends finally takes precedence over the legendary's

temporal ordering structure. The cartographical detail in *Kenelm*, then, is a key to understanding the *SEL*'s complexity. The *SEL* is not a liturgical calendar operating under the auspices of Rome; it is a keystone to English regional and spiritual identity that considers time, place, religion, and the relationship between all three.

Notes

1 All quotations are from D'Evelyn and Mill. For a discussion of alternate prologue traditions, see Liszka, 'The first "A" redaction'.

2 For a discussion of these calculations and their evolution in the classical period, see Arno Bost, *The Ordering of Time: From the Ancient Computus to the Modern Computer*, trans. Andrew Winnard (Chicago: University of Chicago Press, 1993).

3 Kenelm was martyred in the Clent Hills of Worcestershire, but his cult centre of Winchcombe is in Gloucestershire. Both locations are part of the diocese of Worcester.

4 Bede, *A History of the English Church and People*, trans. Leo Sherley-Price (Baltimore: Penguin Books, 1955), II.4 (henceforth quoted by book and chapter number). For the orginal text, see *Bede's Ecclesiastical History of the English Church and People*, ed. Bertram Colgrave and R. A. B. Mynors (Oxford: Clarendon Press, 1969). With respect to the present quotation, Pope John echoes Laurence's sentiment fifteen chapters later when, in a letter to the Scots of 640, he writes, 'certain persons in your province are attempting to revive a new heresy from an old one, contrary to the orthodox faith, and that in the dark cloud of their ignorance they refused to observe our Easter on which Christ was sacrificed, arguing that it should be observed with the Hebrew Passover on the fourteenth day of the moon' (II.19).

5 Nicholas Howe, *Writing the Map of Anglo-Saxon England* (New Haven: Yale University Press, 2008), p. 126.

6 Alan Thacker, '*Loca Sanctorum*: the significance of place in the study of the saints', in Alan Thacker and Richard Sharpe (eds), *Local Saints and Local Churches in the Early Medieval West* (Oxford: Oxford University Press, 2002), pp. 1–44; A. H. Merrils, *History and Geography in Late Antiquity* (Cambridge: Cambridge University Press, 2005); Kathy Lavezzo, *Angels on the Edge of the World: Geography, Literature, and English Community, 1000–1534* (Ithaca: Cornell University Press, 2006); Fabienne Michelet, *Creation, Migration, and Conquest: Imaginary Geography and Sense of Space in Old English Literature* (Oxford: Oxford University Press, 2006).

7 Representations of the zodiac abounded in medieval art/architecture, including carvings on church portals and stained glass windows. Given the popularity of such images, it is unlikely the word 'Taurus' could be

used without evoking the constellation of the zodiac. To read the gloss as a mere translation of the English 'bull' would be to take the gloss out of context.

8　For studies of nationalism in the *SEL* see Hamelinck, 'St Kenelm'; Catherine Cubitt, 'Sites and sanctity: revisiting the cult of murdered and martyred Anglo-Saxon royal saints', *Early Medieval Europe*, 9:1 (2000), 53–83; Thompson, *Everyday Saints*.

9　Jankofsky, 'National characteristics', p. 85; see also Klaus P. Jankofsky, 'Entertainment, edification, and popular education in the *South English Legendary*', *Journal of Popular Culture*, 11:3 (1977), 706–17.

10　Frederick, 'National identity'.

11　Cubitt, 'Sites and sanctity', pp. 68–9.

12　Notable medieval list maps include the Psalter Map (BL Add. MS 28681, fol. 9v), and a reverse T-O map in Bede's *De Natura Rerum* (Exeter Cathedral Library MS 3507, fol. 67r). The Hereford Map represents the fusion of list maps with more illustrative representations of space by providing a relatively accurate geographical worldview, and integrating long descriptions of places or historical events with pictorial representations of place.

13　While translating *drou* as 'draw' is unconventional in standard ME, the dialect of the *SEL* lends itself to this translation, as the word *drou* implies 'to draw' repeatedly throughout the text. In *Edmund of Canterbury*, for instance, Edmund is described as *drou*ing figures all day in powder: 'to arsmetrike he drough / and arsmetrike radde in cours In Oxenford wel faste / and his figurs drough aldai' (II, 500, 224–6).

14　See Evelyn Edson, *Mapping Time and Space: How Medieval Mapmakers Viewed Their World* (London: The British Library, 1997).

15　Edson, *Mapping Time and Space*, p. 18.

16　The present-day location of the well is explored in Mike Smith and David Taylor, 'The crown and the well: the divine king and the re-discovery of a "lost" well', *Mercian Mysteries*, 25 (1995) www.indigo-group.co.uk/edge/Stkenelm.htm (now published as *At the Edge*).

17　Cubitt notes the topographical elements in *Kenelm*, arguing that 'the cults were rooted in the local landscape and not only practised at their ecclesiastical shrines' (p. 54).

18　On the Anglo-Saxon world map, for instance, Rome and the Aegean islands are located centrally. For an image and brief discussion of the Anglo-Saxon world map, see P. D. A. Harvey (ed.), *The Hereford World Map: Medieval World Maps and Their Context* (London: The British Library, 2006), pp. 4–8.

19　For discussions of Worcester's intellectual pursuits, see E. G. Stanley, 'Laȝamon's antiquarian sentiments', *Medium Aevum*, 38 (1969), 23–37; John Frankis, 'Towards a regional context for Lawman's *Brut*: literary activity in the dioceses of Worcester and Hereford in the twelfth century', in Rosamund Allen, Lucy Perry and Jane Roberts (eds), *Laȝamon: Contexts, Language, and Interpretation* (London: King's College London, 2002), pp. 53–78.

20 See *The Rule of Saint Benedict*, ed and trans. Justin McCann (London: Burns and Oates, 1952).

21 Ibid., pp. 110–11. For a detailed account of the Cathedral Priory's holdings, see Glenys Popper (ed.), *Medieval Art and Architecture at Worcester Cathedral* (London: British Archeological Association, 1978).

22 See Christine Franzen, *The Tremulous Hand of Worcester: A Study of Old English in the Thirteenth Century* (Oxford: Clarendon Press, 1991).

23 For a detailed discussion of these grants and tolls, see Nigel Baker and Richard Holt, *Urban Growth and the Medieval Church: Gloucester and Worcester* (Aldershot: Ashgate, 2005), pp. 129–32.

24 Ibid., plate 11. Just as the 'Legend of Saint Kenelm' inscribed the landscape with Kenelm's well and ash tree, Speed inscribed Worcester with a manifestation of culture that best defined the city: a Benedictine cathedral.

16

Visualizing the *South English Legendary*: Bodleian Library, MS Tanner 17

Karen A. Winstead

Oxford, Bodleian Library, MS Tanner 17, produced c. 1400, preserves a substantial portion of the *SEL,* beginning with the prologue and breaking off in the middle of the life of St Augustine of Canterbury.[1] It includes the legends of eighteen martyrs and seventeen confessors, of whom eleven in all are natives of or missionaries to the British Isles, along with the commemorations of five Church feasts: Circumcision, Epiphany, Annunciation, Lent and Holy Cross. Besides these standard *SEL* materials, the manuscript includes Rood poems, a verse account of Christ's passion, and verse lives of Pilate and Judas Iscariot. Tanner 17 was incomplete from at least the sixteenth century;[2] the missing portion's fate is unknown. What remains, however, is a handsome codex, neatly written in a professional textura hand, with initials in gold, blue and red marking the start of each chapter.

What makes the Tanner manuscript truly remarkable is that it is the only known illustrated *SEL* – in fact, the only illustrated manuscript known of any Middle English legendary. About fifty years after the production of the text, forty drawings were added to the ample margins. Five of these are New Testament illustrations: the three kings gazing toward the star that will lead them to Bethlehem (fol. 2), the Annunciation (fol. 46), the cross (fol. 95) and two scenes of the Circumcision (fols 1v, 8). The rest illustrate the manuscript's thirty-five saints' lives, one drawing per saint, with each saint's depiction, except that of Sebastian, placed in the outer margin beside the beginning of his or her life and captioned with the saint's name. Manfred Görlach notes stylistic variations among these images that suggest to him the hands of multiple artists and states that 'the drawings grow in size and naturalistic detail as the volume progresses'.[3] Certainly the later portraits tend to be larger, and some are more detailed than others; however, I see no clear progression in their complexity or naturalism. Moreover,

they are in some ways remarkably uniform: all, with the exception
once again of Sebastian and also of Agnes, are full-length portraits
showing the standing saint, who is never directly facing the viewer
nor in full profile, but always slightly turned, almost always (thirty-
one of thirty-three cases) to the viewer's right. Though they lack
the polish of the illuminations found in high-end continental legendaries and books of hours, they are far from mere marginal doodles.
The consistency of placement and captioning bespeaks planning.
All of the images but one are polychromatic, and most are executed
with meticulous attention to details of clothing, accessories, head-
gear and hairstyle, through which they convey definite social positions: the religious are recognizably popes, bishops, nuns, friars or
abbots, while the lay saints are clearly members of the elite – a king,
two knights and the rest (apart from apostles) arrayed in upper-
class garments. Moreover, certain distinctive features found in all
of the portraits, such as elongated fingers, full lips, wide noses and
large ears, suggest to me the work of a single hand.

In representing the saints with portraits, the Tanner artist varies
from the common practice, in continental legendaries, of showing
scenes from the saint's life, usually episodes so well known that they
identify their subjects: Nicholas resurrecting the three youths from
the vat, Martin dividing his cloak with the beggar, Cuthbert being
fed by the raven. Martyrs are almost always identified through and
with specific violence – Lawrence roasting on his gridiron, Agatha
having her breasts wrenched off, Sebastian thoroughly sagittated.
The margins of Tanner 17 would amply accommodate such scenes;
indeed, as I have noted, most of the images pertaining to the life of
Christ *are* scenes, and those of the Circumcision are quite elaborate, with multiple characters. In their delineation and colouring,
the Tanner saints' portraits are no simpler (usually, indeed, more
elaborate) than those scenes nor than the scenes typically found
in other illustrated continental legendaries; thus we ought not to
attribute the choice of static portrait form to mere expediency or
artistic ineptitude. The more likely motive, I will argue, is a desire
to express a particular concept of sanctity. In its representation both
of martyrs and of confessors, I will show, Tanner 17 celebrates the
saints as citizens of the world with distinct social identities. That
confessors should be clearly identified as monks, nuns, knights,
bishops etc. is not in itself surprising, but the degree of detail the
artist brings to those identifications is extraordinary. Moreover,
the depiction of martyrs stands at odds not only with the standard
iconography of martyrdom but with the emphasis on violence and

nudity in the manuscript's written legends. The Tanner images, I argue, not only 'upgraded' a hagiographical classic but also adapted it to the changing devotional culture of fifteenth-century England.

Identifying signs

Though scenes from the saints' lives were the norm in illustrated legendaries of the later Middle Ages, other devotional books – especially books of hours or psalters – often represented some or all of their saints through portraits.[4] In most instances, even when the saint was identified through a caption or an accompanying prayer, he or she was visually identified by a specific emblem or attribute that had become associated with that saint – usually an object, person, or animal that called to mind a famous event from the saint's life. Some saints – especially martyrs – were associated with multiple attributes.

The Book of Hours of John Lacy (Oxford, St John's College MS 94), an English manuscript produced in 1420, is a good example of how the Tanner artist's contemporaries usually executed portraits of the saints. The intercessionary petitions or suffrages to the saints are laid out in double columns, with a portrait of each of twenty-eight saints painted above his or her suffrage. The long and narrow space allocated to each portrait is comparable to the space the Tanner artist was working with. Each of the Lacy manuscript's saints is represented not only in attire appropriate to his or her profession or station in life but also with an identifying emblem. So, for instance, the viewer need not refer to the suffrages to distinguish Giles from Nicholas from Ignatius, though all were bishops, because a wounded doe is painted at Giles's feet, a pair of lions at Ignatius's and a tub with three boys at Nicholas's (fols 6, 16, 6v).

Six of the seventeen confessors in Tanner 17 are likewise identifiable from their pictures. Viewers would immediately recognize Mary of Egypt by the three loaves of bread she holds, an allusion to the food she brought with her to the desert when she became a penitent (fol. 85). Brendan grasps an oar, an obvious reference to his famous sea voyage (fol. 99v). Julian the Hospitaller, dressed as a knight, steps on the bloody sword he used to kill his parents (fol. 12). Augustine of Canterbury, missionary to the Anglo-Saxons, stands beside a baptismal font (fol. 111).

In the most complex portrait of the manuscript by far, Dunstan grasps in his right hand a chalice and in his left a pair of tongs gripping what looks to be a dragon writhing at his feet (Figure 16.1). Although part of the beast was lost when the manuscript's edges

But as a man of an oþ w[...]
he dede in yrlonde: som[...]
many meracles men han[...]
An abbei he is a rerid: þe[...]
God vs bringe to þat ioy[...]
Eint dunstan w[...]
meracles oure lor[...]
for whan he was[...]
þe were folk at chirche [...]
As he stode alle wiþ her[...]
Sodenli it queinte at o[...]
Rizt as it brente wel: i w[...]
þe folk stode in gret wond[...]
And how it queynte sod[...]
Alle þe folk merueile ha[...]
As þei stode and speke þ o[...]
Seint dunstans modris[...]
As sche it held in hure h[...]
þe folk þat stode þ bi hell[...]
But non wiste when it c[...]
þ of þei tendid al here li[...]
what be tokeney þat bi[...]
And þe folk þat stode a [...]
But þo² þat holi child [...]
Al ingelond schulde be b[...]
þe child was bore iȝ hor[...]
Aftȝ þat oure lord: of y[...]
And þe ferþe zer of þe [...]
his modir inteskyned[...]
þo þis child was bore: h[...]
þei lete it to glastyngb[...]
So reche hi ek þis bi lew[...]
þat child wiþ and wel t[...]
lue zeme he tok of þe w[...]
Eche man þat herde of [...]
þo he was of mannes wi[...]
he made wiþ hi ioie i no[...]
þe erchebischop of cant[...]
þo he seigh of his growd[...]
for deynte þat he hadde o[...]
He fore þe prince of ingel[...]

16.1 Dunstan, Archbishop of Canterbury, MS Tanner 17, fol. 107v were cropped,[5] leaving a jumble of claws, hair, and scales, we can infer from Dunstan's legend that he has some sort of serpentine woman by the nose. According to Dunstan's *vita*, the saint was in the habit of doing metalwork when exhausted by prayer yet unwilling to be idle. While he was alone in his smithy one evening, the devil appeared in the form of a beautiful woman whispering sweet nothings ('truflinge', 206/74),[6] whereupon he grasped the temptress's nose with his blazing hot tongs and would not let go until sure that she had learned her lesson and would never bother him again. Though a chalice is not mentioned in Tanner 17, in other versions of Dunstan's life that is what he was making when the devil visited him.[7]

The only saint identified solely by an attribute that has no connection whatsoever to the accompanying narrative is Cuthbert, who cradles the severed head of King Oswald in his right hand (fol. 42v). The crowned head of the martyred king became an emblem for Cuthbert in the ninth century, when it was placed, for safety, in Cuthbert's tomb. Oswald's head and Dunstan's chalice demonstrate that the artist was willing and able to draw upon broader traditions about the saints, not just the accompanying legends.

A higher proportion of the manuscript's martyrs are identifiable in their images – ten of eighteen. Although the most common emblems for martyrs were instruments employed during their passions, only six of the Tanner martyrs are depicted with such emblems: Blaise holds an iron comb, Alphege an axe, Peter of Verona a clipped-point falchion, and James the Less a fuller's club, while Vincent stands atop what might represent either a gridiron or the bed he was left to die on, and Sebastian is pictured with a bundle of arrows (fols 16v, 89, 93v, 94, 97). Of these six, however, only two – Alphege and Peter – actually show bloody wounds; for the most part, emblems sanitize violence by dissociating the instruments of torture and death from the harm they inflicted. Four other martyrs have emblems unrelated to their violent ends: Longinus holds the spear he used to stab the crucified Christ, and Cyriacus grasps the True Cross (fols 30, 99); Mark stands upon his evangelical lion, and George wears armour decorated with a red cross (fols 92v, 91v). Certain commonplace emblems are conspicuously absent. Though Agatha is almost always pictured with one or both of her breasts either on a platter or grasped in pincers, Tanner 17 represents her simply as a praying woman (fol. 19). Matthias lacks his axe, Philip his cross (fols 25, 93v); and, though George is represented both as a soldier and with his characteristic red cross, there is no dragon at his feet to distinguish him definitively from other soldier saints. What is most remarkable, however, is that eighteen of the thirty-five saints in Tanner 17 are portrayed with no identifying emblems at all.[8]

The Tanner portraits are clearly less concerned with conveying *who* the saints were than *what* they were. Attention is lavished on minutiae of apparel that identify class or profession. Whereas both the narratives of the *SEL* and the contemporary iconography of martyrdom sharply distinguished confessors from martyrs by fixating on the martyrs' grisly passions, the illustrations in Tanner 17 largely erase differences between martyrs and confessors, celebrating the saints more for what they were in life than for how they died.

Episcopal saints

With seven bishops, five archbishops and two popes, episcopal saints form the largest category in the collection, and the artist took particular care in their depiction. Markers of rank are indicated in every portrait but that of Archbishop Alphege: the popes wear tiaras, the bishops and archbishops mitres; the popes hold double-barred cross-staffs, while (with a few exceptions, discussed later) the bishops hold croziers and the archbishops single-barred cross-staffs. Further, most portraits include, besides the mitre, other 'pontificals', those elements of dress – the pontifical ring, gloves, dalmatic, tunicle, buskins and episcopal sandals – that set the vestments of a bishop apart from those of an ordinary priest, and the metropolitan status of Dunstan (Figure 16.1) and Austin is further signalled by their fringed pallia.[9]

Cyriacus is the most elaborately dressed, and the only one displaying all of the pontificals normally visible (Figure 16.2). His blue-green chasuble is lined in scarlet. Beneath it is a fringed red dalmatic, and beneath that an alb appareled at its hem and cuff with blue orphreys embroidered with gold. At his neck, the blue-green orphrey apparel of his amice is embroidered in red. His red episcopal sandals have the typical fork-shaped ornamentation. Over his glove, he wears a pontifical ring with a large red stone on his right thumb; on his middle finger a band. In place of a crozier, Cyriacus grasps his emblem, Christ's cross.

Other bishops are also formally dressed, though the details of their attire vary. If we look at the mitres, for example, Chad's is plain white with yellow bands (the *mitra simplex*, for everyday use),

16.2 Cyriacus, martyr, MS Tanner 17, fol. 99r

and Oswald's is like Chad's but with finialed horns (fols 25v, 28); however, the rest are more ornate, trimmed between the horns' finials with ball tassels or possibly pearls and often decorated between the bands with embroidery (*mitra auriphrygiata*) or, in some cases, what may be jewelled enamel or gold plates (*mitra pretiosa*). Except for Aldhelm, every bishop whose feet are visible is wearing episcopal sandals, with white ornamentation set against red or black. Almost everybody wears an alb, some apparelled with orphreys of different colours and designs. Most wear chasubles and amices whose apparels likewise vary in pattern, sometimes matching the orphreys of their albs. For example, the green chevroned apparel of Aldhelm's amice matches those at the hem and cuffs of his alb (fol. 110). Several of the bishops and archbishops wear dalmatics, again of different colours. Cuthbert's is blue with blue fringe, Hilary's a teal that matches the pillar orphrey of his chasuble and the apparels of his amice and alb (fols 42v, 2). The representation of Chad is harder to make out (Figure 16.3). His dalmatic is white, but it seems to have not the simple side slit that is typical but rather a wide vent with long yellow fringe; at its hem, we see three bands of colour – yellow, red and blue – that may represent either an elaborate border to the dalmatic or the projection of a red tunicle with blue fringe from beneath it.[10]

Though chasubles are the norm among bishops in Tanner 17, not every bishop wears one. Chad wears instead a scarlet cope lined with blue. Patrick and Pope Gregory the Great wear hooded scarlet chimeres over white rochets[11] (fols 31, 29); however, Gregory's hood, unlike Patrick's, is lined with ermine. Wulfstan, Oswald, Alphege and Dunstan are clad in cowled black robes that identify them as Benedictines (fols 3, 25v, 89, 107v). Pope Fabian has a papal mantum secured with a morse (fol. 6).

There are certain peculiarities in the artist's renditions of the prelates' vestments and accessories. Most surprising is that bishops are never shown with the priest's stole and maniple that are routinely found in similarly detailed manuscript illuminations and paintings, as well as on monumental brasses and effigies. Another peculiarity is the representation of Oswald, archbishop of York, with a double-barred cross-staff (fol. 25v). Though such a staff is not inappropriate for an archbishop, within this manuscript it is otherwise reserved for popes.

An apparent error is the artist's representation of Wulfstan, bishop of Worcester, with an archbishop's cross (fol. 3). Might the artist have mistaken St Wulfstan for his more famous uncle

16.3 Chad, Bishop of Lichfield, MS Tanner 17, fol. 28r

Wulfstan, author of the 'Sermo Lupi ad Anglos', who was also
bishop of Worcester before becoming archbishop of York? What
at first appears to be understandable confusion turns out instead
to be scrupulous attention to textual detail, for the accompanying
legend specifically represents the saint as carrying a cross-staff.
In its central incident, Wulfstan is called before King William
and Archbishop Lanfranc, who ask him to resign his see on the
grounds that he is too ill-educated. Wulfstan answers that he will
relinquish his 'crois' (I, 12–13; 119, 130, 141, 145, 147, 161) only to
the one who gave it to him, namely the deceased King Edward the
Confessor.[12] Wulfstan drives his staff into the Confessor's marble
tomb as if into soft sand; only he can withdraw it.

Tanner 17's gallery of bishops reveals much about the artist's
interests and methods. While he is scrupulous about giving each
markers of his proper rank, his bishops, archbishops and popes are
far from generic. Rather, he takes considerable trouble to show not
only the intricacy but the variety of episcopal garb. The scarcity
of identifying emblems makes clear that it is not important to the
artist that the identity of the saint be evident from the portrait; yet
it is important that the image be informed by and consistent with
the saint's story, both as written in the manuscript and as available
elsewhere in the verbal and pictorial traditions.

Other 'holimen' and 'holiwummen'

Matthias, Philip, James the Less and Mark comprise the only
readily identifiable group of saint besides bishops, namely apostles. As was common in the iconography of the time, they are, for
the most part, a shaggy lot clad in relatively simple, loose-fitting
robes, and, in contrast to all other saints in the manuscript, they
are barefoot (where their feet are visible). Even so, the artist cannot
resist gestures towards stylishness in the pleats of the robes worn
by Mark and James and in James's fitted cuffs and neatly trimmed,
pointed beard (fols 92v, 94). As with the bishops, there is no
'generic' apostle; rather, their images reveal a variety of personal
detail. Matthias, the 'junior' apostle chosen to replace Judas, is
a beardless youth with tousled brown hair (fol. 25). Middle-aged
James is the best-groomed of the four (Figure 16.4). Though Mark
and Philip are both much older and grizzled, they look nothing like
each other: the wispy straight hair of Mark's head and forked beard
falls to his waist, whereas Philip's hair is shoulder-length and curly
(fols 92v, 93v).

16.4 James the Less, apostle and martyr, MS Tanner 17, fol. 94r

16.5 Peter of Verona, martyr, MS Tanner 17, fol. 93v

The artist presents the non-episcopal members of religious orders with the same scrupulous attention to attire he shows in portraying the bishops. Peter of Verona is immediately identifiable as a Dominican (fol. 93v) (Figure 16.5); Benedict, with his black cowl and elaborately decorated crosier, is obviously a Benedictine abbot (fol. 43v). Bride of Ireland and Scholastica wear black and grey habits, respectively, their sleeves long and full and the *barbes* at their necks neatly pleated (fols 13v, 21). Brendan, whose order is not specified in his legend, wears a black scapular and hood over a white tunic (fol. 99v). The only member of the clergy not identified by vocation is Vincent (fol. 9). Though identified in the accompanying text as 'dekne' (I, 25, 4) to the bishop of Zaragoza, he not only lacks the dalmatic, stole and maniple of a deacon but appears in shapeless robes and a large red hat that give no indication he is a cleric at all.

The love of detail evident in the portraits of the religious is likewise manifest in most of the artist's portraits of lay saints. Especially striking are the portraits of the highest-ranking saints, King Edward the martyr and the two knights, Julian and George. Edward is arrayed in his regalia, with sword and scepter, ermine shoulder cape over ermine-lined scarlet mantle and a green robe whose hem and cuffs are broidered in gold (Figure 16.6). The portraits of Julian the Hospitaller and George are truly extraordinary (fols 12, 91v). The specialized components of their armour are sedulously drawn – cowters, roundels, coudières, cuissards, greaves, poleyns, sabatons etc. The artist has attended to the tiniest details, from the hinges of the plates of armour, to the finger joints of George's gauntlet (Julian wears no gauntlet), to the decorative swirls on his red cross (Figure 16.7). George, whose open visor reveals his curled moustache, is clearly a knight of the modern world – formidable, dashing, and eminently well equipped for the combat that, as I will discuss later, he never sees in his written legend.

Other distinctly 'modern' saints are Juliana and Longinus (fols 22, 30). Sumptuously dressed in a high-waisted gown whose broad belt and broad green collar match the lining of her houppelande, Juliana looks every bit a wealthy woman 'com of heie men' (I, 62, 1) (Figure 16.8). Though we are given no information in the text about Longinus's condition and lineage, he is also presented as a respectable man of means in his belted and pleated houppelande (Figure 16.9). Longinus's cuffs are fitted, his sleeves puffed. His green boots, with their ornamental pointed toes, match his undergown; his copious scarlet hat matches his collar. Though not as natty as Longinus, Valentine, opposite Juliana, sports a tall red hat that suggests he occupies a place among the well-to-do (fol. 21v).[13] His belt, like Longinus's, is decorated and worn at a slant. Where Longinus's tunic falls just below the knee, Valentine's is the floor-length gown suited to an elderly man.

As a rule, the artist is less detailed in his portraits of women, and apparently less concerned with rank – or perhaps less willing to

16.6 King Edward, martyr, MS Tanner 17, fol. 39v

þe it lai many a day ꝥ ei
ꝥ it was lad to cãiturbe
Alle þe liþe caneþs ꝥ þᵗ le
Aft' þat þe bough gan to
Alle þei deiden in sting d
And sũme deiden feble ꝥ
And sũme bi come cãub
And sũme dreynte in þe
So þ it was sone sene ꝥ þ
ffor þ was non to queyũ
Bidde we alle to seint al
þat we more þõ his lore

Seint George þe l
in þe lond of ca
þe false goddis l
And louede wel iþũ cri
Dacian þe liþe þuce þe
Alle cstene men þ he foi
As he houðed a day his f
Seint george cam i seigh
þe tokne he made of þe ci
And armed hi wiþ þe holi
And wente hi forþ wol b
Do dacian i alle hise þ
Alle false goddis be þe t
ffor oure lord heuē mad
þo dacian herde þis he
And lowred wiþ his seni

16.7 George, martyr, MS Tanner 17, fol. 91v

16.8 Juliana, martyr, MS Tanner 17, fol. 22r

16.9 Longinus, martyr, MS Tanner 17, fol. 30r

accord to women the markers of it. Neither Bride nor Scholastica is shown with an abbess's crozier (fols 13v, 21). Agatha's outfit is far simpler than Juliana's – a plain white gown and a white cloak lined with scarlet – but her gown none the less has the high waist and fitted sleeves that were fashionable during the first decades of the fifteenth century (fol. 19).[14]

Respectability is a governing theme. Mary of Egypt, with her rose gown, green-blue cloak, and black shoes, is well dressed and well shod (Figure 16.10). Her gown, like Agatha's and Juliana's, is fashionably voluminous. Were it not for the three loaves in her arms, we would not recognize her as the hermit whom many late medieval artists depict as a wild woman wearing nothing but her hair. Whereas hats are the most arresting feature of the Tanner artist's lay men, his portraits of lay women always show them with long, flowing hair, never in the fashionable (and much-criticized) headdresses of their time. True, flowing hair can signal virginity, but any such signal here is scrambled by endowing the virgins and reformed prostitute, Mary of Egypt, with identical coiffure. Or is it? The artist's point may have been that the women's common *spiritual* virginity is more important than any physical intactness.[15]

Anomalous portraits: Peter of Verona and Alphege

In the portraits discussed so far, there is little to distinguish the martyrs from the confessors. The martyrs are, for the most part, dissociated from their passions, with few emblems of torture. Only two portraits, those of Alphege and of Peter of Verona (fols 89, 93), depict wounded bodies. Alphege stands holding a bloody axe in one hand and bloodied rocks in the other; blood courses down his face and robes from a wound at the crown of his head (Figure 16.11). Blood also streams from a gash in Peter of Verona's head, and he holds the sword that struck him; a dagger pierces his chest, with more blood flowing from the messy wound (Figure 16.5).

Curiously, the accounts of these two martyrs' passions are some of the *least* violent in the *SEL*. Those who were drawn by the arresting images of violence to the accompanying text would find themselves directed to exceptional legends emphasizing service rather than suffering. The story of Peter is brief and mostly devoted to his preaching career, with his martyrdom at the hands of Lombard heretics tersely narrated:

16.10 Mary of Egypt, reformed prostitute, MS Tanner 17, fol. 85r

16.11 Alphege, Archbishop of Canterbury, martyr, MS Tanner 17, fol. 89r

> After this prechinge on of hom   into a wode him teighte
> Tho he com thuder ther com on   and [mid] a swerd him reighte
> Anouwarde the heved and clef adoun   that brain deop and wide
> With a long knif he smot him ek   thoru out either side.
>
>   (I, 163, 21–24)

(After this preaching, one of them directed him to a wood. When he came there, another came at him and struck downward on his head with a sword, cutting deep and wide into his brain; he also thrust a long knife through his body.)

Peter died, the hagiographer tells us, 'to holde up the rightes of Holi Churche   and the foles forto lere' (I, 163, 26, 'to uphold the rights of Holy Church and to teach fools'). The far longer story of St Alphege also focuses on the saint's career as monk, hermit, abbot, bishop and finally archbishop of Canterbury. He is praised for his 'wisdom' and his 'lore' (I, 150, 48) and for his diligence as a teacher (I, 149, 22). His death at the hands of Danish invaders is peremptorily relayed: his persecutors 'hende him with harde stones' and 'smot him with an ax   in the heved to gronde' (I, 154; 180, 183, 'stoned him with hard stones', 'struck him to the ground with an axe to the head'). The hagiographer shows little interest in whatever gory ordeals might have preceded the saint's martyrdom, saying rather vaguely, 'hi leide him to gronde / And on is feble body made mony harde wonde' (153, 149–50, 'they laid him on the ground and inflicted many severe wounds on his feeble body').

The images of Alphege and Peter of Verona are also unusual in showing the victims of violence without its perpetrators. In fact, the only *perpetrators* of violence among the saints' images are the saints themselves: Julian, his sword stained with the blood of his parents (fol. 12); Longinus grasping the spear with which he pierced the side of Christ (Figure 16.9); and Dunstan subduing the demon (Figure 16.1). There is little attention in the Tanner images to the conflict between good and evil, Christian and pagan, which figures so prominently in the narratives. The absence of that archetypal conflict is perhaps most conspicuous in the two scenes from saints' lives found within the manuscript.

Scenes: Sebastian and Agnes

In scenes drawn from the saint's life story, we would expect to find the closest congruence between text and image. The lives comprising the *SEL* are, for the most part, especially vivid in their descriptions of the violence that dominates the martyrs' passions. Yet the two saints' scenes in the Tanner manuscript, though both of martyrs, avoid showing violence and focus instead on devotional moments peripheral to and scantily described in the narrative. Moreover, what the artist depicts is not quite what the text describes.

In the visual arts, Sebastian's sagittation is by far the most commonly rendered episode of his life. The scene is graphically described in the legend: having had Sebastian tied to a stake, the emperor

. . . let archers to him schete	as it were to a marke
With arwen and with quarels	and made hym wonde starke
Manion wende him thoru out	in a lite wile
Hy stikede on him so thicke	so irchon doth of pile

(I, 17–8, 47–50)

(had archers shoot at him as if he were a target with arrows and bolts, and they inflicted sharp wounds; in a little while, many pierced him. They stuck to him as thick as a hedgehog's spines.)

The Tanner artist portrays not the sagittation but the episode immediately following, when the archers have left Sebastian for dead and the 'Cristene womman' (I, 18, 53) Irene comes to retrieve his body (Figure 16.12). The accompanying text provides few details; in fact, all we're told is that Irene came at night to bury Sebastian but, finding him 'hol and sond   withoute ech maner wonde'(I, 18, 53–6), joyfully led him home with her. The scene's sombre composition evinces none of the text's exaltation. Sebastian's body, though unblemished, shows no signs of life, while Irene, with her eyes downcast and lips drawn, seems to be grieving rather than rejoicing. Her posture – inclined over the supine Sebastian, her hand on his naked breast – is reminiscent of the Pietà, though Irene is standing and thus the martyr's body cannot lie in her lap but must rather hover, somewhat oddly, at the level of her waist. The usual (and often eroticized) sensationalism we find in scenes of Sebastian's martyrdom is wholly absent.[16]

The artist adds details not in the accompanying text. Irene grasps a rope that is twined around a stake on her right, as if she has just unbound the body. More puzzling, Sebastian, though a soldier, wears a bishop's mitre. Endowing Sebastian with a mitre is probably just an error, but it might also be an extreme example of the artist's preoccupation with social identity – Sebastian cannot

16.12 Sebastian, martyr, MS Tanner 17, fol. 6v

simply be a martyr but must have some marker of social station, even if it is wrong.

The placement of the scene is also notable, both because it occurs in the middle of the saint's life rather than at the beginning and because it is placed in an inner margin and lacks a caption. The unusual placement, however, corresponds to the unusual layout of the text. There is a single decorated initial at the beginning of each of Tanner 17's saints' lives, *except* in the case of Sebastian's life, which has a decorated initial not only at the beginning but at the lines introducing Irene: 'A Cristene womman that het Yreine' (I, 18, 53). It is as if the artist read this decorated letter as signalling the beginning of a life of St Irene (she is duly nimbed), even though only four lines of the narrative deal with her, and, whether by design or accident, illustrated Irene's 'life' but not Sebastian's.

The illustration from Agnes's life might at first be taken for a portrait rather than a scene (Figure 16.13). Like Agatha, Agnes is shown gazing toward heaven, her hands clasped in prayer; but, unlike Agatha and other saints in portraits, she is kneeling and bathed in light. Her long golden hair ripples down her back and past her knees. Though this image does not look like a brothel scene, viewers familiar with Agnes's legend would realise that it is exactly that. As related in Tanner 17, the constable of Rome, whose son she had just spurned, 'hure let strupe   so naked so he[o] was ibore' (I, 20, 42, 'had her stripped as naked as she was born') and ordered her to be taken to a brothel. God, however, thwarted his plan to humiliate and deflower her. As soon as she was undressed, her hair grew so long and thick that 'me nemighte for that her   of the body noght yse[o]' (I, 21, 50, 'nobody could see any of her body because of that hair'), and a miraculous light further hid her from view: 'Nemighte noman for lighte hur se[o]' (I, 21, 62, 'Nobody could see her because of the light'). Only after an angel brought her a white robe were the bystanders able to see her: 'Vairor thing nas nevere iseie   thanne this yonge thing tho was' (I, 21, 74, 'a fairer thing than this young thing was never seen').

Some of the key ingredients of the brothel scene are there – the praying saint, the heavenly light and the white garment – but they are not pictured exactly as the legend articulates them. The text has the saint bathed in light *until* the angel brings her clothing: 'Tho he[o] hadde this rochet on   namore ihud he[o] nas' (I, 21, 73, 'when she had this smock on she was no longer hidden'). Also surprising are the ingredients the artist leaves out: he shows neither the angel nor any of the brothel-goers. These elements are present in all of the brothel scenes I have found elsewhere:[17] to my knowledge, the Tanner artist's rendering of Agnes is unique. The conflict between good and evil is wholly erased from this 'scene', as it was from Sebastian's. Narrative itself is absent, as readers are left to

16.13 Agnes, martyr, MS Tanner 17, fol. 7r

contemplate the praying saint. I should note that, though Agnes's hair is long, it is not startlingly long, as it is in other brothel scenes – not long enough to distract from the devotional atmosphere of the image; her plain white gown removes her potentially distracting nudity.[18]

The scenes from the lives of Sebastian and Agnes are on facing pages and, like all the scenes in the manuscript except the Annunciation (fol. 46), appear within the first few folios of the codex. Perhaps the artist planned to illustrate the *SEL* with a mixture of scenes and portraits, then changed his iconographical programme to one of portraits only. Though all the festivals associated with the life of Christ had been illustrated with scenes, the artist chose to illustrate the feast of the Rood on folio 95 not with a Crucifixion but rather with a simple wooden cross punctured by three large nails, an image more in harmony with the iconographical scheme as it had evolved. The images of Agnes and Sebastian are also in harmony with the rest of the manuscript's iconography in their avoidance of violence, sensationalism and nudity. Their anomaly is solely a matter of genre – scenes rather than portraits – yet scenes rendered so static as to be scarcely more than portraits.

Refashioning holiness

The images in Tanner 17 do not so much illustrate the lives they accompany as provide alternative views of the saints – views that, in the case of the martyrs, are very much at odds with the legends. The period during which the *SEL* took shape was marked by a strong association of violence with holiness. The most popular saints of the period were martyrs of the early church, and their stories were being told with increased emphasis on torture and mutilation. Coincident with this fixation on violence was a tendency to portray more vituperative and confrontational saints: while the persecutors heap often sexualized and usually ineffective physical abuse upon the saints, their victims counter with stinging taunts, revelling in their tormentors' impotence. The *SEL* offers prime examples of both of these hagiographical trends.[19] The horrors the saints endure are excruciatingly visual. Of Juliana, for example, we read:

A weol of ire swuthe strang   byvore hure hy caste
Al were the velien aboute   with rasours ystiked vaste
That weol hi turnde al aboute   the maide therbi hi sette.

Dupe wode in hure naked fleiss   the rasors kene iwette
That tho hure vless was al totorne   so deope wode and gnowe
That the bones hy to slitte   and the marrou out drowe.
That marrou sprang out al aboute

(I, 67, 141–7)

(They set a strong iron wheel before her. Razors were affixed all around its rim. They turned the wheel, setting the maiden next to it. The sharpened razors penetrated her naked flesh so deeply that her flesh was torn. They penetrated so deeply that they slit the bones, drawing out the marrow. That marrow sprang out everywhere.)

Juliana and other virgin martyrs, however, meet blows with jeers – and occasionally even blows of their own. Their belligerence, as their foes are quick to point out, is shockingly at odds with norms of femininity. Having been battered and browbeaten by Juliana, the devil wails: 'Nertou corteis and hende? . . . War is the kunde of thi maidenot   that ssolde be[o] milde & stille?' (I, 66, 127, 'Aren't you courteous and gracious? . . . Where's the essence of your maidenhood, which should be mild and quiet?'). Juliana's human persecutor echoes the devil's frustration: 'Ssel a womman with hure wicchinge   us alle overcome?' (I, 68, 182, 'Shall a woman with her hexes overcome us all?'). Certainly, the saints are anything but 'corteis & hende' when flinging epithets: 'develles lime' (I, 20, 37), 'unwreste bouk' (I, 56, 61, 'wicked carcass') and so forth. What's more, but little provocation is needed to set them off. Responding to what seems an innocuous and polite offer of a lucrative marriage, Agnes calls her suitor's father a 'luther dethes fode', accusing him of wanting to 'fouly mi clene lif' (I, 20,24, 'wicked spawn of death'; 'befoul my pure life').

These features of the *SEL*'s representations of virgin martyrs legends have been noted before, but the lives of its male martyrs are equally full of grotesque and sometimes sexualized tortures. Cyriacus's life consists of little more than a catalogue of his sufferings – his hand hewed off, his body roasted, salted and boiled. The life of George boasts one of the bloodiest passions in the collection.[20] As with the virgin martyrs, nudity is explicit:

He let him honge up anhei   in a maner rode
And therto him binde faste naked   mid ropes stronge and gode
With kene oules there binethe   tormentors ther stode
And al todrowe his holy limes   that hi ronne ablode

(I, 156–7, 31–4)

(He had him strung up on high on a sort of cross and bound him naked securely to it with good, strong ropes. Below him the tormentors stood with sharp hooks, and they all tore his holy limbs until they were bloody.)

Even tortures that George does not actually experience are described in grisly detail:

Dacian let make a weol of bras   so strong so he mighte
And ssarpe swerdes thicke aboute   theron faste he pighte
And let nyme this holyman   and ther above him do
That the swerdes ssolde is body   rente and todrawe ato.

(I, 157, 53–6)

(Dacian had the strongest possible wheel of brass made and had sharp swords set thick around its rim and had the holy man taken and placed so that the swords would rend and tear his body in two.)

Readers would surely cringe in anticipation of George's ordeal, even though God smashes the wheel before any damage is done (I, 157, 59–60).

Likewise, although the 'unmaidenly' retorts of the female martyrs are perhaps more shocking, the men are equally caustic to their tormentors. 'Bel amy' ('dear friend'), the emperor remonstrates; 'fol' ('fool') George retorts (I, 156; 25, 27). Threats provoke only jeers from the blessed – 'gidi hound' (I, 179, 9), 'develes tonge' (I, 26, 54) and so forth.

Images of martyrdom that are very much in keeping with the spirit of the SEL flourished during the time of the legendary's heyday – and indeed well beyond. A case in point is Huntington Library HM 3027, an illuminated manuscript of Jacobus de Voragine's Legenda aurea that was produced at roughly the time of the SEL's composition.[21] The Huntington artist focuses on the same facets of the martyr legends as the authors of the SEL, and for most of them furnished scenes of the saints' passions, showing them undergoing the torments so vividly described in the text – Agnes, naked, being burned at a stake (fol. 23v); Agatha, stripped to the waist, having her breasts tugged off (fol. 33). This artist, like the SEL hagiographer, envisions George being tortured on the wheel, and represents him as naked except for a loin cloth, and blood flows from where the wheel's blades have penetrated his groin (fol. 49). Though violence is the dominant theme, the images sometimes also convey the saints' spirited resistance – Juliana binding the devil, for example (fol. 34). A similar focus on violence

dominated the representation of martyrdom in illuminated legendaries into and beyond the period when Tanner 17 was produced.[22]

Though I know of no illuminated legendaries produced in
England, an insular work that is very much in the spirit of the *SEL*
is *Queen Mary's Psalter*, British Library Royal MS 2 B.vii, a lav-
ishly illustrated codex that was produced in England during the
first quarter of the fourteenth century. This psalter's final section
is devoted to saints: fifty-six are represented along the bottom
margins (not counting the eleven thousand virgins and the massa-
cred Innocents!), all but three of them martyrs.[23] The illustrator of
these martyrs, like the *SEL* hagiographer, portrays both defiance
and violence. Each martyr is illustrated at least twice: first facing
his or her judge, then being tortured or executed. The judgement scenes, wherein the saints are clearly remonstrating with,
sometimes even scolding, their persecutors, convey the defiance
also shown by the *SEL*'s martyrs, while the torture and execution
scenes convey the brutality that characterizes the *SEL*'s narratives
– Fabian saggitated, Juliana strung up by her hair, Edward
stabbed, Mark hauled about with a noose, James the Less thrown
from the roof of the temple, Agnes and Valentine beheaded.

The Tanner artist thus departs not only from the dominant
themes in the *SEL* narratives but also from established traditions
in the visual arts by showing the saints, for the most part, neither as
victims nor victors. Where the written legends emphasize nudity,
the Tanner images, as we have seen, emphasize clothing. Emblems
sometimes provide discreet reminders of suffering, but for the
most violent martyr legends even those reminders are absent.
Cyriacus is portrayed grasping the True Cross, even though his
discovery of the cross is mentioned only in passing at the beginning of his lurid passion (I, 179, 4). Invoking the popular legend of
George the dragon-slayer, the artist portrays George as a knight,
even though the only reference to arms in the accompanying narrative may be wholly metaphorical: before confronting the emperor,
George 'armede him thoru the Holi Gost   withinne and eke
withoute' (I, 165, 10).[24]

Most at odds with the written narratives are the Tanner representations of the virgin martyrs. The devout, serene women of
the Tanner illustrations seem divorced from the strident viragos
of the legends; they lack even discreet, emblematic references to
their horrendous passions. I have already discussed the artist's
anomalous portrayal of Agnes. At least as surprising is his portrait
of Juliana – neither spurning her suitor, fighting the devil nor

suffering hideous torments, she is simply a pious reader looking up from her book, her finger marking her place.

Yet the Tanner artist's practices, however at variance with the textual and artistic tradition of legendaries, are fully in keeping with a wider fifteenth-century tendency to make the saints less extraordinary and more human.[25] Both textual and visual representations of the martyrs were becoming less violent, or at least balancing violence with a new interest in the saints as members of their families and communities. Pioneers of the new approach to the writing of saints' lives in England include Osbern Bokenham, John Capgrave and John Lydgate – three of the most prolific and, in Lydgate's case, influential hagiographers of the day.[26] Likewise, though illuminated legendaries, as I noted earlier, retained their traditional focus on violence, elsewhere in the visual arts martyrs were being portrayed more like confessors – as devout Christians rather than as superheroes. Virgin martyrs, for example, were often depicted as readers in religious painting. Thus, whereas *Queen Mary's Psalter* showed *every* martyr being tortured or killed, the *Neville Hours*, produced about a century later, show *no* martyrs actually suffering, while the artist of the Lacy hours, as we have seen, represents all martyrs but Agnes bearing emblems rather than being tortured,[27] and, like the artist of Tanner 17, appears to prefer costumery to gore. Some of the same impulses underlie the images in the Lacy Hours and the Tanner *SEL* – de-emphasizing violence and emphasizing dress, attending to markers of status and profession – although those impulses are more pronounced in the Tanner manuscript.

Much is unknown about Tanner 17's images. Why were they produced? By whom? For whom? It is a fair inference that the owner of the manuscript valued it – why else incur the trouble and expense of having it illustrated? – but its archaic Midlands dialect was likely difficult, if not impossible, for that fifteenth-century owner to read. Quite possibly, then, the images in Tanner 17 were to be experienced not *with* the text they accompany but *instead of* that text, transforming the manuscript from a source of information about the saints and church feasts into an aid to prayer and meditation. These images of static saints, divested of their particular life stories and clothed, literally, in the fifteenth century, were perfectly suited to the reincarnation of the *SEL* as a devotional manuscript – more like a book of hours than a legendary. Readers were invited to see the saints not as denizens of a remote past and an alien culture but as figures of the present, waiting in heaven to hear the prayers of the faithful.

Notes

1 For a description of this manuscript, see Görlach, *Textual Tradition*, pp. 99–100; also Kathleen L. Scott, *Later Gothic Manuscripts 1390–1490*, A Survey of Manuscripts Illuminated in the British Isles, 6, 2 vols. (London: Harvey Miller Publishers, 1996), no. 45.

2 Ibid., p. 100.

3 Ibid.

4 For saints in books of hours, see further Roger S. Wieck, *Time Sanctified: The Book of Hours in Medieval Art and Life* (New York: George Braziller, 1988), pp. 111–23.

5 According to Görlach, 'the pages have been cut down by at least 20 mm' (*Textual Tradition*, p. 100).

6 Because the Tanner version of the texts quoted here does not deviate significantly from the edition, quotations are referenced by volume, page and line number to D'Evelyn and Mill.

7 The 1438 *Gilte Legende* reads, 'the devyl that had to hym grete envye come to hym in the eventyde as he was aboute to make a chalys', *Supplementary Lives in Some Manuscripts of the Gilte Legende,* ed. Richard Hamer and Vida Russell, EETS OS 315 (Oxford: Oxford University Press, 2000), p. 182. Hamer and Russell write that the life 'follows the sequence of that in *SEL* 204–211' (p. 179); however, the chalice is not specified in either D'Evelyn and Mill or Horstmann. In fact, Horstmann's Laud 108 text omits the encounter altogether. The Tanner text, like the D'Evelyn and Mill version, simply reads, 'a tyme he cam to his smytthe   and alone hym fonde / Right as the sonne yede adoun', fol. 108.

8 Those saints are Hilary (fol. 2), Wulfstan (fol. 3), Fabian (fol. 6), Agnes (fol. 7), Julian the Confessor (fol. 11v), Bride of Ireland (13v), Agatha (fol. 19), Scholastica (fol. 21), Juliana (fol. 22), Matthias (fol. 25), Oswald (fol. 25v), Chad (fol. 28), Gregory the Great (fol. 29), Patrick (fol. 31), Edward the Martyr (fol. 39v), Benedict (fol. 43v), Philip (fol. 93v), and Aldhelm (fol. 110).

9 For a useful overview of episcopal attire, see Mary G. Houston, *Medieval Costume in England and France: The 13th, 14th and 15th Centuries* (1939; reprint, New York: Dover, 1996), pp. 19–37.

10 Although the tunicle, worn under the dalmatic, was shorter and thus not ordinarily visible, artists sometimes indicated its presence by allowing it to project beyond the fringe of the dalmatic. See Herbert Druitt, *A Manual of Costume as Illustrated by Monumental Brasses* (London: De La More Press, 1906), p. 73.

11 Unlike the post-Reformation chimere worn by Anglican bishops in choir dress, those of Patrick and Gregory are closed at the front, reflecting the evolution of the chimere from the tabard: see N. F. Robinson, 'The black chimere of Anglican prelates: a plea for its retention and proper use', *Transactions of the St. Paul's Ecclesiological Society*, 4 (1910), 181–220.

12 Although the *MED* indicates that 'crois' can also mean 'a prelate's crosier' (definition 7), the nine examples given do not support that interpretation. Four refer to St Wulfstan's 'crois' in the *SEL*. Another three specifically refer to archiepiscopal staffs, and there is no reason to suppose that these were croziers rather than cross-staffs. The 'crois' that Conscience bears in *Piers Plowman* A, 5.11, is likely to be a cross-staff, since he is performing the archiepiscopal function of preaching to king and nation. Finally, the 'crose' in Capgrave's reference to prelates' 'crosses and croses' is certainly a crozier, but this does not bear on the meaning of 'crois'. The view of the *OED* is that the distinction between crois/croys/cross/crosse and cros/croce/crose was well understood during the Middle Ages (*OED*, *s.v.* 'crose, croce').
    On why Wulfstan is carrying a cross rather than a crosier, see further Emma Mason, 'St. Wulfstan's cross: a legend and its uses', *Medium Aevum*, 53 (1984), 157–79.
13 Illustrations of men's hats similar to those of Longinus and Valentine can be seen in Houston, *Medieval Costume*, pp. 173–6, figures 302, 304 and 305. Iris Brooke discusses the popularity of 'gigantic soft-crowned hats' among men during the second quarter of the fifteenth century in *English Costume from the Early Middle Ages Through the Sixteenth Century* (1936; reprint Mineola, NY: Dover, 2000), p. 136. Examples of hats comparable to those worn by Longinus, Valentine and Vincent are shown on pp. 143, 150, 155 and 165.
14 Agatha's gown resembles that in the monumental brass of Joan Kingstern, reproduced in W. F. Fairholt, *Costume in England: A History of Dress to the End of the Eighteenth Century*, 2 vols, revised and enlarged by H. A. Dillon (London: George Bell and Sons, 1896), vol. 1, p. 169, plate 127. Agatha is not shown wearing a brooch, but her posture and hair would have obscured it, anyway. On the preference for voluminous, high-waisted dresses among women during the first half of the fifteenth century, see Houston, *Medieval Costume*, pp. 159–64.
15 Jocelyn Wogan-Browne discusses the understandings of 'honorary virginity' that flourished in late medieval England in *Saints' Lives and Women's Literary Culture c. 1150–1300: Virginity and its Authorizations* (Oxford: Oxford University Press, 2001), pp. 123–50; for Mary as an honorary virgin, see pp. 137–40. See also Sarah Salih, *Versions of Virginity in Late Medieval England* (Cambridge: D. S. Brewer, 2001), pp. 104–6.
16 Robert Mills discusses the sexualization of Sebastian and other martyrs in *Suspended Animation: Pain, Pleasure and Punishment in Medieval Culture* (London: Reaktion Books, 2005), pp. 156–71.
17 The Morgan-Mâcon Golden Legend (New York, Morgan Library MS M.672–75), a French illustrated legendary from the mid-fifteenth century, for example, shows the naked saint, clothed only in her

ankle-length hair, standing in the courtyard of the brothel. The constable's son lies dead at her feet, while guards on either side clasp her arms; the constable strides towards them (fol. 96v). Less common are renditions of Agnes with only the angel. Any of these images are more in the spirit of the *SEL*'s narrative, with its emphasis on the saint's triumph over those who sought to corrupt her. A decorated initial 'D' in a German antiphonary from circa 1310 (New York, Morgan Library Ms M. 870) shows the angel handing Agnes a cloak. Nakedness is a feature of all of these images, whether the saint's body is wholly exposed or whether a glimpse of her flesh is visible behind her long hair.

18 For example, the Agnes in the Morgan-Mâcon Golden Legend is also praying, but our eyes are drawn to her straight ankle-length hair and the sliver of white flesh visible beneath it.

19 I discuss the *SEL*'s virgin martyr legends in light of these trends in *Virgin Martyrs: Legends of Sainthood in Late Medieval England* (Ithaca: Cornell University Press, 1997), pp. 64–111. On violence in the *SEL*, with particular attention to virgin martyr legends, see also Robert Mills, 'Violence, community and the materialisation of belief', in Salih (ed.), *Companion to Middle English Hagiography*, pp. 87–103. See also Anne B. Thompson, 'Audacious fictions: *Anastasia* and the triumph of narrative', *Assays*, 8 (1995), 1–28, and 'The legend of St. Agnes: improvisation and the practice of hagiography', *Exemplaria*, 13 (2001), 355–97.

20 On the tradition of violence associated with George, see Samantha Riches, *St. George: Hero, Martyr and Myth* (Stroud: Sutton, 2000), pp. 1–67.

21 A description of this manuscript, along with reproductions of each of the miniatures, can be found online at the *Guide to Medieval and Renaissance Manuscripts in the Huntington Library*, http://sunsite3.berkeley.edu/hehweb/HM3027.html. For a discussion of the representation of violence in this manuscript, see Martha Easton, 'Pain, torture and death in the Huntington Library *Legenda aurea*', in Samantha J. E. Riches and Sarah Salih (eds), *Gender and Holiness: Men, Women and Saints in Late Medieval Europe* (London: Routledge, 2002), pp. 49–64.

22 Illuminated manuscripts with similar iconographical programmes include the Morgan-Mâcon Golden Legend (New York, Morgan Library MS M.672–75) mentioned above and numerous manuscripts of Jean de Vignay's translation of the *Legenda aurea* into French. For a general discussion, see Hilary Maddocks, 'Pictures for aristocrats: the manuscripts of the *Légende dorée*', in Margaret M. Manion and Bernard J. Muir (eds), *Medieval Texts and Images: Studies of Manuscripts from the Middle Ages* (Sydney: Harwood, 1991), pp. 1–22.

23 See *Queen Mary's Psalter: Miniatures and Drawings by an English Artist of the 14th Century Reproduced from Royal MS. 2 B VII in the British Museum*, ed. Sir George Warner (London: British Museum, 1912). For the saints, see pp. 46–53 and plates 239–316. The three who are not martyrs are Nicholas, Mary Magdalene and John the Evangelist. John the Evangelist is shown as if he were a martyr – first remonstrating with his judge and then being boiled in oil.

24 On the tradition of George as knight, see Riches, *St. George*, pp. 68–178. The dragon episode, surprisingly, occurs in just one *SEL* manuscript, and only a fragment survives of that account. For an edition and discussion, see E. Gordon Whatley (ed.), with Anne B. Thompson and Robert K. Upchurch, *Saints' Lives in Middle English Collections* (Kalamazoo, MI: Medieval Institute Publications, 2004), pp. 98–101.

25 See my *Virgin Martyrs*, pp. 112–46; pp. 115–16 deal with the Tanner images of Agnes, Agatha and Agnes. On exemplarity in fifteenth-century saints' lives, also see Catherine Sanok, *Her Life Historical: Exemplarity and Female Saints' Lives in Late Medieval England* (Philadelphia: University of Pennsylvania Press, 2007); and Katherine J. Lewis, *The Cult of St Katherine of Alexandria in Late Medieval England* (Woodbridge: Boydell Press, 2000), pp. 175–256.

26 See Winstead, *Virgin Martyrs*, pp. 112–80; and *John Capgrave's Fifteenth Century* (Philadelphia: University of Pennsylvania Press, 2007). For Bokenham, see also Simon Horobin, 'Politics, patronage, and piety in the work of Osbern Bokenham', *Speculum*, 82 (2007), 932–49.

27 Its Agnes is standing amidst the flames in an image that is almost the inverse of Tanner's Agnes. This Agnes is bathed in light from below, Tanner's Agnes from above. With their lack of action, both occupy a middle ground between a scene and a portrait.

17

Conversion, translation and Becket's 'heathen' mother

Robert Mills

Few of the stories collated together in the *SELS* have had greater currency into modern times than the tale of St Thomas of Canterbury's 'heathen' heritage. The earliest version of this legend in English, contained in Bodleian MS Laud Misc. 108, identifies the saint's father as a London burgess, Gilbert Becket, who, as an act of penance, sets out on an expedition to the Holy Land.[1] Captured and locked up by the local 'Amiral' or emir, Gilbert remains in heathendom for two-and-a-half years, during which time he elicits the admiration not only of the Amiral himself but also of the Amiral's beautiful daughter, who pays the prisoner secret visits in his cell. Inspired by the strength of Gilbert's Christian belief, the daughter promises, in exchange for his love, to convert to Christianity, with a view to transforming her father's hostage into a husband; but Gilbert and his fellow captives, fearing treachery on the woman's part, decide to escape from prison that very evening. Gilbert returns to England, the Amiral's daughter follows after and eventually, despite speaking no English, she miraculously ends up in London. Gawped at in the streets – no one understands a word she says – the woman is eventually recognized by one of Gilbert's retainers, a knave who had been with him in the holy land. Reunited with Gilbert, the couple put their case before the bishop of London and five other prelates, who, so long as she is christened first, grant permission for the pair to marry. The night of their wedding the couple conceive a child, Thomas, who will eventually become 'pris-martyr of engelonde' (110, 142). The following day Gilbert departs for the Holy Land for a second time; he returns to London several years later to finds his wife and son Thomas whole and sound. Thus concludes the romance that gave birth to a saint.

Famously, in the prologue inserted at the beginning of later *SEL* manuscripts, secular and sacred modes of biography are presented

as polarized genres. As the version included in Cambridge, Corpus
Christi College, MS 145 makes clear, the stories that people are
so fond of hearing – of battles fought by kings and brave knights
– need to be differentiated from stories about saints from the perspective of their truth value. Whereas the former are, for the most
part, 'lesynge' ('falsehood'), in the legends to which this statement provides an introduction the reader can expect tales of hardy
battles 'that nis no lesinge' ('that are no falsehood') – those of apostles and martyrs who, like 'hardy' knights in battle, suffer evil men
to tear them limb from limb.[2] The myth of Becket's parentage,
built around the adventures of a crusading knight and his eastern
lover, suggests that beneath this ostensible opposition there exists a
good deal of overlap: the tale of England's 'prize-martyr', Thomas
of Canterbury, is rooted in precisely the kind of fabulous story
characterized by the Corpus 145 prologue's narrator as falsehood.

As modern biographers of the saint are quick to point out,
Thomas's parents were actually both of Norman birth and ancestry, Gilbert's wife probably a woman called Matilda from Caen.[3]
Yet this has not prevented the myth of Thomas's mixed descent
from continuing to circulate in the guise of history. No less a sto-
ryteller than Charles Dickens passed the legend off as fact in *A
Child's History of England* (1852), in a chapter on Henry II; this
'most beguiling and romantic legend which is found in a very few
old English histories' provided loose inspiration for the Canadian
author Thomas Costain's best-selling novel *The Black Rose* (1945),
the film version of which, starring Tyron Power and Orson Welles,
was a hit in 1950; Jean Anouilh's play *Becket ou l'honneur de Dieu*
(1959) has King Henry ask Becket whether he is 'ashamed of being
a Saracen girl's son'; written under the pseudonym Jean Plaidy,
Eleanor Hibbert's novel *The Plantagenet Prelude* (1976) incorporated the legend into an account of the life and times of Eleanor
of Aquitaine.[4] Historical romance is the generic hybrid through
which this enduring fascination with Becket's sensational origins is
filtered; but this is also just one more spin on a phenomenon initiated in the *SELS* themselves, which share a collective interest in
facilitating a dialogue between different modes of exemplary biography. The Laud manuscript itself, after all, incorporates within its
binding not only numerous legends of saints but also such texts as
King Horn and *Havelok the Dane* – stories whose themes of exile-
and-return resonate strongly with the experiences of both Gilbert
Becket and his son.[5] This essay seeks to understand this process of
conversion, generic and stylistic, through the lens of translation.

The negotiations of language and identity in which Becket's mother participates can, I will argue, profitably be understood as responses to broader articulations of the interplay between translation and conversion in late medieval England. The fact that this interplay is preserved in a written text reminds us that the *SELS* too are works of translation; that these acts of hagiographic translation perform the work of converting readers; and that conversion, like translation, is predicated on a scene of utter transformation in which the former identity of the converted matter is displaced. What if, I ask, there is an obscure remainder that fails to convert? What 'surplus', if any, do these translations of text and identity leave behind?

The term conversion is derived from the Latin word *conversio*, which refers to the transformation of one thing into another. But this revolution is also cyclical: a mode of change that simultaneously embraces repetition. *Conversio*, related to the rhetorical trope of epistrophe, where words are repeated at the end of clauses (as in the expression 'we're born alone, we live alone, we die alone'), thus carries with it the idea of a recurring pattern. This notion of *conversio* as reverberation sits in tension with ideas of conversion as a single, transformational event. Christian life itself may be comprehended as a string of lesser transformations, of which Thomas Becket's own conversion from worldly administrator to pious archbishop is a prime example; but this notion of change as a cumulative process encodes the risk that the shift is superficial or false, and that something of the former identity remains.[6] The solution, then, is to present conversion as a revolutionary act, breaking once and for all with the trappings of the identity that has been left behind.

Ideas of *translatio*, related to the Latin word *transferre* meaning 'to bring across, transport', encode a parallel tension. Patristic translation theorists such as St Jerome and St Augustine made a case for the need to preserve the textual meaning of the scriptures from the threat of linguistic multiplicity, a model of textual fidelity that underscores the possibility of continuity between an authoritative source text and its exegesis. Yet, as Rita Copeland has demonstrated, this model of translation coexisted with vernacular approaches treating translation as a process of displacement and substitution, which, in keeping with classical rhetorical models, remade texts in ways appropriate to new conditions of understanding. Rather than seeing translation as the faithful rendition of an 'original' or source text in another language, it is the performance of that text in the new language that assumes importance – a performance generating rupture as well as continuity.[7] *Translatio* is thus a performative activity paradoxically centred on destruction and discontinuity, which forecloses the prospect of a return to origins; linguistic translation, traditionally judged in terms of its closeness to the source, possesses its own revolutionary potential when viewed from this perspective. Interpreted as an act of textual *conversio*, translation, like conversion, relies on destruction as much as continuity; yet whereas conversion narratives deliberately highlight the radical possibilities of change, translation disavows or effaces this revolutionary potential, at least according to the dominant model of textual fidelity.

The narrative of Becket's mother in the *SEL* arguably deals with this encounter between *translatio* and *conversio* only by regarding translation in monolingual terms. Rather than acquiring one language from the position of another, the Amiral's daughter is presented as a woman whose apparent lack of language (at least of a language that anyone can understand) is linked indissolubly with her identity as a heathen; Christian conversion is the act that bestows her, finally, with linguistic identity and life. Moving from a place of untranslatability to one of complete assimilation, she comes to embody the very essence of what the Laud narrator calls, in the legend's opening line, 'this Englische tale' (106, 1). This study seeks to situate the mother's story within the various cultural forces potentially motivating such an essentialising outcome.

The fact that the differences between converted and unconverted identities are cast in linguistic terms is apparent in the Laud text's descriptions of the climate within which Gilbert's relationship with the Amiral's daughter develops. We are told that the Amiral invites Gilbert to take meals in his quarters, an act that promotes him above his fellow prisoners, and it is this (we assume) that enables Gilbert to acquire the language of the other. Certainly, by the time the daughter secretly visits Gilbert in prison, their ability to engage in conversation is not hampered by any sense of linguistic barrier: 'Oftesithe heo wold speke with him', we are told, 'hwane heo mighte to bistele' (107, 26, 'Often she would speak with him when she was able to steal away'). In response to the woman's queries about his name, belief and land of origin, and the question of whether he would suffer death for his lord's love, Gilbert answers:

'Of Engelonde Ich am, and cristine man   thei Ich beo nouthe
                                                                                              here;

Mi name is Gilbert Beket   of Londene the cite;
Gladliche Icholde thane deth afongue   for is love that boughte
                                    me,
And for to savi mi Cristinedom   and mine trewe bileve also.'
                                              (107, 34–7)

(I am from England, and a Christian man, though I am now here.
My name is Gilbert Becket, from the city of London. So I would
gladly accept death, for the love of him who bought me and in order
to save my Christendom and also my true belief.)

Various answers were dreamed up in the nineteenth century in
response to the question of how Gilbert manages to communicate
with the Amiral's daughter. Dickens, in his retelling of the episode,
supposes that 'he must have learnt the Saracen tongue himself,
and made love in that language', while a romantic poem by Robert
Buchanan (d. 1901) suggests that the pair fell in love by convers-
ing only in eye-language.[8] The Laud text, with its references to an
exchange of 'wordes' (107, 38), implies that of the two solutions
Dickens is closer to the mark, but this is a conclusion that must be
extrapolated from the narrative by means of guesswork, since the
process of language learning is never explicitly articulated. The
assumption is that Gilbert's ability to communicate in this different culture (emphasized in his own statement that 'Ich beo nouthe
here', 107, 34) is predicated on his ability silently to absorb elements in the culture of his capturer. Yet the core of his identity is
located elsewhere, in 'Engelonde', his 'Cristinedom' and his 'trewe
bileve' (107, 34, 37); his linguistic skills have not affected that fundamental core. For all their ability to talk, Gilbert and the Amiral's
daughter are otherwise divided: the Crusader greets the woman's
marriage proposal with extreme suspicion, his prison-break an
exercise in running the proverbial mile. His ability to converse in
the Amiral's language is not finally an act of assimilation, then, but
conversion – the source of a literal 'turn-around' for the daughter,
as well as the beginning of his own journey home.

The idea that language acquisition facilitates conversion was
hardly novel for the period in which *SEL* manuscripts were
being collated. The Norman polemicist Pierre Dubois completed his treatise *De recuperatione terrae sanctae* around 1306,
two decades or so after the Laud manuscript was copied. This
constitutes an impassioned plea to European rulers, including
Edward I of England, for a crusade to rescue the holy land from
Muslim control. Significantly, however, it includes among the

recommended strategies for accomplishing this end not only war but also language-learning and intermarriage. Dubois promotes his theory of linguistic conversion in a chapter on schooling: children should, he argues, be instructed in Latin, and afterwards Greek or Arabic, 'so that eventually with the help of these youths, trained to speak and write the languages of all peoples, the Roman Church and the Catholic princes as well, may through them communicate with all men and draw them to the Catholic faith and into unity with its head'.[9] He continues by making specific reference to the education of young women. Girls should be instructed in medicine and surgery, he recommends, for with such training they will be adopted as marriage partners by princes in the Holy Land and adjacent places, which would, in turn, 'teach their children and husbands to adhere to the Roman faith and to believe and sacrifice in accordance with it'.[10] In context, these particular remarks appear to be directed more toward converting eastern Christians than converting Muslims.[11] Elsewhere in the treatise, however, Dubois confirms that girls trained in the proposed schools could also 'be given as wives to the Saracen chiefs' and thus persuade their husbands to convert to Roman Christianity; Saracen women would, it follows, be drawn toward 'our manner of life' by the law against polygamy in Christian culture.[12]

Dubois also returns to these themes in a later chapter of *De recuperatione*, apparently meant only for the eyes of the French king Philip IV. This likewise incorporates, among the strategies for assaulting the eastern Christians of Byzantium, language-learning as a means of conversion, assimilation and subjugation. It will be difficult, Dubois writes, to 'dwell in a land whose lettered language and all of whose spoken dialects are unfamiliar to all Frenchmen. It will also be difficult to seek the friendship and alliance of the natives, who naturally are accustomed to hate the Latins and to rule them if they are subjugated, and to mingle with them.' How then, Dubois asks, does one gain the 'love' of the survivors? It will not be sufficient to employ foreign interpreters of their languages: they could prove untrustworthy and, as 'men of a foreign land', would be liable to accepting bribes. Acquiring additional languages personally is the only sure-fire means of conversion, as demonstrated by the example of the apostles themselves:

How could [the apostles] have preached and taught the Gospel of God intelligibly to all barbarian nations, except God himself had granted them the usage of all languages? In no other way could they

have been able to converse with the barbarians. It is in every way
advisable and necessary to procure far in advance men fluent and
well-trained in languages.[13]

In the *SEL* tale of Gilbert Becket the strategies outlined by Dubois
acquire a practical application. Gilbert himself acquires an apostle-
like ability to converse in the language of the other; it is his ability
to render himself intelligible that precipitates the daughter's desire
for conversion and assimilation.

By contrast, the Amiral's daughter herself remains unintelligible
up until the point that she is baptized. Her own physical *translatio*, to England and an English-speaking world, is not accompanied by the capacity to translate or to be translated. In the Laud
text, indeed, her relocation is presented as an event generating a
profound sense of linguistic dislocation. Although she finds a sea-
passage easily enough, this is presented as a divine miracle rather
than the result of any skill on her part: as well as acting as 'hire
lodesman' (108, 54) ('her navigator'), God is also the source of
grace through which 'heo was ilad   with men that onderstoden
hire langage' (108, 55, 'she was guided by men who understood
her language'). God's role as divine translator is emphasized again
when she reaches England and asks how she can get to London:

Ake evere heo axede in hire langage   to Londone for to go.
Mid pilegrimes and thoru grace of God   to Londone heo cam.
And tho heo was thudere icome   thare ne kneu heo no man,
Ne heo ne couthe speke ne hire biseo   bote ase a best that
                                        astrayed were.
Tharefore on hire gapede alday   swythe muche folc there,
Both men and wommen   and children suythe fale –
For hire continaunce was wonderful   and hire speche no man ne
                                        couthe thare
                                                (108, 62–8)

(And repeatedly she asked in her language how to get to London.
With pilgrims and through the grace of God she came to London.
And though she had arrived in that place she knew no one there.
They could neither speak nor look at her, except as a stray animal.
Therefore lots of people there gaped at her all day, men, women
and a large number of children alike – for her countenance was
wonderful and no one there understood her speech.)

This description works to secure the woman's alterity as an effect
of her English-less identity: it is because the sounds she emits from
her mouth are gibberish that she has the appearance of a 'best that

astrayed were'. At the same time, though, that same appearance
elicits wonder: a mixture of fear and fascination.

This ambivalence, vacillating between desire for the other and a
sense of the other's dehumanization, creates the circumstances for
the woman's ultimate assimilation. Wonder, again, generates the
interpretative backdrop against which the Amiral daughter's experiences can be comprehended. After Gilbert has recounted to the
group of bishops the story of his time in 'hethenesse', the bishop of
Winchester expresses the view

> That hit was al thorugh Godes grace   that heo was so fer icome,
> Out of hire owene londe so fer   that heo thoru miseise ne hadde
> ibe nome;
> For heo ne couthe language non   with men for to speke
> With hwan heo mighte iwinnen hire   herboruwe and drinke and
> mete
>
> (109–10, 111–14)

(that it was all through God's grace that she had come so far, so far
out of her own land that she had not been seized with discomfort.
For she knew no language so as to speak with people with whom she
could acquire for herself lodging and drink and food.)

These lines convey a slippage in the narrator's presentation of the
woman's linguistic abilities. From a position in which she can at
least speak 'hire langage' (108, 55, 62), the Amiral's daughter shifts
to a state of 'language non' (109, 113) – no language – which is the
sign, in the bishop's mind, that her journey constitutes a miracle.
Emptied of her previous selfhood, 'so fer' from her land as well
as language, the conditions are finally now ripe for the climax of
the narrative: the woman's baptism. This itself is facilitated by
Gilbert's skills as the converser who converts. For the first time
the narrator explicitly draws attention to the fact that 'Gilbert
couthe [knew] hire language' (110, 135) and so is able to translate,
for the bishops' benefit, the woman's wish to trade conversion for
marriage.

Pierre Dubois, as we have seen, developed a role for women as
missionaries in the Holy Land in which they themselves, educated
in the languages and customs of the Saracens, are attributed with
the capacity to initiate mass conversions. A variation on clerical
debates about the validity of mixed marriages between believers
and unbelievers, Dubois's treatise singles out educated women
as being especially capable in matters of moral persuasion, their
ability to teach being identified as an evangelizing force.[14] This has

similarities with that other plotline commonly found in narratives
of conversion and intermarriage, in which a Christian heroine weds
a pagan ruler and convinces him to accept her faith.[15] The most
familiar of these legends, Chaucer's *Man of Law's Tale*, attributes
the female protagonist Custance's ability to convert to a rather
hazy sense of divine providence: evangelization by intermarriage
is unsuccessful in one instance (Custance's first marriage to the
Syrian Sultan) but mysteriously succeeds in the other (the conversion of and marriage to King Ælle of Northumbria). The *SEL*
narrative reverses this structure but retains the basic underlying
message. Christians are both translatable and translators, whereas
non-Christians, like the Amiral's daughter, fail to understand and
to be understood. Indeed comparison with the *Man of Law's Tale*
reveals what is at stake in Gilbert's own abilities as converser and
converter. Chaucer makes clear that, although, as a Roman emper-
or's daughter, Custance speaks a 'maner Latyn corrupt' when she
lands on the coast of Northumbria, nevertheless 'was sche understonde'.[16] Whereas Gilbert himself is a linguistically able agent, the
object of his converting talents – at least up until the point when
she actually becomes a Christian – is rendered incoherent to the
reader: the Amiral's daughter represents the untranslatable shadow
to Custance's decipherability.

All this changes, of course, with baptism, which effects a linguistic as well as spiritual conversion. Here the emphasis on the
woman's naming is especially significant. Just as 'hire language'
(whatever that is, 108, 57, 62) becomes 'language non' (109, 113),
the daughter's former name is consigned to oblivion by the narrator, who admits that of 'hire hethene name ne I nought telle'
(110, 139). Equally her new name, Alisaundre, bestows her with
identity and life; like the language, English, named in the legend's opening line, it enables her finally to assume a place within
the Christian community. Alisaundre is, of course, a variation on
Alexandria. Christening the woman in this fashion associates her
with a distinct location, the city in Egypt that was, in the early
centuries of Christianity, a centre of theology and church government; Alexandria also provides the setting for the death of St
Katherine at the hands of an idol-worshipping emperor, referred
to as 'Alisaundrie' in the Laud version of the legend (92, 6). Thus
the choice of name itself is potentially significant in linking the
daughter with an identifiable location: baptism gives her a clear
place in the world. This process of securing Alisaundre spatially
is also enhanced by imagery of Christendom as a both a spiritual

and physical home. Christendom is a concept variously defined in the *SELS* as a land and as a state of mind.[17] The daughter's announcement to Gilbert in prison that she wishes to undertake Christendom 'for the love of the' (107, 39) encapsulates the second of these definitions, by expressing a desire for baptism, but in the last analysis this abstract meaning is bound up with its material counterpart. Thus, when interrogated by the bishops on her desire to marry and convert, the woman presents the only alternative as she sees it: 'Yif Gilbert wolde hire weddi   icristned heo wolde ben / And bote he hire weddi wold   heo nolde Cristinedom afonge, / Heo seide heo wolde rather tuyrne agen   into hire owene londe' (110, 132–4, 'If Gilbert would marry her, she would be christened, and unless he would wed her she would not undertake Christendom: she said she would rather return again to her own land'). Christendom here is treated as the equivalent to 'hire owene londe' (109, 112) – a land identified ambiguously, by Gilbert himself, as 'hethenesse' (109, 99). But Christendom the 'londe' finds its material counterpart in England itself: the word 'engelonde' features no less than six times in the Laud Gilbert narrative (106, 6; 107, 34; 108, 57; 109, 95; 110, 42; 112, 194). Translating Alisaundre into England, as well as Christendom, goes hand in hand with Gilbert's conversion of her speech into a language the bishops can understand.

Following baptism, and Gilbert's return to the Holy Land, Alisaundre is assigned a new translator, Gilbert's man Richard, who, having been imprisoned with Gilbert in the Holy Land, 'hire langage couthe [knew]' (111, 177). So Christendom does not bring her immediately to linguistic life. Yet in the main Laud life of St Thomas of Canterbury, which immediately follows the Gilbert legend, this last vestige of Alisaundre's heathen alterity is dramatically effaced: she proceeds to inhabit the role of an archetypal Christian mother by becoming Thomas's educator and moral guardian. Thus the narrator describes how 'His Moder him wolde al day rede' (112, 211), as well as encouraging him to lead a clean life, to forsake lechery and to love God and the Virgin Mary. Like the Virgin's own mother, St Anne, Alisaundre is presented as a reader, book in hand, teaching her child spiritual lessons. No longer linguistically incapable, her conversion is apparently absolute and all-encompassing: implicitly she has acquired the English that eluded her before she was baptized. This miraculous eradication of heathen difference is the final stage in Alisaundre's cultural assimilation, setting the stage for her conception of a future saint and martyr.

Imbrications of gender and genre are especially noteworthy features of this plotline. At the outset, I presented the *SELS* as sites of generic conflict: different modes of exemplary biography may be judged according to their truth-telling capacity. In addition to secular romance, which, with its emphasis on the quest, provides a lens through which to view both Gilbert and Alisaundre's journeys, we need to consider here the role of *chanson de geste*, a genre that was at the height of production and copying in thirteenth-century England. Sarah Kay has identified upwards of twenty *chansons de geste* that include, within their epic stories of unresolved conflict between heathens and Christians, a tale about the daughter of a Saracen emir, who falls in love with a Frankish hero, converts and becomes an exemplary wife; significantly, this conversion also brings extensive estates under Christian rule and attributes the Saracen princess herself with a degree of agency largely lacking in romance.[18] The Laud manuscript's Gilbert legend appears to be committed to a more categorical view of gender than its French intertexts, since Alisaundre's own agency is undermined by the repeated attribution of her ability to manoeuvre in the world to divine miracle; conversely Gilbert is hardly paralysed as a hero, what with his ability to effect conversion and translation even while in prison. Yet the clear parallel with tales of Saracen princesses suggests that hagiography is able to confront a story of conversion from heathen or Muslim to Christian head on only if it deploys such intertextual strategies: seizing upon this gendered structure in the *chansons de geste* enables the Laud hagiographer to associate conversion, implicitly, with stereotypes of female changeability and male constancy (a structure that, as we have seen, reverses that found in the Constance legend).

Another way in which gender potentially inflects the narrative has to do with differences between heathen or Muslim conversion and the conversion of Jews. Elsewhere in this volume, Heather Blurton has drawn attention to anxieties about Jewish conversion in the *passio* of Quiriac and the immediate historical contexts for those anxieties. The notion that some remnant of Jewish identity survives baptism (which may or may not participate in a racial or quasi-racial ideology) seems to have been especially significant in the later Middle Ages. It may be influenced, according to Jonathan Elukin, by the new attention paid, from the twelfth century, to the distinction between interior and exterior expressions of self-hood and identity. Also contributing to these anxieties about the efficacy of baptism was the idea of conversion as ongoing process rather than dramatic shift – a path that Christians themselves were expected to follow.[19] The journey undertaken by Becket's mother is partly represented in these terms; the linguistic challenges she faces encode the fear that her assimilation is doomed to failure. But her untranslatability is a barrier only finally surmounted through the intervention of Gilbert himself and the authorizing bishops, who mediate, in turn, the grace of God. So hers is a story that ultimately revolves around a moment of radical substitution. One unknowable, untranslatable selfhood is displaced, through baptism, by another that is known and understood; heathen non-identity is eclipsed by an identity and name rendered fully coherent for the reader. This presents a contrast with tales of Jewish conversion in the *SELS*, where Jews who convert are depicted in one of two ways. Either they are never really Jewish in the first place, as in the miracle of the so-called 'Jewish Boy', included in the Corpus 145 manuscript, who is identified in the opening line of the story as a 'Giwes child', that is to say the child of a Jew – a grammatical sleight of hand which puts distance between the boy and the Jewishness of his abusive father.[20] Or, as Blurton argues of the Quiriac narrative, there is something potentially counterfeit about that shift. As such, it might be argued that heathen conversion encoded a different set of concerns for the Laud manuscript's makers and receivers from the conversion of Jews. The assimilation and translatability of a non-Christian from 'fer' away is fully realizable, at least through the intervention of God and his representatives; by contrast, Jewish conversion implies the existence of some unassimilable remnant, or that the matter to be converted is already Christian in some essential way.

To the extent that the examples of Jewish conversion are men while the Gilbert legend concerns the baptism of a woman, this is a contrast that manifests itself in starkly gendered terms; again, here, we are confronted with the effects of a gendered sub-plot, the Saracen princess story, borrowed from *chansons de geste*. Then again, the existence of pre-Expulsion Jewish communities in thirteenth-century England, and the continuing presence of Jewish converts in certain parts of the country for many decades following the Expulsion in 1290, may have created additional conditions for this apparent double standard. Because Jewish converts really do appear to have struggled, for predominantly economic reasons, to put their former identities behind them, they may have functioned, in their perceived ongoing Jewishness, as visible guarantors of Christian difference; the opportunities for non-Christian inhabitants of the Holy Land to play this role were presumably less common, although this itself does not preclude the possibility of some Muslim converts living in medieval England during the *SEL*'s heyday.[21]

In this context, it is worth examining a retelling of the Gilbert legend that explicitly draws attention to its relevance as a vantage point from which to reflect on the question of converting Jews. This is a rendition that brings into focus the contradictory impulses surrounding translation and conversion in the period of the *SEL*'s circulation. A Latin sermon, commonly attributed to Thomas Brinton, bishop of Rochester (1373–89), but possibly much earlier in date, contains a summary of the Gilbert legend, which is followed by an extended meditation on the necessity of absolute translation. First the preacher quotes the scriptures, specifically Psalms 79: 9, on how Christ's words represent *Vineam de Egypto transtulisti* ('a vineyard translated out of Egypt'), and Hebrews 7: 12 on how *translato sacerdocio necesse est ut translacio legis fiat* ('for the priesthood being translated it is necessary that a translation also be made of the law').[22] Then the sermon yokes the Gilbert legend to a statement emphasizing the contemporary urgency of these questions. 'Why is it', the preacher wonders, 'that in this glorious city, in which sturdy faith should vigorously flourish, so many faithless Jews are permitted to live with favour, and they are not translated [*transferuntur*] from their errors to the faith of Christ by the persuasions or teachings of so many holy fathers, so many prelates, so many doctors', before going on to argue that 'many Jews would very willingly become Christians, if they did not fear that after their conversion [*post conversionem*] their riches would be lost or scattered'.[23] The reference to contemporary Jews may date the sermon to the decades before the 1290 Expulsion, when there was indeed a policy of confiscating the wealth of Jewish converts in England.[24] The sermon expresses a desire for absolute conversion, akin to the conversion of Becket's mother, but suggests that in the case of contemporary Jews this is simply not possible as a result of the economic ramifications of converting.

This contrast between the conversion of Jews and other non-Christian groups is heightened by the emphasis in the *SEL* Gilbert legend on translation as the mechanism of conversion. If the heathen is materialized at all, it is principally as a confused nothingness. We are afforded no coherent picture of the Amiral's culture, language or religious identity in the Laud text; the Amiral's daughter is effectively translated from nothing into something. This 'nothing' is not fully emptied of significance, of course: it is given a name ('hethenesse', 109, 99) and a location in the Holy Land. In other *SEL* manuscripts, the name itself mutates. In British Library, Harley 2277 (c. 1300), and the closely related Corpus 145 (early fourteenth century), Gilbert goes on a pilgrimage to Jerusalem, where he comes among 'Sarazins'.[25] In the fifteenth-century Bodleian MS Rawl. poet. 225 these Saracens have turned into Jews, with Gilbert and his man Richard being placed in captivity in 'Iewry'. In the latter, also, the mother is endowed with a pre-Christian name – Ysope – which changes to Ione (Joan) following baptism.[26] These modifications mobilize more particularized versions of heathendom, for instance by pressing the narrative into the service of an explicitly Jewish–Christian dichotomy. But even in these later texts the culture of Gilbert's captors is, by and large, an unknown quantity – a threatening spectre of difference rather than a fully intelligible phenomenon. The entry into English goes hand in hand with the entry into Christendom in this scenario: in the land of language – 'Engelonde' – Christian identity and culture lie secure. This process of translation refuses a return to origins. Becket's mother may originate in heathendom but her difference is eradicated completely through baptism. Enmeshed with one another, in this way, conversion and translation work to construct England itself as essentially Christian and monolingual.

Of course, this belies the multilingual situation of England throughout the time in which *SEL* manuscripts were circulating. Latin was the language of the *Legenda aurea* (compiled 1263–73), which, if not the direct 'source' for the *SELS* or the individual legends they contained, appears to have shaped revisions of the collection.[27] French legendaries also circulated or originated in England in the thirteenth century, but the question remains as to whether this created the conditions for a meaningful level of cross-fertilization with individual *SEL* texts. Laud 108 is, for the most part, a monoglot manuscript; linguistic traces of the multilingual environment in which it was produced are, relatively speaking, slight. Yet, as Michelle Warren has recently argued, even mono-lingual texts engage multilingual histories: to the extent that any text (even if it is not, in philological terms, a product of interlingual translation) possesses antecedents and precedents, it may be impli-cated in processes of cultural translation.[28] One indication that the Middle English of the *SELS* operated as a language in contact with others is the inclusion of headings to the Gilbert legend and the Becket legend proper, both of which are rendered in the Laud manuscript in French. The first begins *Ici poez oyer coment seint Thomas de Kaunterbures nasqui. e de quev manere gent de pere e de Mere* ('Here we can see how St Thomas of Canterbury was born, and of the manner of his father's and mother's people'), while the second opens with the announcement that *Hic Isci Comence la vie seint Thomas Erceeueske de Kaunterbury* ('This here begins the life of St Thomas, archbishop of Canterbury'). What these headings convey is evidence not for interlingual translation as such but rather for the kinds of cultural translation that Warren identifies as being central to even predominantly monolingual texts.

Manfred Görlach thinks it unlikely that any of the *SEL* narratives were based directly on French originals, and views the use of occasional French phrases elsewhere in the collection as a manifestation of the authors' and audiences' sociolect. Although acknowledging the French headings in the Laud version of Becket's life, he argues for a Latin source for the Gilbert narrative and sees 'no further evidence of a supplementary French source'.[29] The story of Thomas's parents made its very first appearance in a version of Edward Grim's *Vita Sancti Thomae*. Whereas Grim's original text (completed in the 1170s) contains a preface naming Thomas's mother as a woman called Matilda, the thirteenth-century collection known as the *First Quadrilogus* includes an interpolated copy of Grim's *vita*, which features the more exotic version of events.[30] The Laud legend of Gilbert and the Amiral's daughter follows the *First Quadrilogus* version very closely. The two narratives share a common interest in conversion and translation, and Görlach is right to draw attention to the similarities. But the Laud text differs from its Latin analogue in some small but significant respects. Captured by a pagan *Amiraldi*, Gilbert responds to the daughter's questions about his faith and religion, and his words clearly have the same impact as they do in the English legend. But in the Latin text the daughter is attributed with the ability to use language on her journey: there is one word she has learned from Gilbert, *Londonia*, that enables her to reach her destination by merchant ships.[31] This is also a feature of later *SEL* accounts, which give her one or more words in English: the Corpus 145 text announces that 'heo ne couthe Engliss word non / Bote "Londone, Londone"   to esse woderward gon' ('she knew no English word except "London, London" to ask which way to go'); by the fifteenth century, in Rawl. poet. 225, the vocabulary that facilitates her peregrinations has expanded threefold, to 'Gilbert, Gilbert Beket, Beket   and meri Loundon'.[32] In Laud, though, the ability to speak any word of

English prior to conversion is completely erased. As we have seen, the miracle of her journey is that she has reached England with 'language non' (109, 113). Moreover, in the Latin text there is no reference to the name assigned to the woman after baptism; it is the Laud text that introduces the detail of Alisaundre's naming. This suggests that the Laud translation renders the daughter's conversion starkly as a movement from nothing to something.

In principle, of course, these differences between the Latin and Middle English texts could also indicate a reliance on an intermediary text not identical in every respect to the *First Quadrilogus*. British Library, Harley 978, dated to c. 1261–65, contains an assortment of texts in English, Latin and French, including a Latin rendition of the legend of Becket's parents followed by the first few lines of its translation into French.[33] Although the French rubric in this manuscript differs from that in the Laud manuscript (*Ci comence coment Gilebert beket le pere seint thomas espusa sa femme la mere seint thomas le martir*), it indicates that the Gilbert legend may have circulated independently in French a decade or so before the earliest *SELS* were produced. Yet more significant than any direct French 'source' for the *SEL* tale of Becket's mother is the general influence of French literary culture on the narrative: it is not necessary to revert to a search for origins as a way of comprehending the inclusion of French titles in the text, for the Saracen princess plot appropriated from *chansons de geste* already indicates francophone awareness and suggests a narrative universe for this 'English' saint's life that is, simultaneously, French. The titles themselves, then, might be interpreted not as the untranslated residue of some unidentified French translation of the *First Quadrilogus*, but rather as a means of associating the adventures of a London burgess in the Holy Land with an altogether classier (more 'aristocratic') genre.

Similarly intermittent use of French phrases such as *beau frere* or *bel amy* in the Laud *SEL* is not itself evidence of French source texts. I agree with Görlach that this is probably 'indicative of the jargon rather than the sources'.[34] But the jargon is deployed selectively and arguably in politically resonant ways: these stock phrases tend to be placed in the mouths of wicked pagan tormentors in the legends of Latin martyrs, or sometimes in the mouth of the devil.[35] Thomas Becket himself uses the phrase *beau frere* several times, when he addresses the four soldiers who have come to assassinate him (163, 1993; 164, 2005, 2016). Be that as it may, since Thomas is addressing the 'luthere' (163, 1967, 'evil') knights who themselves have arrived in Canterbury with the king's message 'fram him out of Normandie' (163, 1985), it could be that the saint is simply responding to the Norman assassins in a language they understand: Thomas slips into the *koine* of government and administration associated with his secular career. In any case, even if the use of French vocabulary is not consistently ideological in significance, the general distribution of such phrases may indicate the Laud redactor's investment in staging an encounter between English and French as competing vernaculars. Classical pagan tormentors, implicitly likened to their Norman counterparts, are made to sound just a little bit foreign.

If translation produces a remainder in the *SELS* (of vocabulary or even headings in another language), it is a reminder that the process is neither secure nor total. As in medieval fantasies of Jewish conversion as potentially counterfeit, translations of language, like identity, are liable to produce some sort of remnant – a reminder of the polyglot realities in which this ostensibly 'Englische tale' (106, 1) was read. Presenting translation in terms of conversion affords an opportunity to radicalize the displacement process, by purportedly wiping away the remnant completely. Thus within the Gilbert legend itself there is no visible remainder, no heathen 'surplus', that lingers once Becket's mother finds her place. Notions of an embodied heathen essence do sometimes assume prominence in modern versions of the legend, but these present a marked contrast to the medieval analogues. *Fair Rosamund* (1839), a lengthy historical romance by Thomas Miller, has St Thomas declare to King Henry's lover, Rosamund, 'Thinkest thou that I, who have the hot eastern blood dashing through my veins, have never worshipped at the altar of thy sex', a statement which figures Saracen identity explicitly as a physiological phenomenon.[36] Racial ideologies of this kind seem not to have strongly shaped the *SEL* vision of Thomas Becket's ancestry. His Englishness, as the son of an Englishman and his Anglicized wife, is certainly emphasized; Thomas is explicitly presented as defender of his faith and 'folk'.[37] But a biological concept, akin to the idea of a 'mixed race' identity, seems not to have shaped the *SEL* story of Thomas's birth. What can be detected instead is evidence for the cultural significance of translation itself in thirteenth-century England – a reminder that the *SELS* themselves are the products of translation, of each other and of other texts.

To the extent that the text is structured around recurring motifs of conversion, translation also operates thematically within this single life of Thomas Becket. After all, in so far as it is presented as a dramatic shift from his worldliness (as King Henry's chancellor) to his subsequent holiness (as archbishop), Thomas's own conversion mirrors that of his mother, translating her shift of identity into a model for his own: 'He chaungede everech-del [completely] is lif', the narrator announces, 'and is maneres also' (115, 316). But the narrator also has a stake in downplaying the radicalism of the shift. Although, as Chancellor, Thomas showed fondness for hawking and hunting, 'In is heorte it was anothur   hov-so he him bere; / And evere he was chaste thorugh alle thing   hov-so it evere were' (113, 251–2, 'In his heart it was otherwise, however he conducted himself and he was ever chaste throughout, however it ever was'). This implies that Becket himself keeps the faith with his former self: his transfer to the archbishopric of Canterbury manifests no real break with his inner moral disposition. As in those stories of Jewish conversion emphasizing a distinction between interior and exterior expressions of selfhood, we witness here the tension between ideas of conversion as a revolutionary transformation and those of *conversio* as a reverberating echo. Unlike his mother, whose untranslatability can be resolved only through divine miracle, Thomas's own identity as a convert is predicated on the assumption that he is, and always has been, a martyr in the making.

The contrast between the total conversion of Becket's mother and contemporary anxieties about the intransigence of converted Jews has already been noted in this essay. In both cases, the logic is essentializing. Either the convert's former (non)identity is supplanted by a fully realized Christianity, in which case the agent of translation is God himself; or he or she retains, beneath the veneer of conversion, some visible remnant of that former non-Christian selfhood. The image of *translatio* as *conversio* – an absolute translation in which the point of origin is completely displaced – thus coexists with the recognition that conversion produces repetition as well as rupture; translation is an activity that purports to reproduce what it simultaneously effaces. Reading the tale of Becket's heathen mother from this perspective not only brings into focus contemporary anxieties about language, identity and selfhood in the period of production. It also highlights the status of the *SELS* themselves as translations that convert. The texts' readers are being asked to commit to an illusion of sameness that pits Christian selfhood against its non-Christian opposite. This is a vision that eradicates difference in favour of a unifying paradigm: a fantasy of Christian unity in which every reader is asked to share. But beneath that universal message exists another story, of cultural hybridity, linguistic multiplicity, generic interchange and shifting manuscript contexts. Viewed against this backdrop of change and interchange, translation and transformation, this is the other lesson that the tale of Becket's mother imparts.

Notes

1 For the transmission of the Becket legend in *SEL* manuscripts, see Görlach, *Textual Tradition*, pp. 213–15. For the Laud Gilbert legend, see Horstmann, pp. 106–12. Subsequent references will be to Horstmann by page and line number.

2 D'Evelyn and Mill, I, 3, 60, 62. On reading romance and hagiography collectively as 'forms of exemplary biography', see Jocelyn Wogan-Browne, '"Bet . . . to . . . rede on holy seyntes lyves . . .": romance and hagiography again', in Carol M. Meale (ed.), *Readings in Medieval English Romance* (Cambridge: D. S. Brewer, 1994), pp. 83–97 (85).

3 Frank Barlow, *Thomas Becket* (London: Weidenfeld & Nicolson, 1986), pp. 10–13.

4 Charles Dickens, *A Child's History of England*, 3 vols (London: Bradbury & Evans, 1852), I: 138–40; Thomas B. Costain, *The Black Rose* (New York: Doubleday, 1946), pp. ix–x; Jean Anouilh, *Becket, or, The Honour of God*, trans. Lucienne Hill (London: Samuel French, 1961), p. 21; Jean Plaidy, *The Plantagenet Prelude* (London: Hale, 1976). For a comprehensive overview of nineteenth- and early twentieth-century retellings of the Gilbert legend, see Paul Alonzo Brown, 'The development of the legend of Thomas Becket' (published PhD thesis, Philadelphia: University of Pennsylvania, 1930), pp. 41–50.

5 See further Robert Mills, 'The early *South English Legendary* and difference: race, place, language and belief', in Kimberly K. Bell and Julie Nelson Couch (eds), The *Texts and Contexts of Oxford, Bodleian Library, MS Laud Misc. 108: The Shaping of English Vernacular Narrative* (Leiden: Brill, 2011), pp. 197–221.

6 James Muldoon, 'Introduction: the conversion of Europe', in James Muldoon (ed.), *Varieties of Religious Conversion in the Middle Ages* (Gainesville: University Press of Florida, 1997), pp. 1–10 (1, 4).

7 Rita Copeland, *Rhetoric, Hermeneutics, and Translation in the Middle Ages: Academic Traditions and Vernacular Texts* (Cambridge: Cambridge University Press, 1991). On *translatio* as a mode of genealogical as well as textual transfer, see Zrinka Stahuljak, *Bloodless Genealogies of the French Middle Ages:* Translatio, *Kinship, and Metaphor* (Gainesville: University Press of Florida, 2005).

8 Dickens, *Child's History*, p. 139; Robert Buchanan, 'Gilbert à Becket's troth', discussed in Brown, 'Development', p. 47.

9 Pierre Dubois, *The Recovery of the Holy Land*, trans. Walther I. Brandt (New York: Columbia University Press, 1956), p. 118.

10 Ibid., p. 119.

11 Michael R. Evans, 'Marriage as a means of conversion in Pierre Dubois's *De recuperatione Terre Sancte*', in Guyda Armstrong and Ian N. Wood (eds), *Christianizing Peoples and Converting Individuals* (Turnhout: Brepols, 2000), pp. 195–202.

12 Dubois, *Recovery*, p. 124.

13 Ibid., p. 177. Dubois also expresses enthusiasm for language learning as a means of following in the footsteps of the apostles in another work, *La supplication du pueuble de France au Roy, contre le Pape Boniface le VIII*, in which he criticizes Boniface for not knowing languages when Christ himself had urged his disciples to preach to all men. See ibid., p. 212.

14 See also Sharon Farmer, 'Persuasive voices: clerical images of medieval wives', *Speculum*, 61:3 (1986), 517–43.

15 See further Jennifer R. Goodman, 'Marriage and conversion in late medieval romance', in Muldoon (ed.), *Varieties of Religious Conversion*, pp. 115–28.

16 'Man of Law's Tale', ll. 519–20, in *The Riverside Chaucer*, 3rd edn, ed. Larry D. Benson (Oxford: Oxford University Press, 1987).

17 For the Laud definition of Christendom, see Mills, 'Early *South English Legendary* and difference', pp. 200–7.

18 Sarah Kay, *The* Chansons de geste *in the Age of Romance: Political Fictions* (Oxford: Clarendon, 1995), pp. 30–48.

19 Jonathan Elukin, 'The discovery of the self: Jews and conversion in the twelfth century', in Michael A. Signer and John Van Engen (eds), *Jews and Christians in Twelfth-Century Europe* (Notre Dame: University of Notre Dame Press, 2001), pp. 63–76; Jonathan Elukin, 'From Jew to Christian? Conversion and immutability in medieval Europe', in Muldoon (ed.), *Varieties of Religious Conversion*, pp. 171–89.

20 D'Evelyn and Mill, I, 227, 201.

21 The *Domus Conversorum*, or House of Converts, established in London by Henry III in 1232 was itself a perpetuator of the line separating Jewish converts from other Christians (see Reva Nernan Brown and Sean McCartney, 'Living in limbo: the experience of Jewish converts in medieval England', in Armstrong and Wood (eds), *Christianizing Peoples*, pp. 169–91), and may possibly have provided a home to Muslim converts in the mid-fourteenth century: see Henry Ansgar Kelly, 'Jews and Saracens in Chaucer's England: a review of the evidence', *Studies in the Age of Chaucer*, 27 (2005), 129–69 (133, 145–56).

22 Sermon 91 in *The Sermons of Thomas Brinton, Bishop of Rochester (1373–1389)*, ed. Mary Aquinas Devlin, 2 vols (London: Royal Historical Society, 1954), vol. II, p. 412.

23 'Cur in hac civitate gloriosa in qua debet florere forcius fides firma tot
    perfidi Iudei favorabiliter sunt permissi, nec persuasionibus vel doc-
    trinis tot patrum sanctorum, tot prelatorum, tot doctorum ad fidem
    Christi a suis erroribus transferentur, cum tamen vulgaris opinio
    predicet evidenter quod multi Iudei libentissime fierent Christiani, si
    post conversionem non timerent diviciarum suarum dispendium vel
    iacturam?' (*Sermons of Thomas Brinton*, 413).
24 This was pointed out by H. G. Richardson in his review of Devlin's
    edition of the sermons in *Speculum*, 30:2 (1955), 267–71, though this
    has not prevented the sermon from continuing to be attributed to
    Brinton and being read as evidence for a continuing Jewish population
    in late fourteenth-century England. See, for example, Kelly, 'Jews and
    Saracens', 161–2. If assigned an earlier date, as Richardson suggests,
    the 'glorious city' to which the preacher refers is presumably London.
    Another possibility is that the sermon was delivered by Brinton
    himself at the papal curia in Avignon or Rome, where the bishop was a
    penitentiary in the 1360s and 1370s. See Margaret Harvey, 'Preaching
    in the curia: some sermons by Thomas Brinton', *Archivum Historiae
    Pontificiae*, 33 (1995), 299–301; Lawrence Warner, 'Becket and the
    hopping bishops', *Yearbook of Langland Studies*, 17 (2003), 107–34
    (124–9).
25 For the text of Harley 2277, see *The Life and Martyrdom of Thomas
    Beket, Archbishop of Canterbury*, ed. William Henry Black (London:
    Percy Society, 1845), pp. 1–126; Corpus 145 in *SEL*, ed. D'Evelyn
    and Mill, II, 610, 6.
26 Printed as appendix A in Brown, 'Development of the legend', pp.
    262–8: for the *SEL* textual tradition of the Gilbert narrative, see
    Görlach, *Textual Tradition*, pp. 213–15.
27 Görlach, *Studies*, pp. 25–36.
28 Michelle R. Warren, 'Translation', in Paul Strohm (ed.), *Middle
    English* (Oxford: Oxford University Press, 2007), pp. 51–67.
29 Görlach, *Textual Tradition*, pp. 30–1.
30 The *Quadrilogus* is a composite life of Becket which circulated in two
    versions, the earlier of which dates to the end of the twelfth century.
    Confusingly called the *Second Quadrilogus* by virtue of the fact it
    appeared second in print (in 1682), this does not contain the legendary
    story of Thomas's heathen ancestry. The *First Quadrilogus*, first printed
    in 1495 but originally dating to the thirteenth century, amplifies the
    Quadrilogus with extracts from the expanded version of Grim's *vita*.
    For the text of the *First Quadrilogus* interpolated version of Grim, taken
    from British Library Cotton Vitellius c.xii, see *Materials for the History
    of Thomas Becket*, ed. James C. Robertson and J. B. Sheppard, RS 67,
    7 vols (London: Longman, 1875–85), II: 453–8. For the *Quadrilogus*
    in general, see Anne Duggan, *Thomas Becket: A Textual History of His
    Letters* (Oxford: Clarendon Press, 1980), pp. 15, 205–7, 223–4; Anne

Duggan, 'The Lyell Version of the *Quadrilogus* Life of St Thomas of Canterbury', *Analecta Bollandiana*, 112 (1994), 105–38 (105–7, 112–13).

31 *Materials for the History*, ed. Robertson and Sheppard, p. 455.

32 D'Evelyn and Mill, II, 613, 73–74; Brown, 'Development of the legend', p. 264.

33 See Ruth J. Dean with Maureen B. M. Boulton, *Anglo-Norman Literature: A Guide to Texts and M Manuscripts*, ANTS OPS 3 (London: Anglo-Norman Text Society, 1999), no. 511, and the essay by Sanok in this volume, p. 232, n. 40.

34 Görlach, *Textual Tradition*, p. 31.

35 For examples, see Mills, 'Early *South English Legendary* and difference', pp. 207–9; Thompson, *Everyday Saints*, p. 53. See also Christopher Baswell, 'Multilingualism on the page', in Strohm (ed.), *Middle English*, pp. 38–50.

36 Thomas Miller, *Fair Rosamund, or The Days of King Henry II: An Historical Romance*, 3 vols (London: Henry Colburn, 1839), vol. II, p. 268.

37 Thompson, *Everyday Saints*, pp. 49–50; Thorlac Turville-Petre, *England the Nation: Language, Literature, and National Identity 1290–1340* (Oxford: Clarendon Press, 1996), pp. 62–4.

18

Bodies of belief: MS Bodley 779's *South English Legendary*

Jocelyn Wogan-Browne

In nineteenth- and twentieth-century editions of the *SEL*, manuscripts from the late thirteenth and earlier fourteenth century were
privileged as base texts for their witness to the work's originary
textual tradition.[1] But whether one is counting the twenty-six manuscripts with a very full selection of saints' lives or those containing
smaller selections (Görlach's nineteen 'fragmentary' and eighteen
'miscellany' manuscripts), just over half of the extant *SEL* manuscripts are c. 1400 or later.[2] The fifteenth century sees great variety
in the anthologizing of *SEL* texts: a wider range of other texts
accompany *SEL* selections in the manuscripts, and the prosodic
forms included within the *SEL* become more mixed.[3] It is easy to
see how this situation could be read as one of decline for the *SEL* as
it moved further from its origins. But in a century of such notable
hagiographic production as the fifteenth – the century of saints'
lives by Capgrave, Lydgate, Bokenham, Caxton, and important
anonymous manuscript legendaries – and a century marked by
monastic bids to make hagiography the public voice of letters in
England[4]- the textual state of the *SEL* can as readily be argued to
testify to continuing vigour. Widely dispersed from its south-west
starting point, with significant manuscripts in the north-east, the
SEL is instantiated in various ways in the fifteenth century, at least
twelve times as a very full version of the work, but also with varying
selections appearing in a range of contexts for the needs and interests of different readers.[5] We might see this situation as an effect
of the continuing pertinence of the *SEL*, the energy with which
it was recast for varying purposes among fifteenth-century users
(certainly for the first half of the century), and the capaciousness
of what William Robins discusses in this volume as its 'modular'
form, whereby, as with Chaucer's *Canterbury Tales*, a framing idea
is always present but participated in by different manuscripts and
users in varying ways.

An example of a fifteenth-century *SEL* manuscript with its own particular character is Oxford, Bodleian MS Bodley 779, dated to the first half of the century.[6] Apart from a concluding text of the *Pater noster*, the creed and a short prayer in English on the last leaf, the manuscript contains only *SEL* saints' lives and *temporale* narratives, and its 135 lives make it the single largest *SEL* collection. With a couple of noteworthy exceptions, however, the manuscript remains little studied, probably because of the early established paradigms of *SEL* scholarship and their high valuation of the origins rather than the *mouvance* of the legendary.[7]

That the manuscript *is* a collection in intention has been demonstrated by Thomas Liszka: the compiler went through the liturgical calendar at least twice, adding lives to the legendary's *sanctorale* in a manner neither entirely unsystematic nor unfocused, so that the *SEL* here looks like someone realizing a particular idea or programme as opportunity offered.[8] In spite of a certain amount of misbinding in the deployment of its texts,[9] the manuscript's characteristics give support to the argument that the compiler had an idea of the *SEL*, and that this was a sufficiently capacious and flexible idea not to require forgoing the opportunity of enriching the legendary and adding particular emphases on occasions, even if this meant disrupting strict calendrical order.[10]

In both its *sanctorale* and *temporale*, Bodley 779 witnesses to particular inflections and continuing vigour in the *SEL*. Here I will explore the manuscript's emphasis on a key area of doctrine – papal regulation of kinship, body and blood, in the church, its parishioners and in the Eucharist – as part of an intensified articulation of church authority in the first half of the fifteenth century. As is being increasingly recognized, there is no reason to set saints' lives aside in considering the controversies over late medieval reformist thought in England.[11] Equally, as the texts of Bodley 779 suggest, and as is well recognised in scholarship on Wyclifism and Lollardy, questions of orthodoxy and heresy, let alone heterodoxy, are complex and often only categorizable after the fact.[12] Bodley 779's assertions of orthodoxy reveal a rich account of the paradoxes of human embodiment and show the *SEL* as a continuing participant in the politics of late medieval vernacular doctrine and devotion.

Bodley 779's most distinctive inclusions are its thirteen unique biographies of saintly popes (Table 18.1), together with some particular inclusions in its *temporale* (to be discussed below).[13] Lives of Popes Peter, Clement and to a lesser extent Sylvester are regularly found in earlier *SEL* manuscripts,[14] but in Bodley 779,

Table 18.1 MS Bodley 779: unique papal biographies

---

fols 187r–188v **Seint calston the pope** feast 14 Oct [Calixtus, 217–22], 176 lines.

fols 198v–199v **Seint evarist the pope** 26 Oct [Evaristus, d. c. 107], 108 lines.

fol. 217r–217v **Seint lion the pope the yonge** 28 June [Leo II, feast 3 July, d. 683], 42 lines.

fols. 225r–226r **Seint [s]illu(e)rin the holy pope** 20 June [Silverius, 536–37], 96 lines.

fols 227r–229v **Seint cilvestir the holy pope** 31 Dec [Sylvester, AD 314–35], 308 lines[16]

fol. 231r–231v **Seint anicet the holy pope** 17 April [Anicetus, c. 155-66], 68 lines.

fols 231v–232r **Seint Sother the holy pope** 22 April [Soter, 166–74], 76 lines.

fols 232r–233r **Gay the holy pope** 22 April [Gaius/Caius 283–96], 88 lines.

fols 233v–234r **Seint igin the holy pope** 11 Jan [Hyginus, 138–42], 56 lines.

fols 234r–235r **Melchiades the holy pope** 10 Dec [Miltiades, 311–14], 86 lines.

fol 235r–235v **Seint damas the pope** 11 Dec [Damasus, 366–84], 62 lines.

fols 236v–237v **the holy pope inocent** 28 July [Innocent I, 401–17], 98 lines.

fols 237v–238r **Seint felix the holy pope** 25 Feb (Felix III, 483–92), 76 lines.

---

with the manuscript's characteristic mixture of contingency and selection, the compiler has bunched eleven of its thirteen unique papal biographies together between fols 225 and 238, with only a few interruptions from other types of saints. This non-calendrical ordering principle of grouping by hagiographic type is observable in some other *SEL* manuscripts, and can coexist, as it does here, with calendrical groupings in the runs of saints.[15] (In much the same way, the *Canterbury Tales* 'fragments', to use the nineteenth-century terminology, can be ordered according to various priorities and themes and have varying possible resonance and connections both within and beyond their individual units.)

Before discussing Bodley's papal biographies, it is worth pausing for some general considerations regarding this hagiographic sub-type. Popes and their capacity to make and define the body of the church are symbolically resonant and complicated. Productive tensions between spiritual and biological kinship circle around the figure of the pope: he is at the heart of maintaining and regulating the overlaid relations of biological and spiritual kinship among the members of the church, in the material and spiritual institutional body of the church itself, and in the church's relations with its own members. In these conceptions biology and spirituality both shape and figure each other, and neither is ever simply a metaphor for the other: both are grounded in law, custom and institutional history. A major instrument of papal regulation is canon law, and, as Elizabeth Archibald has explained, one reason why medieval canon law envisages so vast a range of forbidden in-laws is because any act of sexual intercourse is deemed to create lasting relationships with the relatives of any sexual partner.[17] Medieval supplementation of biological kinships by the spiritual affinities created through baptism means that the number of people potentially implicated incestuously in any one sexual act is very great. Questions in the confessors' manuals which do not seem at first glance to offer any threat of in-breeding – have you had sex with the mother of your godchild? With your father's god-daughter? and so on – are, in the view of canon law, all incest questions. Corporeal and spiritual never form a simple binary: as Dyan Elliott has remarked of Christian doctrine in the later Middle Ages, there is always an undertow of recognition that the one thing worse than the excesses of the flesh is the absence of flesh (as in, for instance, angelic and demonic incorporeality). Reconciliation with God *depends* on an incarnate body.[18]

These understandings of biological and spiritual interrelations are marked within and beyond the *SEL* in the association of papal figures and incest. Popes regulate permitted degrees of relationship in romances such as *Emaré*, and popes may themselves embody incest. The most notable example is the life of Pope Gregory the Penitent, widely disseminated in the vernaculars. Gregory's narrative is often found in romance collections, but the boundaries between romance and the *SEL* can be permeable, and Gregory the Penitent is also included alongside *SEL* items in several manuscripts of the legendary.[19] This pope begins as the child of brother – sister incest and goes on to become the husband of his mother. He also becomes, unsurprisingly, a spectacular penitent in later life, a reassurance that *nothing* in the kinship of the church is unrecuperable by true penance within the church's conventions. His is a limit case for how transcendent a saintly life can be of kinship norms, and yet it is also a reaffirmation of the propriety and inevitability of the church's regulation of kinship among its lay members.[20]

The theme of incest in papal lives does not simply signify sexual transgression, but points rather to the extraordinary pontifical embodiment of God's own patriarchal nature and his arrangements for humans. Not only was incest accepted by the early church fathers as necessary to reproduction in the first family created by God, but, as Marc Schell has argued, Christian doctrine's universalist position on the human family whereby all human beings are siblings descended from Adam and Eve means that the same Christian culture that inhibits the practice of incest also represents incest as an ineradicable ideal (in which, for example, the Virgin Mary is sibling, spouse, parent and child in relation to the Holy Trinity).[21] Incest is thus both the zero sum and the *sine qua non* of bodied human progeny, at once a limit case and a resource.[22] As the Vernon manuscript's version of a homily on the feast of Corpus Christi (also used in Bodley 779, pp. 412–14 below) puts it:

Seththhe we han the Modur to preye the sone,
We han the sone to preye the ffader,
tho holy gost we han in wone,
this enteere we have togeder:
What leteth us forte wynne
the Riche blisse is us bi-hote
Bot hit beo ur owne synne?[23]

(Since we have the Mother to pray to the Son, and we have the Son to pray to the Father, and the Holy Ghost in-dwelling, and we have all of this complete and together, what hinders us from winning the rich bliss promised us except for our own sin?)

The papal figure most widely distributed in the *SEL*'s manuscripts after St Peter is Pope Clement,[24] whose mother is accused of adultery with her brother-in-law. This accusation of incest provokes her flight with Clement's young twin brothers, and their subsequent shipwreck sunders Clement from his biological family, leaving him with St Peter. Clement and his family all find each other again and Clement's biological father, Faustinus, and his spiritual father, St Peter, debate their own intellectual and theological positions with Simon Magus, the church's primary figure of inappropriate use of spiritual things for material purposes. After Clement's biological and spiritual fathers are sorted out, and St Peter has been martyred, Clement himself progresses to the papacy. The figure of Clement thus embodies in *SEL* collections the church's concerns with its own organization – with the reproduction of its institutional body in spiritual and material dimensions – and that of the control and reproduction of the human family.

Bodley 779's papal lives regularly emphasize the paternal lineage of each pope, the papal capacity to reproduce the church through the ordination of clergy, and the papal ability to build the institutional church through the regulation of its body of belief and practice (and, less frequently, the material foundation of churches), together with some note of the popes' martyrdom or other death.[25] So, for instance, Pope Calston (Calixtus) is born in Rome, enjoys school and goes straight to the papacy, where his conversion of several high-status laypeople is noted, along with his ordination of clergy, his institution of three fasting Saturdays and his foundation of a church on the Tiber. He continues to make converts after he is imprisoned and when his jailers kill him, his body becomes the site of a church.[26]

The cumulative effect of Bodley's papal lives is to stress regulation as a continuous and collective enterprise: each pope is celebrated for a particular reform or innovation, and together they build a corporate history of doctrine and practice. Pope Anicetus legislates against long-haired priests and clerks (398, 12), ordering under pain of excommunication that every cleric is to learn from monks how to make a crown – i.e. a tonsure (399, 17–20).[27] Pope Leo II's sixth synod is noted as the first held in Rome, and for condemning clerics to death for the heresy 'that al myght was in Crist and namo', instead of the orthodox view that 'in alle cristin workis there were kendus to' (381, 16,18, i.e. two natures, human and divine);[28] while Innocent I is said to combat Pelagius's and Caelestius's arguments against infant baptism by claiming the ritual to be necessitated by Adam's sin (412, 55–63).[29] Thus each pope's biography becomes a reinforcement of institutional norms and of doctrine on the nature of God and humanity.

Complementing the regulation of those who are institutionally included, there is considerable attention to the excluded, notably to Jews and women. Immediately following Bodley's first unique papal life, that of Calixtus, a Jewish convert pope appears (in the calendar and in the manuscript) in the figure of St Evaristus. 'Evarist' is said to have been born near Jerusalem of Jewish kin to a priest, Juda: in an elaboration of the *Liber pontificalis* narrative, the life adds that:

Al [Evaristus'] kyn byleved   al on the Gywerye
So doth yit manyon   and that is gret folye.

A while hit was a lawe   that God lovid swythe,
For they cholde to Jhesu Crist   myd here herte ben blythe,
Bote yif hem ofthenche   that here elderne habbeth iwrought
Jhesu, yif it thy wille be   thereto hem granty thought.
                              (346, 3–8: *Lib. pont.* II, no. 6, p. 13)

(All his kin believed completely in the Jewish religion, as many still do, and that is great folly. At one time it was a faith much loved by God, and they should have welcomed Jesus Christ in their hearts: but if they repent what their elders did, Jesus, if it is your will, grant them the idea of doing so.)

Evaristus converts his father in their nightly debates together, and becomes pope after his father dies. He then lives an ascetic life, beloved of 'Christians, heathens and also Jews' (347, 79) many of whom he converts, until he is beheaded at Diocletian's orders (348, 100). Both in his own life and in the relation of his biography to that of St Calixtus's career in Bodley 779, Evaristus life can be seen as in part a figuration of Christian supercession of older patriarchy and older law by the new, and of Jewish faith by the Christian.

For Bodley 779's Life of Pope Sylvester, a distinctive version, focused on the pope's debates with Jews, is chosen.[30] Sylvester argues that male Jewish circumcision excludes Jewish women and so makes Christianity the more inclusive religion:

. . . youre lawe to wimmen   ne may nothing areche,
For thou ne herdist nevere   in cyte ne in toun
That wymmen in youre lawe   hadde circomsicioun.
Than thou most, me thinketh,   this thing grantin me,
That wimme(n) beth iblessed   other that hy ne be.
Ac Jhesu that alyghte fram hevene   and hadde manhede here,
Wolde that men and women   alle isaved were.
                                         (390, 104–110)

(Your law does not extend to women at all, for you have never heard in city or town that women were circumcised under your law. In that case it seems to me that you must grant me this point: that women are either included in religion or that they are not. But Jesus who came down from heaven and assumed humanity here wanted all men and women to be saved.)

But inclusion only goes so far. Within Christianity, the roles of women are strictly policed. Pope St Sother rules on the question of female ordination:

Gode women mowin wel   in religion ben ido,
Ac icrounyd wit ordre   ne chal be woman none,
For no maner holy lyf   ther ne lyth ther uppone:
Ne the clothus of the auter   ne cholle they handly nought
Bote they ben paraventure   to wasschen hem ibrought.
And yut ic hadde levere   – yif a dekene couthe –
That he wissche the clothus   than eny woman nouthe.
Yut ne chal no wimman   cast encence to the auter,
And yif ye wollith wherfore iwite;   I wol you seggen her:
God was [male] and made   the orderus everychone
And therfore he chal ben [male]   that chal the werkus done:
Ac this Ic wole grantin   wit outin eny respit
That wimman don alle the werkus   that may acolit.

(400, 24–36)[31]

(Women who are good may well be professed in religion, but no woman may be crowned with the tonsure of the orders, for there is no sort of holy life possible in that. Nor should they handle the altar cloths, unless they are brought in to wash them. And yet, I would rather, if a deacon knew how to do it, that he wash the clothes than any woman at all. Nor should any woman cense the altar, and if you want to know why, I will tell you here: God was male and made every one of the orders and therefore he who does their work should be male. But I will allow without any restriction that women may do all the tasks permitted to acolytes.)

A particular version of the institutional body of the Christian church and its boundaries expressive of anxiety about women's participation in the late medieval church is thus built up across this corporate papal biography.[32]

Bodley 779's papal biographies are unsensational, and their thematics are rarely concerned with incest. However their very casting as saints' lives places them in a genre which confronts birth-family structures with alternative models of spiritual affinities and which opens up new ways of seeing lineage and reproduction, social structure and the politics of household and kin group. As Emma Campbell has argued, the very power of kinship to anchor and reproduce heterosexual social formations means that saints' rejections of its limitations open a space for relations and desires which transcend normative assumptions.[33] In the short biography of Pope Evarist noted above, for instance, it is said of the saint's death:

For wel he myghte hopye   to habben good endinge
Whan he cristened his fadir   in his byginnynge.

(347, 45–6)

(For well might he hope to have a good ending when he christened
his father at his beginning.)

Here, 'endinge' and 'beginning' are not filler rhymes but an important rhetorical heightening of the question of origin and supercession as between the individual human line of descent and religion
at large (and as between Judaism and Christianity). The lines, with
their faint suggestion of inbreeding, of a patriarchal line turning
back up into itself in a new version of kinship, carry the power of
hagiography to, as Campbell puts it, 'queer' normative social structures and desires, to move beyond them and to question them. As
with much other hagiography, this does not prevent Bodley 779's
seeking to maintain a stable model of heterosexual reproduction
in the body of believers, its lay audiences. The manuscript's papal
lives, however, both appropriate and rework kinship, defining its
limits in order to claim that God can surpass them.

The nature and status of papal rights and powers was more or
less continuously under debate during the late fourteenth and the
first half of the fifteenth century. Not only were critiques of the
papacy common in reformist thought, but at an international and
institutional level there were continuing battles at the European
councils of the Church from Constance to Basle over conciliarism
as a supplement or alternative to papal regulation.[34] Especially in
the wake of schism, and the continuing influence of new thought
(notably in England, in Ockham's and Wyclif's work, but continued in fifteenth-century reformist writing) on the possibility both
of disobeying and correcting the papacy, the reassertion of the centrality of the pope's role in the church was an issue for lay and cleric
alike.[35] Bodley 779 is not the only late *SEL* manuscript to pay extra
attention to the figure of the pope, though it is particularly notable
for the number and cast of its papal biographies.[36] Alongside the
SELS, moreover, there is the increasing availability of vernacular
historiography's late medieval marshalling of papal and imperial
lives. Responses to the most popular of these, Martinus Polonus's
chronicle of *Emperors and Popes*, occupy the full spectrum of
doctrinal positions.[37] *The Lollard Chronicle*, for example, a late
fourteenth-century Middle English rewriting of Polonus, rewrites
the popes with counter-arguments to the positions adopted by
them in Bodley 779 on matters such as baptism and grace.[38] In
Bodley 779, holy wise children such as Calixtus may go directly to
the papacy, but the *Lollard Chronicle* notes that Grosseteste sent
'a bille' to Pope Innocent the III, 'thoundryng scherply ynouz'

against papal exactions and the appointment of a child kinsman to a canonry in the church at Lincoln.[39]

Bodley 779's extra papal lives can thus be seen as part of a wider late medieval discussion about the nature and prerogatives of the church. Considerable energy is invested here, as elsewhere, in the intertwined themes of the pope's role and the biological and spiritual interrelations of the church, especially in laypeople's understanding of the holy family (the pope's and God's) as modelling both exceptionalism and exemplarity for ordinary lives. The *temporale* feasts of the *SELS* deal extensively with Christ's family and kin, his body and blood and transubstantiation, and, alongside its inclusion of the papal biographies, Bodley 779's *temporale* takes on particular emphases.

The first of the standard *SEL temporale* feasts in the manuscript is the Circumcision (1st January, fols 21v–22r) with its emphasis that Christ 'was man of flesch and blode   to bygge us on the tre' (fol. 21v, 7, 'became a man of flesh and blood to redeem us on the tree') and that

> [New] Yeres Day the holy feste   hy day is and gode
> For thylke day oure swete Lord   schadde fyrst his blode
>
> (fol. 21v, 20–1)

(New Year's Day, the holy feast, is a high and good day, for on that day our sweet Lord first shed his blood.)[40]

Bodley 779's versions of other *temporale* narratives – the Conception of Mary, Birth of Jesus – maintain the themes of body, blood and kinship, while its account of John the Baptist adds a particular emphasis on the Baptist's early family.[41] The manuscript also, unusually, adds the Holy Innocents and the shedding of their blood (fols 265r–266v), and a rare version of the late medieval *Sermo de Corporis Christi* (fols 172v–175r):[42]

> The hyghe feste of Goddus blod   that late was ifounde
> Good is to honoure   in every a stounde . . .
>
> (307, 1–2)

(The high feast of God's blood that was recently established is good to honour at every occasion . . .)

The bulk of the *Sermo* is an extended and colourful defence of transubstantiation, using Christ's body to figure the body of the church, with once again, defining exclusions. Defence of the Eucharist is needed, asserts the *Sermo*, because:

> . . . Jewis and Sarasynus   and some that Cristin is
> Beleveth nought that it is   Goddus blood iwis
>
> (308, 63–4).

(Jews and Saracens and some who are Christian do not believe that
it is truly God's blood.)

The Jews may claim their faith is better because they have the
manna God sent them in the desert, the *Sermo* argues, but manna
rots after two days, whereas the body and blood of the Eucharist
will never rot: the baker is higher than the bread and the manna is
subordinate to Christ (309, 116).[43]

But for all the polemical linking of Jews and Saracens as the
'others' of Eucharistic controversies, it is the doubts and questions
internal to fifteenth-century Christianity that most clearly emerge:

> But al this that the Jewis had   com in thestirnesse
> But we have Cristis oune blood   ryght in soothnesse.
> Lyght is beter than myst   and soth than falsnesse,
> Cristus body than manna   as we scholle bere witnesse.
> O thing me may seyghe   who so wold it wite:
> 'Thou seyst it is Cristus blood: how may I it wite?
> For me thinketh for sothe   flesch non I se
> But me thinkith iwis   bred that it be.
> Win and water also   is in the chalys:
> Blood me thinketh it is naught,   ac ilych it is.'
> Therfore I wile swere,   'For Goddus love leve this
> Other for ryghte sothe   thou levist amys:
> For with mony ensaumplis   I may schewe the
> That thou ondirstond   Goddus flesch that it be.'
>
> (309, 127–40)

(All that the Jews had came in darkness, but we have Christ's own
blood in truth. Light is better than mist, and truth better than
falsity, Christ's body better than manna, as we should bear witness.
One thing may be said, whoever might want to know about it: 'You
say that it is Christ's blood: how can I know that? For truly it seems
to me that I see no flesh: rather it seems to me that it is surely bread.
Wine and water, too, is in the chalice: it doesn't seem to me to be
blood, though it is like it.' I will answer to this: 'For the love of
God, believe this, otherwise, in very truth, you believe falsely. For
with many examples I can show you so that you understand that it
is God's flesh.')

The *Sermo* proceeds vigorously to argue that 'grace is wel
more than kinde' and can suspend nature (310, 185–6), so that

transubstantiation is experientially plausible. Examples are drawn from quotidian experience – the use of water to make ale, or medicinal recipes, for instance: if 'ertheliche' men can do such things, how much more may God, who made everything, make bread out of his flesh when he wills? (311, 213–24). The three kinds of blood shed by Christ in the crucifixion and the devotional and eschatological implications for his human kin are also carefully explained.[44]

Such a focus on Christ's body and blood in Bodley 779's version of the *temporale* is hardly surprising, of course, in a late medieval English text, and indeed this is part of my point: hagiographic collections continue orthodox argument with the same vigour as preaching collections or any other performance genre concerned with lay audiences.[45] Lay belief on these matters was a charged issue: when Margery Kempe is tested at York the interpretation of 'Crescite et multiplicamini' (Gen. 1:22, 121.2–3) is one of the major questions addressed to her. This, as Kathryn Kerby-Fulton points out, was a standard test for Free Spiritist heresy: Kempe passes with the reply that the words are to be 'not vndirstondyn only of begetyng of children bodily but also be purchasing of vertu, which is frute ghostly'.[46] These concerns are already visible in the late fourteenth-century Vernon manuscript, which includes both an *SEL* collection and a version of the Corpus Christi sermon that is reworked by Bodley 779 as part of its *temporale*.[47] So, too, in one of the most influential vernacular sermon collections, John Mirk's late fourteenth-century *Festial*, the relationship of priest and parish is seen, like that of the popes with the church at large, as one that combines corporeality and spirituality: 'my chyldyr yn God' Mirk's priest calls his congregation, while in his instructions for parish priests Mirk stresses that congregations be taught that all those related to a child at baptism 'be cosynes to hym for ay'.[48] In another fifteenth-century sermon collection, parishioners are taught to respect two types of parents –biological and spiritual-ecclesiastical:

> The secound manere of fader and moder is goostliche [spiritual] and been yowre parsoun and yowre vyker as youre goostliche fader . . . Your modir is your parische churches [where you receive sacraments, and especially] the precious and worshipful sacrament of Godis flesche and his blode and therfore this moder, holi churche, ye oweth to honoure and make and amende for to here therinne the servise of God and that ther be nothyng wantyng therinne, nether boke, chalice, ne noon other thynge that schuld be an instrumente

therinne aboute the mynystracioun of the forseide sacramentis to
sauvacioun of your soulis.

(Princeton, MS Garrett 143, fols 10v–11r) [49]

These quotations are from a sermon cycle with Lollard affiliations, but in some ways have more in common with Mirk and
Bodley 779 than either has with us.[50] Open to shades of orthodox
and heterodox thought and feeling, and under pressure, early
fifteenth-century understandings of embodiment – Christ's, the
church's and the faithful – demanded high polemical and imaginative energies for the complex balancing of fleshly and spiritual
relations.

There is no specific provenance known for Bodley 779, and
indeed a variety of purposes for the manuscript can be imagined,
from interested lay collecting to a more programmatic, if une-
venly collected, monastic reassertion of orthodoxy. The compiler-
scribe's dialect is North West Hampshire,[51] but the collection was
made from several sets of exemplars, one of which, given the manuscript's inclusion of a unique *St Oswine*, may very well have come
from the rich Benedictine house of St Albans in Hertfordshire or
its dependent house in Tynemouth, Northumberland.[52] Bodley
779's emphases in its *sanctorale* and *temporale* would fit well into
what is known of contemporary Benedictine response to Wyclifism
and St Albans' activities.[53] The monastery became increasingly
concerned with the religion of the laity and its own relation to the
outside world in the earlier fifteenth century, advocating reform
of the priesthood, the enforcement of canon law and more effective administration of dioceses and parishes: it saw 'the key to the
revival of orthodox piety as being in the monasteries themselves
and in the cult of saints'.[54] But the dialect, the relative amateurism
of the scribe and the presence of other local and regional markers
in the manuscript tell against St Albans or its dependencies as the
place of compilation.[55]

Nevertheless, provenanced or not, the specific character of
Bodley 779 serves to suggest the value of attending to later as
well as earlier manuscript instantiations for our understanding of
the *SEL*. The vigour with which the manuscript articulates the
rich and strange orthodoxies of body and blood shows the *SEL*
still capable, in the first half of the fifteenth century, of vigorous
contemporary cultural work.

Notes

1 Horstmann is based on MS Laud 108 (late thirteenth century); D'Evelyn and Mill is based on Harley 2277 (c. 1300, the earliest 'orderly text of the SEL') and Cambridge, Corpus Christi College 145 (early fourteenth century, with 'the saints' legends in general in the order of the calendar') with variants from Oxford, Bodleian MS Ashmole 43 (second quarter of the fourteenth century) and London, BL Cotton Julius D ix (fifteenth century): the terms are D'Evelyn's (III, *Introduction and Glossary*, pp. 3, 4).

2 Twelve out of Görlach's twenty-five 'complete' manuscripts are dated by him to c. 1400 or later and all but four are dated to the second half of the fourteenth century, while fourteen of his eighteen 'miscellaneous' manuscripts and eight of the nineteen 'fragments' are dated to c. 1400 or later, making (out of Görlach's initial list of sixty-two manuscripts) thirty-four of c. 1400 or later (*Textual Tradition*, pp. viii–x, pp. 70–130). The subsequently discovered Takamiya manuscript (Z) is also fifteenth century: see Oliver S. Pickering and Manfred Görlach, 'A newly-discovered manuscript of the *South English Legendary*', *Anglia*, 100 (1982), 109–23 (p. 111). See further the totals in Thomas R. Liszka, 'The dragon in the *South English Legendary*: Judas, Pilate and the "A(1)" redaction', *Modern Philology*, 100 (2002), 50–9 (51, n. 2). I have taken account of *temporale* manuscripts excluded by Görlach (his Lx and Ux): for the case for including *temporale* manuscripts in *SEL*, see Pickering, '*Temporale* narratives', 429–30, 436–7, 454.

3 For example, Oxford, Bodleian MS Rawl. Poet. 225 (STC 14716), Görlach's Br (*Textual Tradition*, pp. 109–11), contains, alongside *SEL* texts, a life of Barbara in quatrains (fols 2r–5r), a non-*SEL Theophilus* in stanzaic abbacc tail rhyme (fols 11r–15r), a St Nicholas with a continuation in rhymed prose (fols 34v–42v) and a *Margaret* drawn from the *SEL* tradition but with a unique version of the dragon-fight in tail-rhyme stanzas (fols 117v–120r).

4 See Christopher Cannon, 'Monastic productions', in David Wallace (ed.), *The Cambridge History of Medieval English Literature* (Cambridge: Cambridge University Press, 1999), pp. 316–48 (pp. 340–8). Among anonymous legendaries, see (for Oxford, Bodleian MS Douce 114) Jennifer N. Brown, *Three Women of Liège. A Critical Edition of and Commentary on the Middle English Lives of Elizabeth of Spalbeek, Christina Mirabilis, and Marie d'Oignies*, Medieval Women Texts and Contexts 23 (Turnhout: Brepols, 2008); for the East Anglian legendary in Cambridge, Cambridge University Library, Add. MS 2604, see Virginia Blanton and Veronica O'Mara, forthcoming.

5 For the regional distribution of *SEL* manuscripts see maps in Görlach, *Textual Tradition*, pp. 304–5, repr. in his *Studies* as map 2 (p. 28) and fig. 4.2 (p. 39). Other texts (including romance, biblical verse, poems by

Lydgate, lyrics, doctrinal and devotional treatises, theological encyclo-
paedias, homilies etc.) found with the *SEL* in fifteenth-century manuscripts can be compiled from Görlach: see his manuscripts Ax, Az, Cy,
Dy, Hx, Hy, Hz, Ly, Lz, Mz, Ox, Qz, Ry, Tx, Uy and their descriptions (Görlach, *Textual Tradition*, pp. 117–27, also his W, p. 104).

6 For study of another fifteenth-century manuscript, MS Tanner 17, see
Winstead in this volume.

7 The manuscript's unique items are edited by Carl Horstmann,
'Des Ms. Bodl. 779 jüngere Zusatzlegenden zur südlichen
Legendensammlung', in *Archiv für das Studium der neueren Sprachen
und Literaturen*, 82 (1889), 307–53, 369–422 (all except its *temporale*
Holy Innocents). Two lives are edited by Diane Speed, 'Text and
meaning in the "*South English Legendary* Lives of Æthelwold"',
Notes and Queries, 41:3 (1994), 295–301; and 'The Middle English
life of Saint Hilarion', *Parergon*, 29 (1981), 8–14. For its *temporale*
see Pickering, '*Temporale* narratives'; Pickering, 'Expository *temporale*'; Pickering (ed.), *Nativity*; Pickering (ed.), *Ministry*; Pickering
'"Defence of Women"'.

8 Liszka, *SELS*, p. 259 (p. 39 above) and appendix 14; Görlach, *Textual
Tradition*, pp. 76–7. For a valuable new model of *SEL* compilation, see
the essay by Robins in this volume.

9 The group of *temporale* narratives that make up the so-called *Southern
Passion* (see Abbreviations) has been split between fols 241v–241r and
fols 170r–175v. In the latter segment, Whitsun, Corpus Christi and
the Ascension follow each other, between the beginning of 'Matthias'
(abandoned on fol. 170r) and the end of 'Matthias' on fol. 177r, with
175v–177r left blank.

10 Large, thick (312 folios plus two fly leaves) and strongly bound (with
wooden boards, a leather cover and strengtheners, now separately con-
served) added into various quires, and pages of 290 × 200 mm with a
writing area 248 ×157, Bodley 779 is a very big paper manuscript, put
together by someone, who, if not a professional scribe, was familiar
with the conventions of books and book making. The whole work is
written in one hand (though in several stints with changes of ink and
pen), with an initial table of contents (the first half in the same hand
as the manuscript's texts), and capitals and rubrics coloured and often
boxed and flourished in various combinations of red and blue.

11 See, e.g., Karen A. Winstead, *John Capgrave's Fifteenth Century*
(Philadelphia: University of Pennsylvania Press, 2007), ch. 3, esp.
pp. 60–8; Fiona Somerset, 'Here, there and everywhere? Wycliffite
conceptions of the Eucharist and Chaucer's "other" Lollard joke', in
Fiona Somerset, Jill C. Havens and Derek C. Pittard (eds), *Lollards
and Their Influence* (Woodbridge: Boydell Press, 2003), pp. 127–38.

12 For a lucid overview, see Anne Hudson, 'Preface' to Somerset et al.
(eds), *Lollards and Their Influence*, pp. 1–6.

13 Like other late medieval *SEL*s, Bodley 779 adds in native British saints and contains the only extant *SEL* texts of several other saints (see n. 15 below). On the *SEL* and British saints (not discussed here), see the essays by Blanton and Sanok in this volume; Katherine J. Lewis, 'History, historiography and rewriting the past', in Salih (ed.), *Companion to Middle English Hagiography*, pp. 122–40.

14 Görlach, *Textual Tradition*, table, pp. 306–9: Clement appears in seventeen of twenty-four manuscripts, exceeded only by St Peter's twenty-three out of twenty-four. Sylvester occurs in seven (including MS Bodley 779).

15 A run of December saints (from Lucy to John) follows the main insertion of popes in Bodley 779: see Table 18.1 below and Liszka, *SELS*, p. 279 (pp. 61–2 above). Outside the main grouping of papal saints by type (between fols 231r and 238r), Popes Calixtus and Evaristus are included earlier in Bodley 779, in their October calendrical order, along with other unique lives (Winifred, Hilarion, Chrysanthus and Daria, Crispin and Crispinian). The non-papal saints grouped with the main run of popes – Paul the Hermit, Remigius, Emerentiana, Saturnin and Sisinus, Simplicius and Faustinus, Abdon and Sennen, Germanus – are also unique texts. But given the reversion to the calendar for December immediately following in the manuscript (fol. 244v), this is not a case of the compiler's having decided to add in these unique lives after copying the rest of the legendary.

16 This is the same pope but a different version of the life from the Sylvester of the earlier *SEL* (ed. Horstmann, no. 58, pp. 391–2).

17 Elizabeth Archibald, *Incest and the Medieval Imagination* (Oxford: Clarendon Press, 2001), pp. 28–31.

18 Dyan Elliott, *Fallen Bodies: Pollution, Sexuality, and Demonology in the Middle Ages* (Philadelphia: University of Pennsylvania Press, 1999), pp. 137–9.

19 Oxford, Bodleian MS Rawlinson Poet. 225 (later fifteenth century) and London, BL MS Cotton Cleopatra D. ix (fifteenth century) with an *SEL* Becket, Theophilus, Cecilia (see Görlach, *Textual Tradition*, pp. 109–12). *Gregorius* is included in the Vernon manuscript's *SEL* selections (MS Oxford, Bodleian MS Eng. Poet.a.1, c. 1380, fols 44r–47b), see 'Gregorius auf dem Stein aus MS Vernon', ed. Carl Horstmann, *Archiv*, 55 (1876), pp. 405–38; in the Auchinleck MS, fol. 1; and in a Kendal School Grammar Fragment. For Anglo-Norman and continental versions see *La Vie de pape saint Grégoire: huit versions françaises médiévales de la Légende du bon pécheur*, ed. Hendrik Sol (Amsterdam: Rodopi, 1977).

20 For a further spectacular example of a papal penitent included in a fifteenth-century *SEL* collection (Oxford, Bodleian MS Laud Misc. 463), see 'Die Legenden von Celestin und Susanna: I Celestin', ed. Carl Horstmann, *Anglia*, I (1878), 55–85.

21 Marc Shell, 'The want of incest in the human family, or, kin and kind in Christian thought', *Journal of the American Academy of Religion*, 62:3 (1994), 625–50.

22 One distinction between the incorporeality of angels and demons versus humanity's incarnate status in the later Middle Ages is that angels are not created by reproduction as a single angelic race, or derived from a single angel as humans are from one human. Humanity, through its corporeal privilege (the incarnateness shared with its creator) could have access to grace through the remission of sins, even if the body was the very means of transmitting original sin in reproduction: for good angels this was unnecessary; for fallen ones, unavailable. See further Elliott, *Fallen Bodies*, ch. 6, pp. 127–56.

23 '*Sermo in festo corporis Christi*', ed. Carl Horstmann, *Archiv*, 82 (1889), 167- 97 (pp. 186–7, ll. 571–7).

24 See n. 14 above.

25 These features are retained and emphasized from the chief source, the *Liber pontificalis*, accepted as the standard history from the twelfth to the fifteenth centuries. I have used *Liber pontificalis nella recensione di Pietro Guglielmo OSB e del card. Pandolfo, glossato da Pietro Bohier OSB, vescovo di Orvieto*; with Introduction, text, indexes edited by U. Přerovský, *Studia Gratiana* 21, 22, 23 (Rome: Libreria Ateneo Salesiano, 1978).

26 For Calixtus, see Horstmann, 'Des MS Bodl. 779', pp. 328–31 (from whom quotations are henceforth taken for ease of reference, unless manuscript foliation or position is significant); *Liber pontificalis*, II, no. 17, p. 25 (further details taken from the *vita* in AA.SS 14 Oct, p. 439).

27 Unless otherwise noted, all citations are to page and line numbers. Cf *Lib. pont.* II, no. 12, p. 20. The other main events in Bodley's Anicetus biography are his martyrdom at the order of the emperor (Horstmann 'Des MS Bodl. 779', p. 399, ll. 59–60) and his ordination of clergy (p. 399, ll. 63–5).

28 A highly summarized account from *Lib. pont.* II, no. 82, 231–5. Otherwise Leo's life is marked only by the appearance of a blood red moon on 'cher Thorsday' (p. 381, l. 28) and the ordination of clergy (p. 381, ll. 35–6).

29 *Lib. pont.* II, no. 42, pp. 91–4.

30 This is different from earlier *SEL* Lives and largely a debate with twelve Jews; see Horstmann, 'Des MS Bodl. 779', pp. 388–94: much abbreviated from the *vita* in Mombritius, *Sanctuarium*, Milan, 1477, II, fols 279v–293v (at 283v–293v).

31 Much expanded: cf. *Lib. pont.* no. 13, p. 21, ll. 4–5. There is a blank space in Bodley 779 in lines 33–4: Horstmann plausibly supplies 'male'.

32 See Katherine L. French, 'Women in the late medieval English parish', in Mary Erler and Maryanne Kowaleski (eds), *Gendering the Master Narrative: Women and Power in the Middle Ages* (Ithaca: Cornell University Press, 2003), pp. 156–73; also the lyric 'To onpreyse wemen' (IMEV 3782): ed. R. L. Greene, *The Early English Carols*, 2nd edn (Oxford: Clarendon Press, 1977), no. 396, p. 234.

33 Emma Campbell, *Medieval Saints' Lives: The Gift, Kinship and Community in Old French Hagiography* (Woodbridge: D. S. Brewer, 2008), ch. 3, pp. 71–95 (esp. 80, 71).

34 See John Hine Mundy, 'The conciliar movement and the Council of Constance', in *The Council of Constance: The Unification of the Church*, trans. Louise Ropes Loomis, ed. and annotated John Hine Mundy and Kennerly M. Woody (New York and London: Columbia University Press, 1961), pp. 3–51; for an overview of later developments, Nelson H. Minnich, 'From Constance to Trent: a historical overview', in his *Councils of the Catholic Reformation, Pisa I (1409) to Trent (1545–63)* (Aldershot and Burlington, VT: Ashgate, 2007), no. 1, pp. 1–37.

35 On Wyclif's extension of the doctrine of fraternal correction within the church to include the possibility of lay correction of the papacy, see Edwin D. Craun, *Ethics and Power in Medieval English Reformist Writing* (Cambridge: Cambridge University Press, 2010), pp. 86–9, 95–6. See further Vincent Gillespie and Khantik Ghosh (eds), *After Arundel: Religious Writing in Fifteenth-Century England* (forthcoming).

36 See pp. 406–8 above and n. 20.

37 For the *Chronicon* of Polonus (Martin of Troppau, Dominican, d. 1278) see Ludwig Weiland (ed.), *Martini Oppaviensis Chronicon Pontificum et Imperatorum*, MGH SS 22 (Hanover: Impensis Bibliopolii Avlici Hahniani, 1872), 377–482. The *Chronicon* is extant in about 425 manuscripts of which at least ninety-one circulated in England: the text itself draws on the *Liber Pontificalis* as a source. See further Wolfgang-Valentin Ikas, 'Martinus Polonus' *Chronicle of the Popes and Emperors*: a medieval best-seller and its neglected influence on English medieval chroniclers', *English Historical Review*, 116:2 (2001), 327–41.

38 For example, one *Chronicle* manuscript notes apropos Pope Leo's regulations on baptism and godparents that 'natheles Seynt Austyn seith that woxun men, cristened, schulen answere for hemself, nether han nede of godfadres as the lawe techith': *The Chronicles of Rome: An Edition of the Middle English Chronicle of Popes and Emperors and the Lollard Chronicle*, ed. Dan Embree (Woodbridge: Boydell Press, 1998), p. 119, PL 63–5, also Em 67–9 and p. 222 n.

39 Embree, *Chronicles*, p. 138, Em 661.

40 For *temporale* studies and editions, see n. 7 above. Quotations here are from Horstmann, 'Des MS Bodl. 779' by page and line number: or from the manuscript for texts with counterparts elsewhere in *SEL*.

41 Pickering, '*Temporale* narratives', p. 428, n. 8; Bodley 779, St John, fol. 212v, ll. 39–43.

42 Otherwise only in MS Egerton 2810 (Pickering, 'Expository *temporale*', p.12); edited in Horstmann, 'Des MS. Bodl. 779', pp. 307–12.

43 For a more detailed and theologically sophisticated sense of the doubts against which Bodley 779 argues, see e.g. David Aers, 'Walter Brut's theology of the sacrament of the altar', in Somerset et al. (eds), *Lollards and Their Influence*, pp. 115–26.

44 Printed in *Southern Passion*, pp. 60–1, 1,649–1, 670 from Cambridge, Magdalene College, MS Pepys 2344, collated with, *inter alia*, MS Bodley 779. For an earlier version, see Pickering (ed.), *Ministry*, and for the three kinds of blood, ibid., pp. 181(2583)–182(2604). On interest in the Holy Blood in England, see Nicholas Vincent, *The Holy Blood: King Henry III and the Westminster Blood Relic* (Cambridge: Cambridge University Press, 2001), pp. 87–8; Caroline Walker Bynum, *Wonderful Blood* (University Park, PA: Penn State Press, 2007), pp. 85–90.

45 For comparable contemporary arguments see e.g. Nicholas Love, *Treatise on the Sacraments*, in Michael Sargent (ed.), *Nicholas Love, The Mirror of the Blessed Life of Jesus Christ* (Exeter: Exeter University Press, 2005), p. 225, 33–8; p. 227, 8–12; p. 233.

46 Kathryn Kerby-Fulton, *Books Under Suspicion: Censorship and Tolerance of Late Medieval Revelatory Writing in England* (Notre Dame, IN: University of Notre Dame Press, 2006), p. 248. The insistence on testing visions had, as Kerby-Fulton shows, the effect of communicating awareness of the key conciliar issues (see pp. 258–9, 260).

47 In Vernon, the sermon becomes a collective papal biography as the rituals of the mass are elaborated throughout the history of the papacy, see Horstmann, 'Sermo in festo', pp. 183–5, ll. 415–510. For some account of the *SEL* compiler's customizing in the Vernon manuscript, see N. F. Blake, 'Vernon Manuscript: contents and organisation', in D. Pearsall (ed.), *Studies in the Vernon Manuscript* (Cambridge: D. S. Brewer, 1990), pp. 45–59 (48–50).

48 See Sue Powell, 'The *Festial*: the priest and his parish', in Clive Burgess and Eamon Duffy (ed.), *The Parish in Late Medieval England*, Harlaxton Medieval Studies XIV (Donnington: Shaun Tyas, 2006), pp. 160–76 (at 160, 163).

49 First sentence from Oxford, University College MS 97, fol. 89r, others from Princeton, Princeton University Library, MS Garrett 143, fols 10v–11r, both quoted by Jill C. Havens, 'Determining heresy in Middle English texts', in Helen Barr and Ann Hutchison (eds), *Text and Controversy from Wyclif to Bale: Essays in Honour of Anne Hudson* (Turnhout: Brepols, 2005), pp. 340, 345–6.

50 *Myrc's Instructions for Parish Priests*, ed. Edward Peacock, EETS ES 31 (London: Kegan Paul, Trench, Trübner, 1868), p. 6, ll. 163–87.

51 Angus McIntosh et al (eds), *A Linguistic Atlas of Late Mediaeval English*, 4 vols (Aberdeen and New York: Aberdeen University Press, 1986), III, LP 5470. Görlach argued for a consistent superimposition of the compiler's dialect throughout (*Textual Tradition*, p. 76), but Pickering notes that the match is not always even (for instance, the alternative form *hy* rather than this LP's more frequent *þey* for the third person plural pronoun: see Pickering, '"Defence of Women"', p. 161, n. 17). That the *SEL* circulated in Hampshire was established by Görlach (*Textual Tradition*, pp. 78 and map, p. 305): according to an inscription on fols 1v–2r of Cambridge, Corpus Christi College MS 145 (MS C, one of D'Evelyn and Mill's base manuscripts), John Kateryngton, an Augustinian canon of Southwick, Hampshire, gifted this manuscript in the late fourteenth or early fifteenth century to his community. No clear candidate emerges among the North Hampshire religious houses, female or male, for the Bodley 779 scribe, though Titchfield abbey (Premonstratensian) has a medieval catalogue entry thought to refer to the *SEL* ('Legenda sanctorum que dicitur Aurea in anglicis', see David N. Bell (ed.), The *Libraries of the Cistercians, Gilbertines, and Premonstratensians*, Corpus of British Medieval Library Catalogues 3 (London: The British Library, 1992), p. 200).

52 Bodley 779's unique life of St Oswin, king of Deira, d. 651 (fols 208r–212v) ends with a commemoration of Robert de Mowbray (earl of Northumberland, d. 1095, later buried in St Albans abbey, c. 1120), as the founder of Tynemouth (fol. 212v, ll. 31–8; Horstmann, 'Des Ms Bodl. 779', p. 378, ll. 505–12). Oswin was culted at St Albans as well as Tynemouth, but otherwise only (and more contentiously) at Durham, who claimed his relics: Paul Hayward, 'Sanctity and lordship in twelfth-century England: Saint Albans, Durham and the cult of Saint Oswine, king and martyr', *Viator*, 30 (1999), 105–44. On the Oswin life see also Robins, above, pp. 196, 200.

53 See e.g. P. J. Horner, 'Benedictines and preaching in fifteenth-century England', *Revue Bénédictine*, 99 (1989), 313–32; James G. Clark, *A Monastic Renaissance at St Albans: Thomas Walsingham and His Circle, c. 1350–1440* (Oxford: Clarendon Press, 2004), pp. 252–63. Eleven of Bodley 779's unique papal biographies are in the same section of the manuscript as the major abbey saints, St Alban and St Oswin (Pope Leo and two other June saints follow Oswin, and Pope Silverius follows Alban just before the main group of nine popes: Table 18.I above and Liszka, *SELS*, above, p. 61). A rare inclusion for the *SEL*, Bodley 779's *Barlaam and Josaphat* (fols 289v–290v), with its account of a king's hatred of monasticism and the eventual triumph of the monks, also takes on special resonance in the context of a wealthy monastery.

54 Clark, *Monastic Renaissance*, p. 253.

55 The compiler-scribe keeps local references in, for instance, St Frideswide's life (noting her Augustinian priory church and the

Dominicans in Oxford, fol. 281, ll. 19–20). Benedictine nuns are particularly mentioned in the manuscript's *Nativity of Mary and Christ*, with the Virgin born in Jerusalem 'Besyde the yate of Josephat;   that now an abbey is / In the honour of seint Anneth of blake nonnerye' (fol. 271v); and the manuscript makes unique additions to the *Southern Passion*'s 'Defence of Women', arguing that all souls should be brought to individual not gender stereotypical account (see Pickering, '"Defence of Women"', pp. 168–71, 27–54, 62–116; translated in Alcuin Blamires (ed.), *Woman Defamed and Woman Defended: An Anthology of Medieval Texts* (Oxford: Oxford University Press, 1999), pp. 244–8).

Part V
Performance

19

Black humour in the *South English Legendary*

Oliver Pickering

Black humour – by which I mean laughing at someone's death or serious injury – is an aspect of the style of the so-called Outspoken *South English Legendary* Poet, the notably creative writer who made the major contribution to the expansion of the early *SEL* into its more developed form, still before the year 1300. As I have shown elsewhere, he was apparently perfectly capable of writing in the *SEL*'s usual septenary narrative style, but he had the distinctive ability to construct lengthy verse paragraphs with the sense overlapping the usual couplet boundaries, and he characteristically includes lively anecdotes or other incidents which allow him to deploy what I have called his outspoken style.[1] In this exaggerated mode – often drawing on a personal repertoire of stock phrases – he castigates or sardonically mocks bad characters and sympathizes with the persecuted, often with close reference to contemporary medieval daily life. This involvement with his characters is strengthened by the insertion of comments and exhortations addressed explicitly to his audience, an aspect of narrative performance seemingly intended to get them involved also.

A typical example of the poet's black humour is a rather gruesome passage from the life of St Alban, in which the saint's beheader is punished by his eyes falling out:

Ac the tormentour that smot of   Seint Albones heved
He ne dorste noght yilpe therof muche   him were betere habbe
                                     bileved
For tho he smot of is heved   right in thulke stonde
Is eiyne folle out of is heved and ther with he fel to gronde
Is bigete was wel lite ther   it fel doun al byhinde
He mighte segge wanne he comth hom   'War, her comth the
                                       blynde'.[2]
                                          (I, 241, 85–90)

(But the torturer who smote off St Alban's head didn't dare brag about it much – it would have been better for him if he'd believed [in God]. Because when he smote off the saint's head his eyes immediately fell out of his own head and he fell to the ground. His benefit was very small – it was lost in the falling down. He might well say when he arrived home, 'Watch out, here comes a blind man.')

This is fairly crude stuff, underlined by the presence of repetitions and fillers. But it is lively, memorable, sensational and sardonically humorous, helped by the ironic understatements and the clear implication that the torturer's physical blindness signifies that he is also morally and spiritually blind, failing to understand what he has done.

Quite often the bad character whose failure the poet mocks is the devil, and in these cases the term black humour, as defined above, does not quite apply, because the devil is always able to return for a second go. But the striking description of St Margaret's defeat of the devil exhibits marked similarities of phrasing with the passage from St Alban – the same style is at work:

He[o] nom him bi is luther pol   and harde him to gronde caste
And hure right fot sette anon   up is necke bihinde faste
'Thou devel', he[o] sede, 'that ert so strong   fol of prute and
                                                                                      onde
Thou were betere habbe iheved atom   thanne icome me to fonde
Buy doun, thou ert overcome   Ichelle on the stonde
Thou might telle atom that thou were   under a maidens honde.'
Faste he[o] bond this foule wight   and scorgede him wel sore
Grislich he yal and ofte sede,   'Hende maide, thin ore!'
                                                                    (I, 297–8, 177–84)

(She grabbed him by the hair of his wicked head and threw him roughly to the ground, and at once set her right foot firmly on the back of his neck. 'You devil', she said, 'who are so powerful, and full of pride and envy, you would have done better to have stayed at home than come and tested me. Bow down, you have been defeated – I shall stand on top of you. You'll be able to tell them at home that you were under a maiden's control.' She tightly bound this foul creature and scourged him severely. He yelled horribly and frequently said, 'Gracious maid, have mercy!')

Here again we get the formula that it would have been better for the victim to have done something else, in this case (as elsewhere) to have been at home, where it is also envisaged that he will tell his story, as in the passage from St Alban.[3]

Another example, from the life of St Peter, concerns the pagan sorcerer Simon Magus. Peter commands the devils who are bearing Simon Magus aloft to let him go, so that he is dashed to pieces, his death an object of the poet's mockery:

Donward mid thulke worde	he com seily anon
And fel doun that al he todrof	fleiss and fel and bon
'Wat is nou, sire wilde gos?'	woder hadde he ithoght
His fetheren were alle to feble,	is art ne halp him noght
He fel doun to is owe kunde	as he moste nede
'Hail min ape!' wat wolde he ther?	him com sone is mede.

(I, 261–2, 421–6)

(With that word he immediately came sailing downwards, and fell [to earth] so that his flesh, skin and bone were all shattered. 'How are things now, Sir Wild Goose?' – What was he thinking of? His feathers were all too weak; his magic didn't help him. He fell down to join those of his own kind [i.e. in hell], as he was bound to do. 'Hail, my ape!' – What was he trying to do? He soon got his reward.)

The sardonic comments and mocking characterizations (goose, ape), in interjected direct speech, add to the passage's liveliness.

The same style of mockery, again with direct address breaking without warning into the complicated mixture of comment and narrative, is found in a markedly similar episode in the life of St Justine, where the pagan Cyprian, possessed also by the devil, turns himself into a sparrow, flies to the rafters, but then necessarily resumes his proper shape after being spotted by the saint:

He sat and hovede as an ape	ofschamed he was sore
Vor bote he breke his necke	he ne mighte adoun mid al is lore
Yerne he criede and ofte seide	'Justine, now thin ore!'
What wolde this sparewe	whare were hire fetheren tho?
Hail, ape! what wolde he there?	whoder thourte go?
A feble cok he was at roste	whi nolde he adoun vleo?
He mighte sitte and capie there	and is owe schendnesse iseo
'What woste', this maide sede there,	'whi artou so gret ape?
Nere me vor schame ther scholde	mani man on the cape?'[4]

(He sat lurking like an ape, very ashamed, because without breaking his neck he couldn't get down, despite all his learning. He cried out earnestly, and often said, 'Justine, now have mercy!' What was this sparrow meaning to do? Where were his feathers then? 'Hail, ape!' – What did he want up there? Where did he think to go? He was a feeble roosting cock – why wouldn't he fly down? He might as

well sit there and stare, and regard his own shamefulness. 'What are
you thinking of?', this maiden said, 'Why are you such a great fool?
Wouldn't it be shameful for many people to stare at you there?')

But in this case the saint relents and fetches a ladder, so that
Cyprian can climb down safely.

But the bad characters whose downfall is mocked normally
lack special powers, like St Alban's torturer in the first example.
The poet takes particular delight in their wicked devices being
turned against them, as in the life of St Katherine, where (in the
well-known story) an angel with a sword destroys the razor-sharp
wheels that the emperor has set up to tear the saint's flesh, with the
result that thousands of his own men are slain:

> This angel with a drawe swerd   this wheles al toheu
> And the peces flowe aboute   as corn whan me hit seu
> And smyte on this lithere men   wel harde to the grounde
> That four thousend ther were aslawe   in a lute stounde
> Ye, for Gode, that was wel   ther hi mighte lurne
> To fighte aghe Jesu Crist   mid here false querne
> To wende aboute here rasours   the holie maide todrawe
> Hi nemighte hit noght wel biliye   that were ibroght of dawe.
>
> (II, 540, 229–36)

(This angel hacked these wheels to pieces with a drawn sword, and
the pieces flew about like corn when it is sown, and knocked these
wicked men violently to the ground, so that four thousand were slain
there in a short while. Yes, that was good in God's sight – they might
learn there to fight against Jesus Christ with their wicked mill [i.e.
the instrument of torture] and to make their razors ready to tear the
holy maiden's body! Those who were killed couldn't very well deny
the truth of this.)

The lesson that the wicked are to learn from their actions is
expressed ironically as a positive (learn to fight against Jesus
Christ) rather than the expected negative (learn *not* to do so).[5]

In the context of black humour, the verb *biliye* in the final line of
the passage from St Katherine might be thought a form of *bilaugh
/ bilauh*, 'to laugh at', as the *Middle English Dictionary* has it when
quoting the above line from St Katherine (s.v. *bilaughen*, v.), but
this would be unusual dialectally, and it seems better to associate it
with ModE *belie*, 'deny the truth of'.[6] This same rather rare word
(*MED*, s.v. *bilien*, v. (2)) occurs in a passage in the life of St John
the Baptist in which the poet celebrates the death of Herodias and
Salome, and here the meaning 'deny the truth of' is not in question:

And he[o] [i.e. Herodias] fel doun ded anon   as oure Loverd is
                                                                              wreche caste
Me thincth he[o] ne dorste noght bilighe   hure ssreuhede
                                                                              attelaste
[Ne] the foule best hire doghter nother,   for as he[o] yede a day
And pleide upe yse in hure game   as monyman isay
That is tobrak an under hure   and he[o] adreinte anon
And wende forth adevelwey   bothe fleiss and bon . . .
. . . Uvel hy tombede attelaste   nere hom noght so lothe
Nou day [that] hom muche bymene   for ssrewen it were bothe.
                                                              (I, 243–4, 57–62, 65–6)

(And she fell down dead immediately, as our Lord carried out his
vengeance. It seems to me she didn't in the end dare deny the truth
of her villainy, nor the wretched beast her daughter either, because
as she went one day and played a game upon the ice, as many people
saw, the ice broke under her, and she drowned immediately and
went straight to the devil, both flesh and bone . . . They danced
badly in the end; that wouldn't have been so difficult for them. Now
curse those who feel much sorrow for them, for they were both
villains.)

Herodias falls down dead after being blown on by St John's
decapitated head, but Salome dies as the result of a game, playing
upon the ice. The idea of play or game – often with the bad characters matched against the good, and losing – underlies many
of these passages, and is one element of the poet's humorous
technique.[7]

Quite often the poet takes pleasure in the wicked being blinded,
as in the passage quoted first in this essay, from St Alban. There
is another example towards the end of the life of St Anastasia, following the uproarious episode in which a pagan justice mistakenly
assaults dirty pots and pans instead of three Christian virgins and
is then set upon at length by his own men, who take him for a devil
– an example of the humour of humiliation rather than of black
humour, but which includes another instance of the 'he/you were
better . . .' formulation, noticed earlier:

'Oure loverd', hi sede, 'nevere thou nere   thi mighte the is
                                                                              bynome
The were betere atom in helle   thanne amang us habbe icome'
                                                              (II, 587, 47–8)

('You were never', they said, 'our master. You've been stripped of
your power. It were better for you to be at home in hell than to have
come among us here.')

In the blinding episode the saint's victim is the pagan second husband the emperor has forced upon her (the justice's fate is recalled, with relish, at the same time):[8]

> He com ferst to this holy maide   and wolde hure cusse in pleye
> And ar he it evere mighte do   is eiyene wende out beye
> He stod as a witles man   he ne dorste go for eye
> To is maumes he wende anon   ac me ladde him bi the weie
> Me thingth so he moste nede   other he moste steppe amys
> To love hi hadde feble hap   the Justice and he iwis
> The on bedaubed and tobete   and the other suthe ablend
> Lite was, me thingth, hare bigete   hi helde ham bothe issend . . .
> . . . Me ladde thane wrecche hom agen   and as sone as he hom
>   com
> He fel doun ded as a stok   and thane heie wei to helle nom.
>   (II, 589, 89–96, 101–2)

(First he approached this holy maiden intending to kiss her amorously, but before he could do so both his eyes went out. He stood like a man deprived of his senses, and dared not move for fear. He thought at once of his idols, but had to be led along the street – it seems to me he had no choice, or else he would have gone astray. The justice and he certainly had little luck in love, the one covered in dirt and beaten, and the other subsequently blinded. It seems to me their gain was small; they both considered themselves shamed . . . The wretch was led home again, and as soon as he arrived there he fell down dead as a post and took the high way to hell.)

As in other examples, the use of ironic understatement ('had little luck in love', 'their gain was small') reinforces the generally light-hearted tone. The second of these statements ('Lite was, me thingth, hare bigete') is very close to a half-line in the passage from St Alban, 'Is bigete was wel lite ther'.[9]

There is another blinding in the life of St Kenelm, even more similar to that in St Alban, in that the wicked queen's eyes are described as bursting from her head while she reads out a curse from the Psalter:

> For right as he[o] that vers radde   out borste bothe hure eiye
> And falle adoun up hure sauter   as mony men iseie
> And that was, me thincth, wel ido   day that hure bymene
> Heo bylou noght hure tricherie   hure bigete was wel lene.
>   (I, 291, 355–8)

(For as soon as she read that verse, both her eyes burst out and fell down on to the Psalter, as many people saw. That was well done,

it seems to me: curse those who feel sorry for her. She didn't get a
laugh out of her treachery – her benefit was decidedly slender.)

Amongst other familiar sardonic or ironic phrases, the verse form
biliye, argued above to mean 'deny the truth of', now appears
as *bylou* and so may well mean 'laugh at' (*MED*, s.v. *bilaughen*),
as translated here, although the other sense would still fit the
context.[10] If the wicked queen is indeed unable to laugh at what
she has done, the motif is similar to those occasions in Old English
poetry in which a feature of ignominious defeat is that the van-
quished are described as having no occasion to laugh.[11] In the case
of St Kenelm one implication is that we, the audience, are in the
opposite, victorious position of being able to exult at the queen's
plight.

A final example of delight in the blinding of a wicked character –
this time a king – comes from the unpublished life of St Frideswide
of Oxford. Once again there are striking parallels with the passage
from St Alban:

> Anon he ablende ther   as he bigan this strif,
> And bilevede ther the sori wrech   blynd al is lif,
> And wende hom tame inou,   is prowesse was bihynd;
> Me might segge war he com,   'War, her cometh the blynde'.[12]

(He was immediately blinded as soon as he began this hostility, and
the sorry wretch remained blind all his life. He went home tamely
enough; his prowess remained behind. People might say wherever he
came, 'Watch out, here comes a blind man'.)

Line 4 is particularly close to line 6 in the St Alban passage ('He
mighte segge wanne he comth hom   "War, her comth the
blynde" '), though in St Frideswide the scene-setting of 'home'
occurs in the previous line, where there is also a half-line, 'is prow-
esse was bihynd', which recalls 'it fel doun al byhinde' from St
Alban, line 5. And we may also note the presence in St Frideswide
– though it occurs quite often in this poet's contributions to the
SEL – of a formulation similar to a couplet in the life of St Peter
(see above p. 121), where the audience's reaction is also being
invoked or anticipated, namely:

> Nou an alle develwei,   'Amen', seggeth alle,
> And ne come he never in gode stude   in chirch ne in halle!

(Now may he go wholly to the devil: 'Amen', say everybody. May he
never turn up at a favourable time (?) in church or in hall.)

Despite dealing with death and serious maiming, there is little doubt that the passages discussed above were regarded in the late thirteenth century as highly enjoyable. This poet is dealing in entertainment, and one can suppose that the style he adopts both involves the poem's audience emotionally and unites them in mocking opposition to the bad characters and in a shared sense of moral superiority. But although it is stimulating for the modern reader to encounter such a lively and evocative writer so early in the Middle English canon, we have also to admit that this is not sophisticated verse. As is very clear, the poet, when in black humour mode, keeps reusing the same words and phrases. The liveliness, the outspokenness, masks the fact that his style on these occasions is really quite set, dealing in stock characters, to some extent stock situations, and to quite a large degree stock language; although some of his linguistic idiom may well be his own invention.

It is unclear how the characteristic features of his verbal mockery bear on the question of the make-up of the audience for whom he was writing. I have expressed the view that the *South English Legendary*, in its first developed form, was possibly written for the instruction of novice or unlearned religious, but that the audience (or potential audience) had widened by the time the Outspoken Poet became involved – quite likely to include laity, who may in part, or in time, have been readers rather than listeners. It is hard to imagine quite complicated passages of long-lined narrative verse like the episode of St Justine and the sparrow, peppered with comment and direct speech, being read out successfully unless by a skilled and practised performer. It may be that such passages were easier to take in when written on the page – and that phrases like '"Amen", seggeth alle' or 'Wy sitte ye so stille?' are literary devices, designed to give the impression of a listening audience but actually to entertain a readership, while also supplying useful pauses in the narrative.[13]

But leaving such questions aside as ultimately unanswerable, I want to suggest that this style of crude, debunking black humour, distinguished, in the hands of the Outspoken Poet, by great surface liveliness and interplay with a real or imagined audience, is what we might expect from English writing of the late thirteenth century.[14] The style falls far short of the subtlety of a Chaucer or a Gawain-poet (who treats a beheading game very differently), but a hundred years is a long time in terms of Middle English verse composition and, one may think, of audience sophistication.

Before looking at a number of contemporary texts to support this contention, it should be noted that there is of course a long tradition of grotesque or incongruous humour in saints' lives, stretching back to the Anglo-Saxon period and earlier. This commonly involves the torturers being made to look ridiculous by being unable to carry out their threats (because the saints are spiritually stronger),[15] but it sometimes extends to the saint joking with his torturer, as famously in the case of St Laurence, where in Ælfric's version – as also in the *SEL*, and other texts – he suggests to his tormentors that they should roast him on both sides to make sure he is fully cooked.[16] Even the story of the justice in the life of St Anastasia being humiliated by his night-time assault on what turn out to be kitchen pots and pans appears in the *Old English Martyrology*, and elsewhere.[17] It is therefore not surprising, with these traditions behind him, that the Outspoken Poet should play up the black humour in the saints' lives.

The added feature of mockery, of sardonic comment on the failure or defeat of bad characters – sometimes by the narrator, sometimes by the characters themselves or their adversaries – is well known in Old Norse narrative, and is again found from time to time in Old English. Examples include Byrhtnoth laughing when he gains his first success over the Danes during the Battle of Maldon, which, although a laugh of triumph, implies underlying scorn at their defeat, and Ham laughing at Noah's nakedness, surely mockingly, in the poem known as *Genesis A*.[18]

Among other traditions is the human tendency to make fun of people seen as grotesque or sub-human, which leads to laughing at monsters or devils who could do us harm, to bring them down to size; an example from the *SEL* St Margaret was quoted earlier. An inversion of this is when the devils or torturers themselves become the game-players and perpetrators of black humour – as famously in the medieval English mystery plays, but also in Middle English texts of St Patrick's Purgatory, where the devils use the term 'game' in relation to the various torments of hell, and in the *SEL* life of St Juliana, where the pagan justice decides to 'play another game' when his attempts to have the saint killed come to nothing.[19] And in another twist St Vincent, again in the *SEL*, explicitly regards his own torture as a game, to be played out against his torturers over several rounds, with the rules of the game set by him.[20]

For instances of contemporary Middle English texts dealing in sardonic or ironic black humour, it is natural to turn first to the

Chronicle of Robert of Gloucester, who, as I have argued elsewhere, can very likely be equated with the Outspoken Poet, on
the basis of shared stylistic characteristics.[21] Several of the recur-
rent phrases noted above occur there as well, for example the 'it
would have been better if' and 'he/you might say' formulations.
In the *Chronicle*, however, the characters – as befits a largely historical narrative rather than a contest between good and evil – are
not generally laughed at. Those who fail in their enterprises may
attract comment, but more of a rueful, human kind. Thus after
the Scots suffer defeat at the hands of Constantine II the poet
merely remarks: 'Hii mighte segge wan hii come hom   that hii
hor per founde' ('They might say when they arrived home that
they had met their equals'),[22] and his account of the fate of Robert
Courthose, brother of Henry I, has elements almost of lament
(though Robert is criticized in the lines that follow for going
against God's wishes):

> In prison was Roberd al is lif   and yut ich understonde
> Him adde betere abbe ibe king   of the holi londe
> That he vorsoc vor he nolde   in gret travail be
> Tho adde he reste inou   wanne he ne mighte fle
> Awey seli Robelin   seli Courtehese
> In uvele time thou might sege   reste thou dust chese.
>
> (II, 628, 8804–9)

(Robert spent the rest of his life in prison. In my opinion it would
have been better if he'd been king of the Holy Land, which he
declined because he didn't want to be so burdened. He had plenty
of rest afterwards when he wasn't able to escape. Alas, poor little
Robin, poor Courthose. At a wretched time you might well say
you've chosen a life of ease.)

Closer to black humour is the episode of the legendary King
Bladud's unsuccessful attempt to fly, recalling the manner of
Simon Magus's crashing to the ground:

> And tho he was iflowe an hei   and ne couthe noght alighte
> Adoun mid so gret eir   to then erthe he vel and pighte
> That al to peces he torod   that betere him adde ibe
> Abbe bileved ther doune   than ilerned vor to fle.
>
> (I, 49, 672–5)

(And when he had flown up high and wasn't able to alight, he
crashed to earth with such violence that he was dashed to pieces, so
that it would have been better for him to have remained at home than
to have learned how to fly.)

Two further small examples may be given.[23] A little earlier in the narrative, after King Locrine is killed in battle by forces gathered by his abandoned wife, the poet sardonically comments:

> The king mighte segge er   the wule he was olive
> That in a luther time   he strivede with his wive.
>
> (I, 45, 622–3)[24]

(The king might well have said earlier, while he was alive, that he'd quarrelled with his wife at a bad time.)

And later, when King Arviragus slays the wicked Roman commander Hamo, who had treacherously killed Arviragus's brother Guiderius, it is said of the traitor, 'Atte laste is tricherie   wol lute he bilou', I, 106, 1467 ('In the end he got a very small laugh out of his treachery'), a line closely parallel to 'Heo bylou noght hure tricherie' from the passage from St Kenelm quoted above.

Moving away from the Outspoken Poet, the so-called Kildare poems in British Library, MS Harley 913, written in early fourteenth-century Ireland, contain some well-known humour in the form of satire and fantasy, notably in *The Land of Cockaygne*. One example of black humour in a deadpan, understated style comes in the poem satirizing the ruthless Anglo-Irish bounty-hunter Pers of Bermingham, who is described as hunting the native Irish while they are asleep in their beds:

> Of slep he wold ham wake,
> For ferdnis hi wold quake,
>   And fond to sculk awai.
> For the hire of har bedde,
> He toke har hevid to wedde,
> And so he taght ham plai.
>
> (152, 61–6)[25]

(He would wake them from sleep; they would tremble for terror and try to move away stealthily. For the payment for their beds he took their heads as security, and so he taught them to play games.)

Once more beheading is associated with game-playing.[26] Later, when holding a feast for the O'Connors, Pers does them the honour, so the poem says, of making them all special hoods, which Michael Benskin has interpreted, surely correctly, as leather bags in which their heads will be carried to Dublin for reward:[27]

> Sire Pers sei ham com,
> He receivid al and som,

Noght on iwernd nas.
Sith hoodis he let make,
Noght on nas for-sake,
   Bot al he did ham grace.

                                    (156, 115–20)

(Sir Piers saw them come. He received each one, not one was turned
away. Then he caused hoods to be made, not one was refused, but he
did them all honour.)

That is the nearest the poem gets to describing what was a historical massacre. The grim humour – again related to beheading – is
effected by detachment, irony and extreme understatement, with
the perpetrator not explicitly criticized and the author secure
in the knowledge that his audience would interpret the lines
correctly.

Pers of Bermingham is different from the work of the Outspoken
Poet in lacking authorial comment. Closer in style to the latter
is the romance of *Havelok the Dane*, in which the narrator frequently interposes his voice to curse the bad characters, and
at other times uses an understated, ironic mode of narration,
particularly when Havelok's enemies are being slain, as in the
following examples:

Havelok lifte up the dore-tre,
And at a dint he slow he*m* thre:
Was non of hem that hise hernes
Ne lay ther ute ageyn the sternes.

                                 (49, 1807–10)[28]

(Havelok lifted the door-beam, and with one blow he slew the three
of them. There was none whose brains didn't lie out under the stars.)

And smot him sone ageyn the brest,
That havede he nevere sch[r]ifte of prest.

                                 (49, 1829–30)

(And at once smote him on the breast, with the result that he was
never shrived by a priest.)

And smot him on the sholdre so
That he dide thare undo
Of his brinie ringes mo
Than that Ich kan tellen fro.

                                 (75, 2739–42)

(And smote him on the shoulder to such effect that he undid more
rings of his corslet that I can count.)

We might make a connection here between the laconic style of the Old Norse sagas and the partly Scandinavian subject-matter of *Havelok*, but it is also relevant that the romance is told by a distinctive minstrel-like personality, who calls for a drink at the beginning of the text and shows himself to be engaged with the characters of his poem as well as with his audience – that is, the story is presented as if in performance.[29] And *Havelok*, like the *South English Legendary*, is uncourtly and down-to-earth in its tone, its preoccupations, and its narrative details. It is also preserved in one of the earliest *SEL* manuscripts, Bodleian Library, MS Laud Misc. 108. One should not make too much of this because the Laud version of the *SEL* lacks many of the Outspoken Poet's characteristic interventions in the narrative, but the physical association is none the less striking. From a stylistic point of view *Havelok* and the Outspoken Poet's work are clearly linked by a shared sense of performance and by a rather similar style of humour. They may or may not have been delivered orally, but it can be argued that the successful performance of oppositionary narrative at this date needs partisan humour of the kind described to hold and involve an audience that is being invited to take sides.[30]

Notes

1 See particularly my 'The outspoken *South English Legendary* poet', in A. J. Minnis (ed.), *Late-Medieval Religious Texts and Their Transmission: Essays in Honour of A. I. Doyle* (Cambridge: D. S. Brewer, 1994), pp. 21–37 (reprinted in revised form in the present volume), and 'The *South English Legendary*: teaching or preaching?', *Poetica*, 45 (Spring 1996), 1–14.

2 All quotations are from D'Evelyn and Mill.

3 Cf. T. McAlindon, 'The emergence of a comic type in Middle-English narrative: the devil and giant as buffoon', *Anglia*, 81 (1963), 365–71, where there are numerous references to comparable treatment of the devil in the *SEL*, including the citation of a couplet in the life of St Dunstan – the other notable example – clearly in the style of the Outspoken Poet. In McAlindon's translation (p. 367), 'The wicked fellow would have been better to blow his nose at home. He never came there again to be treated for a cold in his head' (I, 207, 91–2). For a more complete extract from this saint's life, see Pickering, 'Outspoken *South English Legendary* poet', p. 36. McAlindon notes the passage from St Margaret on his p. 366 (and n. 4).

4 I quote from a transcription from BL MS Egerton 1993, fol. 205r, kindly made available to me by Professor Manfred Görlach.

5 See also *Matthew* (II, 401, 137–8), quoted on p. 122 above.

6 As do D'Evelyn and Mill (III, glossary, p. 44).
7 Thompson, *Everyday Saints*, discussing this passage (p. 83), notes the pleasure taken by the poet 'in killing off such very bad women'.
8 The two episodes are discussed in detail and with great verve in *Everyday Saints*, pp. 176–80.
9 Compare also the half-line 'is bigete was wel lute' at the end of the mocking description of Lucifer's fall from heaven to hell in part II of the *SEL*'s St Michael, again the work of the Outspoken Poet. The passage is quoted in Pickering, 'Outspoken *South English Legendary* poet', p. 29.
10 The *MED* quotes this line from Kenelm under *bilaughen*. D'Evelyn and Mill, on the other hand, associate *bylou* with *biliye*, 'bely' (III, glossary, p. 44).
11 See Hugh Magennis, 'Images of laughter in Old English poetry, with particular reference to the "hleahtor wera" of *The Seafarer*', *English Studies*, 73 (1992), 193–204 (197), and T. A. Shippey, '"Grim word-play": folly and wisdom in Anglo-Saxon humour', in Jonathan Wilcox (ed.), *Humour in Anglo-Saxon Literature* (Woodbridge: D. S. Brewer, 2000), pp. 33–48 (35).
12 Quoted from Thompson, *Everyday Saints*, p. 174, who transcribes from the text of the legend in Bodleian MS Ashmole 43, fols 155v–157r. Thompson discusses the 'black humour' elements of St Frideswide (*Everyday Saints*, pp. 174–85: the couplet quoted next is also from her p. 174). The phrase 'was bihynd' in the present passage has the additional meaning, 'was found wanting'.
13 For fuller discussion of the above points, see Pickering, 'The *South English Legendary*: teaching or preaching?'.
14 *The Owl and the Nightingale*, the sophisticated exception to this generalization, has its own moment of imagined pleasure in physical suffering: '"VVorp hit ut mid the alre wrste, / That his necke him toberste!" / The Faucun ilefde his bridde / & nom that fule brid a midde, / & warp hit of than wilde bowe, / Thar pie & crowe hit todrowe' ('"Throw out [the owl chick] with all the rubbish, so that its neck breaks in pieces." The falcon left its own birds and seized the filthy bird by the middle, and threw it off the branch to where magpies and crows tore it to bits') (lines 121–6, quoted from *The Owl and the Nightingale*, ed. E. G. Stanley, 2nd edn (Manchester: Manchester University Press, 1972), p. 53). Cruel sardonic humour did not, of course, end with the thirteenth century. It is there, for example, in the English mystery plays.
15 For a general account, see Ernst Robert Curtius, *European Literature and the Latin Middle Ages* (London: Routledge & Kegan Paul, 1953), pp. 425–8.
16 See, for example, Shari Horner, '"Why do you speak so much foolishness?": gender, humour, and discourse in Ælfric's *Lives of Saints*',

pp. 127–36 (128–9), and Hugh Magennis, 'A funny thing happened on the way to heaven: humorous incongruity in Old English saints' lives', pp. 137–57 (146), both in Wilcox (ed.), *Humour in Anglo-Saxon Literature*. For St Vincent in the *SEL*, see below. For other examples of saints laughing 'heroically in their defiance of torture and suffering', see Magennis, 'Images of laughter', p. 196, n. 9.

17 See Horner, 'Why do you speak so much foolishness?', p. 129.

18 Both examples come from Magennis, 'Images of laughter', pp. 195–6.

19 For St Patrick's Purgatory, see T. McAlindon, 'Comedy and terror in Middle English literature: the diabolical game', *Modern Language Review*, 60 (1965), 323–32 (326–8). For St Juliana, see D'Evelyn and Mill, I, 68, 184.

20 Vividly described in Gregory M. Sadlek, 'Laugher, game, and ambiguous comedy in the *South English Legendary*', *Studia Neophilologica*, 64 (1992), 45–54 (50).

21 O. S. Pickering, '*South English Legendary* style in Robert of Gloucester's *Chronicle*', *Medium Aevum*, 70 (2001), 1–18. See also the essay 'Outspoken style . . .' in the present volume.

22 *The Metrical Chronicle of Robert of Gloucester*, ed. William Aldis Wright, 2 vols, RS 86 (London: HMSO, 1887), vol. I, p. 161, 2268.

23 These are not cited in Pickering, '*South English Legendary* style'.

24 The previous line (621) comments on the death of many of Locrine's followers metaphorically: 'So that a luther beverege   to hare biofthe hii browe', i.e. 'So that they brewed a bitter drink for themselves'. The same metaphor occurs at line 6063 with the additional motif of laughter, the reference being to the Danes who had slaughtered St Alphege: 'Ac vewe ther were atte dede   that the beverege bilowe', i.e. 'But there were few at that action who laughed at what they had drunk'. This and the subsequent lines (6064–5) reappear in more extended form in the *SEL* life of St Alphege (I, 155, 219–24).

25 *Pers of Bermingham*, quoted from *Anglo-Irish Poems of the Middle Ages*, ed. and trans. Angela Lucas (Blackrock, Co. Dublin: The Columba Press, 1995), pp. 152–3.

26 For detailed analysis, see Michael Benskin, 'The style and authorship of the Kildare poems – (1) *Pers of Bermingham*', in J. L. Mackenzie and R. Todd (eds), *In Other Words: Transcultural Studies in Philology, Translation and Lexicography Presented to H. H. Meier on the Occasion of his Sixty-Fifth Birthday* (Dordrecht: Foris, 1989), pp. 57–75, esp. pp. 62–3.

27 Benskin, 'Style and authorship', pp. 64–5, summarized in Lucas, *Anglo-Irish Poems*, p. 208.

28 Quoted from *Havelok*, ed. G. V. Smithers (Oxford: Clarendon Press, 1987), by page and line number.

29 Cf. Michael Swanton, *English Literature before Chaucer* (London: Longman, 1987), pp. 195–6. As Swanton notes, the narrator's curses

include phrases like 'May the devil in hell soon take him!' ('The devel of helle him sone take', 446).

30 An earlier version of this paper was given as part of a session on the *South English Legendary* at the International Medieval Congress, University of Leeds, in July 2008.

20

Teaching the *South English Legendaries* at York: performativity and interdisciplinarity

Chloe Morgan, Jocelyn Wogan-Browne and Tim Ayers

Methods and rationale

Saints' lives are multi-dimensional and multi-sensual. They were heard – in song, in prayer, in preaching, in liturgical readings, in legendaries and saints' plays – as well as seen in their various textual forms. In addition, a wealth of visual sources and representations by and on material objects created complex and multifarious cults, some on a small scale for personal use, but others monumental and highly visible within spaces accessible to diverse audiences. This culture is key to the milieu in which the various *SELS* circulated.

While audiences of the *SEL* may not have been directly familiar with the *SEL*'s range of sources, or even aware of the extent to which the collection itself varied in different versions, they would certainly have come into contact with multiple versions of many of the lives that it contained. None of the different audiences that have been suggested for the *SEL*, whether laypeople or religious communities, would have understood its lives in isolation from the broader culture of visual and material hagiography. Though only one manuscript of the *SEL* is illuminated, images of saints were available in parish churches and in more extensive cycles of wall paintings in cathedrals and halls, as statues carried in procession, in stained glass, in breviaries, lectionaries, books of hours and so on.

Studies of individual cults have begun to suggest the hugely varied forms that a single saint's life could take, and the ways that it could be presented for different audiences.[1] Work on narrative in stained glass has begun to unravel the complex relationship between textual and visual narrative.[2] All this, digital and audio resources notwithstanding, can be difficult to convey in the classroom when studying saints' lives through modern editions. These can suggest not only that the text itself is in a fixed form (which the *SEL* emphatically is not) but also that the story takes a particular form, conveying set events in fixed mode to an undifferentiated audience. The *SEL* also needs location within a broader culture, revealing what is particular about it as well as what is unusual. It is not simply a reflex of the *Legenda aurea*: and, in any case, even an influential Latin legendary such as the *Legenda aurea* is itself the reflex of a long tradition of multifarious culting of the saints in various media by both lay and clerical people.

This essay is the product of a series of experimental seminars held for undergraduate and MA students in the History of Art department at the University of York. Taught collaboratively by the authors (members of the History of Art department, the English department and the interdisciplinary postgraduate Centre for Medieval Studies), these seminars sought to explore the multimedia, multi-sensory nature of hagiography in late medieval England, using the *SEL* alongside other sources. First, to show the students that Middle English hagiography is an aural and performative medium as well as a textual one, we performed extracts from the *SEL* as a kind of 'street theatre' in the chapter-house of York Minster. Second, in order to locate the *SEL* within the broader continuum of hagiographical culture, we asked students to use the *SEL* as a comparison narrative in their discussion of the telling of saints' lives in the stained glass of the chapter-house. Our hope was that, together, these interdisciplinary exercises would introduce students to a range of different hagiographical forms, and emphasize how the same story could be told in multiple ways, according to audience and intended function, as well as in varying physical locations and media. Approaching the *SEL* from a perspective which does not privilege textual culture, this collaborative experiment has taught the authors, as well as the students, much about what the *SEL* shares with other kinds of hagiographical culture, as well as what makes it unusual. The *SEL* is often discussed as a distinct, if perplexing entity, but teaching the *SEL* within the broader context of late medieval hagiographical culture, with its almost innumerable contexts, audiences and uses, also places the notorious complexity of the collection itself in perspective.

St Katherine and the chapter-house

Our initial decision was to compare St Katherine in the *SEL* and in the York Minster chapter-house stained glass. This was an opportunistic decision,[3] but, pertinently for our purposes, Katherine is both one of the most popular virgin martyrs in late medieval England and a figure of learning. At least seventeen *SEL* manuscripts contain a text of her life, and many other versions circulated in the later Middle Ages in French, English and Latin.[4] Katherine has a wide spectrum of devotees and her image is reshaped according to their convictions or aspirations in a range of late medieval media and performances.[5] The most celebrated of preaching and debating virgin martyrs, she can also, for instance, be remade into a model of interiorized devotion. [6]

The York Minster chapter-house offers its own distinctive version of Katherine, in a specific architectural context and medium. Built in the last quarter of the thirteenth century, shortly after the earliest redactions of the *SEL* began to circulate, and during the first flush of the *Legenda aurea*'s popularity in Britain, and designed to house the meetings of the Dean and Chapter, the chapter-house is an architectural tour-de-force.[7] Enormous engineering skill is devoted to creating an unusually large octagonal space without a central pillar, so that the sightlines from the Dean and Chapter's seats around the wall both converge in the centre and have unimpeded views of the decorative scheme on the periphery, embracing both the current large multi-light windows and the (formerly present) painted figurative ceiling panels (figure 20.1).[8] Seven impressively large windows were an integral part of the chapter-house's decorative programme. Each consists of five lights, surmounted by tracery, and tells its story in twenty coloured glass medallions which are interspersed with rows of grisaille (painted clear or white glass). Tall and wide, with delicate mullions and a minimum of wall surface between them, these windows encompass and dominate the space within the chapter-house. The Katherine window is the north-west window, followed clockwise by those for St William of York, the Virgin Mary, Christ (now missing), St Peter, St Paul and a window of Sts Thomas Becket, Margaret, Nicholas of Myra and John the Baptist all together. All these saints and/or their relics are elsewhere represented in the Minster, so that the chapter-house gives a summary and overview of the Minster's worship. Arranged around a central, east-facing window depicting the life of Christ, the hagiographical windows powerfully demonstrate that collecting saints' lives was not an exclusively textual mode. The self-contained form and tight iconographical planning of York's polygonal chapter-house provides a particularly clear example of how hagiographical principles could work in visual and physical form.[9]

20.1 Interior of the chapter-house, in a print from Joseph Halfpenny's *Gothic Ornaments in the Cathedral Church of York*, York, 1795.

There is evidence that the glass was designed at the same time as the building, and intended to reflect the interests of the Dean and Chapter, a high-status, educated, exclusively male audience of clerics.[10] Yet over its seven-hundred-year history, the chapter-house has regularly been open to audiences other than the Dean and Chapter. In 1296, almost immediately after the building was completed, the first of several royal parliaments was held there, and, throughout the later Middle Ages, the space was the setting for meetings of the Northern Convocation and York's city government.[11] It has even been suggested that the building was located so that it could, when needed, be 'made available to the laity without compromising the liturgical life of the cathedral'.[12]

The St Katherine window in the chapter-house is not the Minster's only representation of the saint. A second Katherine window was commissioned by Peter de Dene, a canon of the Minster actively involved in the administrative life of the cathedral, and certainly familiar with the chapter-house Katherine, which was probably around twenty years old when, some time before 1310, he chose to donate a window to the north aisle of the recently built nave.[13] But de Dene's window is in no way a copy of the chapter-house Katherine. It conveys its narrative in a much more condensed fashion, its smaller frame containing six narrative panels rather than twenty, with a far greater proportion of the glass given over to heraldry and armorial borders. Its story is simpler and more emblematic, a précis of the most iconographically significant moments of Katherine's life.[14] Located in one of the most public areas of the Minster, the briefer narrative was probably devised with a more diverse, less ecclesiastical audience in mind.[15] De Dene's window is also more personal than those in the chapter-house, containing a prominent donor portrait and an inscription inviting its audience to 'priez pur maistre Piere de Dene ke ceste fenestre fist fere' ('Pray for Master Peter de Dene who had this window made').[16] Close to an altar dedicated to the saint, the window shows a version of St Katherine's narrative which was also part of a broader nexus of worship within the cathedral and across the different communities that used it.[17]

Another, perhaps more dramatic, example of the overlap between different hagiographical cultures and their audiences comes in the slightly later figure of Margery Kempe, who visited the Minster twice in the early fifteenth century.[18] As a member of the lay congregation, Margery would certainly have seen de Dene's window in the nave, and may even have paid it special attention – St Katherine is one of the female saints who regularly appears in her visions.[19] But Kempe would also have seen the windows in the chapter-house, for, after disrupting Sunday services with her 'gret wepyng, boistows sobbyng and lowde crying' (l. 2853), arguing with priests and staying longer than the fourteen days that she had promised, Kempe was summoned to appear before the cathedral's clerks in their 'chapelhows' (l. 2859) or 'chapetilhows' (l. 2864) to be questioned on the articles of the faith. Thus, an outspoken laywoman, illiterate in the modern sense of the word, becomes the centre of attention within the chapter-house, a powerful architectural embodiment of the ecclesiastical authority against which Margery regularly has to prove herself in Kempe's *Book*. This burgher's wife from King's Lynn is able to invoke her own community of saints in order to authorize her personal relationship with Christ:

> Sumtyme owyr Lady spak to hir mend. Sumtyme Seynt Petyr, sumtyme Seynt Powyl, sumtym Seynt Kateryn, er what seynt in hevyn sche had devocyon to aperyd to hir sowle and tawt hir how sche schuld lovyn owyr Lord and how sche schuld plesyn hym.
> (ch. 17, ll. 902–5)[20]

In her various interactions with saints and their narratives – through her visions, shrine visits and the texts read to her by various confessors and guides – Kempe illustrates the diversity of late medieval hagiographical culture. The presence of Kempe in the administrative centre of the chapter-house together with the archbishop's clerks and the wider audience of curious spectators – the 'meche pepil' (2864) who attend Kempe's hearing, curious 'to her and se what schulde ben seyde er do' (2865) – serves to suggest how knitted together the manifestations of this hagiographical culture were.

The *South English Legendary* in the chapter-house

Before the chapter-house seminar on St Katherine, the students had already had several weeks of study on their stained glass course: they had a general knowledge of saints' cults but little experience of textual versions of saints' lives. They were asked to read the *Legenda aurea* Katherine in preparation for the seminar, but, in order to make their primary mode of encountering the *SEL* that of hearing it aloud, they were not given the *SEL* Katherine text till just before the seminar itself. (The life was given to them as a handout of substantial extracts with summaries of omitted passages, its text (based on D'Evelyn and Mill, II, 533–43) transliterated to modern spelling and supplied with marginal glosses.

We gathered under the Katherine window for Tim Ayers's concise indications of the chapter-house's characteristics and then heard Chloe Morgan's exposition of the St Katherine window. She identified damaged subjects and reconstructed their original order (the students were given a diagram handout to supplement the *viva voce* exposition), a point itself demonstrating the possibility of different readings of saints' narratives (table 20.1). She also showed the different ways in which the scenes could be related. If the performance dictates its own order, the many panels in the window are legible potentially in different directions, including horizontally and vertically, left to right, and up or down. Within the chapter-house, the scenes can also be read against other imagery, allowing for the construction of wider narratives across the space. In listening and asking questions as the window was expounded, we were recreating the kind of interpretative community that can occasionally be glimpsed in medieval sources. A sermon of Cardinal Eudes de Chateauroux (d. 1273) for instance refers to a window of the parable of the Good Samaritan, in which a child is instructed by a layman.[21] Several medieval transcriptions of the rhyming inscriptions in the windows of Canterbury Cathedral, preserved in the library there, may have informed their interpretation by the monks. In the continuation of *The Canterbury Tales* constituted by the anonymous fifteenth-century *Tale of Beryn*, a group of pilgrims without a guiding expositor is represented as comically discussing a range of implausible interpretations of the Canterbury windows.[22]

This exposition of the Katherine window revealed the value of an interlocutor in interpreting the imagery. Although the bright colours and clear compositions would originally have made the window more legible than it is today, the height of its upper rows raised questions about visibility for all of us. In this case, familiarity and shared experience of the windows may have made them accessible to the canons of York Minster (individual windows are more readily legible from the canons' seats around the chapter-house walls than from a standing position on the chapter-house floor).

In the chapter-house window, as one might expect, it is St Katherine's ability to model learning and reason that is chiefly foregrounded. Following Morgan's reconstruction of the window's narrative sequence and iconography, the particular emphases of its Katherine narrative clearly emerge (Table 20.2, Figure 20.2).[23] The bottom row of the five-light window, reading from left to right, shows Maxentius's pagan sacrifice, Katherine before him, the saint escorted to prison, Katherine visited there by an angel and

Table 20.1 A suggested order for the York chapter-house Katherine window (after Torre)

8d	8b	8c	8a	8e
Torre 1	Torre 2	Torre 3	Torre 4	Torre 5
Knowles 4/4	Knowles 4/2	Knowles 4/3	Knowles 4/1	Knowles 4/5
(Fig. 23)	**(Fig. 24)**	**(Fig. 25)**	**(Fig. 26)**	**(Fig. 27)**
The Empress and Porphyrius visit Katherine in prison	Christ visits Katherine in prison with angels	Katherine saved from the wheels	Martyrdom of Katherine	Katherine's body taken to Mt Sinai by angels
6d	**6b**	**6c**	**6a**	**6e**
Torre 6	Torre 7	Torre 8	Torre 9	Torre 10
Knowles 3/4	Knowles 3/2	Knowles 3/3	Knowles 3/1	Knowles 3/5
(Fig. 18)	**(Fig. 19)**	**(Fig. 20)**	**(Fig. 21)**	**(Fig. 22)**
Philosophers thrown into the flames	Katherine before Maxentius	The scourging of Katherine	Katherine returned to prison	Maxentius leaves
4d	**4b**	**4c**	**4a**	**4e**
Torre 11	Torre 12	Torre 13	Torre 14	Torre 15
Knowles 2/4	Knowles 2/2	Knowles 2/3	Knowles 2/1	Knowles 2/5
(Fig. 13)	**(Fig. 14)**	**(Fig. 15)**	**(Fig. 16)**	**(Fig. 17)**
Maxentius sends a messenger to gather philosophers	Messenger and Philosophers	Philosophers presented to Maxentius	Katherine brought from prison	Katherine faces Philosophers
2d	**2b**	**2c**	**2a**	**2e**
Torre 16	Torre 17	Torre 18	Torre 19	Torre 20
Knowles 1/4	Knowles 1/2	Knowles1/3	Knowles 1/1	Knowles 1/5
(Fig. 8)	**(Fig. 9)**	**(Fig. 10)**	**(Fig. 11)**	**(Fig. 12)**
Beasts brought to be sacrificed	Katherine before Maxentius	Katherine escorted to prison	An angel visits Katherine in prison	Katherine before Maxentius (?)

Note: CVMA (*Corpus Vitrearum Medii Aevii*) panel numbering (in bold) refers to the current position of scenes in the window. The two columns which have been interchanged (probably in the late seventeenth century) are indicated by shading. The narrative flows from left to right, beginning in the bottom row.

20.2 A view of the St Katherine window (CH nIV)

brought again (probably) before Maxentius. In the second row up of the window, three separate scenes are dedicated to (i) the summoning of the philosophers by the Emperor Maxentius; (ii) the messenger gathering them together; and (iii) their presentation to the emperor (this sequence builds on the to and fro of Katherine's

20.3 The scourging of St Katherine (CH nIV, 6c).

encounters with the secular power in the bottom row of the window, some version of which is present in many representations of the saint, but seldom as emphasized as here). The remaining two scenes of this row show Katherine's own journey from prison and her confrontation with the philosophers. In the third row up the philosophers burn, Katherine is again before Maxentius, she is scourged, returned to prison, and Maxentius leaves (Figure

20.4 St Katherine before the philosophers (CH nIV, 4e).

20.3). The pace and intensity of Katherine's progress to martyrdom quickens in the fourth row of the window: the Empress and Porphyrius, captain of Maxentius's guard, visit Katherine in prison; Christ visits her with angels in prison; she is saved from the wheels; she is then decapitated; and her soul is carried to heaven by angels. In the chapter-house space, dedicated as it is to clerical power and deliberation, Katherine's movement through argument and negotiation towards martyrdom is emphasized, together with the window's strong interest in the role and fate of the converted philosophers. Here the saint works by divine reasoning, through which the philosophers become allied with her against Maxentius's corrupt court. Ecclesiastical authority and its feminine figurehead here assert clerical autonomy as against state intervention, together with an idealized model of debate (Figure 20.4).

Our next move was the reading of the *SEL* narrative. For this first experiment, until we knew how the Art History students would respond, this was done chiefly by Jocelyn Wogan-Browne (once we were sure the students could follow and enjoy reading themselves, subsequent seminars shared out the reading to a greater degree). Wogan-Browne introduced the *SEL* briefly and then gave a semi-dramatized reading of the Katherine life. The students followed by sometimes using their handout texts, but also by looking and listening.

In the *SEL*, Katherine is an eloquent, articulate, public figure. In this version she brings with her many of the questions explored by Catherine Sanok in her account of saints' plays and the problematic exemplarity of virgin martyrs, whose resistance to authority can hardly be mapped on to public space without challenging the late medieval political and religious institutions whereby laywomen in particular were expected to practise a contained and private devotion.[24] But women did participate in guilds and in public spaces and perhaps even in plays, in spite of the prevailing custom of cross-dressing boys or men for female roles.[25] Much cultural investment in enclosing women and female devotion in households and religious communities notwithstanding, Margery Kempe was hardly the only woman to bring devotion into public spaces.[26] The figure of Katherine could speak to varying occupational identities and to different ideological positions.

Against the narrative iconography of the great chapter-house window, voicing the *SEL* Katherine created contrasts and commentary comparable with the scene of Kempe's confrontation there. Several features of the *SEL* Katherine life stood out. The sub-plot of the conversion of Maxentius's wife and his military commander Porphirius is greatly compressed in the chapter-house window. In the *SEL* there is much more focus on the torment of the converted empress at the command of her furious husband: she is led to 'the tounes ende' (II, 541, 244) where her breasts are ripped off with iron hooks 'as me draweth with combes wolle . . . Fram hire bodi mossel mele' ('as one draws wool with combs . . . piecemeal from her body', II, 541, 250) and her body left unburied, until it is interred by Porphiry, himself subsequently executed as 'Mohamed's enemy' outside the town limits (II, 542, 273–4). The window shows Katherine semi-naked and scourged in her reproduction of the iconography of Christ's passion, but is uninterested in the relation between the two women and their martyrdoms. In the *SEL*, the potential of Katherine's convert, the empress, for nourishing her husband Maxentius's lineage is symbolically and actually destroyed, but re-emerges in spiritualized form when the virgin martyr's trunk bleeds milk (breast milk being considered a thickened form of blood in medieval physiology): 'Whit mulc ther orn out of the wounde   and noght o drope of blode' ('White milk ran there out of the wound, and not one drop of blood', II, 542, 296).

The *SEL* Katherine is also very clear about the role of the saint's own agency.[27] No mere mouthpiece for Christ, she seeks out the public commotion of the pagan sacrifice Maxentius has decreed and tackles him directly:

Tho alle the men were thider icome   to don *here lawe*
  when; their; [rituals of] faith
Seinte Katerine *baldeliche*   thiderward gan drawe.   12
  bravely

Heo stod *bihalves* and bihuld   *here gydihede*
  she; to the side; their foolishness
Heo segh honure the *maumetz*   meni Cristene men for drede.
  She saw many Christian people honouring the idols out of fear
Tho hadde heo gret *deol* in hurte: heo *blescede hire* anon
  sorrow; crossed herself
And forth anon to th'emperour   baldeliche gan gon.   16
'Sire *riche* emperor', heo seide,   'thu ert noble & *hende*:
  powerful; gracious
Thu scholdest thi *poer* and thi wit   to som wisdom *wende*.
  power; turn

For the folie ich sigge that   that ich iseo her do
  I say this on account of the foolishness that I see going on here
So moche folc of furrene londe   that thu *clipest* herto   20
  summon
In gret joye and wonder in youre hurte   of this temple ye doth so
  heart
That is ymaked of *lym* and ston;   and of youre *maumetz* also.
  lime (i.e. mortar); idols
Whi *ne biholde ye* the heghe temple   – thereof you wondri mai –
  do you not look at
Of hevene that goth aboute   above you night and dai?   24
Of sonne and mone and of the sterres   that fram the est to the west
Wendeth, and nevere weri *beoth*;   and nevere hi nabbeth rest
  make their way; are
Bithench the bet and turn thi thought   to som wisdom ich *rede,*
  consider better; advise
And whan thyn owene *inwit* the saith   that nowhar nis such a
                                     dede,   28
  And when your own conscience tells you there is nowhere any
  comparable acheivement
Almighti God thu him *holde*   that such wonder can make.
  consider
Tofore alle othere *honure* him;   and youre maumetz thu forsake.'
  Before; worship
Mid other reisouns of *clergie*   that maide preovede also
  With; learning

That *here* godes *nothing nere*   that hi anourede hem to.   32
  That their gods were nothing that they should give them such worship
           (D'Evelyn and Mill, II, 533–4, 11–32)[28]

Under the chapter-house roof, Katherine's contrast of God's heavens with Maxentius's temple and 'maumets' of lime and stone had extra subversive power. Equally striking was the clipped cogency of the saint's speech and her appeal to Maxentius's own innate intelligence as a created being: 'thyn owene inwit the saith ('your own conscience tells you', II, 534, 28), and the narrative endorsement that the saint is using 'resouns of clergie' ('learned reasons') and that she 'preovede hem' ('proved them', II, 534, 31).

When it came to the full debate commissioned by Maxentius between his philosopher-clerks and the saint, the *SEL* remained striking and powerful, even under the monumental treatment of the saint and the philosophers in the huge Katherine window. The vigour and pungency of the *SEL* arguments are still clearer when read aloud, as is the relatively surprising level of doctrinal sophistication:

God hadde evere, and evere schal   with him his godhede,
And for love of ous in oure flesch,   he *nom* his *manhede*.
Of two things he was ymaked,   aither moste his cunde afonge
For in cunde of manhode ous to bugge,   he tholede deth stronge:
Ac to bileve ded hit was   age cunde of godhede.
Therfore he aros fram deth to lyve,   tho he hadde ido al his dede,
Thurf the stronge deth that thurf Adam   we were on ibroght
Thurf godhede ymengd in oure kunde   nede moste beo iboght.
                    (II, 536–7, 107–114)

(God ever had, and ever shall have his divinity with him, and he took his humanity in the flesh for love of us. He was formed of two things, each of which had to receive his nature: for in the nature of humankind he suffered violent death in order to redeem us, but it was against the nature of divinity to remain dead, and so he arose from death to life when he had completed his deed. Because of the compulsion of death into which we were brought through Adam, we had necessarily to be redeemed by divinity mingled with our nature.)

This may be didactic, but it is also, as debate, a form of spectator sport.

For the undergraduate students, engaged upon their own spectator sport in watching and listening to the rendition of the *SEL* life, the narrative in the St Katherine window was given a new energy by the performance at its foot. The Middle English was remarkably accessible: the dramatic directness and humour left the students applauding Katherine's bravery in the face of Maxentius's impotent violence. Unlike the medieval minster canons, the students were mostly female, underlining the openness of this strand of the narrative to both men and women. In a subsequent follow-up seminar in their Art History course, what the students said they appreciated most was the discovery of the unfamiliar, an insight into the relative value of different kinds of storytelling – oral, written and depicted – in a culture unlike our own. Each medium has its conventions, whether in word, gesture, line or colour, but the students recognized similarities between the performance and the window in the simplified props, clear characterization and vigorous poses of the painted figures. In his pioneering study of the relationship between medieval drama and narratives in stained glass, Wolfgang Kemp explored similar issues in positing a relationship between earlier narrative windows on the continent and the jongleurs.[29] Like the exposition of the window, the reading of the *SEL* life was in some ways a version of medieval performance and group response.

The student response encouraged us to continue, and we further explored the chapter-house narratives in a second group of sessions with MA students. This time we experimented with the St Peter window and the *SEL* St Peter, using the same preparation and seminar activities as with St Katherine, but this time having the students perform some of the parts themselves, as well as comparing the narratives in glass and text. The *SEL Peter* has still stronger inscriptions of audience response and more explicit street theatre scenes: it offers vivid performativity and a more highly contrasted set of emphases in relation to the chapter-house version. Again, it made an immediate impact on students without prior experience of Middle English. The St Peter window has been much rearranged and there is no proven original order (it may well be irretrievable), so in a subsequent seminar two groups of students were invited to reorder it. This was partly to be done on art-historical grounds, but also to be informed by the narrative structures that they had discussed in the chapter-house itself. These possible narrative orderings were used to group dramatic episodes and to organize the scenes within the repeating grid of geometrical frames.

In both sets of seminars, the cross-media comparison was greeted as clearly beneficial by the Art History students. This suggests that it would be worth designing further seminars along similar lines and with still more student participation. Ideally Art

History and Literature students would join together in such seminars and exchange across their disciplines. While other legendaries could be experimented with, the *SEL*'s intense performativity
makes it particularly suitable: moreover it is itself further revealed
in performance contexts as a very rewarding work.[30]

The *South English Legendary* and performance

Imagining further performance spaces for *SELS* obviously requires
far more detailed and wide-ranging research, re-creation and
experimentation than our opportunistic use of the chapter-house
venue. Textual scholarship on the *SEL* manuscripts has revealed
something of their provenance and ownership, but the specific
social spaces in which the manuscripts' texts might have been read
and heard are of course not necessarily the same thing and are
much harder to elicit and reconstruct. However recent studies of
medieval urban performance culture make the idea of *SEL* performance in a range of locations more readily conceivable than previously.[31] Parish guilds, urban guildhalls, parish churches, church
yards might perhaps provide venues in addition to Samson's existing suggestions regarding chamber reading and reading in hall.[32]
While the sheer scale of the *SEL* in its fullest versions makes it
hard to imagine as a communal performance, the mystery cycles
provide an obvious analogy for extended civic engagement in para-
liturgical performance, distributed, to use William Robins's term
(p. 205 above), in a modular way, pageant by pageant.[33]

At first sight, the extant material traces of the *SELS* suggest
that their texts are best understood as scripts dependent on their
full realization through the voices and gestures of readers. With
only one of its manuscripts containing images of saints, the forms
in which the *SEL* comes to us do not offer the complex somat-
ics of reading visual and textual codes together, shown by much
recent work on books of hours, psalters and other books to be an
important aspect of medieval reading performances (physical and
figurative).[34] Moreover, so strongly have issues of textual transmission modelled our account of the *SEL* as a phenomenon created by
clerics and given to lay people, that, even when these accounts have
envisaged a degree of lay–clerical interaction or shared agendas, it
is initially difficult to imagine that *SEL* texts could be attempts to
control and smooth out a communally mounted performance of
some kind.

Yet numerous aspects of the *SEL* would respond to such a paradigm, and so prompt the question whether what we have is not sometimes the codified version of still more vigorous imaginings and actions. Carol Symes has recently suggested that we might stand the evidence that constructs the relations we have assumed between extant texts and their medieval perfomance, on its head:

> [Rather than imagining that a given text is the starting-point for any inquiry] . . . we will be getting closer to the truth if we posit that a text may be trying to control, to censor, or to proscribe existing practices, modalities, and behaviors . . . pre-modern scripts are more likely to function in this way than they are to offer careful prescriptions of what was supposed to occur or faithful transcriptions of what did.[35]

Whether or not further detailed work would make it possible to show the *SEL* as a collaborative lay and clerical phenomenon, it seems possible that the experience of performance contributed to the *SEL* as it developed, and that taking such possibilities into account can modify our sense of the work. An example is the Corpus-Harley *temporale* account of the Rogationtide Litany procession for St Mark's Day (25 April). This *temporale* narrative has the apparent function of teaching the greater importance of the Rogationtide or 'Greater Litany' in comparison with the Lesser Litanies for the 'Gangdawes' (walking-days), the three days before Ascension 'wanne me aboute veldes goth' ('when one goes around the fields', I, 161, 11–12). The lesser litany, says the *SEL*, was founded by a mere bishop in the city of Vienne (Bishop Mamertius c. 470, I, 162, 35–6), the greater litany by a greater man in a greater place at greater need (I, 161 15–16): Pope St Gregory of Rome ordained it because the Romans, having fasted for Lent, succumbed to gluttony and lived in lechery as soon as Easter came. God's vengeance on them was to have them drop dead in their debauchery as they yawned and sneezed in the fields, and this is why we bless ourselves when we yawn and sneeze – 'for drede of that sodeyn deth'. It is also why, given that these 'wretched evils' happened after Easter

> . . . we maketh oure vastynge   the nexte day of echon
> That cometh after Ester   and bivore nevere mo
> As a sein Markes day   that yconfermed was tho
>
> (I, 161, 30–2)[36]

(. . . we hold our fasts on the days following the one after Easter and no longer beforehand – that day was confirmed at that time as St Mark's Day)

Liszka has examined the analogies and correspondences between the Sarum Consuetudinary for the Rogantiontide procession, the *Legenda aurea* account of the procession and the *SEL*, concluding that 'the *SEL*'s readers could have drawn on their experience of actual Rogationtide and Ascension Day processions to understand what the redactor was doing'.[37] But the origin-story in the *SEL*'s account makes it possible to imagine this relationship reversed: the procession for the new double Litany might be seen as a clerical response to rumbustious observance, rather than a didactic prescription teaching laypeople how to hold Rogationtide. The Litany and its accompanying celebrations may well have been too vigorously pursued: now, with the monitory tale of the divine punishment given the Romans, a more decorous version is urged:

... for the frut an eorthe   that God let it wel sprynge
And god weder give therto   and to oure vode forth it bringe.
Thanne me maketh processions   with baners arered
That is as oure Louerdes ost   to make the devel aferd.
The baners that me bereth bivore   bitokneth victorie
That oure Louerd is al above   and ywonne hath the maistrie;
The dragon that me bereth   bitokneth oure luther fo
The devel that is bihinde ibroght   and worth evere mo;
So mote it bi him evere be[o]   ne be[o] he nevere above!
Nou swete Jesus it grante us   for his moder love
That we holde so this procession   and the vastinge withoute sunne
That frut an eorthe come wel vorth   to helpe of mankunne.
                                                                (I, 162, 39–50)

(... for the sake of the earth's fruit, and so that God may allow it to blossom well and give good weather for it and bring it forth for our food. Then we form processions as our Lord's army with banners raised to make the devil fearful. The banners we carry in front signify victory, that our Lord has completely conquered and won the mastery; the dragon we carry behind signifies our wicked enemy the devil, who is dragged behind, and will for ever be. May it always be like this for him, let him never conquer! Now may sweet Jesus grant it to us for the love of his mother that we hold this procession and the fasting without sin in such a way that the earth's fruit may come forth to the help of humankind.)

Some scenes in the *SEL* are quite as suited for 'street theatre' as, say, the celebrated fights of Noah and his wife in the Wakefield Master's versions of mystery cycle pageants. For example, St Juliana's disposal of a squealing devil in a disused public latrine after exposing and shaming him all over the marketplace is robust comic action, involving nice lexical play with courtly registers (most egregiously the euphemizing and ironic French 'chambre foreyne' for 'outside lavatory'), and the inversion of social codes for modesty and embarrassment – all the while maintaining the underlying typological resonances of virginity's defeat of the devil:

> This maide *nom* this foule best   and efter hure it *drou:*
> > > > *took; dragged*
> 'Leove levedy', he sede, 'thin *ore!*   *Yssend* Ich am inou!   124
> > > > *dear; mercy; ruined*
> Ne make namo men gawe on me   – *nertou* corteis and *hende!*
> > > > *you are not; gracious*
> Thench that maidens ssolde milde beo   – and bring me of this
> > > bende!
> > > > *bonds*
> War is the *kunde* of thi maidenot   that ssolde beo milde and stille?
> > > > [*proper*] *nature*
> And thou ert agen me so sterne –   hou mightou *habbe the wille?*' 128
> > > > *desire this*
> > So longe he on this maide cride   as heo him drou and ladde
> Afte hure thoru the *chepinge,*   that *reuthe* of him *heo* hadde.
> > > > *marketplace; pity; she*
> A *chambre foreyne* heo *sey*   al up touward the strete:
> > > > *latrine; saw*
> *Fol* it was of *fulthhede,*   old and al *forlete*   132
> > > > *full; filth; abandoned*
> This maide nom this foule thing,   and caste it al amide.
> *Daythat him* wolde *ricchore* bed   bisech other bidde!
> > > *Curses to anyone who begs or asks for a nobler bed for him!*
> For it was *god inou to* him   withinne and *eke* aboue –
> > > > *good enough for; also*
> *Wat segge ye? Segge ich soth?*   *Ne lieth noght for* is *love!*
> > *What do you say? Do I tell the truth? Now, don't lie for love of* him!]
> > > > (I, 66, 123–36)

Oliver Pickering has argued that the creation of a vigorous narrative persona soliciting audience response (as in lines 134–6 here) and the free use of enjambement in the *SEL* couplet (lines 129–30) reveals the 'outspoken poet' at work revising the *SEL* (pp. 106–28 above). But such a writer may be revising performance rather than text, and there is room to see the development of the *SEL* as collaborative and not solely as the work of a gifted cleric. The even more knockabout scene of the confrontation between St Peter and Simon Magus's dog vividly dramatizes the topos of the holy man's ability to exercise Adamic power over sub-rational animals, while also, in the lynch mob that reads the dog's instinctive response as a licence for its own response, suggesting something of the communal forces that performance can both evoke and control:

> Symon hadde a gret dogge,   *kennore ne mihte beo non:*
> *there could be none fiercer*
> He teide him *bivore* a dore   *there* Peter *ssolde gon.*   376
> *in front of; where; was to go*
> 'Icholde,' he sede, 'that this *trichor*   herevorth sone wende:
> *I believe: traitor*
> *Me thencheth wonder bote* this dogge   is olde limes torende.'
> *It will seem a marvel to me if this dog doesn't tear his limbs to pieces.*
> The dogge, *tho* seinte Peter com,   *vaunede* on him anon
> *when; fawned*
> And lickede him with gret joie   and *wolde* with him gon.   380
> *wanted*
> *Tho* seinte Peter him hadde unteid,   forth with him; he wende
> *when*
> *A vot he nolde fram him gon*   *woder so* he kende,
> *Not a foot would he go from him; wherever*
> So that Symon agen him com   and *chidde wis honde.*
> *scolded his dog*
> The dogge *sturte* anon to him   and *braid* him doun to gronde. 384
> *leaped: knocked*
> *Astrangli he wolde* him anon   ac Peter *agen him drou*
> *to choke to death; he wanted; but; drew him back*
> *Is clothes he hadde er todrawe*   *with ssennesse inou.*
> *He had already torn his clothes with damage enough.*
> Ac evere *me thencheth al to lite*   that he nadde forbite his throte.
> *it seems to me all too little*
> Hou thencheth you, segge ich soth?   nadde it noht beo note? 388
> *How does it seem to you, do I say the truth?*
> *Wouldn't that have been fitting?*
> That folk and yonge children ek   than wrecche bigone to *poune;*
> *beat/crush*
> *Mid ssennesse* as it were a wolf   hi drive him out of toune.   390
> *ignominy*
> Now *an alle develwey,*   *and ne come he nevere agen!*
> *Now by the devil, let him never come back!*
> Wy sitte ye so stille?   Wy ne segge ye 'Amen!'?
> *Why are you sitting so quietly? Why don't you say Amen?*
>   (I, 260, 375–92)

These ideas are offered here as frankly speculative for the moment, but it can at least be securely asserted that Symes's argument for the importance of performance as a category in the analysis of texts is of great potential for the *SEL*.[38] When more performances of the work, in classrooms or anywhere else, have been experienced by modern students, their teachers and perhaps wider audiences, we will have many important new dimensions to our experience of the *SEL* and new questions and paradigms of enquiry to bring to it.

Notes

1 See e.g. Katherine J. Lewis, *The Cult of St Katherine of Alexandria in Late Medieval England* (Woodbridge: Boydell Press, 2000); Christopher Norton, *St William of York* (Woodbridge: York Medieval Press, 2006); Virginia Blanton, *Signs of Devotion: The Cult of St Æthelthryth in Medieval England, 695–1615* (University Park, PA: Pennsylvania University Press, 2007); Anthony Bale (ed.), *St Edmund, King and Martyr: Changing Images of a Medieval Saint* (Woodbridge: York Medieval Press, 2009).

2 Wolfgang Kemp, *The Narratives of Gothic Stained Glass* (Cambridge: Cambridge University Press, 1997); Colette Manhes-Deremble with Jean-Paul Deremble, *Les vitraux narratifs de la cathédrale de Chartres: étude iconographique* (Paris: Léopard d'or, 1993); Madeline H. Caviness, 'Biblical stories in windows: were they bibles for the poor?', in Bernard S. Levy (ed.), *The Bible in the Middle Ages: Its Influence on Literature and Art* (Binghamton, NY: Medieval & Renaissance Texts & Studies, 1992), pp. 103–47); Alyce A. Jordan, *Visualizing Kingship in the Windows of the Sainte-Chapelle* (Turnhout: Brepols, 2002).

3 Some later manuscripts of the *SEL* circulated in fifteenth-century Yorkshire (see Görlach, *Textual Tradition*, map, p. 305), but there is no known direct relationship between them and York.

4 See Lewis, *Cult of St Katherine* for a detailed study, also Jacqueline Jenkins and Katherine Lewis (eds), *St Katherine of Alexandria: Texts and Contexts in Western Medieval Europe*, Medieval Women Texts and Contexts 8 (Turnhout: Brepols, 2003); Christine Walsh, *The Cult of St Katherine in Early Medieval Europe* (Aldershot: Ashgate, 2007), esp. ch. 7.

5 Lewis, *Cult of St Katherine*, pp. 161–74; Ruth Kennedy, ed., *Three Middle English Alliterative Poems*, EETS OS 321 (Oxford: Oxford University Press, 2003), pp. 1–9 (for a prayer probably composed by a Carmelite for Stamford's Parish Guild of St Katherine). On the surviving traces of the long tradition of Katherine plays, see Clifford Davidson, 'The Middle English saint play and its iconography', in his (ed.), *The Saint Play in Medieval Europe* (Kalamazoo, Michigan: Medieval Institute Publications, 1986), pp. 31–122 (46–52).

6 See e.g. Jacqueline Jenkins, 'Lay-devotion and women readers of the Middle English prose life of St Katherine (MS. Harley 4012)', in Jenkins and Lewis (eds), *St Katherine of Alexandria*, pp. 153–70.

7   On the evidence for the dating of the chapter-house, see Sarah Brown, *'Our Magnificent Fabrick': York Minster: An Architectural History c. 1250–1500* (Swindon: English Heritage, 2003), 51–5 and 294–7. On the *Legenda Aurea* and the *SEL* see Görlach, *Textual Tradition*, pp. 25–9. For the suggestion that the *Legenda Aurea* influenced narrative modes in stained glass, see Richard Marks, 'Medieval stained glass: recent and future trends in scholarship', *The Journal of Stained Glass*, 24 (2000), 62–79 (70).

8   Christopher Norton, 'The medieval paintings in the chapter house', *Friends of York Minster Annual Report*, 67 (1996), pp. 34–51. On the implications of the chapter-house's form, see Chloe Morgan, 'A life of St Katherine of Alexandria in the chapter-house of York Minster', *Journal of the British Archaeological Association*, 162 (2009), 146–78 (149).

9   On the glass as a unit, see Brown, *'Our Magnificent Fabrick'*, p. 79. The structuring principle of the *SEL* itself has been metaphorically compared by Sadlek to a rose window, where 'the coherence of the legendary is assured by the typological connection of each of the saints to a mental image of Christ at "the centre of the wheel"': Sadlek's metaphor is made material in the chapter-house windows (Gregory M. Sadlek, 'The image of the devil's five fingers in the *South English Legendary*'s "St Michael" and Chaucer's Parson's Tale', in Jankofsky, pp. 49–64, p. 10).

10 See Morgan, 'A life of St Katherine', pp. 147–51.

11 Brown, *Architectural History*, pp. 51, 58.

12 Ibid., p. 58.

13 On de Dene, see C. Winston and W. S. Walford, 'On a heraldic window in the north aisle of York Cathedral', in *Memoirs Illustrative of the Art of Glass Painting by the Late Charles Winston* (London: Murray, 1865), pp. 256–84, at pp. 265–72; A. B. Emden, *A Biographical Register of the University of Oxford to AD 1500*, 3 vols (Oxford: Clarendon Press, 1957–59) III, pp. 2168–9; F. D. Logan, *Runaway Religious in Medieval England c. 1240–1540* (Cambridge: Cambridge University Press, 1996), 34–41. For the window's dating see further Brown, *Architectural History*, p. 90.

14 The scenes show Katherine before the emperor, Katherine converting the philosophers, the philosophers' martyrdom, Katherine visited in prison, Katherine tortured, Katherine executed.

15 The adjacent 'Bell Founder's' window, for instance, was donated by Richard Tunnoc, a wealthy goldsmith who served as mayor of York in 1327, and prominently features his wares (see Brown, *Stained Glass*, p. 34).

16 Reconstructed in Winston and Walford, 'Heraldic window', p. 258.

17 See Brown, *'Our Magnificent Fabrick'*, p. 122; W. J. Sheils, 'The altars in York Minster in the early sixteenth century', in R. N. Swanson

(ed.), *Continuity and Change in Christian Worship*, Studies in Church History 35 (Woodbridge: Boydell Press for the Ecclesiastical History Society, 1999), pp. 104–15 (109, 111); E. A. Gee, 'The topography of altars, shrines and chantries in York Minster', *Antiquaries Journal*, 64 (1984), 337–50 (348, 341).

18 Lynn Staley (ed.), *The Book of Margery Kempe* (Kalamazoo, MI: Medieval Institute Publications, 1996), bk I, chapters 10 and 50–2.

19 The saint is mentioned, for example, at lines 903, 1161, 1187, 2029, 2625, 5002–4, 5118. The Mayor of Leicester contrasts Kempe with Katherine at 2625. For some of the images of saints visible in the Minster at the time of Kempe's visits, see www.holycross.edu/depart-ments/visarts/projects/kempe/parish/whtshsw.htm.

20 Margery also refers to Margaret on several occasions, and gives the reason for her visit to York as a 'pilgrimage to offyr at [the shrine of] Seynt William' (2873–4). Almost all the saints in the chapter-house are also mentioned in Kempe's *Book*.

21 Ibid., pp. 71– 2.

22 M. A. Michael, *Stained Glass of Canterbury Cathedral* (London: Scala, 2004), p. 14; *The Tale of Beryn*, ed. F. J. Furnivall and W. G. Stone, EETS ES 105 (London: Kegan Paul, Trench, Trübner and Henry Froude for Oxford University Press, 1909), p. 6, ll. 147–62.

23 The account here draws heavily on Morgan, 'A life of St Katherine', pp. 158–67.

24 Catherine Sanok, 'Performing feminine sanctity in late medieval England: parish guilds, saints' plays and the *Second Nun's Tale*', *Journal of Medieval and Early Modern Studies*, 32 (2002), 269–303.

25 Sanok, 'Performing feminine sanctity', pp. 286–7, but see also P. J. P. Goldberg, 'Craft guilds, the Corpus Christi play and civic govern-ment', in Sarah Rees Jones (ed.), *The Government of Medieval York: Essays in Celebration of the 1396 Royal Charter*, Borthwick Studies in History 3 (York: University of York, 1997), pp. 141–63 (145–8 and tables, 161–3).

26 Cloistered abbesses and prioresses routinely entered public space on the socio-economic business of their houses (see further Marilyn Oliva, *The Convent and the Community in Late Medieval England: Female Monasteries in the Diocese of Norwich 1350–1540* (Woodbridge: Boydell Press 1998)), while Carolyn Collette has shown that the figure of the pious married laywoman, the 'chaste matron', had important public and political dimensions: Carolyn P. Collette, *Performing Polity: Women and Agency in the Anglo-French Tradition, 1385–1620* (Turnhout: Brepols, 2006).

27 For a discussion of the tensions surrounding the (predominant) rep-resentation of Katherine as learned and not merely a vessel of God's word, see further Lewis, *Cult of St Katherine*, pp. 134–40.

28 Quotations without translations in this essay are reproduced from the

handouts given to students in the seminar: i.e. with glosses but not
with translations.

29 Kemp, *Narratives of Gothic Stained Glass*, pt 2, ch. 6 (pp. 145–53).

30 As Thompson's *Everyday Saints* and Pickering's two essays of stylistic analysis in the present volume in particular show, the *SEL* offers
abundant materials for the recreation of performative readings, and, as
noted above (Introduction, p. 4 and n 6), recent TEAMS editions such
as those by Reames, Blalock and Lawson and by Whatley, Thompson
and Upchurch make entire *SEL* texts available.

31 On medieval urban locations for the performance culture of towns
(locations often less amenable to censorship and regulation than, for
instance, early modern theatres) see Carol Symes, *A Common Stage*:
Theater and Public Life in Medieval Arras (Ithaca and London:
Cornell University Press, 2007), esp. pp. 277–82.

32 For valuable nuancing and a consideration of the changing conditions
here see Sanok, 'Performing feminine sanctity', pp. 278–80, 286; for
gentry reading, see Samson, 'Constructing a context'.

33 On the relation of pageants and urban confraternities, see the important revisionist account by Sheila K. Christie, 'Bridging the jurisdictional divide: the masons and the York Corpus Christi Play',
in Margaret Rogerson (ed.), *Reflections on the York Mystery Cycle*
(Woodbridge and York: York Medieval Press, 2011), pp. 53–74.

34 For the extension of such thinking away from para-liturgical books
and into other kinds of texts, see Pamela Sheingorn, 'Performing
the illustrated manuscript: great reckonings in little books', in Elina
Gertsman (ed.), *Visualizing Medieval Performance: Perspectives,
Histories, Contexts* (London and Burlington, VT: Ashgate, 2008), pp.
57–82. On the one *SEL* manuscript with illustrations, see the essay by
Winstead above.

35 Carol Symes, 'The medieval archive and the history of theatre: assessing the written and unwritten evidence for pre-modern performance
practice', in *Theatre Survey* 52.1 (2011), 29–58 (at 33).

36 D'Evelyn and Mill's text lacks six lines between lines 29 and 30
omitted in its manuscripts: these are printed in Pickering, 'Expository
temporale', p.8.

37 Thomas R. Liszka, 'The dragon in the *South English Legendary*: Judas,
Pilate, and the "A(1)" redaction', *Modern Philology*, 100:1 (2002), 50–9
(at 55–6, 58).

38 See further Carol Symes, 'The appearance of early vernacular plays:
forms, functions, and the future of medieval theater', *Speculum*, 77
(2002), 778–831 (esp.779 on emergent form).

Part VI
Afterword

21

Where next?

Anne B. Thompson

When, in the late 1980s, I began thinking about the *SEL* it seemed to me that not very much had been written. Two names, however, did stand out: Manfred Görlach, whose detailed examination of *SEL* textual tradition opened up the collection for study in a way not previously possible, and O. S. Pickering, the first writer to pay close attention to stylistic aspects of the *SEL* as though they mattered. Then in 1992, Klaus Jankofsky published the first collection to attempt a critical assessment of the *SEL*, and my own book appeared in 2003. Although the field had by then expanded considerably, with many essays treating the collection in different and interesting ways, I want to begin my response using Jankofsky's book and mine as jumping off points for a consideration of what I see as newest and most valuable about *Rethinking the South English Legendaries*. The essays in the Jankofsky collection for the most part treated individual items from a textual, thematic, or literary-critical perspective. My book treated the *SEL* as one more or less coherent narrative in order to concentrate, following my own interests, on a close reading of its style and content. Both these books have proved valuable in drawing attention to the collection, but both are limited in a number of ways, not least because of their reliance on the two published editions of the *SEL*. In this respect, Thomas Liszka's 2001 essay on the '*South English Legendaries*' (reprinted here along with other very useful earlier work by Frankis, Heffernan and Pickering), is groundbreaking in its attention to the multiple and misleading ways in which these editions have created the idea of a single unified collection which (following Görlach's thesis) could be imagined, if not demonstrated, as tracing back to a lost 'original'.

There are several significant ways in which the present book breaks the mould of earlier scholarship. First, while many essays focus on English saints, all of them vastly complicate the meaning of

'Englishness', which earlier scholars have identified with 'nationalistic' attitudes in the *SEL*; second, it brings together essays which often treat the same saint, but from different perspectives, drawing on a more detailed attention to history and cultural context: it is a particular pleasure to see how they engage, so to speak, in mutually enriching conversations with one another; third, following Liszka, is the attempt to take in many more aspects of the different *SEL* manuscripts, some of which have received virtually no mention in the past. In surveying the collection as a whole, I am impressed by how much more venturesome and knowledgeable all of these scholars have become with regard to bringing other fields and other knowledge to bear on our study of the *SEL*. The comments below are intended to highlight just a few of the insights to be found within the pages of this book.

In his essay about the Christianization of England in the seventh century, Gordon Whatley shows how the *SEL* takes Pope Gregory to its heart, transforming him into a beloved English saint, while Austin (Augustine), who actually made the difficult and unpleasant journey across Europe in order to carry out the work of conversion, is portrayed in more problematic terms, especially in comparison to good King Ethelbert, who receives the lion's share of the credit. In this legend, Whatley suggests, the *SEL* encourages its audience to enhance its own self-image by reclothing a famous Roman pope in English garb but Heather Blurton's essay about Quiriac, a converted Jew and the first bishop of Jerusalem, martyred during the reign of Julian the Apostate casts Englishness in a darker light. The legend seemingly has nothing to do with England and the English, yet Blurton links it convincingly both to a late thirteenth-century coin-clipping scandal in England, which resulted in the hanging of 269 Jews, and to the deepening suspicion of converted Jews more generally.

The legend of the child martyr Kenelm, murdered by his tutor, has attracted considerable attention in the past, with its riveting assemblage of folkoric and supernatural details: a wicked sister, prophetic dreams, a magical white cow who persists in sitting by the burial site until villagers take note, and finally, most glorious of all, a dove who delivers the truth to the pope in a document which, however, he cannot understand because it is written in English. Jocelyn Wogan-Browne, Chloe Morgan and Sarah Breckenridge all make use of interdisciplinary methods to shed new and very original light on Kenelm's meaning, moving well beyond previous assessments of the legend as a simple example of

English nationalism, and disputing what has been seen as a general feature of the *SEL*, its participation in an anti-textual, anti-urban culture. Each essay brings a wealth of new information garnered from the authors' knowledge of the specific historical or cultural contexts of the *SEL*, and, though none depends on the others for an understanding of its individual thesis, together they weave a rich composite tapestry. All three essays, for instance, illuminate the significance of the dove's document, with its golden letters, in slightly different ways. Chloe Morgan uses it to make a point about the way the *SEL* engages texts and the written word. Far from being hostile to textual culture, the narrative draws attention to the importance of texts as physical objects, whose power for lay people did not always depend on reading. For Jocelyn Wogan-Browne, the word 'writ' itself draws the audience's attention to the new importance of legal documents, helping to ground the legend in a moment of 'emergent civic literacy and identity'. This moment is further grounded very specifically in Winchcombe where Kenelm's body is finally enshrined. Sarah Breckenridge demonstrates the centrality of Winchcombe/Worcestershire to the legend's meaning: when the people of the diocese of Worcester are better able to read and interpret the dove's writ than the pope, the map of the world undergoes a seismic shift whereby Rome must give way to Worcester as the '*precise* centre of Christendom'.

Three different essays take up the legend of Thomas Becket, England's most famous saint. Sherry Reames, whose extensive knowledge of English liturgical manuscripts has greatly increased our understanding of the *SEL*'s use of them as both source material and model, looks at possible liturgical models for the translation of Thomas. Catherine Sanok considers the idea of community in the overall form of the *SEL* as well as within the legend of Thomas itself. With regard to the custom of a Tuesday fast in St Thomas's honour, which concludes the legend, Reames and Sanok make separate but related points. In comparing the *SEL* narrative to its likely liturgical model, Reames shows how the *SEL* has privileged the role of King Henry III over that of the archbishop in bringing about Thomas's translation and also how a change in the order of events narrated emphasizes the possibility of the hypothetical audience's participation in this custom. Sanok sees the same moment as a reminder that the unity suggested by the ritual commemoration of a Tuesday fast is not only temporary, but demonstrates the impossibility of reconciling the claims of ecclesiastical and regnal authority. In other words, both essays

once again engage the question of Englishness, while unpacking
the complexities and the tensions that belie the notion of a simple
nationalism. Finally, in an essay which concentrates on the mythical account of Becket's parentage, Robert Mills explores this narrative of a Crusader knight wooed by an emir's heathen daughter.
Ultimately the princess becomes Christian through baptism, and
learns English from Becket's mother, thus allowing the narrative
to 'construct England itself as essentially Christian and monolingual', yet the displaced 'other' (e.g. *not* only Christian, *not* just one
language) remains as a source of anxiety, once more eroding any
simple sense of Englishness.

Despite the continued usefulness of the two printed editions
of the *SEL* (Horstmann and D'Evelyn and Mill) many of the
essays in this collection allude to texts and manuscripts not found
in them. Essays by Karen Winstead and Jocelyn Wogan-Browne
introduce the reader to two relatively late manuscripts, lending
support to Liszka's thesis that the *SEL* was both constructed and
understood in different ways. 'Late', following Görlach, is usually
considered to mean also of lesser interest, yet MS Tanner 17 and
MS Bodley 779 offer excellent insights into the fifteenth-century
cultural context that produced them. Tanner 17 is the only illustrated *SEL* manuscript and its portraits of saints (wonderfully
reproduced here), with their de-emphasis on torture, and detailed
attention to clothing, suggest a shift towards these saints as objects
of devotion and emblems of community. In MS Bodley 779, with
its many additional lives of popes, we see a new emphasis placed
by the fifteenth-century compiler on the politics of church doctrine
and church authority. Taken together these manuscripts also demonstrate the continuing vitality of the *SEL* well beyond the period
of its initial composition.

Is there more work to be done? Of course, and I trust that the
impetus provided by this collection will lead to further scholarship along similar lines. There is, for instance, much still to be
learned from studying the many unprinted manuscripts. Gender
has received less attention here, probably because it was one of the
first aspects of the *SEL* to receive close attention in the hands of
contemporary scholars, but there is certainly more to be said. The
final section of this book also reminds me of two crucial aspects of
the *SEL*: first, that it's funny, entertaining and eminently suitable
for both reading aloud and performing once the language barrier
is surmounted; and second, following from the first, that it can be
made accessible even to undergraduates. Somewhat to my surprise,

I have found undergraduates very receptive to working with the *SEL*, introducing them to manuscript studies through the use of *SEL* microfilms (which I obtained for my own work). With this in mind – and as a teacher who spent her working life at an undergraduate institution – I confess that my thoughts tend to centre on how the *SEL* can be made both more available and more accessible to undergraduates: I would love to see editions of individual legends, especially those not printed in either Horstmann or D'Evelyn and Mill. Sherry Reames offers an excellent model for such editions in her *Middle English Legends of Female Saints* where, for example, she prints two different versions of the *SEL* 'Frideswide' with an excellent introduction and a full and user-friendly textual apparatus. Something along the lines of the Norton Critical Editions would also be welcome and useful. I'm thinking, for instance, of the legend of Kenelm, printed together with Chaucer's 'Nun's Priest's Tale', again with full textual apparatus, but also accompanied by a variety of critical essays. I believe there is a continuing need for contemporary readers to understand Chaucer as both part of, and influenced by, the broader contexts of medieval literature. We pay lip service to this idea, but the *SEL* offers an especially good opportunity to see it at work. Reading the *SEL* alongside of Chaucer is a way of encouraging readers to take the *SEL* seriously, both for its influence and even more importantly for its richness and readability on its own terms.

To conclude: as previously noted, many of the essays in this collection contest the earlier idea that the *SEL* displays a strongly nationalistic representation of 'a time-transcending English community rooted in a pastoral countryside' (Wogan-Browne). Morgan alludes to how the *SEL* has repeatedly frustrated attempts to place it in terms of geographical original, target audience or ideological allegiances. Yet I think that these essays do none the less affirm Englishness, both local and national, in the following ways (not all of which are positive): yes to Worcester/Winchcombe, yes to urban civic culture, yes to underlying anxieties about who is in and who is out when Englishness is named, and yes to an English audience who may not be fully literate but are very much aware of the importance of texts and the different ways they can signify. Indeed, once we stop trying to pin down through manuscript evidence exactly where and when the *SEL* originated, we are freed up to see just how much we actually know: a knowledge that was always already there, waiting to be discovered, of just how specifically the *SEL is* contextualized with regard to time, place and culture, both secular and religious. The nature of this discovery reminds me of the knight's quest in Browning's *Childe Roland* when, after years of toil and close to despair he looks up towards the horizon: 'Burningly it came on me all at once, / this was the place!' 'With these essays I think we have arrived at just such another place and it seems fair to say that *SEL* studies have come of age.

Works Cited

Manuscripts

Aberystwyth, National Library of Wales, MS 5043
Cambridge, Cambridge University Library, Additional MS 2604
  MS Ff.5.48
Cambridge, Corpus Christi College, MS 145
Cambridge, Magdalene College, MS Pepys 2344
Cambridge, St John's College, MS 28
  MS B.6
Cambridge, Trinity College, MS 323 (B.14.39)
  605 (R.3.25)
Dublin, Trinity College, MS 172
Exeter, Exeter Cathedral Library, MS 3507
Hereford, Hereford Cathedral Library, MS P.7.vi
Karlsruhe, Badische Landesbibliothek, MS St. Georgen 12
London, British Library, Additional MS 10626
  28681
  32427
  43406
  46919
  70513
MS Cotton Appendix 23
  Caligula A.xi
  Cleopatra D. ix
  Julius D.ix
  Nero E.i
  Otho D.ix
  Tiberius E.i
  Vespasian A.xxii
  Vitellius C.xii
MS Egerton 1993
  2810
MS Harley 913
  1808

2277
4012
MS Stowe 949
London, College of Arms, MS Arundel 127
London, Lambeth Palace, MS 223
    522
Oxford, Bodleian Library, MS Additional C. 38
    Ashmole 43
    Bodley 779
    Digby 86
        112
    English Poetry A.1
    Lat. lit.c.36
    Lat.lit.e.39
    Laud Misc. 108
        463
    Rawlinson A.287
    Rawl. Poet. 225
    Tanner 15
Oxford, Corpus Christi College, MS 237
Oxford, Jesus College, MS 29
Oxford, St John's College, MS 94
    190
Oxford, University College, MS 97
Paris, Bibliothèque nationale, fonds fr. 24766
Princeton, Princeton University Library, MS Garrett 143
Winchester, Winchester College, MS 33

South English Legendary editions

Acker, Paul, 'Saint Mildred in the *South English Legendary*', in Jankofsky
    (ed.), *South English Legendary*, pp. 140–53.
Braswell, Laurel, 'Saint Edburga of Winchester: a study of her cult, A.D.
    950–1500, with an edition of the fourteenth-century Middle English and
    Latin lives', *Mediaeval Studies*, 33 (1971), 292–333.
The Early South-English Legendary or Lives of Saints, ed. Carl Horstmann,
    EETS OS 87 (London: Trübner, 1887; reprint, Millwood, NY: Kraus,
    1987).
*An East Midland Revision of the South English Legendary: A Selection from
    Ms. C.U.L. Add. 3039*, ed. Manfred Görlach, Middle English Texts 4
    (Heidelberg: Winter, 1976).
Horstmann, Carl (ed.). 'Des Ms. Bodl. 779 jüngere Zusatzlegenden
    zur südlichen Legendensammlung', *Archiv für das Studium
    der neueren Sprachen und Literaturen*, 82 (1889), 167–97, 307–53,
    369–422.

———, 'Sermo in festo corporis Christi', ed. Carl Horstmann, Archiv, 82 (1889), 175–88.

———, Leben Jesu, ein Fragment und Kindheit Jesu, zwei altenglishe Gedichte, I. Theil, Leben Jesu (Münster, 1873).

Lapidge, Michael and Michael Winterbottom (eds), 'The Middle English "Life of Adelwolde"', in Michael Lapidge and Michael Winterbottom (eds), The Life of St. Æthelwold (Oxford: Clarendon Press, 1991), pp. 87–92.

Liszka, Thomas R., 'The South English Legendary: a critical edition of the Prologue and the Lives of Saints Fabian, Sebastian, Gregory the Great, Mark, Quiriac, Paul, and James the Great' (PhD dissertation, Northern Illinois University, 1980).

Nagy, Michael S., 'Saint Æþelberht of East Anglia in the South English Legendary', The Chaucer Review, 37:2 (2002), 159–72.

Pickering, Oliver S. (ed.), 'The "Defense of Women" from the Southern Passion: a new edition', in Jankofsky (ed.), South English Legendary, pp. 154–76.

Reames, Sherry L. (ed.), 'Shorter South English Legendary Life of St Frideswide' and 'Longer South English Legendary Life of St Frideswide', in Reames et al. (eds), Middle English Legends of Women Saints, pp. 27–36, 37–49 (see under Other Published Primary Texts).

The South English Legendary, Edited From Corpus Christi College Cambridge MS 145 and British Museum MS Harley 2277, ed. Charlotte D'Evelyn and Anna J. Mill, 3 vols, EETS OS 235, 236, 244 (London: Oxford University Press, 1956–59).

The South English Ministry and Passion, ed. Oliver S. Pickering, Middle English Texts 16 (Heidelberg: Carl Winter, 1984).

The South English Nativity of Mary and Christ, ed. Oliver S. Pickering, Middle English Texts 1 (Heidelberg: Carl Winter Universitätsverlag, 1975).

The Southern Passion, ed. Beatrice Daw Brown, EETS OS 169 (London: Oxford University Press, 1927).

Speed, Diane, 'Text and meaning in the "South English Legendary Lives of Æthelwold"', Notes and Queries, 41:3 (1994), 295–301.

———, (ed.), 'The Middle English life of Saint Hilarion', Parergon, 29 (1981), 8–14.

Whatley, E. Gordon (ed.), with Anne B. Thompson and Robert K. Upchurch, 'Saint George and the Dragon in the South English Legendary', in Whatley et al (eds), Saints' Lives in Middle English Collections, pp. 98–101 (see under Other Published Primary Texts).

Other published primary texts

Acta Sanctorum quotquot toto orbe coluntur. . ., ed. G. Henschen and D. Papenbroeck, 68 vols (Antwerp and Brussels, 1643–1940) [http://acta.chadwyck.com/].

Altenglische Legenden, ed. Carl Horstmann (Paderborn: Schöningh, 1875).

Altenglische Legenden. Neue Folge, ed. Carl Horstmann (Heilbronn: Henninger, 1881).

Ancrene Wisse, ed. J. R. R. Tolkien, EETS OS 249 (London: Oxford University Press, 1962).

Anglo-Irish Poems of the Middle Ages, ed. Angela Lucas (Blackrock, Co. Dublin: The Columba Press, 1995).

Annales Monastici, ed. Henry Richards Luard, 5 vols, RS 36 (London: HMSO, 1864–69).

Anouilh, Jean, *Becket, or, The Honour of God,* trans. Lucienne Hill (London: Samuel French, 1961).

Augustine, *Ennarationes in psalmos I,* CCSL 38 (Turnhout: Brepols, 1956).

——, trans. James Tweed in James Tweed, Thomas Scratton, Henry Musgrave Wilkins et al. (eds), *Expositions on the Book of Psalms,* Library of the Fathers of the Holy Catholic Church nosg 24, 30, 32, 39 (Oxford: John Henry Parker, 1847–57).

Bede's Ecclesiastical History of the English Church and People, ed. Bertram Colgrave and R. A. B. Mynors (Oxford: Clarendon Press, 1969).

Bede, *Expositio Actuum Apostolorum,* trans. L. T. Martin as *Commentary on the Acts of the Apostles,* Cistercian Study Series 117 (Kalamazoo, MI: Cistercian Publications, 1991).

——, *Expositio Actuum Apostolorum,* ed. M. L. W. Laistner, CCSL 121 (Turnhout: Brepols, 1983).

——, *A History of the English Church and People,* trans. Leo Sherley-Price (Baltimore: Penguin Books, 1955).

Bell, Alexander (ed.), 'The Anglo-Norman *Description of England*: an edition', in Ian Short (ed.), *Anglo-Norman Anniversary Essays,* ANTS OPS 3 (London: ANTS, 1993), pp. 31–47.

Blamires, Alcuin, (ed.), *Woman Defamed and Woman Defended: An Anthology of Medieval Texts* (Oxford: Oxford University Press, 1999).

Bodleian Library MS Fairfax 16, ed. J. Norton-Smith (London: Scolar Press, 1979).

Borough Customs, ed. Mary Bateson, Surtees Society 18 (London: Quaritch, 1904–6).

Breviarium ad usum insignis ecclesiae Eboracensis, ed. Stephen W. Swayley, 2 vols, Surtees Society 71, 75 (Durham: Andrews, 1880–83).

Breviarium ad usum insignis ecclesiae Sarum, ed. Francis Procter and Christopher Wordsworth, 3 vols (Cambridge: Cambridge University Press, 1879–86).

Brown, Carleton (ed.), *English Lyrics of the XIIIth Century* (Oxford: Clarendon Press, 1932).

Brown, Jennifer M., *Three Women of Liège. A Critical Edition of and Commentary on the Middle English Lives of Elizabeth of Spalbeek, Christina Mirabilis, and Marie d'Oignies,* Medieval Women Texts and Contexts 23 (Turnhout: Brepols, 2008).

Chaucer, Geoffrey, *The Riverside Chaucer*, 3rd edn, ed. Larry D. Benson (Oxford: Oxford University Press, 1987).

The Chronicle of William de Rishanger, of the Barons' Wars, ed. J. O. Halliwell (London: Camden Society, 1840).

The Chronicles of the Reigns of Stephen, Henry II and Richard I, ed. Richard Howlett, RS 82 (London: Longman & Co., 1885).

The Chronicles of Rome: An Edition of the Middle English Chronicle of Popes and Emperors and the Lollard Chronicle, ed. Dan Embree (Woodbridge: Boydell Press, 1998).

Crick, Julia (ed.), *Charters of St Albans* (Oxford: Oxford University Press for the British Academy, 2007).

Cursor Mundi: A Northumbrian Poem of the XIVth Century, ed. Richard Morris, 7 vols, EETS OS 57, 59, 62, 66, 68, 99, 101 (London: N. Trübner for EETS, 1874–93).

Damasus I, *Epigrammata Damasiana*, ed. Antonio Ferrua (Rome: Pontifico Istituto di Archeologia Christiana, 1942).

The Dialogues of Saint Gregory, Surnamed the Great. . ., ed. and trans. Edmund G. Gardner (London: Warner, 1911).

Dickens, Charles, *A Child's History of England*, 3 vols (London: Bradbury & Evans, 1852).

Die me. Thomas Beket-legende des Gloucesterlegendars, ed. Hermann Thiemke (Berlin: Mayer and Müller, 1919).

Dockray-Miller, Mary (ed. and trans.), *Saints Edith and Æthelthryth: Princesses, Miracle Workers, and Their Late Medieval Audience: The Wilton Chronicle and the Wilton Life of St Æthelthryth*, Medieval Women Texts and Contexts 25 (Brepols: Turnhout, 2009).

Documents of the Baronial Movement of Reform and Rebellion 1258–1267, ed. R. E. Treharne and I. J. Sanders (Oxford: Clarendon Press, 1973).

Dominic of Evesham, 'Dominic of Evesham: *Vita S. Ecgwini Episcopi et Confessoris*', ed. Michael Lapidge, *Analecta Bollandiana*, 96 (1978), 65–104.

Dubois, Pierre, *The Recovery of the Holy Land*, trans. Walther I. Brandt (New York: Columbia University Press, 1956).

The Earliest Life of Gregory the Great, ed. Bertram Colgrave (1968; reprint, Cambridge: Cambridge University Press, 1985).

The Early English Carols, ed. Richard Leighton Greene (Oxford: Clarendon Press, 1935).

English Wycliffite Sermons, ed. Anne Hudson, 5 vols (Oxford: Clarendon Press, 1983–96), vol. I (1983).

Facsimile of Oxford, Bodleian Library, MS Digby 86, with an introduction by Judith Tschann and M. B. Parkes, EETS SS 16 (Oxford, 1996).

Flores Historiarum, ed. Henry Richards Luard, RS 95 (London: Eyre & Spottiswode for HMSO, 1890).

Gaimar, *Lestorie des Engleis*, ed. T. D. Hardy and C. T. Martin, 2 vols, RS 91 (London: Eyre and Spottiswode, 1888–89).

Geoffrey of Monmouth, *Historia Regum Brittanniae*, ed. Neil Wright, vol. I (Woodbridge and Dover, NH: D. S. Brewer, 1985).

Gervase of Canterbury, 'Mappa mundi' in W. Stubbs (ed.), *The Historical Works of Gervase of Canterbury*, 2 vols, Royal Society 73 (London: Longman, Brown, Green, Longmans & Roberts, 1879–80), vol. II, pp. 414–49.

The Golden Legend: or, Lives of the Saints, as Englished by William Caxton, ed. F. S. Ellis (London: J. M. Dent, 1900).

Gregory of Tours, *Life of the Fathers*, trans. E. James, *Translated Texts for Historians* 1 (Liverpool, 1986).

——, 'Vita patrum', ed. B. Krusch in *Gregorii Episcopii Turonensis Opera*, MGH: Scriptores Rerum Merovingicarum (Hanover: Hahn, 1885), pp. 661–743.

Havelok, ed. G. V. Smithers (Oxford: Clarendon Press, 1987).

Henry of Huntingdon, *The History of the English People, 1000–1154*, trans. Diana Greenway (Oxford: Oxford World Classics, 2002).

——, *Historia Anglorum: The History of the English People*, ed. and trans. Diana Greenway (Oxford: Clarendon Press, 1996).

The Hereford Breviary, Edited from the Rouen Edition of 1505 with Collation of Manuscripts, ed. Walter H. Frere and L. E. G. Brown, 3 vols, HBS 26, 40, 46 (London: Henry Bradshaw Society, 1904–15).

Horstmann, Carl (ed.), 'Die Legenden von Celestin und Susanna: I Celestin', *Anglia*, I (1878), 55–85.

——, 'Gregorius auf dem Stein aus MS Vernon', ed. Carl Horstmann, *Archiv*, 55 (1876), pp. 405–38.

——, 'Die Sprüche des h. Bernhard und die Vision des h. Paulus nach Ms. Laud 108', *Archiv für das Studium der Neueren Sprachen und Literaturen*, 52 (1874), 33–8.

——, 'King Horn nach Ms. Laud 108', *Archiv für das Studium der Neueren Sprachen und Literaturen*, 50 (1872), 39–58.

Jacobus de Voragine, *Golden Legend*, trans. William Granger Ryan, 2 vols (Princeton, NJ: Princeton University Press, 1993).

——, *The Golden Legend*, trans. William Granger Ryan and Helmut Ripperger (New York: Longmans, 1941).

Jerome, *Letters of St. Jerome*, ed. F. A. Wright, Loeb Classical Library 262 (London: Heinemann, 1954).

John the Deacon, *Sancti Gregorii Magni Vita* (BHL 3641), in *Patrologia Latina* 75: 59–242.

The Kalendre of the New Legende of England, ed. Manfred Görlach (Heidelberg: Carl Winter Universitätsverlag, 1994).

Kennedy, Ruth, ed., *Three Middle English Alliterative Poems*, EETS OS 321 (Oxford: Oxford University Press, 2003).

King Horn, Floriz and Blauncheflur, the Assumption of Our Lady, First ed. in 1866, by J. Rawson Lumby, and now re-ed. from the manuscripts, ed.

George McKnight, EETS OS 14 (London: Oxford University Press, 1901).

Kingsford, C. L. (ed.), *The Song of Lewes* (Oxford: Clarendon Press, 1890).

Landboc sive Registrum monasterii beatae Mariae virginis et sancti Cenhelmi de Winchelcumba, ed. David Royce, 2 vols, Bristol and Gloucestershire Archaeological Society Publications (Exeter: William Pollard, 1892, 1903).

Langland, William, *Piers Plowman: The B Version, Will's Vision of Piers Plowman, Do-Well, Do-Better, and Do-Best*, ed. G. Kane and E. T. Donaldson (London: Athlone Press, 1988)

Lapidge, Michael (ed.), *The Lives of St. Oswald and St. Ecgwine* (Oxford: Oxford University Press, 2009).

The Latin Charters of the Anglo-Saxon Period, ed. F. M. Stenton (Oxford: Clarendon Press, 1955).

Layamon, Brut or Historia Brutonum, ed. W. R. J. Barron and S. C. Weinberg (Harlow, Essex: Longman, 1995).

Legenda Exon, Exeter Chapter MSS. 3504 and 3505, ed. J. N. Dalton, HBS 63, vol. 3 (London: Harrison and Sons, 1926).

Legends of the Holy Rood: Symbols of the Passion and Cross-Poems in Old English of the Eleventh, Fourteenth, and Fifteenth Centuries, ed. Richard Morris, EETS OS 46 (London: N. Trübner for EETS, 1881).

Liber pontificalis nella recensione di Pietro Guglielmo OSB e del card. Pandolfo, glossato da Pietro Bohier OSB, vescovo di Orvieto, ed. U. Přerovský, *Studia Gratiana* 21, 22, 23 (Rome: Libreria Ateneo Salesiano, 1978).

The Life and Martyrdom of Thomas Beket, Archbishop of Canterbury, ed. William Henry Black (London: Percy Society, 1845).

Love, Nicholas, *Treatise on the Sacraments*, in Michael Sargent (ed.), *Nicholas Love, The Mirror of the Blessed Life of Jesus Christ* (Exeter: Exeter University Press, 2005).

Love, Rosalind C. (ed.), *Three Eleventh-Century Anglo-Latin Saints' Lives: Vita S. Birini, Vita et Miracula S. Kenelmi and Vita S. Rumwoldi* (Oxford: Oxford University Press, 1996).

Lydgate, John, 'The Virtues of the Mass', in H. N. MacCracken (ed.), *The Minor Poems of John Lydgate*, Pt II, EETS ES 107 (London: Kegan Paul, Trench, Trübner, 1911), pp. 87–115.

Manuscript Bodley 638: A Facsimile, ed. P. Robinson (Norman, Oklahoma: Pilgrim Books, 1982).

Materials for the History of Thomas Becket, ed. James C. Robertson and J. B. Sheppard, 7 vols, RS 67 (London: Longman, 1875–85).

Matthew Paris, *Chronica majora*, ed. Henry Richards Luard, RS 57, 7 vols (London: 1872–83).

The Metrical Chronicle of Robert of Gloucester, ed. William Aldis Wright, 2 vols, RS 86 (London: HMSO, 1887).

Miller, Thomas, *Fair Rosamund, or The Days of King Henry II: An Historical Romance*, 3 vols (London: Henry Colburn, 1839).

Milton, John, *The History of England* (London: R. Chiswell, 1695).

The Monastic Breviary of Hyde Abbey, Winchester, ed. John B. L. Tolhurst, 6 vols, HBS 69–71, 76, 78, 80 (London: Harrison and Sons, 1932–42).

Moore, Grace Edna (ed.), 'The Middle English Verse Life of Edward the Confessor' (PhD dissertation, University of Pennsylvania, 1942).

Myrc's Instructions for Parish Priests, ed. Edward Peacock, EETS ES 31 (London: Kegan Paul, Trench, Trübner, 1868).

Nova Legenda Anglie, ed. Carl Horstmann (Oxford: Clarendon Press, 1901).

Orderic Vitalis, *Historia Ecclesiastica*, ed. and trans. Marjorie Chibnall, 7 vols (Oxford: Oxford University Press, 1980).

Ordinale Exon., ed. J. N. Dalton, HBS 63, 4 vols (London: Harrison and Sons, 1926).

Oschinsky, Dorothea (ed.), *Walter of Henley and Other Treatises on Estate Management and Accounting* (Oxford: Clarendon Press, 1971).

The Owl and the Nightingale, ed. E. G. Stanley, 2nd edn (Manchester: Manchester University Press, 1972).

The Owl and the Nightingale, Reproduced in Facsimile from the Surviving Manuscripts, introduction by N. R. Ker, EETS OS 251 (London: Kegan Paul, Trench, Trübner, 1963).

Passio SS, Xysti et Laurentii, in 'Récherches sur le légendier romain', ed. Hippolyte Delehaye, *Analecta Bollandiana*, 51 (1933), 72–98.

Patrologia Latina cursus completus series latina, ed. J. P. Migne (Paris, 1841–64).

Paul the Deacon, Sancti Gregorii Magni Vita (BHL 3640) in *Patrologia Latina*, 75: 41–59.

The Philobiblon of Richard de Bury, ed. and trans. E. C. Thomas (Oxford: Blackwell, 1960).

Plaidy, Jean, *The Plantagenet Prelude* (London: Hale, 1976).

Polonus, Martinus, *Chronicon*, in *Martini Oppaviensis Chronicon Pontificum et Imperatorum*, ed. Ludwig Weiland, MGH SS 22 (Hanover: Impensis Bibliopolii Avlici Hahniani, 1872), pp. 377–482.

Polychronicon Ranulfi Higden monachi Cestrensis, ed. J. R. Lumby, 9 vols, RS 41 (London: Longman, Green, Longman, Roberts and Green, 1865–86).

Prudentius, *Aurelii Prudenti Clementis Carmina*, ed. M. P. Cunningham, CCSL 126 (Turnhout: Brepols, 1966).

——, *The Poems of Prudentius*, trans. Sister M. Clement Eagan, The Fathers of the Church 43 (Washington: Catholic University of America Press, 1962).

Queen Mary's Psalter: Miniatures and Drawings by an English Artist of the 14th Century Reproduced from Royal MS. 2 B VII in the

British Museum, ed. Sir George Warner (London: British Museum, 1912).

Ragman Roll, ein spätmittelenglisches Gedicht, ed. Andreas Freudenberger (Erlangen: Junge, 1909).

Reames, Sherry L., with Martha G. Blalock and Wendy L. Larson (eds), *Middle English Legends of Women Saints* (Kalamazoo, MI: Medieval Institute Publications, 2003).

Reichl, Karl, *Religiöse Dichtung im englischen Hochmittelalter: Untersuchung u. Edition d. Handschrift B. 14. 39 d. Trinity College in Cambridge* (Munich: Fink, 1973).

Robbins, R. H. (ed.), *Secular Lyrics of the Fourteenth and Fifteenth Centuries* (Oxford: Clarendon Press, 1952).

Robert Mannyng of Brunne, *Handlyng Synne*, ed. Idelle Sullens (Binghamton, NY: Medieval and Rennaissance Texts and Studies, 1983).

The Rule of Saint Benedict, ed. and trans. Justin McCann (London: Burns and Oates, 1952).

Sammlung Altenglischer Legenden, ed. Carl Horstmann (Heilbronn: Gebr. Henniger, 1878).

The Sermons of Thomas Brinton, Bishop of Rochester (1373–1389), ed. Mary Aquinas Devlin, 2 vols (London: Royal Historical Society, 1954).

Shewings of Julian of Norwich, ed. Georgia Ronan Crampton (Kalamazoo, MI: Medieval Institute Publications, 1994).

Sir Orfeo, ed. A. J. Bliss (Oxford: Oxford University Press, 1954).

Staley, Lynn (ed.), *The Book of Margery Kempe* (Kalamazoo, MI: Medieval Institute Publications, 1996).

Stengel, E., *Codicem Manu Scriptum Digby 86* (Halle: Libraria Orphanotrophei, 1871).

Stephen of Ripon, *The Life of Bishop Wilfrid*, ed. Bertram Colgrave (Cambridge: Cambridge University Press, 1927).

Supplementary Lives in Some Manuscripts of the Gilte Legende, ed. Richard Hamer and Vida Russell, EETS OS 315 (Oxford: Oxford University Press, 2000).

The Tale of Beryn, ed. F. J. Furnivall and W. G. Stone, EETS ES 105 (London: Kegan Paul, Trench, Trübner and Henry Froude for Oxford University Press, 1909).

Thomas of Marlborough, *History of the Abbey of Evesham*, ed. Jane E. Sayers and Leslie Watkiss (Oxford: Clarendon Press, 2003).

The Vernon Manuscript: A Facsimile of Bodleian Library, Oxford, Ms Eng. Poet A.1, ed.A. I. Doyle (Cambridge: D. S. Brewer, 1987).

Verses in Sermons: Fasciculus Morum and Its Middle English Poems, ed. Siegfriend Wenzel (Cambridge, MA: Medieval Academy of America, 1978).

La Vie de pape saint Grégoire: huit versions françaises médiévales de la Légende du bon pécheur, ed. Hendrik Sol (Amsterdam: Rodopi, 1977).

The Vita Wulfstani of William of Malmesbury, ed. Reginald R. Darlington (London: Royal Historical Society, 1928).

Wace, *Wace's Roman de Brut: A History of the British*, ed. and trans. Judith Weiss (Exeter: University of Exeter Press, 1999).

Whatley, E. Gordon (ed.), with Anne B. Thompson and Robert K. Upchurch, *Saints' Lives in Middle English Collections* (Kalamazoo, MI: Medieval Institute Publications, 2004).

Whitelock, Dorothy, *English Historical Documents Volume 1, c. 500–1042* (London: Routledge, 1996).

William of Malmesbury, *Gesta pontificum Anglorum*, ed. and trans. M. Winterbottom and R. M. Thomson (Oxford: Clarendon Press, 2007).

——, *Saints' Lives*, ed. and trans. M. Winterbottom and R. M. Thomson (Oxford: Clarendon Press, 2002).

——, *Gesta Regum Anglorum*, ed. and trans. R. A. B. Mynors, R. M. Thomson and M. Winterbottom, 2 vols (Oxford: Clarendon Press, 1998).

Wright, T., *The Latin Poems of Walter Mapes*, Camden Society OS 16 (London: J. B. Nichols, 1841).

Secondary works

Aers, David, 'Walter Brut's theology of the sacrament of the altar', in Somerset et al. (eds), *Lollards and Their Influence*, pp. 115–26.

Allen, J. B., *The Friar as Critic: Literary Attitudes in the Later Middle Ages* (Nashville: Vanderbilt University Press, 1971).

Appadurai, Arjun, *Modernity at Large: Cultural Dimensions of Globalization* (Minneapolis: University of Minnesota Press, 1996).

Archibald, Elizabeth, *Incest and the Medieval Imagination* (Oxford: Clarendon Press, 2001).

Ashton, Gail, *The Generation of Identity in Medieval Hagiography: Speaking the Saint* (London: Routledge, 2000).

Baert, Barbara, *A History of Holy Wood: The Legend of the True Cross in Text and Image*, trans. Lee Preedy (Leiden: Brill, 2004).

Baker, J. H., *Manual of Law French*, 2nd edn, (Aldershot: Scolar Press, 1990).

Baker, Nigel and Richard Holt, *Urban Growth and the Medieval Church: Gloucester and Worcester* (Aldershot: Ashgate, 2005).

Bale, Anthony, (ed.), *St Edmund, King and Martyr: Changing Images of a Medieval Saint* (Woodbridge and York: York Medieval Press, 2009).

——, *The Jew in the Medieval Book* (Cambridge: Cambridge University Press, 2007).

Barlow, Frank, *Thomas Becket* (London: Weidenfeld & Nicolson, 1986).

Bassett, Steven, 'In search of the origin of Anglo-Saxon kingdoms', in Steven Bassett (ed.), *Origins of Anglo-Saxon Kingdoms* (Leicester: Leicester University Press, 1989), pp. 3–27.

Baswell, Christopher, 'Multilingualism on the page', in Strohm (ed.), *Middle English*, pp. 38–50.

Baxter, Stephen, 'Archbishop Wulfstan and the administration of God's property', in M. Townend (ed.), *Wulfstan, Archbishop of York: The Proceedings of the Second Alcuin Conference* (Turnhout: Brepols, 2004), pp. 161–205.

Bedingfield, M. B., *The Dramatic Liturgy of Anglo-Saxon England* (Woodbridge: Boydell Press, 2002).

Bell, David N. (ed.), *The Libraries of the Cistercians, Gilbertines, and Premonstratensians*, Corpus of British Medieval Library Catalogues 3 (London: The British Library, 1992).

Bell, Kimberly K. and Julie Nelson Couch (eds), *The Texts and Contexts of Bodleian Library, MS Laud Misc. 108: The Shaping of English Vernacular Narrative* (Leiden: Brill, 2011).

Bemont, Charles, *Simon de Montfort Earl of Leicester, 1208–1265*, trans. E. F. Jacob (Oxford: Clarendon Press, 1930).

Bennett, J. A. W., completed by Douglas Gray, *Middle English Literature* (Oxford: Clarendon Press, 1990).

——, and G. L. Smithers, *Early Middle English Verse and Prose* (Oxford: Clarendon Press, 1966; 2nd edn, 1968; 2nd rev. edn, 1982).

Benskin, Michael, 'The style and authorship of the Kildare poems – (1) *Pers of Bermingham*', in J. L. Mackenzie and R. Todd (eds), *In Other Words: Transcultural Studies in Philology, Translation and Lexicography Presented to H. H. Meier on the Occasion of his Sixty-Fifth Birthday* (Dordrecht: Foris, 1989), pp. 57–75.

Biddick, Kathleen, *Typological Imaginary: Circumcision, Technology, History* (Philadelphia: University of Pennsylvania Press, 2003).

Binski, Paul, *Westminster Abbey and the Plantagenets: Kingship and the Representation of Power* (New Haven: Yale University Press, 1995).

Bjelland, Karen, 'Defining the *South English Legendary* as a form of drama', *Comparative Drama*, 22 (1988), 227–43.

——, 'Franciscan versus Dominican responses to the knight as societal model: the case of the *South English Legendary*', *Franciscan Studies*, 48 (1988), 11–27.

Blackburn, Bonnie and Leofranc Holford-Strevens, *The Oxford Companion to the Year: An Exploration of Calendar Customs and Time-Reckoning* (Oxford: Oxford University Press, 1999).

Blake, N. F., 'Vernon Manuscript: contents and organisation', in Pearsall (ed.), *Studies in the Vernon Manuscript*, pp. 45–59.

Blanton, Virginia, *Signs of Devotion: The Cult of St. Æthelthryth in Medieval England, 695–1615* (University Park: Penn State Press, 2007).

Boenig, Robert, 'Chaucer and St. Kenelm', *Neophilologus*, 84 (2000), 157–64.

Boffey, Julia and A. S. G. Edwards, *A New Index of Middle English Verse* (London: British Library, 2005).

Bond, C. J., 'The estates of Evesham Abbey: a preliminary survey of medieval topography', *Vale of Evesham Historical Society Research Papers*, 4 (1973), 1–62.

Bond, Francis, *Dedications and Patron Saints of English Churches: Ecclesiastical Symbolism, Saints and Their Emblems* (London: Oxford University Press, 1914).

Bonnier, C., 'List of English towns in the fourteenth century', *English Historical Review*, 16 (1901), 501–2.

Bost, Arno, trans. Andrew Winnard, *The Ordering of Time: From the Ancient Computus to the Modern Computer* (Chicago: University of Chicago Press, 1993).

Boureau, A. 'How law came to the monks: the use of law in English society at the beginning of the thirteenth century', *Past and Present*, 167 (2000), 29–74.

Boyd, Beverly, 'The enigma of Bodleian Library MS Laud Misc. 108 (circa 1300)', *Manuscripta*, 39 (1995), 131–6.

——, Review of *The Textual Tradition of the South English Legendary*, by Manfred Görlach, *Speculum*, 52 (1977), 678.

——, 'A new approach to the *South English Legendary*', *Philological Quarterly*, 47 (1968), 494–8.

——, 'New light on the *South English Legendary*', *Texas Studies in English*, 37 (1958), 187–94.

Boyle, Leonard, 'Dominican lectionaries and Leo of Ostia's *Translatio S. Clementis*', *Archivum Fratrum Praedicatorum*, 28 (1958), 362–94.

Brand, Paul, 'Jews and the law in England, 1275–90', *The English Historical Review*, 115:464 (2000), 1138–58.

Braswell, Laurel, 'The South English Legendary collection: a study in Middle English religious literature of the thirteenth and fourteenth centuries' (PhD dissertation, University of Toronto, 1964).

Brewer, Derek, *English Gothic Literature* (London: Macmillan, 1983).

Bright, William, *Chapters of Early English Church History*, 3rd edn (Oxford: Clarendon Press, 1897).

British Museum, *Catalogue of the Stowe Manuscripts in the British Museum*, 2 vols (Hildesheim: Olms, 1973).

Britnell, Richard, 'French in towns', in Wogan-Browne et al. (eds), *Language and Culture in Medieval Britain*, pp. 81–9.

Brooke, Iris, *English Costume from the Early Middle Ages through the Sixteenth Century* (1936; reprint Mineola, NY: Dover, 2000).

Brown, Carleton, *A Register of Middle English Religious & Didactic Verse, Part I: List of Manuscripts* (Oxford: Oxford University Press, 1916).

Brown, Michelle P., *The Lindisfarne Gospels: Society, Spirituality and the Scribe* (London: University of Toronto Press, 2003).

——, and Carol A. Farr (eds), *Mercia: An Anglo-Saxon Kingdom in Europe* (Leicester: Leicester University Press, 2001, repr. Continuum, 2005).

Brown, Paul Alonzo, 'The development of the legend of Thomas Becket' (published PhD thesis, Philadelphia: University of Pennsylvania, 1930).

Brown, Reva Nernan and Sean McCartney, 'Living in limbo: the experience of Jewish converts in medieval England,' in Guyda Armstrong and Ian N. Wood (eds), *Christianizing Peoples and Converting Individuals* (Turnhout: Brepols, 2000), pp. 169–91.

Brown, Sarah, *'Our Magnificent Fabrick': York Minster: An Architectural History c. 1250–1500* (Swindon: English Heritage, 2003).

Bullock-Davies, Constance, *Professional Interpreters and the Matter of Britain* (Cardiff: Wales University Press, 1966).

——, 'Marie, Abbess of Shaftesbury, and her brothers', *English Historical Review*, 80 (1965), 314–22.

Burrow, J., 'Bards, minstrels and men of letters', in D. Daiches and A. Thorlby (eds), *Literature and Civilization: The Medieval World* (London: Aldus, 1973), pp. 347–70.

Bynum, Carolyn Walker, *Wonderful Blood* (University Park, PA: Penn State Press, 2007).

Calendar of Entries in the Papal Register Relating to Great Britain and Ireland: Papal Letters, A.D. 1198–1304, ed. W. H. Bliss (London: Eyre & Spottiswoode, 1893).

Calendar of the Patent Rolls, Edward I A.D. 1277–1281 (London: Eyre & Spottiswoode, 1901).

Camille, Michael, 'The book as flesh and fetish in Richard de Bury's *Philobiblon*', in Frese and O'Keeffe, *The Book and the Body*, pp. 34–77.

Campbell, Emma, *Medieval Saints' Lives: The Gift, Kinship and Community in Old French Hagiography* (Woodbridge: D. S. Brewer, 2008).

Cannon, Christopher, *Middle English Literature* (Cambridge: Polity Press, 2008).

——, 'Monastic productions', in Wallace (ed.), *Cambridge History of Medieval English Literature*, pp. 316–48.

Carpenter, D. A., 'Simon de Montfort: the first leader of a political movement in English history', *History: The Journal of the Historical Association*, 246 (1991), 3–23.

Carruthers, Mary J., 'Reading with attitude, remembering the book', in Frese and O'Keeffe, *The Book and the Body*, pp. 1–33.

Caviness, Madeline H., 'Biblical stories in windows: were they bibles for the poor?', in Bernard S. Levy (ed.), *The Bible in the Middle Ages: Its Influence on Literature and Art* (Binghamton, NY: Medieval & Renaissance Texts & Studies, 1992), pp. 103–47.

Cerquiglini, Bernard, *Éloge de la variante: histoire critique de la philologie* (Paris: Seuil, 1989).

Chapman, Alison, 'Now and then: sequencing the sacred in two Protestant calendars', *Journal of Medieval and Early Modern Studies*, 33 (2003), 91–123.

Cheney, C. R., *Medieval Texts and Studies* (Oxford: Clarendon Press, 1973).

Christie, Sheila K., 'Bridging the jurisdictional divide: the masons and the York Corpus Christi Play', in Margaret Rogerson (ed.), *Reflections on the York Mystery Cycle* (Woodbridge and York: York Medieval Press, 2011), pp. 53–74.

Clanchy, M. T., *From Memory to Written Record: England 1066–1307*, 2nd ed. (Oxford: Blackwell, 1993) (originally published London: Blackwell, 1979).

Clark, James G., *A Monastic Renaissance at St Albans: Thomas Walsingham and His Circle, c. 1350–1440* (Oxford: Clarendon Press, 2004).

Cohen, Jeremy, *Living Letters of the Law: Ideas of the Jew in Medieval Christianity* (Berkeley: University of California Press, 1999).

Coleman, Janet, *English Literature in History, 1350–1400* (London: Hutchinson, 1981).

Collette, Carolyn P., *Performing Polity: Women and Agency in the Anglo-French Tradition, 1385–1620* (Turnhout: Brepols, 2006).

Connolly, Margaret and Linne R. Mooney (eds), *Design and Distribution of Late Medieval Manuscripts in England* (Woodbridge and York: York Medieval Press, 2008).

Copeland, Rita, *Rhetoric, Hermeneutics, and Translation in the Middle Ages: Academic Traditions and Vernacular Texts* (Cambridge: Cambridge University Press, 1991).

Coss, P. R., 'Sir Geoffrey de Langley and the crisis of the knightly class in thirteenth-century England', in T. H. Aston (ed.), *Landlords, Peasants and Politics in Medieval England* (Cambridge: Cambridge University Press, 1987), pp. 166–202.

——, 'Aspects of cultural diffusion in medieval England', *Past and Present*, 108 (1985), 35–79.

——, and S. D. Lloyd (eds), *Thirteenth Century England I* (Bury St Edmunds: Boydell Press, 1986).

Costain, Thomas B., *The Black Rose* (New York: Doubleday, 1946).

Cothren, M. W., 'The iconography of Theophilus windows in the first half of the thirteenth century', *Speculum*, 59 (1984), 308–41.

Cox, D. C., 'The Vale estates of the Church of Evesham c.700–1086', *Vale of Evesham Historical Society Research Papers*, 5 (1975), 25–50.

Crane, Susan, *Insular Romance: Politics, Faith, and Culture in Anglo-Norman and Middle English Literature* (Berkeley: University of California Press, 1986).

Craun, Edwin D., *Ethics and Power in Medieval English Reformist Writing* (Cambridge: Cambridge University Press, 2010).

Crick, Julia, 'St. Albans, Westminster, and some twelfth-century views of the Anglo-Saxon past', *Anglo-Norman Studies*, 25 (2003 for 2002), 65–83.

Cubitt, Catherine, 'Folklore and historiography: oral stories and the writing of Anglo-Saxon history', in Ross Balzaretti and Elizabeth Tyler (eds), *History and Narrative* (Turnhout, Brepols, 2006), pp. 189–223.

——, 'Sites and sanctity: revisiting the cult of murdered and martyred Anglo-Saxon royal saints', *Early Medieval Europe*, 9:1 (2000), 53–83.

Curtius, Ernst Robert, *European Literature and the Latin Middle Ages* (London: Routledge & Kegan Paul, 1953).

Davidson, Clifford, 'The Middle English saint play and its iconography', in Clifford Davidson (ed.), *The Saint Play in Medieval Europe* (Kalamazoo, MI: Medieval Institute Publications, 1986), pp. 31–122.

Dean, Ruth J. with Maureen B. M. Boulton, *Anglo-Norman Literature: A Guide to Texts and Manuscripts*, ANTS OPS 3 (London: Anglo-Norman Text Society, 1999).

Delano-Smith, Catherine and Roger J. P. Kain, *English Maps: A History* (London: British Library, 1999).

Delany, Sheila, *Impolitic Bodies: Poetry, Saints, and Society in Fifteenth-Century England, the Work of Osbern Bokenham* (Oxford: Oxford University Press, 1998).

Derrida, Jacques, *Of Grammatology*, trans. Gayatri Spivak, 2nd edn (Baltimore and London: Johns Hopkins University Press, 1999).

D'Evelyn, Charlotte and Frances A. Foster, 'Saints' legends', in J. Burke Severs (ed.), *A Manual of the Writings in Middle English, 1050–1500 II* (New Haven: Connecticut Academy of Arts and Sciences, 1970), pp. 410–57.

Dobson, E. J., *The Origins of Ancrene Wisse* (Oxford: Clarendon Press, 1976).

Donovan, Claire, *The de Brailes Hours: Shaping the Book of Hours in Thirteenth-Century Oxford* (Toronto and Buffalo: University of Toronto Press, 1991).

Druitt, Herbert, *A Manual of Costume as Illustrated by Monumental Brasses* (London: De La More Press, 1906).

Duggan, Anne, *Thomas Becket: Friends, Networks, Texts and Cult* (Aldershot: Ashgate, 2007).

——, 'The Lyell Version of the *Quadrilogus* Life of St Thomas of Canterbury', *Analecta Bollandiana*, 112 (1994), 105–38.

——, *Thomas Becket: A Textual History of His Letters* (Oxford: Clarendon Press, 1980).

Dumville, D. N., *Liturgy and the Ecclesiastical History of Late Anglo-Saxon England: Four Studies* (Woodbridge: Boydell Press, 1992).

Dunn-Lardeau, Brenda (ed.), *Legenda Aurea: sept siècles de diffusion: actes du colloque international sur la Legenda aurea, texte latin et branches vernaculaires à l'Université du Québec à Montréal, 11–12 mai 1983* (Montreal: Bellarmin; Paris: J. Vrin, 1986).

Earle, J. W., 'Typology and iconographic style in early medieval hagiography', *Studies in the Literary Imagination*, 8 (1977), 15–46.

Easton, Martha, 'Pain, torture and death in the Huntington Library *Legenda aurea*', in Samantha J. E. Riches and Sarah Salih (eds), *Gender and Holiness: Men, Women and Saints in Late Medieval Europe* (London: Routledge, 2002), pp. 49–64.

Edson, Evelyn, *Mapping Time and Space: How Medieval Mapmakers Viewed Their World* (London: The British Library, 1997).

Edwards, A. S. G., 'Fifteenth-century English collections of female saints' lives', *Yearbook of English Studies*, 33 (2003), 131–41.

——, 'The contexts of the Vernon romances', in Pearsall (ed.), *Studies in the Vernon Manuscript*, pp. 159–70.

Elliott, Dyan, *Fallen Bodies: Pollution, Sexuality, and Demonology in the Middle Ages* (Philadelphia: University of Pennsylvania Press, 1999).

Elukin, Jonathan, 'The discovery of the self: Jews and conversion in the twelfth century', in Michael A. Signer and John Van Engen (eds), *Jews and Christians in Twelfth-Century Europe* (Notre Dame: University of Notre Dame Press, 2001), pp. 63–76.

——, 'From Jew to Christian? Conversion and immutability in medieval Europe', in Muldoon (ed.), *Varieties of Religious Conversion*, pp. 171–89.

Emden, A. B., *A Biographical Register of the University of Oxford to AD 1500*, 3 vols (Oxford: Clarendon Press, 1957–59).

Erler, Mary C. and Maryanne Kowaleski (eds), *Gendering the Master Narrative: Women and Power in the Middle Ages* (Ithaca: Cornell University Press, 2003).

Evans, Michael R., 'Marriage as a means of conversion in Pierre Dubois's *De recuperatione Terre Sancte*', in Guyda Armstrong and Ian N. Wood (eds), *Christianizing Peoples and Converting Individuals* (Turnhout: Brepols, 2000), pp. 195–202.

Evans, Ruth, Andrew Taylor, Nicholas Watson and Jocelyn Wogan-Browne, 'The notion of vernacular theory', in Wogan-Browne et al. (eds), *The Idea of the Vernacular*, pp. 314–30.

Fairholt, W. F., *Costume in England: A History of Dress to the End of the Eighteenth Century*, 2 vols, revised and enlarged by H. A. Dillon (London: George Bell and Sons, 1896).

Farmer, Sharon, 'Persuasive voices: clerical images of medieval wives', *Speculum*, 61:3 (1986), 517–43.

Finberg, H. P. R., *Early Charters of the West Midlands* ([Leicester]: Leicester University Press, 1961).

Finnegan, Ruth, *Oral Poetry: Its Nature, Significance, and Social Context* (Cambridge: Cambridge University Press, 1977).

Forey, A. J., 'The military order of St. Thomas of Acre', *English Historical Review*, 92 (1977), 481–503.

Frankis, John, 'Towards a regional context for Lawman's *Brut*: literary activity in the dioceses of Worcester and Hereford in the twelfth century', in Rosamund Allen, Lucy Perry and Jane Roberts (eds), *Laʒamon: Contexts, Language, and Interpretation* (London: King's College London, 2002), pp. 53–78.

Frantzen, Allen J., *Before the Closet: Same-Sex Love from* Beowulf *to* Angels in America (Chicago: University of Chicago Press, 1998).

Franzen, Christine, *The Tremulous Hand of Worcester: A Study of Old English in the Thirteenth Century* (Oxford: Clarendon Press, 1991).

Frederick, Jill, 'The *South English Legendary*: Anglo-Saxon saints and national identity', in Donald Scragg and Carole Weinburg (eds), *Literary Appropriations of the Anglo-Saxons from the Thirteenth to the Twentieth Century* (Cambridge: Cambridge University Press, 2000), pp. 57–73.

French, Katherine L., 'Women in the late medieval English parish', in Erler and Kowaleski (eds), *Gendering the Master Narrative*, pp. 156–73.

Frese, Dolores Warwick and Katherine O'Brien O'Keeffe (eds), *The Book and the Body* (Notre Dame, IN: University of Notre Dame Press, 1996), pp. 34–77.

Freyer, A., 'Theophilus the penitent as represented in art', *Archaeological Journal*, 92 (1935), 287–333.

Fryde, E. B. *Handbook of British Chronology*, 3rd edn repr. with corr. (Cambridge: Cambridge University Press, 1996).

Furnivall, F. J., 'Original and extra series books, 1893–5', in *The Minor Poems of the Vernon Manuscript*, ed. Carl Horstmann, EETS OS 98 (London: Trübner, 1892).

——, 'Early English Text Society: statement for 1887 and 1888', in *The Lives of Women Saints of Our Contrie of England*, EETS OS 86 (London: Trübner, 1886).

Gameson, Fiona, 'Goscelin's *Life* of Augustine of Canterbury', in Richard Gameson (ed.), *St Augustine and the Conversion of England* (Stroud: Sutton, 1999), pp. 391–409.

Gameson, Richard and Fiona Gameson, 'From Augustine to Parker: the changing face of the first Archbishop of Canterbury', in Simon Keynes and Alfred P. Smyth (eds), *Anglo-Saxons: Studies Presented to Cyril Roy Hart* (Dublin: Four Courts, 2006), pp. 13–38.

Geary, Patrick, *Furta sacra: Thefts of Relics in the Central Middle Ages* (Princeton: Princeton University Press, 1978, repr. 1990).

Gee, E. A. 'The topography of altars, shrines and chantries in York Minster', *Antiquaries Journal*, 64 (1984), 337–50.

Gellrich, Jesse M., *The Idea of the Book in the Middle Ages: Language Theory, Mythology and Fiction* (Ithaca: Cornell University Press, 1985).

Gillespie, Vincent and Ghosh, Kantik, *After Arundel: Religious Writing in Fifteenth- Century England* (Turnhout: Brepols, forthcoming).

Godden, Malcolm, 'Were it not that I have bad dreams: Gregory the Great and the Anglo-Saxons on the dangers of dreaming', in Rolf H. Bremmer, Jr, Kees Dekker and David F. Johnson (eds), *Rome and the North: The Early Reception of Gregory the Great in Germanic Europe*, Mediaevalia Groningana, New Series 4 (Paris; Sterling, VA: Peeters, 2001), pp. 93–113.

Goldberg, P. J. P., 'Craft guilds, the Corpus Christi play and civic government', in Sarah Rees Jones (ed.), *The Government of Medieval York: Essays in Celebration of the 1396 Royal Charter*, Borthwick Studies in History 3 (York: University of York, 1997), pp. 141–63.

Goodman, Jennifer R., 'Marriage and conversion in late medieval romance,' in Muldoon (ed.), *Varieties of Religious Conversion*, pp. 115–28.

Görlach, Manfred, *Studies in Middle English Saints' Legends*, Anglistische Forschungen 257 (Heidelberg: Winter, 1998).

——, 'Middle English legends, 1220–1530', in Guy Philippart (ed.), *Hagiographies: International History of the Latin and Vernacular Hagiographical Literature in the West from Its Origins to 1550* (Turnhout: Brepols, 1994), pp. 427–85.

——, 'The *Legenda aurea* and the early history of *The South English Legendary*', in Dunn-Lardeau (ed.), *Legenda Aurea*, pp. 301–16.

——, *The Textual Tradition of the South English Legendary*, Leeds Texts and Monographs NS 6 (Leeds: School of English, University of Leeds, 1974).

Gransden, Antonia, *Historical Writing in England c. 550 to c. 1307* (Ithaca: Cornell University Press, 1974).

Greenhill, E. S., 'The child in the tree: a study of the cosmological tree in Christian tradition', *Traditio*, 10 (1954), 323–71.

Green, Richard F., *Poets and Princepleasers: Literature and the English Court in the Late Middle Ages* (Toronto: University of Toronto Press, 1980).

Gretsch, M., 'Die Wintney-Version der *Regula Sancti Benedicti*', *Anglia*, 96 (1978), 310–48.

Hamelinck, Renee, 'St. Kenelm and the legends of the English saints in the *South English Legendary*', in N. H. G. E. Veldhoen and H. Aertson (eds), *Companion to Middle English Literature* (Amsterdam: Free University Press, 1988), pp. 21–30.

Hampson, R. T., *Medii Aevi Kalendarium* (London: Henry Kent Causton, 1841).

Hanna, Ralph, III, 'Miscellaneity and vernacularity: conditions of literary production in late medieval England', in Stephen G. Nichols and

Siegfried Wenzel (eds), *The Whole Book: Cultural Perspectives on the Medieval Miscellany* (Ann Arbor: University of Michigan Press, 1996), pp. 37–51.

——, 'Leeds University Library, MS Brotherton 501: a redescription', *Manuscripta*, 26 (1982), 38–42.

Harper, John, *The Forms and Orders of Western Liturgy from the Tenth to the Eighteenth Century* (Oxford: Clarendon Press, 1991).

Hart, C. R., *The Early Charters of Northern England and the North Midlands* (Leicester: Leicester University Press, 1975).

Harvey, Margaret, 'Preaching in the curia: some sermons by Thomas Brinton', *Archivum Historiae Pontificae*, 33 (1995), 299–301.

Harvey, P. D. A. (ed.), *The Hereford World Map: Medieval World Maps and Their Context* (London: The British Library, 2006).

Havens, Jill C., 'Determining heresy in Middle English texts', in Helen Barr and Ann Hutchison (eds), *Text and Controversy from Wyclif to Bale: Essays in Honour of Anne Hudson* (Turnhout: Brepols, 2005).

Hayward, Paul, 'Gregory the Great as "Apostle of the English" in post-Conquest Canterbury', *Journal of Ecclesiastical History*, 55 (2004), 19–57.

——, 'Sanctity and lordship in twelfth-century England: Saint Albans, Durham and the cult of Saint Oswine, king and martyr', *Viator*, 30 (1999), 105–44.

——, 'The idea of innocent martyrdom in late tenth- and eleventh-century English hagiology', in D. Wood (ed.), *Martyrs and Martyrologies*, Studies in Church History, 30 (Oxford: Basil Blackwell, 1993), pp. 81–92.

Heffernan, Thomas, 'Dangerous sympathies: Simon de Montfort, politics, and the *South English Legendary*', in Jankofsky (ed.), *South English Legendary*, pp. 1–18 (reprinted in this volume).

——, *Sacred Biography: Saints and Their Biographers in the Middle Ages* (New York: Oxford University Press, 1988).

——, 'Additional evidence for a more precise date of the "South English Legendary"', *Traditio*, 35 (1979), 345–51.

Heuser, W., *Die Kildare-Gedichte* (Bonn, 1904; reprint, Darmstadt: Wissenschaftliche Buchgesellschaft, 1965).

Hiatt, Alfred, *The Making of Medieval Forgeries: False Documents in Fifteenth-Century England* (Toronto: University of Toronto Press, 2004).

Hillaby, Joe, 'The Worcester Jewry, 1158–1290: portrait of a lost community', *Transactions of the Worcestershire Archaeological Society*, 3rd series 12 (1990), 73–122.

Hill, Betty, 'Oxford, Jesus College MS 29', *Notes and Queries*, 220 (1975), pp. 98–105.

——, 'Cambridge, Fitzwilliam Museum Manuscript McClean 123', *Notes and Queries*, 210 (1965), 87–90.

———, 'The *Luue-Ron* and Thomas de Hales', *Modern Language Review*, 59 (1964), 321–30.

Hohler, Christopher, 'Reflections on some manuscripts containing 13th-century polyphony', *Journal of the Plainsong and Medieval Music Society*, 1 (1978), 2–38.

Holsinger, Bruce, 'Cultures of performance', *New Medieval Literatures*, 6 (2003), 271–311.

Horner, P. J., 'Benedictines and preaching in fifteenth-century England', *Revue Bénédictine*, 99 (1989), 313–32.

Horner, Shari, '"Why do you speak so much foolishness?": gender, humour, and discourse in Ælfric's *Lives of Saints*', in Jonathan Wilcox (ed.), *Humour in Anglo-Saxon Literature* (Woodbridge: D. S. Brewer, 2000), pp. 127–36.

Horobin, Simon, 'Politics, patronage, and piety in the work of Osbern Bokenham', *Speculum,* 82 (2007), 932–49.

Horstmann, Carl, 'Die Legenden des Ms. Laud 108', *Archiv für das Studium der Neueren Sprachen und Literaturen*, 49 (1872), 395–414.

Houston, Mary G., *Medieval Costume in England and France: The 13th, 14th and 15th Centuries* (1939; reprint New York: Dover, 1996).

Howe, Nicholas, *Writing the Map of Anglo-Saxon England* (New Haven: Yale University Press, 2008).

Hudson, Anne, 'Preface' in Somerset et al. (eds), *Lollards and Their Influence*, pp. 1–6.

———, *Lollards and Their Books* (London: Ronceverte, 1985).

———, 'Tradition and innovation in some Middle English manuscripts', *Review of English Studies*, NS 17 (1966), 359–72.

Ikas, Wolfgang-Valentin, 'Martinus Polonus' *Chronicle of the Popes and Emperors*: a medieval best-seller and its neglected influence on English medieval chroniclers', *English Historical Review*, 116:2 (2001), 327–41.

James, M. R., *A Descriptive Catalogue of the Manuscripts in the Library of Lambeth Palace* (Cambridge: Cambridge University Press, 1932).

Jankofsky, Klaus P. (ed.), *The South English Legendary: A Critical Assessment* (Tübingen: Francke, 1992).

———, 'National characteristics in the portrayal of English saints in the *South English Legendary*', in Renate Blumenfeld-Kosinski and Timea Szell (eds), *Images of Sainthood in Medieval Europe* (Ithaca: Cornell University Press, 1991), pp. 81–93.

———, '*Legenda Aurea* materials in the *South English Legendary*: translation, transformation, and acculturation', in Dunn-Lardeau (ed.), *Legenda Aurea*, pp. 317–30.

———, 'Entertainment, edification and popular education in the *South English Legendary*', *Journal of Popular Culture*, 11 (1977), 706–17.

——, 'Personalized didacticism: the interplay of narrator and subject matter in the *South English Legendary*', *Texas A & I University Studies*, 10 (1977), 69–77.

Jeffrey, David L., *The Early English Lyric and Franciscan Spirituality* (Lincoln: University of Nebraska Press, 1975).

Jenkins, Jacqueline, 'Lay-devotion and women readers of the Middle English prose life of St. Katherine (MS. Harley 4012)', in Jacqueline Jenkins and Katherine Lewis (eds), *St. Katherine of Alexandria: Texts and Contexts in Western Medieval Europe*, Medieval Women Texts and Contexts 8 (Turnhout: Brepols, 2003), pp. 153–70.

Johnson, Lesley, 'The Anglo-Norman *Description of England*: an introduction', in Ian Short (ed.), *Anglo-Norman Anniversary Essays*, ANTS OPS 3 (London: ANTS, 1993), pp. 11–30.

Johnson, Lesley and Jocelyn Wogan-Browne, 'National, world and women's history: writers and readers of English in post-Conquest England', in Wallace (ed.), *Cambridge History of Medieval English Literature*, pp. 92–121.

Johnson, Willis, 'Between Christians and Jews: the formation of anti-Jewish stereotypes in medieval England' (PhD dissertation, University of California, Berkeley, 1997).

——, 'Textual sources for the study of Jewish currency crimes in thirteenth-century England', *British Numismatic Journal*, 66 (1990), 21–32.

Jordan, Alyce A., *Visualizing Kingship in the Windows of the Sainte-Chapelle* (Turnhout: Brepols, 2002).

Kay, Sarah, 'The sublime body of the martyr: violence in early romance saints' lives', in Richard W. Kaeuper (ed.), *Violence in Medieval Society* (Woodbridge: Boydell Press, 2000), pp. 3–20.

——, *The* Chansons de geste *in the Age of Romance: Political Fictions* (Oxford: Clarendon, 1995).

Kelly, Henry Ansgar, 'Jews and Saracens in Chaucer's England: a review of the evidence', *Studies in the Age of Chaucer*, 27 (2005), 129–69.

Kelly, S. 'Anglo-Saxon lay society and the written word', in R. McKitterick (ed.), *The Uses of Literacy in Early Medieval Europe* (Cambridge: Cambridge University Press, 1990), pp. 36–65.

Kemp, Wolfgang, *The Narratives of Gothic Stained Glass* (Cambridge: Cambridge University Press, 1997).

Kennedy, Edward Donald, 'Chronicles and other historical writings', in Albert E. Hartung (ed.), *A Manual of the Writings in Middle English VIII* (Hamden: Connecticut Academy of Arts and Sciences, 1989), pp. 2597–956.

Kerby-Fulton, Kathryn, *Books Under Suspicion: Censorship and Tolerance of Late Medieval Revelatory Writing in England* (Notre Dame, IN: University of Notre Dame Press, 2006).

Ker, N. R., *Medieval Libraries of Great Britain* (London: Offices of the Royal Historical Society, 1964).

——, *English Manuscripts in the Century after the Norman Conquest* (Oxford: Clarendon Press, 1960).

——, *Catalogue of Manuscripts Containing Anglo-Saxon* (Oxford: Clarendon Press, 1957).

Keynes, Simon, 'Mercia and Wessex in the ninth century' in Brown and Farr (eds), *Mercia*, pp. 310–28.

——, *The Diplomas of King Æthelred 'the Unready' (978–1016): A Study in Their Use as Historical Evidence* (Cambridge: Cambridge University Press, 1980).

Kienzle, B. M., 'The typology of the medieval sermon and its development in the Middle Ages: report on work in progress', in X. Hermand and J. Hamesse (eds), *De l'Homélie au Sermon: Histoire de la Prédication Médiévale: Actes du Colloque International de Louvain-la-Neuve (9–11 Juillet 1992)* (Louvain-la-Neuve: Institut d'Études Médiévales de l'Université Catholique de Louvain, 1993), pp. 83–101.

King, Pamela M., *The York Mystery Cycle and the Worship of the City* (Woodbridge: D. S. Brewer, 2006).

Knowles, Clive H., 'Provision for the families of the Montfortians disinherited after the Battle of Evesham', in Coss and Lloyd (eds), *Thirteenth Century England I*, pp. 124–7.

Kowaleski, Maryanne, bibliography of *Town Records*, www.fordham.edu/frenchofengland/bibliography.html.

Kruger, Stephen, *The Spectral Jew: Conversion and Embodiment in Medieval Europe* (Minneapolis: University of Minnesota Press, 2006).

Laing, Margaret, *Catalogue of Sources for a Linguistic Atlas of Early Medieval English* (Cambridge: D. S. Brewer, 1993).

Långfors, A., *Un jeu de société du moyen age, Ragemon le Bon* (Helsinki: Annales Academiae Scientiarum Fennicae, 1920).

Lapidge, Michael, 'The career of Aldhelm', *Anglo-Saxon England*, 36 (2007), 15–70.

——, *Anglo-Latin Literature, 900–1066* (London: Hambledon Press, 1993).

——, 'The Digby-Gotha Recension of the Life of St. Egwine', ed. Michael Lapidge, *Vale of Evesham Historical Society Research Papers*, 7 (1979), 39–55.

——, 'The medieval hagiography of St. Ecgwine', *Vale of Evesham Historical Society Research Papers*, 6 (1977), 77–93.

——, J. Crook, R. Deshman and S. Rankin (eds), *The Cult of St Swithun* (Oxford: Clarendon Press, 2003).

Larson, Wendy, 'Who is the master of this narrative? Maternal patronage of the cult of St. Margaret', in Erler and Kowaleski, *Gendering the Master Narrative*, pp. 94–104.

Latham, R. E., *Revised Medieval Latin Word-List from British and Irish Sources* (London: British Academy, 1965).

Lavezzo, Kathy, *Angels on the Edge of the World: Geography, Literature, and English Community, 1000–1534* (Ithaca: Cornell University Press, 2006).

Lees, Clare A., 'In Ælfric's words: conversion, vigilance and the nation in Ælfric's *Life of Gregory the Great*', in Hugh Magennis and Mary Swan (eds), *A Companion to Ælfric* (Leiden: Brill, 2009), pp. 271–96.

Legge, M. D., *Anglo-Norman Literature and Its Background* (Oxford: Clarendon Press, 1963).

——, *Anglo-Norman in the Cloisters: The Influence of the Orders upon Anglo-Norman Literature* (Edinburgh: Edinburgh University Press, 1950).

——, 'The Anglo-Norman sermon of Thomas of Hales', *Modern Language Review*, 30 (1935), 212–18.

Lewis, Katherine J., 'History, historiography and rewriting the past,' in Salih (ed.), *Companion to Middle English Hagiography*, pp. 122–40.

——, 'Anglo-Saxon saints' lives, history and national identity in late medieval England', in Helen Brocklehurst and Robert Phillips (eds), *History, Nationhood and the Question of Britain* (New York: Palgrave, 2004), pp. 160–70.

——, *The Cult of St Katherine of Alexandria in Late Medieval England* (Woodbridge: Boydell Press, 2000).

Lifshitz, Felice, 'Beyond positivism and genre: hagiographical texts as historical narrative', *Viator*, 25 (1994), 95–113.

Liszka, Thomas R., 'The dragon in the *South English Legendary*: Judas, Pilate and the "A(1)" redaction', *Modern Philology*, 100:1 (2002), 50–9.

——, 'The *South English Legendaries*', in Thomas R. Liszka and Lorna E. M. Walker (eds), *The North Sea World in the Middle Ages: Studies in the Cultural History of North-Western Europe* (Dublin: Four Courts Press, 2001), pp. 243–80 (reprinted in this volume).

——, 'Manuscript G (Lambeth Palace 223) and the early *South English Legendary*', in Jankofsky (ed.), *South English Legendary*, pp. 91–101.

——, 'MS Laud Misc. 108 and the early history of the *South English Legendary*', *Manuscripta*, 33 (1989), 75–91.

——, 'The first "A" redaction of the *South English Legendary*: information from the "Prologue"', *Modern Philology*, 82:4 (1985), 407–13.

Logan, F. D., *Runaway Religious in Medieval England c. 1240–1540* (Cambridge: Cambridge University Press, 1996).

Long, Mary Beth, 'Corpora and manuscripts, authors and audiences', in Salih (ed.), *Companion to Middle English Hagiography*, pp. 47–69.

Maddocks, Hilary, 'Pictures for aristocrats: the manuscripts of the *Légende dorée*', in Margaret M. Manion and Bernard J. Muir (eds), *Medieval*

Texts and Images: Studies of Manuscripts from the Middle Ages (Sydney: Harwood, 1991), pp. 1–22.

Magennis, Hugh, 'A funny thing happened on the way to heaven: humorous incongruity in Old English saints' lives', in Jonathan Wilcox (ed.), *Humour in Anglo-Saxon Literature* (Woodbridge: D. S. Brewer, 2000), pp. 137–57.

——, 'Images of laughter in Old English poetry, with particular reference to the "hleahtor wera" of *The Seafarer*', *English Studies*, 73 (1992), 193–204.

Manhes-Deremble, Colette, with Jean-Paul Deremble, *Les vitraux narratifs de la cathédrale de Chartres: étude iconographique* (Paris: Léopard d'or, 1993).

Manning, Warren F., 'The Middle English life of Saint Dominic: date and source', *Speculum*, 31 (1956), 82–91.

Marks, Richard, 'Medieval stained glass: recent and future trends in scholarship', *The Journal of Stained Glass*, 24 (2000), 62–79.

Marner, Dominic, *St Cuthbert: His Life and Cult at Medieval Durham* (London: British Library, 2000).

Mason, Emma, 'St. Wulfstan's cross: a legend and its uses', *Medium Aevum*, 53 (1984), 157–79.

Matheson, L. M., *The Prose 'Brut': The Development of a Middle English Chronicle* (Tempe, AZ: MRTS, 1998).

McAlindon, T., 'Comedy and terror in Middle English literature: the diabolical game', *Modern Language Review*, 60 (1965), 323–32.

——, 'The emergence of a comic type in Middle-English narrative: the devil and giant as buffoon', *Anglia*, 81 (1963), 365–71.

McDonald, Nicola F., 'A polemical introduction', in Nicola F. McDonald (ed.), *Pulp Fictions of the Middle Ages: Essays in Popular Romance* (Manchester: Manchester University Press, 2004), pp. 1–21.

McIntosh, Angus, M. L. Samuels, Michael Benskin, with Margaret Laing and Keith Williamson (eds), *A Linguistic Atlas of Late Mediaeval English*, 4 vols (Aberdeen and New York: Aberdeen University Press, 1986).

McKenna, J. W., 'Popular canonization as political propaganda: the cult of Archbishop Scrope', *Speculum*, 45:1 (1970), 608–23.

Merrils, A. H., *History and Geography in Late Antiquity* (Cambridge: Cambridge University Press, 2005).

Meyer, Paul, 'Notice et extraits du MS 8336 de la bibliothèque de Sir Th. Phillipps à Cheltenham', *Romania*, 13 (1884), 497–541.

Michael, M. A., *Stained Glass of Canterbury Cathedral* (London: Scala, 2004).

Michelet, Fabienne, *Creation, Migration, and Conquest: Imaginary Geography and Sense of Space in Old English Literature* (Oxford: Oxford University Press, 2006).

Miller, B. D. H., 'The early history of Bodleian MS Digby 86', *Annuale Medievale*, 4 (1963), 23–56.

Millett, Bella, 'The audience of the saints' lives of the Katherine-Group', in *Saints and Saints' Lives: Essays in Honour of D. Hugh Farmer*, Reading Medieval Studies, 16 (1990), 12–56.

Mills, Robert, 'The early *South English Legendary* and difference: race, place, language and belief', in Bell and Couch (eds), *The Texts and Contexts of Bodleian Library, MS Laud Misc. 108*, pp. 197–221.

——, *Suspended Animation: Pain, Pleasure and Punishment in Medieval Culture* (London: Reaktion Books, 2005).

——, 'Violence, community, and the materialisation of belief', in Salih (ed.), *Companion to Middle English Hagiography*, pp. 87–103.

Minnich, Nelson H., 'From Constance to Trent: a historical overview', in Nelson H. Minnich, *Councils of the Catholic Reformation, Pisa I (1409) to Trent* (1545–63) (Aldershot and Burlington, VT: Ashgate, 2007), no. 1, pp. 1–37.

Minnis, A. J. (ed.), *Late-Medieval Religious Texts and Their Transmission: Essays in Honour of A. I. Doyle* (Cambridge: D. S. Brewer, 1994).

Mitchell, Sarah, '"We englisse men": construction and advocacy of an English cause in the Chronicle of Robert of Gloucester', in Erik Kooper (ed.), *The Medieval Chronicle: Proceedings of the 1st International Conference on the Medieval Chronicle, Driebergen/Utrecht, 13–16 July 1996* (Amsterdam: Rodopi, 1999), pp. 191–201.

Morgan, Chloe, 'A life of St Katherine of Alexandria in the chapter-house of York Minster', *Journal of the British Archaeological Association*, 162 (2009), 146–78.

Morgan, Nigel, *The Lambeth Apocalypse: Manuscript 209 in Lambeth Palace Library* (London: Harvey Miller, 1990).

Morson, J., 'The English Cistercians and the Bestiary', *Bulletin of the John Rylands Library*, 39 (1956–57), 146–70.

Muessig, Carolyn (ed.), *Preacher, Sermon and Audience in the Middle Ages* (Leiden: Brill, 2002).

Muir, Laurence, 'The Southern Temporale', in J. Burke Severs (ed.), *A Manual of the Writings in Middle English, 1050–1500* (New Haven: Connecticut Academy of Arts and Sciences, 1970), II: 403–7.

Muldoon, James, 'Introduction: the conversion of Europe,' in Muldoon (ed.), *Varieties of Religious Conversion*, pp. 1–10.

——, (ed.), *Varieties of Religious Conversion in the Middle Ages* (Gainesville: University Press of Florida, 1997).

Mundill, Robin, *England's Jewish Solution: Experiment and Expulsion, 1262–1290* (Cambridge: Cambridge University Press, 1998).

Mundy, John Hine, 'The conciliar movement and the Council of Constance', in *The Council of Constance: The Unification of the Church*, trans. Louise Ropes Loomis, ed. and annotated John Hine Mundy and

Kennerly M. Woody (New York and London: Columbia University Press, 1961), pp. 3–51.

Mynors, R. A. B., *A Catalogue of the Manuscripts of Balliol College* (Oxford: Clarendon Press, 1963).

Nilson, Benjamin J., *Cathedral Shrines of Medieval England* (Woodbridge: Boydell Press, 2001).

Norton, Christopher, *St William of York* (Woodbridge and York: York Medieval Press, 2006).

——, 'The medieval paintings in the chapter house', *Friends of York Minster Annual Report*, 67 (1996), pp. 34–51.

O'Doherty, Marianne, 'Old stories and new contexts: constructions of the figure and reign of Edward the Confessor in Robert of Gloucester's verse *Chronicle*' (MA dissertation, Centre for Medieval Studies, University of Leeds, 1997).

O'Keeffe, Katherine O'Brien, *Visible Song: Transitional Literacy in Old English Verse* (Cambridge: Cambridge University Press, 1990).

Oliva, Marilyn, *The Convent and the Community in Late Medieval England: Female Monasteries in the Diocese of Norwich 1350–1540* (Woodbridge: Boydell Press, 1998).

Opie, Iona and Peter Opie, *The Singing Game* (Oxford: Oxford University Press, 1985).

Orchard, Andy 'Parallel lives: Wulfstan, William, Coleman and Christ', in Julia Barrow and Nicholas Brooks (eds), *St. Wulfstan and His World* (Aldershot: Ashgate, 2005), pp. 39–58.

Orme, Nicholas, *Medieval Schools from Roman Britain to Renaissance England* (New Haven: Yale University Press, 2006).

Parkes, M. B., 'On the presumed date of the manuscript of the *Orrmulum*', in E. G. Stanley and D. Gray (eds), *Five Hundred Years of Words and Sounds: A Festschrift for E. J. Dobson* (Cambridge: D. S. Brewer, 1983), pp. 115–27.

——, 'The literacy of the laity', in D. Daiches and A. Thorlby (eds), *Literature and Civilization: The Medieval World* (London: Aldus, 1973), 555–77.

Pearsall, Derek, (ed.), *Studies in the Vernon Manuscript* (Cambridge: D. S. Brewer, 1990).

——, *Old English and Middle English Poetry* (London: Routledge & Kegan Paul, 1977).

Pfander, H. G., 'Medieval friars and some alphabetical reference-books for sermons', *Medium Aevum*, 3 (1934), 19–29.

Pickering, Oliver, '*South English Legendary* style in Robert of Gloucester's *Chronicle*', *Medium Aevum*, 70 (2001), 1–18 (revised version in this volume).

——, 'The *South English Legendary*: teaching or preaching?' *Poetica*, 45 (Spring 1996), 1–14.

——, 'The outspoken *South English Legendary* poet', in Minnis (ed.), *Late-Medieval Religious Texts*, pp. 21–37 (revised version in this volume).

——, 'The *Southern Passion* and the *Ministry and Passion*: the work of a Middle English reviser' *LSE*, NS 15 (1984), 33–56.

——, 'The expository *temporale* poems of the *South English Legendary*', *LSE*, NS 10 (1978), 1–17.

——, 'Three *South English Legendary* nativity poems', *LSE*, NS 8 (1975), 105–19.

——, 'The *temporale* narratives of the *South English Legendary*', *Anglia*, 91 (1973), 425–55.

——, and Manfred Görlach, 'A newly-discovered manuscript of the *South English Legendary*', *Anglia*, 100 (1982), 109–23.

Popper, Glenys (ed.), *Medieval Art and Architecture at Worcester Cathedral* (London: British Archeological Association, 1978).

Powell, Sue, 'The *Festial*: the priest and his parish', in C. Burgess and E. Duff (ed.), *The Parish in Late Medieval England*, Harlaxton Medieval Studies XIV (Donnington: Shaun Tyas, 2006), pp. 160–76.

Powicke, Sir Maurice, *The Thirteenth Century, 1216–1307*, 2nd edn (Oxford: Clarendon Press, 1962).

——, *King Henry III and the Lord Edward: The Community of the Realm in the Thirteenth Century*, 2 vols (Oxford: Clarendon Press, 1947).

Prothero, George, *Life of Simon de Montfort, Earl of Leicester* (London: Longmans, 1877).

Quinn, W. A. and A. S. Hall, *Jongleur: A Modified Theory of Oral Improvisation and Its Effects on the Performance and Transmission of Middle English Romance* (Washington, DC: University Press of America, 1982).

Ranger, F. (ed.), *Prisca Munimenta: Studies in Archival and Administrative History Presented to A. E. J. Hollaender* (London: University of London Press, 1973).

Reames, Sherry L., 'Unexpected texts for saints in some Sarum breviary manuscripts', in George H. Brown and Linda Ehrsam Voigts (eds), *The Study of Medieval Manuscripts of England: A Festschrift in Honor of Richard Pfaff* (Tempe AZ: MRTS, 2010), pp. 163–84.

——, 'Late medieval efforts at standardisation and reform in the Sarum lessons for saints' days', in Connolly and Mooney (eds), *Design and Distribution*, pp. 91–117.

——, 'Lectionary revision in Sarum breviaries and the origins of the early printed editions', *Journal of the Early Book Society*, 9 (2006), 95–115.

——, 'Reconstructing and interpreting a thirteenth-century office for the Translation of Thomas Becket', *Speculum*, 80 (2005), 118–70.

——, *The Legenda Aurea: A Reexamination of Its Paradoxical History* (Madison: University of Wisconsin Press, 1985).

Rees Jones, Sarah, 'Cities and their saints in England, c. 1150–1300: the development of bourgeois values in the cults of Saint William of York', in Caroline Goodson, Anne E. Lester and Carol Symes (eds), *Cities, Texts, and Social Networks, 400–1500* (Aldershot: Ashgate, 2010), pp. 193–214.

——, *York between the Conquest and the Black Death* (Oxford: Oxford University Press, forthcoming).

Renna, Thomas, 'The Jews in the Golden Legend', in Michael Frassetto (ed.), *Christian Attitudes Toward the Jews in the Middle Ages: A Casebook* (New York: Routledge, 2007), pp. 137–50.

Rice, Nicole R., *Lay Piety and Religious Discipline in Middle English Literature* (Cambridge: Cambridge University Press, 2009).

Richards, M. P., 'BL MS Cotton Vespasian A.xxii, the Vespasian Homilies', *Manuscripta*, 22 (1978), 97–103.

Richardson, H. R., Review of Sister Mary Aquinas Devlin, O.P. (ed.), *The Sermons of Thomas of Brinton, Bishop of Rochester, Speculum*, 30:2 (1955), 267–71.

Riches, Samantha, *St. George: Hero, Martyr and Myth* (Stroud: Sutton, 2000).

Rigg, A. G., 'Golias and other pseudonyms', *Studi Medievali*, 18 (1977), 65–109.

Robbins, R. H., 'The authors of the Middle English religious lyric', *Journal of English and Germanic Philology*, 39 (1940), 230–8.

——, 'The earliest carols and the Franciscans', *Modern Language Notes*, 53 (1938), 239–45.

Roberts, Jane, *Guide to Scripts Used in English Writings up to 1500* (London: British Library, 2005).

Robertson, M., 'The shallow clerk: a morphology of *The South English Legendary*', *Comparison*, 10 (1970), 36–65.

Robins, William, 'Towards a disjunctive philology', in S. Echard and S. Partridge (eds), *The Book Unbound* (Toronto: University of Toronto Press, 2004), pp. 144–77.

Robinson, N. F., 'The black chimere of Anglican prelates: a plea for its retention and proper use', *Transactions of the St. Paul's Ecclesiological Society*, 4 (1910), 181–220.

Rokeah, Zefirah, 'Money and the hangman in late 13th century England: Part II', *Jewish Historical Studies*, 32 (1990–92), 159–218.

——, 'Money and the hangman in late 13th century England: Jews, Christians, and coinage offenses alleged and real', *Jewish Historical Studies*, 31 (1988–90), 83–109.

Rollason, D. W., 'The cult of murdered royal saints', *Anglo-Saxon England*, 11 (1983), 1–22.

——, 'Lists of saints' resting-places in Anglo-Saxon England', *Anglo-Saxon England*, 7 (1978), 61–93.

Rouse, Robert Allen, *The Idea of Anglo-Saxon England in Middle English Romance* (Cambridge: D. S. Brewer, 2005).

Rubin, Miri, *Gentile Tales: The Narrative Assault on Late Medieval Jews* (New Haven: Yale University Press, 1999).

Russell, Delbert, 'The Campsey collection of Old French Saints' lives: a re-examination of its structure and provenance', *Scriptorium*, 57 (2003), 51–83.

Russell, Josiah Cox, 'The canonization of opposition to the king in Angevin England', in C. H. Taylor and J. L. La Monte (eds), *Haskins Anniversary Essays in Medieval Studies* (Boston: Houghton Mifflin, 1929), pp. 279–90.

Sadlek, Gregory M., 'The image of the devil's five fingers in the *South English Legendary*'s "St Michael" and in Chaucer's Parson's Tale', in Jankofsky (ed.), *South English Legendary*, pp. 49–64.

——, 'Laughter, game, and ambiguous comedy in the *South English Legendary*', *Studia Neophilologica*, 64 (1992), 45–54.

——, 'The archangel and the cosmos: the inner logic of the *South English Legendary*'s "St Michael"', *Studies in Philology*, 85 (1988), 177–91.

——, 'The *South English Legendary* as rose window', *Ball State University Forum*, 25:4 (1984), 3–17.

——, 'Three basic questions in literary studies of the *South English Legendary*' (PhD dissertation, Northern Illinois University, 1983).

Salih, Sarah, 'Introduction: saints, cults and *Lives* in late medieval England', in Salih (ed.), *Companion to Middle English Hagiography*, pp. 1–23.

——, (ed.), *A Companion to Middle English Hagiography* (Cambridge: D. S. Brewer, 2006).

——, *Versions of Virginity in Late Medieval England* (Cambridge: D. S. Brewer, 2001).

Salmon, Pierre, *The Breviary Through the Centuries*, trans. Sister David Mary (Collegeville, MN: Liturgical Press, 1962).

Salter, E., 'A complaint against blacksmiths', *Literature and History*, 5 (1979), 194–215.

Samson, Annie, 'The *South English Legendary*: constructing a context', in Coss and Lloyd (eds), *Thirteenth Century England I*, pp. 185–95.

Sanok, Catherine, *Her Life Historical: Exemplarity and Female Saints' Lives in Late Medieval England* (Philadelphia: University of Pennsylvania Press, 2007).

——, 'Performing feminine sanctity in late medieval England: parish guilds, saints' plays and the *Second Nun's Tale*', *Journal of Medieval and Early Modern Studies*, 32 (2002), 269–303.

Sargent, Michael, 'What do the numbers mean?: a textual critic's observations on some patterns of Middle English manuscript transmission', in Connolly and Mooney (eds), *Design and Distribution*, pp. 205–44.

Sayers, J., '"Original" cartulary and chronicle: the case of the Abbey of Evesham', in *Fälschungen im Mittelalter. Internationaler Kongress Der Monumenta Germaniae Historica, München, 16–19 September 1986*, MGH 33 (Hanover: Hansche Buchhandlung, 1988), vol. IV, pp. 371–95.

Scahill, John, with Margaret Rogerson, *Middle English Saints' Legends*, Annotated Bibliographies of Middle English Literature 8 (Woodbridge: D. S. Brewer, 2005).

Scattergood, V. J. and J. W. Sherborne (eds), *English Court Culture in the Later Middle Ages* (London: Duckworth, 1983).

Schechner, Richard, 'What is performance studies anyway?' in Peggy Phelan and Jill Lane (eds), *The Ends of Performance* (New York: New York University Press, 1998), pp. 357–62.

Schofield, B., 'The provenance and date of *Sumer is icumen in*', *Music Review*, 9 (1948), 81–6.

Scott, Kathleen L., *Later Gothic Manuscripts 1390–1490*, A Survey of Manuscripts Illuminated in the British Isles, 6, 2 vols (London: Harvey Miller Publishers, 1996).

Serjeantson, Mary J., 'The index of the Vernon manuscript', *Modern Language Review*, 32 (1937), 222–61.

Sharpe, Richard, *A Handlist of the Latin Writers of Great Britain and Ireland before 1540*, Publications of the Journal of Medieval Latin 1, corrected edition (Turnhout: Brepols, 2001).

——, 'Charters, deeds, and diplomatics', in F. A. C. Mantello and A. G. Rigg (eds), *Medieval Latin: An Introduction and Bibliographic Guide* (Washington, DC: Catholic University Press of America, 1996).

Sheils, William J., 'The altars in York Minster in the early sixteenth century', in R. N. Swanson (ed.), *Continuity and Change in Christian Worship*, Studies in Church History 35 (Woodbridge: Boydell Press for the Ecclesiastical History Society, 1999), pp. 104–15.

Sheingorn, Pamela, 'Performing the illustrated manuscript: great reckonings in little books', in Elina Gertsman (ed.), *Visualizing Medieval Performance: Perspectives, Histories, Contexts* (London and Burlington, VT: Ashgate, 2008), pp. 57–82.

Shell, Marc, 'The want of incest in the human family, or, kin and kind in Christian thought', *Journal of the American Academy of Religion*, 62:3 (1994), 625–50.

Shippey, T. A., '"Grim wordplay": folly and wisdom in Anglo-Saxon humour', in Jonathan Wilcox (ed.), *Humour in Anglo-Saxon Literature* (Woodbridge: D. S. Brewer, 2000), pp. 33–48.

Skemer, Don, 'King Edward's articles of inquest on the Jews and coin clipping, 1279', *Historical Research*, 72:177 (1999), 1–26.

Slocum, Kay Brainerd, *Liturgies in Honour of Thomas Becket* (Toronto: University of Toronto Press, 2004).

Smith, Lesley, 'The theology of the twelfth and thirteenth-century Bible', in R. Ganeson (ed.), *The Early Medieval Bible: Its Production, Decoration and Use* (Cambridge: Cambridge University Press, 1994), pp. 223–32.

Smith, Mike and David Taylor, 'The crown and the well, the divine king and the re-discovery of a "lost" well', *Mercian Mysteries*, 25 (1995), now published as *At the Edge*: www.indigogroup.co.uk/edge/Stkenelm.htm.

Somerset, Fiona, 'Here, there and everywhere? Wycliffite conceptions of the Eucharist and Chaucer's "other" Lollard joke', in Somerset et al. (eds.), *Lollards and Their Influence*, 2003), pp. 127–38.

Somerset, Fiona, Jill C. Havens and Derek C. Pittard (eds), *Lollards and Their Influence* (Woodbridge: Boydell Press, 2003).

Speed, Diane, 'The construction of the nation in medieval English romance', in Carol Meale (ed.), *Readings in Medieval English Romance* (Cambridge: D. S. Brewer, 1994), pp. 135–57.

Stacey, Robert C., 'The conversion of the Jews to Christianity in thirteenth century England', *Speculum*, 67 (1992), 263–83.

Stafford, Pauline, 'Political women in Mercia, eighth to early tenth centuries', in Brown and Farr (eds), *Mercia*, pp. 35–49.

Stahl, Alan, 'Coin and punishment in medieval Venice', in Ruth Mazo Karras, Joel Kaye and E. Ann Matter (eds), *Law and the Illicit in Medieval Europe* (Philadelphia: University of Pennsylvania Press, 2008), pp. 164–79.

Stahuljak, Zrinka, *Bloodless Genealogies of the French Middle Ages: Translatio, Kinship, and Metaphor* (Gainesville: University Press of Florida, 2005).

Stanley, E. G., 'Laȝamon's antiquarian sentiments', *Medium Aevum*, 38 (1969), 23–37.

Steiner, Emily, '*Piers Plowman*, diversity, and the medieval political aesthetic', *Representations*, 91 (2005), 1–25.

——, *Documentary Culture and the Making of English Literature* (Cambridge: Cambridge University Press, 2003).

Stein, Robert M., 'Making history English: cultural identity and historical explanation in William of Malmesbury and Laȝamon's *Brut*', in Sylvia Tomasch and Sealy Gilles (eds), *Text and Territory: Geographical Imagination in the European Middle Ages* (Philadelphia: University of Pennsylvania Press, 1998), pp. 97–115.

Strohm, Paul (ed.), *Middle English* (Oxford: Oxford University Press, 2007).

Swanton, Michael, *English Literature before Chaucer* (London: Longman, 1987).

Symes, Carol, 'The medieval archive and the history of theatre: assessing the written and unwritten evidence for pre-modern performance practice', in *Theatre Survey* 52.1 (2011), pp. 29–58.

——, *A Common Stage: Theater and Public Life in Medieval Arras* (Ithaca: Cornell University Press, 2007).

——, 'The appearance of early vernacular plays: forms, functions, and the future of medieval theater', *Speculum*, 77 (2002), 778–831.

Taft, Robert F., *The Liturgy of the Hours in East and West*, 2nd revised edn (Collegeville, MN: Liturgical Press, 1993).

Taylor, Andrew, *Textual Situations: Three Medieval Manuscripts and Their Readers* (Philadelphia: University of Pennsylvania Press, 2002).

Thacker, Alan, '*Loca sanctorum*: the significance of place in the study of the saints', in Alan Thacker and Richard Sharpe (eds), *Local Saints and Local Churches in the Early Medieval West* (Oxford: Oxford University Press, 2002), pp. 1–44.

——, 'In Gregory's shadow? The pre-Conquest cult of St Augustine', in Richard Gameson (ed.), *St Augustine and the Conversion of England* (Stroud: Sutton, 2000), pp. 373–90.

Thompson, Anne B., *Everyday Saints and the Art of Narrative in the South English Legendary* (Aldershot: Ashgate, 2003).

——, 'The legend of St. Agnes: Improvisation and the practice of hagiography', *Exemplaria*, 13 (2001), 355–97.

——, 'Audacious fictions: *Anastasia* and the triumph of narrative', *Assays*, 8 (1995), 1–28.

——, 'Narrative art in the *South English Legendary*', *Journal of English and Germanic Philology*, 90 (1991), 20–30.

Thompson, John J., *The Cursor Mundi: Poem, Texts and Contexts* (Oxford: The Society for the Study of Medieval Languages and Literatures, 1998).

Tiller, Kenneth H., *Laʒamon's Brut and the Anglo-Norman Vision of History* (Cardiff: University of Wales Press, 2007).

Tilley, Morris Palmer, *A Dictionary of the Proverbs in England in the Sixteenth and Seventeenth Centuries* (Ann Arbor: University of Michigan Press, 1950).

Tinti, F., 'From episcopal conception to monastic compilation: Hemming's cartulary in context', *Early Medieval Europe*, 11:3 (2002), 233–61.

Tomasch, Sylvia, 'Postcolonial Chaucer and the virtual Jew', in Jeffrey Jerome Cohen (ed.), *The Postcolonial Middle Ages* (New York: Palgrave Macmillan, 2000), pp. 243–60.

Trenholme, N. M., 'Evesham: a history of the borough', in J. W. Willis-Bund and William Page (eds), *The Victoria History of the County of Worcester* (London: Constable & Co., 1906), vol. II, pp. 371–96.

Tuck, Anthony, *Crown and Nobility 1272–1461: Political Conflict in Late Medieval England* (Oxford: Blackwell, 1986).

Turville-Petre, Thorlac, *England the Nation: Language, Literature and National Identity 1290–1340* (Oxford: Clarendon Press, 1996).

Vicaire, M. H., *Saint Dominic and His Times*, trans. Kathleen Pond (New York: McGraw Hill, 1964).

The Victoria History of the County of Gloucester, II, ed. William Page (London: Constable, 1907).

Vincent, Nicholas, *The Holy Blood: King Henry III and the Westminster Blood Relic* (Cambridge: Cambridge University Press, 2001).

Wallace, David (ed.), *The Cambridge History of Medieval English Literature* (Cambridge: Cambridge University Press, 1999).

Walsh, Christine, *The Cult of St Katherine in Early Medieval Europe* (Aldershot: Ashgate, 2007).

Warner, Lawrence, 'Becket and the hopping bishops', *Yearbook of Langland Studies*, 17 (2003), 107–34.

Warren, Michelle R., 'Translation', in Strohm (ed.), *Middle English*, pp. 51–67.

Waters, Claire, *Angels and Earthly Creatures: Preaching, Performance and Gender in the Later Middle Ages* (Philadelphia: University of Pennsylvania Press, 2004).

Watt, J. A., 'The papacy', in David Abulafia (ed.), *The New Cambridge Medieval History, V: c. 1198–c. 1300* (Cambridge: Cambridge University Press, 1999), pp. 107–63.

Wells, John Edwin, *A Manual of the Writings in Middle English: 1050–1400* (London: Oxford University Press, 1916).

Wells, Minnie E., 'The *South English Legendary* and its relation to the *Legenda aurea*', *PMLA*, 51:2 (1936), 337–60.

Whatley, E. Gordon, 'Acta Sanctorum', in Frederick M. Biggs, Thomas D. Hill, Paul E. Szarmach and E. Gordon Whatley (eds), *Sources of Anglo-Saxon Literary Culture*, vol. 1 (Kalamazoo, MI: Medieval Institute Publications, 2001), pp. 22–486.

——, 'John Lydgate's *Saint Austin at Compton*: the poem and its sources', in Siân Echard and Gernot Wieland (eds), *Anglo-Latin Literature and its Heritage: Essays in Honour of A.G. Rigg on His 64th Birthday*, Publications of the Journal of Medieval Latin 4 (Turnhout: Brepols, 2001), pp. 191–227.

Whiting, B. J. and H. W., *Proverbs, Sentences and Proverbial Phrases from English Writings Mainly before 1500* (Cambridge, MA: Belknap Press, 1968).

Wieck, Roger S., *Time Sanctified: The Book of Hours in Medieval Art and Life* (New York: George Braziller, 1988).

Wilkinson, B., *The Later Middle Ages in England 1216–1485* (New York: McKay, 1969).

Wilson, E. (ed.), *A Descriptive Index of the English Lyrics in John of Grimestone's Preaching Book* (Oxford: Blackwell, 1973).

Winstead, Karen A., *John Capgrave's Fifteenth Century* (Philadelphia: University of Pennsylvania Press, 2007).

——, *Virgin Martyrs: Legends of Sainthood in Late Medieval England* (Ithaca: Cornell University Press, 1997).

Winston, C. and Walford, W.S., 'On a heraldic window in the north aisle of York Cathedral', in *Memoirs Illustrative of the Art of Glass Painting by the Late Charles Winston* (London: Murray, 1865), pp. 256–84.

Wogan-Browne, Jocelyn, *Saints' Lives and Women's Literary Culture, c. 1150–1300: Virginity and Its Authorizations* (Oxford: Oxford University Press, 2001).

——, 'The apple's message: some post-Conquest hagiographic accounts of textual transmission', in Minnis (ed.), *Late-Medieval Religious Texts*, pp. 39–53.

——, '"Bet . . . to . . . rede on holy seyntes lyves . . .": romance and hagiography again', in Carol M. Meale (ed.), *Readings in Medieval English Romance* (Cambridge: D. S. Brewer, 1994), pp. 83–97.

——, with Carolyn Collette, Maryanne Kowaleski, Linne Mooney, Ad Putter and David Trotter (eds), *Language and Culture in Medieval Britain: The French of England c. 1100–c. 1500* (Woodbridge and York:York Medieval Press, 2009).

——, Nicholas Watson, Andrew Taylor and Ruth Evans (eds), *The Idea of the Vernacular: Middle English Literary Theory 1280–1530* (University Park, PA: Penn State Press, and Exeter: Exeter University Press, 1999).

Wolpers, Theodor, *Die Englische Heiligenlegende des Mittelalters* (Tübingen: Niemeyer, 1964).

Wood, Ian, 'The mission of Augustine of Canterbury to the English', *Speculum*, 69 (1994), 1–17.

Woolf, Rosemary, *The English Religious Lyric in the Middle Ages* (Oxford: Clarendon Press, 1968).

Wormald, Patrick, 'Lordship and justice in the early English kingdom: Oswaldlaw revisited', in *Legal Culture in the Early Medieval West: Law as Text, Image and Experience* (London: Hambledon Press, 1999).

——, *The Making of English Law: King Alfred to the Twelfth Century* (Oxford: Blackwell Publishers, 1999).

Wright, C. E., *English Vernacular Hands from the Twelfth to the Fifteenth Centuries* (Oxford: Clarendon Press, 1960).

Yeager, Stephen M., 'Poetic properties: legal forms and literary documents in early English literature' (PhD dissertation, University of Toronto, 2009).

Index

Note: *SEL* represents *South English Legendary/ies*. Illustrations are marked in italic.